NEUROPSYCHOLOGICAL ASSESSMENT IN CLINICAL PRACTICE

NEUROPSYCHOLOGICAL ASSESSMENT IN CLINICAL PRACTICE

A GUIDE TO TEST INTERPRETATION AND INTEGRATION

Gary Groth-Marnat, Editor

John Wiley & Sons, Inc.

New York • Chichester • Weinheim • Brisbane • Singapore • Toronto

ISBN 0-471-19325-9

Printed in the United States of America.

10 9 8 7 6 5 4

In memory of
Barbara Banks Groth-Marnat

Contributors

Jeffrey T. Barth, PhD
Professor and Chief, Medical
  Psychology/Neuropsychology
University of Virginia Health Sciences
  Center
Charlottesville, VA

Thomas J. Boll, PhD
Professor of Psychology, Pediatrics, and
  Neurological Surgery
School of Medicine
University of Alabama
Birmingham, AL

Donna K. Broshek, PhD
Division of Neuropsychology
Department of Psychiatric Medicine
University of Virginia Health Sciences
  Center
Charlottesville, VA

John Edward Fowler, Professor
Chief, Medical Psychology &
  Neuropsychology
Division of Neuropsychology
Department of Psychiatric Medicine
University of Virginia Health Sciences
  Center
Charlottesville, VA

Michael D. Franzen, PhD
Director, Neuropsychology
Associate Professor of Psychiatry
Department of Psychiatry ANI-AGH
Pittsburgh, PA

Shawna M. Freshwater, MA
Center for Psychological Studies
Nova Southeastern University
Fort Lauderdale, FL

Roberta E. Gallagher, PhD
Clinical Neuropsychologist
Department of Neuropsychology
Spaulding Rehabilitation Hospital
Boston, MA

Carlton S. Gass, PhD
Director, Neuropsychology Section
Department of Veterans Affairs Medical
  Center
Miami, FL

Charles J. Golden, PhD
Center for Psychological Studies
Nova Southeastern University
Fort Lauderdale, FL

Gary Groth-Marnat, PhD
Senior Lecturer, Clinical Health
  Psychology
School of Psychology
Curtin University
Perth, WA, Australia

James B. Hale, PhD
Assistant Professor, Psychology
Psychology Department
Plattsburgh State University of New York
Plattsburgh, NY

Edward Helmes, PhD
Associate Professor, Psychology
School of Psychology
Edith Cowan University
Joondalup, Australia

Daniel Holland
Clinical Assistant Professor
Department of Physical Medicine and
   Rehabilitation
Division of Clinical Health Psychology
   and Neuropsychology
University of Missouri-Columbia
Columbia, MO

Grant L. Iverson, PhD
Assistant Professor
Department of Psychiatry
University of British Columbia
Vancouver, BC, Canada

Brick Johnstone, PhD
Director, Division of Clinical Health
   Psychology and Neuropsychology
Department of Physical Medicine and
   Rehabilitation
University of Missouri-Columbia
Columbia, MO

Edith Kaplan, PhD
Diplomate in Clinical Neuropsychology
Professor of Psychology, Clinical
   Development Program
Suffolk University
Boston, MA
Adjunct Professor of Neurology
   (Neuropsychology)
Boston University School of Medicine
Boston, MA

Patricia Lacks, PhD
Private Practice
Santa Barbara, CA

Carmen Larimore, PhD, CCCP
Department of Educational and
   Counseling Psychology
University of Missouri-Columbia
Columbia, MO

**Carolyn M. Lemsky, PhD, C. PSYCH,
ABPP/ABCN**
Community Head Injury Resources
   Services of Metropolitan Toronto
Etobicoke, Ontario, Canada

Marnie J. Nadolne, PsyD
Research Fellow
Department of Rehabilitation Medicine
Emory School of Medicine
Emory University
Atlanta, GA

Jennie L. Ponsford
Associate Professor, Department of
   Psychology
Monash University
Director, Bethesda Rehabilitation
   Research Unit
Epworth Hospital
Melbourne, Australia

**Robert J. Sbordone, PhD, ABCN,
ABPN, ABAP**
Private Practice
Irvine, CA

Michael Selby, PhD
Associate Professor of Psychology
Psychology and Human Development
California Polytechnic State University
San Luis Obispo, CA

Anthony Y. Stringer, PhD
Associate Professor
Department of Rehabilitation Medicine
Emory School of Medicine
Emory University
Atlanta, GA

Jyothi Vayalakkara, MA
Center for Psychological Studies
Nova Southeastern University
Fort Lauderdale, FL

Mark A. Williams, PhD
Assistant Professor
Division of Neuorsurgery
University of Alabama School of
   Medicine
University of Alabama
Birmingham, AL

Preface—————————————————————

Welcome to *Neuropsychological Assessment in Clinical Practice: A Practical Guide to Test Interpretation and Integration*. I hope you find the book useful, interesting, and relevant to your clinical work. If my efforts have been successful, the following pages should enable you to work through the various phases of neuropsychological assessment. These phases begin with understanding the context of different referral settings, selecting tests, understanding basic neurology, and conducting an assessment interview (Part One). Formal assessment involves administering relevant tests, which might be in the form of a formal test battery (Part Two) or might be more individual tests organized around various domains of a client's functioning (Part Three). Finally, the data is organized into a psychological report, which typically involves integrating the data into a treatment plan (Part Four). Throughout the book, bold-faced terms indicate those that are defined in the Glossary at the end of the book. My goal is to present these procedures in a way that is logical and easy to follow. I hope that the information gives credence both to relevant research and to the pragmatic realties of dealing with clients and referral sources.

My search for this book began many years ago when I began practicing as a neuropsychologist. There were no books that provided a comprehensive guide to neuropsychological assessment. By that, I mean that there was nothing that helped me through the pragmatics of test selection, interpretation, and report writing. Certainly there were manuals on how to interpret single tests and, later, books on interpreting some of the more comprehensive batteries. There was also Lezak's (1976, 1983, 1995) outstanding, comprehensive, in-depth text, which was followed by two editions (1990, 1998) of Spreen and Strauss. However, both Lezak and Spreen and Strauss were compendiums, sort of encyclopedias on neuropsychological assessment. Although I found them invaluable in reviewing tests, in providing information helpful for test selection, and in including relevant norms, they still did not provide a practitioner's guide to actual test interpretation and integration. My need for and search for such a book became more urgent when I began teaching courses on clinical neuropsychology. After waiting for the book that never emerged, I decided to bring together authors to create such a book.

The theoretical orientation behind the book is purposely eclectic. This is not to say that individual authors do not have quite clear orientations. Some are proponents of the fixed battery approach whereas others prefer a hypothesis-testing approach. My feeling is that each approach has various strengths and weaknesses and that it is up to the individual readers to choose the approach that works best for them, their clients, and their assessment contexts. I prefer a fixed-core battery with additional tests tailored toward the needs of the referral question and the characteristics of the client (so-called fixed-flexible approach). I like to look at both quantitative scores and qualitative responses, which can be used to more fully understand unique features of clients and the reasons why they made certain responses. Research reviews suggest that the greatest segment of practicing neuropsychologists also take such an approach. Thus I hope the book will particularly appeal to that large number of fixed-flexible eclectic practitioners, as well as to those who are more strongly invested in a particular theoretical orientation.

The preparation of *Neuropsychological Assessment in Clinical Practice* has been a group effort. I feel pleased, thankful, and proud that such a distinguished group of authors agreed to contribute. I especially appreciated their compliance with my many nit-picky and repeated requests for revisions ("Oh no, he's not sending it back for more revisions!"). I'm sure that many authors thought they had seen the last draft of their chapter only to have it returned once again. And each time, they revised it with never a complaint. I hope they agree that the requested changes helped to fine-tune an outstanding product rather than to merely satisfy the ceaseless needs of an overcontrolling, highly compulsive editor. Thanks to all of you. I also much appreciate Dawn Erickson for her tolerance, her support, and her help with the glossary.

My thanks especially go to the outstanding team at Wiley and primarily my editor Jennifer Simon. Her support, humor, cheerfulness, rapid response to my many questions, and incredible patience with (yet another) request for an extension will always be appreciated. The book would not have been possible nor would it have been as enjoyable to create without her.

GARY GROTH-MARNAT

Contents

Chapter 6   The Wechsler Memory Scales   195
Michael D. Franzen and Grant L. Iverson

Chapter 7   The Halstead-Reitan Neuropsychological Test Battery   223
Donna K. Broshek and Jeffrey T. Barth

Chapter 8   The Luria Nebraska Neuropsychological Battery   263
Charles J. Golden, Shawna M. Freshwater, and Jyothi Vayalakkara

PART ONE

Overview and Introduction to Neuropsychological Assessment

Chapter 1

INTRODUCTION TO NEUROPSYCHOLOGICAL ASSESSMENT

GARY GROTH-MARNAT

OVERVIEW OF NEUROPSYCHOLOGICAL ASSESSMENT

Neuropsychology is the study of brain-behavior relationships. Clinical neuropsychological assessment is the application of this knowledge to evaluate and to intervene in human behavior as it relates to normal and abnormal functioning of the central nervous system. Neuropsychology involves assessing such areas as memory, abstract reasoning, problem solving, spatial abilities, and the emotional and personality consequences of brain dysfunction. The result of a neuropsychological assessment is ideally a clear, coherent description of the impact that brain dysfunction has had on a person's cognitions, personality, emotions, interpersonal relationships, vocational functioning, educational potential, and ability to enjoy life. The practical importance of this knowledge consists of assisting with case management, rehabilitation planning, and the monitoring of progress, as well as the enlarging of the discipline's research base. Over the past 50 years, clinical neuropsychology has evolved from and represented a synthesis of psychometric testing, clinical psychology, and behavioral neurology. However, it is also distinctly different from the emphasis in neurology: Whereas neurologists might explain how the *brain* is functioning, the neuropsychologist assesses how the *person* is functioning *as a result of changes in the brain.*

The major purposes of neuropsychological assessment are to provide answers related to the following four areas: (1) differential diagnosis, (2) treatment planning, (3) rehabilitation, and (4) legal proceedings. *Differential diagnosis* most typically occurs within medical contexts when practitioners are asked to discriminate between neurological disorders and psychiatric disorders. For example, a neurologist with a patient having unexplained seizures might wish to know whether the patient's psychological characteristics are consistent with conversion disorder. This information would then be used to help decide whether the patient should be referred for further medical evaluation or for psychotherapy. The most frequent referral within a general psychiatric context is for assessment of the possible presence of organic functioning as a result of changes in the brain. An invaluable contribution of neuropsychological assessment is detecting and evaluating cerebral dysfunction in the absence of clear anatomical evidence of alterations. Such a condition is most likely to occur following exposure to neurotoxic substances, cognitive decline associated with substance abuse, the behavioral impact of cardiac surgery, and cognitive changes associated with chronic obstructive pulmonary disease. An increasingly important type of differential diagnosis is determining whether an older person who presents with memory complaints is suffering from the early signs of dementia or is merely experiencing the cognitive disruption of depression.

Treatment planning involves various decisions related to the nature and the extent of brain dysfunction. A person who had a stroke might consider returning to work. If the person does decide to return to work, he or she might be helped by the development of some awareness regarding the likely job complications that may occur due to the presence of specific mild deficits. Another patient might have had a mild head injury and is experiencing a variety of psychosocial complications. Assessment might focus on his or her readiness for psychotherapy by considering awareness of deficits, motivation to change, and capacity for abstract reasoning. Another patient with a more serious but moderate head injury might need to be evaluated to determine capacity for self-care.

Patients with brain dysfunction are frequently considered for neuropsychological *rehabilitation.* This typically involves a careful consideration of their relative strengths and weaknesses, thereby enabling rehabilitation practitioners to ideally capitalize on the patients' strengths and improve their weaknesses. Unless these areas are clearly evaluated, rehabilitation efforts may be ineffective. For example, patients with poor awareness of their deficits might be placed in a module to improve their attention. Because they are only minimally aware of their deficits, they might be poorly motivated, which could result in little improvement. Another patient might be experiencing a number of brain-related personality changes. This person's rehabilitation might include working with the family to accommodate these changes. A school-age child who is experiencing learning difficulties would require evaluation to more fully understand the nature of his or her difficulties. Once these difficulties are understood in more detail, special education teachers can focus their interventions around the child's difficulties. Finally, monitoring a patient's progress as she or he works through and is later discharged from a program is an important role of neuropsychology. This monitoring role might have important implications for the patient, but it would also help researchers to more fully evaluate specific types of programs for different types of patients.

Neuropsychologists have become increasingly involved in *legal proceedings.* One of their primary roles has been to document the causes, nature, and severity of brain dysfunction in personal injury cases. For example, litigation might stem from damage allegedly caused by a car accident in which the injury was caused by another driver who has been found to be at fault. Alternatively, a large company might not have taken appropriate safety measures to protect employees from exposure to neurotoxic substances. A neuropsychologist might be requested to assess the possible presence and extent of brain dysfunction as well as the patient's potential for recovery. Another scenario might involve neuropsychological assessment to determine the capacity of patients to defend themselves during legal proceedings. Another patient might have committed a violent crime and need to be assessed to determine whether there were mitigating organic factors such as epilepsy that might have influenced the patient's actions.

These four areas demonstrate the wide variety of information related to neuropsychological assessment. It should be apparent that such evaluations involve considerably more than just psychological testing. The competent neuropsychologist needs to draw on a wide variety of knowledge areas including abnormal psychology, psychological testing, functional neuroanatomy, neurological disorders, disability issues, community resources, and vocational and educational options. Competent evaluations also involve taking a flexible, creative, problem-oriented approach toward working with individual clients.

The field of neuropsychological assessment has traditionally been organized around the following perspectives: specialized neuropsychological tests, domains of functioning, types of disorders, or a functional assessment of the different lobes of the brain. Each of these facets or angles of approach has various strengths and weaknesses. The emphasis in this book is on developing a working knowledge of the most frequently used neuropsychological tests. This approach is familiar to most psychologists, provides relative ease of learning, and can potentially cover a wide band of areas. The danger is that practitioners learning neuropsychology from such a test-oriented focus might rely too much on tests rather than on having the tests function as tools to assist in solving client-related problems. Thus their reports might end up being "test driven" rather than "person driven." Efforts are made throughout the book to correct for this by emphasizing the importance of integrating information from a wide variety of sources, including history, behavioral observations, and medical records. In addition, there is an emphasis on refining the referral question(s) to assist in making decisions related to a client. Further emphasis is given to presenting data according to functional domains (memory, executive functions, etc.) as well as to providing answers to specific referral questions. It is believed that this emphasis will keep clinicians focused on people and their lives rather than on the tools-tests used to understand these people.

Clinicians should also broaden their competencies by becoming familiar with other perspectives of clinical neuropsychology. In particular, client functions, and the tests that measure these functions, can be organized according to different domains, the most important of which are memory and learning, mental activity (attention and processing speed), visuoconstructive abilities, verbal functions and academic skills, motor performance, executive functions, and emotional status (see Groth-Marnat, 1999; Lezak, 1995). This approach has the advantage of organizing a client's functions into logical groupings which can relate both to specific tests as well as to client problems. Accordingly, this domain-based approach is also emphasized throughout the book. Test descriptions and test selection focus on functional domains as do issues related to treatment planning and the format of psychological reports.

One perspective is to focus either on knowledge of specific types of clinical syndromes or on different types of disorders, along with how these syndromes or disorders might be assessed. For example, various syndromes might include aphasia, alexia, agraphia, acalculias, body scheme disturbances, agnosia, or neglect (see Heilman & Valenstein, 1993). Information might also be organized according to the considerations that are relevant for such disorders including head injuries, learning disabilities, epilepsy, stroke, or exposure to neurotoxic substances. Through an understanding of these syndromes-disorders, a clinician can be guided through the interview-and-assessment process. In some instances, the nature of the disorder is emphasized above and beyond issues related to measurement. In other cases, specialized batteries have been developed for assessing specific syndromes. This is especially true for aphasia, dementia, and neurotoxicity.

Yet another approach is to understand the client and the assessment procedures according to the different lobes of the brain (see Kolb & Whishaw, 1996; Walsh, 1991). Knowledge essential for this approach is understanding the types of symptoms that might emerge from damage to a particular lobe as well as the procedures used to assess for these symptoms. For example, parietal lobe injury frequently results in such difficulties as deficits in naming things from touch (tactile **agnosia**), difficulty constructing (**constructional apraxia**), disorders of drawing, and right-left confusion. Specific tests to measure these functions might include tests of drawing (Bender Visual Motor Gestalt Test, Rey-Osterrith Complex Figure Test), ability to recognize objects from touch (Tactual Performance Test, Sensory Perceptual Examination), or measures of the ability to distinguish right from left. Competent neuropsychological assessment requires a working knowledge of each of the perspectives mentioned previously.

ORGANIZATION OF THE BOOK

When working with a client, neuropsychologists typically become involved with a series of processes. This begins with clarifying the referral question, developing initial hypotheses, conducting an interview, selecting and administering tests, interpreting test results, and integrating relevant information into a case-focused, problem-oriented psychological report. Accordingly, the book is organized around each of these steps in such a way as to guide practitioners through the different stages of neuropsychological assessment. Chapters 1 and 2 cover basic orienting information related to such areas as understanding the context of neuropsychological assessment, refining the referral question, selecting appropriate tests, and general guidelines for assessment. Chapter 3 briefly reviews basic information on neurological disorders and neurological methods of diagnosis. Chapter 4 covers both unstructured and structured methods of obtaining relevant client information through interview.

Chapters 5 to 14 (the central and major portion of the book) introduce, review, and provide interpretative guidelines on the most frequently used tests and test batteries in clinical neuropsychology. The major test batteries, in order of presentation in the book, are the Wechsler intelligence scales, Wechsler Memory Scales, Halstead-Reitan Neuropsychological Test Battery, and the Luria-Nebraska Neuropsychological Test Battery. Frequently used tests according to functional domains are the Rey Auditory Verbal Learning Test and Rey-Osterrith Complex Figure Test (memory and learning); Boston Naming, Woodcock-Johnson Psychoeducational Battery Wide Range Achievement Test and Controlled Oral Word Association Test (language functions and academic skills); Paced Auditory Serial Addition Test and Stroop (mental activities); Bender Visual Motor Gestalt (visuoconstructive abilities); and the Minnesota Multiphasic Personality Inventory (emotional functioning). Each chapter includes discussions of strategies for assessing the respective domain of functioning. These discussions define the domains themselves along with ways that other tests and procedures can be used to further assess the domain. Often tests will be referred to which were included in the chapters on test batteries. For example, the chapter on memory and learning (Chapter 9) discusses the Wechsler Memory Scales along with the Digit Symbol/Coding subtests from the Wechsler intelligence scales. An additional chapter on executive functions has been included due to the importance of this aspect of assessment (Chapter 13). However, no specific tests have been included due to the multifaceted nature of assessing executive abilities and to the fact that specific tests have not been found to be particularly helpful.

Over the past 15 years, neuropsychological rehabilitation has become progressively more important. Along with this emphasis has emerged knowledge on test results and treatment planning. Accordingly, Chapter 15 provides a systematic approach to tailoring client information around client management and rehabilitation planning. The last chapter (Chapter 16) provides a format for integrating test results into a concise, case-focused neuropsychological report. Examples of reports from the three most frequently encountered contexts (differential diagnosis, treatment planning, legal) have been included.

PATTERNS OF TEST USE IN NEUROPSYCHOLOGY

During the past 30 years, surveys in the general area of professional psychology have carefully documented the patterns of test use. Noteworthy findings are that these patterns have changed little and that often the selection of tests is based more on perceived clinical utility and tradition than on the strength of empirical support. The most frequently used tests have consistently been the Wechsler intelligence scales, Minnesota Multiphasic Personality Inventory, Bender Visual Motor Gestalt, Rorschach, Thematic Apperception Test, Projective drawings (all kinds), Millon Multiaxial Clinical Inventory, California Psychological Inventory, and the Beck Depression Inventory (Lubin, Larsen, & Matarazzo, 1984; Piotrowski & Zalewski, 1993; Watkins, Campbell, Nieberding, & Hallmark, 1995).

In contrast to the general field of professional psychology, neuropsychology has not been surveyed until relatively recently. Existing surveys indicate that test use varies according to whether the professionals surveyed are specialty neuropsychologists (versus more general practitioners who also offer neuropsychological services), the region (U.S. patterns versus international patterns), context (forensic versus general neuropsychological), or theoretical orientation. Summarizing across surveys indicates that the two tests that most frequently emerge are the Wechsler Adult Intelligence Scale-Revised (WAIS-R) and the Wechsler Memory Scale (revised and original forms). Other frequently used tests are the following: partial Halstead-Reitan Battery (particularly Trail Making and Finger Tapping), Minnesota Multiphasic Personality Inventory, Wide Range Achievement Test, Rey Auditory Verbal Learning Test, Bender Visual Motor Gestalt, full Halstead-Reitan Battery, Luria Nebraska Battery, Wisconson Card Sorting, and the Rey-Osterrith Complex Figure (Butler, Retzlaff, & Vanderploeg, 1991; Guilmette, Faust, Hart, & Arkes, 1990; Lees-Haley, Smith, Williams, & Dunn, 1995; Retzlaff, Butler, & Vanderploeg, 1992; Sullivan & Bowden, 1997; Sweet, Moberg, & Westergaard, 1996). Most neuropsychologists use a core battery comprised of either their preferred tests or a formally developed battery, particularly the Halstead-Reitan. They also routinely supplement their assessments with additional tests of memory, of speech and language, and of visuospatial, psychomotor, executive, and personality functioning. The selection of these supplemental tests is based on the type of additional information that needs to be obtained. In order to collect actual test data, the majority (between 59% and 69%) of neuropsychologists use technicians, although nearly all of them (97%) conduct the interview themselves (Sweet et al., 1996).

A more detailed analysis of test usage has been derived by considering theoretical orientation. Specifically, different patterns of test usage have been found associated with eclectic, hypothesis testing, process, and Halstead-Reitan orientations (Retzlaff et al., 1992). All orientations were consistent in giving strong support for using the Wechsler intelligence scales. As would be expected, neuropsychologists endorsing an eclectic orientation (34% of persons surveyed) did not endorse any one test or test battery but instead selected tests from a wide variety of options. Thirty-one percent of respondents endorsed a hypothesis testing approach and were more likely to avoid the Halstead-Reitan tests and to instead use the Wide Range Achievement Test, Rey Auditory Verbal Learning Test, Rey-Osterrith Complex Figure Test, Wechsler Memory Scales, Boston Naming, California Verbal Learning Test, Wisconson Card Sorting, Controlled Oral Word Association Test, and Token Test. Neuropsychologists using a process approach (25% of those surveyed) were most likely to use Trail Making, Finger Tapping, Wide Range Achievement Test, Wechsler Memory Scales, California Verbal Learning Test, Rey-Osterrith Complex Figure Test, Wisconsin Card Sorting, Boston Naming, Boston Diagnostic Aphasia, and the Rey Auditory Verbal Learning Test. The Halstead-Reitan approach was endorsed by 20% of respondents, who, as would be expected, were most likely to use the Halstead-Reitan battery along with the Minnesota Multiphasic Personality Inventory, Wide Range Achievement Test, and, to a lesser extent, the Wechsler Memory Scales. The preceding discussion strongly indicates that the clearest clusters are the Halstead-Reitan approach on the one hand and the hypothesis-testing and the process approaches on the other hand. These two latter approaches seemed to have considerable overlap in the tests they preferred to use. It should also be noted that a recent survey indicates that the fixed-battery approach is now used by only 14% of those surveyed (Sweet et al., 1996). This suggests that flexible, hypothesis-testing approaches are becoming the dominant trend in neuropsychology. The existing surveys also suggest that there is more diversity in neuropsychology than in the more general area of clinical psychology.

HISTORY AND DEVELOPMENT OF CLINICAL NEUROPSYCHOLOGY

Neuropsychological assessment as a well-defined discipline began in the 1950s with the work of Halstead, Reitan, and Goldstein in the United States, Rey in France, and Luria in the Soviet Union. Within the United States, the experimental and statistical orientation of American psychology was clearly reflected in test design and use. Norms were refined and used for comparisons with an individual patient's performance. Optimal cutoff scores were developed to distinguish impaired from normal performance. In particular, the Halstead-Reitan Neuropsychological Test Battery (HRB) grew out of Ward Halstead's selection of 27 tests that he believed measured cerebral functioning and "biological intelligence." Halstead reduced the 27 tests to 10 tests, which Reitan (1955) later reduced to 7. Cutoff scores were developed on these tests, and, based on the proportion of tests in the impaired range, an Impairment Index was calculated. Downward extensions have been developed for children aged 9 to 15 (Halstead Neuropsychological Test Battery for Children and Allied Procedures) and aged 5 to 9 (Reitan-Indiana Neuropsychological Test Battery for Children).

Early success was achieved with the HRB in distinguishing not only the presence of brain damage, but also the location and nature of existing lesions (Reitan, 1955). During the days before sophisticated neuroradiological techniques, this was extremely useful information. These efforts emerged into an emphasis on what has sometimes been referred to as the three L's of neuropsychology: Lesion detection, Localization, and Lateralization. In contrast, there was relative neglect in the study of diffuse impairment in favor of the stronger emphasis on focal involvement.

Concomitant with the developments in the United States was the work of Alexander Luria in the Soviet Union and of Rey in France. Luria and Rey relied extensively on close patient observation and in-depth case histories. They were not so much interested in what score a person might have obtained but rather in why he or she performed in a certain manner. Their work emphasized and laid the groundwork for the flexible pathognomonic sign or qualitative approach. Rather than developing a series of quantitatively oriented tests with optimal cutoff scores, Luria developed a series of procedures that he believed would help the client to express relevant behavioral domains. As such, his approach relied far more heavily on clinician expertise and observation than on formal psychometric data. A.-L. Christensen (1979) later organized Luria's procedures into a flexible, hypothesis-testing format, which has been summarized into a text, manual of instructions, and test cards. Golden, Purisch, and Hammeke (1985) also formalized Luria's procedures into the standardized but less flexible Luria-Nebraska Neuropsychological Battery.

From these early beginnings, there emerged two distinct strategies of approaching neuropsychological assessment. One was the comprehensive battery approach epitomized by Halstead and Reitan and formalized into the HRB. The other was a more flexible, qualitative, hypothesis testing strategy as represented by Rey, Goldstein, and Luria. Each of these approaches has different strengths and weaknesses (see Bauer, 1995; Jarvis & Barth, 1994; Russell, 1995, 1998). The battery approach has the advantages of providing an assessment of a broad spectrum of behaviors and assessing both strengths and weaknesses. It is easier to use for research, is more extensively normed and researched, can be administered by trained technicians, and is easier for students to learn. Its disadvantages are that it is typically quite time consuming, may overlook the underlying reasons why a client obtained a specific score, and is more difficult to tailor toward the unique aspects of the client and the referral question. The advantages of the contrasting qualitative hypothesis-testing approach are that it can be tailored to the specifics of the client and the referral question, emphasizes the processes underlying a client's performance rather than a final score, and is quite time efficient. Measurements of a client's strengths and weaknesses or of certain reasons for ambiguous responses can be pursued in more depth according to decisions made by the examiner. Weaknesses frequently attributed to this approach are that, in practice, it focuses on a client's weaknesses, relies too extensively on clinician expertise, is more difficult to research, is not as extensively researched, and provides a narrower slice of a client's domains of functioning.

The preceding description is somewhat polarized in that it does not do justice to the fact that in actual practice most practitioners use a combination of approaches. Whereas HRB practitioners focus extensively on test scores, they also consider various hypotheses along with relevant qualitative responses (client response to failure, quality of drawings, etc.). Similarly, practitioners emphasizing a flexible, hypothesis-testing approach test not only to further understand the idiosyncrasies of client responses, but also to pay close attention to the scores clients achieve. Thus, it is more a question of emphasis than of blind adherence to a given tradition. In addition, there is increasing support within the neuropsychological community for a flexible-fixed battery comprised of a relatively short fixed or core battery combined with additional flexible tests that are selected based on the uniqueness of the client and the specifics of the referral questions (Benton, 1992; Sweet et al., 1996). Consistent with this integration of approaches is the finding of Retzlaff et al. (1992) that the greatest percentage of neuropsychologists (34%) identify with an eclectic orientation. A further development that suggests an integration between the approaches has been the development of objective, in-depth, computerized scoring systems that can help to understand the underlying qualitative processes a client makes in responding to test items (i.e., scoring for the California Verbal Learning Test; Delis, Kramer, Kaplan, & Ober, 1987).

Perhaps reflective of this integration of traditions is the process approach, which in many ways is a synthesis between the qualitative, hypothesis-testing approach and formal psychometric methods. The process approach relies on neuropsychological tests with strong psychometric properties. However, its main distinction is the development of procedures to evaluate the process a client undergoes when responding to the test materials. As such, it is quite closely aligned with the qualitative, hypothesis-testing approach. One of the major developments of the process approach has been specialized administrations and analyses of the WAIS-R (WAIS-R Neurological Impairment or WAIS-R NI; Kaplan, Fein, Morris, & Delis, 1991) and WISC-III PI (Kaplan, Fein, Morris, Kramer, & Delis, 1999). For example, administration of the Block Design subtest includes a superimposed grid to determine if this external structure enhances performance. Information retrieval difficulties might be assessed by using a multiple-choice adjunct to the information subtest. Patients who once knew the answers but had difficulty retrieving them would be expected to perform considerably better on the multiple-choice version, which requires recognition, a task that is easier than retrieval.

Concurrent with the development of the early testing procedures and batteries, there was also an emphasis on brief screening instruments. The Bender Visual Motor Gestalt Test, or simply the Bender Gestalt Test, was one of the earliest of these. It was first developed by Lauretta Bender in 1938 and is comprised of nine designs that a client is requested to reproduce. A similar but more complex visuoconstructive test was originally devised by Rey in 1941 and was expanded by Osterrith in 1944 (Osterrith, 1944; Rey, 1941). It has since been refined and is referred to as the Rey-Osterrith Complex Figure Test. Patients are requested first to complete the drawing while it is directly in front of them and then to make a second reproduction of the drawing from memory. Rey also developed the Rey Auditory-Verbal Learning Test (Rey, 1964), which screens for difficulties with short-term verbal memory. Clients are instructed to listen to a series of items that is read to them and then to repeat back as many of the items as possible. One final example of an early screening test for attentional difficulties is the Stroop procedure (Stroop, 1935). This test presents clients with a series of color names that are written in colored ink different from the written name of the color given. For example, the name green might be written in red ink. The client is then requested to read through the list and give the name of the color of the ink (i.e., red) rather than merely reading the word (i.e., green).

During the 1970s and 1980s, many screening procedures were combined to form short assessment batteries. For example, Wysocki and Sweet (1985) developed a seven-test battery comprised of Trail Making, finger-tapping speed, drawing a Greek cross, the Pathognomonic Scale of the Luria-Nebraska Neuropsychological Battery, the Stroop, and the Logical Memory and Visual Reproduction subtests of the Wechsler Memory Scale. Total administration time is approximately 60 minutes. Another representative screening system is the BNI Screen for Higher Cerebral Functions (Prigatano, Amin, & Rosenstein, 1992). The test is given to determine if a patient is capable of taking other neuropsychological tests, to evaluate their level of self-awareness, to provide qualitative information regarding cognitive functioning, and to assess a wide range of cerebral functions. The entire procedure typically takes 10 to 15 minutes to complete. There have also been two abbreviated versions of the HRB by Golden (1976) and Erickson, Caslyn, and Scheupbach (1978). Such tests are currently undergoing careful empirical scrutiny to determine which ones are relatively more sensitive for various types of patients (i.e., Chouinard & Braun, 1993).

During the 1980s and into the 1990s, clinical neuropsychology moved from being primarily an assessment discipline to becoming increasingly concerned with interventions primarily within the context of rehabilitation. A 1995 survey indicated that 64% of neuropsychologists were involved with treating patients with brain dysfunction (Sweet et al., 1996). Rehabilitation has typically occurred within the context of multidisciplinary teams often in day-treatment settings. Neuropsychological activities have included cognitive retraining, memory training, visual-spatial training, and individual, group, and family therapy. These activities have typically occurred and been integrated with interventions from psychiatrists and physiatrists along with speech, occupational, physical, and recreational therapists. However, many interventions have not been fully validated and frequently suffer from outcome measures unrelated to ecological validity. Clinical neuropsychology is currently in the process of carefully evaluating which methods do or do not have demonstrated benefits to patients (Carney et al., 1999).

CURRENT TRENDS AND PATTERNS

New technology, emerging research, the impact of managed health care, and legal challenges have combined to create several current trends in clinical neuropsychology. These include computerized approaches, greater emphasis on understanding the nature of deficits (versus presence of brain damage), greater focus on application, organization of results around functional domains, and the development of test batteries specific to certain conditions. In particular, computerized techniques hold considerable promise (Groth-Marnat & Schumaker, 1989; Kane & Kay, 1992). They have the potential to reduce costs by reducing direct clinician (or technician) contact through computerized administration. They might also reduce clinician time through computers assisting clinicians during assessment to generate hypotheses and, based on these hypotheses, to select future optimal assessment procedures (Hammainen, 1994). Tailoring item presentation based on previous responses in combination with various decision rules might result in a highly efficient means of gathering information. In addition, computer-assisted interpretation enables tentative interpretations to be based on a large database. As a result, several fully automated batteries are routinely used particularly in large organizational contexts such as the military and the Federal Aviation Administration (see Kane & Kay, 1992). Often these batteries have focused on particular types of problems. For example, COGSCREEN has been used in the selection of airline pilots; the military's UTCPAB was developed to assess the impact of drugs on the workplace; and the Neurobehavioral Evaluation System is particularly sensitive to the impact of environmental toxins.

Computerized batteries are being used more frequently, but they currently do not have the extensive validation associated with the more traditional tests such as the Halstead Reitan batteries. Even though computerized administration and interpretation procedures hold considerable promise, they still are not being used nearly as often as the more familiar individually administered neuropsychological tests or test batteries (Butler et al., 1991; Lees-Haley et al., 1995; Lezak, 1995). Furthermore, computerized administrations may not necessarily produce the same results as their clinician-administered versions (Van Schijndel & van der Vlugt, 1992). A further issue is that computer-generated interpretations need to be treated with considerable caution. Clinicians should consider all interpretations within the unique context of each client; they should avoid potentially obsolete software; and they should critically evaluate how the interpretations were generated within the software itself (Groth-Marnat, 1985; Groth-Marnat & Schumaker, 1989). Computer-based interpretations, then, should not be used to replace the clinician, but more appropriately to widen the number of interpretive possibilities.

Throughout the earlier history of clinical neuropsychology, a typical goal was to differentiate between organic difficulties and functional difficulties. Thus, a referral question was sometimes expressed in terms of "ruling out organicity" or of "differentiating" between organic and functional causes. More recently, the appropriateness of this goal, and the assumptions behind it, has been questioned. Leonberger (1989) has pointed out that there has been a gradual disintegration of the distinction between many functional and organic disorders. For example, early conceptualizations of schizophrenia considered it to be functional. In contrast, current research supports the presence of strong biochemical and structural correlates in a substantial portion of people with schizophrenia (Heinrichs, 1993; Raz & Raz, 1990; Weinberger & Berman, 1988). In addition, recent advances in neuroradiological and other neurologically oriented techniques have greatly refined the diagnosis of brain damage. As a result, the use of neuropsychological techniques in diagnosis has become deemphasized. In contrast, referrals from neurologists and psychiatrists are more likely to request information regarding the nature of already identified lesions. This is consistent with a 1990 survey that identified that the second most frequent reason to conduct a neuropsychological assessment is evaluating a client's work capacity (Guilmette et al., 1990). Finally, the biopsychosocial model for understanding disfunction emphasizes the dynamic interplay between biological, psychological, and social factors.

A further change over time has been that, rather than focusing on measurement, there has been greater emphasis on application (Johnstone & Farmer, 1997; Ponsford, 1988). Thus it is no longer sufficient to merely state that a client is experiencing cognitive deficits in certain areas. Instead, more functionally relevant areas are being evaluated, such as the client's employability, responsiveness to rehabilitation, and the need for certain types of environmental supports. This change in emphasis can be clarified by considering the differences between impairment and disability. *Impairment* typically reflects normative comparisons and test data. In contrast, the more functionally relevant term *disability* more closely takes into account the context of the client, including his or her circumstances, environment, and interests. For example, a client might be statistically in the mildly impaired range on tests requiring sequencing. If he or she was a computer programmer, this difficulty would result in a disability. In contrast, another client with different interests might not find this problem to be a disability. This means that there are increasing expectations on clinicians to work with both the test data and the specifics of the client to translate the impact of any test-related impairment on the level to which they might be disabled. This may also require using methods of analysis other than psychological tests, such as the ratings of relatives, ward observation charts, and simulations (Knight & Godfrey, 1996; Ponsford, 1988; Sbordone & Long, 1996).

Because the preceding questions related to a client's real-life functioning are becoming more important, neuropsychology is working to more clearly address the empirical basis for the inferences clinicians make from test scores to client functioning (Matarazzo, 1990). In other words, test results can actually predict how a specific client will adapt to a vocational, community, educational, interpersonal or, rehabilitation context. Whereas neuropsychologists are typically quite comfortable discussing test data, it is often necessary to stretch the meaning and empirical basis between scores and areas of real-life functioning. This difficulty often becomes most noticeable during legal proceedings when neuropsychologists are challenged to provide empirical support for their inferences. This is particularly an issue when a patient claims significant deficits with little corresponding objective medical evidence (i.e., computerized tomography scans indicating lesions, loss of consciousness surrounding the injury). The issue of test scores not relating sufficiently to real-life behaviors has been an important and welcome trend in neuropsychology since it has forced neuropsychologists to integrate past research and generate new research into establishing the ecological validity of assessment procedures. Currently there are available reviews of the ability of neuropsychological assessment to predict real-life behavior for such areas as attentional capacity, executive functions, perceptual abilities, memory, and personality (see Acker, 1990; Bowman, 1996; Crepeau & Scherzer, 1993; Groth-Marnat & Teal, in press; Sbordone & Long, 1996; Vilkki et al., 1994). Some of the research is quite supportive, whereas other literature indicates that neuropsychology needs to make considerable progress.

Consistent with issues related to ecological validity is that more recent emphasis has not been so much on measuring the presence of brain damage but rather on assessing different functional domains, which might include such areas as memory, visuoconstructive abilities, mental activity, verbal functions, executive functions, and emotional status. Thus "brain sensitive" screening tests should not be considered to be tests of brain damage but rather tests of certain functions that *may* be consistent with central nervous system (CNS) involvement. Clearly this means that, instead of using single tests, neuropsychological assessment should ideally use several instruments that assess different domains. Thus, the emphasis throughout this book is to organize and integrate the assessment results around different functional domains. Such an organization more easily allows clinicians to make inferences related to the client's functioning within vocational, community, educational, or interpersonal contexts.

One issue with this domain-based approach is that typically neuropsychological tests do not clearly fit into specific, well-delineated domains. A test such as Digit Symbol-Coding measures a wide variety of abilities, including processing speed, visual short-term memory, rote learning, flexibility, and sequencing. Although Digit Symbol-Coding is often categorized as a measure of processing speed, it might arguably be placed into another domain category, such as visuospatial ability or memory. More importantly, one patient might have the same score on Digit Symbol-Coding as another one but the reason for the score might be quite different (i.e., slow processing speed versus poor memory). Dodrill (1997) has provided psychometric support related to poor test specificity by emphasizing that the median correlation for common neuropsychological tests *within* domain groupings was .52, whereas the median correlation *between* groupings was .44. If the tests were specific to certain abilities (and not to others), it would be expected that the median correlations within groupings would be higher and that median correlations between groupings would be lower. This clearly suggests that the primary tools for assessment are not measuring specific domains/abilities as clearly as practitioners conceptualize them as doing.

In the past, most clinical neuropsychologists were content to use a selection of their preferred tests on most clients whom they assessed. More recently, there has been the development of recommended collections of tests for specific types of disorders. An important rationale for this is that there are often certain tests that are either quite sensitive to the presence of a particular condition or that provide essential information related to that condition. Each battery will usually use a combination of previously developed tests such as Trail Making and portions of the WAIS-III. For example, specialized batteries for the evaluation of neurotoxicity are the California Neuropsychological Screening Battery (Bowler, Thaler, & Becker, 1986), Pittsburgh Occupational Exposure Test (Ryan, Morrow, Parkinson, & Branet, 1987), and the Individual Neuropsychological Testing for Neurotoxicity Battery (Singer, 1990). Assessment and monitoring of some of the more important domains of dementia might be achieved with the CERAD Battery (Morris et al., 1989) or the Dementia Assessment Battery (Corkin et al., 1986). A similar specialized battery for detecting the early signs of AIDS-related dementia is the NIMH Core Neuropsychological Battery (Butters et al., 1990). It is likely that there will be the continued development of additional batteries tailored to optimally assess specific disorders or conditions.

Neuropsychologists have traditionally attempted to understand brain functioning by measuring cognitive changes following lesions to specific regions of the brain. This tradition was set in the early 1800s by Broca who noted that patients with lesions on the lateral slope of the left prefrontal cortex typically experienced difficulties with symbol formation along with difficulties producing speech in an orderly manner. Although this "lesion behavior" correlational approach is well established, it does not reflect developments in a wide variety of technologies. Indeed, clinical neuropsychology is struggling to integrate the findings and implications from diverse technologies that include not only the older electroencephalograms (EEGs) and computerized tomography (CT) but also more recent techniques, such as magnetic resonance imaging (MRI), event-related potentials (ERPs), cerebral blood flow (CBF), positron emission tomography (PET), and single positron emission tomography (SPECT; Bigler, 1991). For example, Chase et al. (1984) used PET scans to study the glucose metabolism associated with various performances on the WAIS-R. They found Block Design performance was associated with greater metabolism in the right postereoparietal region. In contrast, performance on the Comprehension subtest was primarily associated with increased metabolism in the left hemisphere but with some associated right hemisphere activation associated with right hemisphere speech and language centers. A somewhat similar strategy found that cognitive processes associated with generating the names for objects were associated with activation of the frontal cortex (Zelkowicz, Herbster, Nebes, Mintun, & Becker, 1998). As more techniques are focused on specific clinical phenomenon, neuropsychology may not only undergo considerable advances in knowledge, but may even alter how patients are assessed. One technique that holds considerable promise is "importance modeling," which rates different brain structures on a continuum based on their relative importance to performance measures (Turkheimer, Yeo, & Bigler, 1990).

THE STATUS OF CLINICAL NEUROPSYCHOLOGY

During the past 30 years, clinical neuropsychology has evolved from a minor subspecialty of professional psychology to a well-developed, major, international discipline. There are now more than six journals devoted exclusively to clinical neuropsychology. Neuropsychology is also extremely multidisciplinary and draws from the knowledge base of neurology/neurosurgery, psychiatry, rehabilitation, occupational therapy, speech therapy, physical therapy, and neuroscience, as well as physiological, clinical, counseling, cognitive, and developmental psychology. Thus, neuropsychologists are likely to be involved with treatment teams or, if not directly involved with treatment teams, typically network with a variety of different health professionals. Whereas the discipline was initially concerned with assessment, more recently it has become progressively focused on methods of psychotherapy and rehabilitation. The dominant assessment methodology has become either an eclectic or a flexible-battery approach (Retzlaff et al., 1992; Sweet et al., 1996).

Many neuropsychologists believe training should most appropriately occur at the postdoctoral level and should be a proficiency stemming from clinical psychology (Sweet et al., 1996). In contrast, recent guidelines emphasize that neuropsychology as a speciality should begin at the doctoral level and extend into an internship and residency (Hannay et al., 1998). Additional guidelines are being developed for subspecialities within neuropsychology, which will most likely include child, pediatric, geriatric, and rehabilitation. Within the United States, it is estimated that specialty doctoral, internship, and postdoctoral programs graduate a combined total of over 400 neuropsychology graduates per year (Mathews, 1996).

The preceding overview attests to neuropsychology as a vital, robust, growing discipline. However, the bedrock of any discipline ultimately depends on the extent to which it is has sufficient scientific support. This has become a particular issue in neuropsychology due to challenges to such vital areas as the reliability and validity of judgments, value of training in increasing judgment accuracy, and the appropriateness of neuropsychologists appearing as expert witnesses (Faust, 1991; Faust, Guilmette, Hart, Arkes, & Fishburn, 1988; Faust, Ziskin, & Hiers, 1991). The result has been that clinical neuropsychology has been through and continues to undergo a clear, sobering, and often critical reevaluation. Areas of particular importance are the reliability and validity of clinical judgment, ecological validity of measures, the importance of clinical experience, and the ability to detect malingering.

Reliability for judgments based on standardized neuropsychological tests is good to excellent (Garb & Schramke, 1996). Representative results indicate that interrater reliability for judging the presence or absence of impairment ranged from a low of .65 to a high of .94, and the rating of laterality of impairment was .84 (Garb, 1998; Garb & Schramke, 1996). More specific interrater ratings for cognitive domains were somewhat lower but still good (high of .88 for intelligence to a low of .53 for attention; Brown, Del Dotto, Fisk, Taylor, & Breslau, 1993). Intertest ratings between the HRB/WAIS and LNNB were .64 for the presence of brain damage, .72 for identifying the hemisphere involved, and .65 for ratings of more specific locations (left frontal, right temporal, etc.; Diamont & Hijmen, 1981). The preceding data refers to standardized battery approaches. Due to wide variation in using flexible approaches, no reliability data is currently available.

Validity for test batteries and for individual tests varies according to each test and according to the purpose and population for which it is being used. For example, WAIS-R factor scores (Verbal Comprehension, Perceptual Organization, Freedom from Distractibility) have good construct validity based on correlations with relevant neuropsychological tests (Sherman, Strauss, Spellacy, & Hunter, 1995). A meta-analytic review of tests indicated that the Stroop, Facial Recognition, Wechsler Memory-Visual delayed subtest, Grooved Pegboard, and Rey-Osterrith Complex Figure tests were particularly good at detecting diffuse damage (Chouinard & Braun, 1993). Another meta-analysis of 77 studies by Christensen, Hadzi-Pavlovic, and Jacomb (1991) found that neuropsychological tests were quite effective at differentiating patients with mild, moderate, or severe dementia from older people without dimentia (effect size = .68). The differentiations made with neuropsychological tests are quite clearly far more accurate than differentiations based on interviews or informal observations (i.e., Roca, Klein, & Vogelsang, 1982; S. Schwartz & Wiedel, 1981). More detailed information on test validity can be found and reviewed in the following chapters on each of the tests.

Clinical neuropsychologists typically make judgments in which they rely heavily on test results. In order to research this process, it has been necessary to standardize information given to each judge prior to the making of final conclusions. In many ways, this is an artificial task because it means clinicians are not given relevant behavioral observations, details related to the context of the assessment, or additional idiosyncratic features of the subject. The result might be that judgment accuracy is likely to be significantly lower in the artificial research situation than in actual clinical contexts. A further issue with this line of research is the ultimate yardstick or "Gold standard" to compare clinician judgments. For example, CT scans might indicate focal lesions but might miss diffuse damage. Clinicians requested to localize a lesion might have their judgment confounded if the client under question has not only diffuse impairments but also specific lesions. In these cases clinicians might technically be considered "wrong" according to CT records but might be quite accurate in that they have detected a wide range of complications above and beyond the focal ones indicated by CTs. Finally, comparison group selection can greatly alter the accuracy of judgments. If patients with moderate to severe impairments are being compared to healthy comparison groups, judgment accuracy for presence of brain damage is likely to be high. In contrast, distinguishing patients with subtle deficits from healthy controls might be a considerably more difficult task resulting in much less accuracy. Somewhat similarly, differentiating people with severe psychiatric complaints from people with brain damage might be a relatively difficult task as well. These caveats should be taken into consideration when evaluating the following conclusions of research on clinical judgment.

Validity of judgments can be organized around detecting the presence of impairment, specifying lesion location, and identifying the process and etiology of the disorder. Reviews found that the overall hit rate (correct positives + correct negatives) for detecting impairment was a respectable 84% (Garb, 1998; Garb & Schramke, 1996). However, the level of accuracy across studies varied considerably. In addition, 21% of subjects were false positives (nonimpaired incorrectly classified as impaired) with a false negative rate of 14% (unimpaired incorrectly identified as impaired). As would be expected, clinicians who made the finer distinction of location of impairment (diffuse, right, left, left-anterior, etc.) had lower average hit rates, ranging from 68% to 70% (Garb, 1998; Garb & Schramke, 1996). Hit rates were a lower 60% to 64% when evaluating whether the condition was static or progressive. However, it should be noted that in practice the hit rates for acute/static differentiation should be considerably higher if the client is given repeat testing to monitor changes over time. Considerable variation has been reported when judgments were made on the specific etiology of the impairment (i.e., head injury, Alzheimer's disease, partial-complex seizures). Filskov and Goldstein (1974) reported a hit rate of 85%, and Reitan (1964) reported a similarly high hit rate of 84%. In contrast, Faust, Guilmette, et al. (1988) reported a much lower hit rate of only 23%.

The emphasis on validity refers primarily to neuropsychology's role in differential diagnosis. More recently, this focus has changed to emphasize ecologically important dimensions such as a patient's level of functioning in vocational, educational, interpersonal, and community contexts. The ability of neuropsychological procedures to predict such areas has been somewhat variable. An important reason for this is that the assessment session itself can be somewhat artificial; it is typically focused on specific tests given in a relatively structured, distraction-free environment. In contrast, real-life situations often present multiple demands on patients and require them to initiate and to organize their own behavior rather than to respond to tasks structured by the examiner. In addition, some symptoms occur intermittently and, thus, may not actually occur within the evaluation session. All this is further complicated by the fact that patients with impairments often can neither recall certain types of difficulties nor articulate them adequately, nor do they have much awareness regarding their deficits.

Although it is not possible to review all areas of ecological validity in neuropsychology, assessment of attention, memory, executive functions, and personality deserve particular comment. Attention is crucial to a wide range of everyday activities.

However, formal assessment of attention is often so narrow in its focus that the multiple demands of everyday life are not taken into account (see Chapter 11). For example, a patient might temporarily perform well on a Digit Span type task but, in real life, is relatively easily distracted by two or more competing demands. This means assessment should not only take into account traditional test scores but should also consider more demanding, complex tasks along with patient self-reports and descriptions by significant others (Kerns & Mateer, 1996). The ecological validity of memory assessment has been enhanced with the development of tests of everyday memory functions. For example, the Rivermead Behavioral Memory Test (Wilson, Cockburn, & Baddeley, 1985) includes activities such as remembering a hidden object, an appointment, faces, or details from a newspaper article. Representative validity indicates good correlations with self and family ratings (Williams, 1987), with detection of patients with formal memory disorders (Kotler-Cope, 1990), and with ability to predict degree of independence following closed head injury (Wilson, 1991).

Executive functions refer to a person's ability to anticipate behavior, to select relevant goals, to sequence his or her actions, to monitor self-behavior, and to be actually motivated to perform certain behaviors (see Chapter 13). One of the crucial features of executive functions is self-awareness. However, assessing executive function is particularly problematic because it requires approaching the client from a variety of angles. This is further complicated by the fact that there are few formal procedures that adequately or specifically measure frontal lobe/executive functioning (Bigler, 1988; Reitan & Wolfson, 1994) although the new Behavioral Assessment of Dysexecutive Symdrome (BADS; Wilson, Alderman, Burgess, Emslie, & Evans, 1999) shows some potential for fulfilling this need. The clinical literature is filled with examples of normal-looking test performance in which the client still has significant executive dysfunction (i.e., Cripe, 1996). This has resulted in no clearly accepted assessment methodology with each clinician often using idiosyncratic qualitative approaches. Consistent with this is the fact that there is little research related to the ecological validity of the assessment of executive functions despite its acknowledged research and clinical importance.

In contrast to the limited strategies for assessing executive functions, there is body of research some of which supports the importance of using tests of emotional functioning in predicting relevant everyday functioning. For example, MMPI performance among people with neuropsychological impairments has been found to predict vocational function at least as accurately as cognitive assessment (Heaton, Beade, & Johnson, 1978). Similarly, California Personality Inventory performance (Social Presence, Self Acceptance, Capacity for status) predicted job performance among patients with epilepsy, especially if combined with WAIS scores (M. Schwartz, Denneril, & Lin, 1968). More recent work has included developing more specific instruments for assessing emotional functioning among people with neuropsychological impairments (Judd & Fordyce, 1996).

It would be expected that accuracy of clinical judgment would increase with additional training and experience. However, this has been given only limited research support. A supportive study by Goldstein, Deysach, and Kleinknecht (1973) found that, following training with the Halstead-Reitan Neuropsychological Test Battery, clinician accuracy increased from 53% to 95%. In contrast, other studies found that various measures of training (hours of practicum training, percentage of internship spent on neuropsychology, completion of specialized postdoctoral fellowship, ABPP qualification) did not predict accuracy of ratings for presence/absence, location, or etiology of impairment (Faust, Guilmette, et al., 1988; Heaton, Beade, et al., 1978). One caution in interpreting the preceding equivocal results is that accuracy might be related to setting (Garb & Schramke, 1996). This would mean that under research conditions where neuropsychologists are given the same objective sets of data, there may be little opportunity for expertise to emerge. However, these same clinicians, working in their own specific clinical settings, might be able to enhance their accuracy, especially when compared with lesser trained professionals unfamiliar with the setting.

In legal contexts, particularly with personal injury and compensation cases, some patients might benefit from faking symptoms. Thus, it is crucial for neuropsychologists to be able to differentiate between actual and faked performances. However, the ability to do so has been controversial. Most formal studies have used simulated sets of faked test results and real test results that have then been ranked by neuropsychologists. The results have been generally disappointing (Faust, Hart, Guilmette, 1988; Faust, Hart, Guilmette, & Arkes, 1988; Heaton, Smith, et al., 1978; Schacter, 1986). Although these results question the ability of neuropsychologists to detect malingering, they should be accepted with considerable caution. First of all, numerous strategies have been specifically developed to detect malingering, yet they were not used in the aforementioned studies. One strategy is the use of forced choice items in which *below chance performance* indicates deliberate exaggeration of symptoms (i.e., Hiscock & Hiscock, 1989). Research has also indicated that event-related potentials could be used to detect actual from simulated memory complaints (Allen, Iacono, & Danielson, 1992; Rosenfeld et al., 1998). In order to adequately evaluate clinically relevant detection rates, these techniques need to be included as part of a test battery. In addition, neuropsychologists typically evaluate malingering within the context of the referral question. If there is the potential for malingering due to potential gain (i.e., higher compensation) combined with certain client characteristics (i.e., antisocial features), then a closer examination is warranted. This might involve careful history, ward observations, relevant personality testing, identification of patterns of inconsistent performance, symptoms that do not make neuroanatomical sense, and informal clinical testing for faking. Thus the ultimate test of a clinician's ability to detect faking should be made within the context of the referral question along with specialized techniques.

SUMMARY

Neuropsychological assessment has undergone considerable growth over the past 20 years. It has gone from a discipline primarily concerned with neuropsychodiagnosis to one which has become progressively involved with understanding the functional significance of assessment results and taking a larger responsibility for client care particularly in the rehabilitation context. Current trends also include the use of computer-assisted assessment, the development of more specialized assessment batteries, integration of knowledge from other disciplines, improving clinical judgment, ecological validity, and the accurate detection of malingering. Future challenges will be coping with the restrictions imposed by managed care (Sweet, Westergaard, & Moberg, 1995), demonstrating the financial efficacy of neuropsychological assessment (Groth-Marnat,

1999), improving treatment planning, incorporating new technologies from a wide number of areas, and re-defining the role of the clinician given developments both within the profession and changes in the delivery of health care.

RECOMMENDED READING

Garb, H.N., & Schramke, C.J. (1996). Judgment research and neuropsychological assessment: A narrative review and meta-analysis. *Psychological Bulletin, 120,* 140–153.

Heilman, K.M., & Valenstein, E. (Eds.)(1993). *Clinical neuropsychology* (3rd ed.). New York: Oxford University Press.

Kolb, B., & Whishaw, l.Q. (1996). *Fundamentals of human neuropsychology* (4th ed.). New York: W.H. Freeman.

Lezak, M. (1995). *Neuropsychological assessment* (3rd ed.). New York: Oxford University Press.

Sbordone, R.J., & Long, C.J. (1996). *Ecological validity of neuropsychological testing.* Delray Beach, FL: GR/St. Lucie Press.

Walsh, K.W. (1991). *Understanding brain damage: A primer of neuropsychological evaluation* (2nd ed.). Edinburgh: Churchill Livingstone.

REFERENCES

Acker, M.B. (1990). A review of the ecological validity of neuropsychological tests. In D.E. Tupper & K.D. Cicerone (Eds.), *The neuropsychology of everyday life: Assessment and basic competencies.* Boston: Kluwer Academic.

Allen, J.J., Iacono, W.G., & Danielson, K. (1992). The identification of concealed memories using the event-related potential and implicit behavioral measures: A methodology for prediction in the face of individual differences. *Psychophysiology, 29,* 504–522.

Bauer, R.M. (1995). The flexible battery approach to neuropsychological assessment. In R.D. Vanderploeg (Ed.), *Clinician's guide to neuropsychological assessment.* Hillsdale, NJ: Erlbaum.

Benton, A.L. (1992). Clinical neuropsychology: 1960–1990. *Journal of Clinical and Experimental Neuropsychology, 14,* 407–417.

Bigler, E.D. (1988). Frontal lobe damage and neuropsychological assessment. *Archives of Clinical Neuropsychology, 3,* 279–297.

Bigler, E.D. (1991). Neuropsychological assessment, neuroimaging, and clinical neuropsychology: A synthesis. *Archives of Clinical Neuropsychology, 6,* 113–132.

Bowler, R.M., Thaler, C.D., & Becker, C.E. (1986). California neuropsychological screening battery (CNC/B I & II). *Journal of Clinical Psychology, 42,* 946–955.

Bowman, M.L. (1996). Ecological validity of neuropsychological and other predictors following head injury. *Clinical Neuropsychologist, 10,* 382–396.

Brown, G.G., Del Dotto, J.E., Fisk, J.L., Taylor, H.G., & Breslau, N. (1993). Analyzing clinical ratings of performance on pediatric neuropsychological tests. *Clinical Neuropsychologist, 7,* 179–189.

Butler, M., Retzlaff, P., & Vanderploeg, R. (1991). Neuropsychological test usage. *Professional Psychology: Research and Practice, 22,* 510–512.

Butters, N., Grant, L., Haxby, J., Judd, L.L., Martin, A., McClleland, J., Pequgnat, W., Schacter, D., & Stover, E. (1990). Assessment of AIDS-related cognitive changes:

Recommendations of the NIMH Workgroup on neuropsychological approaches. *Journal of Clinical and Experimental Neuropsychology, 12,* 963–978.

Carney, N., Chestnut, R.M., Maynard, H., Mann, N.C., Patterson, P., & Helfand, M. (1999). Effect of cognitive rehabilitation on outcomes for persons with traumatic brain injury: A systematic review. *Journal of Head Trauma Rehabilitation, 14,* 277–307.

Corkin, S., Growden, J.H., & Sullivan, E .V. (1986). Assessing treatment effects: A neuropsychological battery. In L.W. Poon (Ed.), *Handbook for clinical assessment of older adults.* Washington, DC: American Psychological Association.

Chase, T.N., Fedio, P., Foster, N.L., Brooks, R., DiChio, G., & Mansi, L. (1984). Wechsler adult intelligence scale performance: Cortical localization by flurodeoxyglucose F18-positive emission tomography. *Archives of Neurology, 41,* 1244–1247.

Chouinard, M.J., & Braun, C.M.J. (1993). A meta-analysis of the relative sensitivity of Neuropsychological screening tests. *Journal of Clinical and Experimental Neuropsychology, 15,* 591–607.

Christensen, A.-L. (1979). *Luria's neuropsychological investigation* (2nd ed.). Denmark: Munksgaard.

Christensen, D., Hadzi-Pavlovic, D., & Jacomb, P. (1991). The psychometric differentiation of dementia from normal aging: A meta-analysis. *Psychological Assessment, 3,* 147–155.

Crepeau, F., & Scherzer, P. (1993). Predictors and indicators of work status after traumatic brain injury: A meta-analysis. *Neuropsychological Rehabilitation, 3,* 5–35.

Cripe, L.I. (1996). The ecological validity of executive function testing. In R.J. Sbordone & C.J. Long (Eds.), *Ecological validity of neuropsychological testing.* Delray Beach, FL: GR Press/St. Lucie Press.

Delis, D.C., Kramer, J.H., Kaplan, E., & Ober, B.A. (1987). *California verbal learning test: Adult version.* San Antonio, TX: Psychological Corporation.

Diamont, J.J., & Hijmen, R. (1981). Comparison of test results obtained with two neuropsychological test batteries. *Journal of Clinical Psychology, 37,* 355–358.

Dodrill, C.B. (1997). Myths of neuropsychology. *Clinical Neuropsychologist, 11,* 1–17.

Erickson, R.C., Caslyn, D.A., & Scheupbach, C.S. (1978). Abbreviating the Halstead-Reitan neuropsychological test battery. *Journal of Clinical Psychology, 42,* 946–955.

Faust, D. (1991). Forensic neuropsychology: The art of practicing a science that does not exist. *Neuropsychology Review, 2,* 205–231.

Faust, D., Guilmette, T.J., Hart, K., Arkes, H.R., & Fishburn, F.J. (1988). Neuropsychologists training, experience, and judgment accuracy. *Archives of Clinical Neuropsychology, 3,* 145–163.

Faust, D., Hart, K., & Guilmette, T.J. (1988). Pediatric malingering: The capacity of children to fake believable deficits on neuropsychological testing. *Journal of Clinical and Consulting Psychology, 56,* 578–582.

Faust, D., Hart, K., Guilmette, T.J., & Arkes, H.R. (1988). Neuropsychologists ability to detect adolescent malingerers. *Professional Psychology, 19,* 508–515.

Faust, D., Ziskin, J., & Hiers, J.B. (1991). *Brain damage claims: Coping with Neuropsychological evidence.* Los Angeles: Law & Psychology Press.

Filskov, S.B., & Goldstein, S.G. (1974). Diagnostic validity of the Halstead-Reitan neuropsychological battery. *Journal of Consulting and Clinical Psychology, 42,* 382–388.

Garb, H.N. (1998). *Studying the clinician: Judgment research and psychological assessment.* Washington, DC: American Psychological Association.

Garb, H.N., & Schramke, C.J. (1996). Judgment research and neuropsychological assessment: A narrative review and meta-analysis. *Psychological Bulletin, 120,* 140–153.

Golden, C.J. (1976). The identification of brain damage by an abbreviated form of the Halstead-Reitan neuropsychological battery. *Journal of Clinical Psychology, 32,* 821–826.

Golden, C.J., Purisch, A.D., & Hammeke, T.A. (1985). *Luria-Nebraska neuropsychological battery: Forms I and II (Manual).* Los Angeles: Western Psychological Services.

Goldstein, S.G., Deysach, R.E., & Kleinknecht, R.A. (1973). Effect of experience and amount of information on identification of cerebral impairment. *Journal of Consulting and Clinical Psychology, 41,* 33–34.

Groth-Marnat, G. (1985). Evaluating and using psychological testing software. *Human Resource Management Australia, 23,* 16–21.

Groth-Marnat, G. (1999). *Handbook of psychological assessment* (3rd Rev. ed.). New York: Wiley.

Groth-Marnat, G. (1999). Financial efficacy of clinical assessment: Rational guidelines and issues for future research. *Journal of Clinical Psychology, 55,* 813–824.

Groth-Marnat, G., & Schumaker, J. (1989). Computer-based psychological testing: Issues and guidelines. *American Journal of Orthopsychiatry, 59,* 257–263.

Groth-Marnat, G., & Teal, M. (in press). *Ecological validation of the WAIS-R block design subtest: Ability to predict everyday spatial performance. Perceptual and Motor Skills.*

Guilmette, T.J., Faust, D., Hart, K., & Arkes, H.R. (1990). A national survey of psychologists who offer neuropsychological services. *Archives of Clinical Neuropsychology, 5,* 373–392.

Hammainen, L. (1994). Computerized support for neuropsychological test interpretation in clinical situations. *Clinical Neuropsychologist, 8,* 167–185.

Hannay, H.J., Bieliauskas, L.A., Crosson, B.A., Hammeke, T.A., Hamsher, K deS., & Koffler, S.P. (1998). Proceedings of the Houston conference on specialty education and training in clinical neuropsychology. *Archives of Clinical Neuropsychology, 13,* 157–250.

Heaton, R.K., Beade, L.E., & Johnson, K.L. (1978). Neuropsychological test results associated with psychiatric disorders in adults. *Psychological Bulletin, 85,* 141–162.

Heaton, R.K., Smith, H.H., Lehman, R.A.W., & Vogt, A.T. (1978). Prospects for faking believable deficits on neuropsychological testing. *Journal of Clinical and Consulting Psychology, 46,* 892–900.

Heilman, K.M., & Valenstein, E. (Eds.). (1993). *Clinical neuropsychology* (3rd ed.). New York: Oxford University Press.

Heinrichs, R.W. (1993). Schizophrenia and the brain: Conditions for a neuropsychology of madness. *American Psychologist, 48,* 221–233.

Hiscock, M., & Hiscock, C.K. (1989). Refining the forced-choice method for the detection of malingering. *Journal of Clinical and Experimental Neuropsychology, 11,* 967–974.

Johnstone, B., & Farmer, J.E. (1997). Preparing neuropsychologists for the future: The need for additional training guidelines. *Archives of Clinical Neuropsychology, 12,* 523–530.

Jarvis, P.E., & Barth, J. (1994). *The Halstead-Reitan neuropsychological battery: A guide to interpretation and clinical application.* Odessa, FL: Psychological Assessment Resources.

Judd, T., & Fordyce, D. (1996). Personality tests. In R.J. Sbordone & C.J. Long (Eds.), *Ecological validity of neuropsychological testing.* Delray Beach, FL: GR Press/St. Lucie Press.

Kane, R.L., & Kay, G.G. (1992). Computerized assessment in neuropsychology: A review of tests and test batteries. *Neuropsychology Review, 3,* 1–117.

Kaplan, E., Fein, D., Morris, D., & Delis, D. (1991). *WAIS-R as a neuropsychological instrument.* San Antonio, TX: The Psychological Corporation.

Kerns, K.A., & Mateer, C.A. (1996). Walking and chewing gum: The impact of attentional capacity on everyday activities. In R.J. Sbordone & C.J. Long (Eds.), *Ecological validity of neuropsychological testing.* Delray Beach, FL: GR Press/St. Lucie Press.

Knight, R.G., & Godfrey, H.P.D. (1996). Psychosocial aspects of neurological disorders: Implications for research in neuropsychology. *Australian Psychologist, 31,* 48–51.

Kolb, B., & Whishaw, L.Q. (1996). *Fundamentals of human neuropsychology* (4th ed.). New York: Freeman.

Kotler-Cope, S. (1990). *Memory impairment in older adults: The relationship between objective and subjective, clinical everyday measures.* Paper presented at the annual meeting of the Southern Society for Philosophy and Psychology, Louisville, KY.

Lees-Haley, P.R., Smith, H.H., Williams, C.W., & Dunn, J.T. (1995). Forensic neuropsychological test usage: An empirical survey. *Archives of Clinical Neuropsychology, 11,* 45–51.

Leonberger, L.R. (1989). The question of organicity: Is it still functional? *Professional Psychology: Research and Practice, 20,* 411–414.

Lezak, M.D. (1976). *Neuropsychological assessment.* New York: Oxford University Press.

Lezak, M.D. (1983). *Neuropsychological assessment* (2nd ed.). New York: Oxford University Press.

Lezak, M.D. (1995). *Neuropsychological assessment* (3rd ed.). New York: Oxford University Press.

Lubin, B., Larsen, R.M., & Matarazzo, J.D. (1984). Patterns of psychological test usage in the United States: 1935–1982. *American Psychologist, 39,* 857–861.

Matarazzo, J.D. (1990). Psychological assessment versus psychological testing: Validation from Binet to the school, clinic, and courtroom. *American Psychologist, 45,* 999–1017.

Mathews, C.G. (1996). Slouching toward the millennium: Some survival prescriptions for neuropsychology. *Archives of Clinical Neuropsychology, 11,* 261–269.

Morris, J.C., Heyman, A., Mobs, R.C., Hughes, J.P., van Belle, G., Fillenbaum, G., Mellits, E.D., Vlark, C., & the CERAD investigators. (1989). The consortium to establish a registry for Alzhimer's disease. *Neurology, 39,* 1159–1165.

Osterrith, P.A. (1993). Le test de copie d'une figure complexe (J. Corwin & F.W. Byslma, Trans.). *Clinical Neuropsychologist, 7,* 9–15. (Original work published 1944)

Piotrowski, C., & Zalewski, C. (1993). Training in psychodiagnostic testing in APA approved PsyD and PhD clinical training programs. *Journal of Personality Assessment, 61,* 394–405.

Ponsford, J. (1988). Neuropsychological assessment: The need for a more pragmatic approach. *Australian Psychologist, 23,* 349–360.

Prigatano, G.P., Amin, K., & Rosenstein, L.D. (1992). *Manual for the BNI screen for higher cerebral functions.* Phoenix, AZ: Barrow Neurological Institute.

Raz, S., & Raz, N. (1990). Structural brain abnormalities in the major psychosis: A quantitative review of the evidence from computerized imaging. *Psychological Bulletin, 108,* 93–108.

Reitan, R.M. (1955). Certain differential effects of left and right cerebral lesions in human adults. *Journal of Comparative and Physiological Psychology, 48,* 474–477.

Reitan, R.M. (1964). Psychological deficits resulting from cerebral lesions in man. In J.M. Warren & K.A. Akert (Eds.), *The frontal granular cortex and behavior* (pp. 295–312). New York: McGraw-Hill.

Reitan, R.M., & Wolfson, D. (1994). A selective and critical review of neuropsychological deficits and the frontal lobes. *Neuropsychological Review, 4,* 161–198.

Retzlaff, P., Butler, M., & Vanderploeg, R.D. (1992). Neuropsychological battery choice and theoretical orientation: A multivariate analysis. *Journal of Clinical Psychology, 48,* 666–672.

Rey, A. (1964). *The clinical exam in psychology.* Paris: Presses Univsitaires de France.

Rey, A. (1993). Psychological examination of traumatic encephalopathy (J. Corwin & F.W. Bylsma, Trans.). *Clinical Neuropsychologist,* 4–9. (Original work published 1941)

Roca, R.P., Klein, L.E., & Vogelsang, G. (1982). Inaccuracy in diagnosing dementia among medical inpatients. *Clinical Research, 30,* 305A.

Rosenfeld, J.P., Reinhart, A.M., Bhatt, M., Ellwanger, J., Gora, K., Sckera, M., & Sweet, J. (1998). P-300 correlates of simulated amnesia in a matching-to-sample task: Topographic analysis of deception versus truthtelling responses. *International Journal of Psychophysiology, 28,* 233–247.

Russell, E.W. (1995). The cognitive-metric, fixed battery approach to neuropsychological assessment. In R.D. Vanderploeg (Ed.), *Clinician's guide to Neuropsychological assessment.* Hillsdale, NJ: Erlbaum.

Russell, E.W. (1998). In defense of the Halstead-Reitan battery: A critique of Lezak's review. *Archives of Clinical Neuropsychology, 13,* 365–381.

Ryan, C.M., Morrow, L., Parkinson, D., & Branet, E. (1987). Low level lead exposure and neuropsychological functioning in blue collar males. *International Journal of Neuroscience, 36,* 29–39.

Sbordone, R.J., & Long, C.J. (1996). *Ecological validity of neuropsychological testing.* Delray Beach, FL: GR Press/St. Lucie Press.

Schacter, D.L. (1986). On the relation between genuine and simulated amnesia. *Behavioral Sciences and the Law, 4,* 47–64.

Schwartz, M.L., Denneril, R.D., & Lin, Y. (1968). Neuropsychological and psychosocial predictors of employability in epilepsy. *Journal of Clinical Psychology, 24,* 174–177.

Schwartz, S., & Wiedel, T.C. (1981). Incremental validity of the MMPI in neurological decision-making. *Journal of Personality Assessment, 45,* 424–426.

Sherman, E.M.S., Strauss, E., Spellacy, F., & Hunter, M. (1995). Construct validity of WAIS-R factors: Neuropsychological test correlates in adults referred for evaluation of possible head injury. *Psychological Assessment, 7,* 440–444.

Singer, R.M. (1990). *Neurotoxicity guidebook.* New York: Van Nostrand-Reinhold.

Spreen, O., & Strauss, E. (1990). *A compendium of neuropsychological tests: Administration, norms, and commentary.* New York: Oxford University Press.

Spreen, O., & Strauss, E. (1998). *A compendium of neuropsychological tests: Administration, norms, and commentary* (2nd ed.). New York: Oxford University Press.

Stroop, J.R. (1935). Studies of interference in serial verbal reactions. *Journal of Experimental Psychology, 18,* 643–662.

Sullivan, K., & Bowden, S.C. (1997). Which tests do neuropsychologists use? *Journal of Clinical Psychology, 53,* 657–661.

Sweet, J.J., Moberg, P.J., & Westergaard, C.K. (1996). Five-year follow-up survey of practices and beliefs of clinical neuropsychologists. *Clinical Neuropsychologist, 10,* 202–221.

Sweet, J.J., Westergaard, C.K., & Moberg, P.J. (1995). Managed care experiences of clinical neuropsychologists. *Clinical Neuropsychologist, 9,* 214–218.

Turkheimer, E., Yeo, R.A., & Bigler, E.D. (1990). Basic relations among lesion location, lesion volume and neuropsychological performance. *Neuropsychologia, 28,* 1011–1019.

Van Schijndel, F.A.A., & van der Vlugt, H. (1992). Equivalence between classical neuropsychological tests and their computer version: Four neuropsychological tests put to the test. *Journal of Clinical and Experimental Neuropsychology, 14,* 45.

Vilkki, J., Ahola, K., Holst, P., Obman, J., Servo, A., & Heiskanen, O. (1994). Prediction of psychosocial recovery after head injury with cognitive tests and neurobehavioral ratings. *Journal of Clinical and Experimental Neuropsychology, 16,* 325–338.

Walsh, K.W. (1991). *Understanding brain damage: A primer of neuropsychological evaluation* (2nd ed.). Edinburgh: Churchill Livingstone.

Watkins, C.E., Campbell, V.L., Nieberding, R., & Hallmark, R. (1995). Contemporary practice of psychological assessment by clinical psychologists. *Professional Psychology: Research and Practice, 26,* 54–60.

Weinberger, D.R., & Berman, K.F. (1988). Speculation on the meaning of cerebral metabolic hypofrontality in schizophrenia. *Schizophrenia Bulletin, 14,* 157–163.

Williams, J.M. (1987). *Cognitive behavior rating scales. Manual research edition.* Odessa, FL: Psychological Assessment Resources.

Wilson, B.A. (1991). Long-term prognosis of patients with severe memory disorders. *Neuropsychological Rehabilitation, 1,* 117–134.

Wilson, B.A., Alderman, N., Burgess, P., Emslie, H., & Evans, J.J. (1999). *Manual for the Behavioral Assessment of the Dysexecutive Syndrome.* Odessa, FL: Psychological Assessment Resources.

Wilson, B.A., Cockburn, J., & Baddeley, A. (1985). *The Rivermead behavioral memory test.* Gaylord, MI: National Rehabilitation Services.

Wysocki, J.J., & Sweet, J.J. (1985). Identification of brain-damaged schizophrenic, and normal medical patients using a brief neuropsychological screening battery. *International Journal of Clinical Neuropsychology, 7,* 40–44.

Zelkowicz, B.J., Herbster, A.N., Nebes, R.D., Mintun, M.A., & Becker, J.T. (1998). An examination of regional cerebral blood flow during object naming tasks. *Journal of the International Neuropsychological Society, 4,* 160–166.

Chapter 2

NEUROPSYCHOLOGICAL ASSESSMENT: CONTEXTS FOR CONTEMPORARY CLINICAL PRACTICE

Anthony Y. Stringer and Marnie J. Nadolne

The 1990s brought dramatic changes in health care. Reimbursement for services and career opportunities shrank for many professionals. Neuropsychology was not immune to these changes. A recent survey of 259 clinical neuropsychologists revealed that a third had experienced reductions in income, reimbursement rates, referral sources, and numbers of patients referred to their practices (Sweet, Westergaard, & Moberg, 1995). More than half had been excluded from participation in managed care plans. Those receiving managed care referrals reported increased paperwork and a loss of autonomy.

One creative response to these challenges is to seek innovative contexts in which to practice. Of the myriad of health care professionals feeling the pinch of managed care, neuropsychologists may have the most options for developing alternative practices. The clinical contexts in which neuropsychologists practice have never been more varied. The expertise of neuropsychologists has never been more in demand. In this chapter, we survey the settings in which neuropsychological assessment occurs, including both well-established (e.g., the neurology clinic) and newly developing (e.g., the prison death-row cell block) contexts for contemporary practice. Using clinical vignettes, we discuss referral issues, special diagnostic considerations, and some of the test batteries specific to each assessment context.

Finally, we present a comprehensive list of neuropsychological tests in Table 2.1. It lists and describes commonly used neuropsychological tests, the various functional domains they assess, and the context(s) within which they may be used. The information included in Table 2.1 should not be viewed as restrictive. It serves only as a general guideline for instrument selection depending on the context or the domain of interest to the clinician. The complexity of many of the tests included in the table may allow them to be used in ways other than we have suggested.

Table 2.1 does not include normative data; however, this information may be found in the publication manuals associated with the various tests. Compilations of norms are also available (e.g., Lezak, 1995; Mitrushina, Boone, & D'Elia, 1999; Spreen & Strauss, 1998), and a web site (www.normativedata.com) is available which enables neuropsychologists to compare raw scores to selected norms. Test performance can be affected by many factors other than brain damage. Neuropsychologists, in part, rely on norms when

Table 2.1. Commonly used neuropsychological tests grouped by functional domain and context

	Neurol	Rehab	Psych	Surg	Voc/Ed	Judicial
Composite Batteries						
Halstead-Reitan Neuropsychological Test Battery—Assesses a broad range of cognitive, perceptual, and motor abilities to localize brain damage and to describe functional abilities.	✓	✓	✓		✓	✓
Luria-Nebraska Neuropsychological Battery—Assesses a broad range of cognitive, perceptual, and motor abilities utilizing the tasks (but not the methods) developed by Aleksandr Luria.	✓	✓	✓			✓
Intellectual						
Wechsler Intelligence Scales (WASI/WAIS-III, WISC-III)—Measure intellectual functioning using a combination of verbal and perceptually based subtests, some of which are supplementary.	✓	✓	✓		✓	✓
Kaufman Brief Intelligence Test—Provides brief screening of vocabulary and ability to solve visual analogies, yielding IQ score.	✓	✓	✓		✓	✓
Premorbid Ability						
Barona Estimate of Premorbid Intelligence—Predicts IQ based on demographic data (age, sex, education, etc.).	✓	✓			✓	✓
National Adult Reading Test—Predicts IQ based on current reading ability.	✓	✓			✓	✓
Oklahoma Premorbid IQ Estimate—Predicts IQ based on combination of demographic data and WAIS-R performance.	✓	✓			✓	✓
Learning and Memory						
Wechsler Memory Scale-III—A compilation of subtests that measure various aspects of verbal and visual memory.	✓	✓	✓			✓
Rey Auditory Verbal Learning Test—Assesses verbal learning and memory.	✓	✓	✓			✓
California Verbal Learning Test—Measures verbal learning and memory.	✓	✓	✓			✓
Rey-Osterreith Complex Figure Test—Assesses visuoconstructional ability and visual memory.	✓	✓	✓			✓
Benton Visual Retention Test-Revised—Assesses Visual memory, visual perception, and visual construction skills.	✓	✓	✓			✓
Memory Assessment Scales—Memory assessment battery that measures various aspects of verbal and visual learning and recall.	✓	✓	✓			✓
Rivermead Behavioural Memory Test—Assessment battery that assesses memory for everyday events and situations.	✓	✓	✓			✓
Verbal and Academic Abilities						
Wide Range Achievement Test-3—Measures achievement in the areas of reading, spelling, and mathematics.		✓			✓	
Woodcock Johnson-R—Assesses academic ability and achievement.			✓		✓	

(continued)

Table 2.1.   *(Continued)*

	Neurol	Rehab	Psych	Surg	Voc/Ed	Judicial
Language and Academic Abilities (continued)						
Controlled Oral Word Association Test —Measures verbal fluency by asking patients to rapidly produce words which begin with particular letters.	✓	✓	✓			✓
Boston Naming—Assesses ability to verbally identify objects from pictures.	✓	✓	✓	✓		✓
Aphasia Screening Test—A brief screen of language functions that assesses classic aphasia syndromes.	✓	✓	✓	✓		✓
Peabody Individual Achievement Test-Revised—Assesses achievement in the areas of reading, spelling, mathematics, and general information.		✓			✓	
Peabody Picture Vocabulary Test-Revised—Assesses auditory comprehension of object names.	✓	✓	✓			✓
Attention and Orientation						
Trail Making A and B—Measures speed of visual search and visuospatial sequencing.	✓	✓	✓			✓
Stroop—Assesses visual attention and concentration.	✓	✓	✓		✓	✓
Paced Auditory Serial Addition Test—Assesses sustained and divided attention.	✓	✓	✓		✓	✓
Symbol Digit Modalities Test—Assesses complex scanning and visual tracking.	✓	✓	✓		✓	✓
Galveston Orientation and Amnesia Test—Measures orientation and presence of post-traumatic amnesia.	✓	✓		✓		✓
Visuoconstructive						
Bender-Gestalt Test—Measures ability to reproduce a series of designs; measures visual perception and visual construction skills.	✓		✓		✓	
Rey-Osterreith Complex Figure Test—Assesses visuoconstructive ability; also measures visual memory.	✓	✓	✓			✓
Benton Visual Retention Test—Assesses ability to draw a series of designs; measures visual perception and visual construction; also measures visual memory.	✓	✓	✓			✓
Hooper Visual Organization Test—Assesses ability to conceptually arrange parts to make a whole.	✓	✓	✓			✓
Benton Facial Recognition Test—Assesses identification and discrimination of novel faces.	✓	✓	✓			✓
Benton Visual Form Discrimination—Assesses ability to match and discriminate figures.	✓	✓	✓			✓
Executive and Motor						
Trail Making Tests A and B—Assesses executive functioning using alphabetic and numeric sequencing tasks.	✓	✓	✓			✓
Wisconsin Card Sorting—Assesses concept formation and mental flexibility; can be computerized or hand-administered.	✓	✓	✓		✓	✓
Benton Motor Impersistence—Measures ability to maintain postures and movements.	✓	✓	✓			✓

Table 2.1. *(Continued)*

	Neurol	Rehab	Psych	Surg	Voc/Ed	Judicial
Executive and Motor (continued)						
Finger Tapping Test —Assesses motor speed and coordination.	✓	✓	✓		✓	✓
Grooved Pegboard Test —Assesses fine motor control and speed.	✓	✓	✓		✓	✓
Hand Dynamometer—Measures grip strength.	✓	✓	✓		✓	✓
Luria Motor Programs—Tests which measure motor planning and control, derived form Luria's Neuropsychological Investigation.	✓	✓	✓			✓
Emotional						
Minnesota Multiphasic Personality Inventory (MMPI-2/MMPI-A)—Measures affect and personality; a multiple choice test.	✓	✓	✓		✓	✓
Beck Depression Inventory-II—A brief objective instrument which measures physical and mood-related symptoms of depression (note also *Children's Depression Inventory* and the *Geriatric Depression Scale*).	✓	✓	✓		✓	✓
California Psychological Inventory—Measures personality and interpersonal patterns; a multiple choice test.		✓	✓		✓	
Millon Clinical Multiaxial Inventory-3—Multiple choice inventory which profiles Axis II personality styles and Axis I patterns.	✓	✓	✓			✓
Validity						
Portland Digit Recognition Test —Forced choice test which measures digit recognition and permits comparison of performance to chance recognition.	✓	✓	✓			✓
Rey 15-Item Memory Test —Assesses recall of 15 easy-to-remember items.	✓	✓	✓			✓
Victoria Symptom Validity Test —Computerized visual forced choice test which measures digit recognition and permits comparison of performance to chance.	✓	✓	✓			✓
Vocational						
McCarron Dial System—Neuropsychologically oriented instrument which assesses vocational skill and ability.		✓			✓	
Self-Directed Search—Manual or computer-administered test which assesses vocational interests, and yields a description of interest patterns and occupational choices.		✓			✓	
Strong-Campbell Interest Inventory—Assesses vocational interests, yielding a description of interest patterns and occupational choices (computer-scored).		✓			✓	
Specialized Batteries						
Consortium to Develop a Registry for Alzheimer's Disease (CERAD) Neuropsychological Battery—Evaluates dementia through a screening battery that includes tests of mental status, verbal fluency, naming, praxis, and verbal learning and memory.	✓		✓			

(continued)

Table 2.1.   *(Continued)*

	Neurol	Rehab	Psych	Surg	Voc/Ed	Judicial
Specialized Batteries (ocntinued)						
Emory Clinic Wada Protocol—Provides alternate forms for assessing language and memory functioning pre- and post-injection of intracarotid amobarbital in candidates for epilepsy surgery.				✓		
Emory Clinic Language Mapping Protocol—A set of 20 confrontational naming item sets, matched for difficulty, which measures language functioning in various areas of the brain during intraoperative electrocortical stimulation.				✓		
Mayo Clinic Wada Protocol—Screens patients for epilepsy surgery by utilizing brief language and memory tasks administered during intracarotid amobarbital injection.				✓		
National Institute of Mental Health (NIMH) Core Battery—Assesses cognitive deterioration in patients HIV+ utilizing conventional neuropsychological measures and computerized attention and processing speed tasks.	✓					

attempting to distinguish the effects of age, education, gender, and other factors from the effects of brain lesions. Unfortunately, only in some instances do the available norms take into account performance differences due to age, education, and gender (e.g., Heaton, Grant, & Matthews, 1991). Rarer still are normative tables that account for the influence of such factors as cultural differences, language barriers, the presence of psychiatric illness, atypical brain lateralization (whether due to heredity or pathology), motor limitations unrelated to brain damage, and so forth. Ultimately, the expansion of neuropsychology into ever new clinical domains must be matched by an equivalent growth in the sophistication of the norms that guide neuropsychological diagnosis.

NEUROPSYCHOLOGICAL ASSESSMENT IN THE NEUROLOGY CLINIC

O.T. is a 50-year-old, right-handed woman whose vehicle consecutively struck three other cars and a dog while she was being directed at slow speed through a traffic-congested road by a police officer. She did not stop the car immediately following the accidents, but surrendered her keys when requested by the police. O.T. was wearing a seat belt, but reported that she may have hit her head on the car roof. She never lost consciousness, but later she could recall only one of the three collisions. She was taken to an emergency room where computed tomography (CT) and magnetic resonance imaging (MRI) scans were obtained. These revealed an old infarction in the right frontal lobe and a left parietal infarction of uncertain age. Despite the CT and MRI findings, O.T. had never been evaluated or treated for stroke and had been neurologically asymptomatic until her accident. A neuropsychological evaluation was sought to help determine whether she had suffered a brain injury or a stroke coincident with her accident.

Neuropsychology emerged in the era when clinical acumen was the neurologist's main diagnostic tool. The field developed as a more objective adjunct to the neurological examination. Its initial focus was on determining the presence, lateralization, location, and, to a lesser degree, the etiology of brain damage (Hartman, 1991). Though the historical accuracy of this characterization has been questioned (Reitan, 1989), the centrality of lesion detection is evident in the early neuropsychology batteries. The hallmark of the Halstead-Reitan Battery, neuropsychology's oldest and most researched testing approach (see Chapter 7), is the indices that predict the presence, nature, and location of brain damage. Additional tests appropriate to the neurology context are listed in Table 2.1.

The advent of sophisticated neuroradiologic procedures that sometimes permit direct observation of brain lesions has helped to shift neuropsychology away from the art and science of lesion detection (Lezak, 1995). Increasing emphasis is placed on description of functional strengths and weaknesses. This shift in focus also reflects the success of neuropsychological science. Dissemination of its knowledge base has influenced neurology and other applied fields, altering examination methods and enhancing diagnostic efficacy (e.g., see Strub & Black, 1993). Despite these changes in healthcare, neuropsychologists continue to play an important role in unraveling the diagnostic puzzlers that present in the neurology clinic.

The opening case for this section illustrates the complex issues confronting neuropsychologists in the context of an undiagnosed neurologic disease. A grasp of neurologic diseases of the brain is essential for neuropsychologists working in these settings (see Chapter 3). Referral questions may center on whether a patient has neurologic disease when radiologic and other diagnostic procedures yield negative or equivocal results. Furthermore, the neuropsychologist may be asked to distinguish between the effects of several possible etiologies or to monitor a patient over time (see Sample Report 1: The Neurology Clinic). The ability of the neuropsychologist to answer these referral questions is dependent on the diagnostic efficacy of neuropsychological tests, particularly when compared to other procedures.

Despite the technological advances in the past few decades, neuropsychological testing continues to fare well in its ability to detect brain abnormality in conditions that do not always produce structural lesions detectable by CT scan (e.g., mild traumatic brain injury and alcoholism; K. Adams et al., 1993; Shores et al., 1990). Radiologic procedures that are sensitive to brain function (e.g., functional MRI, positron emission tomography—PET) correlate better with neuropsychological performance than do procedures designed solely to detect structural lesions (Ichise et al., 1994; Levin, Williams, Eisenberg, High, & Guinto, 1992; Ruff et al., 1994; J. Wilson et al., 1988). Even in comparison to functional radiologic procedures, neuropsychological testing provides nonredundant and clinically useful information. Though treatment of neuropsychological deficits more often occurs in rehabilitation settings than in the neurology context, neurologists must concern themselves with the functional consequences of their patients' deficits. Functional scanning techniques do not provide this type of information, at least not to the extent that neuropsychological examinations do. Thus, even in cases where the etiology and the distribution of brain damage is known, neuropsychological examinations will be needed to determine if return to work or school is feasible, if the patient requires supervision at home, if the patient can safely operate a vehicle, and if the patient requires cognitive rehabilitation. In addition, the burgeoning field of restorative neurology (Dimitrijevic, 1989; L. Goldstein & Davis, 1990; Greenwood, 1992), with its emphasis on treating both cause and consequence of neurologic disease, is apt to increase the need for neuropsychological consultation in neurology clinic settings.

NEUROPSYCHOLOGICAL ASSESSMENT IN THE REHABILITATION CONTEXT

W.J. is a 17-year-old girl who sustained a basal skull fracture and brain injury in a motor vehicle accident 2 years ago. There was a one-week period of unresponsiveness after the accident and a three-month period of post-traumatic amnesia. She was hydrocephalic and required a shunt to drain excess fluid from her cerebral ventricles. An electroencephalogram (EEG) obtained 5 months after the accident showed right frontotemporal slowing, and a CT scan showed moderate loss of brain volume. Two years post-injury, W.J. continued to have such severe cognitive impairment that she could not reenter school. She was referred for evaluation and treatment of her persistent cognitive deficits.

In rehabilitation settings, diagnosis of a patient's disease has generally already occurred by the time the neuropsychologist is consulted. What is left is identification of cognitive and behavioral deficits and discussion of their effects on the patient's ability to carry out activities of daily living. Though the discussion of functional implications has not historically been the neuropsychologist's domain (Diller, 1987), contemporary neuropsychologists are uniquely positioned to contribute to the understanding of a patient's real-world potential. Rehabilitation neuropsychology integrates psychosocial and biological information to create realistic scenarios for acute rehabilitation care as well as for long-term vocational and life care planning. In the initial phases of rehabilitation, neuropsychological assessment typically addresses three issues: premorbid ability, global level of impairment, and performance pattern (G. Goldstein & Ruthven, 1983).

As rehabilitationists cannot hope to make patients perform better than they did before their brain injury, the goals of therapy are based on the patient's premorbid status. Assessment of premorbid ability involves the integration of medical, educational, and social history data with empirically based measures. Often, an interview and inspection of past school records is all that is necessary to determine preexisting learning deficits and premorbid intellectual and achievement status. When such information is not readily available, regression-based methods (e.g., Barona, Reynolds, & Chastain, 1984) can be used to estimate premorbid IQ from demographic factors. Alternatively, premorbid ability may be estimated from current performance in ability domains that are unaffected by the patient's brain damage. Versions of the *National Adult Reading Test* (Crawford, Parker, & Besson, 1988; Nelson, 1982) and the *Wide Range Achievement Test* (see Chapter 10) have been used for this purpose. Finally, demographic factors may be combined with current ability measures to obtain a premorbid estimate (Krull, Scott, & Sherer, 1995).

Once premorbid status has been determined, neuropsychological assessment focuses on the patient's current pattern of impairments and strengths. This provides a baseline from which future gains can be measured. From this data, the rehabilitation team plans a program of therapy. When planning for discharge and community and vocational reentry, rehabilitation professionals focus on "disability" rather than on "impairment." An impairment only becomes a disability when it limits a person's ability to function in his or her environment. Neuropsychologists can help to minimize a patient's disability by recommending environmental alterations and accommodations that allow a patient to function with greater independence.

Ecological validity—the ability of neuropsychological data to predict real-world performance—is of obvious importance in rehabilitation where the focus is on enhancing practical, everyday skills. To augment their ecological validity, several contemporary neuropsychological batteries incorporate tasks drawn from the everyday environment. The Rivermead Behavioural Memory Test (B. Wilson, Cockburn, & Baddeley, 1985), for example, assesses memory for names, faces, an appointment, object pictures, the location of a belonging, prose, and a route. The Rivermead has been shown to correlate with ratings of memory based on direct patient observation. The Memory Assessment Scales (J. Williams, 1991) and the third revision of the Wechsler Memory Scale (Wechsler, 1997) similarly incorporate everyday memory items.

In addition to the cited tests, Table 2.1 lists some traditional measures that do not incorporate everyday items and for which ecological validity has yet to be established. Research supports incorporating everyday tasks in neuropsychological batteries. In a direct comparison of a traditional visual memory task (memory for a complex design) and a simulated everyday memory task (memory for a route depicted on slides), Nadolne and Stringer (1996) found that recall of the simulated route correlated higher with patients' ability to find their way through a building. Hence, neuropsychologists working in the rehabilitation context may want to select tests for which ecological validity has been demonstrated or that at least incorporate everyday items.

Within the rehabilitation context, neuropsychologists expand their role beyond assessment to include planning and implementation of cognitive treatment paradigms. Cognitive rehabilitation (see Chapter 15) focuses on restoring or retraining diminished cognitive skills and on providing patients with compensatory strategies to circumvent permanent impairments (León-Carrión, 1997). Such treatments may begin in the initial weeks or even days after an injury, but they can still be valuable even further out from the brain injury. In the case of W.J., neuropsychological assessment 2 years after her brain injury led to her participation in cognitive rehabilitation. Because after 2 years she was not expected to show further recovery of her cognitive ability, treatment focused on helping her to compensate for possibly permanent cognitive limitations. Environmental changes were introduced to minimize distractions while she worked. She learned to use mnemonic strategies (Harrell, Parenté, Bellingrath, & Lisicia, 1992; B. Wilson, 1987) for remembering practical information, and she practiced step-by-step methods of problem solving (Hayes, 1981). By the end of treatment, W.J. had made sufficient progress that she was able to enroll and to participate in General Educational Diploma (GED) examination courses and was expected to successfully obtain her high school equivalency certificate.

NEUROPSYCHOLOGICAL ASSESSMENT IN PSYCHIATRIC-PSYCHOLOGICAL PRACTICE

M.G. is a 29-year-old man who was in a minor car accident 3 years ago. In the accident, he struck his head on the seat in front of him but suffered no loss of consciousness. He noted changes in memory and concentration over the next few days and complained of headaches, sensitivity to noise and light, inability to sleep, and a change in the taste and smell of food. He did not seek medical attention. Over the next several months, M.G. deteriorated in his behavior, becoming disheveled and neglecting hygiene. His speech became incoherent, and he exhibited many disturbing and bizarre behaviors, including turning furniture upside down, tying ropes around furniture, leaning beds against walls, and throwing away valuables. In interview, M.G. admitted to drug abuse (LSD, cocaine, and marijuana) since age 19. Since then, he has had periods when his speech becomes disorganized and incoherent. M.G. attended college but did not graduate. He worked numerous jobs, but none for long. He does not date and has few friends.

If medical specialties tend to be organized around organ systems, psychiatry was once a specialty without an organ. Neurology had a firmer claim on the brain than psychiatry. Hence, the role of neuropsychological testing in psychiatric settings was to diagnose *organicity*—behavioral disturbance due to a diseased brain rather than to an unbalanced psyche. Distinguishing the organic brain syndrome from "functional" psychiatric syndromes was useful to the extent that such cases could be better treated in a neurology setting. Advances in biological psychiatry have rendered the organic-functional distinction moribund for schizophrenia, major mood disorders, and obsessive-compulsive disorder. Indeed, there are fewer and fewer psychiatric disorders that have not been considered from a neurobiological perspective. The brain increasingly is being shared by neurology and psychiatry. Along with this trend has come an expanded role for neuropsychology in the diagnosis and treatment of patients with psychiatric disorders.

Though it is no longer meaningful to speak of organic and functional disorders, it continues to be important to identify undiagnosed neurologic disease in patients with psychiatric disorders and undiagnosed psychiatric disease in patients with neurologic disorders. The patient who is convinced that familiar people have been replaced by imposters may have been suffering from paranoid delusions or may have Capgras Syndrome due to a stroke or some other disease process (Forstl, Almeida, Owen, Burns, & Howard, 1991). Knowing this is more than a matter of academic interest. If a stroke has been the cause of the disorder, treatment is not limited to the delusions but must also address the complications of the stroke and the prevention of future strokes. Without knowing the etiology, an important aspect of treatment will not be initiated. Similarly, the older patient with failing memory may have Alzheimer's Disease or a depression that is secondarily suppressing memory functions (McAllister, 1983). Distinguishing a primary degenerative dementia from a pseudodementia due to depression affects both prognosis and treatment. The prognosis in pseudodementia is much more hopeful if the underlying depression is treated.

Reviews are available of neurological syndromes that may be mistaken for purely psychiatric disorders and psychiatric syndromes that mimic neurologic disorders (see

Stringer, 1996). For example, **abulia** (marked decrease in motivation), **moria** (euphoric mood), and **somatoparaphrenia** (delusions regarding the ownership of one's limbs) are three disorders that have neurologic etiology but that may be misidentified as psychiatric in nature (Stringer, 1996). Conversely, **psychogenic unresponsiveness** (decrease in alertness due to psychological causes) and **pseudodementia** (decrease in cognitive function due to a factor such as depression) are disorders that are psychological in nature but that may appear neurologic (Stringer, 1996). These disorders can be thought of as potential false positives in neurologic and psychiatric diagnosis. Detection of these false positives is partly a function of conducting a skillful and comprehensive interview. The neuropsychological interview should encompass developmental, educational, occupational, forensic, cultural, familial, psychiatric, and neurologic factors that may play a role in the patient's presentation (see Chapter 4). Furthermore, the interview should elicit symptoms and complaints that form the basis for hypothesis testing about the presence or absence of cognitive, affective, and behavioral syndromes of either neurologic or psychiatric origin. Structured interviews and questionnaires can be helpful in this regard (e.g., the Neuroemotional-Neuroideational-Neurobehavioral Symptom Survey; Stringer, 1996), as are traditional personality and psychological tests (see Table 2.1 and Chapter 14). When using such tests, the neuropsychologist must be careful to consider the ways in which neurologic symptoms may alter test interpretation. For example, stroke and brain injury symptoms may inflate Minnesota Multiphasic Personality Inventory protocols, a finding that has led to the development of neurocorrective factors that purportedly increase the interpretability of results (Gass, 1991, 1992).

Detection of malingering requires specialized tests and procedures. Forced choice symptom validity tests compare the performance of patients over a series of trials to the level of performance that would be expected by chance (Stringer, 1996). Such tests work because most people do not know what a chance level of performance would be across a large series of trials. Performing worse than chance suggests an intentional strategy of feigning impairment. A variety of such tests are available to detect malingering of sensory and memory disturbances (see Table 2.1) (Binder & Willis, 1991; Hiscock & Hiscock, 1989).

Detection of pseudoneurologic syndromes also relies on the patient's not having sufficient information to be able to intentionally or unintentionally mimic the effects of neurologic disease. For example, patients who feign unarousability may resist when the examiner attempts to raise their closed eyelids, unaware that comatose patients do not show such resistance (Plum & Posner, 1980). Similarly, pseudoamnestic patients may do poorly on tests they perceive as effortful even when the memory demands of such tests are actually minimal (Stringer, 1996). Naive patients also show atypical patterns of memory test performance, such as doing worse on recognition than on recall tests of memory (see Chapters 6 and 9).

The case of M.G. illustrates the complex presentation of patients evaluated by neuropsychologists in psychiatric settings. His history suggests that both psychiatric and neurologic factors are involved. Hence, the neuropsychologist's objective is not so much to distinguish these components as to ascertain their relative contribution to the patient's clinical presentation. Accomplishing this requires familiarity with the neuropsychological profile produced by various psychiatric and neurologic etiologies.

Characteristic patterns of neuropsychological performance have been described for alcoholism, schizophrenia, aggressive psychopathy, affective disorder, obsessive-compulsive disorder, and hysteria (Becker & Kay, 1986; Flor-Henry, 1983). This provides a foundation for determining whether a patient's presentation is typical of that seen in patients with psychiatric disease or in patients with additional deficits, which are better accounted for by a neurologic etiology.

In his accident, M.G. appeared to have suffered a mild concussion, but that could not account for his slowly progressive decline in hygiene, speech, and behavior over the course of several months. Neuropsychological testing revealed deficits more typical of psychiatric disorder than of postconcussion syndrome. Accordingly, the neuropsychologist directed treatment efforts toward the psychiatric disorder, which was judged to be playing a greater role in M.G.'s clinical presentation. In this regard, neuropsychological assessment is useful in determining the prognosis for pharmacologic treatment in patients with psychiatric disorders. For example, neuropsychological performance is related to the response of patients with schizophrenia to neuroleptics and patients with attention deficit disorder to stimulants (Becker & Kay, 1986). In patients with a history of alcoholism, the degree and pattern of neuropsychological impairment on the Halstead-Reitan Battery is associated with the likelihood of dropping out of treatment and relapse (Parsons & Farr, 1980). Finally, cognitive deficits also show a strong association with the need for hospitalization following psychiatric emergency (Galankyer & Harvey, 1992).

NEUROPSYCHOLOGICAL ASSESSMENT IN THE SURGERY SUITE

B.J. is a 50-year-old, left-handed man with a seventh-grade education who worked as a truck driver. He has been disabled for many years due to intractable complex partial seizures, which began in infancy following a high fever. MRI scans show left midtemporal sclerosis and left frontotemporal atrophy. PET scans show a left temporal decrease in brain activity (hypometabolism). EEG recordings obtained both between and during seizures establish that the abnormal brain activity begins within the left temporal lobe. Neuropsychological examination revealed borderline intellectual functioning, mild aphasia, memory that is below average for his age, poor right-hand psychomotor performance, and severely impaired problem solving. B.J. was considered a candidate for a left temporal lobectomy to control his seizures. Further neuropsychological consultation was requested to determine language lateralization and localization and to gauge the risk of surgery adding to the patient's disability.

Neurosurgical interventions stop advancing disease processes within the brain when less invasive medical procedures cannot accomplish the same outcome. This includes surgical ablation of an expanding tumor, insertion of a shunt to drain excess cerebrospinal fluid, removal of plaque from a narrowed artery, and the isolation and extirpation of diseased brain tissue. Surgical interventions are directed at disabling and often life-threatening disease processes. Rarely or never is the goal solely to improve cognitive functioning. Nevertheless, the cognitive consequences of surgery, be they positive or negative, have long been recognized. Hence, neuropsychological consultation may be sought before or, more typically, after surgery to document cognitive outcome. In this context, the neuropsychologist attempts to answer a question that is not substantially different from questions that may arise in other clinical contexts: Are there documentable cognitive impairments that have consequences for the patient's everyday existence? Assessment strategies to address this type of question are discussed elsewhere in this chapter and are listed in Table 2.1.

More unique questions arise when the neurosurgeon wants to predict the outcome of surgery. This becomes an issue when large amounts of brain tissue must be removed to effectively arrest the disease. Large tissue-volume loss means greater potential loss of functioning. Hence, predicting the outcome of surgery is crucial to the patient's ability to make an informed choice about whether to risk surgery or to face the consequences of an unarrested disease. When the predicted consequence of surgery is further loss of functioning, the neurosurgeon may attempt to better the outcome by decreasing the amount of tissue removed or by avoiding removal of critical brain areas. In this instance, the neuropsychological examination guides the surgical ablation by specifying the areas that the surgeon must spare. These uniquely challenging referral questions warrant further discussion.

Prediction of the outcome of a lobectomy became possible with the development of techniques for inducing local cerebral anesthesia. A unilateral injection of sodium amobarbital into the internal carotid artery (the "Wada Test") will anesthetize one hemisphere for 10 to 12 minutes with no or only transitory effects seen in the uninjected hemisphere (Wada & Rasmussen, 1960). After a brief period of general lethargy, the patient will become sufficiently alert for the neuropsychologist to test language and memory functions (Milner, Branch, & Rasmussen, 1962). Procedural variability is the norm with regard to the language and memory assessment (Trenerry, Loring, Petersen, & Sharbrough, 1996), though most protocols in use are based on procedures developed at the Montreal Neurological Institute or at the Mayo Clinic.

The Wada Test has been adopted by epilepsy surgery centers across the United States for patients who are candidates for unilateral temporal lobectomy. Successful recall of pictures presented following injection of the epileptic hemisphere is associated with the absence of amnesia after removal of the diseased temporal lobe (Blume, Grabow, Darley, & Aronson, 1973). Poor memory performance after injection of the epileptic hemisphere predicts a poorer surgical outcome (Jones-Gotman, 1992; Wyllie, Naugle, Awad, et al., 1991). Better picture memory performance when the nonepileptic hemisphere is injected suggests the diseased hemisphere is playing an important role in memory. In this instance, surgical ablation may result in poorer memory (Kneebone, Chelune, Dinner, Naugle, & Awad, 1995).

With respect to language functions, the absence of aphasia after injection of the diseased hemisphere predicts the absence of postsurgical aphasia. When aphasia is present following injection, a more limited surgical excision may still spare the patient from postsurgical language impairment (Blume et al., 1973). Wada Test results are also useful in determining the laterality of seizure onset (Perrine et al., 1995; Wyllie, Naugle, Chelune, et al., 1991). Finally, differences in postinjection performance of the two hemispheres is predictive of the degree of postoperative seizure control (Loring et al., 1994; Perrine et al., 1995; Sperling et al., 1994).

Case B.J. underwent Wada Testing and was found to have preserved memory following injection of 125 milligrams of amobarbital into the epileptic left hemisphere. A similar injection into the right hemisphere resulted in poor memory performance. Left temporal lobectomy should, therefore, not result in an amnestic syndrome because the right hemisphere appears to be mediating memory functions with little or no input from the diseased left temporal lobe. B.J.'s language results were less clear. He had mild aphasia at baseline, a slight worsening of his aphasia after left hemisphere injection, and marked worsening after right hemisphere injection. The right hemisphere appeared to be playing the larger role in mediating language, but a left hemisphere contribution could not be ruled out given the baseline aphasia and the effect of the amobarbital in the left hemisphere. Language mapping prior to the left temporal lobectomy was recommended.

Neurosurgeons traditionally relied on clinico-anatomical correlates to guide resections in the language dominant hemisphere. Sparing the superior temporal gyrus, for example, decreases the likelihood of postsurgical aphasia. Unfortunately, even when classic language areas are avoided during surgery, aphasic syndromes can still occur (Heilman, Wilder, & Malzone, 1972). Intraoperative language mapping decreases the likelihood of postsurgical aphasia by providing an individualized map of brain-language relationships. Language mapping is accomplished following a craniotomy on an awake patient under local anesthesia.

The effect of cortical surface electrical stimulation on a standardized, repeatable language test is observed in order to draw the language map. In their classical studies of the effects of brain electrical stimulation, Penfield and Roberts (1959) reported that focal stimulation at some association cortex sites blocked ongoing object naming. Subsequent research established that postsurgical aphasia is more likely when the resection encroaches on areas in which naming is interrupted by electrical stimulation (Ojemann, 1993). Hence, naming tasks have become standard in language mapping protocols (Ojemann, Ojemann, Lettich, & Berger, 1989). Some posterior language sites, however, do not produce **anomia** to electrical stimulation. When a posterior resection is contemplated, sentence reading tasks may be more useful in detecting language zones (Ojemann, 1989; Ojemann & Mateer, 1979).

In 117 patients undergoing language mapping with naming and reading tasks, variability in the localization of language occurred with high frequency (Ojemann, 1993). Some patients had language areas identified in regions classically considered "safe" for resection based on clinico-anatomical relationships established in lesion studies. No anatomical area could be identified that had a reliable relationship to language functioning across patients. Regardless of whether this variability in language organization is normal or is due to the effects of a disease process on the brain, it underscores the importance of neuropsychological techniques in the surgical suite. Case B.J. had four language sites identified through a naming protocol. Avoidance of these sites during surgery spared him any further decline from his baseline status of mildly aphasic communication.

The preceding discussion has focused on epilepsy surgery because this is the most common context in which neuropsychologists and neurosurgeons collaborate. However, it is important to mention the other surgical contexts for neuropsychological assessment. Testing may be initiated before or after surgery, and sometimes both, in cases of tumor resections, shunt placement for hydrocephalus, endarterectomy, and cerebrovascular bypass surgery. The neuropsychology-neurosurgery collaboration has been a fruitful one and is likely to experience continued growth.

NEUROPSYCHOLOGICAL ASSESSMENT IN VOCATIONAL AND EDUCATIONAL CONTEXTS

A.U. is a 20-year-old woman who sustained a severe traumatic brain injury at age 11 in a motor vehicle accident. At the time she was referred for neuropsychological assessment, A.U. was a high school senior. She was struggling to complete high school due to ongoing physical limitations (i.e., left hemiparesis, bilaterally decreased coordination, tremulousness, decreased balance) and severe cognitive impairment. A.U. stated that her goal was to work in a computer-related field. She and her parents believed the school system was unable to accommodate her special needs and was failing to prepare her for a computer career. In contrast, the school system asserted that they were making all reasonable accommodations but that A.U. was too physically and cognitively impaired to master entry-level computer skills.

Vocationally oriented neuropsychological examinations address four main questions with regards to patient functioning:

1. Can the patient return to his or her previous job or school program?
2. What other jobs might the patient be able to perform if he or she cannot return to the previous one?
3. What training or therapy is needed for the patient to make a successful school or work reentry?
4. What changes, supports, and accommodations in the job or school setting are necessary for the patient to make a successful reentry?

Addressing these questions requires that the traditional neuropsychological battery be supplemented with tests that measure academic achievement (see Chapter 10) and behavioral domains relevant to work (see Table 2.1). The patient's capacity for emotional and behavioral self-regulation can be as important as his or her cognitive ability in successfully returning to work; hence specialized tests of executive function (see Chapter 13) are an essential part of a vocational neuropsychology evaluation (see Sample Report 2: The Vocational/Rehabilitation Context). Finally, the neuropsychologist must sample the domain of skills required by the school and work environments. General descriptions of the aptitudes and the percentage of U.S. occupations that require each of them are available (Lees-Haley, 1990). Most jobs require attention, memory, and communication ability even when they do not require specialized, technical skills. Managerial, professional, and technical positions may require not only specialized knowledge but also general problem solving, reasoning, organization, and planning ability. Fields as diverse as architecture, cartography, and radiology require high-level perceptual abilities.

As a minimum, the neuropsychologist must have a clear understanding of the nature of the patient's work and the skills required so that the examination can be tailored to assess the relevant cognitive domains. The U.S. Department of Labor (1986) *Dictionary of Occupational Titles* provides concise descriptions of virtually every job performed in the United States. As the specific duties of jobs bearing the same job title can vary across companies, generic job descriptions should be supplemented by the patient's description of his or her work and, when available, by a description from the patient's supervisor or co-workers.

The McCarron Dial System (MDS; Blackwell, Dial, Chan, & McCollum, 1985; McCarron & Dial, 1972), a battery of sensory, motor, psychosocial, and cognitive measures, was developed specifically to predict work-related behavior. It does so successfully in populations with mental retardation and has also been shown to discriminate patients with brain damage from healthy controls (Dial, Chan, & Norton, 1990). Besides this specialized battery, various versions of the Halstead-Reitan Battery have shown potential in predicting employment (Barth et al., 1983; Dikman & Morgan, 1980; McSweeney, Heaton, Prigatano, & Adams, 1985; Newman, Heaton, & Lehman, 1978). The addition of measures of emotional and psychosocial functioning (e.g., the Minnesota Multiphasic Personality Inventory or the California Personality Inventory) improves the ability of neuropsychological batteries to predict work performance (Heaton, Chelune, & Lehman, 1978; Newman et al., 1978; Schwartz, Dennerll, & Lin, 1968).

Information from standardized test batteries goes only so far in predicting job performance. Often, direct observation of the patient as he or she attempts work-related tasks is required. Such tasks can at times be simulated in the examiner's office. For example, simulation of clerical and computer-related tasks can be accomplished with materials available in most neuropsychological offices. At other times, a trip to the work or the school environment is necessary. This provides a rare opportunity for the neuropsychologist to collaborate with other professionals (e.g., teachers, vocational evaluators, rehabilitation engineers) in conducting and interpreting the parts of the examination that involve direct observation. Such collaborations can yield a richer characterization of the patient and his or her academic and vocational abilities. Guilmette and Kastner (1996) offer general guidelines for conducting and interpreting vocational neuropsychological evaluations that will be helpful to the practitioner just beginning to work in this area (also see Chapter 15).

Translating neuropsychological findings into recommendations that will be helpful to patients, teachers, co-workers, and supervisors provides a daunting challenge. With regard to case A.U., the range and the severity of motor and cognitive impairment required that she receive such a specialized program that it exceeded the school system's resources. The challenge in such cases is to develop recommendations that will work in the real world where there are limits in resources and in the willingness of employers and school principals to accommodate special needs. The line is often obscured between what is a legally required and reasonable accommodation and what is too costly and unwieldy for a school system or an employer to implement.

Reasonable recommendations for school systems include allowing students with brain injuries to take fewer courses per semester and to progress at a slower rate. Most school systems and colleges will allow access to instructor notes or to tape recording of lectures. Support in the form of tutors and study groups for students with disabilities are available in some systems, but it may have to be arranged outside the school by parents.

The schools are usually willing to cooperate and are appreciative of the specialized help provided by such outside tutors. Recommendations to allow students to take examinations privately and without time limits are also often accepted.

Employers vary in how willing they are to accommodate a returning employee's disability. Part-time work or job sharing may be helpful in some cases. In others, a job coach or co-worker mentor can greatly facilitate work reentry. Job coaches typically require an outside payor source, whereas a co-worker mentor would be unpaid. However, employers may balk at any decreases in the productivity of a co-worker mentor while they are engaged in helping the returning employee. Employers should be willing to remove any physical barriers that would prevent a person from getting to and performing a job for which they are otherwise capable. Opportunities to work in quieter surroundings, limits on work interruptions and time pressures, and permitting more frequent rest periods can often be negotiated.

When deficits are too severe and accommodations too expensive and cumbersome to permit the patient to perform the previous job, the neuropsychologist may be able to sketch, in general terms, the types of work the patient can still perform. This must be done with concern for the patient's dignity. A person who cannot return to a legal firm as an attorney cannot be expected to return to work as a secretary. A physician with brain injury who cannot practice medicine must not be recommended for a position as a janitor even if such work is within his or her physical capacity. The standard must be whether the patient can return to work that is comparable in status and pay. If not, then it should be determined whether parts of the previous job can be performed in such a way that it benefits both the patient and the employer.

NEUROPSYCHOLOGICAL ASSESSMENT IN THE JUDICIAL SYSTEM

J.W. is a 30-year-old man convicted of murder and awaiting sentencing. The district attorney indicated his intent to seek the death penalty. Following his conviction, J.W.'s attorney became aware of two incidents in which J.W. sustained head trauma. He was in a motor vehicle accident 5 years ago in which he lost consciousness and suffered a chin laceration. He was struck in the back of the head 9 years ago, resulting in contusion and acute muscle strain, but no other symptoms. Furthermore, at age 15, J.W. swallowed excessive amounts of an unknown medication causing confusion, disorientation, and lethargy. He was seen in the emergency room where his stomach was pumped, and he was hospitalized for observation. J.W.'s attorney sought neuropsychological consultation to determine if any of these incidents had resulted in brain damage that would mitigate a death penalty.

Neuropsychological evidence may be sought and introduced in many court proceedings, including personal injury, criminal, or competency hearings. The patient with a brain injury caused by a motor vehicle accident is probably the most common type of patient seen by neuropsychologists (see Sample Report 3, The Judiciary System) (R. Adams & Rankin, 1996). Patients with work-related brain injuries and toxic exposure are also frequently encountered. Less common are evaluations of medical malpractice suits investigating alleged iatrogenic injuries. The sensitivity of neuropsychological tests allows them to provide essential evidence in legal trials. However, the admissibility of neuropsychological data has been challenged on a number of grounds (Giuliano, Barth, Hawk, & Ryan, 1997; Guilmette, Faust, Hart, & Arkes, 1990). To date, neuropsychologists have successfully defended their methods in the courtroom. Most states allow testimony of neuropsychologists regarding the presence of brain dysfunction, and Alabama and Florida permit testimony about the cause of brain dysfunction (R. Adams & Rankin, 1996). Neuropsychologists may base testimony on their own test data, as well as on a review of medical, educational, employment, and other relevant records (Laing & Fisher, 1997). Neuropsychologists can also act as consultants in court cases to review the data of other neuropsychologists and to assist with the preparation of cross-examination questions.

To maximize the admissibility of neuropsychological data, neuropsychologists must be especially careful when selecting test batteries. The tests used should be relevant to the legal issue and to the patient population. In addition, standardized tests that are in common and accepted use in the field are, in forensic contexts, preferable to instruments that may be more experimental (A. Williams, 1997). Tests should have established and documented sensitivity, specificity, reliability, and validity and a solid basis for normative interpretation. Tests appropriate to the judicial context are noted in Table 2.1. The Halstead-Reitan Battery is commonly cited in legal settings because of its long-established history (see Chapter 7). This should not discourage clinicians from using newer batteries as they gain increasing empirical support (see Chapter 8 for a discussion of the Luria Nebraska Battery).

Forensic neuropsychologists often face the question asked of psychiatrists—whether a patient is exaggerating symptoms. Methods discussed previously for detecting feigned disorders are especially applicable in examinations conducted for legal purposes. In addition, there are well-known patterns of performance shown by people who malinger in the context of a personal injury claim. Heaton, Smith, Lehman, and Vogt (1978) administered the Halstead-Reitan Battery to 38 patients, half of whom did not have head injuries and were instructed to feign neuropsychological deficits and half of whom were nonlitigants with documented brain injuries. The patients who were intentionally exaggerating symptoms tended to be more impaired on motor and sensory perceptual tasks, such as the Speech Sounds Perception Test, Finger Tapping Test, and Grip Strength. Nonlitigating patients with brain injuries performed more poorly on subtests with a higher "cognitive load," such as the Category Test, Trail Making B, and the Tactual Performance Test. Mittenberg, Azrin, Millsaps, and Heilbronner (1993) described patterns of performance of malingerers on the Wechsler Memory Scale-Revised. Test results of patients with documented brain injuries were compared with results of age-matched controls who were instructed to fake deficits. Patients with brain injuries had significantly higher Attention-Concentration indices than General Memory indices, whereas the opposite held true in the malingering group.

Malingering may also occur in criminal cases where the patient faces severe penalties if found competent and responsible for his or her crime. These issues become especially acute in the assessment of inmates suspected of capital murder. Neuropsychological consultation may be sought when questions arise about an inmate's ability to participate in his or her own defense and to understand the consequences if convicted. Mental retardation and brain injury are considered mitigating factors in some states and can mean the difference between a life sentence or the death penalty for a convicted inmate. In J.W.'s case, the central issue was whether there was sufficient neuropsychological impairment present to mitigate a death sentence. Given the stakes involved for both the individual and society, such decisions call for the solid, empirical foundation that the established neuropsychological batteries offer.

CONCLUSION

This review outlined the traditional contexts in which clinical neuropsychologists practice and the novel contexts that offer new opportunities and challenges. Traditional test batteries were discussed which were applicable across multiple clinical contexts as well as tests designed for highly specific clinical situations. Sources for currently available test norms were provided along with the need for increasingly sophisticated norms that take into account a wider range of confounding factors.

The chapters that follow amplify the themes that were introduced in a necessarily cursory fashion in this review. What should be clear from this introduction is the continued variety and vitality within the practice of neuropsychology. It is a vitality that should secure for this field a place in the 21st century.

RECOMMENDED READING

Adams, R.L., Parsons, O.A., Culbertson, J.L., & Nixon, S.J. (1996). *Neuropsychology for clinical practice: Etiology, assessment, and treatment of common neurological disorders.* Washington, DC: American Psychological Association.

Lezak, M.D. (1995). *Neuropsychological assessment* (3rd ed.). New York: Oxford University Press.

Sbordone, R.J., & Long, C.J. (1996). *Ecological validity of neuropsychological testing.* Delray Beach, FL: GR/St. Lucie Press.

Stringer, A.Y. (1996). *A guide to adult neuropsychological diagnosis.* Philadelphia: F.A. Davis.

REFERENCES

Adams, K.M., Gilman, S., Koeppe, R.A., Kluin, K.J., Brunberg, J.A., Dede, D., Berent, S., & Kroll, P.D. (1993). Neuropsychological deficits are correlated with frontal hypometabolism in positron emission tomography studies of older alcoholic patients. *Alcoholism, Clinical and Experimental Research, 17,* 205–210.

Adams, R.L., & Rankin, E.J. (1996). A practical guide to forensic neuropsychological evaluations and testimony. In R.L. Adams, O.A. Parsons, J.L. Culbertson, & S.J. Nixon (Eds.) *Neuropsychology for clinical practice* (pp. 455–488). Washington, DC: American Psychological Association.

Barona, A., Reynolds, C.R., & Chastain, R. (1984). A demographically based index of premorbid intelligence for the WAIS-R. *Journal of Consulting and Clinical Psychology, 52,* 855–857.

Barth, J.T., Macciocchi, S.N., Giordani, B., Rimel, R., Jane, J.A., & Boll, T.H. (1983). Neuropsychological sequelae of minor head injury. *Neurosurgery, 13,* 529–533.

Becker, B., & Kay, G.G. (1986). Neuropsychological consultation in psychiatric practice. *Psychiatric Clinics of North America, 9*(2), 255–265.

Binder, L.M., & Willis, S.C. (1991). Assessment of motivation after financially compensable minor head trauma. *Psychological Assessment, 3,* 175–181.

Blackwell, S., Dial, J., Chan, F., & McCollum, P. (1985). Discriminating functional levels of independent living: A neuropsychological evaluation of mentally retarded adults. *Rehabilitation Counseling Bulletin, 29,* 42–52.

Blume, W.T., Grabow, J.D., Darley, F.L., & Aronson, A.E. (1973). Intracarotid amobarbital test of language and memory before temporal lobectomy for seizure control. *Neurology, 23,* 812–819.

Crawford, J.R., Parker, D.M., & Besson, J.A.O. (1988). Estimation of premorbid intelligence in organic conditions. *British Journal of Psychiatry, 153,* 178–181.

Dial, J.G., Chan, F., & Norton, C. (1990). Neuropsychological assessment of brain damage: Discriminative validity of the McCarron-Dial system. *Brain Injury, 4,* 239–246.

Dikman, S., & Morgan, S.F. (1980). Neuropsychological factors related to employability and occupational status in persons with epilepsy. *Journal of Nervous and Mental Disease, 168,* 236–240.

Diller, L. (1987). Neuropsychological rehabilitation. In M. Meier, A. Benton, & L. Diller (Eds.), *Neuropsychological rehabilitation* (pp. 3–17). New York: Guilford Press.

Dimitrijevic, M.R. (1989). Restorative neurology of head injury. *Journal of Neurotrauma, 6,* 1989.

Flor-Henry, P. (1983). Neuropsychological studies of patients with psychiatric disorders. In K.M. Heilman & P. Satz (Eds.), *Neuropsychology of human emotion* (pp. 193–220). New York: Guilford Press.

Forstl, H., Almeida, O.P., Owen, A.M., Burns, A., & Howard, R. (1991). Psychiatric, neurological and medical aspects of misidentification syndromes: A review of 260 cases. *Psychological Medicine, 21,* 905–910.

Galankyer, I., & Harvey, P.D. (1992). Neuropsychological screening in the psychiatric emergency room. *Comprehensive Psychiatry, 33,* 291–295.

Gass, C.S. (1991). MMPI-2 interpretation of closed-head-trauma: A correction factor. *Journal of Consulting and Clinical Psychology, 3,* 27–31.

Gass, C.S. (1992). MMPI-2 interpretation of patients with cerebrovascular disease: A correction factor. *Archives of Clinical Neuropsychology, 7,* 17–27.

Giuliano, A.J., Barth, J.T., Hawk, G.L., & Ryan, T.V. (1997). The forensic neuropsychologist: Precedents, roles, and problems. In R.J. McCaffrey, A.D. Williams, J.M. Fisher, & L.C. Laing (Eds.), *The practice of forensic neuropsychology: Meeting challenges in the courtroom* (pp. 1–27). New York: Plenum Press.

Goldstein, G., & Ruthven, L. (1983). *Rehabilitation of the brain-damaged adult.* New York: Plenum Press.

Goldstein, L.B., & Davis, J.N. (1990). Restorative neurology: Drugs and recovery following stroke. *Stroke, 21,* 1636–1640.

Greenwood, R. (1992). Neurology and rehabilitation in the United Kingdom: A view. *Journal of Neurology, Neurosurgery and Psychiatry, 55*(Suppl.), 51–53.

Guilmette, T.J., Faust, D., Hart, K., & Arkes, H.R. (1990). A national survey of psychologists who offer neuropsychological services. *Archives of Clinical Neuropsychology, 5,* 373–392.

Guilmette, T.J., & Kastner, M.P. (1996). The prediction of vocational functioning form neuropsychological data. In R.J. Sbordone & C.J. Long (Eds.), *Ecological validity of neuropsychological testing* (pp. 387–412). Delray Beach, FL: GR/St Lucie Press.

Harrell, M., Parenté, F., Bellingrath, E.G., & Lisicia, K.A. (1992). *Cognitive rehabilitation of memory: A practical guide.* Gaithersburg, MD: Aspen.

Hartman, D.E. (1991). Reply to Reitan: Unexamined premises and the evolution of clinical neuropsychology. *Archives of Clinical Neuropsychology, 6,* 147–165.

Hayes, J.R. (1981). *The complete problem solver.* Hillsdale, NJ: Erlbaum.

Heaton, R.K., Chelune, G.J., & Lehman, A.W. (1978). Using neuropsychological and personality tests to assess the likelihood of patient employment. *Journal of Nervous and Mental Disease, 166,* 408–416.

Heaton, R.K., Grant, I., & Matthews, C.G. (1991). *Comprehensive norms for an expanded Halstead-Reitan battery. Demographic corrections, research findings, and clinical applications.* Odessa, FL: Psychological Assessment Resources.

Heaton, R.K., Smith, H.H., Jr., Lehman, R.A.W., & Vogt, A.J. (1978). Prospects for faking believable deficits on neuropsychological testing. *Journal of Consulting and Clinical Psychology, 46,* 892–900.

Heilman, K., Wilder, B., & Malzone, W. (1972). Anomic aphasia following anterior temporal lobectomy. *Transactions of the American Neurology Association, 97,* 291–293.

Hiscock, M., & Hiscock, C.K. (1989). Refining the forced-choice method for the detection of malingering. *Journal of Clinical and Consulting Psychology, 11,* 967–974.

Ichise, M., Chung, D.G., Wang, P., Wortzman, G., Gray, B.G., & Franks, W. (1994). Technetium-99m-HMPAO SPECT, CT and MRI in the evaluation of patients with chronic traumatic brain injury: A correlation with neuropsychological performance. *Journal of Nuclear Medicine, 35,* 217–226.

Jones-Gotman, M. (1992). Neuropsychological techniques in the identification of epileptic foci. *Epilepsy Research Supplement, 5,* 87–94.

Kneebone, A.C., Chelune, G.H., Dinner, D.S., Naugle, R.I., & Awad, I.A. (1995). Intracarotid amobarbital procedure as a predictor of material-specific memory change after anterior temporal lobectomy. *Epilepsia, 36,* 857–865.

Krull, K.R., Scott, J.G., & Sherer, M. (1995). Estimation of premorbid intelligence from combined performance and demographic variables. *Clinical Neuropsychologist, 9,* 83–88.

Laing, L.C., & Fisher, J.M. (1997). Neuropsychology in civil proceedings. In R.J. McCaffrey, A.D. Williams, J.M. Fisher, & L.C. Laing (Eds.), *The practice of forensic neuropsychology: Meeting challenges in the courtroom* (pp. 117–130). New York: Plenum Press.

Lees-Haley, P.R. (1990). Vocational neuropsychological requirements of U.S. occupations. *Perceptual and Motor Skills, 70,* 1383–1386.

León-Carrión, J. (1997). *Neuropsychological rehabilitation. Fundamentals, innovations, and directions.* Delray Beach, FL: GR/St. Lucie Press.

Levin, H.S., Williams, D.H., Eisenberg, H.M., High, W.M., Jr., & Guinto, F.C., Jr. (1992). Serial MRI and neurobehavioral findings after mild to moderate closed head injury. *Journal of Neurology, 55,* 255–262.

Lezak, M.D. (1995). *Neuropsychological assessment* (3rd ed.). New York: Oxford University Press.

Loring, D.W., Meador, K.J., Lee, G.P., King, D.W., Gallagher, B.B., Murro, A.M., & Smith, J.R. (1994). Stimulus timing effects on Wada memory testing. *Archives of Neurology, 51,* 806–810.

McAllister, T.W. (1983). Overview: Pseudodementia. *American Journal of Psychiatry, 140,* 528–533.

McCarron, L., & Dial, J.G. (1972). Neuropsychological predictors of sheltered workshop performance. *American Journal of Mental Deficiency, 77,* 244–250.

McSweeney, A.J., Heaton, R.K., Prigatano, G.P., & Adams, K.M. (1985). Relationship of neuropsychological status to everyday functioning in healthy and chronically ill persons. *Journal of Clinical and Experimental Neuropsychology, 7,* 281–291.

Milner, B., Branch, C., & Rasmussen, T. (1962). Study of short-term memory after intracarotid injection of sodium amytal. *Transactions of the American Neurological Association, 87,* 224–226.

Mitrushina, M.N., Boone, K., & D'Elia, L.F. (1999). *Handbook of normative data for neuropsychological assessment.* New York: Oxford University Press.

Mittenberg, W., Azrin, R., Millsaps, C., & Heilbronner, R. (1993). Identification of malingered head injury on the Wechsler memory scale—revised. *Psychological Assessment, 5,* 34–40.

Nadolne, M.J., & Stringer, A.Y. (1996). Ecologic validity in neuropsychological assessment: Prediction of wayfinding. *Archives of Neuropsychology, 12,* 375.

Nelson, H.E. (1982). *The national adult reading test (NART): Test manual.* Windsor, Berks, UK: NFER-Nelson.

Newman, O.S., Heaton, R.K., & Lehman, R.A.W. (1978). Neuropsychological and MMPI correlates of patients' future employment characteristics. *Perceptual and Motor Skills, 46,* 635–642.

Ojemann, G.A. (1989). Some brain mechanisms for reading. In C. Vol Euler, I. Lundberg, & G. Lennerstrand (Eds.), *Brain and reading* (pp. 47–59). New York: Macmillan.

Ojemann, G.A. (1993). Functional mapping of cortical language areas in adults. In O. Devinsky, A. Beriecllal, & M. Dogali (Eds.), *Electrical and magnetic stimulation of the brain and spinal cord* (pp. 155–163). New York: Raven Press.

Ojemann, G.A., & Mateer, C. (1979). Human language cortex: Localization of memory, syntax and sequential motor-phoneme identification systems. *Science, 205,* 1401–1403.

Ojemann, G.A., Ojemann, J., Lettich, E., & Berger, M. (1989). Cortical language localization in left-dominant hemisphere. *Journal of Neurosurgery, 71,* 316–326.

Parsons, O.A., & Farr, S.P. (1980). The neuropsychology of alcohol and drug use. In S.B. Filskov & T.J. Boll (Eds.), *Handbook of clinical neuropsychology* (pp. 320–365). New York: Wiley-Interscience.

Penfield, W., & Roberts, L. (1959). *Speech and brain mechanisms.* Princeton: Princeton University Press.

Perrine, K., Westerveld, M., Sass, K.J., Devinsky, O., Dogal, I.M., Spencer, D.D., Luciano, D.J., & Nelson, P.K. (1995). Wada memory disparities predict seizure laterality and postoperative seizure control. *Epilepsia, 36,* 851–856.

Plum, F., & Posner, J. (1980). *Diagnosis of stupor and coma* (3rd ed.). Philadelphia: F.A. Davis, 1980.

Reitan, R.M. (1989). A note regarding some aspects of the history of clinical neuropsychology. *Archives of Clinical Neuropsychology, 4,* 385–391.

Ruff, R.M., Crouch, J.A., Troster, A.I., Marshall, L.F., Buchsbaum, M.S., Lottenberg, S., & Somers, L.M. (1994). Selected cases of poor outcome following a minor brain trauma: Comparing neuropsychological and positron emission tomography assessment. *Brain Injury, 8,* 297–308.

Schwartz, M.L., Dennerll, R.D., & Lin, Y. (1968). Neuropsychological and psychosocial predictors of employability in epilepsy. *Journal of Clinical Psychology, 24,* 174–177.

Shores, A., Kraiuhin, C., Zurynski, Y., Singer, A., Gordon, E., Marosszeky, J., & Fearnside, M.R. (1990). Neuropsychological assessment and brain imaging technologies in evaluation of the sequelae of blunt head injury. *Australian and New Zealand Journal of Psychiatry, 24,* 133–138.

Sperling, M.R., Saykin, A.J., Glosser, G., Moran, M., French, J.A., Brooks, M., & O'Connor, M.J. (1994). Predictors of outcome after anterior temporal lobectomy: The intracarotid amobarbital test. *Neurology, 44,* 2325–2330.

Spreen, O., & Strauss, E. (1998). *A compendium of neuropsychological tests* (2nd ed.). New York: Oxford University Press.

Stringer, A.Y. (1996). *A guide to adult neuropsychological diagnosis.* Philadelphia: Davis.

Strub, R.L., & Black, F.W. (1993). *The mental status examination in neurology* (3rd ed.). Philadelphia: Davis.

Sweet, J.J., Westergaard, C.K., & Moberg, P.J. (1995). Managed care experiences of clinical neuropsychologists. *Clinical Neuropsychologist, 9,* 214–218.

Trenerry, M.R., Loring, D.W., Petersen, R.C., & Sharbrough, F.W. (1996). The Wada test. In E. Wyllie (Ed.), *The treatment of epilepsy: Principles and practice* (2nd ed.), (pp 1000–1005). Baltimore: Williams & Wilkins.

U.S. Department of Labor. (1986). *Dictionary of occupational titles* (3rd ed.). Washington, DC: Superintendent of Documents.

Wada, J., & Rasmussen, T. (1960). Intracarotid injection of sodium amytal for the lateralization of cerebral speech dominance: Experimental and clinical observations. *Journal of Neurosurgery, 17,* 266–282.

Wechsler, D. (1997). *Wechsler memory scale* (3rd ed.). San Antonio, TX: The Psychological Corporation.

Williams, A.D. (1997). Fixed versus flexible batteries. In R.J. McCaffrey, A.D. Williams, J.M. Fisher, & L.C. Laing (Eds.), *The practice of forensic neuropsychology: Meeting challenges in the courtroom* (pp. 57–67). New York: Plenum Press.

Williams, J.M. (1991). *Memory assessment scales professional manual.* Odessa, FL: Psychological Assessment Resources.

Wilson, B.A. (1987). *Rehabilitation of memory.* New York: Guilford Press.

Wilson, B.A., Cockburn, J., & Baddeley, A. (1985). *The Rivermead behavioral memory test manual.* Bury St. Edmunds, England: Themes Valley Test Company.

Wilson, J.T., Wiedmann, K.D., Hadley, D.M., Condon, B., Teasdale, G., & Brooks, D.N. (1988). Early and late magnetic resonance imaging and neuropsychological outcome after head injury. *Journal of Neurology, Neurosurgery and Psychiatry, 51,* 391–396.

Wyllie, E., Naugle, R., Awad, I., Chelune, G., Luders, H., Dinner, D., Skibinski, C., & Ahl, J. (1991). Intracarotid amobarbital procedure: I. Prediction of decreased modality-specific memory scores after temporal lobectomy. *Epilepsia, 32,* 857–864.

Wyllie, E., Naugle, R., Chelune, G., Luders, G., Morris, H., & Skibinski, C. (1991). Intracarotid amobarbital procedure: II. Lateralizing value in evaluation for temporal lobectomy. *Epilepsia, 32,* 865–869.

Chapter 3

OVERVIEW OF NEUROLOGY

Michael J. Selby

THE RELATIONSHIP BETWEEN NEUROLOGY AND NEUROPSYCHOLOGY

Neurology is the branch of medicine that deals with the nervous system, in particular, the central nervous system, and damage or diseases affecting it. The neurologist employs nonpsychometric methods to study observable behavioral deficits to diagnose brain pathology. The subdiscipline of behavioral neurology is based on clinical-anatomical correlations from which the nature, extent, and evolution of brain lesions can be inferred by identifying the associated signs and symptoms of behavioral disorders. One of the main approaches of behavioral neurology is behavioral observation in a clinical setting. In contrast, clinical neuropsychology employs psychometric instruments to examine the effects of brain function on behavior. The neuropsychologist is interested in quantitatively describing and explaining the degree of behavioral dysfunction produced by brain impairment in terms of practical and psychosocial implications for the patient.

Both the neurologist and neuropsychologist must have a thorough knowledge of brain structure and function, as well as of behaviors characteristically associated with neurological disorders to provide meaningful interpretation of clinical behavioral observations and test findings. Figure 3.1 provides a comparison of the neurological and neuropsychological methods of diagnosis. Medical, psychosocial, and behavioral assessment are essential to both specialties.

Where brain injury has occurred or is suspected, the patient is generally initially seen by a neurologist who conducts a behavioral and physical examination of the central nervous system. The neurologist may then request neuroimaging studies of the brain to aid in formulating a diagnostic impression. At this point, the neuropsychologist may be called upon to assist in diagnostic clarification (e.g., identification of early signs of dementia), or to provide a more complete understanding of the effect of brain pathology on a number of psychological domains.

When testing a patient who has not received a prior evaluation by a neurologist, the neuropsychologist may wish to conduct a formal neurological examination to rule out any of a variety of neurobehavioral disorders. Also, while the focus of neurological assessment is largely one of medical diagnosis of brain pathology, portions of the neurological examination may be used to confirm or support psychometric findings. For

Neurology	Neuropsychology
History (Medical)	History (Medical/Psychosocial)
Neurological Physical Exam	Psychometric testing
12 cranial nerves	
Motor exam	
Mental Status Exam	Behavioral observation/
	behavioral ratings
Neuroimaging and Laboratory Tests	
CT/MRI/PET Scan	
Angiogram	
CBF	
EEG	
Lumbar puncture	

Figure 3.1.   Comparison of diagnostic methods

example, the cranial nerve examination can reveal information regarding cortical functioning not readily available on neuropsychological measures. Neurological assessment provides the neuropsychologist with important data to supplement the neuropsychological test findings. For example, test performance could be significantly affected by a previous history of drug and alcohol abuse, pre- and postnatal problems, childhood illnesses, mental illness, and so on. The subject's mental status at the time of testing (e.g., attention/concentration, mood) may complicate test performance.

An overview of neuropsychological impairment as it relates to the structure and function of the neocortex is followed by a description of the most common neurological conditions and the neuropsychological sequallae associated with them. The neurological examination is then described, explaining the hierarchical structure and purpose of both the mental status and physical components. Finally, neuroimaging techniques used in the assessment of neurological damage and diseases are discussed.

NEUROPSYCHOLOGICAL IMPAIRMENT: OVERVIEW

Although brain structures are interconnected and often have multiple functions, research in behavioral neurology and neuropsychology has shown that certain portions of the brain play a larger role in the production of specific behaviors (e.g., language) than others. The following sections will briefly describe the primary behavioral function and dysfunction associated with the occipital lobe, parietal lobe, temporal lobe, and frontal lobe.

Occipital Lobes

The primary area of the occipital lobes (also known as the **striate cortex**) is responsible for visual processing. Bilateral destruction causes cortical blindness, but isolated lesions result in discrete blind spots in the corresponding parts of the visual fields yet do not disrupt the ability to comprehend visual stimuli. Patients with acute cortical blindness may develop **Anton's syndrome,** an active denial of vision loss in which the patient behaves as though he or she had sight, and will construct elaborate explanations for their poor performance on visual tasks.

Damage to the association areas of the visual cortex can produce visual agnosias. Patients suffering from **apperceptive agnosia** may have normal visual acuity, but they cannot successfully recognize objects visually by their shape. For example, a brain-damaged patient studied by Benson and Greenberg (1969) was initially believed to be blind but was subsequently observed to navigate his wheelchair around the halls of the hospital. Testing revealed that his visual fields were normal as demonstrated by his being able to pick up threads placed on a sheet of white paper. However, although he could discriminate among stimuli that differed in size, brightness, or hue, he could not distinguish those that differed only in shape.

A common symptom of apperceptive visual agnosia is **prosopagnosia,** an inability to recognize particular faces. That is, patients can recognize that they are looking at a face but cannot say whose face it is—even if it belongs to a close friend. On the other hand, a person with **associative visual agnosia** can perceive normally but cannot name who they have seen. In fact, they seem to be unaware of these perceptions. These patients are capable of copying the shapes of objects, but unable to recognize or name what they have drawn.

Another visual syndrome is **Balint's syndrome,** caused by damage to the region bordering the parietal and occipital lobes. Balint's syndrome consists of three major symptoms: optic ataxia, ocular apraxia, and simultanagnosia. All three symptoms are related to spatial perception. **Optic ataxia** is a deficit in reaching for objects under visual guidance. The patient might be able to perceive and recognize an object, but when he or she tries to reach for it, the movement is often misdirected. **Ocular apraxia** is a deficit of visual scanning. If the patient looks around a room filled with objects, he or she will see an occasional item and will be able to perceive it normally. However, the patient will not be able to maintain fixation: his or her eyes will begin to wander and another object will come into view for a time. Thus, the person is unable to make a systematic scan of the contents of the room and will not be able to perceive the location of the objects he or she sees. **Simultanagnosia** refers to the inability of Balint's syndrome patients to perceive more than one object at a time. For example, if an examiner holds either a comb or a pen in front of a patient's eyes, the patient will recognize the object. But if the examiner holds a pen and a comb together (for example, so that they form the legs of an X), the patient will see either the comb or the pen, but not both.

Parietal Lobes

The primary area of the parietal cortex is known as the **somatosensory cortex,** and is responsible for processing touch, changes in temperature, and presence of pain. The secondary or posterior parietal cortex integrates visual, tactile, and auditory input. The left parietal lobe has many connections which integrate visual perception with motor processes needed to reproduce drawings, write, perform mathematical operations, or to carry out any type of constructional task. In 1924, Josef Gerstmann described a number of neurobehavioral symptoms observed in a patient suffering from left parietal lobe stroke. These included **agraphia** (inability to write), **finger agnosia** (inability to recognize fingers on either hand), **acalculia** (inability to perform mathematical operations), and left-right confusion. The lesion was said to focus in the **angular gyrus,** an association area in the left parietal lobe where the temporal, parietal, and occipital lobes meet. These four neuropsychological symptoms came to be known as **Gerstmann's syndrome,** and initiated a heated debate as to whether these symptoms occur together, and whether these symptoms are the only symptoms. With regard to the latter, later research has shown that damage to the left parietal lobe produces a number of other symptoms including constructional difficulties (**constructional apraxia**), **alexia,** and language disorders.

The right parietal lobe has significantly greater visuospatial capabilities than the left, and allows the correct reading of maps and blueprints. In addition, the right parietal area is involved with the integration of both visual and tactile information necessary for dressing. Common right parietal syndromes are (1) constructional apraxia, (2) dressing apraxia , (3) geographic disorientation, and (4) denial and/or **neglect** of the left side of the environment and body (termed **contralateral neglect**). In contralateral neglect there is typically neglect of visual, auditory, and somatosensory stimulation on the side and/or space opposite to the lesion, which may be accompanied by denial of the deficit. Although the exact location of the lesion is difficult to pinpoint, the area of most overlap among lesion studies has been the inferior parietal lobe.

Temporal Lobes

Language

The temporal lobes not only contain the primary auditory cortex, but also have the primary role in language reception. Damage to the left hemisphere often produces **aphasia** (disturbance in language formulation or comprehension). As language and speech rely on the interaction between various cortical and subcortical regions, it is impossible to localize a particular syndrome to a single structure. However, it is generally the case that aphasias are cortical in nature, and predominantly involve the left hemisphere.

Damage to the left posterior temporal lobe may result in **Wernicke's Aphasia.** Wernicke's aphasia is primarily a comprehension deficit, however, the nature of the syndrome necessarily affects both spoken and written language. Located in the posterior, superior temporal lobe,Wernicke's area processes speech sounds and transforms these sounds into meaningful words. In the typical Wernicke's patient, speech is fluent and well-articulated with correct syntax and prosody. However, patients display significant word finding problems (**anomia**) on confrontation and in conversation. Also present are **neologisms** (made up words) or literal **paraphasias** (e.g., "ioliphant" for "elephant") and semantic paraphasias (e.g., "binoculars" for "spectacles").

Because of impaired comprehension of speech, even one's own, the patient is often unaware of (**anosognosic** for) these problems. Reading and writing is also impaired with regard to content, however, the letters are generally well formed. There is usually preservation of social conventions such as awaiting one's turn to speak, nodding the head at the right moment.

Memory

The medial temporal lobes contain the hippocampus and the amygdala which are essential to the consolidation of new memories. Damage to these areas often produces **anterograde amnesia** (inability to consolidate new memories) or **retrograde amnesia** (inability to retrieve information from long-term storage). Specifically, lesions in the left temporal lobe produce verbal memory deficits with lesions in the right temporal lobe producing nonverbal memory deficits (e.g., memory for designs, faces, melodies, spatial material).

Frontal Lobes

Owing to the size (one third of the human cerebral cortex) and number of connections with other brain structures, much of frontal lobe functioning remains a mystery. The following paragraphs briefly describe what is known about areas of neuropsychological function and dysfunction associated with the frontal cortex.

Motor Function

The primary motor cortex, located anterior to the central sulcus, executes programs for movement developed in the supplementary motor cortex. Thus, it has a number of connections with subcortical motor structures (e.g., basal ganglia, cerebellum) necessary for initiating motor sequences. Damage to the primary motor cortex reduces the speed, accuracy, and force of movements. Interestingly, damage does not produce hemiparesis due to the fact that (1) subcortical structures have the ability to initiate behavioral sequences, and (2) some motor pathways bypass the motor cortex altogether.

The supplementary or secondary motor cortex creates the motor programs sent to the adjacent primary motor cortex. Lesions to this area cause motor movements to be performed out of sequence. Thus, the patient suffering from secondary motor impairment will exhibit difficulty performing simple motor commands such as, "take this paper in your left hand, fold it in half, and place it on the floor." Patients may also show difficulty copying a series of rapidly executed hand movements.

Memory and Cognition

Patients with damage to the prefrontal cortex may exhibit memory or other cognitive deficits, but these appear to be the result of a lack of impetus to recall information rather than the presence of a specific cognitive disorder. In fact, when damage is limited to the frontal lobes, there typically appears to be little or no impairment on most widely used neuropsychological memory tests (Janowsky, Shimamura, & Squire, 1989). However, it should be kept in mind when evaluating patients with known or suspected frontal lobe damage that there may be major dissociations between well-preserved memory and other cognitive abilities which subsequently severely impair utilization of those abilities in real-life situations. Although patients will often score within normal limits on standard memory tests (e.g., WMS-III), close relatives will report significant everyday memory problems (e.g., misplacing keys, personal effects, leaving the television or lights on when leaving a room). This failure to remember is a common feature of frontal lobe syndromes.

Finally, there is considerable evidence that one factor which contributes to the memory difficulties of patients with frontal lobe damage is susceptibility to interference (e.g., Benson, 1993; Milner, Petrides, & Smith, 1985). Distraction by irrelevant stimuli and failure to inhibit irrelevant responses may have a profound impact on memory and other cognitive abilities of patients with frontal lobe damage. Thus, the frontal lobe patient might be described as one whose cognitive abilities are intact, but who is unable to utilize them in real-life situations.

Language

The left frontal lobe appears to play an important role in various aspects of language processing, including combining speech sounds into complete sentences (Damasio, 1991). Other frontal regions (cingulate gyrus and supplementary motor area), are involved in the affective and motor control of speech production.

The best known language deficit is **Broca's Aphasia.** Located in the posterior portion of the inferior frontal cortex, Broca's area is involved in the development of motor programs for speech production. Neural word representations originating in Wernicke's area are sent to Broca's area via a group of axons called the **arcuate fasciculus,** and transformed into words. True manifestation of Broca's aphasia requires damage to adjacent motor and premotor areas together with underlying white matter, the basal ganglia, and the insula. Thus, the condition normally improves when damage is restricted to the frontal cortex.

True Broca's aphasia ranges from complete muteness to slowed, deliberate speech which is also nonfluent, effortful, dysarthric (slurred), and agrammatic, with abnormal prosody (rhythm). Further, word order is abnormal, with omission of articles (e.g., the, a) and prepositions. On the other hand, the ability to use content words (e.g., apple, tree, bear) is generally intact. Repetition, reading, and writing are also disordered. Unlike Wernicke's aphasia, insight and awareness are usually retained. Clear focal signs typically accompany Broca's aphasia, such as right side motor deficits and ideomotor apraxia (knowledge of how to perform a motor movement). **Verbal fluency,** as measured by verbal association tests, may also be impaired by frontal lobe damage. Decreased verbal fluency and impoverishment of spontaneous speech tend to be associated with left frontal lobe lesions, although mildly depressed verbal fluency also occurs with right frontal lobe lesions (Shallice & Burgess, 1991). The work of Milner (1964) and Benton (1968) indicates that impairment in fluency is not associated with verbal learning defects, suggesting the relative independence of the mechanism underlying fluency.

Cognitive Flexibility

Testing of the ability to initiate, stop, and modify behavior in response to changing stimuli has traditionally been part of the evaluation for frontal lobe dysfunction. A widely used measure of cognitive abstraction and flexibility is the Wisconsin Card Sorting Test (WCST; Berg, 1948). In one of the earlier studies, Milner (1963) documented a consistent and severe impairment on the WCST in patients who had undergone prefrontal lobectomies for treatment of epilepsy. Although subsequent studies also found that, as a group, frontal lobe damaged subjects tended to perform worse than subjects with focal non-frontal damage, these investigations showed substantial variability in WCST performance across subjects (Drewe, 1974; Heaton, 1981). In a more recent study (Anderson, Damasio, Jones, & Trannel, 1991), no differences were found between subjects with focal frontal vs. focal non-frontal lesions. Clearly, scores on the WCST must be interpreted within a broad neuropsychological context rather than be specifically limited to frontal lobe function. Performance on the WCST is correlated with age, education, and IQ and the combined findings of several studies suggest that time since onset is a critical factor, with considerable improvement occurring over time (Heaton, Grant, & Matthews, 1996).

HEAD TRAUMA

Traumatic brain injury (TBI) is the most common cause of brain damage. In the United States, head injuries account for approximately 500,000 hospitalizations or deaths per year. Most head injuries occur to victims between the ages of 15 and 24, with falls being the leading cause. In other age groups, motor vehicle accidents account for 50% of head injuries. Men sustain twice as many head injuries as do women. Ninety percent of all head injuries are closed head injuries (i.e., there is no significant skull damage) as opposed to penetrating injuries (e.g., skull fractured) (Parker, 1990).

In general, injury to the brain may be either primary or secondary, and may have either acute or long-term effects. Primary injury is that which severs or destroys axons in the brain. If axons are completely severed or destroyed, damage is often permanent and tissue is lost. An example of this would be a gunshot wound, in which the bullet makes a path through the brain from the point of entry, severing and destroying tissue in its path. Secondary brain damage is caused by the after-effects of the primary injury. Hemorrhage causes oxygen deprivation leading to cell death. Edema (brain-swelling), hemorrhage, and infection may all cause increased cranial pressure which may effectively "squeeze off" areas of brain functions. In addition to damage produced within the immediate location of head trauma, there may also be damage to more distal areas due to disconnection of neuronal pathways or bruising of opposite sides of the brain against the skull (coup and contra-coup injuries). Generally, damage to the brain takes the form of lesions; neuronal shearing, stretching and tearing, or oxygen deprivation.

Brain lesions are any pathological or traumatic discontinuity of brain tissue. Lesions are holes or cavities in the brain and are almost always associated with the loss of function. Depending on their size and location, lesions result in minor or major behavioral effects. Lesions may be caused by trauma such as punctures from bullet wounds, fragments of bone from skull fractures, or other foreign objects entering the brain. Neurons which are completely severed will soon degenerate, causing the tissue surrounding them to shrink and die within hours. Cerebrospinal fluid then fills the cavity. Surrounding brain tissue may collapse the cavity with time, which may result in concomitant distortions of other areas of the brain or ventricles, depending on the size of the lesion. Dead neuronal debris are engulfed by glial cells which then block or interrupt neural transmission.

Neuronal shearing, stretching and tearing most often results from rapid acceleration and deceleration of the brain caused by the brain being shaken within the cranial cavity, as in the case of closed head injury, in which the head impacts another object or is suddenly thrown back in a whiplash injury. Only those neurons which are not completely severed may re-sprout axonal projections. New axonal sprouting may bypass damaged areas and restore function. However, neurons may also form unwanted connections resulting in behavioral disturbances.

Oxygen deprivation (or **anoxia**), for more than a few minutes, can cause permanent brain damage. Damage can also be caused by **hypoxia** (reduced oxygen flow), resulting from a more long term but intermittent deprivation or a lower oxygen saturation in the blood. The most common causes of anoxia are cardiopulmonary failures associated with heart attacks, complications of anesthesia, or accidents such as near-drowning episodes. Most anoxic episodes appear to result in damage to subcortical and limbic areas, the frontal lobes and the cerebellum.

Postconcussion Syndrome

Postconcussion syndrome is usually defined as a rapid acceleration/deceleration of the brain resulting in a period of amnesia, and followed by a number of neurophysiological and neuropsychological symptoms including headache, poor memory, difficulties in attention and concentration, and anxiety/depression. In the past, it was believed that concussion was a transient state in which no organic damage resulted, although it is now clear that with careful examination, microscopic damage can be found.

Early symptoms (those of which the patient complains immediately after regaining full consciousness) include: headache, dizziness, vomiting, nausea, drowsiness, and blurred vision. Long-term symptoms (those that are reported at clinical visits several weeks later) include memory and concentration problems, fatigue, depression, anxiety, irritability, insomnia, and poor hearing and vision.

Neuropsychological functioning gradually returns to normal within four to six weeks although the recovery period may take up to a year depending on the age, post traumatic amnesia, job stress, use of alcohol, mental exertion, previous history of head trauma, and personality. In a study by Russell (1971), 93% of patients under the age of 40 and 78% of those over 40 were working two months after injury. Another factor which may increase recovery time, found with work-related injuries and automobile accidents, is whether financial compensation is involved. For example, H. Miller (1966) found that 90% of his subjects made a complete recovery after a settlement had been reached. Further, Wrightson and Gronwell (1981) reported that subjects injured in sports contests had significantly fewer prolonged complaints compared to subjects with equally severe job or car-related injuries. However, malingering or exaggeration of head injury is considered to affect only a small proportion of head trauma cases regardless of litigation or other circumstances.

Assessment of Head Trauma

In the early stages of TBI, the neuropsychologist can employ the Galveston Orientation and Amnesia Test (GOAT) which allows the evaluator to determine the duration and severity of post-traumatic amnesia (PTA) as well as the duration of retrograde amnesia. Such an evaluation is important as PTA has been found to be a predictor of recovery. Other tests that make minimal demands on the patient are (1) simple response time tasks (to measure speed of information processing), (2) picture naming (to measure visual recognition/name retrieval), (3) verbal fluency (to measure strategic memory search/name retrieval), and (4) letter cancellation (to measure spatial name retrieval). In the later stages of recovery, a more formal neuropsychological evaluation should be completed which would include administration of standard clinical measures such as the Wechsler intelligence scales, Wechsler Memory Scale, and measures of executive functioning. Executive functioning is a term that refers to a number of behaviors mediated by the frontal cortex including behavioral goal selection, planning/organization, execution, and assessment of performance. A number of measures have been developed to assess various aspects of frontal lobe functioning. For example, The Category Test and Wisconsin Card Sorting Test were designed to measure cognitive flexibility, hypothesis generation, and response shifting. When assessing verbal initiation and divergent thinking, The Controlled Oral Word Association Test is often employed. Finally, the Porteus Maze Test, Tower of London Test, and Rey-Osterrieth Complex Figure Test are useful in the assessment of planning and organizational ability.

TBI patients are usually evaluated at least three times in the postacute recovery period and thus it is important to use some repeatable tests that are relatively resistant to test-retest or "practice" confounds. Long-term recovery is usually assessed by evaluating the degree of improvement over at least one year postinjury. In addition to the neuropsychological measures, other indices of recovery, such as functional independence in activities of daily living, employability, school performance, family and community adjustment, and other social functions should be assessed.

Recovery from Head Injury

The recovery process of the brain is individual and depends upon a number of variables. Statistically, the following factors affect the prognosis for recovery:

1. *Location and extent of damage.* For example, a lesion in the frontal cortex will have less of an effect on adaptive behavior than damage to the thalamus, brain stem, or basal ganglia.

2. *Duration of time since the injury.* The longer the time since the injury, the greater the probability of recovery, with the greatest proportion of recovery occurring within the first year.

3. *Age.* Younger individuals tend to recover faster, particularly in the first ten years of life when the brain is most plastic (flexible) and intact brain structures can compensate for injured portions.

4. *Premorbid intellectual level.* Individuals with greater cognitive ability tend to show the greatest amount of recovery. For example, a person with an IQ of 120 who lost 20 points due to head trauma would have greater cognitive resources for adaptive functioning than a person with a premorbid IQ of 85 who suffered a similar 20 point loss of cognitive ability.

5. *Gender/handedness.* Females and left handed persons tend to recover better. This appears to be due to the greater number of neural connections between hemispheres for these groups.

6. *Medical and emotional health.* Those with fewer medical and mental health problems have greater resources for recovery.

7. *Personality.* Individuals who are optimistic and motivated for recovery tend to recover better than less motivated, negative persons.

8. *Social support.* Individuals with strong support systems tend to recover more successfully than persons with weak or no support systems.

NEUROLOGICAL DISEASES

It is essential for the clinical neuropsychologist to be familiar with basic neuropathology to provide a context for evaluating patient history, behavior, and test performance. For example, if a patient shows significant memory deficits, the clinician must be acquainted with the various patterns produced by different neurological conditions (e.g., cerebrovascular disease, multi-infarct dementia, and Alzheimer's disease) to provide an accurate diagnostic interpretation and useful treatment recommendations. While there are a wide number of neurological diseases, the ones most frequently encountered by neuropsychologists include cerebral vascular disease, Parkinson's disease, Huntington's disease, brain tumors, epilepsy, and dementia (Alzheimer's disease, multi-infarct dementia, AIDS-related dementia).

Cerebral Vascular Disease

Cerebral vascular disease (CVD) results from stroke, either ischemic (lack of oxygen) or hemorrhagic (bleeding). Both types of stroke can produce a wide variety of neurobehavioral impairments depending on the site and/or extensiveness of the lesion (see Brown, Baird, Shatz, & Bornstein, 1996). A summary of cerebrovascular accidents is provided in Figure 3.2.

Types of Cerebrovascular Accident		
Obstructive Stroke Thrombotic Embolic	Transient Ischemic Attack	Hemorrhagic Stroke Aneurysm Hypertension
Neurobehavioral Symptoms		
Artery	Symptoms	
Anterior choroidal	Acute confusion, inattention, neglect, anosognosia	
Anterior cerebral artery	Akinetic mutism, transcortical motor aphasia	
Middle cerebral artery	Aphasia, aprosodia, personality change, apraxia, Gerstmann syndrome, neglect and inattention, pure word deafness, alexia with agraphia	
Basilar artery	Locked-in syndrome, amnesia	
Posterior cerebral	Achromatopsia, prosopagnosia, pure alexia, Anton's syndrome	
Boundary zone	Transcortical aphasias, Balint's syndrome	

Figure 3.2.   Types and symptoms of cerebrovascular accidents

Ischemic Strokes

Ischemic strokes are most commonly associated with cerebral **atherosclerosis** (build-up of lipid deposits in cerebral arteries), **thrombosis** (formation of a blood clot on an atherosclerotic plaque), or **embolism** (plaque originally formed in the heart is discharged into the circulation and subsequently blocks a cerebral artery). These conditions produce anoxia (loss of blood/oxygen flow) or hypoxia (reduced blood/oxygen flow) resulting in either a **transient ischemic attack** or **cerebral infarction.**

Transient Ischemic Attacks   Transient ischemic attacks (TIAs) result from reduced blood flow to the brain in the early stages of vascular damage. Associated neurological deficits have a sudden onset and last for a period of a few minutes to as long as 24 hours. Symptoms are generally due to loss of blood flow to the carotid or vertebral-basilar arterial systems. TIAs resulting from insufficiency in the carotid system often produce recurring symptoms such as blindness or dimness of vision in one eye, transient language disturbances or deficits in visuospatial abilities. TIAs involving the vertebral-basilar system produce occipital headaches, dimness of vision, facial weakness, tinnitus, nausea, feelings of numbness, and ataxia. TIAs are a warning that the patient may suffer a major stroke at a later time.

Cerebral Infarction   The most common cause of cerebral infarction is occlusion of an artery by thrombosis or embolism which produces an **infarct** (cell death). The majority of infarcts involving cerebral vessels occur in patients with atherosclerosis producing arterial **stenosis** (narrowing) resulting in **hypoxia** (reduced oxygen flow), or complete arterial blockage resulting in **anoxia** (complete loss of oxygen). Cerebral infarction most commonly originates within the internal carotid and vertebral arteries.

    Neurobehavioral symptoms vary depending on the adequacy of collateral circulation and the size of the occluded vessel. Approximately 50% of patients exhibit significant symptoms (e.g., TIAs) prior to stroke onset. In acute onset, the patient becomes stuporous or comatose. A variety of other neurological signs may develop including body paralysis or weakness, language impairment, and facial weakness.

Hemorrhagic Strokes

Subarachnoid Hemorrhage   Subarachnoid hemorrhage usually results from a rupture of a cerebral **aneurysm** (dilated blood vessel), most commonly in an artery at the base of the brain. Bleeding quickly disseminates throughout the subarachnoid space and leads to a sudden increase in intracranial pressure. If bleeding is contained early, the patient may show few signs of cognitive impairment (Ogden, Mee, & Henning, 1993).

Intracerebral Hemorrhage   Intracerebral hemorrhage is usually caused by hypertension. It usually occurs as the result of the rupture of blood vessels at the base of the cerebral hemispheres causing impairment of the thalamus, basal ganglia, and brain stem. Blood is released into the brain under arterial or capillary pressure and causes dysfunction of a localized area. Most patients with intracerebral hemorrhage (70%–80%) die as a result of the initial episode because of the release of blood into the brain tissue under high pressure causing widespread destruction of brain tissue. Surviving patients are always left with residual motor impairment and memory dysfunction.

Neuropsychological Impairment

The type and extent of neuropsychological deficits seen in stroke patients is determined by the arterial vessel(s) involved. For example, partial occlusion of a major cerebral artery will cut supply to its entire field, resulting in an extensive infarct. However if a collateral blood supply from other arterial systems is available, the infarct will be restricted, and will cause significantly less neuropsychological impairment. A brief description of the type of neuropsychological impairment associated with the major arterial fields follows.

Anterior Cerebral Artery (ACA) The ACA supplies blood to much of the medial part of the cerebral hemispheres, including the frontal and parietal lobes, and corpus callosum. An infarction of the ACA is uncommon because it is provided with collateral blood supply from the anterior communicating artery.

If total occlusion of the ACA does occur, it can produce severe loss of motor function on the contralateral (opposite) side of the infarct. Unilateral damage of the dominant hemisphere may result in disturbances in language and voluntary movement. Damage to the secondary motor cortex of the frontal lobes will cause deficits in initiating and controlling voluntary movements. Left frontal lobe damage may produce a **transcortical motor aphasia,** a language disturbance characterized by a paucity of spontaneous speech, but with relatively preserved repetition and comprehension. Damage to the orbital frontal area may result in personality change, disinhibition, and apathy (see J. Cummings, 1993).

Middle Cerebral Artery (MCA) The MCA supplies blood to a large number of lateral surface areas of the neocortex including the frontal, temporal, and parietal lobes. Thrombosis and embolism are the most common causes of occlusion and subsequent infarct. Complete occlusion will cause loss of muscle tone/control which is most pronounced in the face and arm. If the lesion affects the dominant hemisphere, the patient may exhibit disruption of language, left-right disorientation, problems with simple arithmetic calculations, and an inability to recognize fingers.

Posterior Cerebral Artery (PCA) The PCA arises from the basilar artery supplying blood to the thalamus, portions of the temporal lobes, and most of the occipital lobes. Occlusions of this artery commonly result in visual field deficits. Dominant hemisphere PCA infarcts may cause reading without writing problems as well as deficits in recognizing visual stimuli. Lesions which affect the medial temporal area of the dominant hemisphere may produce severe learning and memory deficits. Lesions involving the occipitotemporal area can produce **transcortical sensory aphasia,** a language disorder producing severe comprehension deficits while having no influence on speech fluency. Nondominant hemisphere damage has been associated with lack of awareness of sensory information to the side of the body opposite the lesion, and visuoconstructional deficits.

Parkinson's Disease

Parkinson's disease (PD) is one of the most common neurological diseases in elderly patients. It is characterized by a number of physiological and neuropsychological symptoms including tremor, muscular rigidity, abnormal gait, anxiety, depression, and dementia. Age of onset is typically between 50–65 years and males are twice as commonly affected as females (J. Cummings, 1992; Shoulson & Kurlan, 1993). PD is progressive and without remissions or exacerbations, though progress can in some cases be very slow. Genetic and environmental factors have been implicated in its etiology, however, the cause remains unknown. The neuropathology of PD is characterized by loss of dopaminergic neurons in the substantia nigra and locus coeruleus leading to diminished activity of dopamine in the basal ganglia. Death occurs in approximately 10 years, although treatment with levodopa (the precursor molecule to dopamine) can reduce symptoms and significantly extend life expectancy.

Neuropsychological Impairment

Although PD was originally thought to be largely a disorder of motor functioning, recent clinical research and the longer survival of patients have revealed significant cognitive declines over the course of the disease. In the area of language, word finding difficulties and generation of words beginning with a particular letter or within a particular category (e.g., animals) has been reported (Globus, Mildworf, & Melamed, 1985; Levin, Llabre, & Weiner, 1989). These deficits are most likely due to deficits in frontal lobe functioning. Visuospatial deficits are commonly reported and include impaired performance on tasks measuring visual analysis and synthesis, visual discrimination, and visuoconstructional abilities (see Huber, Shuttleworth, Paulson, Bellchambers, & Clapp, 1986; Levin et al., 1989).

Memory   In the area of memory, *recognition* for most kinds of material, verbal or visuospatial, is less impaired than *recall*. The research literature has consistently shown deficits on tasks measuring verbal list learning and the recall of both complex verbal and nonverbal material (see Beatty, Staton, Weir, Monson, & Whitaker, 1989; A. Taylor, Saint-Cyr, & Lang, 1986). The fact that such deficits are present even in early-onset PD indicates that they are not merely an artifact of aging. Recall, even of remote memory, is affected and may parallel the development of dementia. In contrast, the ability to register, consolidate, and store information appears to remain intact.

Dementia   The frequency of dementia in PD is higher than in the general population, and may reach 20% (Hammond-Tooke & Pollock, 1992). It is classified as a **subcortical dementia** which means that it is identified by mental slowing, poor recall with intact recognition, mood alterations, reduced levels of attention, and frontal lobe deficits (executive dysfunction) typified by an inability to initiate activities, develop successful problem-solving strategies, and cognitive inflexibility. This is in contrast to a **cortical dementia** which is typified by Alzheimer's disease (DAT) and involves deficits in object naming, comprehension, memory recall, recognition, object recognition, and ability to perform skilled motor tasks (Dubois, Boller, Pillon, & Agid, 1991). For example, when compared to DAT patients, PD patients have been found to perform significantly worse on measures of list learning, orientation, verbal fluency, drawing, and timed aspects of attentional tests (Richards, Cote, & Stern, 1993).

Executive Function   Frontal or "executive" functions are particularly affected as evidenced by difficulties with goal/strategy development and maintaining and shifting attention (Bradshaw et al., 1993). PD patients also demonstrate problems with cognitive flexibility as evidenced by their performance on the Wisconsin Card Sorting Test and Stroop Color and Word Test (Richards et al., 1993). There are also problems of verbal initiation, generating solutions to novel problems without the help of external guidance, and temporal organization/sequencing (see Pirozzolo, Swihart, Rey, Mahurin, & Jankovic, 1993; M. Taylor, 1993). Finally, although PD patients obviously exhibit symptoms which suggest poor executive abilities, they usually continue to have insight and concern over their behavior, do not perseverate, and they can still inhibit their actions. This suggests that loss of dopaminergic influence in the frontal cortex produces deficits in the dorsolateral prefrontal cortex while sparing the orbitofrontal region.

Psychiatric   The most common psychiatric disturbance in PD is depression. The frequency of depression is uncertain, perhaps reaching 40%, but not correlating with age or gender. A review of the literature shows a wide range of prevalence rates for depression ranging from 12% to 90% (Starkstein, Mayberg, Leiguarda, Preziosi, & Robinson, 1992). It is generally believed that depression among PD patients is much lower than in DAT. Debate continues as to whether it is reactive to the disease or endogenous and integral to the disorder, though the latter possibility seems the more likely. The endogenous nature of the depression is consistent with changes to neurotransmitter systems and the presence of a long, prodromal Parkinsonian personality of depression, introversion, pessimism, rigidity, stoicism, and reduced affect (Stacy & Jankovic, 1992). Some depressive symptoms found in PD are related to the disease process itself (e.g., loss of facial expression, psychomotor retardation), a fact which requires the examiner to establish the presence of a depressed mood and anhedonia in order to make a definitive diagnosis.

Huntington's Disease

Huntington's disease is a progressive, neurodegenerative disorder characterized by the insidious onset of minor motor incoordination followed by uncontrollable movements, cognitive deterioration, and affective and psychiatric symptoms with personality change. Memory and speech deficits appear, along with abnormal eye movement. There is no cure, and death occurs within 15 years of diagnosis typically from pneumonia or heart failure (S. Folstein, 1989). Typical age of onset is 40, although the disease can begin in childhood (Bryois, 1989). Late onset generally produces more severe motor deficits but milder cognitive impairment (R. Myers et al., 1991). It is an autosomal dominant disorder, so that a child of an affected parent has a 50% chance of developing the disease irrespective of gender. Huntington's disease is also referred to as Huntington's Chorea.

Symptomatology

The first clinical signs of HD are typically affective, involving depression, anxiety, irritability, emotional ability, impulsivity, and aggression (Pirozzolo et al., 1993). These are soon followed by restlessness, clumsiness, incoordination, forgetfulness, personality changes, altered speech, and writing disturbances, then by problems with fine motor dexterity, steadiness, and speed. Motor dysfunction may initially present as minor tics and twitches, developing into abrupt jerks that occur randomly in place and time, interspersed with periods of normalcy. Motor impairment activity usually decreases during sleep and increases with stress and voluntary movements like walking. Speech becomes dysarthric (slurred), with disturbed rate and rhythm leading to unintelligibility. Bursts of words are emitted with pauses in midsentence. Gait becomes awkward, resembling alcoholic intoxication with short, slow steps, irregular rhythm, problems in turning, impaired balance, and sudden falls.

Neuropathology

The neuropathology of HD is typified by the progressive atrophy of the striatum (basal ganglia). Atrophy begins at the head of the caudate, followed by the dorsal putamen and then the tail of the caudate (Vonsattel, 1992). The role of the striatum is to modify cortical activity and patterns of movement by timing, ordering, and sequencing movements via a complex communication network with motor, prefrontal, orbitofrontal and cingulate structures. The caudate receives extensive nonmotor (i.e., limbic and prefrontal) inputs, and it is dysfunction of this particular basal ganglia-frontal circuit that accounts for the characteristic cognitive symptoms of HD. However, the frontal lobe also shows a 20% to 30% cell loss. Prefrontal involvement accounts for the disinhibition, apathy, cognitive inflexibility, and strategy-related problems observed in HD, whereas hippocampal dysfunction explains the other cognitive and memory deficits. Finally, loss of gamma-amino butyric acid (GABA) neurons in the basal ganglia leads to disinhibition and abnormal movements. The resulting imbalance of dopaminergic and gabaminergic neurons in the striatum can be somewhat compensated for through the use of GABA agonists or dopaminergic antagonists.

Neuropsychological Impairment

Cognitive decline may parallel or precede motor decline (Brandt, 1991). HD patients develop a subcortical dementia resembling that of PD, and consequently patients retain good orientation to place and time with preserved recognition of friends and family, insight, sense of humor, and social intelligence (Woodcock, 1992).

Frontal lobe deficits are indicated by impairment in the development and execution of mental plans, difficulties with insight, judgment, and problem-solving ability, perseveration, cognitive inflexibility, apathy, and disinhibition (S. Folstein, Brandt, & Folstein, 1990). In addition, concentration and attention both decline and consequently simple tasks are performed slowly and require significant effort (Koroschetz, Myers, & Martin, 1992).

Memory deficits appear early in HD and tend to be more visual than verbal, and involve short- rather than long-term memory, and recall rather than encoding. The most impaired aspects of memory have been found to be paragraph recall and associative word learning which measure verbal learning ability (Butters, Sax, Montgomery, & Tarlow, 1978). However, when comparing Alzheimer's (DAT) patients with HD patients, DAT patients have been found to perform worse than HD patients on memory tests, while the HD patients performed more poorly than DAT patients on tests of initiation and attention (Salmon, Kwo-on-Yuen, Heindel, Butters, & Thal, 1989).

Deficits in receptive and expressive language are rarely seen, which is in marked contrast to DAT, and is suggested as an important distinguishing feature between the cortical and subcortical dementias (J. Cummings, 1990). In fact, speech comprehension is well retained, even after total loss of intelligible production and thus television watching behavior may continue into the late stages of the disease. Observed language deficits appear to be related to frontal lobe functioning as evidenced by diminished performance on visual confrontation naming tasks, limited verbal initiation, response latency, reduced sentence complexity, and impairment on both letter and category fluency tasks (Monsch et al., 1994).

Visuospatial difficulties occur early and are generally more severe than language impairment. HD patients have been found to perform significantly worse than normal controls on tasks measuring general visuospatial processing, mental rotation and manipulation, and geographical location (Bylsma, Brandt, & Strauss, 1990; Mohr et al., 1991).

With regard to affect, signs of increased levels of irritability, anger and aggression, frustration, explosive outbursts, anxiety, apathy and withdrawal are present often before motor difficulties (Koroschetz et al., 1992). Depression, suicidal tendencies, and panic all occur, and seem not to be merely reactive to HD diagnosis. As the disease progresses, inappropriate sexual, eating, alcohol, and drug-related behaviors are common, which reflect dysfunctional pathways between the frontal and striate cortex. Paranoia and schizophrenic-like psychosis, delusions, hallucinations, and confabulation reflect disruption of dopaminergic activity and are amenable to neuroleptic treatment.

Brain Tumors

Tumors are classified into two major groupings: **infiltrative** tumors, which take over the body and destroy nerve tissue, and **noninfiltrative** tumors, which cause dysfunction by compression and displacement of tissue. **Glioblastoma** is the most common form of infiltrative tumor and arises from the aberrant growth of glial cells which provide support and nutrients to nerve cells. This type of tumor typically forms in middle age and is usually found in the cerebral hemispheres. Growth rate is rapid and results in early neurological symptoms. **Astrocytomas** are a type of infiltrative tumor arising from abnormal astrocyte cells (a type of glial cell), and are generally more slow-growing than the glioblastomas, and consequently allow for greater cerebral compensation and neuropsychological functioning. **Meningiomas** are the most common extrinsic, noninfiltrative tumors, and account for about 15% of all cases of cerebral tumors. These tumors are called extrinsic because they arise from the meninges, or outer coverings of the brain. **Metastatic** tumors are infiltrative tumors that migrate to the brain from carcinomas that occur initially in another part of the body, most commonly in the lungs, breasts, adrenal system, and lymphatic system. They are generally fast-growing tumors and because these tumors are multiple in nature, the overall behavioral and cognitive effects can be much more severe.

Neuropsychological Impairment

Brain tumors impair brain function by increasing intracranial pressure, inducing seizures, destroying brain tissue by secreting hormones or by changing endocrine patterns that affect a variety of body functions. The degree of neuropsychological impairment is dependent on the size, location, and rate of growth of the tumor. In **frontal lobe tumors,** there is usually impairment of executive functions, or the brain's capacity to plan and organize goal-directed behavior. Performance deficits are commonly seen on neuropsychological tests of frontal lobe functioning (e.g., Halstead Category Test, Wisconsin Card Sorting Test, and Stroop Color-Word Test). Other cognitive disturbances include loss of spontaneity, and a generalized slowing of mental efficiency. Affective symptoms include depression, euphoria and apathy. Changes in personality are also seen which include irresponsibility, disinhibition, lack of insight and indifference to the current situation. In **temporal lobe tumors,** language disturbances are common if the tumor is located in the middle to posterior region of the dominant hemisphere. Changes in mood are also common including anger outbursts, anxiety, depression and irritability. **Parietal lobe tumors** may produce aphasia or apraxia if the tumor is located in the dominant hemisphere. Tactile, kinesthetic and proprioceptive disorders may also be seen, and include the loss or inability to analyze sensation, locate body parts, and recognize objects by touch. Emotional or personality changes are rare.

Epilepsy

Epilepsy is a common disorder, affecting approximately one percent of the population, and may involve individuals of any age. The term encompasses a diverse and complex set of behaviors produced by abnormal electrical activity in the brain. The causes of epilepsy are numerous and include head trauma, cerebrovascular disorder, developmental abnormalities, disease, and toxicity. Although many seizures produce **convulsions** (motor seizures), **clonus** (tremors), and **tonus** (rigidity), some involve subtle changes of thought, mood, or behavior that are not easily distinguishable from normal activity.

Some epileptics experience peculiar psychological changes just before a convulsion. These changes, called **auras,** may take many different forms, for example, a bad smell, a specific thought, a vague feeling of familiarity, a hallucination, or a tightness of the chest. Epileptic auras are important for two reasons. First, the nature of the auras provides clues concerning the location of the epileptic focus. Second, since the epileptic auras experienced by a particular patient are often similar from attack to attack, they warn the patient of an impending convulsion.

The classification of epilepsy is complicated due to multiple etiologies as well as the often fluctuating symptom pattern. For a more comprehensive review of classification systems, the reader is referred to Thompson and Trimble (1996). In general, seizures are divided into **partial** forms that begin in localized areas in the cerebral cortex, and **generalized** forms that begin in subcortical structures and spread to involve both hemispheres simultaneously.

Partial Seizures

A partial seizure is a seizure that does not involve the entire brain. The specific behavioral symptoms of a partial seizure depend on where the disruptive discharges begin and into which structures they spread. **Simple partial** seizures include focal motor seizures, with or without a **Jacksonian march** (beginning in one part of the body and spreading to adjacent parts), elementary sensory symptoms (visual, auditory, and somatosensory hallucinations), autonomic symptoms (respiratory, cardiac, and gastrointestinal disturbances), and a combination of these.

Complex partial seizures are distinguished from simple partial seizures by impairment of consciousness, amnesia for the seizures, and the complex nature of the ictal (seizure) events. Behavioral characteristics are diverse. Alterations of language, memory, cognition, emotion, sensation, or behavior are common. Aphasia can occur as a manifestation of seizure activity and may be the only indication of the seizure. Memory distortions are common, including *deja vu.* Dreamy states and depersonalization are characterized by a sense of detachment and loss of contact with the environment or the self. Psychomotor automatism (behaviors carried out without the individual being aware of it) are usually simple, perseverative, poorly executed, purposeless motor behaviors. Typical examples are pushing, groping, chewing, lip smacking, and plucking.

Generalized Seizures

Generalized seizures are seizures that involve the entire brain. Some begin as focal discharges that gradually spread through the entire brain. In other cases, the discharges seem to begin almost simultaneously in all parts of the brain. Like partial seizures, generalized seizures occur in many forms. One type is the **grand mal** seizure. The primary symptoms of grand mal seizure are loss of consciousness, loss of equilibrium, and a violent tonic-clonic convulsion. Tongue biting, urinary incontinence, and **cyanosis** (turning blue from excessive extraction of oxygen from the blood during the convulsion) are common manifestations.

A second major category of generalized seizure is the **petit mal** seizure. The primary behavioral symptom is **absence,** a disruption of consciousness that is associated with a cessation of ongoing behavior, a vacant look, and sometimes fluttering eyelids. Petit mal seizures are most common in children, and they frequently cease at puberty.

Neuropsychological Impairment

Previous research has reported that epilepsy which occurs early in life or is associated with an identifiable cause (e.g., tumor), results in lower levels of cognitive functioning. If generalized absence seizures are frequent, this often results in significant educational delays. Also, patients with generalized seizures tend to show more deficits of attention and concentration than patients with focal seizures (Hermann & Whitman, 1984).

Patients with epilepsy frequently complain of memory difficulties. While often this is related to problems of concentration and attention, some studies have reported that epilepsy patients perform worse on memory tests than control subjects without epilepsy (Thompson, 1991). However, the literature also points out that research findings are mixed. This appears to be due to the types of measures used (verbal vs. nonverbal) and the predominance of temporal lobe epilepsy patients in test populations. For example, a great deal of research has been conducted on patients undergoing temporal lobectomy, where careful testing of memory function prior to surgery is mandatory. However, findings are confounded by the fact that memory functioning in some individuals may decline following removal of the impaired lobe yet improved in others, due to increasing control of seizures. In addition, it has been noted that differences in mood (e.g., levels of depression) may significantly affect memory performance in epilepsy patients (L. Goldstein & Polkey, 1992).

The effect of antiepileptic drugs on cognitive function has been investigated in recent years. Generally, findings indicate the presence of greater cognitive impairment with phenytoin and phenobarbital as compared to the newer drugs carbamazepine, sodium valproate and vigabatrin (e.g., Smith, 1991; Thompson, Huppert, & Trimble, 1981).

Dementia

Today, more than 11% of the U.S. population, nearly 26 million people, are older than 65 years, compared to only 4% in the early 1900s. In the year 2030, there will be 55 million Americans older than 60, constituting approximately 20% of U.S. citizens. While 1% to 2% of the population between 60 and 70 years old are estimated to suffer from dementia, by age 85 the prevalence of dementia increases to approximately 18% (G. Myers, 1990). Clinical neuropsychologists, by their role in distinguishing normal aging from dementia, play an important role in healthcare decision making. One important function is early diagnosis and monitoring. Neuropsychologists can also help assure that neither too much nor too little care has been given in relation to a particular elderly patient's actual needs.

Dementia is a *syndrome,* or cluster of behavioral symptoms, which may or may not point to a disease, but is not a disease entity in and of itself. The various subcategories of dementia are usually based on the suspected cause or primary site of the damage (e.g., cortical vs. subcortical). There may be well over 50 causes of dementia, a sampling of which are listed in Table 3.1.

Among the most well-known are the primary degenerative dementias caused by a progressive and unrelenting disease process such as Alzheimer's, Huntington's, or Parkinson's diseases. These disease processes have traditionally been categorized as cortical, subcortical or mixed, depending on the degree to which they have been purported to affect gray or white matter areas of the brain. Vascular, infectious, and toxic conditions, as well as a variety of other brain conditions may also result in a dementia. Some of these conditions may be progressive, while others, such as dementia resulting from herpes encephalitis, may be static and do not continue to worsen over time.

While most dementing conditions encountered by neuropsychologists represent persistent and/or progressive states, "reversible" or temporary dementia has also been suggested. Reduced metabolic efficiency accompanies aging and makes older individuals especially susceptible to conditions and substances that may be better tolerated by younger people. Additionally, symptoms of dementia can occur due to adverse reactions to medications (e.g., sedative-hypnotics, anticholinergic drugs); nutritional disorders (e.g., thiamine deficiency, pernicious anemia); metabolic disorders (hypoglycemia, hypercalcemia, kidney failure); psychiatric disorders (e.g., severe mood disorders, psychosis); and other conditions such as anesthesia or surgery.

Alzheimer's Disease

Epidemiology and Etiology This disorder is the most common and most devastating form of the dementias representing 50% or more of dementia cases (W. Cummings & Benson, 1992). Dementia of the Alzheimer's type (DAT) is estimated to affect between 1.5 to 3 million people in the United States over age 65, and approximates 50% of all dementia patients over age 85 (Katzman & Kawas, 1994). About twice as many women as men in the older population have DAT, but it is not clear if this represents a gender preference or a predominantly female elderly population. Those with more education

Table 3.1.   Causes of dementia

Cortical Dementias
    Alzheimer's disease
    Pick's disease
    Wilson's disease
Subcortical Dementias
    Huntington's disease
    Parkinsons's disease
    Progressive supranuclear palsy
Mixed Dementias
    Lewy body dementia
    Vascular dementias
    Binswanger's disease
Infectious Conditions
    AIDS Dementia
    Creutzfeld-Jacob disease
Static Dementias
    Alcoholic dementia
    Heavy metal poisoning
    Herpes encephalitis
    Tumor
    Head trauma
Reversible Dementias
    Addison's disease
    Thyroid disorders
    Drug Toxicity
Pseudodementia
    Depression

seem to be less likely to develop DAT, but again this is probably more a marker of continued intellectual activity through life. Family history of DAT in a first-degree relative has been shown to increase the risk of developing dementia by as much as 400% (van Duijn, Hofman, & Kay, 1991). In support of the presence of a genetic factor in the development of DAT, individuals born with Down's syndrome, resulting in an abnormality on chromosome 21, inevitably develop a dementia, usually by age 40, and experience brain changes similar to those seen in DAT (i.e., neurofibrillary tangles and senile plaques). Other risk factors identified have included head trauma and exposure to neurotoxins (Katzman & Kawas, 1994).

Neuropathology   DAT is considered a "cortical dementia" because major areas of the cerebral cortex are involved resulting in massive cell loss and brain shrinkage. However, major subcortical limbic system structures are also affected, particularly in the areas of the hippocampus and amygdala. Specifically, the major pathways to and from the hippocampus are destroyed. Thus the hippocampus is cut off from direct connections to association cortices so that the most direct feedback system to the brain fails to work.

Two types of lesions are particularly characteristic of DAT: neuritic (senile) plaques and neurofibrillary tangles (Clark & Goate, 1993). Neuritic plaques are round aggregates of "cellular trash" that have a particular affinity for the regions where the majority of synapses are located. The synapses eventually disintegrate leaving holes and misshapen neurons where there were once synaptic connections. In the cortex, plaques are likely to be concentrated in the frontal and temporal regions (Goedert, 1993) whereas subcortically they occur predominantly in the terminals of cholinergic neurons of the hippocampus and amygdala. Neurofibrillary tangles resemble entwined and twisted pairs of rope within the cytoplasm of swollen cell bodies. Tangles and plaques are not specific to DAT. They are also seen in normal aging without evidence of dementia, as well as in other degenerative diseases. It is the pattern and quantity of these markers which point to DAT.

DAT patients experience significant loss of cholinergic neurons in various parts of the cortex. The greatest loss occurs in the temporal lobe, whereas the cingulate cortex and primary visual cortex remain relatively unaffected (Moore, 1990). There is also substantial cholinergic cell loss in the basal forebrain. For example, a comparison of the number of cells in the basal forebrain of age related normals and Alzheimer's patients showed the former group to have a 50% reduction compared to a 95% reduction for the latter group (Terry, Katzman, & Bick, 1994). Interestingly, DAT does not affect the large populations of cholinergic neurons in the basal ganglia, the nuclei of the cranial and spinal motor nerves, or the cholinergic cells of the autonomic nervous system. Some loss of noreadrenergic and serotoninergic cells in the locus coeruleus and raphe nucleus have also been reported (Clark & Goate, 1993).

Neuropsychological Profile   DAT is often missed or is difficult to classify in its early stages because the initial symptoms vary from person to person and their significance may not be recognized by the individual, the family, or health professionals. The diagnostic problem is made even more difficult because people with DAT are typically poor historians who give sparse or inaccurate accounts of the progression of their symptoms. It may also be that there are subtypes of DAT which present somewhat differently.

Although the clinical presentation of DAT patients can vary, there are characteristic patterns which are common to many. The most consistent deficits across patients with autopsy-documented DAT are memory and a fluent anomic aphasia (Nebes, 1992). Visual-spatial difficulties are also characteristic. Initially, some frontal areas appear relatively spared which corresponds with neuropsychological testing and clinical observation indicating that despite severe memory impairment, many Alzheimer's patients retain an appropriate "social facade," do not have a Brocas type aphasia, and retain normal strength and simple motor speed until the end stages of the disease.

Memory   Memory dysfunction in DAT patients is probably the most global and profound of any patient group. New declarative learning at all levels (i.e., encoding storage and retrieval), and retention over time will usually be the problems first noticed. On tests of free recall, whether the material is meaningful (e.g., stories) or rote (e.g., word lists) DAT patients perform significantly worse than controls. DAT patients also do not appear to benefit from repetition or cuing. Recent memory will be particularly affected with no initial impairment in immediate short-term memory span but with significant deficits in the recall of material after a short retention interval. Finally, short term memory span, names of family members, and familiar stories become impaired. Interestingly, learning ability for simple motor and skill tasks is relatively preserved. For example, in one motor skill learning task, rotary pursuit, subjects must learn over repeated trials to maintain contact between a stylus held in the preferred hand and a small metallic disk on a rotating turntable. In a study by Heindel, Salmon, and Butters (1990) it was found that DAT and amnestic patients demonstrated systematic and equivalent improvement in contrast to Huntington's patients who were severely impaired in skill acquisition.

Memory functioning in everyday life is observed in the patient's forgetting appointments and the location of objects. In addition, there will be numerous attempts to cope, with "memory" notes littering the house. There will be frequent confabulation, false recognition, misidentification, a general inability to integrate past and present so as to anticipate the future, and severe acquisition deficits. Finally, self-awareness is significantly compromised early in the disease process, and continues to decline as memory deficits increase.

Language/Speech   DAT patients suffer early loss in the quality, quantity, and meaningfulness of speech and in verbal comprehension. However, they do not show language problems that can be neatly characterized with other classical aphasias, as the aphasia progressively worsens both in degree and type. Early in the disease process, patients show an anomic aphasia, characterized chiefly by word-finding and naming difficulties (W. Cummings & Benson, 1992). For example, on a test requiring examinees to name pictures (e.g., Boston naming test), DAT patients are more likely to say "tool" for "hammer," or "piano" for "harmonica" indicating that the semantic category is recognized but only the general category or the wrong example from the same category can be retrieved. This type of anomic problem suggests a **semantic anomic aphasia** which represents a semantic knowledge breakdown and not a classic aphasia. In normal conversation DAT patients appear to have intact conversational fluency and comprehension. Only careful observation may reveal circumlocutions or sparsity of content. However, as the dementia progresses, comprehension problems begin to appear, followed by problems in repeating information. Lastly, declines in fluent conversational output may appear which resemble a global aphasia (Zec, 1993).

Visual-Spatial Functioning   Visual-spatial problems are evident by the middle stages of Alzhiemer's disease, if not before. In daily living, this deficit is evidenced in the patient's inability to orient to familiar environments such as his or her neighborhood and home. On neuropsychological examination, DAT patients will show poor performance on tests of line orientation (e.g., Benton Judgment of Line Orientation test), spatial construction tasks (e.g., WAIS-III Block Design), copying (e.g., Rey Osterreith complex figure test, Bender Gestalt), drawing (e.g., Clock Drawing Test), and visual integration (e.g., Hooper Visual Organization Test). It appears that complex tasks such as the Rey Osterreith Complex Figure are more sensitive to impairment in the early stages of the disease than are simple drawing tasks (Zec, 1993).

General Intellectual Functioning   DAT, like other dementias, is often said to result in a "decline in general cognitive functioning." Usually what is meant by this is that a large number of separate functions have declined from previous levels so that when DAT patients are administered global tests of IQ such as the WAIS-III, their Full Scale IQ (FSIQ) has declined from previous estimates. However, all functions do not decline at the same rate, so it is more useful to consider the sub-components of the test.

Abstract reasoning ability is often impaired even in mild DAT (Zec, 1993). Verbally the patient may be unable to determine how two objects or concepts, such as a phone and a radio, are alike (e.g., WAIS-III Similarities). Visually, the patient may be unable to ascertain a common principle which relates multiple figures (e.g., Category test, Ravens Progressive Matrices). This can be understood as a problem in conceptualization and conceptual reasoning. For this reason people with DAT do poorly on a number of tasks which require reasoning and problem solving.

Executive Functioning   Problems in executive functioning may be seen in daily life in several ways. For example, in an attempt to compensate for memory loss, patients may write notes as reminders to themselves. However, without an adequate executive strategy, increased disorganization may result in these notes being scattered in various places around the house or listed tasks started but left unfinished. Perseveration of thought is often noticed by family members because stories are related over and over, or questions are asked repeatedly. Many apparent "personality changes" may actually be the result of frontal impairment. For example, the emergence of apparent obsessive personality traits, such as checking and rechecking, may be the combined effect of a poor memory and increased perseveration. Further, DAT patients appear to lose self-awareness or the ability to monitor their own behavior and performance. They are often described by clinicians as having little insight into their own deficits.

Problems in the ability to organize, plan and use appropriate strategies for problems solving in DAT patients are often seen on tests designed for the purpose of evaluating strategic processing (e.g., Tower of London) and qualitatively on tests designed for other purposes such as visual-spatial problem solving (e.g., Block Design test of WAIS-III). In addition, **perseverations** (inappropriate recurrence of a response) are often seen on memory testing, and on tests which require flexible problem solving (e.g., Wisconsin Card Sorting Test or Trails B).

Motor/Sensory   In relation to other areas of functioning, motor and sensory areas are relatively preserved in DAT. Simple motor speed and strength are preserved until later in the course of the dementia, but more complex motor behavior, which may involve co-ordination or skilled movement, is affected earlier.

Sensory functioning, that is visual, auditory and tactile acuity, appear to be spared by the disease process. Olfaction is the only primary sensory area seemingly affected. It has been observed that sense of smell is compromised even in the mild stages of the disease (Jones & Richardson, 1990).

Psychiatric Symptoms   In some cases, psychiatric symptoms can be explained via the cognitive difficulties accompanying DAT. For example suspiciousness and even frank paranoid delusions can occur as a manifestation of memory dysfunction. One 70 year-old woman reported that her husband had begun accusing her of stealing his glasses and other personal items. He also accused her of having an affair (after 50 years of marriage). On questioning, it became apparent that he was accusing her of taking things he was misplacing. Because of his impaired time estimation, five minutes could seem like an hour, or an hour like five minutes. He had little insight into his memory difficulties and in trying to make sense of a frustrating situation, externalized the problem and blamed his wife.

Symptoms which indicate a significant change in personality usually alert family members, thus these patients are most likely to be seen by mental health professionals. However, psychiatric symptoms which are exacerbations of premorbid personality styles make recognizing change extremely difficult. A person who was always considered to be impulsive and destructible, flighty or disorganized, may appear at first to be simply eccentric when he or she begins to loose track of daily memories. Early coping styles and defense mechanisms which were characteristic of earlier time are likely to become exaggerated and may often be used to deal with memory loss. For example, a person concerned with order, timeliness or organization premorbidly may obsessively check dates, doctor's appointments, medications, memos and lists as memory becomes less reliable.

Approximately 40% of those with DAT may also suffer from depression or symptoms of depression, although major depressive episodes are relatively rare (J. Cummings, 1992). One of the more common differential diagnostic issues consulting neuropsychologists deal with is the referral to distinguish between depression and dementia in elderly patients. The term **pseudo dementia** has often been applied to cases in which the patient complains of progressive memory loss and other cognitive changes that eventually are found to be the result of a mood disturbance rather than true dementia. Although this is clearly a challenging diagnostic problem due to the fact that both conditions share similar symptoms, there are a number of unique features of the demented patient which can be identified with careful examination of psychosocial history, behavior, and test performance. For example, in contrast to the pseudo demented patient, the psychosocial history will generally reveal a lack of previous psychiatric history and gradual onset of symptoms. Behavioral observations during the evaluation will show the demented patient to report few complaints of cognitive loss, struggle with evaluation tasks, and display minimal emotion. Further, evaluation findings will often show the demented patient to demonstrate consistently impaired performance while the pseudo demented patient will show inconsistent performance, particularly in the area of memory (see Strub & Black, 1993).

Multi-Infarct Dementia

Multi-infarct dementia (MID) is the term applied to progressive dementia in a cardiovascular patient. It is due to the cumulative effect of repetitive infarcts widely scattered through the central nervous system (Strub & Black, 1988). Patients with MID frequently show (1) episodic and fluctuating intellectual deterioration (versus the slow, progressive deterioration seen in Alzheimer's disease); (2) a history of TIAs; (3) episodes of aphasia, apraxia or ataxia followed by rapid recovery; (4) focal neurological signs and lateralized neurological deficits, such as hemiparesis; (5) patchy reduction of cerebral blood flow; (6) evidence of atherosclerosis or other signs of vascular disease (e.g., hypertension, hypotension); and (7) preserved memory abilities relative to other areas of cognitive functioning.

Dementia Associated with AIDS

The AIDS dementia complex is classified as a subcortical dementia which occurs in the later stages of the disease and is characterized by cognitive and psychomotor slowing, impaired concentration and attention, and memory disturbances (E. Miller et al., 1990). As described in earlier sections, these symptoms are common to other subcortical dementias such as Huntington's and Parkinson's disease, and indicates damage to neuronal pathways between the frontal and striate cortex.

Over the years, a great deal of research has been conducted to identify the early signs of the AIDS dementia complex (see Bornstein, 1994; Van Gorp, Lamb, & Schmitt, 1993). Some research studies have found no impairment in the early stages of the disease while others have found the presence of mild impairment in asymptomatic, seropositive patients. A review of the literature (White, Heaton, Monsch, & the HNRC Group, 1995) reported that of 57 studies comparing neuropsychological performance in asymptomatic seropositive and seronegative subjects, 47% found no significant neuropsychological differences, 21% found inconclusive results, and 32% found significant differences between experimental and control subjects. In examining the relationship between methodology and outcome for the various studies, it was found that studies which employed a comprehensive neuropsychological test battery were three times more likely to find performance deficits in the experimental groups than were those using less comprehensive batteries.

Neuropsychology of Aging

The aging brain normally undergoes structural changes such as decreased size, flattening of the cortical surface, and increasing amounts of intracranial space. Loss of neurons, changes in normal size, altered dendritic processes, and an increased frequency of neurofibrillary tangles and senile plaques have also been reported. However, this does not mean that the patient necessarily suffers from a form of dementia. Many areas of the brain, such as the striate cortex and parietal cortex, do not appear to lose a significant number of neurons over the life span. By contrast, 15% to 20% of neurons in the neostriatum and in the frontal cortex are lost between young adulthood and old age.

In evaluating older adults, it is necessary for the neuropsychologist to differentiate between cognitive changes associated with normal aging and pathology. In normal aging, predictable decline is most pronounced in three areas of intellectual activity, all of which are considered fluid markers of intelligence: new learning, abstract and complex new problem solving, and behavioral slowing (Horn & Donaldson, 1976). In general, long-term memory, or stored knowledge and habitual ways of solving problems (i.e., **crystallized intelligence**), are resistant to the effects of aging whereas novel reasoning and the ability to solve new problems or comprehend abstract ideas (i.e., **fluid intelligence**) decline with age. Since these declines are also present in dementias such as Alzheimer's disease, it is important to differentiate whether these changes indicate the beginning of a progressive dementia or are qualitatively different.

ALCOHOL/SUBSTANCE ABUSE AND EXPOSURE TO TOXIC CHEMICALS

Alcohol

Chronic alcohol abusers have consistently shown neuropsychological impairment, particularly in the area of memory (Grant, 1987). Other commonly observed cognitive deficits include difficulties with abstraction, problem-solving, complex perceptual-motor functioning, and new learning (Grant 1987; Leckliter & Matarazzo, 1989). These functions have been associated with the frontal and fronto-parieto-temporal brain regions. Neuropathological and neuroradiological studies have revealed sulcal widening and brain tissue shrinkage among chronic alcohol abusers (Ron, 1987). Cortical atrophy tends to be more evident bilaterally in frontal and frontal-temporal-parietal areas of the brain (Golden et al., 1981). Some research suggests that the right hemisphere is more vulnerable to the effects of alcohol than the left (Berglund et al., 1987) while other findings support frontal lobe and generalized dysfunction models (see Goldstein & Shelly, 1982; Parsons & Leber, 1981). Studies examining the relationship between length of excessive drinking and neuropsychological impairment have been mixed. Parsons and Stevens (1986) reported, in their review of the literature, that 57% of studies showed significant correlations between length of alcohol abuse and neuropsychological test performance while 43% did not.

Alcoholic Dementia

Dementia associated with alcohol is usually observed first in patients who have a 15 to 20 year history of excessive drinking. The initial signs are a progressive lack of interest and concern for events in the environment, carelessness about personal appearance, impairment of judgment and attention, and slowed mentation. Most of these abnormalities are associated with frontal lobe disease. On formal neuropsychological testing, the most pronounced defects are seen in measures of abstract reasoning, learning and memory, and perseveration.

Wernicke-Korsakoff's Disease

Wernicke's disease and Korsakoff's psychosis are not separate diseases but essentially represent a sequential process of a single disease. Wernicke's disease results from thiamine (vitamin B1) deficiency. Thiamine is found in many foods and is absorbed through the small intestine, but only small quantities are stored in the body. Thus, malnutrition among chronic alcoholics may cause Wernicke's disease, a condition characterized by mental confusion, ocular disturbances and ataxia. Treatment is intramuscular or intravenous thiamine, and recovery is usually rapid with only a 20% mortality rate in the acute stage (Victor, Adams, & Collins, 1971). However, among the survivors, Korsakoff's syndrome becomes manifest in approximately 80% of patients. Korsakoff's psychosis is a state characterized by profound anterograde and retrograde amnesia and impaired planning and organizational ability. In addition, patients frequently demonstrate little insight into their disability, are generally apathetic, and, surprisingly, are no longer interested in alcohol. Other neuropsychological functions such as constructional ability and language functions appear to be relatively unaffected.

Prognosis for Korsakoff's syndrome is good with at least 20% to 50% recovering completely, and another 20% to 30% showing significant improvement in memory function. The neuropathology of Korsakoff's syndrome indicates that neuropsychological deficits are due to lesions in the dorsomedial nucleus of the thalamus and the mammillary bodies of the hypothalamus (Brierly, 1977). Finally, it is important to note that Korsakoff's syndrome occurs in only a small percentage of chronic alcoholics. One explanation is that lesions to the thalamus and hypothalamus are caused by chronic thiamine deficiency, and that most alcoholics may consume enough thiamine to prevent severe neuropsychological impairment.

Other Psychoactive Drugs

Research examining the neuropsychological functioning of individuals who use other substances is limited because of several factors. Among these is the difficulty of obtaining single drug use subjects; problems with cross sectional designs; unreliable self reports of drug use; and failure to employ multi-variate statistical approaches (see Carlin & O'Malley, 1996). Since most psychoactive drugs are illegal to use or possess, it is difficult to establish adequate testing populations while ruling out potential confounds.

Cannabis

A recent review of the literature indicates the presence of a residual effect from use of cannabis (marijuana, hashish), following a 12- to 14-hour period of abstinence. These include deficits in the areas of attention, psychomotor tasks, and short-term memory (Pope, Gruber, & Yurgelun-Todd, 1996). There is no evidence to support the presence of long-term residual effects among users.

Cocaine and Other Stimulants

Studies among chronic cocaine abusers have yielded conflicting results. Several well-controlled studies (e.g., Mittenberg & Motta, 1993; O'Malley, Adams, Heaton, & Gawin, 1992; Selby, Azrin, Ireland, Quiroga, & Malow, 1995) have failed to reveal any residual neuropsychological deficits. Other studies have reported impairments in attention, visuospatial processing speed, verbal memory, visual memory, executive and overall neuropsychological functioning (e.g., Berry, 1991; Sevy, Kay, Opler, & van Praag, 1990). Importantly, there is no evidence documenting irreversible neuropsychological dysfunction among cocaine abusers (Reed & Grant, 1990). In fact, some studies (e.g., O'Malley et al., 1992; Sevy et al., 1990) have shown cocaine users performed significantly better than controls on measures of verbal initiation and visual attention/concentration.

Heroin

Several studies have examined neuropsychological functioning in heroin abusers. Hill, Reyes, Michael, and Ayre (1979) found the neuropsychological test performance of a group of heroin abusers fell between that of a group of alcohol abusers and controls. Other studies (e.g., Hendler, Cimini, Ma, & Long, 1980; Strang & Gurling, 1989) found no evidence for the presence of residual neuropsychological impairment.

Polysubstance Abuse

Although the exact nature and impact of specific drugs on neuropsychological functioning is presently unknown, the detrimental effect of polysubstance abuse on the brain is well documented. For example, in a recent study (Selby & Azrin, 1998) examining the differential effects of alcohol, cocaine, and polysubstance abuse on neuropsychological functioning, the polysubstance abuse group was found to perform significantly worse compared to the alcohol, cocaine and control subjects in the areas of short-term memory, long-term memory, and visual motor ability. In addition, the polysubstance abuse group showed minimal improvement in performance with abstinence (5 of 15 variables) compared to the alcohol group (9 of 15 variables). The cocaine group showed no improvement with abstinence, but was not impaired compared to controls.

Toxic Chemicals

There are approximately 50,000 chemicals currently in use in the United States and more than 1,000 others are developed each year (EPA, 1986). A brief overview of studies examining the effects of toxic chemicals on neuropsychological functioning follows.

Lead

Individuals are exposed to lead in food, beverages, drinking water, and in air contaminated by automobile exhaust. Symptoms of lead intoxication include anemia, abdominal pain, vomiting, persistent headache, drowsiness, mood changes, depression, muscle weakness, paralysis, seizures, and even coma and death. Neuropathology includes brain swelling, increased cerebrospinal fluid pressure, inflammation of the meninges, and dilation of capillaries. Although workers exposed to lead generally perform within normal limits on neuropsychological tests compared to controls, the degree of abnormal performance has been shown to increase with the amount of lead exposure. For example, Baker et al. (1984) found that increased levels of lead in the blood was negatively correlated with tests of verbal intelligence, mental control, and reports of anger, depression, fatigue, and confusion.

Organic Solvents

The euphoric intoxicating effects of solvents have led to their abuse. Sniffing of solvent-containing substances such as lacquer thinner, spot remover, glues, styrene, and even marker pens has been widely reported in the literature (see Watson, 1980). However, it remains controversial as to whether there exists an "organic solvent syndrome" which arises from chronic exposure to organic solvents. Support for the existence of this syndrome comes from neuroimaging studies of house painters describing cerebral atrophy in almost 80% of those with measured intellectual impairment (Arlien-Soborg, Henriksen, Gade, Gyldensted, & Paulson, 1982). Solvent exposure has also been implicated in the etiology of several neurological diseases including Parkinson's and multiple sclerosis. In a study of Finnish car painters and railway workers (Husman & Karli, 1980), it was found that car painters performed significantly worse on tests of verbal intelligence, visual-spatial intelligence, verbal memory, visual memory, and psychomotor function. However, studies conducted in Britain and the United States have not supported the presence of an organic solvent syndrome (see Cherry, Hutchins, Pace, & Waldron, 1985).

Pesticides

The worldwide number of pesticide-related illnesses has been estimated to be between 500,000 and 2.9 million per year (Coye, 1985). Although the short-term central nervous effects of pesticides are well documented (see Anger, 1992) the existence and nature of long-term neuropsychological effects remain controversial and unresolved. For example, Savage et al. (1982) found significantly worse performance scores on the Halstead-Reitan battery for persons exposed to pesticides compared to normal controls. However, Maizlish, Schenker, Weisskopf, Seiber, and Samuels (1987), using a computer assisted neurobehavioral battery, found no significant performance differences between pesticide applicators and nonapplicators.

Styrene

A number of studies have investigated the neuropsychological effects of styrene exposure, a chemical used in the manufacture of plastics and resins (e.g., boats, storage tanks, surfboards). In a review of the literature, Groth-Marnat (1993) noted that a large number of studies have found a consistant relationship between exposure to high doses of styrene and slowing of reaction time. Other studies were reported to have found neuropsychological deficits in the areas of attention/concentration, visuo-motor accuracy, psychomotor speed, verbal and nonverbal memory, and visual problem solving. The author concluded that the available data indicated that a number of variables increased vulnerability to long-term neuropsychological deficits from syrene exposure including increased exercise, exposure to other solvents, the presence of cuts or abrasions, use of drugs or alcohol, absorbent skin, and relative physiological sensitivity to the effects of styrene.

THE NEUROLOGICAL EXAMINATION

The neurological examination typically includes both a mental status exam and a neurological physical exam. The purpose of this examination is to identify behavioral signs of central nervous system disorders. Although the neuropsychologist typically administers a wide battery of quantitative measures of brain function to identify behavioral deficits (and strengths), a preliminary assessment of cognitive and motor processes can not only provide valuable information regarding the type, location, and extent of impairment, but can often aid in clarifying results gathered from psychometric tests. Such an examination typically includes behavior, affect and mood, thought content, language, ambulation, motor function, strength, accuracy, learned acts, sensory function, language, memory, and constructional skills. Although initially such an examination can appear to be somewhat arduous and lengthy, with practice it can be completed in 20 to 30 minutes. In addition, depending upon the condition of the patient, certain aspects can be abbreviated or eliminated.

The Mental Status Exam

The mental status exam was first introduced into American psychiatry by Adolf Meyer in 1902. Based on the physical exam model, the mental status exam was designed to assess various aspects of psychiatric functioning. Over the years, a number of guidelines for conducting a mental status exam have been published (see Rogers, 1995; Strub & Black, 1993; M. Taylor, 1993). Mental status examinations have ranged from unstructured to comprehensive structured versions such as the North Carolina Mental Status Examination (Ruegg, Ekstrom, & Golden, 1990) which is composed of 36 items covering the areas of physical appearance, behavior, speech, thought processes, thought content, mood, affect, cognitive functioning, orientation, recent memory, immediate recall, and remote memory. Currently, the most widely used mental status instruments are structured but non-comprehensive. An example is the Mini Mental Status Examination (MMSE: M. Folstein, Folstein, & McHugh, 1975) which is composed of 11 items assessing orientation, registration, attention, calculation, and language. In a recent study (Roper, Bieliauskas, & Peterson, 1996), the MMSE was found to be as sensitive to cognitive impairment as the Neurobehavioral Cognitive Status Examination (Kiernan, Mueller, Langston, & Van Dyke, 1987), a more comprehensive screening measure of cognitive abilities (see Chapter 4 for additional mental status examination formats).

The mental status examination is organized in a systematic and hierarchical fashion. Since the higher cognitive functions (e.g., verbal abstraction or calculating ability) rely on the integrity of more basic functions (e.g., attention and language), impairment of these basic functions will interfere with the ability to validly assess higher functions. For example, the patient with disturbed attention and vigilance secondary to an acute confusional state will be unable to perform validly on most parts of the mental status exam because of the inability to concentrate and assimilate details. Similarly, verbal memory or other functions relying on language cannot be objectively evaluated in patients with aphasia. Thus, it is essential that the examiner not haphazardly sample various aspects of neurobehavioral functions as this will result both in confusing results and in potentially erroneous conclusions. Consequently, the following mental status outline has been organized hierarchically in keeping with neurobehavioral theory. For a more comprehensive review of the administration, interpretation, and clinical implications of the mental status exam in neurology see Strub and Black (1993).

Behavior

Systematic observation of the patient's appearance, behavior, and mood is important because:

1. Some behavioral syndromes are associated with particular neurologic lesions (e.g., the denial and neglect syndrome associated with right hemispheric lesion);
2. It is helpful in making the differential diagnosis between functional and organic processes; and
3. These factors may negatively affect patient performance on formal neuropsychological testing (e.g., a floridly schizophrenic patient will perform poorly on structured memory testing due to inattention, tangential thinking, and intrusions).

Affect and Mood

Is there evidence of depression, mania, euphoria, agitation, or rage? If the patient is depressed, is there a cause? Are the patient's speech and mannerisms congruent with the affect displayed?

Thought Content

Does the patient display loose tangential thinking? Are there obsessions, compulsions, phobias, or rituals present?

Language

The examiner should note whether conversational speech appears normal or whether there appears to be verbosity or paucity of content. Are straightforward aphasic deficits present? Is there perseveration of topics in speech? Disorders of language frequently accompany diffuse cerebral disorders as well as disorders more focally affecting the dominant hemisphere.

Memory

Memory should be briefly evaluated in terms of immediate recall (i.e., simple digit span); memorization of four words (pen, table, house, dictionary), recent memory (current events in news; how did the patient get to the office or hospital), and remote memory (date of birth, names of past presidents, names of parents, spouse, or children). Typically, recent memory is the type most affected in organic disease, but the examiner must rule out the possibility that memory impairment may be due to other factors such as mood state (e.g., depression), deficits in attention and concentration, or substance use (including alcohol, drugs, or prescription medications). This can be done by conducting a thorough psychosocial history, evaluating the patient's mood during the evaluation, and being alert to unexpected performance on neuropsychological tests. For example, the patient may demonstrate variable scores on attention and concentration tasks (i.e., perform worse on timed versus untimed tests or perform better on more complex tasks than on simple ones).

Ambulation

Formal evaluation of ambulation should include having the patient walk in a normal fashion for a distance of fifteen to twenty feet, first moving away from the examiner and then back. The examiner should observe for the presence/absence of motor symmetry, presence of ataxia or spasticity. If ataxia is present, further delineation may be obtained by having the patient walk on tiptoes or heels. Disturbance of cerebellar or vestibular function can frequently be observed by testing tandem gait (walking heel-to-toe). Posture may be affected by extrapyramidal or cerebellar disorders. Ability to initiate movement may be disturbed, as seen in various diseases of the frontal lobes or in generalized disorders. The Romberg test requires the patient to stand erect with feet together. Swaying, losing posture, or falling with eyes open suggest the presence of cerebellar lesion.

Lateral Dominance

The Reitan-Klove (see Reitan & Wolfson, 1993) lateral dominance examination has been found to be a rapidly administered and effective measure of hand, foot, and eye dominance. Briefly, this test requires the patient to perform or explain how he or she would perform various tasks with either the hands, eyes, or feet. For example, the patient would be asked: "With which hand do you write? Flip a coin? Throw a ball?" The patient might then be asked to act out tasks such as look through a telescope, aim a pistol, or kick a ball.

Motor Function

Fasciculations (abnormal muscle twitches) occur usually as a result of peripheral (lower motor neuron) disease. Spasm is typified by brief episodes of extensor rigidity, usually associated with upper motor neuron disease of the spinal cord. **Myoclonus** (clonic muscle spasm) is characterized by jerking of a limb or muscle group and is usually associated with serious progressive diseases of the central nervous system, the most common being myoclonic epilepsy and Jakob-Creutzfeldt disease. Tremor may develop at rest as seen in Parkinson's disease or with intention, as commonly seen with cerebellar disease. **Choreatic** movements are defined as quick, inappropriate movements that consist of arm flailing and random thrusting along with similar purposeless movements of the head and lower extremities. They are commonly associated with Huntington's disease or Sydenham's chorea in childhood. **Athetosis** is a writhing, nondeforming movement of the extremities typically associated with cerebral palsy. **Dystonia** is closely allied to athetosis, differing in that its duration of position abnormality is longer. Disorders of the basal ganglia are frequently implicated in dystonia.

Strength

The hand dynamometer is commonly used to measure strength of grip in each hand. Typically, the examiner gives two or three trials for each and records an average grip strength. The dominant hand tends to be 8% to 12% stronger than the nondominant hand.

Accuracy

The finger oscillation test (finger tapping) is a simple test of fine motor control and speed. The patient places the index finger with palm down on a lever that will register a count each time it's depressed. The patient is instructed to depress the lever as fast as possible over a ten-second period. A normal score is typically 45 or higher, with the dominant hand performing the task at tapping speeds 8% to 12% greater than the nondominant hand. Accuracy can also be tested by having the patient touch his finger to his nose, alternating fingers to thumb and other rapid alternating movements. Finger oscillating speed deficits imply possible contralateral posterior frontal lobe dysfunction.

Learned Acts (Praxis)

Praxis refers to skilled, learned, and purposeful movements that require integrative control, normal strength, and intact dexterity. Examples of this are ability to copy (draw) figures, use simple tools, put on clothes, or use some type of utensil. The two most common forms of apraxia are described below.

- *Ideomotor Apraxia.* Ideomotor apraxia represents the most common form of apraxia. The patient is simply unable to carry out a previously learned motor act. To assess for this deficit, the examiner should first give the patient commands by verbal instruction. If the patient fails, the examiner should display or pantomime the act, and have the patient imitate it. Sample commands used to test for apraxia are listed in Table 3.2.

A variety of lesion sites may produce ideomotor apraxia. This is because a considerable amount of cortex is necessary to process a command (receptive areas of dominant hemisphere), retrieve memories for motor movement (frontal, temporal, and parietal lobes), and perform the movement (frontal lobe), which, in turn, depends on kinesthetic and proprioceptive (parietal lobe) feedback to be executed efficiently .

- *Ideational Apraxia.* Ideational praxic functions are considered to require a higher level of cortical organization than ideomotor functions. Ideational aparaxia occurs when there is a deficit in following a verbal command to perform a motor task that requires linkage of various skilled movements (such as folding a letter and placing it in an envelope, sealing it, and placing a stamp on it). Other examples of commands that may reveal ideational apraxia are "Pour coffee into a cup, add sugar, stir, and drink." "Take a toothbrush, squeeze toothpaste onto the brush from a tube, and brush your teeth." Ideational apraxia is commonly found in patients with more generalized or diffuse brain disorders, and consequently, is frequently seen in degenerative diseases.

Sensory Function

The Reitan-Klove Sensory-Perceptual Examination (SPE) is a comprehensive series of tests that examine visual, auditory, and somesthetic functioning (see Reitan & Wolfson,

---

Table 3.2.   Samples of commands used to test apraxia

Buccofacial Movement
1. Show me how to blow out a match
2. Drink through a straw
3. Cough

Limb Movement
1. Flip a coin
2. Comb your hair
3. Throw a ball
4. Kick a ball
5. Use a screwdriver
6. Hammer a nail
7. Salute
8. Cut paper
9. Squash a bug

Bilateral Limb Movement
1. Play a piano
2. File fingernails

Whole-Body Movement
1. Stand like a boxer, golfer, batter, diver
2. Shovel dirt
3. Take a bow

1993). The visual sections of this test have already been described. The remainder of the exam is described below.

- *Tactile Double (Bilateral) Simultaneous Stimulation (DSS).* Once it is established that there is no serious unilateral sensory loss, the patient is instructed to close his or her eyes. The examiner then touches one hand, and the patient is to indicate whether the right or left hand was touched. Touch should be brief and light. The hands are then unilaterally stimulated in a random fashion initially, and then the stimulation is interspersed with bilateral (double) stimulation. Extinction occurs when touch to one side is not perceived when DSS is applied. Such unilateral suppression suggests pathology in the contralateral cerebral hemisphere, usually in the parietal lobe.

- *Tactile Finger Recognition.* Tactile finger recognition tests the ability of the patient to identify individual fingers when they are touched. First the fingers are numbered in serial fashion with the thumb being number one and so on (if for some reason numbers are a problem, the actual names may be substituted, for instance, thumb and index, middle, ring, and little finger). The patient then closes his or her eyes. Each finger is randomly touched, and the patient's responses are recorded. The examiner should make sure that the fingers are not moved because proprioceptive cues may provide adventitious feedback that obscures results. A deficit in finger recognition is referred to as **finger agnosia.** Unilateral finger agnosia implies dysfunction in the contralateral hemisphere, again typically the parietal region.

- *Stereognosis.* Stereognosis refers to the ability to distinguish form with the tactile sense. In the Reitan-Klove SPE, stereognosis is evaluated by tests of tactile coin recognition (penny, nickel, dime) and tactile form recognition (plastic shapes of circle, cross, triangle, and square). Other common items such as a paper clip, hair pin, or safety pin, may be used. Deficits in form perception also indicate cortical impairment to the contralateral side, usually the parietal region.

- *Visual Agnosia.* Visual agnosia implies that the patient cannot visually recognize or identify objects, given that visual acuity is normal and that the deficit cannot be ascribed to purely aphasic disorder or blindness. Although the patient may not be able to visually identify the object, the object may be readily identified with other sensory or kinesthetic cues. Thus, the patient may be able to hold the object and easily identify it. **Prosopagnosia** (the inability to recognize common faces, even members of the patient's immediate family) and color agnosia are also common forms of visual agnosia. Visual agnosias are typically found in association with posterior parieto temporal lesions, occipital lesions, or both.

Language Skills

Comprehensive language evaluation may be accomplished using a variety of assessment batteries which are covered in other chapters of this book. In the context of a comprehensive neurological examination, it is recommended that the examiner use either the aphasia screening test modified by Reitan (see Reitan & Davison, 1974) or the aphasia exam proposed by Strub and Black (1993). A summary of language disturbances is provided in Table 3.3.

Table 3.3.   Language disturbances

Function	Condition	Damaged Site
Naming	Anomia	Left posterior temporal lobe
Repetition	Conduction aphasia	Left peri-sylvian zone
Comprehension	Transcortical sensory aphasia	Left temporo- parietal, occipital
Fluency	Transcortical motor aphasia	Left frontal lobe, thalamus
Reading	Alexia	Left occipital lobe
Writing	Agraphia	Left frontal lobe
Prosody	Aprosodia	Right hemisphere
Gesture	Pantomime agnosia	Left occipital

Constructional Skills

The ability to copy or reproduce by drawing is a non-verbal, complex, higher cerebral function. Deficits in constructional abilities are typically suggestive of parietal lobe dysfunction, and there is a somewhat higher incidence of right hemisphere pathology, particularly right parietal, responsible for the deficit. The Reitan-Indiana exam has a number of items which test for constructional ability. Drawing a tobacco pipe, flower pot, house, bicycle, and Necker cube have also been used in testing. The Bender Visual-Motor Gestalt test (Bender, 1938; see Chapter 12) is also a test designed specifically to examine constructional ability, although there are significant limitations with the sole use of this instrument (see Bigler, 1981; Bigler & Ehrfurth, 1980). An additional test is the Block Design subtest from the Wechsler Adult Intelligence Scale, as this test correlates highly with the presence of constructional apraxia. The Benton Visual Retention Test (Benton, 1974), and the Rey-Osterrieth Complex Figure Test (Osterrieth, 1944) may also be used in the assessment of constructional ability.

The Neurological Physical Exam

Although the cranial nerve exam is normally performed by a physician, understanding cranial nerve function and pathology is critical to understanding integrated neural systems. In addition, the neuropsychologist will often be referred patients who have not received a neurological examination and are presenting symptoms suggesting a neurological disorder associated with cranial nerve involvement. Finally, cranial nerve dysfunction may alter performance on various neuropsychological measures and possibly lead to a misinterpretation of findings. For example, damage to the second or third or fourth cranial nerve may result in visual deficits which significantly affect all performance-based tasks. A brief summary of cranial nerve function is provided in Table 3.4.

- *First Cranial Nerve (Olfaction).* In testing for olfaction the main concern is for the appreciation of smell and not necessarily for the precise discrimination between odors. Aromatic but nonirritating odors such as coffee, peppermint, or cloves should be used. Each nostril should be tested separately. The patient should also be asked if there has been any change in their appreciation of taste. Any patient who is suspected of having frontal lobe disease or who has suffered head trauma should be tested.

Table 3.4.   Cranial nerve function

Number	Name	Function
I	Olfactory	Smell
II	Optic	Vision
III	Oculomotor	Horizontal and vertical eye movement
IV	Trochlear	Vertical eye movement
V	Trigeminal	Facial sensation and mastication
VI	Abducens	Horizontal eye movement
VII	Facial	Facial movement and taste
VIII	Auditory/vestibular	Hearing and balance
IX	Glossopharyngeal	Pharyngeal sensation
X	Vagus	Autonomic function, swallowing, voice
XI	Accessory	Head turning, flexion, and extension
XII	Hypoglossal	Tongue movement

- *Second Cranial Nerve (Vision).* Each eye can be tested for visual acuity, typically using a Snellen eye chart. Visual fields are tested by having the patient fix his or her gaze on the examiner's nose, and then identifying a small object when it enters the visual field periphery. Each quadrant should be tested separately. Simultaneous visual stimulation is tested by having the patient fix his or her gaze on the examiner's nose; the examiners arms are placed into the lateral extent of either the superior or inferior quadrant; the examiner then discretely moves one hand (finger) or both simultaneously. If the patient perceives stimulation in either quadrant with singular stimulation, but does not perceive stimulation in one quadrant or entire visual field with simultaneous stimulation, this pattern is considered to be a sign for contralateral dysfunction in the visual system. The lack of perception in one aspect of the visual field has been termed **simultagnosia.**

- *Third Cranial Nerve (Pupils).* Shining a light in one eye normally leads to constriction of both pupils. Unilateral pupillary dilation is seen with defects in third nerve functioning and is common in moderate to severe traumatic injury to the brain. The pupillary light reflex involves a direct pathway to the midbrain from the optic tract.

- *Third, Fourth, and Sixth Cranial Nerves (Ocular Motility).* The third and fourth cranial nerve function can be assessed by having the patient follow a target up (third nerve) and down (third and fourth nerves). Damage to the sixth cranial nerve often produces **diplopia** (double vision) because it significantly affects lateral eye movement.

- *Fifth Cranial Nerve (Facial).* This nerve is divided into sensory and motor sections. The motor division can be tested by palpating the masseter and temporal muscles simultaneously while the jaw is clenched. The examiner should also test for any deviation in movement of the mouth on opening. To test sensation, the patient's perception of a light touch with a wisp of cotton to the upper jaw, lower jaw, and forehead should be tested.

- *Seventh Cranial Nerve (Facial).* The seventh cranial nerve innervates those muscles of the face not innervated by the fifth cranial nerve. Examination should include inspection for any asymmetry in facial musculature at rest, as well as spontaneous movement and movement on command (e.g., wrinkle forehead, frown, smile).

- *Eighth Cranial Nerve (Hearing).* Hearing can be screened by determining if the patient can hear a wrist watch ticking, a common word being whispered, or by light rubbing or snapping of fingers. To test for auditory extinction (suppression) the examiner should simultaneously stimulate each ear by lightly rubbing the fingers together very quickly. However, it should be noted that the finding of auditory extinction (or suppression with double simultaneous stimulation to one side) may also be indicative of contralateral temporal dysfunction rather than cranial nerve impairment.

- *Ninth, Tenth, and Twelfth Cranial Nerves (Brain Stem).* Symmetric deviation of the palate, symmetric gag reflex, normal quality of speech, and normal swallowing all indicate intact functioning of the ninth and tenth cranial nerves. The twelfth cranial nerve innervates the tongue and is tested by examining the tongue for any asymmetry, wasting, or fasciculations.

- *Eleventh Cranial Nerve (Motor).* The nerve is tested by having the patient shrug his shoulders, turn his head to each side, and bow his head.

NEUROIMAGING TECHNIQUES

A major role of early clinical neuropsychologists was to predict the location of brain pathology on the basis of behavioral data. However, clinicians today have access to a variety of advanced neuroimaging techniques which are far superior to neuropsychological assessment in identifying lesion sites. The primary methods for examining brain structure, function, and pathology include computerized tomography, magnetic resonance imaging, positron emission tomography, single photon emission computed tomography, and functional magnetic resonance imaging.

Electroencephalography

The electroencephalogram (EEG) is a gross measure of the electrical activity of the brain. It is recorded through large electrodes by a device called an electorencephalograph. Electrodes, generally eight or fewer, are attached with adhesive to various locations on the surface of the scalp. The electrodes do not record the activity of any one neuron, but an average of the whole population of cells in the area under the electrode. EEG abnormalities may be divided into two types: distortion, alteration, and disappearance of both normal and abnormal waves, and the appearance of abnormal rhythms with or without the disturbance of normal electrical activity. Abnormalities in the EEG recording may suggest the presence of epilepsy, tumor, or other medical problem. However, abnormality on a EEG tracing may not be clinically significant and may only represent a long-standing electrical disturbance not related to a disease process. Also, a normal EEG does not exclude significant underlying neurological disease. In many patients with significant brain lesions the EEG is normal. EEG is most helpful when it is done during the early course of the patient's evaluation, after an acute, unexplained change in the patient's neurological status, and sequentially for comparison of findings on different EEG examinations (Sharbrough & Sundt, 1982).

Computerized Tomography

Available since the early 1970s, computerized tomography (CT) is the most well-established and widely used of the modern neuroimaging techniques. CT scanning provides a visual reconstruction of brain structure by measuring tissue density. This visual picture of the brain is obtained by placing the patient on a table and inserting his or her head into the middle of a doughnut-shaped ring. An X-ray source is moved in a circular path around the head and at each position it delivers a small amount of X-radiation which passes through the head. How much of this radiation is absorbed within the head depends on the density of the tissue. A ring of detectors opposite the X-ray source analyzes the amount of X-radiation that has passed through the head. The X-ray tube and detectors are then moved to a new position, and the process is repeated until a composite picture can be constructed by a computer on the basis of many X-ray views from different angles around the head. By passing X-ray beams through the head from many different angles on a single plane, a slice of brain tissue can be reconstructed. A series of horizontal slices are obtained at regular intervals which together provide an image of brain structure. In a standard CT image, hypodense structures such as bone appear white, structures such as the ventricles appear black, and the various neuronal tissues appear as different shades of gray. Cerebral pathology is detected as a change in the normal density of specific brain structures. CT scans can reveal brain atrophy, tumors, and enlarged ventricles.

Magnetic Resonance Imaging (MRI)

Magnetic Resonance Imaging generates pictures that reveal structural details in the living brain without exposure to X-rays. MRI involves placing the patient within a large magnet which causes the nuclei of some molecules in the body to spin with a particular orientation. When a radio frequency wave is then passed through the brain, these nuclei emit radio waves of their own, because different molecules emit energy at different frequencies. The MRI scanner is tuned to detect the radiation from hydrogen molecules. Because these molecules are present in different concentrations in different tissues, the scanner can use the information to prepare pictures of slices of the brain.

Unlike CT scans, which are limited to the horizontal plane, MRI scans can be taken in the sagittal or frontal planes as well. There are a number of advantages to the use of MRI over CT. First, MRI produces a superior picture of brain tissue which allows for the identification of smaller lesions than CT. Second, it has the ability to distinguish between white and grey matter. Third, MRI has the ability to detect ischemic changes in brain tissue within 45 minutes post-onset, whereas CT can only detect the full extent of tissue damage after several days (Donnan, 1992). Fourth, there is no interference from bone which enables the clinician to examine structures which are otherwise obscured (e.g., pituitary gland, eyeballs, and spinal cord). Finally, MRI is capable of detecting neuropathology produced by some degenerative neurological disorders such as the formation of plaque in multiple sclerosis. Limitations of MRI imaging are the substantially higher cost compared to CT, and the length of time required to complete the assessment (approximately 15 minutes). In addition, MRI images can reveal only stationary structures, not movement. Like CT scans, an MRI image can reveal structural defect such as enlarged ventricles or an atrophied cortex.

Positron Emission Tomography (PET)

In contrast to CT and MRI imaging techniques, PET provides information on the activity of neural mechanisms underlying behavior, and thus provides understanding of the functioning of the normal or damaged brain. PET is based on the assumption that an increase in the level of neuronal activity in a particular region will be accompanied by an increase in physiological changes in the brain (e.g., cerebral blood flow, regional glucose metabolism, and regional oxygen consumption).

First, the patient receives an injection of a chemical (usually glucose) which contains a radioactive label. The radioactive half-lives of these chemicals range from 110 seconds to two minutes. Because their half-lives are so short, they must be made in a cyclotron near the PET scanner. Cyclotrons are very large and expensive, and consequently PET scans are available only at the largest research hospitals. The chemical chosen for injection depends upon the nature of the investigation. Glucose, for example, will go to the most active areas of the brain, so that the "scans" can then identify which areas of the brain are experiencing the most activity at a given moment.

As a radioactive label decays, it releases a positron, which immediately collides with a nearby electron. When a positron and electron collide, they emit two gamma rays in exactly opposite directions. The patient's head is surrounded by a set of gamma ray detectors. When the detectors record two gamma rays at the same time, they identify a spot halfway between them as the point of origin of the gamma rays. Using this information, a computer can determine how many gamma rays are coming from each spot in the brain, and therefore, how much of the radioactively labeled chemical is located in each area (Phelps & Mazziotta, 1985). PET scans enable physicians to localize tumors, certain types of epilepsy, and other disorders that alter the metabolic rate of a given brain area.

Single Photon Emission Computed Tomography (SPECT)

Although the use of radioactive isotopes that have a relatively short half-life allows the PET imaging process to obtain several images from a single individual, the need for ready access to a cyclotron makes the total cost prohibitive. A more affordable alternative is SPECT which uses photon-emitting isotopes that have a relatively long half-life and can therefore be produced commercially at distant sites. Another advantage of SPECT is that once the radioactive isotopes enter brain tissue, their metabolites remain trapped for several hours. Thus, images reflecting regional cerebral blood flow (rCBF) at the time of injection can be taken up to several hours later (Prichard & Brass, 1992). The disadvantage of SPECT is that spatial resolution is poor compared to PET.

Functional MRI (fMRI)

This technique has permitted researchers and clinicians to obtain images of functional activity using MRI. Like PET and SPECT, fMRI is based on the measurement of changes in rCBF that accompany local variations in the level of neural activity. Increases in rCBF exceed the oxygen demands of cells in active areas, thereby resulting in a net increase in local blood oxygen levels. The amount of oxygen bound to hemoglobin affects the magnetic properties of the latter, and rapid MRI methods are sensitive to these hemodynamic changes. There are several advantages of fMRI. First, the signal is obtained from the blood, which acts as an endogenous contrast agent; injection of radioactive isotopes is therefore unnecessary. Second, fMRI provides functional images that can be used in conjunction with structural images from static MRI, thereby permitting extremely accurate localization of activity. Finally, fMRI has a relatively high spatial resolution, and has been already used to study patterns of neural activity accompanying primary sensory and motor functions, language, and visual imagery (Cohen & Bookheimer, 1994).

RECOMMENDED READING

Grant, I, & Adams, K.M. (1996) (2nd Ed.). *Neuropsychological assessment of neuropsychiatric disorders.* New York: Oxford University Press.

Mesulam, M.M. (1990). *Principles of behavioral neurology.* (Ed.) Philadelphia: F.A. Davis.

Strub, R.L., & Black, W.F. (1993). *The Mental status examination in neurology* (3rd ed.). Philadelphia: F.A. Davis company.

Woodcock, J.H. (1992). *Movement disorders in neurology and neuropsychiatry.* Oxford: Blackwell.

Zec, R.R. (1993). *Neuropsychology of Alzheimer's disease and other dementias.* Oxford: Oxford University Press.

REFERENCES

Anderson, S.W., Damasio, H., Jones, R.D., & Trannel, D. (1991). Wisconsin card sorting test performance as a measure of frontal lobe damage. *Journal of Clinical and Experimental Neuropsychology, 13,* 909–922.

Anger, W.K. (1992). Assessment of neurotoxicity in humans. In H. Tilson & L. Mitchell (Eds.), *Neurotoxicology.* New York: Raven Press.

Arlien-Soborg, P., Henriksen, L., Gade, A., Gyldensted, C., & Paulson, O.B. (1982). Chronic painter's syndrome. *Acta Neurologica Scandinavica, 60,* 149–156.

Baker, E.L., Feldman, R.G., White, R.A., Harley, J.P., Niles, C.A., Dinse, G.E., & Berkey, C.S. (1984). Occupational lead neurotoxicity: A behavioral and electrophysiologial evaluation: Study design and year one results. *British Journal of Industrial Medicine, 41,* 352–361.

Beatty, W.W., Staton, R.D., Weir, W.S., Monson, N., & Whitaker, H.A. (1989). Cognitive disturbances in Parkinson's disease. *Journal of Geriatric Psychiatry and Neurology, 2,* 22–23.

Bender, L.A. (1938). A visual motor Gestalt test and its clinical use. *American Orthopsychiatric Association Research Monographs,* (No. 3).

Benson, D.F. (1993). Prefrontal abilities. *Behavioural Neurology, 6,* 75–81.

Benson, D.F., & Greenberg, J.P. (1969). Visual form agnosia. *Archives of Neurology, 20,* 82–92.

Benton, A.L. (1968). Differential effects of frontal lobe disease. *Neuropsychologia, 6,* 53–60.

Benton, A.L. (1974). *The revised visual retention test* (4th ed.). New York: Psychological Corporation.

Berg, E.A. (1948). A simple objective treatment for measuring flexibility in thinking. *Journal of General Psychology, 39,* 15–22.

Berglund, M., Hagstadius, S., Risberg, J., Johanson, T.M., Bliding, A., & Mubrin, Z. (1987). Normalization of regional cerebral blood flow in alcoholics during the first 7 weeks of abstinence. *Acta Psychiatrica Scandinavica, 75,* 202–208.

Berry, J.C. (1991). Neuropsychological deficits in abstaining cocaine abusers. *Dissertation Abstracts International, 52,* 3284B.

Bigler, E.D. (1981). The continued inappropriate singular use of the Bender visual motor Gestalt test. *Professional Psychology, 12,* 562–569.

Bigler, E.D., & Ehrfurth, J.W. (1980). Critical limitations of the Bender-Gestalt test in clinical neuropsychology: Response to Lacks. *Clinical Neuropsychology, 2,* 88–90.

Bornstein, R.A. (1994). Methodological and conceptual issues in the study of cognitive change in HIV infection. In I. Grant & A. Martin (Eds.), *Neuropsychology of HIV infection* (pp. 146–160). New York: Oxford University Press.

Bradshaw, J.L., Waterfall, M.L., Phillips, J.G., Iansek, R., Mattingley, J.B., & Bradshaw, J.A. (1993). Reorientation of attention in Parkinson's disease: An extension to the vibrotactile modality. *Neuropsychologia, 31,* 51–66.

Brandt, J. (1991). Cognitive impairments in Huntington's disease: Insights into the neuropsychology of the striatum. In F. Boller & J. Grafman (Eds.), *Handbook of neuropsychology* (Vol. 5, pp. 241–261). Amsterdam, The Netherlands: Elsevier.

Brierly, J.B. (1977). Neuropathology of amnesic states. In C. Whitty & O. Zangwill (Eds.), *Amnesia* (2nd ed., pp. 199–223). Boston: Butterworth.

Brown, G.G., Baird, A.D., Shatz, M.W., & Bornstein, R.A. (1996). The effects of cerebral vascular disease on neuropsychological functioning. In I. Grant & K.M. Adams (Eds.), *Neuropsychological assessment of neuropsychiatric disorders* (2nd ed., pp. 342–378). New York: Oxford University Press.

Bryois, C. (1989). The length of survival and cause of death in Huntington's chorea. *Schweizer Archiv fur Neurologie und Psychiatrie, 140,* 101–115.

Butters, N., Sax, D.S., Montgomery, K., & Tarlow, S. (1978). Comparison of the neuropsychological deficits associated with early and advanced Huntington's disease. *Archives of Neurology, 35,* 585–589.

Bylsma, R.W., Brandt, J., & Strauss, M.E. (1990). Aspects of procedural memory are differentially impaired in Huntington's disease. *Archives of Clinical Neuropsychology, 5,* 287–297.

Carlin, A.S., & O'Malley, S. (1996). Neuropsychological consequences of drug abuse. In I. Grant, & K.M. Adams (Eds.), *Neuropsychological assessment of neuropsychiatric disorders* (2nd ed., pp. 486–503). New York: Oxford University Press.

Cherry, N., Hutchins, H., Pace, T., & Waldron, H.A. (1985). Neurobehavioral effects of repeated occupational exposure to toluene and paint solvents. *British Journal of Industrial Medicine, 42,* 291–300.

Clark, R.F., & Goate, A.M. (1993). Molecular genetics of Alzheimer's disease. *Archives of Neurology, 50,* 1164–1172.

Cohen, M.S., & Bookheimer, S.Y. (1994). Localization of brain function using magnetic resonance imaging. *Trends in Neurosciences, 17,* 268–277.

Coye, M.J. (1985). The health effects of agricultural productions: 1. The health of agricultural workers. *Journal of Public Health Policy, 6,* 349–370.

Cummings, J.L. (1990). *Subcortical dementia.* New York: Oxford University Press.

Cummings, J.L. (1992). Parkinson's disease and parkinsonism. In A.B. Joseph & R.R. Young (Eds.), *Movement disorders in neurology and neuropsychiatry* (pp. 195–203). Oxford, England: Blackwell Scientific.

Cummings, J.L. (1993). Frontal-subcortical circuits and human behavior. *Archieves of Neurology, 50,* 873–879.

Cummings, W.R., & Benson, D.F. (1992). *Dementia: A clinical approach* (2nd ed.). Boston: Butterworth-Heinemann.

Damasio, H. (1991). Neuroanatomical correlates of the aphasias. In M.T. Sarno (Ed.), *Acquired aphasia* (pp. 45–72). San Diego: Academic Press.

Donnan, G.A. (1992). Investigation of patients with stroke and transient ischemic attacks. *Lancet, 339,* 473–477.

Drewe, E.A. (1974). The effect of type and area of brain lesions on Wisconsin card sorting test performance. *Cortex, 10,* 159–170.

Dubois, B., Boller, F., Pillon, B., & Agid, Y. (1991). Cognitive deficits in Parkinson's disease. In F. Boller & J. Grafman (Eds.), *Handbook of neuropsychology* (pp. 195–240). Amsterdam, The Netherlands: Elsevier.

Environmental Protection Agency, Office of Toxic Substances. (1986). *Core activities of the office of toxic substances* (Report no. 560/4-76-005). Washington, DC: Author.

Folstein, M.F., Folstein, S.E., & McHugh, P.R. (1975). Mini-mental state. *Journal of Psychiatric Research, 12,* 189–198.

Folstein, S.E. (1989). *Huntington's disease: A disorder of families.* Boston: John Hopkins University Press.

Folstein, S.E., Brandt, J., & Folstein, M.F. (1990). Huntington's disease. In J.L. Cummings (Ed.), *Subcortical dementia* (pp. 87–107). New York: Oxford University Press.

Globus, M., Mildworf, B., & Melamed, E. (1985). Cerebral blood flow and cognitive impairment in Parkinson's disease. *Neurology, 35,* 1135–1139.

Goedert, M. (1993). Tauprotein and the neurofibrillary pathology of Alzhiemer's disease. *Trends in the Neurosciences, 16,* 460–465.

Golden, C.J., Graber, B., Blose, L., Berg, R., Coffman, J., & Bloch, S. (1981). Difference in brain densities between chronic alcoholic and normal control patients. *Science, 211,* 508–510.

Goldstein, G., & Shelly, C. (1982). A multivariate neuropsychological approach to brain lesion localization in alcoholism. *Addictive Behaviors, 7,* 165–175.

Goldstein, L.H., & Polkey, C.E. (1992). Everyday memory after unilateral temporal lobectomy or amygdalohippocampectomy. *Cortex, 28,* 189–201.

Grant, I. (1987). Alcohol and the brain: Neuropsychological correlates. *Journal of Consulting and Clinical Psychology, 55,* 310–324.

Groth-Marnat, G. (1993). Neuropsychological effects of styrene exposure: A review of current literature. *Perceptual and Motor Skills, 77,* 1139–1149.

Hammond-Tooke, G.D., & Pollock, M. (1992). Depression, dementia, and Parkinson's disease. In A.B. Joseph & RR. Young (Eds.), *Movement disorders in neurology and neuropsychiatry* (pp. 221–229). Oxford, England: Blackwell Scientific.

Heaton, R.K. (1981). *Wisconsin card sorting test (WCST).* Odessa, FL: Psychological Assessment Resources.

Heaton, R.K., Grant, I., & Matthews, C.G. (1996). Demographic influences on neuropsychological test performance. In I. Grant, & K.M. Adams (Eds.), *Neuropsychological assessment of neuropsychiatric disorders* (2nd ed., pp. 141–163). New York: Oxford University Press.

Heindel, W.C., Salmon, D.P., & Butters, N. (1990). Pictorical priming and cued recall in Alzhiemer's and Huntington's disease. *Brain and Cognition, 13,* 282–295.

Hendler, N., Cimini, C., Ma, T., & Long, D. (1980). A comparison of cognitive impairment due to benzodiazepines and to narcotics. *American Journal of Psychiatry, 137,* 828–830.

Hermann, B.P., & Whitman, S. (1984). Behavioral and personality correlates of epilepsy: A review, methodological critique, and conceptual model. *Psychological Bulletin, 95,* 451–497.

Hill, H.E., Reyes, R.B., Michael, J., & Ayre, F. (1979). A comparison of alcoholics and heroin abusers: Computerized transaxial tomography and neuropsychological functioning. *Currents in Alcoholism, 5,* 187–205.

Hoeppner, J.B., Garron, D.C., Wilson, R.S., & Koch-Weser, M.P. (1987). Epilepsy and verbosity. *Epilepsi, 28,* 35–40.

Horn, & Donaldson, G. (1976). On the myth of intellectual decline in adulthood. *American Psychologist, 31,* 701–719.

Huber, S.J., Shuttleworth, E.C., Paulson, G.W., Bellchambers, M.G.J., & Clapp, L.E. (1986). Cortical vs. subcortical dementia: Neuropsychological differences. *Archives of Neurology, 43,* 392–394.

Husman, K., & Karli, P. (1980). Clinical neurological findings among car painters exposed to a mixture of organic solvents. *Scandinavian Journal of Work, Environment & Health, 6,* 33–39.

Janowsky, J.S., Shimamura, A.P., & Squire, L.R. (1989). Source memory impairment in patients with frontal lobe lesions. *Neuropsychologia, 27,* 1043–1056.

Jones, A.W.R., & Richardson, J.S. (1990). Alzhiemer's disease: Clinical and pathological characteristics. *International Journal of Neuroscience, 50,* 147–168.

Katzman, R., & Kawas, C. (1994). The epidemiology of dementia and Alzheimer disease. In R.D. Terry, R. Katzman, & K.L. Bick (Eds.) *Alzhiemer disease* (pp. 105–122). New York: Raven Press.

Kelly, M.D., Grant, I., Heaton, R.K., Marcotte, T.D., & and the HNRC Group. (1996). Neuropsychological findings in HIV infection and AIDS. In I. Grant & K.M. Adams (Eds.), *Neuropsychological assessment of neuropsychiatric disorders* (2nd ed., pp. 403–422). New York: Oxford University Press.

Kiernan, R.J., Mueller, J., Langston, J.W., & Van Dyke, C. (1987). The neurobehavioral cognitive status examination: A brief but differentiated approach to cognitive assessment. *Annals of Internal Medicine, 107,* 481–485.

Koroschetz, W.J., Myers, R.H., & Martin, J. (1992). The neurology of Huntington's disease. In A.B. Joseph & R.R. Young (Eds.), *Movement disorders in neurology and neuropsychiatry* (pp. 167–177). Oxford, England: Blackwell Scientific.

Leckliter, I.N., & Matarazzo, J.D. (1989). The influence of age, education, IQ, gender, and alcohol abuse on Halstead-Reitan neuropsychological test battery performance. *Journal of Clinical Psychology, 45,* 485–512.

Levin, B.E., Llabre, M.M., & Weiner, W.J. (1989). Cognitive impairments associated with early Parkinson's disease. *Neurology, 39,* 557–561.

Maizlish, N.A., Schenker, M., Weisskopf, C., Seiber, J., & Samuels, S. (1987). A behavioral evaluation of pest control workers with short-term, low-level exposure to the organophosphate diazinon. *American Journal of Industrial Medicine, 12,* 153–172.

Miller, E.N., Selnes, O.A., McArthur, J.C., Satz, P., Becker, J.T., Cohen, B.A., Sheridan, K., Machado, A.M., Van Gorp, W.G., & Visscher, B. (1990). Neuropsychological performance in HIV-I-infected homosexual men: The multicenter AIDS cohort study (MACS). *Neurology, 40,* 197–203.

Miller, H. (1966). Mental after-effects of head injury. *Procedural Research in Social Medicine, 59,* 257–263.

Milner, B. (1963). Effects of different brain lesions on card sorting. *Archives of Neurology, 9,* 9–100.

Milner, B. (1964). Some effects of frontal lobectomy in man. In J.M. Warren & K. Akert (Eds.), *The frontal granular cortex and behavior.* New York: McGraw-Hill.

Milner, B., Petrides, M., & Smith, M.L. (1985). Frontal lobes and the temporal organization of memory. *Human Neurobiology, 4,* 137–142.

Mittenberg, W., & Motta, S. (1993). Effects of chronic cocaine abuse on memory and learning. *Archives of Clinical Neuropsychology, 8,* 447–461.

Mohr, E., Brouwers, P., Claus, J.J., Mann, U.M., Fedio, P., & Chase, T.N. (1991). Visuospatial cognition in Huntington's disease. *Movement Disorders, 6,* 127–132.

Monsch, A.U., Bondi, M.W., Butters, N., Paulsen, J.S., Salmon, D.P., Brugger, P., & Swenson, M.R. (1994). A comparison of category and letter fluency in Alzheimer's and Huntington's disease. *Neuropsychology, 8,* 25–30.

Moore, R.Y. (1990). Subcortical chemical neuroanatomy. In J.L. Cummings (Ed.), *Subcortical dementia* (pp. 44–58). New York: Oxford University Press.

Myers, G.C. (1990). Demography of aging. In R.H. Binstock & L.K. George (Eds.), *Handbook of aging and the social sciences* (3rd. ed., pp. 19–44). San Diego: Academic Press.

Myers, R.H., Sax, D.S., Koroshetz, W.J., Mastromauro, C., Cupples, L.A., Kiely, D.K., Pettengil, F.K., & Bird, E.D. (1991). Factors associated with slow progression in Huntington's disease. *Archives of Neurology, 48,* 800–804.

Nebes, R.D. (1992). Cognitive dysfunction in Alzheimer's disease. In F.I.M. Craik & T.A. Salthouse (Eds.), *The handbook of aging and cognition* (373–446). Hillsdale, NJ: Erlbaum.

Ogden, J.A., Mee, E.W., & Henning, M. (1993). A prospective study of impairment of cognition and memory and recovery after subarachnoid hemorrhage. *Neurosurgery, 33,* 1–15.

O'Malley, S., Adamse, M., Heaton, R.K., & Gawin, F.H. (1992). Neuropsychological impairment of chronic cocaine abusers. *American Journal of Drug and Alcohol Abuse, 18,* 131–144.

Osterrieth, P.A. (1944). Le test de popie d'une fugure complexe. *Archives de Psychologie, 30,* 206–256.

Parker, R.S. (1990). *Traumatic brain injury and neuropsychological impairment: Sensorimotor, cognitive, emotional, and adaptive problems of children and adults.* New York: Springer-Verlag.

Parsons, O.A., & Leber, W.R. (1981). The relationship between cognitive dysfunction and brain damage in alcoholics: Causal, interactive, or epiphenomenal? *Alcoholism: Clinical and Experimental Research, 5,* 326–343.

Parsons, O.A., & Stevens, L. (1986). Previous alcohol intake and residual cognitive deficits in detoxified alcoholics and animals. *Alcohol and Alcoholism, 21,* 137–157.

Phelps, M.E., & Mazziotta, J.C. (1985). Positron emission tomography: Human brain function and biochemistry. *Science, 228,* 799–809.

Pirozzolo, F.J., Swihart, A.A., Rey, G.J., Mahurin, R., & Jankovic, J. (1993). Cognitive impairments associated with Parkinson's disease and other movement disorders. In J. Jankovic & E. Tolosa (Eds.), *Parkinson's disease and movement disorders* (2nd ed., pp. 493–510). Baltimore: Williams & Wilkins.

Pope, H.G., Gruber, A., & Yurgelun-Todd, D. (1996). The residual neuropsychological effects of cannabis: The current status of research. *Drug and Alcohol Dependence, 38,* 25–34.

Prichard, J.W., & Brass, L.M. (1992). New anatomical and functional imaging methods. *Annals of Neurology, 32,* 395–400.

Reed, R.J., & Grant, I. (1990). The long-term neurobehavioral consequences of substance abuse: Conceptual and methodological challenges for future research. *National Institute on Drug Abuse Research Monograph, 101,* 10–56.

Reitan, R.M., & Davison, L.A. (1993). *Clinical neuropsychology: Current status and applications.* Washington, DC: Winston.

Richards, M., Cote, L.J., & Stern, Y. (1993). Executive function in Parkinson's disease: Set shifting or set maintenance? *Journal of Clinical and Experimental Neuropsychology, 15,* 266–279.

Ron, M.A. (1987). The brain of alcoholics: An overview. In O.A. Parsons, N. Butters, & P.E. Nathan (Eds.), *Neurpsychology of alcoholsim: Implications for diagnosis and treatment* (pp. 11–20). New York: Guilford Press.

Rogers, R. (1995). *Diagnostic and structured interviewing: A handbook for psychologists.* Odessa, FL: Psychological Assessment Resources.

Roper, B.L., Bieliauskas, L.A., & Peterson, M.R. (1996). Validity of the mini-mental state examination and the neurobehavioral cognitive status examination in cognitive screening. *Neuropsychiatry, Neuropsychology and Behavioral Neurology, 9,* 54–57.

Ruegg, R.G., Ekstrom, D.E., & Golden, R.N. (1990). Introduction of standardized report form improves the quality of mental status examination reports by psychiatric residents. *Academic Psychiatry, 14,* 157–163.

Russell, W.R. (1971). *The traumatic amnesias.* London: Oxford Press.

Saint-Cyr, J.A., & Taylor, A.E. (1993). Cognitive dysfunction in Parkinson's disease. In J.S. Schneider & M. Gupta (Eds.), *Current concepts in Parkinson's disease research* (pp. 41–58). Seattle: Hogrefe & Huber.

Salmon, D.P., Kwo-on-Yuen, P.F., Heindel, W.C., Butters, N., & Thal, L.J. (1989). Differentiation of Alzhiemer's disease and Huntington's disease with the dementia rating scale. *Archives of Neurology, 46,* 1204–1208.

Savage, E.P., Keefe, T.J., Mounce, L.M., Lewis, J.A., Heaton, R.K., & Parks, L.H. (1982). *Chronic neurological sequelae of acute organophosphate pesticide poisoning: An epidemiologic study.* Fort Collins: Colorado Epidemiologic Pesticide Studies Center.

Selby, M.J., & Azrin, R.L. (1998). Differences in neuropsychological functioning among alcohol, cocaine and polysubstance abusing males. *Drug and Alcohol Dependence, 50,* 39–45.

Sevy, S., Kay, S.R., Opler, L.A., & van Praag, H.M. (1990). Significance of cocaine history in schizophrenia. *Journal of Nervous and Mental Disease, 178,* 642–648.

Shallice, T., & Burgess, P. (1991). Higher-order cognitive impairments and frontal lobe lesions in man. In H.S. Levin, H.M. Eisenberg, & A.L. Benton (Eds.), *Frontal lobe function and dysfunction* (pp. 231–246). New York: Oxford University Press.

Sharbrough, F.W., & Sundt, Jr., T.M. (1982). Electroencephalography. In J.R. Youmans (Ed.), *Neurological surgery* (pp. 195–230). Philadelphia: Saunders.

Shoulson, I., & Kurlan, R. (1993). Inherited disorders of the basal ganglia. In R.N. Rosenberg, S.B. Prusiner, S. DiMauro, R.L. Barchi, & L.M. Kunkel (Eds.), *The molecular and genetic basis of neurological disease* (pp. 753–763). Boston: Butterworth-Heinemann.

Smith, D.B. (1991). Cognitive effects of antiepileptic drugs. In D.B, Smith, D.M. Treiman, & M.R. Trimble (Eds.), *Advances in neurosurgery: Neurobehavioral problems in epilepsy* (pp. 197–212). New York: Raven Press.

Stacy, J., & Jankovic, J. (1992). Differential diagnosis of Parkinson's disease and the Parkinsonian plus syndromes. *Neurologic Clinics, 10,* 341–359.

Starkstein, S.E., Mayberg, H.S., Leiguarda, R., Preziosi, T.J., & Robinson, R.G. (1992). A prospective longitudinal study of depression, cognitive decline, and physical impairments in patients with Parkinson's disease. *Journal of Neurology, Neurosurgery, and Psychiatry, 55,* 377–382.

Strang, J., & Gurling, H. (1989). Computerized tomography and neuropsychological assessment in long-term high-dose heroin addicts. *British Journal of Addiction, 84,* 1011–1019.

Strub, R.L., & Black, W.F. (1988). *Neurobehavioral disorders: A clinical approach.* Philadelphia: Davis.

Strub, R.L., & Black, W.F. (1993). *The mental status examination in neurology* (3rd ed.). Philadelphia: Davis.

Stuss, D.T., & Benson, D.F. (1984). Neuropsychological studies of the frontal lobes. *Psychological Bulletin, 95,* 3–28.

Taylor, A.E., Saint-Cyr, J.A., & Lang, A.E. (1986). Frontal lobe dysfunction in Parkinson's disease. The Cortical focus of neostriatal outflow. *Brain, 109,* 845–883.

Taylor, M.A. (1993). *The neuropsychiatric guide to modern everyday psychiatry.* New York: Free Press.

Terry, R.D., & Katzman, R., & Bick, K.L. (1994). *Alzheimer disease*. New York: Raven Press.

Thompson, P.J. (1991). Memory function in patients with epilepsy. In D.B. Smith, D.M. Treiman, & M.R. Trimble (Eds.), *Advances in neurology* (Vol. 55, pp. 369–384). New York: Raven Press.

Thompson, P.J., Huppert, F.A., & Trimble, M.R. (1981). Phenytoin and cognitive functions: Effects on normal volunteers. *British Journal of Social and Clinical Psychology, 20*, 155–162.

Thompson, P.J., & Trimble, M.R. (1996). Neuropsychological aspects of epilepsy. In I. Grant & K.M. Adams (Eds.), *Neuropsychological assessment of neuropsychiatric disorders* (2nd ed., pp. 263–287). New York: Oxford University Press.

van Duijn, C.M., Hofman, A., & Kay, D.W. (1991). Risk factors for Alzheimer's disease: A collaborative re-analysis of case-control studies. *International Journal of Epidemiology, 20*(Suppl. 2), No. 2.

Van Gorp, W.G., Lamb, D.G., & Schmitt, F.A. (1993). Methodologic issues in neuropsychological research with HIV-spectrum disease. *Archives of Clinical Neuropsychology, 8*, 17–33.

Victor, M., Adams, R.D., & Collins, G.H. (1971). *The Wernicke-Korsakoff syndrome*. Philadelphia: Davis.

Vonsattel, J.P. (1992). Neuropathology of Huntington's disease. In A.B. Joseph & R.R. Young (Eds.), *Movement disorders in neurology and neuropsychiatry* (pp. 186–194). Oxford, England: Blackwell Scientific.

Watson, J.M. (1980). Solvent abuse by children and young adults: A review. *British Journal of Addiction, 75*, 27–36.

White, D.A., Heaton, R.K., Monsch, A.U., & the HNRC Group. (1995). Neuropsychological studies of asymptomatic human immunodeficiency virus-type 1 infected individuals. *Journal of the International Neuropsychological Society, 1*, 304–315.

Woodcock, J.H. (1992). Behavioral aspects of Huntington's disease. In A.B. Joseph & R. Young (Eds.), *Movement disorders in neurology and neuropsychiatry* (pp. 178–185). Oxford, England: Blackwell Scientific.

Wrightson, P., & Gronwell, P. (1981). Time off work and symptoms after minor head injury. *Injury, 12*, 445–451.

Zec, R.R. (1993). Neuropsychological functioning in Alzhiemer's disease. In R.W. Parks, R.R. Zec, & R.S. Wilson (Eds.), *Neuropsychology of Alzheimer's disease and other dementias* (pp. 3–80). Oxford, England: Oxford University Press.

Chapter 4

THE ASSESSMENT INTERVIEW IN CLINICAL NEUROPSYCHOLOGY

Robert J. Sbordone

Patients are referred for neuropsychological testing for a variety of different purposes: diagnostic (e.g., does the patient have an organic versus a functional disorder?), descriptive (e.g., what are the cognitive and behavioral manifestations of the brain insult?), evaluative (e.g., how much improvement or deterioration has occurred?), treatment-rehabilitation (e.g., what type of treatment or rehabilitation services are needed?), or forensic (e.g., are the patient's deficits the result of a specific accident or injury?) (Lezak, 1995). Although many psychologists rely heavily on the patient's neuropsychological test data to answer these questions, such data is frequently confounded by a variety of factors that necessitate that the psychologist proceed with caution to avoid arriving at any diagnostic, descriptive, evaluative, treatment, or forensic impressions without a full appreciation of the impact of these factors. The following case example illustrates this:

A 35-year-old man was referred for neuropsychological testing by his treating physician after he had been involved in a motor vehicle accident 6 months earlier. The physician wanted to know if the patient's symptoms were organic or functional because there was no clear evidence that the patient had ever been rendered unconscious or had ever struck his head during the accident. The patient complained of numerous cognitive problems, severe low-back pain, constant headaches, insomnia, and significant psychiatric difficulties. The patient underwent an 8-hour battery of neuropsychological tests. After reviewing the test data, the psychologist concluded that the patient had severe cognitive impairments that were most likely caused by a head injury the patient sustained during the motor vehicle accident.

The referring physician was unhappy with the psychologist's opinions and referred the patient to another psychologist. The second psychologist took a very careful and lengthy history from the patient that revealed that the patient had had a preexisting history of severe cluster headaches, chronic low-back pain, prior head trauma, and attention deficit-hyperactivity disorder (which resulted in the patient being placed in special education classes throughout elementary school and junior high school). The patient had an extensive history of drug and alcohol abuse, had only worked a total of 3 years during the past 10 years, had been arrested and convicted of two felonies (e.g., grand theft and fraud), and had served a total of 5 years in prison. The psychologist also learned that the patient had a preexisting psychiatric disorder, had begun receiving psychiatric treatment during his late adolescence for a bipolar disorder, and was currently taking Haldol, Vicodin, Klonopin, Desyrel, Lithium, and Imitrex. The patient also had a very rebellious childhood, which included gang involvement, reckless disregard for the welfare of others, frequent arrests and fights, repeated lying, poor judgment, impulsivity, and consistent irresponsibility. The patient was in considerable pain and discomfort after having injured his lower back as a result of falling down a flight of stairs the previous week while intoxicated. The patient had also had a verbal and physical altercation with his wife that morning after she informed him that she wanted a divorce.

This case example illustrates the numerous confounding factors present at the time the patient arrived for his neuropsychological examination, any one of which, alone or in combination, would have negatively impacted his neuropsychological test performance, regardless of whether he had sustained a brain injury in his motor vehicle accident. Given these factors, this patient would have most likely performed poorly on many, if not all, of the neuropsychological tests that were administered to him. Thus, although the test data would technically be considered valid, the presence of the numerous confounding factors described would have rendered the first psychologist's interpretation of the etiology of the patient's neuropsychological deficits inaccurate.

Sbordone and Purisch (1996) have listed a number of factors that can produce poor performance on neuropsychological tests (see Table 4.1). This list is not meant to be exhaustive nor is a discussion of these factors meant to be more than cursory.

Table 4.1. Factors that can significantly affect a patient's neuropsychological test performance

 1. Prior brain injury or insult.
 2. Congenital or preexisting neurological conditions.
 3. Absences (seizures).
 4. Acute pain.
 5. Symptoms and impairment secondary to physical injuries.
 6. Peripheral sensory impairment.
 7. Peripheral motor impairment.
 8. Current and chronic medical illness.
 9. Sleep deprivation and excessive fatigue.
10. Alcohol-drug abuse.
11. Medication use.
12. Psychiatric illness.
13. Recent psychosocial stressors.
14. Suboptimal motivation and malingering.
15. Negative patient-examiner interaction.
16. Cultural-linguistic discrepancies.
17. Vocational and avocational background.
18. Test sophistication and practice effects.

Sbordone & Purisch (1996).

CONFOUNDING FACTORS

Prior Brain Injuries and Congenital Neurological Conditions

It is generally well known that a number of congenital and preexisting congenital disorders, such as attention deficit-hyperactivity disorder, anoxia, febrile illnesses, mental retardation, epilepsy, learning disability, cerebral palsy, and neurological disorders, can produce poor performance on neuropsychological tests (Boucagnani & Jones, 1989; McCaffrey, Williams, Fisher, & Laing, 1993). Unless such disorders are identified, the neuropsychologist may erroneously attribute the patient's neuropsychological test data to a recent brain insult.

Pain and Physical Conditions

Patients who have severe headaches or who are sleep deprived, excessively fatigued, or in acute pain will most likely exhibit deficits on tests of attention, concentration, and recent memory. Unless the psychologist is aware that the patient has any of these conditions, the patient's neuropsychological test performance may be inaccurately attributed to a brain insult. Similarly, if the patient has sustained any musculoskeletal injuries that affect the peripheral nervous system, the psychologist may erroneously conclude that the patient has sustained a brain insult. For example, a psychologist who is unaware that the patient sustained a crush injury to his or her left arm might erroneously conclude that the patient has a right hemisphere brain injury.

Medical Illnesses

In general, patients with medical illnesses frequently exhibit impaired functioning on neuropsychological tests. For example, a variety of systemic medical disorders, as well as specific medical conditions and treatments, have been associated with neuropsychological dysfunction, including **hyponatremia** (Atchinson et al., 1993), **hypoxemia** (Gutierrez, Atkinson, & Grant, 1993), multiple sclerosis (Grant, 1987), renal dialysis (Gutierrez et al., 1993), cancer treatment (Adams, Queseda, & Gutterman, 1984), HIV infection (Dalakas, Wichman, & Sever, 1989), thyroid disorder (Trzepacz, McCue, & Klein, 1988), cardiac problems (Garcia, Tweedy, & Blass, 1984), cortisol deficits (Basavaraju & Phillips, 1989), **porphyria** (Grabowski & Yeragani, 1987), **Wilson's disease** (Goldstein, Ewert, & Randall, 1968), epilepsy (Homan, Paulman, & Devous, 1989), systemic lupus erythematosus (Adelman, Saltiel, & Klinenbert, 1986), vitamin B-12 deficiency (Hector & Burton, 1988), and folate deficiency (Martin, 1988).

Alcohol-Drug Abuse and Medication Use

Research has shown that acute alcohol use can produce mild neuropsychological impairments, particularly on tasks involving short-term memory recall, concept formation, and mental flexibility (e.g., Rourke & Loberg, 1996). Chronic alcohol abuse has been shown to produce significant impairments on tasks involving learning, recent memory, mental flexibility, problem solving, and executive functions (Ryan & Butters, 1980). Although the chronic neurological and neuropsychological effects of street drugs are confounded by a variety of methodological issues, the adverse effect of chronic polysubstance abuse is generally well accepted (Sweeney, Meisel, & Walsh, 1989). Although specific studies are currently ongoing to assess the chronic effects of street drugs on cognitive functioning, Strickland et al. (1993) have reported that casual cocaine use can produce neuropsychological impairments and abnormal Single Positron Emission Tomography (SPECT) scan findings.

A number of medications have been reported to produce cognitive impairments. For example, a variety of anticonvulsants, particularly phenytoin (Dilantin), phenobarbital, and Primidone, have been shown to produce a dose-dependent impairment on neuropsychological tests of attention, concentration, memory, perception, and psychomotor performance (Wroblewski, Glenn, Whyte, & Singer, 1989). Psychiatric medications, particularly antidepressants such as amitriptyline (Elavil), have been shown to produce impairments on neuropsychological measures of reaction time, vigilance, psychomotor coordination, learning, and memory (LaRue, D'Elia, Clark, Spar, & Jarvik, 1986; Thompson & Trimble, 1982). Lithium (Glenn & Joseph, 1987) and antipsychotic medications (Cardenas, 1987) have also been found to produce similar adverse effects on a patient's neuropsychological test performance. Stein and Strickland (1998) have recently reviewed the neuropsychological effects of commonly used prescription medications. They found that the patient's psychomotor functioning, concentration, and memory are commonly affected by such medications. However, it should also be stressed that the effects of the aforementioned medications-drugs tend to be relatively mild compared with the typical impact that results from brain damage.

Psychiatric Disorders

Patients with psychiatric disorders have been found to display a wide range of cognitive impairments on neuropsychological measures. For example, patients with depression (Burt, Zembar, & Niederehe, 1995; Goulet-Fisher, Sweet, & Smith, 1986; Miller, 1975; Newman & Silverstein, 1987) or schizophrenia (Walker, Lucas, & Lewine, 1992) frequently exhibit a wide range of cognitive impairments (attention, concentration, recent memory, problem solving, and executive functions, etc.) during neuropsychological testing.

Recent Psychosocial Stressors

A variety of significant psychosocial stressors, such as divorce, marital conflicts, financial difficulties, recent arrest, serious illness, altercations with others, physical abuse or assault, sexual abuse, or significant emotional losses, can affect a patient's performance on neuropsychological testing, particularly on tests of attention, concentration, vigilance, and short-term and recent memory. Furthermore, as a result of these stressors, patients are likely to experience significant sleep difficulties and high levels of anxiety and/or depression, which may cause them to increase their consumption of alcohol and/or drugs or to take medications that can adversely affect their neuropsychological test performances (Stein & Strickland, 1998).

Suboptimal Motivation and Malingering

Suboptimal motivation can occur when a patient experiences pain, fatigue, or depression. These patients may perform poorly, without any voluntary intention to do so, as a result of physical and/or emotional factors. However, individuals who are seeking financial compensation for their alleged injuries following an accident may be motivated to perform poorly while undergoing neuropsychological testing. When this is done in an exaggerated manner, it constitutes malingering. Although individuals who have a history of antisocial, narcissistic, or borderline personality disorder are likely to have a lower threshold to engage in malingering than do individuals who do not have such disorders (Sbordone, 1991), the clinician should realize that *anyone* can engage in malingering when financial issues or external incentives are present. Furthermore, malingering on neuropsychological testing does not preclude the possibility that the patient may have genuine neuropsychological deficits (Pancratz & Binder, 1997). Finally, the interaction between the patient and the examiner may become troublesome when negative interactions result in anger, anxiety, and passive-aggressive behavior. These interactions may significantly affect the patient's motivation and level of performance.

Demographic Discrepancies

Individuals with limited intellectual functioning and/or low educational levels typically perform more poorly on neuropsychological testing than do individuals with normal intelligence or higher educational levels (Ardila, Rosselli, & Ostrosky-Solis, 1992). Thus, if the psychologist utilizes norms derived from a population in which the subjects were of average intelligence or were high school graduates, he or she may erroneously diagnose as brain damaged those patients who have low premorbid IQs. Conversely, because individuals with superior intellectual functioning typically perform better than individuals with average intelligence on neuropsychological tests (Dodrill, 1988), the psychologist may not identify a patient with high premorbid intellectual functioning as impaired if his or her test performances fall within the normal range.

Prior Experience and Practice

A patient's performance on a neuropsychological test can be influenced by prior experience or familiarity with the tests he or she is administered. For example, well-developed mechanical or visuoconstructional skills that are acquired as a result of one's vocation or avocation may enhance a patient's performance on assembly-constructional tasks and thereby mask her or his visuoconstructional deficits. Similarly, prior testing with identical or similar tests can result in "practice effects," which may artificially enhance the level of the patient's test performance (e.g., Lezak, 1995) and erroneously be interpreted as evidence of recovery following a brain insult or of improvement as a result of treatment intervention.

THE CLINICAL INTERVIEW

The clinical interview process provides the psychologist with an opportunity to gather data about the patient's presenting problems and background in order to rule out any of the confounding factors described in the preceding section and to permit the psychologist to accurately interpret the patient's neuropsychological test data. It also provides the psychologist with an excellent opportunity to formulate hypotheses about the patient's underlying cognitive and behavioral deficits, which can later be evaluated after testing is completed. For this reason, the clinical interview should precede neuropsychological testing.

Because many patients who are referred for neuropsychological testing are poor historians as a result of their brain insult, a family member or significant other should also be interviewed (Sbordone, Seyranian, & Ruff, 1998). These individuals will frequently identify the cognitive and behavioral problems that the patient exhibits, but is unaware of, as well as furnish historical information about the patient's development and functioning in unstructured and real-world settings (e.g., home, work, school). This is particularly important when frontal lobe pathology or dementia is suspected.

A detailed chronological history of the patient's brain insult, including a history of the patient's symptoms, should be taken. This information should assist the psychologist in assessing the patient's cognitive and behavioral functioning and the etiology of the patient's symptoms independent of the results of neuropsychological testing. For example, patients with traumatic brain injuries are typically unable to provide a highly detailed chronological recollection of the events that immediately preceded, followed, or occurred during an accident or injury, particularly if the patient lost consciousness and does not appear distressed when discussing the accident. In contrast, patients who sustain post-traumatic stress disorders typically provide highly detailed and emotionally charged recollections of the events surrounding their trauma (Sbordone & Liter, 1995). Patients with Alzheimer's disease are poor historians for recent events and become extremely confused when they are asked to provide such information. Although patients with Pick's disease are able to provide fairly detailed histories, the chronological order of their histories is typically inaccurate. Patients with frontal lobe pathology will frequently exhibit circumstantial and tangential thinking and **confabulate.** Patients with temporal lobe epilepsy frequently exhibit viscosity; that is, they appear to be stuck on a particular topic. Thus, the patient's ability to provide a history of his or her illness or symptoms can provide valuable insights into the etiology of the patient's neurological or neuropsychological disorder.

Table 4.2 presents the pertinent information that should be directly obtained from a patient suspected of having a brain insult and from assisting collateral sources (e.g., spouse, parents, siblings, significant others). This information tends to be more reliable if it can be obtained during the clinical interview, rather than from a questionnaire. For example, patients tend to underreport problems such as alcoholism, sexual difficulties, drug abuse, psychiatric problems, or academic or learning difficulties when they are asked to complete a clinical history questionnaire or symptom checklist, particularly if they are below average intelligence, have a limited educational background, have problems with English, or have reading difficulties. The examiner should

Table 4.2.   Possible areas for a neuropsychological history

Clinical History

Complaints of patient and significant others
History of injury or illness
Onset and duration of symptoms
Neurological findings
Hospitalization history
Treatment-rehabilitation history
Current residual problems
Change in patient's condition during the past year

Effect of injury on patient and significant others
Expectations of the patient and significant others
History of medication use
Psychiatric or emotional problems since injury

Background History and Factors

Developmental

Problems or drugs during pregnancy
Place of birth
Birth order
Birth weight
Problems during delivery
Developmental milestones
Childhood diseases
Emotional problems during childhood and adolescence

History of learning disabilities
History of health problems
History of attention deficit disorder and/or hyperactivity
History of physical or emotional trauma
History of head trauma
History of neurological diseases

Dominance

Initial preference
Changes in preference
Familial history of sinistrality

Tasks performed with dominant and non-dominant hands

Language

First language spoken
Other languages spoken
Preferred language

History of speaking or language difficulties and treatment

Education

Highest grade completed
Grades attained
Best-preferred courses
Worst-least preferred courses
Extracurricular activities
Awards and achievements
Courses or grades completed

History of remedial training
History of conduct disturbances or expulsions
Reasons for leaving school
Additional schooling or nonacademic training

Military Service

Branch and dates of service
Jobs held within service
Training received while in service
Combat history

Rank at discharge
Type of discharge
Service connected disabilities

Occupational

Present occupation
Job duties
Salary
Last job held

Previous occupations
Longest job held
History of job termination or promotions
Job aspirations

Table 4.2.   *(Continued)*

Legal

Arrest history

Type of criminal offenses

Time served in jail

Current legal problems

Prior history of litigation

Prior history of disability claims

Current court cases

Cultural Background

Country of birth

Ethnic background of patient and family

History of discriminations

Religion

Religious background

Recent changes in religious beliefs

Church attendance

History of religious discrimination

Religious customs observed, beliefs, etc.

Marital History

Marital status

Number of years married

History of previous marriages

Age, education, and occupation of spouse

Spouse's expectations

Previous and current marital difficulties

Current marital stability and conflicts

Number and ages of children

Physical and emotional health of children

Living status of children

Effects of children on patient

Current support system

Sexual

Sexual preference

Changes in sexual preference

History of sexual problems

Changes in libido

History of extra-marital affairs

History of venereal disease

Family

Parents

Age and education

Occupation

Personality

Marital status and history

Alcohol- and substance-abuse history

Psychiatric history

Criminal history

Health history

Relationship with patient

History of neurological disorders

Stability of patient's marriage

History of divorce and/or separation

Siblings

Number and ages of siblings

Education and occupation

Personality

Marital status and history

Alcohol- and substance-abuse history

Psychiatric history

Criminal history

Health history

History of neurological disorders

History of divorce and/or separation

Relationship with patient

Psychiatric

History of previous emotional or psychiatric
difficulties

History of suicidal ideation or behavior

History of psychiatric treatment

History of psychiatric hospitalization

History of psychiatric medications

Family history of psychiatric illness or
treatment

(continued)

Table 4.2.   *(Continued)*

Current Stressors

Death or loss of spouse or family member	Recent accidents
Divorce or marital separation	Recent injuries or illnesses
Marital difficulties	Recent relocation of self or family
Job difficulties or termination	Recent travel
Financial difficulties	Recent problems with law enforcement
Sexual difficulties	authorities
Loss of friends	Pending litigation
Conflicts with others	Recent problems of family members or
Academic difficulties	significant others
Business difficulties	Recent problems with IRS

Medical

History of major hospitalizations	Previous surgery
Prior health or medical problems	

History of any of the following problems:

Alcoholism	Hyponatremia
Anoxia or hypoxia	Hypoxemia
Arteriosclerosis	Liver disease
Cancer	Motor difficulties
Cancer treatment	Pernicious anemia
Cerebral vascular disease	Porphyria
Coronary dysfunction	Renal dialysis
Cortisol deficiency	Respiratory problems
Deficiency (e.g., folate, B_{12}, etc.)	Seizures
Diabetes	Sleep apnea
Gastrointestinal disorders	Substance abuse
Genital or urinary problems	Syncope
Headaches	Systemic lupus erythematosus
Head trauma	Toxic or heavy metal exposure
HIV	Vascular disease
Hypertension	Vertigo
Hypoglycemia	

also be sensitive to the potential for purposeful omission of such information in medi-legal cases.

BACKGROUND INFORMATION

Information obtained from the patient and from family members and significant others is helpful in formulating a working hypothesis of the patient's premorbid level of functioning. Information about the patient's occupational and educational attainments and those of other family members may provide an estimate of the patient's premorbid level of intellectual and cognitive functioning and genetic potential. Information regarding self-professed handedness and familial sinistrality may shed light on subtle differences in brain organization. Information about past and familial neurological disorders or brain insults may provide the clinician with valuable insights into the patient's premorbid strengths and deficits as well as the possible influence of genetic and environmental etiological factors to explain the patient's present symptoms and behavior.

Developmental and Educational

The clinician should obtain information about the patient's birth and developmental history, which should include language and motor milestones, particularly with respect to a childhood history of developmental slowness, hyperactivity, or learning disability. Information about the patient's educational background and achievements (or lack thereof) may be helpful in assessing the patient's premorbid cognitive strengths and may shed light on the patient's premorbid personality characteristics. Information should be obtained about the patient's childhood to determine whether a patient was exposed to physical, psychological, or sexual abuse, which may help the clinician understand the patient's premorbid coping skills, psychological defense mechanisms, and vulnerability to stress. It may also help predict how the patient might be expected to cope with a significant alteration in his or her coping skills as a result of impaired cognitive functioning.

Vocational, Marital, and Substance Use

Information about the patient's employment history and military service background may shed light on the patient's premorbid personality traits, motivation, relationship with authority figures, level of responsibility, and ability to tolerate stress. Information about the patient's marital background may permit the clinician to identify prior and current psychological stressors, and the patient's ability to form and maintain meaningful relationships and to act responsibly, and premorbid and current sexual functioning. Information about the patient's intake of alcohol and recreational and/or prescribed drugs should also be obtained in order to determine how the patient had previously coped with stress and whether such substances have significantly compromised the patient's cognitive, emotional, and behavioral functioning.

Psychiatric

Furthermore, the psychologist should inquire whether the patient had a prior history of depression, anxiety, or psychotic, violent, or suicidal behavior and if the patient had ever received treatment for such problems. The psychologist should also inquire whether there is a familial history of psychiatric illness.

PATIENT'S COMPLAINTS AND SYMPTOMS

The clinical interview should begin with the patient's presenting cognitive, behavioral, physical, and psychological complaints and symptoms. This should include information about when such complaints or behaviors initially began because such information may be of considerable importance in arriving at a differential diagnosis. For example, patients with Alzheimer's disease or frontal lobe pathology will minimize or deny their cognitive and behavioral deficits, even though such deficits are readily apparent to others. In contrast, neurologically intact patients who are depressed and/or anxious will frequently complain of numerous cognitive problems (e.g., "My memory is terrible!"), but yet provide rather detailed examples of such problems. Thus, the patient's description of his or her cognitive and behavioral symptoms can provide the psychologist with valuable information about the possible etiology of the patient's underlying neuropsychological disorder.

Although some clinicians prefer to utilize symptom checklists to determine the patient's presenting complaints and symptoms, the clinician should not use such checklists as a substitute for an interview because the interview can provide rich information about the patient's perception of his or her symptoms, particularly their effect on his or her life, employment, marriage, family, social relationships, and everyday functioning (e.g., activities of daily living and driving skills). This type of information is often difficult to obtain by means of a checklist or a questionnaire.

Family Input

The psychologist should interview family members and/or significant others during the neuropsychological examination. Such information will frequently reveal the kinds of problems and difficulties the patient has exhibited since the onset of the brain insult. In many cases, the family will disclose significant alterations in the patient's premorbid, cognitive, behavioral, and psychological functioning. For example, many family members will describe dramatic changes in the patient's personality; irritability, temper outbursts, rapid changes in mood, poor judgment, and impulsive behavior; impaired problem-solving skills; diminished frustration tolerance; impaired interpersonal skills; strained relationships with others; diminished motivation and initiative; a loss of sensitivity to the needs and welfare of others; loss of libido; diminished motivation and incentive; apathy; significant memory deficits; and poor awareness of his or her cognitive and behavioral deficits.

Because the family or significant others typically have the benefit of having known the patient well prior to the brain insult, they are frequently able to detect relatively subtle changes in the patient's behavior that may not be detected by health professionals lacking this knowledge. Because the home or family environment tends to be fairly unstructured, patients with brain impairments are likely to exhibit cognitive, behavioral, and emotional deficits in these environments that they may not exhibit within the structured environment of a psychologist's or a physician's office.

There are two problems psychologists face when utilizing the information obtained from family members and/or significant others. The first problem is its potential accuracy because the emotional reactions or problems of the informants may color their perception of the patient's functioning. For example, the patient's family may exaggerate the patient's cognitive, behavioral, or emotional problems for purposes of potential financial gain if the patient is planning on filing a lawsuit or if there is pending litigation. The other problem is that the family may minimize the patient's problems because of the denial arising out of their own emotional problems as a result of their grief in coping with the patient's brain insult. For example, families who utilize denial as a way of coping with their loved one's traumatic brain injury typically appear emotional, distraught, and tired but are generally pleasant. They will frequently state, "Our son's doing great. He's been home now for nearly a week, and we haven't noticed any problems in him. We plan on sending him back to school next week." These statements may be made irrespective of the fact that the patient exhibited severe cognitive and behavioral problems while hospitalized, after having been comatose for 3 months! However, over time, the family's denial and use of repression will frequently sap the family's emotional resources and may result in a psychiatric crisis and hospitalization of family members.

BACKGROUND FACTORS

Developmental

Low birth weight or prematurity suggests that the patient's mother may have smoked, drank, or was ill during pregnancy. In some cases, forceps were used to remove the child from the birth canal, which may have produced a brain injury. Individuals with such histories not infrequently have a history of attentional problems, hyperactivity, learning difficulties, frequent temper tantrums, poor self-esteem, and behavioral difficulties. Many patients with brain insults have a childhood history of terrifying nightmares, bedwetting, or severe psychological abuse. A surprising number of individuals with brain insults grow up in broken homes or in families where they were often physically and/or sexually abused.

Dominance

Approximately 85% of people are right-handed. Virtually all of these individuals have their centers for language located in their left hemisphere. Approximately two-thirds of left-handed individuals also have their language centers located in the left hemisphere. Even though there are more right-handed women than men, the brains of women are less lateralized with respect to language than the brains of men. Thus, patients who are left-handed or who have a family history of sinistrality frequently make a better recovery of their language skills following an injury to the left hemisphere of their brain than those who are right-handed (Cummings, 1986). Furthermore, any changes in dominance during childhood may reflect the compensatory use of the nondominant hand following an ipsilateral brain injury. Such changes can also reflect considerable pressure (including harsh discipline) during the patient's childhood by family members to force the patient to use his or her right hand. In other words, knowledge of lateral dominance and its history can help the psychologist evaluate the patient's neuropsychological test data and prognosticate on the recovery of language functioning following a brain insult.

Language

Further information about the patient's linguistic background allows a clinician to weigh the possible contribution of linguistic and/or cultural factors on interpreting neuropsychological test data. For example, patients who have been raised in a different culture or who speak a different language will typically perform poorly on many standardized IQ tests. Unless this factor is considered, the patient's low IQ score may be inaccurately interpreted as evidence of brain damage or significant intellectual deterioration.

Education

A substantial number of patients with an acquired brain injury have a preexisting history of poor academic performance, learning difficulties, hyperactivity, truancy, expulsions, and/or conduct disorders. Thus, a review of the patient's academic records may provide valuable insights into the patient's premorbid level of intellectual and cognitive functioning. However, poor grades in school can reflect a variety of nonneurological factors such as divorce, physical or sexual abuse, economic difficulties, and chronic medical illnesses. Therefore, the clinician should determine why the patient performed poorly in school. However, because many patients provide inaccurate information about their grades or academic achievements, the psychologist should never assume that the academic history furnished by the patient is accurate unless it is corroborated by the patient's academic records.

Military Service

Many adult men have served in the military. Some of them may have been wounded in combat and/or experienced the atrocities of war. As a consequence, some of these individuals may have a preexisting history of post-traumatic stress disorder. Some individuals may have failed their physical examinations at the time of their enlistment or may have been given undesirable or medical discharges after enlisting. In such cases, the psychologist should determine the basis for the patient's rejection or undesirability for military service because these prior problems could have significant bearing on the patient's present complaints or symptoms. The patient's rank at discharge is often helpful in determining whether the patient had ever been court-martialled or demoted. This information may provide the psychologist with valuable insights into the patient's preexisting personality traits and character.

Occupational

Knowledge of the patient's occupational history and the job duties performed permits the clinician to estimate the patient's premorbid cognitive strengths and weaknesses. Furthermore, a careful description of the patient's job duties and demands prior to the onset of the brain insult can be helpful in assessing the patient's ability to return to work. For example, individuals who have poor premorbid work histories are unlikely to successfully return to work in the absence of a brain insult (Sbordone & Guilmette, in press).

Legal

A significant number of individuals who sustain traumatic brain insults have a history of problems with law enforcement authorities. Many of these individuals have been arrested and/or convicted for crimes such as burglary, embezzlement, grand theft, attempted murder, drug abuse and/or sales, or assault and battery. These individuals are at greater risk to engage in malingering in medi-legal cases as a result of their antisocial personality traits. The psychologist should determine if the patient had been a party in a prior lawsuit or had filed a worker's compensation claim in the past. The psychologist should become suspicious about the patient's underlying motivation if he or she has a history of prior personal injury lawsuits, particularly if the patient has not been gainfully employed for several years.

Cultural Background

Cultural background may influence the manner in which patients describe their symptoms, as well as the manner in which their family is likely to cope with the alterations in their cognitive, behavioral, and emotional functioning. For example, the patient and/or family may not divulge specific problems (e.g., past history of legal involvement, loss of libido) for fear of violating the norms of their culture. In addition, many individuals who grew up in a particular cultural background may feel anxious or distrustful toward individuals whom they perceive to be outsiders. Thus, their family may withhold important information about the patient's cognitive and behavioral functioning prior to and/or following a brain insult.

Religion

Patients' religious views may influence their motivation and attitude toward neuropsychological assessment. This may be reflected in the patient's or the family's unwillingness to divulge problems that are caused by a brain insult, not to mention their reluctance to follow up if they are referred for psychological or psychiatric treatment. Furthermore, many individuals who are raised in strict or fundamentalist religions may be at higher risk of developing psychiatric problems following a brain insult.

Marital Status and History

A brain insult will frequently aggravate the patient's preexisting marital conflicts, which may give rise to the development of such problems as extramarital affairs, incest, alcoholism, drug abuse, and psychiatric illness in their spouses and/or other family members. Because divorce is common following a brain insult, a patient may lose his or her support system through separation or divorce. Should this occur, the patient is likely to become depressed or possibly even suicidal.

Sexual

Sexual difficulties are common following a brain insult. For example, patients who sustain a traumatic brain injury, hypoxic encephalopathy, or stroke or who have progressive neurological disorders such as Alzheimer's or Parkinson's diseases typically experience a significant reduction in libido. To complicate matters even further, many of the medications that are commonly prescribed for patients with brain impairment to alleviate their mental confusion or depression may also cause sexual difficulties (Stein & Strickland, 1998). Patients who develop temporal lobe epilepsy often exhibit alterations in their sexual conduct (e.g., hyposexuality or homosexuality) or may report becoming sexually aroused by inanimate objects. Patients who sustain frontal lobe insults may demonstrate hypersexuality, characterized by excessive sexual activity including extramarital affairs and frequent masturbation. Thus, alterations in sexual functioning are typically the rule rather than the exception following a brain insult. The clinician, however, should proceed with caution in this area because many patients may deny any change in their sexual functioning or interest following a brain insult. As a consequence, the clinician should interview the patient's spouse to determine if any changes in the patient's sexual behavior have been observed.

Medical

Because a variety of medical disorders are known to affect the integrity of a patient's cognitive and behavioral functioning, it is essential that the clinician obtain a careful medical history. Unfortunately, many patients with brain insults may provide inaccurate or incomplete medical histories. As a consequence, the psychologist should carefully review the patient's medical records rather than rely on the medical history provided by the patient. It is also important to determine how the patient has coped with his or her medical problems in the past. Unfortunately, many psychologists, partly because of their lack of medical training, fail to inquire into the patient's prior medical history or fail to recognize the symptoms of a particular medical or neurological disorder (e.g., hypothyroidism) that can significantly affect the patient's cognitive, behavioral, and emotional functioning. Should this occur, the psychologist should contact the patient's physician and/or review appropriate medical or neuropsychiatric textbooks (e.g., Fogel, Schiffer, & Rao, 1996) to appreciate the possible role such illnesses may play in the patient's cognitive and behavioral functioning.

Psychiatric

Some patients who sustain brain insults have a preexisting history of psychiatric illness, which may include suicidal ideation and/or attempts, psychiatric hospitalizations, and outpatient treatment, which commonly includes taking psychotropic medications. Such preexisting disorders may confound the psychologist's understanding of the patient's current symptoms and their etiology. Because there is growing evidence that many psychiatric disorders (particularly depression, manic-depressive illness, and schizophrenia) are to a large extent genetically determined, it is essential that the clinician obtain a careful patient and family history of psychiatric illness with the assistance of the patient's family and/or significant others.

Current Stressors

Patients who are referred for neuropsychological testing frequently are undergoing significant stressors in their lives, which are likely to create a number of rather disabling psychological symptoms that can affect their neuropsychological test performance. Such stressors would include the death or the abandonment of a family member, divorce or marital separation, marital difficulties, job difficulties or termination, financial difficulties, loss of important relationships, academic or business difficulties, or sexual difficulties. These stressors should be identified so that appropriate psychotherapeutic intervention can be made.

Family

Obtaining information about the patient's family may provide the clinician with valuable insights into the patient's complaints and current psychological or even medical problems. This information should include the ages of both parents and stepparents; their educational background, occupations, health status, and personalities; and a description of how they interacted with the patient during the patient's formative years, adolescence, and adulthood. It should also include the patient's perception of his or her parents, stepparents, siblings, and stepsiblings, as well as information about the family's history of alcohol and substance abuse, psychiatric difficulties, and neurological disorders. Obtaining this information can also be important in treatment planning because many individuals who sustain significant brain insults typically are forced to reside with their families. The patient's disruptive behavior is quite stressful for most families, and may create emotional conflicts that can exacerbate the patient's cognitive, behavioral, and psychological difficulties. Identifying these stressors is frequently quite helpful in planning treatment and rehabilitation programs, particularly if the level of psychopathology in the family is so severe that the patient's needs may be best served by placing the patient in a long term-rehabilitation and/or psychiatric facility.

Siblings

The patient's siblings can serve as a rough index of the patient's premorbid neuropsychological functioning and potential, particularly if the patient and his or her siblings are roughly comparable in terms of their educational achievements, size, attitudes, personalities, and abilities prior to the patient's brain insult.

THE MENTAL STATUS EXAMINATION

The mental status examination is an integral part of the neuropsychological assessment process (Rogers, 1995; Strubb & Black, 1993). It consists of observing the patient's behavior in a highly subjective manner and gathering information from the patient and his or her significant others about the patient's symptoms; their onset, duration, frequency, and severity; and their impact on the patient and his or her significant others. During the mental status examination, the clinician should listen carefully to what is being said and *not* being said and should look for discrepancies between the patient's description of his or her symptoms and the symptoms observed by significant others. The clinician should also strive to form a therapeutic alliance with the patient and his or her significant others so that these individuals can feel comfortable in expressing themselves and in sharing personal information (Trzepacz & Baker, 1993).

The skilled clinician will usually attend to both the content (overtly communicated material) and the process (how the material is being communicated) of the patient's symptoms. For example, many histrionic patients will complain of numerous and extremely severe cognitive difficulties without appearing troubled by their symptoms. Given this observation, the clinician should inquire into such discrepancies in a gentle and nonthreatening manner, without alienating the patient. Furthermore, open-ended questions permit the clinician to observe the patient's comprehension, language, memory, organizational, and verbal problem-solving skills. The clinician should also strive to write his or her observations of the patient's behavior in as objective a manner as possible, using terminology that is nonprejudicial and nonjudgmental. Such terminology will help in communicating to other professionals how the patient appeared and behaved during the examination. Table 4.3 presents the behavioral factors that the psychologist should observe during the clinical interview.

Behavioral Observations

During the clinical interview, the examiner should note the patient's physical appearance (grooming, dress, physical characteristics, and disabilities), attitude toward the assessment process (cooperative, suspicious, guarded, etc.), mental status (level of arousal, attention, orientation to surroundings, etc.), affect and mood (anxiety, depression, hostility, euphoria, suicidal or homicidal ideation, emotional lability, irritability, poor frustration tolerance, paranoia/suspiciousness, depression, etc.), personality traits (eccentric, dramatic, labile, etc.), insight and coping mechanisms (awareness versus denial of problems or illness, reactions to errors or mistakes, etc.), and psychiatric disorder (hallucinations, delusions, paranoia, etc.).

Attention

The clinician should observe whether the patient is oriented in all spheres (person, place, time, and purpose). He or she should also note whether the client appears bored, disinterested, distractible (unable to screen out irrelevant stimuli such as noise), delirious (marked, rapid alterations in cognitive functioning ranging from lucidity to confusion), internally preoccupied with their thoughts (hallucinations, ruminative thinking), or is autistic (displays a lack of interest in communicating with the examiner and plays with inanimate objects).

Age and Posture

The clinician should determine to what extent the patient appears his or her age. For example, patients who are manic, immature, or narcissistic or who have undergone cosmetic surgery frequently appear younger than their stated age. On the other hand,

Table 4.3.   Behavioral observations

Behavioral Observations	

Appearance:

Attire and grooming
Facial expression
Physical characteristics
Movements
Posture
Eye contact
Mannerisms
Disabilities

Attitude toward Assessment:

Cooperation
Motivation

Mental Status:

Arousal level
Attention
Orientation to surroundings
Speech
Comprehension
Memory
Cognition
Self-regulation
Ability to recognize and self-correct errors
Judgment
Problem-solving skills
Executive functions

Affect and Mood:

Affect
Anxiety
Depression
Hostility
Euphoria
Suicidal or homicidal ideation
Irritability
Poor frustration tolerance
Paranoia or suspiciousness

Insight or Coping Mechanisms:

Awareness or denial of problems or illnesses
Reactions to errors or mistakes

Personality Traits:

Eccentric
Dramatic
Labile
Erratic
Demanding
Manipulative
Anxious
Compulsive
Histrionic
Grandiose
Perfectionistic
Paranoid
Narcissistic
Antisocial

Psychiatric:

Hallucinations
Delusions
Paranoia
Bizarre thinking
Schizophrenia
Viscosity
Concrete thinking
Circumstantial
Perseveration
Flight of ideas
Manic-depressive illness
Depression
Loose associations
Tangential thinking

(continued)

Table 4.3.   *(Continued)*

Behavioral Observations

Personality Traits: (continued)
Avoidant
Obsessional
Suspicious
Intellectual
Oppositional
Dependent
Controlling
Detached or withdrawn

Speech and Language:
Voice
Articulation
Prosody
Rhythm
Rate
Anomia
Circumlocution
Paraphasic errors
Neologisms
Echolalia
Paucity or empty speech
Comprehension

patients who appear older than their stated age often have a history of alcohol or drug abuse, excessive psychological and/or financial hardships, or poor health. The patient's posture can often provide valuable insights into their emotional and neurological functioning. For example, patients with Parkinson's disease frequently appear stiff and rigid. Patients who are wheelchair bound frequently have a history of central nervous system injury or disease. Patients who appear to be slumped over or who slouch during the interview are often depressed, whereas patients who present as cross-legged are likely to be anxious.

Attire and Grooming

The patient's attire and grooming can reflect their socioeconomic status, medical condition, psychiatric status, or a brain insult. For example, poor personal hygiene is frequently seen in patients who have organic brain syndromes or dementia or who are psychotic. Individuals with antisocial personality traits or psychiatric illness often present in bizarre attire. Individuals who shave only one side of their face may have a neglect syndrome. Individuals who present as fastidiously groomed, in the face of numerous cognitive and somatic complaints, are frequently histrionic.

Eye Contact and Physical Characteristics

The degree or lack of eye contact is likely to reflect the patient's current psychiatric or neurological functioning. For example, patients who are depressed, anxious, or psychotic frequently have difficulty maintaining eye contact. Patients who have a history of attention deficit disorder or hyperactivity are frequently observed to rapidly scan the environment, whereas patients with frontal lobe pathology may exhibit scanning difficulties or have difficulty maintaining eye contact because of their propensity to become distracted easily. The physical characteristics of the individual may shed light on the patient's medical condition, personality, psychiatric illness, or neurologic status. For example, individuals who present with tattoos and needle marks frequently have a history of antisocial behavior and drug abuse. Individuals who present with obesity and excessive sweating often have a history of thyroid disease. Individuals who present with amputated legs frequently have a history of prior injuries. Patients' skin color is often a reflection of their medical condition, nutritional status, and personal hygiene. For example, unpleasant body odor can be caused by a variety of medical illnesses, alcohol abuse, poor hygiene, psychiatric illness, **anosmia,** or organic brain syndrome.

Level of Consciousness

The patient's level of consciousness should be carefully observed. For example, in contrast to individuals who are awake and alert, a patient who appears hypervigilant or hyperaroused may have a history of mania, anxiety, or cocaine and/or amphetamine abuse or of medical conditions such as hyperthyroidism. Individuals who present as hypoaroused (e.g., lethargic, drowsy, obtunded, stuporous, or comatose) may have a history of sleep deprivation, drug intoxication, cerebral edema, epilepsy, concussion, CNS infection, or intracranial hematoma.

Attitude

The patient's attitude (e.g., friendly, trusting, suspicious, childlike) may provide the clinician with insight into the patient's medical condition and neurologic or psychiatric functioning. For example, patients with frontal lobe pathology frequently appear immature and childlike and often make facetious remarks or inappropriate statements. The presence of hostility, suspicion, guardedness, and vigilance suggest that the information being provided to the clinician is likely to be unreliable or incomplete.

Activity Level

The patient's activity level (hyperactive, active, **bradykinesia,** psychomotor retardation, catatonic, or comatose) is often pathognomic of the patient's neurological or psychiatric functioning. For example, individuals who have a history of attention deficit disorder, hyperthyroidism, or drug abuse will frequently present as hyperactive and restless. Bradykinesia is a frequent manifestation of subcortical diseases such as

Parkinson's. Individuals who present as catatonic frequently have a history of psychiatric illness.

Movements

The patient's movements can also reflect neurologic or psychiatric illnesses. For example, individuals who present with weakness of one or both limbs or their facial muscles **(paresis)** are likely to have peripheral CNS disease. Individuals who present with motor paralysis are likely to have a history of central nervous system disease or injury. Individuals who display a lack of motion despite intact motor strength **(akinesia)** frequently have a history of psychiatric illness. **Hypokinesia** can be due to the side effects of a variety of medications, depression, diffuse axonal brain injury, catatonia, and subcortical diseases.

Clinicians should note whether the patient exhibits any tremors (oscillating movements that have a fairly consistent rhythm). For example, patients with Parkinson's disease typically exhibit a resting tremor of 3 to 8 cycles per second. This tremor disappears whenever the body part that is exhibiting the tremor is used. Individuals who present with **action tremors,** which are frequently caused by hyperthyroidism, drug toxicity, alcohol abuse, withdrawal from sedative-hypnotic medications, neurosyphilis, or anxiety, typically exhibit a tremor when a particular body part is used or is held in a fixed posture. However, this tremor disappears when the body part is not in use or is relaxed. Individuals with **intentional tremors** (made when the patient is asked to perform specific fine motor movements such as touching the nose with the finger) are typically caused by diseases of the cerebellum or its connections to the brain, multiple sclerosis, **Wilson's disease,** drug and alcohol abuse, or anticonvulsant medication toxicity.

Dystonias represent involuntary increases in muscle tone, which produce sustained contractions of the patient's posture or physical movements. Dystonias often reflect the side effects of antipsychotic medications for a variety of neurological diseases such as Huntington's disease, Parkinson's disease (see Chapter 3), Wilson's disease, or hypoxic brain damage. Simple or complex involuntary movements that seem purposeless or bizarre (e.g., lip smacking, walking from one room to another, saluting, or undressing) may be the result of simple **complex partial seizures** (see Chapter 3) or **fugue states.** Individuals who exhibit involuntary movements or vocalizations that they are unable to resist except with considerable effort (e.g., blinking, facial grimacing, neck jerks, throat clearing, and/or vocalization of profanities and obscenities **[coprolalia]**), may be exhibiting manifestations of **Tourette's disease,** excessive caffeine use, or obsessive-compulsive disorder.

MENTAL STATUS QUESTIONNAIRES

A number of relatively short and easy-to-administer mental status questionnaires have been developed and are widely used in psychiatric settings by mental health professionals (Rogers, 1995). The primary reason to use structured mental status examinations (MSE) is the tendency for clinicians to overlook critical information about the patient (Palmateer & McCartney, 1985). In fact, Ruegg, Ekstrom, Dwight, and Golden (1990) reported that the use of a detailed mental status questionnaire significantly improved the assessment and recording of the clinician's behavioral observations. In a critical evaluation, the use of such questionnaires among psychiatric residents and faculty found that whereas both groups tended to utilize such questionnaires within a psychiatric evaluation, more experienced clinicians were less inclined to employ standardized mental status examinations (Rodenhauser & Fornal, 1991). Some clinicians, however, have expressed strong criticisms over the use of structured mental status examinations. For example, Yager (1989) felt that they were often too mechanical and insensitive, whereas Rosen and Fox (1986) felt that the potential for misuse by clinicians was considerable. Nonetheless, the use of structured mental status examinations, if done in a cautious manner and in conjunction with a careful and detailed clinical history, should help the clinician formulate hypotheses about the patient's underlying neuropsychological deficits, which can be later evaluated by neuropsychological testing.

The following instruments have been developed to gather relevant clinical data about the patient's mental status: The Mental Status Evaluation Record (Spitzer & Endicott, 1970), the Missouri Mental Status Examination (Sletten, Ernhart, & Ulett, 1970), the MSE Checklist (Othmer & Othmer, 1989), and the North Carolina MSE (Ruegg et al., 1990).

Mental Status Evaluation Record

The Mental Status Evaluation Record (Spitzer & Endicott, 1970) permits clinicians to systematically rate clinical data using a 5-point rating scale (none, slight, mild, moderate, and marked). The distinguishing characteristic of this test is its emphasis on observational data because nearly one-third of the test can be completed strictly on detailed clinical observations. Although the test was designed to provide systematic ratings of the patient's psychopathology, it does pay some attention to the patient's cognitive deficits. The test consists of 172 items in which 50 clinical ratings of each patient are made. The major categories addressed are the reliability and the completeness of the information and the patient's appearance, motor behavior, general attitude and behavior, mood and affect, quality of speech and thought, contents of speech and thought, somatic functioning and concern, perception, sensorium, cognitive functions, judgment, potential for suicide or violence, and insight and attitude toward illness. The chief shortcoming of this instrument is its poor interrater reliability (Endicott, Spitzer, & Fleiss, 1975; Rogers, 1995).

Missouri Mental Status Examination

The Missouri Mental Status Examination was designed to serve as a standardized mental status examination (Sletten et al., 1970). The patient's symptoms are rated according to their severity on a 4-point scale (absent, mild, moderate, and severe). The initial part of the test is devoted to clinical observations regarding the patient's appearance, motor activity, speech, and behavior during the interview. Other sections of the examination assess the patient's mood and affect, disturbances in thinking, thought content, obsessions, sexual preoccupation, delusions, hallucinations, and cognitive abilities (sensorium and intellect). Although reliability studies have demonstrated a 69% agreement with the

Diagnostic and Statistical Manual of Mental Disorders, 2nd edition (DSM-II), diagnoses for psychiatric residents, this instrument has been found to have poor interrater reliability, which clearly limits its clinical applications.

MSE Checklist

The MSE Checklist provides clinicians with an excellent format for their clinical observations (Othmer & Othmer, 1989). By utilizing highly specific criteria, it rates the patient's clinical characteristics as either present or absent. The final section of this checklist focuses on the patient's cognitive functioning, which is assessed through a variety of brief cognitive tests (Digit Span, Serial Seven Subtraction, naming the months backward, spelling words backward, and brief tasks to assess the patient's memory, which appear to be truncated versions of standardized memory tests). The greatest potential use for this checklist is the patient's neuropsychological symptoms. However, the major limitation of this instrument is that no reliability studies have ever been done to support its use.

North Carolina MSE

The North Carolina MSE (Ruegg et al., 1990) assesses the patient's mental status with 36 items that are rated on a 3-point scale (not present, slight or occasional, marked or repeated). This instrument focuses on the patient's physical appearance, behavior, speech, thought process, thought content, mood, affect, cognitive functioning, orientation, recent memory, immediate recall, and remote memory. At the present time, no interrater reliability studies have been done to assess its reliability, nor has any formal attempt been made to assess its content validity.

COGNITIVE MENTAL STATUS EXAMINATIONS

In the past three decades, cognitive mental status examinations have been developed to assist psychiatrists in screening for possible cognitive dysfunction and organic involvement. The following cognitive mental status examinations have been designed specifically for this purpose: The Mental Status Questionnaire (Kahn, Goldfarb, Pollack, & Peck, 1960), the Short Portable Mental Status Questionnaire (Pfeiffer, 1975), the Mini-Mental State Examination (Folstein, Folstein, & McHugh, 1975), the Cognitive Capacity Screening Examination (Jacobs, Bernhard, Delgado, & Strain, 1977), the Cambridge Cognitive Examination (Roth et al., 1986), and the Neurobehavioral Cognitive Status Examination (Kiernan, Mueller, Langston, & Van Dyke, 1987).

Mental Status Questionnaire

The Mental Status Questionnaire (Kahn et al., 1960) was designed as a brief screening measure for older people, particularly with respect to identifying organicity in this population. The questionnaire consists of 10 items and focuses on patients' verbal responses to questions regarding their orientation to time and place and long-term memory of personal (age, date, year of birth) and public (current president and his predecessor) information. Reliability studies by Foster, Sclan, Welkowitz, Boksay, and Seeland (1988) found that the interrater reliability of this questionnaire was very high for both psychiatrists and research assistants. Although this questionnaire appears to have greater validity for patients with little or no cognitive impairment and with moderate to severe cognitive impairment (Kahn et al., 1960), it appears to be ineffective at detecting mild cognitive deficits (Reisberg, Ferris, DeLeon, & Crook, 1982). Additionally, hearing loss may confound the validity of this questionnaire as a measure of cognitive decline (Ohta, Carlin, & Harmon, 1981).

Short Portable Mental Status Questionnaire

The Short Portable Mental Status Questionnaire (Pfeiffer, 1975) was developed to provide an overall measure of cognitive impairment in older people. This questionnaire evaluates the patient's orientation to time (day of the week and date) and place (name of the place and street address), his or her memory of personal and public information (birth date, age, telephone number, and mother's maiden name; current president and his predecessor), and concentration (serial three addition). Based on the patient's educational levels, this questionnaire tends to categorize the patient's intellectual functioning into one of four categories (intact, mild, moderate, and severe impairment). Reliability studies have yielded high interrater reliability coefficients, whereas other studies (e.g., Foreman, 1987) have reported high internal consistency. Validity studies (e.g., Symer, Hofland, & Jonas, 1979) found this questionnaire to be accurate in making broad categorizations about the patient's intellectual functioning but found the questionnaire to be relatively poor in identifying individuals with mild impairment. These studies have suggested that this questionnaire should only be used as a screening tool to identify older patients with moderate and severe cognitive impairment. However, other studies have suggested that the usefulness of this questionnaire as a screening measure for organicity is questionable (e.g., Dalton, Pederson, Blom, & Holmes, 1987) because patients with mild dementia or delirium are unlikely to be detected. Thus, psychologists should avoid concluding that a patient is cognitively intact when his or her scores on this questionnaire fall into the nonimpaired range.

Mini-Mental State Examination

The Mini-Mental State Examination (MMSE; Folstein et al., 1975) was designed to provide a quantitative assessment of the patient's cognitive functioning. The 11-item questionnaire assesses the patient's orientation (time and place, naming of objects, and the ability to perform serial sevens, to remember objects, to follow directions, to write a sentence, and to copy a geometric figure). The overall reliability of this questionnaire has been found to be consistently high (Foster et al., 1988). Although this questionnaire has been found to be valid, Folstein, Anthony, Parhad, Duffy, and Gruenberg (1985) have recommended that it should be employed as a screening device rather than as a tool to diagnose a patient's suspected dementia. This questionnaire has been found to be sensitive to global and left hemisphere deficits, but not to right hemisphere deficits (Rogers, 1995; Tombaugh, McDowell, Krisjansson, & Hubley, 1996).

The MMSE has been criticized by Tombaugh and McIntyre (1992) for its failure to discriminate between patients with mild dementia and normal controls, as well as its bias against patients with low educational backgrounds. In response to these problems, several attempts have been made to modify the MMSE. For example, Teng, and Chui (1987) added four additional subtests (date and place of birth, word fluency, similarities, and delayed recall of words) and modified its scoring procedure, which increased the maximum score from 30 to 100 points. Tombaugh et al. (1996) compared the standard and the modified versions and found that although both tests yielded comparable reliability estimates, the inclusion of the verbal fluency test in the modified version increased the sensitivity of the test.

Cognitive Capacity Screening Examination

The Cognitive Capacity Screening Examination (Jacobs et al., 1977) provides a more extensive mental status examination than the Mental Status Questionnaire, the Short Portable Mental Status Questionnaire, and the MMSE. It evaluates the patient's orientation, concentration, serial sevens, repetition, verbal concept formation, and short-term recall, but it places greater emphasis on the patient's recall of numbers (forward and backward) and ability to perform simple calculations. In addition, the patient's abstract thinking is assessed through antonyms (three simple items) and similarities. Although this questionnaire consists of 30 items, it does not assess the patient's long-term memory based on their personal history or common knowledge. Its test-retest reliability has been found to be high at one-week intervals (Haddad & Coffman, 1987), but poor after a two-hour interview (Carnes, Gunter-Hunt, & Rodgers, 1987). Validity studies have found that this questionnaire has good sensitivity and specificity in identifying organic patients (e.g., Kauffman, Weinberger, Strain, & Jacobs, 1979). While psychologists may feel comfortable using this questionnaire as a brief screening instrument for cognitive impairment, they should not equate the absence of observed deficits with normal functioning.

Cambridge Cognitive Examination

The Cambridge Cognitive Examination (Roth et al., 1986) provides a comprehensive assessment of older people through the use of diagnostic interviews, collateral interviews, medical procedures, and a structured interview. It utilizes 11 items from the MMSE along with 43 additional items to assess the patient's cognitive functioning (orientation, language, memory, praxis, attention, abstract thinking, and perceptual and arithmetic skills). It has been found to have high interrater reliability and high sensitivity and specificity in identifying organic patients and differentiating them from normal patients and older patients with depression.

Neurobehavioral Cognitive Status Examination

The Neurobehavioral Cognitive Status Examination (Kiernan et al., 1987) was developed to assess the patient's language, constructional, memory, mental calculations, and reasoning abilities. It consists of 64 items, most of which can be scored as either passed or failed. It was primarily devised to screen for specific cognitive dysfunctions of a relatively mild severity, which are often overlooked by the vast majority of mental status examinations. Although no tests of reliability have been reported, validation studies have reported modest detection rates (Roper, Bielauskas, & Peterson, 1996; Schwamm, Van Dyke, Kiernan, Merrin, & Mueller, 1987). This test has been criticized for tending to "overdiagnose cognitive impairment" (McBride-Houtz, 1993). Whereas it appears to offer psychologists a means to measure discrete forms of cognitive impairment, it should only be employed as a screening measure for cognitive dysfunction, even though it appears to have considerable potential for differentiating dementia from other disorders.

NEUROPSYCHOLOGICAL STATUS QUESTIONNAIRES

Within the past several years, questionnaires have been developed specifically for neuropsychologists to assist them in identifying the patient's symptoms, premorbid functioning, developmental history, medical history, physical status, emotional status, family history, cognitive status, personal history (marital, educational, occupational, military, recreational), substance abuse history, and results of neuropsychological and neurodiagnostic testing. The most frequently used questionnaires are the Neurobehavioral Assessment Format, the Child Neuropsychological Questionnaire, the Adult Neuropsychological Questionnaire, the Child Neuropsychological History Questionnaire, the Adult Neuropsychological History Questionnaire, the Neuropsychological History Questionnaire, and the Neuropsychological Status Examination.

One of the main functions of these questionnaires is that they provide a systematic means of collecting information so that most major topics are covered. If portions are completed by the patient or the patient's caregivers, interview time can also be reduced. However, the questionnaires should not be used as the final source of information about the patient. Rather, clinicians should use them as vehicles to flexibly explore relevant aspects of the patient's symptoms and history. In particular, such inquiries should focus on the onset, duration, frequency, intensity, and severity of the patient's symptoms. Structured questionnaires are also useful for training clinicians how to conduct neuropsychological interviews. Beginning clinicians can use the questionnaires to help decide which questions to ask and to identify that topics need to be covered.

Neurobehavioral Assessment Format

The Neurobehavioral Assessment Format (Siegal, Schechter, & Diamond, 1996) was designed to identify the patient's presenting complaints (types, duration, frequency, mode of onset, associated symptoms), history of present illness (age of onset, course, factors that ameliorate or exacerbate the illness, current and past treatments, and current medications), medical history, developmental history, mental status, neurobehavioral symptoms, physical characteristics, motor behavior, psychomotor reactivity, posture, gait, carriage anomalies, respiration, communicative functions, thought organization, orientation, consciousness, perceptual functions, behavioral programming, language, conceptual functioning, calculations, memory, psychiatric symptoms, and physical appearance.

Although this questionnaire permits the clinician to gather information on almost every conceivable dimension, its primary limitation is that it requires 3 to 5 hours for the clinician to complete. Its usefulness in most clinical settings is clearly impractical, but it does offer psychologists in medi-legal settings an excellent opportunity to rule out a variety of possible confounding factors that may influence the patient's neuropsychological test performance. The use of this instrument, however, requires that the clinician have a strong background in neuropsychology and a good understanding of psychiatry and neurology.

Child Neuropsychological Questionnaire

The Child Neuropsychological Questionnaire (Melendez, 1978, Psychological Assessment Resources, Inc.) was developed to be a part of an overall evaluation of youngsters who are suspected of having brain dysfunction. It was designed as a set of points of inquiry and contains 41 questions that can be answered by the patient's parent or by the child in a simple yes-or-no fashion. The questionnaire was designed to be only part of a very extensive battery that includes neuropsychological testing and pediatric neurological examinations. Although the questionnaire does not furnish any diagnostic answers, it was designed to urge the clinician to think about the child in terms of alternative problems in order to make appropriate referrals for further studies.

Adult Neuropsychological Questionnaire

The Adult Neuropsychological Questionnaire (Melendez, 1978, Psychological Assessment Resources, Inc.) contains 59 items that can be answered in a simple yes-or-no manner in approximately 10 minutes. These questions evaluate the patient's general health; substance abuse; psychiatric problems; general neurological functioning; right and left hemisphere functioning; subcortical, cerebellar, and spinal functioning; and sensory and perceptual functioning. The questionnaire was designed to aid clinicians who are generally unsophisticated about neuropsychological phenomena but are nonetheless placed in a position of having to evaluate patients with neuropsychological deficits. It is recommended that the questionnaire should only be used as an adjunct to a general intake interview and that the information gathered from the patient should lead to appropriate referrals to medical practitioners. Although the questionnaire is self-administered, it is best if the clinician asks the questions and makes the appropriate inquiries.

Child and Adult Neuropsychological
History Questionnaires

The Child and the Adult Neuropsychological History questionnaires (Greenberg, 1990, International Diagnostic Systems, Inc.) were designed to be completed by the patient or by the patient's significant other. Both questionnaires inquire into the patient's symptoms, particularly whether the symptom has occurred within the past year or at least one year ago in the following areas: problem solving, speech, language, math skills, nonverbal skills, concentration awareness, memory, motor and coordination skills, and sensory, physical, and behavioral functioning. Both questionnaires explore the patient's early history and developmental background, but the childhood questionnaire does this more extensively. Both questionnaires examine the patient's health and medical history, family history, and background. Clinicians should not rely entirely on the information produced by the questionnaire but instead should interview the patient and the patient's significant other to supplement the information contained in the questionnaire. Inexperienced neuropsychologists may find the questionnaires helpful in providing them with guidelines for gathering information about the patient's current symptoms, premorbid functioning, and medical and neurological functioning. It may also help the neuropsychologist to identify extraneous factors that could significantly compromise the patient's neuropsychological test performance. In medi-legal cases, however, the clinician is cautioned to avoid relying on the accuracy of the information completed by the patient unless such information is corroborated by the patient's educational, medical, or occupational records.

Neuropsychological History Questionnaire

The Neuropsychological History Questionnaire (Wolfson, 1985) consists of a detailed 38-page questionnaire which is completed by the patient. It attempts to obtain comprehensive information about the referral source and issues, the patient's general background, and academic, developmental, social, behavioral, emotional, and medical history, as well as the patient's current functioning in the home, workplace, and community. It also asks the patient to compare his or her current functioning in a variety of areas (thinking, concentration, memory, energy level, depression, temper/impulse control, social relationships, physical, alcohol use, etc.) to his or her pre-injury or pre-illness level. While this questionnaire is quite comprehensive in scope, it appears to be limited by the patient's intellectual functioning, cultural and linguistic background, reading skills, and cognitive impairments. With respect to the latter issue, Sbordone et al. (1998) found that patients who had sustained mild traumatic brain injuries approximately two and a half years earlier were often unaware of their cognitive, emotional, or behavioral impairments, or tended to minimize them. Thus, this questionnaire may be limited in its usefulness if the patient is cognitively impaired unless the patient's significant other assists the patient complete the questionnaire.

Neuropsychological Status Examination

The Neuropsychological Status Examination (Schinka, 1983) was designed to provide the clinician with the format for comprehensive data collection, as well as with a detailed outline for the generation of a complete clinical report. It was also designed to be utilized with the Neuropsychological Symptom Checklist (Schinka, 1983), a two-page screening inventory that is given to the patient to complete and that is later reviewed by the examiner.

RECOMMENDED READING

Rogers, R. (1995). *Diagnostic and Structured Interviewing: A Handbook for Psychologists*. Odessa, FL: Psychological Assessment Resources.

Spreen, O., & Strauss, E. (1998). *A Compendium of Neuropsychological Tests, Second Edition.* New York: Oxford.

Taylor, M.A. (1981). *The Neuropsychiatric Mental Status Examination.* New York: SP Medical and Scientific Books.

Trzepacz, P.T., & Baker, R.W. (1993). *The Psychiatric Mental Status Examination.* New York: Oxford.

REFERENCES

Adams, F., Queseda, J.R., & Gutterman, J.V. (1984). Neuropsychiatric manifestations of human leukocyte interferon therapy in patients with cancer. *Journal of the American Medical Association, 252,* 938–941.

Adelman, D.C., Saltiel, E., & Klinenbert, J.R. (1986). The neuropsychiatric manifestations of systemic lupus erythematosus: An overview. *Seminars in Arthritis and Rheumatology, 15,* 185–199.

Ardila, A., Rosselli, M., & Ostrosky-Solis, F. (1992). Socio-educational. In A.E. Puente & R.J. McCaffrey (Eds.), *Handbook of neuropsychological assessment: A biopsychosocial perspective.* New York: Plenum Press.

Atchinson, J.W., Wachendorf, J., Haddock, D., Mysiw, J., Gribble, M., & Corrigan, J.D. (1993). Hyponatremia associated cognitive impairment in traumatic brain injury. *Brain Injury, 7,* 347–352.

Basavaraju, J., & Phillips, S.L. (1989). Cortisol deficient state: A state of reversible cognitive impairment and delirium in the elderly. *Journal of the American Geriatrics Society, 37,* 49–51.

Boucagnani, L.L., & Jones, R.W. (1989). Behaviors analogous to frontal lobe dysfunction in children with attention deficit hyperactivity disorder. *Journal of Clinical Neuropsychology, 4,* 161–173.

Burt, D.B., Zembar, M.J., & Niederehe, G. (1995). Depression and memory impairment: A meta-analysis of the association, its pattern, and specificity. *Psychological Bulletin, 117,* 285–305.

Cardenas, D. (1987). Antipsychotics and their use after traumatic brain injury. *Journal of Head Trauma Rehabilitation, 2*(4), 43–49.

Carnes, M., Gunter-Hunt, G., & Rodgers, E. (1987). The effect of an interdisciplinary geriatrics clinic visit on mental status. *Journal of the American Geriatrics Society, 35,* 1035–1036.

Cummings, J.L. (1986). *Clinical neuropsychiatry.* New York: Grune & Stratton.

Dalakas, M., Wichman, A., & Sever, J. (1989). AIDS and the nervous system. *Journal of American Medical Association, 261,* 2396–2399.

Dalton, J.E., Pederson, S.L., Blom, B.E., & Holmes, N.R. (1987). Diagnostic errors using the short portable mental status questionnaire with a mixed clinical population. *Journal of Gerontology, 42,* 512–514.

Dodrill, C.B. (1988, August). *What constitutes normal performance in clinical neuropsychology?* Paper presented at American Psychological Association, Atlanta.

Endicott, J., Spitzer, R.L., & Fleiss, J.L. (1975). The mental status evaluation record (MSER): Reliability and validity. *Comprehensive Psychiatry, 16,* 285–301.

Fogel, B.S., Schiffer, R.B., & Rao, S.M. (1996). *Neuropsychiatry.* Baltimore: Williams & Wilkins.

Folstein, M.F., Anthony, J.C., Parhad, I., Duffy, B., & Gruenberg, E.M. (1985). The meaning of cognitive impairment in the elderly. *Journal of the American Geriatrics Society, 33,* 228–235.

Folstein, M.F., Folstein, S.E., & McHugh, P.R. (1975). Mini-mental state: A practical method of grading cognitive state of patients for the clinician. *Journal of Psychiatric Research, 12,* 189–198.

Foreman, M.D. (1987). Reliability and validity of mental status questionnaires in elderly hospitalized patients. *Nursing Research, 36,* 216–220.

Foster, J.R., Sclan, S., Welkowitz, J., Boksay, I., & Seeland, I. (1988). Psychiatric assessment in medical long-term care facilities: Reliability of commonly used rating scales. *International Journal of Geriatric Psychiatry, 3,* 229–233.

Garcia, C.A., Tweedy, J.R., & Blass, J.P. (1984). Underdiagnosis of cognitive impairment in a rehabilitation setting. *Journal of the American Geriatrics Society, 32,* 339–342.

Glenn, M.B., & Joseph, A.B. (1987). The use of lithium for behavioral and affective disorders after traumatic brain injury. *Journal of Head Trauma, 2,* 68–76.

Goldstein, N.P., Ewert, J.C., & Randall, R.V. (1968). Psychiatric aspects of Wilson's disease (hepatolenticular degeneration): Results of psychiatric tests during long term therapy. *American Journal of Psychiatry, 124,* 113–119.

Goulet-Fisher, D., Sweet, J.J., & Smith, E.A. (1986). Depression and neuropsychological impairment. *International Journal of Clinical Neuropsychology, 8,* 14–18.

Grabowski, J., & Yeragani, V.K. (1987). Porphyria and psychosis: A case report. *Canadian Journal of Psychiatry, 32,* 393–394.

Grant, I. (1987). Alcohol and the brain: Neuropsychological correlates. *Journal Consulting Clinical Psychology, 55,* 310–324.

Grant, I., McDonald, W.I., & Trimble, M.R. (1989). Neuropsychological impairment in early multiple sclerosis. In L. Knudsen, E. Stenager, et al. (Eds.), *Mental disorders and cognitive deficits in multiple sclerosis* (pp. 17–26). London: Libbey Press.

Greenberg, G.D. (1990a). *Adult neuropsychological history.* Worthington, OH: International Diagnostic Systems.

Greenberg, G.D. (1990b). *Child neuropsychological history.* Worthington, OH: International Diagnostic Systems.

Gutierrez, R., Atkinson, J.H., & Grant, I. (1993). Mild neurocognitive: Needed addition to the nosology of cognitive impairment (organic mental) disorders. *Journal of Neuropsychiatry, 5,* 161–177.

Haddad, L.B., & Coffman, T.L. (1987). A brief neuropsychological screening exam for psychiatric geriatric patients. *Clinical Gerontologist, 6,* 3–10.

Hector, M., & Burton, J.R. (1988). What are the psychiatric manifestations of vitamin B12 deficiency? *Journal of the American Geriatrics Society, 36,* 1105–1112.

Homan, R.W., Paulman, R.G., & Devous, M.D. (1989). Cognitive function and regional cerebral blood flow in partial seizures. *Archives of Neurology, 46,* 964–970.

Jacobs, J.W., Bernhard, M.R., Delgado, A., & Strain, J.J. (1977). Screening for organic mental syndromes in the medically ill. *Annals of Internal Medicine, 107,* 481–485.

Kahn, R.K., Goldfarb, A.I., Pollack, M., & Peck, A. (1960). Brief objective measures for the determination of mental status in the aged. *American Journal of Psychiatry, 117,* 326–328.

Kauffman, D.M., Weinberger, M., Strain, J.J., & Jacobs, J.W. (1979). Detection of cognitive deficits by a brief mental status examination. *General Hospital Psychiatry, 1,* 247–255.

Kiernan, R.J., Mueller, J., Langston, J.W., & Van Dyke, C. (1987). The neurobehavioral cognitive screening examination: A brief but quantitative approach to cognitive assessment. *Annals of Internal Medicine, 107,* 481–485.

LaRue, A., D'Elia, L.F., Clark, E.O., Spar, J.E., & Jarvik, L.F. (1986). Clinical tests of memory in dementia, depression and healthy aging. *Psychology of Aging, 1,* 69–77.

Lezak, M.D. (1995). *Neuropsychological assessment* (3rd ed.). New York: Oxford Press.

Martin, D.C. (1988). B12 and folate deficiency dementia. *Clinical Geriatric Medicine, 4,* 841–851.

McBridge-Houtz, P. (1993). *Detecting cognitive impairment in older adults: A validation study of selected screening instruments.* Unpublished doctoral dissertation, University of North Texas, Denton.

McCaffrey, R.J., Williams, A.D., Fisher, J.M., & Laing, L.C. (1993). Forensic issues in mild head trauma. *Journal of Head Trauma Rehabilitation, 8,* 38–47.

Melendez, F. (1978a). *Adult neuropsychological questionnaire.* Odessa, FL: Psychological Assessment Resources.

Melendez, F. (1978b). *Child neuropsychological questionnaire.* Odessa, FL: Psychological Assessment Resources.

Miller, W. (1975). Psychological effects of depression. *Psychology Bulletin, 238–260.*

Newman, P.J., & Silverstein, M.L. (1987). Neuropsychological test performance among major clinical subtypes of depression. *Archives of Clinical Neuropsychology, 2,* 115–125.

Ohta, R.J., Carlin, M.F., & Harmon, B.M. (1981). Auditory acuity and performance on the mental status questionnaire in the elderly. *Journal of the American Geriatrics Society, 29,* 476–478.

Othmer, E., & Othmer, S.C. (1989). *The clinical interview using DSM-III-R.* Washington, DC: American Psychiatric Press.

Palmateer, L.M., & McCartney, J.R. (1985). Do nurses know when patients have cognitive deficits? *Journal of Gerontological Nursing, 11,* 6–16.

Pancratz, L., & Binder, L.A. (1997). Malingering on intellectual and neuropsychological measures. In R. Rogers (Ed.), *Clinical assessment of malingering and deception* (2nd ed., pp. 223–236). New York: Guilford Press.

Pfeiffer, E. (1975). A short portable mental status questionnaire for the assessment of organic brain deficit in elderly patients. *Journal of the American Geriatrics Society, 23,* 433–441.

Reisberg, B., Ferris, S.H., DeLeon, M.J., & Crook, T. (1982). The deterioration scale for assessment of primary degenerative dementia. *American Journal of Psychiatry, 139,* 1136–1139.

Rodenhauser, P., & Fornal, R.E. (1991). How important is the mental status examination? *Psychiatric Hospital, 22,* 21–24.

Rogers, R. (1995). *Diagnostic and structured interviewing: A handbook for psychologists.* Odessa, FL: Psychological Assessment Resources.

Roper, B.L., Bielauskas, L.A., & Peterson, M.R. (1996). Validity of the mini-mental status examination and the neurobehavioral cognitive status examination in cognitive screening. *Neuropsychiatry, Neuropsychology, and Behavioral Neurology, 9,* 54–57.

Rosen, A.M., & Fox, H.A. (1986). Tests of cognition and their relationship to psychiatric diagnosis and demographic variables. *Journal of Clinical Psychiatry, 47,* 495–498.

Roth, M., Tym, E., Montjoy, C.Q., Huppert, F.A., Hendrie, H., Verma, S., & Goddard, R. (1986). CAMDEX: A standardized instrument for the diagnosis of mental disorders in the elderly with special reference to the early detection of dementia. *British Journal of Psychiatry, 149,* 698–709.

Rourke, S.B., & Loberg, T. (1996). The neuropsychological correlates of alcoholism. In I. Grant & K.M. Adams (Eds.), *Neuropsychological assessment of neuropsychiatric disorders* (2nd ed., pp. 423–485). New York: Oxford University Press.

Ruegg, R.G., Ekstrom, D.E., Dwight, L., & Golden, R.N. (1990). Introduction of a standardized report form improves the quality of mental status examination reports by psychiatric residents. *Academic Psychiatry, 14,* 157–163.

Ryan, C., & Butters, N. (1980). Learning and memory impairments in young and old alcoholics: Evidence for the premature aging hypothesis. *Alcoholism: Clinical and Experimental Research, 4,* 288–293.

Sbordone, R.J. (1991). *Neuropsychology for the attorney.* Orlando, FL: Deutsch Press.

Sbordone, R.J., & Guilmette, T.J. (1999). Ecological validity: Predictions of everyday and vocational functioning from neuropsychological test data. In J. Sweet (Ed.), *Forensic neuropsychology: Fundamentals and practice* (pp. 223–250). New York: Swets.

Sbordone, R.J., & Liter, J. (1995). Post-concussive and post-traumatic stress disorders: Two mutually incompatible disorders. *Brain Injury, 9,* 405–412.

Sbordone, R.J., & Purisch, A.D. (1996). Hazards of blind analysis of neuropsychological test data in assessing cognitive disability: The role of confounding factors. *Neurorehabilitation, 1,* 15–26.

Sbordone, R.J., Seyranian, G.D., & Ruff, R.M. (1998). Are the subjective complaints of traumatically brain-injured patients reliable? *Brain Injury, 12,* 505–515.

Schinka, J.A. (1983). *Neuropsychological status examination.* Odessa, FL: Psychological Assessment Resources.

Schwamm, L.H., Van Dyke, C., Kiernan, R.J., Merrin, E.L., & Mueller, J. (1987). The neurobehavioral cognitive status examination: Comparison with cognitive capacity screening examination and the mini-mental state examination in a neurosurgical population. *Annals of Internal Medicine, 107,* 486–491.

Siegal, A.W., Schechter, M.D., & Diamond, S.P. (1996). Neurobehavioral assessment format. In R.J. Sbordone & C.J. Long (Eds.), *Ecological validity of neuropsychological testing* (pp. 429–504). Delray Beach, FL: St. Lucie Press.

Sletten, I.W., Ernhart, C.B., & Ulett, G.A. (1970). The Missouri automated mental status examination: Development, use and reliability. *Comprehensive Psychiatry, 11,* 315–327.

Spitzer, R.L., & Endicott, J. (1970). *The mental status evaluation record (MSER).* New York: Biometrics Research.

Stein, R.A., & Strickland, T.L. (1998). A review of the neuropsychological effects of commonly used prescription medications. *Archives of Clinical Neuropsychology, 13,* 259–284.

Strickland, T.L., Mena, I., Villaneuva-Meyer, J., Miller, B., Cummings, J., Mehringer, C.M., Satz, P., & Meyers, H. (1993). Cerebral perfusion and neuropsychological consequences of chronic cocaine use. *Journal of Neuropsychiatry Clinical Neuroscience,* 419–427.

Strub, R.L., & Black, F.W. (1993). *The mental status examination in neurology.* (3rd ed.). Philadelphia: Davis.

Sweeney, J.A., Meisel, L., & Walsh, V.L. (1989). Assessment of cognitive functioning in polysubstance abusers. *Journal of Clinical Psychology, 45,* 346–350.

Symer, M., Hofland, B., & Jonas, E. (1979). Validity study of the short portable mental status questionnaire for the elderly. *Journal of the American Geriatrics Society, 27,* 263–269.

Teng, E.T., & Chui, H.C. (1987). The modified mini-mental state (3MS) examination. *Journal of Clinical Psychiatry, 48,* 314–318.

Thompson, P.J., & Trimble, M.T. (1982). Non-MAOI antidepressant drugs and cognitive functions: A review. *Psychological Medicine, 12,* 530–548.

Tombaugh, T.N., McDowell, I., Krisjansson, B., & Hubley, A.M. (1996). Mini-mental state examination (MMSE) and the modified mini-mental status examination (3MS): Psychiatric comparisons and normative data. *Psychological Assessment, 8,* 48–59.

Tombaugh, T.N., & McIntyre, N.J. (1992). The mini-mental state examination: A comprehensive review. *Journal of the American Geriatrics Society, 40,* 922–935.

Trzepacz, P.T., & Baker, R.W. (1993). *The psychiatric mental status examination.* New York: Oxford University Press.

Trzepacz, P.T., McCue, M., & Klein, I. (1988). Psychological response to propranolol in Graves disease. *Biol Psychiatry, 23,* 243–249.

Walker, E., Lucas, M., & Lewine, R. (1992). Schizophrenic disorders. In A.E. Puente & R.J. McAffrey (Eds.), *Handbook of neuropsychological assessment: A biopsychosocial perspective* (pp. 309–334). New York: Plenum Press.

Wolfson, D. (1985). *Neuropsychological history questionnaire.* Tucson, AZ: Reitan Neuropsychological Laboratory.

Wroblewski, B., Glenn, M.B., Whyte, J., & Singer, W.D. (1989). Carbamezepine replacement of phenytoin, phenobarbital and primidone in a rehabilitation setting: Effects on seizure control. *Brain Injury, 3,* 149–156.

Yager, J. (1989). Specific components of bedside manner in general hospital psychiatric consultation: 12 concrete suggestions. *Psychosomatics, 30,* 209–212.

PART TWO

TEST BATTERIES IN NEUROPSYCHOLOGICAL ASSESSMENT

Chapter 5

THE WECHSLER INTELLIGENCE SCALES

Gary Groth-Marnat, Roberta E. Gallagher, James B. Hale, and Edith Kaplan

Intelligence has been described as the "global capacity of the individual to act purposefully, to think rationally, and to deal effectively with the environment" (Wechsler, cited in Matarazzo, 1972, p. 79). The earliest intelligence tests were aimed at describing an individual's capacities for problem solving and level of adaptive functioning, relative to others of the same age, for optimal placement within school and institutional settings. The Wechsler Intelligence scales have also demonstrated substantial sensitivity to the functional consequences of brain damage and cognitive impairments. As a result, they have become the most frequently used instruments in neuropsychological evaluations (Sullivan & Bowden, 1997; Sweet, Moberg, & Westergaard, 1996). The Wechsler Scales have a long tradition of careful development and technical refinement, with each subsequent revision receiving extensive clinical and empirical examination. These revisions advance the field of intellectual assessment by providing clinicians with sophisticated instruments that aid in the diagnosis of cognitive and neuropsychiatric disorders, while providing researchers with psychometrically sound measures of intellectual processes to increase the understanding of brain-behavior relations.

HISTORY AND DEVELOPMENT

Although concepts of differential endowment of mental faculties are quite old, Binet pioneered formal assessment in the early years of the 20th century as a means of predicting which children would have difficulty learning in traditional instructional environments. Binet's early scales (1905, 1908) developed scores that could compare a person's chronological age (CA) and mental age (MA). Later conceptualizations and versions of the Binet scales by Terman (1916, 1937) refined this as the intelligence quotient (IQ) based on the formula $IQ = MA/CA \times 100$. The most recent versions (1960, 1986) used Wechsler's concept of the deviation quotient to more accurately and usefully make age-related comparisons.

Whereas the early (and later) Binet scales measured children's abilities, Wechsler was initially interested in the measurement of adult intelligence. During the 1930s, he developed his first battery for intellectual assessment by incorporating elements from a range of existing instruments, including the Stanford-Binet and Army entrance examinations. This eventually led to the development of the Wechsler-Bellevue Scale (Wechsler, 1939), which was followed by various versions for adults and children (see Table 5.1). The children's versions were primarily downward extensions of the adult scales. Each revision of the tests were done to update the norms, modify the stimulus materials, add new subtests, and align the scales with relevant research, especially related to factor structure.

The current versions of the Wechsler scales, the Wechsler Pre-School and Primary Scale of Intelligence-Revised (WPPSI-R; Wechsler, 1989), Wechsler Intelligence Scale for Children-Third Edition (WISC-III; Wechsler, 1991), and Wechsler Adult Intelligence Scale-Third Edition (WAIS-III; Wechsler, 1997a, 1997b), are tools for multidimensional, individualized psychological evaluations. An advantage of the Wechsler IQ Scales is that IQs, indexes, and scaled scores are all based on the same statistical scale. Thus, deviations from the mean on the normal distribution are theoretically the same for the standardization population as for a clinical population. This allows comparison of the examinee's performance on one subtest with another, as well as comparisons with the normative sample. In theory, comparison with z-scores or t-scores on a wide range of additional instruments should also be possible. In reality, however, these other measures have been normed on other populations, compromising comparability, since it is not known how the normative distribution of one study sample actually maps on to that of another. To a certain extent this problem was addressed in the co-norming of the WAIS-III with the Wechsler Memory Scale-Third Edition (WMS-III; Wechsler, 1997b) and the Wechsler Individual Achievement Test (Wechsler, 1992) so that the same subject pool formed the standardization sample for both test instruments. Direct comparisons can therefore be made among an examinee's performances on these tests.

Almost from the beginning, the Wechsler intelligence scales were used for the assessment of cognitive dysfunction. This is logical given that many of the abilities measured by the Wechsler Intelligence scales (memory, speed of information processing, abstract reasoning, attention, etc.) are relevant to neuropsychological assessment. When Halstead and Reitan developed their battery (Reitan, 1956) of 10 (later reduced to 7) "brain sensitive" tests, they emphasized that assessment was to include the Wechsler-Bellevue scales. Many other authors have affirmed the Wechsler intelligence scales to be essential for neuropsychological assessment. Such assessments have typically focused on both quantitative (IQ scores) as well as qualitative (types of errors) aspects of performance, both of which lead to specific hypotheses regarding individual strengths and needs (Milberg, Hebben, & Kaplan, 1996). From a practitioner's

Table 5.1.   Chronology for the development of the Wechsler intelligence scales

Adult Scales	Child Scales	Primary/Preschool
Wechsler-Bellevue (1939)	WISC (1949)	WPPSI (1967)
WAIS (1955)	WISC-R (1974)	WPPSI-R (1989)
WAIS-R (1981)	WISC-III (1991)	
WAIS-III (1997)		

perspective, ecological (concurrent) and treatment validity have been overriding concerns in any interpretative process (Reschly, 1997).

Various methods of interpreting the Wechsler scales have recognized and utilized advances in cognitive and neuropsychological theory and research. For example, Horn and Cattell's (Horn, 1994) theories of crystalized versus fluid intelligence have been used to categorize and subsequently analyze the different Wechsler subtests. In addition, Luria's (1980) distinction between sequential and simultaneous methods of information processing has also been used to organize the subtests based on the extent to which they emphasize these modes of processing (see Groth-Marnat, 1999b; Kaufman, 1990, 1994; Kaufman & Lichtenberger, 1999). Kaplan and her colleagues have developed procedures to more fully understand the reasons (or underlying processes) why an examinee obtains a particular score. These procedures have been formalized in the WAIS-R as a Neuropsychological Instrument (WAIS-R NI; Kaplan, Fein, Morris, & Delis, 1991) and, more recently, in the WISC-III as a Process Instrument (WISC-III PI; Kaplan, Fein, Morris, Kramer, & Delis, 1999). The standard WAIS-III has incorporated some of Kaplan et al.'s (1991) process features in the form of optional procedures, primarily on the Digit Symbol subtest. In addition, Lezak (1995) has elaborated on various methods of testing hypotheses to determine the reasons for different levels of performance.

Kaufman (1990, 1994) developed an additional method of Wechsler interpretation that tests hypotheses by exploring both the relations between patterns of Wechsler subtests as well as additional subtests external to the Wechsler scales. To test various patterns of Wechsler scores, the clinician notes the consistencies/inconsistencies between subtests. For example, a low WISC-III Coding score might be due to low speed of information processing, poor visual memory, or difficulties with visual processing. Clinicians would determine which of these hypotheses were correct by noting high and low scores among other Wechsler subtests. If, for example, other subtest scores with a significant visual memory component were high, it suggests that poor visual memory was not the reason for the low Coding score. The second strategy of Kaufman's method is to administer additional non-Wechsler tests. For example, to determine if an examinee's low Coding scores were due to poor visual processing, the Visual Processing subtests of the Woodcock Johnson-R might be given. If these yielded high scores, then it would argue that this was not the reason why the Coding scores were low. Thus, Kaufman has placed considerable emphasis on investigating clusters of subtests as well as hypothesis testing through using subtests external to the Wechsler scales. In contrast, Kaplan and her colleagues primarily emphasized variations on the administration of the Wechsler subtests themselves (as well as using some external tests) to probe the examinee's underlying cognitive processes.

Many controversies surround intelligence testing. These include questions about the precise nature of what it is that is being measured; the social, educational, and moral implications of labeling individuals; and the validity of applying norms to an increasingly diverse population (see Weinberg, 1989). One of the crucial controversies relevant to neuropsychology relates to the extent to which individual Wechsler subtests can and should be interpreted. On one extreme, Lezak (1988, 1995) presents each of the Wechsler subtests separately and disparages the usefulness of the global IQ ("IQ:RIP"). She states that "When the many and various neuropsychological observations elicited by so-called 'intelligence' tests are lumped and leveled into a single IQ score—or even three—the product of this unholy conversion is a number that, in referring to everything, represents nothing" (Lezak, 1988, p. 352). She, along with a number of other authors, uses procedures that conceptualize and work to understand and parse the multivariate cognitive complexity of each examinee. These assessment profiles of test scores represent various cognitive strengths and weaknesses. The resulting interpretations are useful in providing a range of information about an examinee, and can often be used more effectively in making inferences about competencies in the real world.

In contrast to the above approach, other authors recommend that clinicians avoid subtest interpretation and focus instead on global IQs (McDermott, Fantuzzo, & Glutting, 1990, p. 522). Their rationale is that Wechsler subtests are not sufficiently reliable, valid, and specific (McDermott, Fantuzzo, & Glutting, 1990; Glutting, McDermott, Watkins, Kush, & Konold, 1997). They argue that lack of specificity is of particular importance and that instead, most of the variance in subtest performance can be accounted for by a general factor (g) which is hypothesized to underlie all intellectual activities.

The debate on subtest interpretation is far from being settled. It does, however, highlight that interpretations need to be made cautiously and should follow careful guidelines. In particular, subtest scores should not be interpreted when there are only mild differences between high and low scores. Such differences need to be tested to make sure that they have achieved sufficient levels of significance. The process approach outlined in this chapter and elsewhere (Kaplan, 1988; Kaplan et al., 1991, 1999; Milberg et al., 1996), can also be used to parse the reason(s) why an examinee achieved a particular score. In addition, hypothesis testing can be used to search for patterns among different subtests as well as note data external to the Wechsler scales themselves (behavioral observations, history, other test scores).

A further controversy is that IQ scores (and the Wechsler subtests in particular) have often been used to explain too much of a person's behavior. This controversy (and misuse) has occurred because IQ scores have been clearly demonstrated to accurately predict a number of highly relevant behaviors such as academic and occupational performance (Neisser et al., 1996). However, there are a large number of behaviors that are not adequately measured by the Wechsler scales, but are still of considerable interest to neuropsychologists. Noteworthy among these is the observation that poor executive functions may not be reflected in Wechsler performance (see Chapter 13). Thus, it might be possible for a client to have performed quite well on virtually all areas of the WAIS-III/WISC-III and yet be significantly impaired due to executive dysfunction. Unless a neuropsychologist specifically assessed executive function, the impairment might go unnoticed. To a certain extent, alternative administrations and careful qualitative observations can help clinicians be more sensitive to indications of possible executive dysfunction on the WAIS-III/WISC-III (see section on "Wechsler subtests"). There are also a wide number of other areas related to intelligence that are relevant to a person's functioning, but are not measured by the Wechsler intelligence scales. These include creativity, common sense, skills in daily living, musical ability, kinesthetic ability, planning, and long-term memory for recently learned material.

Related to these issues has been the controversy over whether or not there are unique "brain damage" Wechsler profiles. Wechsler (1958) distinguished between "no hold" subtests (Digit Span, Digit Symbol, Similarities, Block Design), which were quite sensitive to the effects of deterioration, versus "hold" subtests (Information,

Object Assembly, Picture Completion, Vocabulary). Theoretically a person's performance on the "hold" subtests could be used to assess premorbid level of functioning, whereas performance on "no hold" subtests could indicate the presence and level of impairment. Even though some subtests are clearly more sensitive to deterioration (see section on "Wechsler subtests"), brain impairment is much too diverse to be able to classify subtest patterns easily. This means that diagnoses made on this simple hold/no hold distinction are likely to result in numerous misclassifications. Specifically, the hold/no hold distinction does not take into account such crucial factors related to brain functioning as age, handedness, education, recency of the injury (acute versus chronic), lesion site, and environmental factors. There are also many important abilities related to brain functioning that are not measured by the Wechsler intelligence scales. In essence, there is no one pattern, or even a cluster of patterns, that are consistently diagnostic of brain damage.

A final controversy relevant to neuropsychology is that the Wechsler scales generally do not have sufficient research supporting inferences related to everyday behaviors (ecological validity). Despite this, clinicians are often expected to make ecologically relevant inferences such as how well examinees might perform in employment settings, the impact of brain injury on interpersonal relationships, and what might be an optimal treatment plan. Recently this issue has become highlighted in the field and efforts are being made to extend validity studies on the Wechsler scales into a wide number of ecologically relevant areas (Groth-Marnat & Teal, in press; Sbordone & Long, 1996).

Despite these only partially resolved issues, intelligence testing has been widely accepted as a reliable, objective source of information about a broad spectrum of individual skills and aptitudes. When placed in the proper context, such measures can be extremely valuable in understanding and predicting an examinee's level of performance and adaptation.

PSYCHOMETRIC PROPERTIES

Extensive data are provided in the most recent Wechsler manuals (Wechsler, 1989, 1991, 1997a) as well as in numerous additional studies using the Wechsler scales. Based on this material, as well as actual experience with the scales, thorough reviews can be found on the WAIS-III (Groth-Marnat, 1999b; Kaufman & Lichtenberger, 1999; Sattler & Ryan, 1999; Tulsky, Zhu, & Prifitera, in press) and WISC-III (Bracken & McCallum, 1993; Cooper, 1995; Edwards & Edwards, 1993; Jones & James, 1993; Kaufman, 1993, 1994; Sattler, 1992). The general conclusion is that the Wechsler intelligence scales have some of the best psychometric properties in the field. In addition, the manuals provide mostly clear, straightforward administration and scoring instructions.

WAIS-III

The 1997 WAIS-III was standardized on a large sample of 2,450 adults screened for medical and psychiatric conditions. The 100 men and 100 women in each age group (except ages 80–89, where the total sample size was 250) were stratified by race/ethnicity, education level, and geographic region. The WAIS-III manual (Wechsler, 1997a) provides documentation of the sample's demographic characteristics, which accurately reflects the 1995 U.S. census data. The manual also describes an additional study to test for item bias using African-American and Hispanic subjects and two studies to ensure protocol scoring accuracy.

One feature of the 1997 revision was that the age range was from 16 to 89 years. This extended the age norms upward relative to the WAIS-R, which only went to 74 years. Also, an extended number of minority subjects have been included (i.e., "oversampling"). However, the mean IQs and Index scores were not included for the various ethnic groups. The WAIS-III contains the same six WISC-III Verbal and Performance subtests along with Symbol Search (derived from the WISC-III), Matrix Reasoning, and Letter-Number Sequencing. Pilot studies revealed the new Matrix Reasoning subtest was technically adequate and provided a good measure of Performance and Perceptual Organization (PO). As a result, the WAIS-III development team decided to replace Object Assembly (now optional) with this measure to enhance the scale's measurement of fluid intelligence. In addition, the Letter-Number Sequencing subtest was added to strengthen the Working Memory Index (WM; conceptually replacing WISC-III Freedom from Distractibility or FD). Other changes included a reduced emphasis on processing speed on some Performance subtests, extension of subtest floors and ceilings, and updated artwork with larger pictures and the addition of color.

Reliability coefficients are reported in the manual for each age group and averages are provided across the sample. Average internal consistency coefficients are excellent for the Full Scale, Verbal, and Performance IQs (range = .90 to .95) as well as the four indexes (Verbal Comprehension/VC, .96; Perceptual Organization/PO, .93; Working Memory/WM, .94; Processing Speed/PS, .88). The WAIS-III subtests have lower average reliabilities, ranging from a low of .70 for Object Assembly to a high of .93 for Vocabulary. Since Picture Arrangement (.74), Letter-Number Sequencing (.79), and Object Assembly (.70) all have relatively low reliabilities, they should be interpreted with caution. Test-retest reliabilities are reported for four age groups and are fairly high for the IQs (range = .88 to .97) and Indexes (range = .83 to .96). Similar to the other Wechsler scales, average stability coefficients are generally higher for core Verbal (range = .81 to .94) as compared to Performance (range = .69 to .82) subtests.

Confidence intervals are calculated using estimated true scores, instead of actual scores, to take into account regression to the mean. The standard errors of measurement (SEMs), presented by age group, are relatively low for the average Full Scale (2.29), Verbal (2.50), and Performance IQs (3.75). Factor Indexes have higher average SEMs, with VC lowest (3.03), PO (3.79), WM (3.84) are intermediate (3.03 and 3.79, respectively), and PS highest (5.36). The least confidence can be placed in subtests with the highest SEMs. For example, Vocabulary with a SEM of .79 can be interpreted with more confidence than Picture Arrangement with a much larger SEM of 1.60.

Each subtest has moderate to high correlations with the relevant indexes. For the Verbal Comprehension Index (VC), simple correlations are high for Information (.90), Similarities (.90), and Vocabulary (.93). The PO Index subtests of Picture Completion (.81), Block Design (.85), and Matrix Reasoning (.83) have somewhat lower correlations. Arithmetic (.83), Digit Span (.83), and Letter-Number Sequencing (.85) correlated equally well with WM. Strong correlations between PS and Coding (.91), and Symbol Search (.91) were obtained. High intercorrelations are reported for many of the subtests at each age level and several have significant relationships across Verbal and Performance domains.

For the WAIS-III factor structure, five age groups were created and exploratory factor analyses using principal component analysis with an oblique rotation and confirmatory factor analyses were conducted. According to exploratory analyses across age groups, a four-factor solution best fits the data sets. Only the 75 to 89 age group presents a significant deviation from the collapsed sample, with several PO subtests loading on PS. Similar to the WISC-III, Vocabulary (.89), Similarities (.76), Information (.81), and Comprehension (.80) load on the VC factor and substantially lower loadings are observed for Arithmetic (.22) and Picture Arrangement (.27). Picture Completion (.56), Block Design (.71), Picture Arrangement (.47), and Matrix Reasoning (.61) load on the PO factor. Small PO loadings included the Symbol Search (.16), Arithmetic (.15), and Similarities (.10) subtests. The WAIS-III PO factor is probably somewhat different than its WISC-III counterpart, as Object Assembly was not included in the analyses. The WAIS-III WM factor was comprised of Arithmetic (.51), Digit Span (.71), and Letter-Number Sequencing (.62) subtests and Matrix Reasoning had a minor loading (.21). Finally, Processing Speed was comprised of Coding (.68) and Symbol Search (.63) subtests, with minor loadings for Picture Completion (.17) and Letter-Number Sequencing (.13). Confirmatory analyses of one through five factor models support the four-factor model for each of the age groups, with significant reductions in chi-square and goodness-of-fit indexes observed at each level (except from four to five factors). The confirmatory results provide regression scores for the latent factors, and results suggest both Comprehension and Picture Arrangement contribute little additional variance and were therefore excluded from VC and PO, respectively. Caruso and Cliff (1999) also found support for the four factor model (VC, WM, PO, PS) but suggest that a two factor model comprised of *GF* and *Gc* are more appropriate than the traditional Verbal-Performance distinction.

A number of concurrent construct validity studies were conducted to evaluate various measures of cognitive and neuropsychological functioning. Although the manual provides demographic data and IQ results for these samples, no subtest relationships are presented. WAIS-III correlations with the WAIS-R and WISC-R Full Scale (.84 and .91), Verbal (.85 and .90), and Performance IQs (.82 and .90) are adequate. The Full Scale (.84), Verbal (.78), and Performance IQs (.83) appear to be related to fluid intelligence as measured by the Standard Progressive Matrices test (Raven, 1976). IQ correlations with the MicroCog (Powell et al., 1993) Information Processing Accuracy (.59 to .77) and the Dementia Rating Scale (Mattis, 1988; .58 to .61) were somewhat lower although this is not surprising considering the limited crystalized aspects of these measures. There are no other studies reported using other measures of intellectual functioning.

The extensive WAIS-III neuropsychological validity studies are broken down into measures tapping attention and concentration, memory, language, fine motor skills, visuospatial abilities, and executive functioning. The WMS-R Attention/Concentration Index was highly correlated with the Working Memory Index (.66) and, as would be expected, had much lower correlations with VC (.36), PS (.38), and PO (.46). Consistent with the visuospatial and executive function demands of the Halstead-Reitan Trails A and Trails B subtests, Trails A was primarily related to PO (−.53) and PS (−.49); whereas, Trails B was related to PO (−.62), WM (−.65), and PS (−.55). The MicroCog Attention/Mental Control Index was primarily related to WM (.65), PS (.60), and PO (.58).

In addition to their widespread use in clinical assessment, the Wechsler intelligence scales have been used extensively in neuropsychological research with a broad range of clinical populations. These studies have been important in characterizing the cognitive concommitants of clinical syndromes, aiding in differential diagnosis, and helping the clinician understand the presentation and course of different syndromes for the purposes of treatment planning. Although many years of research have established patterns of WAIS-R responses across a variety of clinical populations, it is important to remember that the WAIS-III is a distinct instrument that may or may not produce similar patterns; only empirical evidence from this specific version will reveal this.

Although the Wechsler manuals provide excellent information about test-retest reliability in a normal sample, these issues are less clear when using Wechsler intelligence scales to monitor recovery or decline of function in a neuropsychological setting. For example, the same inferences for a normal population about practice effects cannot necessarily be made for an examinee with a cognitive impairment. It is possible that individuals with attention, learning, or memory problems may profit less from prior exposure, yet it is important to avoid attributing gains made on the basis of practice to recovery of function. Practice could also mitigate the apparent effects of subtle decline. A related issue is that it is important to note whether an examinee has moved into a new normative age cohort at the time of the repeated evaluation. This may result in an apparent improvement in scaled scores, or may disguise a decline that would be apparent in comparing raw scores.

Concerns about the appropriateness of applying the standard norms and assumptions of the Wechsler intelligence tests to examinees from minority, socioeconomically disadvantaged, culturally or linguistically different backgrounds, are magnified in the context of neuropsychological assessment. Little is known about how these factors may interact with compromised cognitive function.

It is also important to evaluate whether assumptions about the predictive value of the WAIS-III hold true in clinical populations. For example, in the structured, interactive testing environment, some patients with intact language and visuospatial skills but with acquired deficits in areas such as long-term memory or executive functions may obtain relatively strong scores that would erroneously predict more successful adaptive functioning than their actual deficits would allow in more demanding real-life situations. Several separate validity studies were conducted with special populations. Although the sampling procedures are described in the appendixes, subtype analyses were not conducted on many of the samples and no discriminate analyses were reported. Therefore, the following conclusions must be considered anecdotal. For adults with suspected Alzheimer's disease, relatively lower mean IQ scores were obtained but VC was the highest (93) with somewhat lower scores on WM (87), PO (85), and PS (80). Patients with Huntington's disease showed lower PS (69), WM (83), and PO (85) as compared to VC (98). This is similar to the pattern found among patients with Parkinson's disease (VC = 97, PO = 85, WM = 90, PS = 82). Individuals with Traumatic Brain Injury showed relatively spared VC (90), PO (92), and WM (90) as compared to their extremely low PS (73) scores. Adults diagnosed with mild mental retardation (VIQ = 60; PIQ = 64; FSIQ = 58) appeared to be higher functioning than those with moderate mental retardation (VIQ = 55; PIQ = 55; FSIQ = 51). Individuals diagnosed with ADHD had relatively average scores (VC = 105; PO = 101; WM = 97), except for PS (93), which was slightly lower. This was somewhat different than the trend observed for individuals diagnosed with Math and Reading disabilities, who performed poorly on WM (89 and 91), as compared to their VC (102 and 98), PO (102 for both) and PS (95 and 96).

A wide variety of short forms or abbreviated scales have been proposed (see Campbell, 1998 and Groth-Marnat, 1999b, pp. 200–204 and 726–727). These fulfill the desire of many clinicians to approximate an IQ score in a shorter time than the full Wechsler scales require. Typically, these short forms consist of administering a small number (usually between 2 and 5) of the subtests and prorating the results into Full Scale, Verbal, and Performance IQs based on the mean of the tests actually administered. Conversion formulae have also been proposed. One option for the WAIS-III is to give all the subtests necessary for calculating the index scores and then prorate them to form the three IQs. Ryan and Ward (1999) have developed two seven subtest short forms (Short Form 1: Information Digit Span, Arithmatic Similarities, Picture Completion, Block Design, Digit Symbol-Coding; Short Form 2: the same except Matrix Reasoning is substituted for Block Design). These short forms have high correlations with the Full Scale (.97), Verbal (.96) and Performance (.92) IQs and have fairly low Standard Errors of Measurement (Short Form 1 = 2.80; Short Form 2 = 2.72). Alternatively, Satz and Mogel (1962) and Adams, Smigielski, and Jenkins (1984) have published data on a short form that samples each domain by giving every other or every third item within each subtest (except for Digit Span and Digit Symbol, which are administered in full).

Although use of short forms may be tempting for clinicians working under time constraints, these are short cuts that should be used only with caution in working even with normal examinees, and are particularly questionable in a neuropsychological setting. Although many short forms have been reported to have high correlations with the WAIS-III/WISC-III (based on the normative data), they typically have a wider band of error than do the actual IQ scores. The short form approach also tends to imply primacy of the IQs and ignores the factor structure underlying the Wechsler scales. Perhaps most serious is the loss of the range of clinical observations afforded by administering the scale in its entirety. Those who choose to use a short form should always indicate clearly that the reported scores are based on incomplete data.

The Psychological Corporation, cognizant that there are times that psychologists, clinicians, and researchers need a short and reliable measure of intelligence, addressed this issue by developing the Wechsler Abbreviated Scale of Intelligence (WASI; The Psychological Corporation, 1999). The WASI consists of four WAIS-III subtests: Vocabulary, Similarities, Block Design, and Matrix Reasoning similar in format to the WAIS-III but with different content items. The choice of the WASI subtests was consistent with evidence suggesting bilateral hemispheric activation on most complex cognitive tasks (Goldberg & Costa, 1981; Springer & Deutsch, 1998), and so tap crystalized, fluid and executive function abilities (Hale, 1996). Despite this, the WASI continues to yield a Verbal (crystalized), and Performance (fluid) dichotomy as well as a Full Scale IQ based on the subtests with the highest loadings on general intellectual functioning (g). It was nationally standardized on a population aged 6 to 89 and, because it was linked to the WISC-III and WAIS-III, the subtests that were chosen permit obtaining reliable estimates of full WISC-III and WAIS-III IQs. Should there be a need to further reduce administration time, a two-subtest form (Vocabulary and Matrix Reasoning) can be administered, cutting administration time in half (approximately 15 minutes); however this two-subtest version yields only a FSIQ estimate.

WISC-III

The 1991 revision of the Wechsler scale for children (age range from 6 to 16 years, 11 months) is one of the most commonly used measures in the neuropsychological assessment of children (Donders, 1996; Sullivan & Bowden, 1997; Sweet et al., 1996). Like its predecessor, it contains the same six Verbal and six Performance subtests, along with the new Symbol Search subtest. The WISC-III was standardized on a sample of 2,200 children. The 100 boys and 100 girls in each age group were stratified by race/ethnicity, parent education level, and geographic region. The WISC-III manual has an extensive demographic characteristics section, which reflects the sample's congruence with 1988 U.S. Census data.

WISC-III reliability coefficients are excellent for the Full Scale, Verbal, and Performance IQs (ranging between .91 and .96) as well as the four indexes (Verbal Comprehension/VC, .94; Perceptual Organization/PO, .90; Freedom from Distractibility/FD, .87; Processing Speed/PS, .85). Test-retest reliabilities are reported for three age groups, and are fairly high for the IQs (range = .85 to .96) and Indexes (range = .71 to .95). As would be expected, the stability coefficients are higher for the Verbal (range = .73 to .89) than Performance (range = .57 to .81) subtests, probably because of greater practice effects or loss of novelty for the performance subtests. Long-term stability over a 2.8-year interval has been found to be high (Full Scale IQ = .91, Verbal IQ = .87, Performance IQ = .87) but much lower for the individual subtests (Canivez & Watkins, 1998). While an examination of subtest intercorrelations reveals shared variance among the subtests, subtest specificity is ample or adequate for a majority of subtests (Sattler, 1992). Because Block Design, Picture Arrangement, Picture Completion, Digit Span, Coding, and Mazes have ample specificity at most age levels, interpretations of unique strengths and weaknesses can be made with appropriate caution on these subtests. For the remainder of the subtests, specificity must be examined at each age prior to making interpretations of unique patterns of subtest strengths and weaknesses.

Several WISC-III factor analyses have been performed, and it is unclear whether the measure is best represented by a one-factor (Carroll, 1997; Glutting, Youngstrom, Ward, & Ward, 1997; Macmann & Barnett, 1994), two-factor (Kush, 1996), three-factor (Allen & Thorndike, 1995; Little, 1992; Sattler, 1992), or four-factor solution (Donders, 1996, 1997; Kamphaus, Benson, Hutchinson, & Platt, 1994; Konold, Kush, & Canivez, 1997; Tupa, Wright, & Fristad, 1997). The WISC-III manual reports the results of a maximum likelihood factor solution with a varimax rotation for the entire sample and four age groups. Two- and four-factor solutions are presented, and summary statistics are provided for confirmatory factor analyses. While the WISC-III confirmatory factor analyses suggest the four-factor solution provides the best fit of the data, Sattler (1992) provides convincing exploratory evidence that a three-factor solution (without the FD factor) more accurately represents the latent factor structure of the WISC-III.

Subsequent studies have confirmed the utility of a four-factor solution for children with disabilities or psychiatric disorders (Konold et al., 1997; Newby, Recht, Caldwell,

& Schaefer, 1993; Schwean, Saklofske, Yackulic, & Quinn, 1993; Tupa et al., 1997). Given the previously recognized utility of the WISC-R FD factor (Kaufman, 1994), and the limitations of exploratory factor analysis (Joreskog & Sorbom, 1989), a four-factor interpretation appears to be warranted in most cases. However, as noted earlier, the clinician is encouraged to examine an individual's pattern of performance and subtest variability before determining whether any IQ or Index score is interpretable.

One useful psychometric finding is that Symbol Search may be a better subtest and predictor of PO, Performance IQ, and g than Coding (Kaufman, 1994; Roid, Prifitera, & Weiss, 1993) and clinicians may therefore choose to use Symbol Search instead of Coding when computing Performance IQs. Reynolds, Sanchez, and Willson (1996) provide useful normative tables for determining WISC-III Full Scale and Performance IQs when Symbol Search is substituted for Coding.

The WISC-III manual reports validity studies with the WISC-R, WAIS-R, and WPPSI-R (discussed in WAIS-III section), Differential Ability Scales (DAS; Elliott, 1990), Benton Visual Retention Test-Revised (BVRT-R; Benton, 1974), Wide Range Achievement Test-Revised (WRAT-R; Wilkenson, 1993), and school grades. The WISC-III and WISC-R IQs are fairly comparable (Full Scale $r = .89$; Verbal Scale $r = .90$; Performance Scale $r = .81$). This suggests that much of the validity research with the WISC-R may be applicable to the WISC-III. As would be expected given the general increase in intellectual functioning over time (Flynn, 1999), WISC-III Full Scale, Verbal, and Performance IQs are lower than the WISC-R (5, 2, and 7 points, respectively).

A wide variety of WISC-III validity studies have been conducted on persons with learning disabilities, Attention Deficit Hyperactivity Disorder (ADHD), mental retardation, reading disabilities, and language difficulties. Unfortunately, one of the major studies using a neuropsychological population collapsed the sample of children with ADHD and Learning Disabilities (LD) as defined by discrepancy criteria. As a result, the findings may not be generalizable (Fletcher, Francis, Rourke, & Shaywitz, 1992). The results, however, do provide preliminary evidence of the relationship between the WISC-III and neuropsychological constructs. As would be expected, absolute value correlations of the neuropsychological measures are stronger for the Performance scale (range = .37 to .64) than for the Verbal Scale (range = .01 to .40). Trails A Time (−.51 to −.59) and Trails B Time (−.36 to −.40) were related to PO, FD, and PS as was the Tactual Performance Test (TPT) Total Time (range = −.32 to −.61), Memory (.45), and Localization (.42). The Number Correct on the Benton Revised Visual Retention Test was most related to Performance (.47) and Full Scale IQs (.37) as well as PO (.38), and FD (.37). The poor correlations with the Verbal Scale are not surprising, given that the neuropsychological tasks primarily measure visuospatial, tactile, and motor functioning (Batchelor, Sowles, Dean, & Fischer, 1991).

The WISC-III Verbal Scale has better predictions of achievement such as the Differential Abilities Scales (DAS; range = .54 to .55) and WRAT-R (range = .41 to .61) than the Performance Scale (DAS range = .29 to .41; WRAT-R .11 to .40). However, a comparison of WISC-III factor scores and the DAS and WRAT-R achievement subtest scores suggest this simple relationship may not be predictive of academic competence. For the DAS Basic Number Skills subtest and WRAT-R Arithmetic subtest, VC (.46

and .52), FD (.49 and .68), and PS (.39 and .73) appear to accurately reflect math computation skills. Both DAS Word Reading and WRAT-R Reading subtests show similar relationships with VC (.54 and .55), FD (.61 and .67), and PS (.53 and .55). DAS Spelling is more related to VC (.49), FD (.59), and PS (.55) than is the WRAT-R Spelling subtest, where only FD (.51) has a substantial correlation with spelling performance. These findings have been essentially replicated using other WRAT-R samples (Slate, 1995) and on the WRAT-3 (Vance & Fuller, 1995). While WISC-III Indexes predict Wechsler Individual Achievement Test (WIAT) scores better than IQs do, covarying the Full Scale IQ reduces their importance (Glutting et al., 1997), which is not surprising considering the shared variance between the IQs and Indexes. The WISC-III criterion-related validity study correlations with student grade point average and English, reading, spelling, and mathematics grades were generally consistent across IQs (range = .28 to .48) and Indexes (range = .24 to 42).

Although separate validity studies with special populations included children diagnosed as gifted, mildly mentally retarded (MR), LD, reading disabled (RD), ADHD, conduct disordered (CD), epileptic, speech/language delayed (SL), and hearing impaired (HI), no subtype analyses were performed on these exceptional samples. Except for PS (110), children identified as gifted received IQ and Index scores just below the gifted range (123 to 129). Children with MR received IQ and Index scores in the expected range (56 to 63), but this time PS was relatively higher (70). For the children with LD, RD, and ADHD, most IQ and Index scores were in the average range (range = 98 to 105), and FD (range = 87 to 93) and PS (range = 89 to 95) were generally lower, similar to the results for other LD and ADHD samples (Anastopolous, Spisto, & Maher, 1994; Riccio, Cohen, Hall, & Ross, 1997; Schwean et al., 1993). However, the collapsed LD group had somewhat lower Verbal, Full Scale, and VC scores (range = 92 to 94). Full or partial ACID profiles (**A**rithmetic, **C**oding, **I**nformation, and **D**igit Span; were frequently more depressed in the LD/RD (25%) and ADHD (39%) samples than the standardization sample (7%). The children with CD received low overall IQs (78 to 82). Children with epilepsy scored low on the IQs (range = 74 to 77), and PS (73; Donders, 1997). Finally, as predicted, children with SL delays were lower on the Verbal (69) than the Performance (78) IQs and individuals who were HI also performed lower on the Verbal (81) as compared to the Performance (106) IQ. Although these results suggest average Performance scores in the HI population, WISC-III Performance scores were significantly lower than those obtained on the WISC-R in another study (Slate & Fawcett, 1995).

For language functioning, the Boston Naming Test (Kaplan, Goodglass, & Weintraub, 1983) correlated with the VC (.49) and PO (.43; because of its pictorial stimuli), the Controlled Oral Word Association Test (COWAT; Benton & Hamsher, 1989), and the Token Test (De Renzi & Vignolo, 1962) all correlated with VC (.57, .62, .59 respectively). However, the COWAT also correlated moderately with WM (.54) and PS (.55), providing support for their relationship with executive functions. For motor functioning, the MicroCog Reaction Time Index was primarily related to WM (.85), and, to a lessor extent, to PO (.63) and PS (.59). No meaningful Index differences were observed for the nonsignificant Finger Tapping Test and significant Grooved Pegboard (Kløve, 1963) correlations.

Profile analysis should take into account the factorial complexity of the WISC-III subtests, subtest reliabilities and specificities, significant differences between subtests, and base rates for subtest differences found in the standardization sample. Profile analysis is not as affected by floor and ceiling effects, and significant differences for the IQs and Indexes are broken down by age in the manual. However, significant differences on subtest scaled scores are collapsed across ages and the simple difference score method is used instead of the Standard Error of Difference (SED); therefore, the clinician may wish to calculate the SED for a given age, using the .01 or .05 level of significance. The WISC-III manual also has base rate intersubtest scatter data for various IQs and Indexes, and base rate information for significant strengths and weaknesses, collapsed for all ages. As Digits Forward and Digits Backward measure different cognitive constructs, base rate information is provided for each in the WISC-III manual.

Several resources are available to aid the clinician choosing to perform profile analysis (Groth-Marnat, 1999b; Kaufman, 1994), including interpretation for different age groups (McGrew & Wrightson, 1997) and subtest constructs (Siegel & Piotrowski, 1994). Although limited in neuropsychological interpretation, Groth-Marnat (1999b), Kaufman (1994), and Sattler (1992) present comprehensive texts on WISC-III interpretation and profile analysis. After consulting these resources, it is critical that the clinician does not automatically equate certain constructs with certain test scores, since subtests do not measure the same constructs equally for all children. The astute clinician can develop hypotheses about subtest profiles only after careful examination of test-taking behaviors and the examinee's responses to individual test items (see "Interpretation" section). The validity of these hypotheses should be examined by testing the limits with the standardized WISC-III PI before generalizations about a child's performance are made.

ASSETS AND LIMITATIONS

The Wechsler intelligence scales provide a broad assessment of a wide range of abilities. The procedures are well standardized and the results are presented in a clear, objective manner. Standardization closely reflects U.S. census data. In addition, the Wechsler scales have been translated into and used by many language groups throughout the world. Each new version of the scales has resulted in improvements in areas such as standardization, ease of handling, age range, greater IQ ceiling/floor, guidelines for interpretation, reliability, and validity. These versions have increasingly utilized advances in cognitive and neuropsychological theory and research. The development of indexes for the WAIS-III and WISC-III have been a clear strength that allows for more detailed interpretations of particular relevance among neuropsychological populations.

One of the strongest assets of the Wechsler intelligence scales is the extensive research that has been done with or on them. Indeed, the Wechsler intelligence scales are the most extensively researched of all psychological tests. This research base allows practitioners to more fully understand the meanings behind the performances of individuals as well as various population groups. Some of this research has been reviewed in the previous section. However, far more research needs to be done on ecologically relevant domains, particularly for the various subtests. For example, little research has actually studied whether low scores on Digit Span or WM/FD indexes predict difficulty with such day-by-day activities as remembering telephone numbers, following instructions, or being able to follow directions for operating a simple sequence on a computer. Current research on various aspects of the WAIS-III is limited, but this should change considerably over the next few years as progressively more research is published.

Although the Wechsler intelligence scales cannot be considered formal tests of personality, they have been designed in such a way to informally assess important personality variables. This information is typically obtained by noting relevant behaviors as well as qualitative responses on some of the items. For example, a cautious, reflective problem-solving style can be observed in how the examinee approaches the tasks. Such a style is also likely to lower performance on speeded tasks. Often qualitative responses on test items can also reveal aspects of personality. For example, an examinee who states that he or she would "soak the stamp off" an envelope found on the street may be revealing antisocial tendencies. These behavioral observations and qualitative responses can often be crucial in increasing both the accuracy of interpretations, as well as developing and testing out various hypotheses related to personality.

Even though the Wechsler manuals provide mostly clear, objective scoring guidelines, clinicians have been found to make a surprisingly high number of administrative and scoring (mainly clerical) errors (Slate, Jones, & Murray, 1991). These errors are due to factors such as carelessness, lack of proper instruction, and work overload. A further reason is that some of the subtests (Vocabulary, Comprehension, Similarities) require more judgment than others such that an "easy" scorer may develop higher subtest and possibly IQ and Index scores than a "hard" scorer. This issue underscores the importance of rigorous, closely supervised training (see Fantuzzo, Blakey, & Gorsuch, 1989).

A number of improvements have occurred each time the Wechsler scales have been revised. Representative, up-to-date standardization has been one of these noteworthy features. In addition, the WISC-III introduced the Symbol Search subtest which, when paired with Coding, allowed the fourth Processing Speed Index to emerge. This tradition was continued with the WAIS-III, which included not only an adult version of Symbol Search, but also included the new subtests Letter-Number Sequencing and Matrix Reasoning. Similar to the WISC-III, this yielded four Index scores. The advantage for the clinician is that the Index scores allow for greater precision regarding an examinee's relative strengths and weaknesses. The new WAIS-III (and earlier WISC-III) Processing Speed Index has been found to be particularly sensitive to neuropsychological impairment. The WAIS-III profile form also provides tables to facilitate calculating subtest scores and especially to determine whether or not the subtest scaled scores represent significant variations from the means of Verbal, Performance, or total subtests. A further feature of the WAIS-III and WISC-III is that subtest scaled scores are based on comparisons with a subject's age-related peers. The earlier WAIS-R did not automatically make age-related comparisons on the subtest profile sheet, which increased the likelihood that clinicians would erroneously interpret profile interpretations without taking these age-related comparisons into account. The WAIS-III has developed a greater range of IQs (45–155) as well as increased the age for norms to include persons up to the age of 89. This co-norming means that more accurate comparisons can be made between an examinee's performance on these additional important tests. Finally, the essential structure of the earlier versions of the Wechsler scales have been maintained which is reflected in high correlations between IQs on the new and previous versions. As a result, much of the research derived from the earlier versions can be cautiously transferred to the newer WAIS-III and WISC-III.

While few would dispute that the Wechsler intelligence scales often reveal crucial examinee information, the amount of face-to-face clinician time is often considerable. This is particularly true for patient groups (particularly those with cognitive impairment) where administration times are longer (Ryan, Lopez, & Werth, 1998) and can sometimes extend beyond two hours. If variations on administration are given such as those for the WAIS-R NI or WISC-III PI, this extends the administration time even further. This level of time commitment is likely to be carefully scrutinized by managed care organizations and raises issues related to financial and treatment efficacy (Groth-Marnat, 1999a). Thus, practitioners need to carefully evaluate and possibly defend whether the time spent on the Wechsler scales is actually needed for a particular individual.

The essential strategy for Wechsler revisions has been to make relatively minor changes and to adhere to the IQ tradition as originally developed by the early Stanford Binet and Wechsler Scales. However, theories of intelligence have undergone significant changes (see Harrison, Flanagan, & Genshaft, 1997) and these changes generally have not been reflected in the structure or strategies underlying the Wechsler scales. More recent theories include Luria's (1980) PASS model (Planning-Attention-Successive-Sequencing), common sense problem solving (Sternberg, Wagner, Williams, & Horvath, 1995), Gardner's multiple intelligences (Gardner, 1993), and emotional intelligence (Bar-On, 1998). This has led Sternberg and Kaufman (1998) to point out that the Wechsler scales have not responded to many of the more current views of intelligence.

ADMINISTRATION

The WAIS-III and WISC-III manuals generally provide clear guidelines for administration and scoring. Examiners should be thoroughly trained in these procedures prior to assessing neuropsychological populations. Typically, training involves carefully reading the manual, several live or videotaped administrations in which the clinician receives feedback, and ongoing supervision of cases (see training guidelines in Fantuzzo et al., 1989). Developing competent administration skills is a particular issue given that research has consistently noted that even experienced clinicians make far more administrative and clerical errors than would be desired (Moon, Blakely, Gorsuch, & Fantuzzo, 1991; Slate et al., 1991).

Even though Wechsler administration and scoring procedures should be adhered to as closely as possible, standardization procedures must sometimes be violated when working with neuropsychologically impaired patients. Logistically, because of fatigue, hospital schedule, and so on, the patient may have to be tested in multiple sessions which breaks up the flow of the subtests in a manner discrepant from standardization procedures. In addition, instructions or presentation of the stimuli may have to be modified in nonstandard ways when the nature of the subject's impairments so dictate. While this has the advantage of increasing an examinee's motivation and obtaining clinically valuable information, it also may compromise the comparability of scores due to the nonstandardized administrations.

INTERPRETATION

The interpretive approach outlined and recommended in this section involves working through five successive steps (see Table 5.2). These steps are a summary and integration of procedures developed by Groth-Marnat (1999b), Kaufman (1990, 1994), Kaufman and Lichtenberger (1999), Naglieri (1993), and Sattler (1992). The various interpretive steps begin with the most general levels (Full Scale IQ) and proceed to more detailed and specific aspects of performance (subtest scatter, qualitative responses). It should be stressed that this approach provides information on quantitative scores as well as procedures for understanding the underlying processes clients went through in responding to the stimuli. During Level II and III interpretation (interpretation of Indexes and subtests), readers can consult information on the various subtests included in the next section ("Wechsler subtests"). This will provide relevant information on subtests including possible interpretive hypotheses, neuropsychological implications, and various strategies on how to parse underlying client processes.

The interactive nature of Wechsler intelligence scale tasks provides the examiner with many opportunities to observe clinically meaningful strategies, whether adaptive or maladaptive, as well as other relevant behaviors. This allows the clinician to generate and test hypotheses about ways in which modifications of the structure of certain tasks might facilitate performance. This is of particular importance for assessments in which the referral involves questions regarding brain-behavior relation. However, it should be cautioned that the Wechsler intelligence scales were not originally designed to assess

---

Table 5.2. Successive five-level WAIS-III/WISC-III interpretive procedures

Level I. Full Scale IQ

Level II. Verbal-Performance, Index Scores, and Additional Groupings

    (a) Verbal-Performance discrepancies.

    (b) Index scores: Verbal Comprehension, Perceptual Organization, Working Memory/ Freedom from Distractibility, Processing Speed.

    (c) Additional Groupings: Bannatyne's Categories, ACID/SCAD profiles, Horn groupings.

Level III. Subtest variability

    (a) Determining subtest scatter.

    (b) Hypothesis testing.

    (c) Integrate subtest hypothesis with additional information.

Level IV. Intrasubtest variability

Level V. Qualitative analysis

Adapted from Groth-Marnat (1999b).

neurocognitive deficits in individuals with known or suspected central nervous system dysfunction. Kaplan and her colleagues have produced an extensive, formalized corpus of practical modifications, the WAIS-R as a Neuropsychological Instrument (WAIS-R NI; Kaplan et al., 1991) and the WISC-III as a Process Instrument (WISC-III PI; Kaplan et al., 1999). These modifications are outlined after each of the various subtests and provide alternative administration formats of the same content, and additional scoring procedures to allow parsing the subcomponents of a given subtest to help identify which subcomponent underlies the problem(s). Expansions of two WISC-III subtests provide more opportunities to assess a child's abilities, and new subtests were added to further explore areas such as sequencing and planning ability. The WISC-III PI, unlike the WAIS-R NI, provides a norm-referenced assessment of the component processes as well as base rates for given qualitative responses.

A crucial feature of intelligence testing is that it relies on the clinical examination of all relevant variables affecting an individual's current level of functioning and pattern of performance. In utilizing the Wechsler intelligence scales, the clinician must always marshal as much information as possible about developmental history, education, prior level of functioning, motivation, emotional issues, and potential confounds such as fatigue and medication. Interpreting scores and performances should only be made within this context. This is particularly true in a neuropsychological setting. This means that any "interpretation" listed in the following sections should be considered tentative and should also be supported by a larger number of sources of evidence.

Level I. The Full Scale IQ

The Full Scale IQ is the most reliable and valid score. It is an excellent measure of general ability in that it predicts behaviors such as academic and work performance (Neisser et al., 1996). It is often useful to transform IQ scores into percentile equivalents and IQ classifications since these are more likely to be understood by a wider range of persons. Some clinicians also prefer to include the SEM to indicate that the IQ is an estimate of a person's ability and there is an expected range of error.

Within neuropsychological populations, a person's Full Scale IQ is often lowered following brain damage. A general rule of thumb is that if the Full Scale IQ is lower than would be expected given the person's academic and employment history, brain damage might be suspected. However, in some instances, an examinee's Full Scale IQ is seemingly not affected despite what appears to be a significant disability. This is likely to be particularly true for impaired attentional (see Chapter 11) or executive functions that typically occur in association with frontal lobe damage (see Chapter 13). In other cases, there might be significant lowering in a few of the selected subtests but overall they are not enough to impact the Full Scale IQ to any great extent.

Although Full Scale IQs may be useful to report when subtest scatter is minimal, thoughtful interpretation requires careful review of the IQs and Index scores to determine if they accurately reflect an individual's level of performance (Messick, 1995). When subtest scaled scores (M = 10, SD = 3) are relatively homogeneous, a Full Scale IQ is useful. However, significant IQ (Verbal-Performance), Index, or subtest differences indicate variable patterns of performance so that collapsing subtests that vary significantly into a single IQ would be misleading (Kaplan, 1988; Lezak, 1988). In these cases, it is necessary to consider both additional assessment strategies, as well as more detailed analysis of other aspects of the WAIS-III/WISC-III scores themselves.

Level II. Verbal-Performance IQs, Index Scores, and Additional Groupings

Level IIa. Verbal-Performance IQs

If there is a significant difference between the Verbal and Performance IQs, the Full Scale IQ should be interpreted with caution. The magnitude of Verbal-Performance (V-P) discrepancy required for statistical significance varies somewhat for different ages but is generally 9 points for the WAIS-III and 12 points for the WISC-III. A higher Verbal IQ indicates that the client's verbal abilities (verbal memory, verbal fluency, ability to work with abstract symbols, extent of educational background) are superior whereas a higher Performance IQ indicates higher abilities such as visuospatial skills, nonverbal contact with environment, speed of information processing, integration of perceptual information. It should, however, be noted that a Verbal-Performance (V-P) discrepancy of 9 (WAIS-III) or 12 (WISC-III) is a fairly common occurrence even in the WAIS-III and WISC-III standardization samples. This means that V-P discrepancies should not be over-interpreted and they should especially not be overpathologized. The need for interpreting this difference becomes more urgent as the difference increases, especially if the difference is 25 or more points.

Verbal-Performance differences can occur for a number of reasons including cognitive style, different types of interests, difficulty/strength working under time constraints, deficiency/strength in information processing, emotional disturbance, sensory deficits, or brain damage (see interpretive hypotheses in Verbal Scales and Performance Scales sections). One of the traditional interpretations among neuropsychological populations is that a higher Verbal than Performance IQ (V > P) suggests unilateral right hemisphere impairment whereas higher Performance than Verbal (P > V) suggests unilateral left hemisphere damage. There is some evidence that persons with unilateral right hemisphere damage have an average of a 9-point V > P difference and persons with unilateral left hemisphere damage have an average of a 4-point P > V difference (Kaufman, 1990). However, these differences are mediated to a large extent by age (children typically do not show V-P differences with unilateral damage), gender (V-P differences are greater among males), education (higher SES groups have relatively higher verbal scores, conversely lower SES groups have higher performance scores), and type and recency/location of lesion (V-P differences are most pronounced with acute, focal, posterior lesions). These issues and various interpretive hypotheses are discussed in further detail in the sections on Verbal Scales and Performance Scales.

Sometimes even significant V-P differences are not particularly useful in understanding the client's intellectual functioning. This occurs when either the subtests cluster around various Indexes (or other groupings) or when subtest variability is quite high (generally 9+ scaled score points or more between the highest and lowest subtest scaled scores for Verbal or 9+ points for Performance subtests). These conditions indicate that the IQs are not unitary constructs. It is then incumbent on the clinician to understand the meanings behind the discrepant scores.

Level IIb. Index Scores

Factor analyses of the WAIS-III/WISC-III typically have resulted in a four-factor solution that has been used to cluster subtests around Index scores. The Indexes are purer measures of functions than either the Verbal or Performance IQs. Using tables and worksheets provided in the manuals, discrepancies can be determined to see if differences between the Indexes are sufficient for interpretation. A summary of abilities assessed by the Indexes follows:

- *Verbal Comprehension.* This is similar to the Verbal IQ in that it measures a person's verbal-related knowledge, verbal fluency, and verbal reasoning while minimizing demands on working memory.
- *Perceptual Organization.* This index measures nonverbal, fluid reasoning, attention to detail, and visual-motor integration. It is somewhat similar to the Performance IQ, but speed of information processing is less important.
- *Working Memory (WAIS-III)/Freedom from Distractibility (WISC-III).* The subtests comprising Working Memory/Freedom from Distractibility require the examinee to listen to oral information, hold and process the information, and develop a correct response. As such, it measures short-term memory, concentration, attention, and the ability to work with numbers. Each of the tasks also involves sequencing. Executive functions may also be involved since examinees must make mental shifts and monitor their behavior. Since attention and memory are crucial, Working Memory/Freedom from Distractibility are often lowered by brain damage. It is also comprised of those subtests that are most sensitive to anxiety.
- *Processing Speed.* This index measures the mental and motor speed required for the examinee to solve visuospatial problems. Good performance also means that they must plan, organize, and follow through with relevant strategies. It is typically the lowest index for examinees with Alzheimer's disease, Huntington's disease, traumatic brain injury, and ADHD (Wechsler, 1997a). Performance can also be lowered due to low motivation or a cautious, overly reflective problem solving style.

Level IIc. Additional Groupings: Bannatyne's Categories,
ACID/SCAD Profiles, Horn Groupings

Bannatyne's Categories   Bannatyne's categories were originally developed as a means of organizing subtests according to those that were believed to reflect patterns among persons with learning disabilities (Bannatyne, 1974). The central idea behind the categorization was that spatial abilities that require simultaneous, holistic processing of information would be highest. Verbal conceptualization would be intermediate, and Sequencing and Acquired Knowledge would be lowest (Spatial > Verbal Conceptualization > Sequential > Acquired Knowledge). Traditionally these have been determined by merely calculating the means for the following clusters of scaled scores:

Spatial (Picture Completion, Block Design, Object Assembly, and possibly Matrix Reasoning from the WAIS-III)
Verbal Conceptualization (Vocabulary, Comprehension, Similarities)

Sequential (Digit Span, Arithmetic, Digit Symbol-Coding, and probably Letter-Number Sequencing from the WAIS-III)

Acquired Knowledge (Information, Vocabulary, Arithmetic)

Even though inserting the new WAIS-III subtests of Matrix Reasoning and Letter-Number Sequencing is speculative, their inclusion is conceptually consistent with what these tests seem to be measuring. For the WISC-III, Bannatyne's categories can be further refined by calculating standard scores (M = 100, SD = 15) using the following formulas developed by Kaufman (1994):

Spatial: 2.0 (PC + BD + OA) + 40

Verbal Conceptualization: 1.9 (V + C + S) + 43

Sequential: 2.3 (DSp + A + Coding) + 31

Acquired Knowledge: 1.9 (I + V + A) + 43

After these standard scores have been calculated, clinicians need also to determine whether or not the differences between the derived standard scores are significant. To calculate these differences, examiners should first find the mean of the standard scores and then determine the difference between each of the standard scores and the mean. The following values can be used to determine whether or not the standard scores vary at the .05 level:

Spatial: 10

Verbal Conceptualization: 12

Sequential: 12

Acquired Knowledge: 8.5

Formulas for developing standard scores and required differences for the WAIS-III are not yet available.

Although it was hoped that the above categorizations could classify learning disabled persons, only 20% to 25% of learning disabled persons typically have the Spatial > Verbal Conceptual > Sequential > Acquired Knowledge pattern (Katz, Goldstein, Rudisin, & Bailey, 1993). For example, sometimes bright, highly motivated persons with learning disabilities will compensate by learning a large amount of information. The result is that their Acquired Knowledge category might be quite high even though their Sequential abilities might be low. Since many learning disabled persons do not have the classic Bannatyne pattern, it should not be used for diagnostic purposes. Despite this, the value of Bannatyne's categorization is that, regardless of a person's diagnosis, it does provide a means of further understanding Wechsler subtests (see Groth-Marnat, in press).

SCAD Profile   The SCAD profile is composed of those subtests (**S**ymbol Search, **C**oding/Digit Symbol, **A**rithmetic, **D**igit Span) that learning disabled persons frequently perform poorly on. This is conceptually similar to Bannatyne's categories in that the subtests involve a combination of sequencing, working memory, perceptual speed, and acquired knowledge. The new Letter-Number Sequencing subtest on the WAIS-III is conceptually consistent with the above cluster. Thus, it might be speculated that it could either be included in the SCAD profile, or might substitute for one of the subtests. There is some support for the use of the SCAD profile (Kaufman, 1994; Wechsler, 1997a) but, as with Bannatyne's categories, interpretations should be made cautiously since many learning disabled persons still do not have the expected SCAD pattern.

Horn Groupings   The Horn Groupings have been organized around the conceptual distinction between *fluid* and *crystalized* intelligence (Horn, 1994). Since fluid intelligence is more closely tied to brain functioning than crystalized intelligence, it is sensitive to many types of cerebral impairment. The Horn categories for the WAIS-III include those subtests concerned with fluid intelligence (Matrix Reasoning, Block Design, Object Assembly, Similarities, Picture Arrangement, Arithmetic) versus crystalized intelligence (Information, Vocabulary, Comprehension, Similarities, Picture Arrangement). Somewhat similarly, the WISC-III fluid intelligence grouping is comprised of Picture Arrangement, Block Design, Object Assembly, Similarities, and Arithmetic. In contrast, crystalized intelligence comprises Information, Similarities, Vocabulary, Comprehension, and Picture Arrangement. Picture Arrangement and similarities have been included on both since there are aspects of fluid and crystalized intelligence involved in performance on these subtests. A further category, *Achievement* (Information, Similarities, Arithmetic, Vocabulary, Comprehension, Picture Arrangement) is also sometimes included. Standard scores ($M = 100$, $SD = 15$) for the WISC-III can be calculated with the following formulas (Kaufman, 1994):

WISC-III Fluid Intelligence: 1.3 (S + A + PA + BD + OA)

WISC-III Crystallized Intelligence: 1.3 (I + S + V + C + PA) + 35

WISC-III Achievement: 0.85 (I + S + A + V + C + PA) + 49

To determine if differences are significant, the mean of the standard scores for the above categories should be determined and then the differences from the mean calculated for each category. To be significant at the .05 level, differences should be 8.5 points for Fluid Intelligence, 9 points for Crystalized Intelligence, and 8.5 points for Achievement. Corresponding formulas have not yet been developed for the WAIS-III.

Level III. Interpreting Subtest Variability

Individual subtest scores are highly correlated with overall IQ in normal individuals, possibly due to a hypothesized general intelligence factor *(g)* that may underlie the structure of the scale. This hypothesized general factor is sometimes undermined in the presence of brain damage, where variability among subtests can be substantial (Kaufman, 1990; Lezak, 1995). When marked variability occurs, reporting IQ scores is likely to average out intersubtest scatter and present an overall index that obscures the individual's strengths and weaknesses. It is important, therefore, to focus on specific patterns of scatter among a patient's scaled scores on the subtests. However, it should be noted that high intersubtest scatter should not necessarily be used as a sign of brain impairment. Ryan, Paolo, and Smith (1992) found that degree of intersubtest scatter was no greater among a population of brain-damaged persons than for the WAIS-R standardization sample. Demographics can have a considerable impact on scatter. For example, elderly, well-educated persons were found to have a particularly high degree of subtest scatter (Mitrushina & Satz, 1995) whereas persons with low education and low IQs were found to have a low amount of scatter (Wechsler, 1997a).

The approach to subtest interpretation that follows takes into account both psychometric considerations as well as various hypothesis testing strategies. Hopefully clinicians will be able to take into account and integrate the best of these traditions. The ultimate goal is interpretations that do justice to the complexity of examinee's abilities, take into account multiple sources of information, and do so within the bounds of empirically and clinically supported guidelines. The following strategies and considerations emphasize measuring the extent of scatter along with various hypothesis testing strategies.

Level IIIa. Determining Subtest Scatter   Subtest interpretation should only be undertaken if there is sufficient subtest scatter. If little scatter exists, then there is no need to interpret subtest scores. This means that when little scatter is present, interpretations will rely on the IQ or Index scores (and possibly intrasubtest variability and qualitative features of the client's responses). It is, however, incumbent on each clinician to make sure that subtests do deviate sufficiently from the IQs (see Appendix A). The general principle is that the higher the reliability, the fewer points will be needed for a significant discrepancy to occur. For example, the highly reliable WISC-III Vocabulary subtest only needs 3 points to deviate significantly (.05 level) from the mean of all subtests. In contrast, the much less reliable Object Assembly subtest needs a full 4.5 points to deviate at the .05 level.

Another issue is the amount of subtest specificity. Only those subtests with sufficient subtest specificity can be interpreted with confidence. In general, the WAIS-III subtests with good to ample subtest specificity are Arithmetic, Digit Span, Information, Digit Symbol-Coding, Block Design, Matrix Reasoning, and Picture Completion (see Sattler & Ryan, 1998). The WISC-III subtests with ample subtest specificity are Digit Span, Coding, Picture Arrangement, Picture Completion, and Block Design. Object Assembly has inadequate specificity and the remaining six subtests have adequate specificity. However, the extent of specificity can vary according to age (see Kaufman, 1990, 1994; Kaufman & Lichtenberger, 1999; Sattler, 1992).

Level IIIb. Hypothesis Testing   Any test score is *at best* a hypothesis. The interpretations will depend on integrating and evaluating that score within the context of other information. The relevance of an interpretation will then be further determined by the referral question. The three general strategies for testing hypotheses are to evaluate the consistencies/inconsistencies among different subtests, use alternative administrations of subtests, and integrate scores with additional sources of information (scores from other tests, behavioral observations, medical history, etc.).

Consistencies/Inconsistencies among Subtests   The presence of a significantly high (or low) score on a subtest does not explain why that performance occurred. Examiners who merely note the high/low scores and list the abilities as if they were "interpretations" are likely to make interpretations that are not only inaccurate, but have the potential to be damaging. One method of determining the underlying meaning of a subtest score is to check other subtests for consistencies and inconsistencies. For example, Digit Symbol is a subtest that requires a multitude of different abilities especially visual memory and psychomotor speed. If a patient obtains a low score, it is important to understand why. If other speeded subtests (Symbol Search, Picture Arrangement, Block Design) produced high scores, then it would argue that psychomotor speed was not the reason for the low score.

Many clinicians do this type of hypothesis testing in an informal, even intuitive manner. A more formal way is by following the procedures in Appendix B. *This should not be done in a mechanical way.* At times, it might be necessary to accept an interpretation which is not quite supported by the procedures in Appendix B. This might be particularly true if medical history and behavioral observations support the interpretation. At other times, it might be necessary to discount an "interpretation" made through Appendix B if there is insufficient support from behavioral observations or medical history.

Alternative Administrative Procedures (WAIS-R NI and WISC-III PI)   Various alternative administrations have been developed to investigate the underlying processes an examinee undergoes when responding to the subtests. The importance of this is that two examinees might obtain the same score, but might do so for quite different reasons. Kaplan et al. (1991) illustrate this by noting that a Korsakoff patient with amnesia, a schizophrenic with attentional deficits, and a left parietal stroke patient with acalculia may all get the same score on Arithmetic. However, the final raw score obscures very important differences in the reason for the score. Thus, it is important to understand these differences in more depth since this might make a difference in diagnosis or treatment recommendations.

At the end of each subtest description (see section on Wechsler Scales), alternative procedures are summarized from the WAIS-R NI and WISC-III PI. These procedures are not necessary for every examinee, rather they can be tailored to the examinee's needs and the clinician's understanding of the patient. For example, a patient who is performing below the expected level on Information might be given the multiple-choice version. If the examinee did quite well on this alternative administration, it would support the hypothesis that the difficulty was primarily related to retrieval deficits. Careful questioning and behavioral observations are also important. In the above example, asking the patient if he or she once knew the information that was originally requested might not only help support the hypothesis of retrieval deficits, but also assist in deciding whether or not to give the multiple-choice administration. These procedures can assist in understanding the nature of cognitive deficits, identifying the location of possible sites of impairment, tailoring treatment programs to address certain cognitive processes, and monitoring recovery. One caution is that the inferences related to locus of damage are more likely to be valid for right-handed persons since persons with left-handedness are more likely to have anomalous brain organization (i.e., mixed dominance, language center in the right hemisphere).

Each section on alternative administrations includes a rationale, a description of the procedures, and a listing of possible interpretive hypotheses associated with various types of errors. It should be stressed that the hypotheses are *not* interpretations but merely interpretive possibilities. It would be necessary for clinicians to carefully observe the examinee's behavior, note similar errors on other subtests, and possibly administer additional tests to confirm/disconfirm the hypotheses. A more complete description of errors can be found in the WAIS-R NI and WISC-III PI manuals (Kaplan et al., 1991; Kaplan et al., 1999). A major caution, however, is that with so many *possible* indicators of deficits, clinicians may err in the direction of overpathologizing. This is a particular concern given clinicians' reported predilection to develop hypotheses and then test them out in such a way as to confirm them (a combination of primacy effects and confirmatory bias; see Garb, 1998). Even intact, normally functioning examinees are likely to have a few of the errors suggestive of "impairment."

The alternative administrations described for the WAIS-R are for this earlier version and not for the WAIS-III. However, since there is considerable overlap for some of the WAIS-R and WAIS-III subtests, multiple choice items from the WAIS-R NI (e.g., Information and Vocabulary) can be used to test clinical limits with the WAIS-III. Qualitative scoring for Digit Span and Block Design also inform the clinician with regard to specific processing deficits. Future research as well as single case, process-oriented studies will provide a better understanding of the comparability between the WAIS-R NI procedures and the WAIS-III. Note that there are plans for a WAIS-III NI.

Level IIIc. Integrate Subtest Hypotheses with Additional Information As with any test score, the clinician should also confirm subtest interpretations by searching for consistencies or inconsistencies with outside information. This might include other test scores, behavioral observations, history (medical, psychiatric, academic, vocational), or qualitative responses to test items (Level V). For example, a client who does poorly on speeded subtests might have attentional deficits, but might alternatively have a cautious, perfectionistic problem-solving style. This can often best be determined by close behavioral observation, trying to understand responses to failure, and asking family members about the examinee's problem-solving style. Poor motivation due to lack of interest or malingering are also possibilities. This process necessarily goes well beyond empirical guidelines but is clearly an essential part of understanding subtest interpretation.

Level IV. Intrasubtest Variability

Most persons taking the WAIS-III/WISC-III will provide correct answers on the early, easy items and, as the items get more and more difficult, will miss progressively more of them. An unusual pattern arises when an examinee misses early easier items but then succeeds on more difficult items. This might suggest memory difficulties or attentional deficits consistent with central nervous system dysfunction, especially with diffuse damage (Mittenberg, Hammeke, & Rao, 1989). The manual for the WAIS-R NI provides scoring systems and tables to evaluate the relative extent of scatter. It should also be stressed that, in addition to cerebral dysfunction, subtest scatter might occur due to conscious malingering.

Level V. Qualitative Analysis

Unique responses to test items can often assist in understanding the examinee's cognitive and personality processes. For example, perseveration might be noted if an examinee "contaminates" a response by including details from previous items. Examinees might also be "pulled" to the sound of items such as stating that "ponder" means to "pound" or to "plunder" (clang responses). Personality variables such as impulsiveness, antisocial tendencies, or suspiciousness might also be reflected in responses to items especially on Vocabulary, Comprehension, and Similarities. The error categories and possible meanings at the end of the subtest descriptions can be used to more fully understand qualitative responses related to neuropsychological populations.

THE WECHSLER SUBTESTS

Verbal Scale

The Verbal scales measure a person's ability to work with abstract symbols, verbal fluency, verbal memory abilities, and the degree to which they have benefited from education. They are generally considered to be more influenced by culture than the Performance scales. Within neuropsychological populations, standard administration of the Verbal subtests may be difficult, if not impossible, for patients with severe language or certain other cognitive impairments. Instead of omitting a test, the clinician may choose to present modified adaptations in testing clinical limits. This should be done only with the understanding that such testing provides the examinee with additional information and cues and is not really comparable to a standard administration. As long as it is understood that this violates the validity of the test norms and that the procedures are being modified to elicit information that would be otherwise inaccessible, this is a reasonable course. As noted previously, however, the WISC-III PI is norm referenced, and it is thus possible to compare scaled scores.

Considerable discussion and research have emerged in an attempt to understand the meanings associated with significant differences (usually 9 points for the WAIS-III and 12 IQ points for the WISC-III) between an examinee's Verbal and Performance IQs. A Verbal IQ that is significantly higher than Performance IQ (V > P) suggests the following interpretive possibilities (see Kaufman, 1990, 1994; Kaufman & Lichtenberger, 1999; Sattler, 1992; Sattler & Ryan, 1998):

- Possible over achievement.
- High educational level.
- Difficulty with practical tasks.
- Psychomotor slowing due to depression.
- Deficits in performance abilities.
- Poor visual-motor integration.
- Slow, reflective problem-solving style (resulting in slower performance on speeded tasks).
- Quick, impulsive problem-solving style (resulting in more errors on performance tasks).

Specific populations more likely to have V > P are persons from professional backgrounds, high IQs, highly educated persons, psychiatric populations, patients with

Alzheimer's disease, and persons with motor coordination problems. Determining which of the above possibilities is accurate involves integrating other test results, behavioral observations, relevant history, and qualitative responses.

Reviews of research on patients with unilateral right hemisphere impairment have found that, on average, their Verbal IQs are 9 points higher than Performance (Kaufman, 1990, 1994; Kaufman & Lichtenberger, 1999; Reitan & Wolfson, 1993; Sattler, 1992). The V > P discrepancy is likely to be most pronounced among adult, educated (12+ years), Caucasian males with acute, focal unilateral lesions due to tumors or strokes toward the posterior (versus frontal/anterior) regions. The following list summarizes relevant considerations and research in understanding V > P discrepancies:

- *Age.* Since children have greater brain symmetry and plasticity, the V > P difference should not be used to make inferences regarding brain laterality. However, studies with adults have consistently found the V > P discrepancy to be associated with unilateral right hemisphere impairment.

- *Education.* Persons with higher educations will typically have higher Verbal scores anyway which will serve to further exaggerate the V > P discrepancy with brain damage. In contrast, many persons from lower educational backgrounds have relatively higher Performance scores, decreasing the V > P difference usually associated with right hemisphere impairment.

- *Race.* Since Hispanics and Native Americans are more likely to have higher premorbid Performance abilities than Verbal, the V > P discrepancy is likely to be less for them following unilateral right hemisphere damage. In contrast, the V > P difference is likely to be more pronounced among European Americans and African Americans due to their premorbidly higher relative Verbal abilities.

- *Gender.* Following unilateral right hemisphere impairment, the V > P discrepancy is likely to be greater for males (M = 11.8 points) than females (M = 6.7; Kaufman, 1990). This may be because males have greater cerebral asymmetry along with females being more likely to more effectively use verbally mediated strategies to solve visuospatial tasks. This suggests that females may be able to compensate more effectively for the impact of right hemisphere lesions.

- *Recency of lesion.* The more acute the lesion (less than 12 months), the more likely that the V > P difference will be more pronounced. This is because over time patients have natural recovery from their deficits and learn to adapt by using compensatory strategies.

- *Type and location of lesion.* Right focal (i.e., from strokes, tumors), posterior lesions are more likely to produce V > P differences. Right temporal lobe epileptics are also likely to have the expected V > P discrepancy. In contrast, frontal lobe lesions have little effect on V > P.

The following sections elaborate on WAIS-III and WISC-III subtests. Note that under the headings for each subtest, the functions involved in performing well on the subtest are listed. Each discussion also includes a listing of possible interpretations associated with high and low scores (see Level III interpretation). The listing of functions and possible interpretations are derived from reviews and interpretive resources (Groth-Marnat, 1999b; Kaufman, 1990, 1994; Kaufman & Lichtenberger, 1999; Sattler, 1992; and Sattler & Ryan, 1998). However, it should be stressed that the interpretations are extremely tentative and need to be investigated further. To assist with this hypothesis testing, a description of the WAIS-R NI and WISC-III PI alternative administrations along with error categories and possible meanings associated with these categories are provided as a means of parsing the underlying processes involved with the client responses.

Information

> Range of general factual knowledge*
>
> Long-term memory
>
> Alertness to day-to-day world
>
> Curiosity, need to collect factual knowledge
>
> Extent of learning/schooling

This subtest taps an examinee's fund of general verbal knowledge about the world, drawn from literature, geography, history, and science, and represents semantic knowledge retained from prior learning. The format of this multifactorial subtest requires the comprehension of a spoken question, retrieval of the required information from remote memory, and organization and articulation of an oral response. Test performance on Information is considered a good index of premorbid functioning in many assessment contexts. This is primarily because it is highly resistant to deterioration. Information is highly correlated with education, socioeconomic status, and occupational history (Matarazzo, 1972). Designed to represent a range of material familiar to individuals living in the United States, it may be biased in assessing persons from other cultures, or minority subcultures within the United States. However, various foreign language adaptations have been developed that include information items relevant to the country in which the adaptation has been made.

Some individuals with language problems may be unable to verbalize their responses to the Information questions even when their actual knowledge is spared. This is likely to be particularly true for persons with retrieval deficits who may retain latent knowledge, but may be unable to access it readily. Many clinicians attempt to circumvent these problems by offering multiple-choice options. Systematic multiple-choice questions on the WAIS-R NI (see below) have been developed to eliminate the variability among clinicians in identifying multiple-choice options. A qualitative review of an individual's pattern of performance may reveal scatter, such that some easy items are missed while other, more difficult ones are passed, suggesting deterioration from a higher premorbid level. Sometimes a high degree of intrasubtest scatter may also suggest poor motivation or even malingering. In other cases, one may observe a selective deficit in a particular domain of information.

High scores suggest excellent long-term memory, good general verbal ability, extensive educational background, cultural interests, positive attitude toward learning, or possible intellectualizing tendencies. *Low scores* suggest difficulties with memory retrieval,

---

* Abilities followed by an asterisk (*) indicate specific abilities and traits strongly associated with the subtest under discussion.

poor long term memory, superficiality of interests, low intellectual curiosity, cultural deprivation, or simply lack of familiarity with Western (especially American) culture.

WAIS-R NI Information Multiple Choice   The choices for incorrect items on multiple-choice version of the standardized information subtest was based on actual errors frequently made by patients with central nervous system (CNS) dysfunction. It enables examinees who cannot articulate a verbal response or have difficulty activating retrieval mechanisms to access stored information. Such examinees may perform substantially better when the task requires only recognition of the correct response. In a study of nonclinical adults between the ages of 50 and 89, raw scores on the standard administration of Information declined and standard deviations increased with age, particularly after the age of 70. In contrast, performance on the WAIS-R NI Multiple Choice Information subtest remained stable across age (see Milberg et al., 1996).

At least six different information content areas may be analyzed separately (e.g., number facts, geography, history, literature), with selective difficulty suggesting specific developmental or acquired domain problems. The WAIS-R NI and WISC-III PI manuals provide detailed error analyses which are summarized below according to various content (and other) areas, types of errors, and possible meanings:

- *Facts related to numbers.* Number facts may be disturbed as a result of aphasia (i.e., patient responds with an incorrect number yet knows the correct one, reflecting "semantic paraphasia"). Gross overestimation or underestimation when guessing may reflect the poor judgment consistent with frontal system impairment.

- *Directions.* Poor responses when providing answers related to directions might suggest spatial relation disturbances (primary visual-perceptual impairment, right-left confusion, specific topographic difficulties).

- *Classic writings.* Errors related to knowledge about literature may be secondary to school difficulties, possibly learning disabilities.

- *Names of famous people.* Incorrect responses may indicate anomic language disturbances.

- *Poor control of mental processes.* Poor mental control can be reflected in perseverations (intrusions of information from responses provided on a previous item) or "pull" toward one portion of stimulus (i.e., question on theory of relativity may result in a response about relatives).

- *Generally poor retention of general information.* If an examinee knows the information but doesn't provide a correct answer it might be due to poor attention, negativism, poor motivation, hypoactivity, distractibility, or depression.

WISC-III PI Information Multiple Choice   The incorrect WISC-III Information multiple-choices have been taken from the errors made by cognitively intact as well as clinical populations of children from the WISC-III standardization and clinical validity samples. The content categories here are quantitative, calendar, science, geography, and history. For normally developing children, the correlation between standard WISC-III Information scaled scores and the WISC-III PI multiple-choice scaled scores is moderate to high ($r = .75$). A significant discrepancy between standard Information and multiple choice favoring multiple choice was found to occur for children with developmental language impairments. Children with specific learning disabilities may show a selective difficulty with certain content areas. Occasionally, children from some clinical groups tend to be distracted by the choices, therefore performing more poorly on multiple choice than on the standard administration. Again, the WISC-III PI manual presents a detailed error analysis. Error categories relevant for both the WAIS-III (listed previously) and the WISC-III include those related to numbers, poor control of mental processes, and generally poor retention of general information. Additional categories listed in the WISC-III PI manual include asking for repetition of an item, no response, recall of calendar information, science, geography (directions), and history.

- *Asks for repetition.* If a child requests the examiner to repeat more items than would be expected for his or her age (see scoring and norms for "Asks for Repetition" over four subtests: Information, Arithmetic, Vocabulary, and Digit Span) it suggests language comprehension or attentional difficulties (i.e. reading and/or writing disabilities, ADHD, language impairment, or closed head injury).
- *No response.* No or minimal responses suggests the child is giving minimal effort, dislikes exerting him or herself, is oppositional, or is experiencing difficulty retrieving verbal information.
- *Poor recall of calendar, science, geography, or history.* Poor performance on these areas might suggest poor exposure to or difficulties with these areas. Overall poor performance might reflect poor learning associated with a learning disability.

Vocabulary

Word knowledge*

Language development*

Extent of educational background

General verbal ability

Estimate of the client's optimal intellectual efficiency

Ability to articulate ideas and accumulated verbal learning

Range of interests, ideas, experiences

Similar to Information, Vocabulary assesses an individual's established semantic knowledge. The examinee must orally define words of increasing difficulty. Vocabulary correlates highly with general intelligence, and is relatively resistant to many types of neuropsychological deficits. The Vocabulary subtest is often stable even in the presence of cognitive impairment. Vocabulary, along with Information and Picture Completion, is considered a good estimate of premorbid intelligence. An exception to this is that it is often the lowest subtest among brain impaired children (Reitan & Wolfson, 1992). Despite the typical resilience of Vocabulary, performance can be adversely affected by a variety of cognitive, social, and emotional factors such as poor educational opportunity, poor attention in school, or selective language impairment. It is generally of little use to administer Vocabulary to severely impaired individuals, especially patients with aphasia. Regardless of the internal semantic knowledge that such patients might have, they would be unlikely to retrieve a synonym or organize an adequate definition, and scoring guidelines penalize vague or impoverished responses.

Testing limits can therefore involve multiple choices of alternative definitions, presented orally and in print.

Qualitative responses to Vocabulary (and Comprehension) can often reveal information related to an examinee's thought processes, life experiences, background, and ability to cope with frustration. Sometimes brain-injured patients think in concrete terms. For example, they might respond to "winter" by acting as if they were shivering and stating "cold, wet." Or they may demonstrate stimulus bound behavior by responding to the sensory auditory stimulus value of the words (e.g., saying "cucumber" for "encumber"; or "headache" for "migrate"). Other responses might suggest bizarre associations or over inclusive reasoning.

High scores suggest high general intelligence, a wide range of interests, high need for achievement, good fund of general information, and good ability to recall past ideas and form concepts relating to these ideas. In contrast, *low scores* suggest low general intelligence, poorly developed language abilities, limited educational background, little familiarity with English, and/or low motivation.

WAIS-R NI Vocabulary Multiple Choice   The rationale for the WAIS-R NI Vocabulary multiple-choice format is to better assess word knowledge in persons with expressive language problems, particularly word finding difficulties. Such patients might do quite poorly on the standard administration, but may do much better with multiple-choice, which minimizes the need for retrieving, organizing, and articulating a response. Five choices are offered for each word, for the most part selected from the manual as 2-, 1-, and 0-point answers as well as responses that neurologically impaired patients commonly give in the standard free-response method. In addition, for each of the words, one error choice phonetically corresponds to the target word. Examinees with stimulus bound behaviors tend to show a predilection for these similar sounding foils.

A summary of error types and their possible meanings is provided below:

- *Difficulty retrieving words* (on standard administration). This type of error might be revealed if a client extensively uses words like "thingy," "something," "situation," or other overly vague and general language. This may reflect anomia which is often more pronounced for retrieving nouns. Despite this, a patient might struggle with articulating a correct definition of the word, indicating good underlying comprehension and word knowledge.

- *Circumstantial/tangential definitions.* Overly detailed, circumstantial, verbose, or overly personalized responses might reflect temporal lobe epilepsy, right hemisphere involvement, frontal lobe dysfunction dementia, or psychiatric disturbance.

- *Clang association.* Sometimes examinees are bound by the stimulus properties of the word and provide phonetically similar words (i.e., "assemble" means to "resemble" or "conceal" meaning "to close an envelope").

- *Perseveration.* Perseverations may occur in the form of a persisting influence of previous words or responses or even repetition of previous definitions. This might indicate frontal system dysfunction.

WISC-III PI Vocabulary Multiple Choice and Picture Vocabulary   In addition to multiple choice (four choices per item), a four-choice picture vocabulary subtest was also constructed for the same words. The distracters represent related concepts, share a perceptual feature, or represent a phonetically confusable word. Scaled scores for standard administration, multiple choice, and picture vocabulary allow the clinician to make comparisons and to differentiate retrieval problems from lack of word knowledge, as well as difficulty organizing and articulating a verbal response. In the standardization study's clinical groups, the group with language impairment had mean scaled scores that moved from the impaired range in the standard free response administration to the average range on both multiple choice and picture vocabulary. Error categories previously described for the WAIS-III NI might also be relevant in understanding the WISC-III. Additional error categories are outlined next:

- *Asks for repetition.* An unusually high number (see norms in WISC-III PI manual) of requests for repetition (summed over Information, Arithmetic, Vocabulary, Digit Span) suggests attentional difficulties or problems with language comprehension. This may be consistent with ADHD, reading/writing disabilities, closed head injuries, or language impairment (see also Information).
- *No response.* An unusually high number of no responses (see norms in WISC-III PI manual) suggests that the child was oppositional, impulsive, afraid to admit to ignorance, provided minimal effort, gave up too easily, or had poor self-monitoring.
- *Preference for first or last choices* (on multiple-choice formats). A disproportionate number of responses from either the first or last choices suggests a passive or impulsive response style.
- *Phonemic errors.* A large number of phonemic errors (i.e. being pulled toward distracters which are phonetically similar to the stimulus word) suggests that the child is not hearing the words correctly. It might therefore be advisable to refer for evaluation of the child's hearing and auditory discrimination.

Similarities

Logical abstract reasoning*

Associative ability combined with verbal ability

Verbal concept formation

Differentiating essential from nonessential details

The examinee must apply categorical verbal reasoning and concept formation skills to identify similarities between pairs of objects or concepts. Abstract, precise responses are scored the highest. A higher level of abstraction is required for the last few items. Many brain-damaged individuals have difficulty grasping or retaining the precise task. Others may have difficulty inhibiting a tendency to respond with a difference rather than a similarity, to simply report some noteworthy feature of each pair, or to report some concrete or inconsequential similarity (e.g., praise and punishment, both begin with a "p"). When a patient fails this task, the examiner may test limits by modeling the beginning of a response sentence, such as "a dog and a lion are both. . . ."

Similarities is one of the verbal tests most sensitive to brain damage. This is particularly true for damage to the left temporal and frontal regions (McFie, 1975). Populations who do particularly poorly on Similarities may be rigid thinkers, schizophrenics, or persons with dementia (LaRue & Jarvik, 1987). However, patients in the sub-acute phases of head trauma (Correll, Brodginski, & Rokosz, 1993) or polysubstance abusers who are undergoing detoxification (Sweeny, Meisel, Walsh, & Castrovinci, 1989) have been reported to have Similarities as their highest score.

High scores reflect good verbal concept formation and possible tendencies toward intellectualization. *Low scores* might indicate inflexible thinking, poor abstracting abilities, and left hemisphere lesions (especially left temporal and/or left frontal). The interpretation of difficulties with verbal reasoning and verbal concept formation is strengthened if Information and Vocabulary are also lowered.

Similarities Multiple Choice (WAIS-R NI Only)   As with previous multiple-choice administrations, error choices were selected from the protocols of neurological patients. The rationale for the multiple-choice version was to provide an alternative means of presenting the material (visual/written rather than auditory) for use with patients having auditory language difficulties. In addition, the recognition format helps to determine whether the examinee's difficulty is due to a retrieval/organization impairment rather than problems with concrete reasoning.

Qualitative errors are listed below along with possible meanings:

- *Concrete responses.* In addition to poor education or low premorbid IQ, concrete responses might indicate an impairment in the examinee's ability to perform at an abstract level.
- *Loss of set/perseveration.* Sometimes examinees will lose track of the task, which will be reflected in providing differences rather than similarities, or they will get "pulled" to one of the words (usually the first) more than the other (i.e., "Steam and fog are alike in that they are both hot"). Perseveration may be expressed in responses which carry over the answers or stimuli from a previous item. Both loss of set and perseveration are consistent with frontal system involvement.
- *Minimal responses.* Minimal responses (i.e., "nothing") might reflect problems with arousal, functional or initiation difficulties, poor motivation, passivity, resistance, or paranoia.

Arithmetic

Computational skill*

Sequencing ability

Concentration and attention/low distractibility

Auditory memory

Acquired knowledge from early school learning

Logical analysis, abstract reasoning, and analysis of numerical problems (later items)

Numerical reasoning and speed of arithmetical manipulations

Working memory

Mental computations are presented in a "story problem" format. In addition to calculation skill, significant demands are placed on auditory processing, concentration, ability to manipulate information actively in working memory, and ability to convert the verbal problems to the required operations. Since Arithmetic is timed and requires concentration, it is more challenging than either Vocabulary or Information. Distractible, anxious examinees often have a difficult time with Arithmetic. It is sometimes useful to determine whether the person did poorly because they lacked the required skills. This can be determined by re-administering each of the items the examinee missed but providing paper and pencil and allowing as much time as is needed. Under these conditions, a person who has the underlying arithmetical knowledge but is merely distractible may perform the re-administered items correctly.

Since the orally administered Arithmetic problems involve such a strong reliance on memory and concentration, the score can be lowered due to a number of different central nervous system disorders. Some of the more important possibilities include Alzheimer's disease, acute head injuries, early Huntington's disease, multiple sclerosis, chronic alcoholism, and left hemisphere damage (Kaplan, Gallagher, & Glosser, 1998; Lezak, 1995).

Persons with *high scores* might be alert, able to concentrate, have good short-term auditory memory, can resist distractions, and have good math skills. In contrast, *low scores* may suggest poor arithmetical abilities, low concentration, distractibility, difficulties with auditory short-term memory, or a low level of education. If Digit Span is lowered along with Arithmetic, it strengthens the interpretation of poor concentration and attention that might be consistent with left hemisphere impairment. It is often crucial to investigate the examinee's academic background to screen out the possibility of either a pre-existing math disability or poor educational instruction.

WAIS-R NI and WISC-III PI Arithmetic Modifications   The rationale for providing modifications in Arithmetic is to determine whether the examinee has done poorly due to the attention and memory demands of the task or to deficits in computational ability. The modifications work to systematically reduce the demands of concentration and memory. Thus, a printed version (WAIS-R only) serves to eliminate the need to hold the problem in working memory. If performance significantly improves with the printed version, then it suggests that attention and/or memory were the reasons for the previous poor performance.

Systematic testing of clinical limits consists of presenting the task as follows: (1) allowing the examinee to read the test items (with help from the examiner if needed) to reduce attention and working memory demands; (2) providing paper and pencil so that calculations can be written, to reduce mental control demands; and (3) directly assessing computational ability by eliminating the verbal story context and converting the task to one of simple written calculation.

The following analysis of errors may elucidate the examinee's cognitive processes:

- *Difficulties with the spatial layout (written version).* This might occur when an examinee places numbers in the incorrect column or loses track of columns (spatial acalculia), and suggests right hemisphere involvement.
- *Impaired ability to perform simple calculations.* Impaired arithmetical ability (primary acalculia) which is not due to poor spatial organization suggests left hemisphere involvement. This might be due to a Gerstmann syndrome (see Chapter 3); to investigate this possibility the other elements of this syndrome should be examined (finger agnosia, right-left disorientation, agraphia).

- *Confuses operational signs.* Confusing operational signs might suggest poor attention or, if a simpler operation is used (addition rather than multiplication), might indicate inability to perform the more complicated procedure. Knowledge of this difficulty might be used in remediation activities.
- *Failure to work from right to left.* Failure to work from right to left might indicate either right-left confusion or visuospatial difficulties.

Digit Span

Immediate rote recall*

Reversibility; ability to shift thought patterns (from digits forward to digits backwards)*

Attention and concentration

Auditory sequencing

Rote learning

The examinee repeats a fixed random series of numbers of increasing length spoken by the examiner. A backward span is then evaluated by having the examinee repeat digits in reverse order. These are then summed to derive a single Digit Span raw score. This summation may obscure clinically important information, since the two tasks sample different cognitive functions. Digits forward tests immediate auditory memory and repetition and is very sensitive to the ability to establish and sustain a focus of attention. This is also true of Digits backward, but the latter task also requires an active manipulation of digits in the working memory buffer. The difference in the demands of the two tasks may lead in some cases to highly discrepant performances that are apparent only when norms for forward and backward conditions are examined separately. Qualitative examination of errors may provide information such as a tendency to repeat all the presented digits but with sequencing errors. Greater span for digits backward than forward may suggest variability in deploying attention. Sometimes "pull" to stimulus occurs in the form of the examinee losing the set and starting to repeat the digits in the forward direction even after repeated reminders to repeat the digits backward.

Examinees with significant language involvement are unable to perform Digit Span in a valid manner. If desired, an analog to this task is to present the digits from 1 to 9 on a card and to have the examinee point to the sequence spoken by the examiner. This procedure can be confounded by the tendency of some patients with paraphasia to point to one number while being unable to inhibit saying a different one so that their intended response is unclear. It may be helpful if the clinician insists on silence or attends only to the pointing response.

On the surface, Digit Span appears to be a measure of auditory short-term memory. However, severely amnestic patients can do quite well on Digit Span if they are able to focus their attention for the brief time it takes to repeat the digits (Butters & Cermak, 1980). Thus, the attention component is probably more essential than memory. A further anomaly is that patients with transcortical sensory aphasia do not comprehend the stimuli, but can nonetheless repeat them quite adequately (Goodglass & Kaplan, 1983). In contrast, patients with conduction aphasia typically have excellent comprehension, but their ability to repeat digits is profoundly impaired. Clients can also do poorly due to anxiety or poor motivation.

High scores suggest excellent attention and the absence of significant levels of anxiety. The examinee may also have good short-term auditory memory. It should be stressed, however, that just because a client's performance on Digit Span is good, it does not then necessarily mean that memory for complex (rather than simple) auditory information will also be good. Examinees also may not necessarily have good memory for other modalities (i.e., visual).

Low scores on Digit Span may indicate one of the following: difficulty concentrating or the presence of anxiety. One important consideration is the relation between Digits Forward versus Digits Backward. Digits Backward is a far more difficult task than the more straightforward Digits Forward. As a result, Digits Backward is more sensitive to deterioration. Both the WAIS-III and WISC-III manuals provide data on unusual discrepancies between digits forward and backward. As a general rule, a difference of five or more digits in favor of Digits Forward can be considered unusual. Laterality differences have been noted in that Digits Forward is more likely to be lowered by left hemisphere involvement whereas Digits Backward is more likely to be impaired with either diffuse or right frontal involvement (Lezak, 1995; Swierchinsky, 1978). The low Digits Backward performance with right hemisphere involvement is most likely because some examinees try to accomplish the reversals by forming visual images of them and then "reading" them backward. Such a visualization strategy is more likely to be impaired by right hemisphere damage. This is consistent with Rudel and Denckla (1974), who found that children with developmental disorders of the right hemisphere have impaired performance on Digits Backward while Digits Forward may well be at or above grade level. Examinees with learning disabilities are likely to have difficulty with Digit Span (see Groth-Marnat, in press) as are persons with the diffuse damage associated with exposure to solvents (Groth-Marnat, 1993; Morrow, Furman, Ryan, & Hodgson, 1988). Patients with impaired executive function may have difficulty with Digits Backward secondary to problems switching set.

WAIS-R NI and WISC-III PI (WAIS-R NI and WISC-III PI Verbal and Spatial Spans)   Error analysis of the standard administration of Digit Span can often be quite informative. The WAIS-R NI manual details a variety of errors that have diagnostic relevance, the main ones of which are outlined below:

- *Sequencing errors.* Sequencing errors on shorter spans might suggest a developmental learning disability. To explore this hypothesis further, check the examinee's academic history and other subtests involving sequencing particularly the verbal/auditory sequencing tasks of Arithmetic and Letter-Number Sequencing but possibly also the visual sequencing tasks of Picture Arrangement, Digit Symbol-Coding, and Mazes.
- *Digit omissions/additions.* Digit omissions or additions suggest the examinee has not adequately appreciated the acoustic frame of the digit sequence.

- *Perseveration.* Types of perseveration might include placing a digit in the same slot over repeated trials, repeating digits from a previous trial, and repeating digits from the same trial.
- *Stimulus-bound responses.* Automatically reporting sequences according to an overlearned series (i.e., 2-4-6-8 or 4-3-2-1). Perseveration is consistent with frontal system damage.
- *Errors at the beginning of a sequence.* This might indicate a passive style of responding in which the client merely repeats the most recently heard digits (at the end of the series read by the examiner). Such errors might either suggest delayed attentional processes or retroactive interference or frontal system echo phenomenon.
- *Errors at the end of the sequence.* Errors at the end of the digit series might indicate the client was rehearsing earlier portions of the sequence, but then forgot the later portions due to proactive interference.
- *Reversals.* Reversing the order of two or more digits suggests poor attention in which the examinee has momentarily forgotten the task or, with Digits Backward, they have over rehearsed the forward digits and then been unable to reverse them as required by the instructions.
- *Digits Backward performance superior to Digits Forward.* This atypical pattern might occur when a person needs the greater challenge of the backward task to apply sufficient attention to meet the challenge. It may occur with depression, attention and activation problems, or oppositional, poorly motivated persons.

Spatial Span is a visual analogue to Digit Span that requires the examinee to tap a randomly arranged array of cubes in the same sequence that the examiner demonstrates. Spatial errors can be analyzed in the same manner as Digit Span. In addition, the location of errors (right versus left side of space) can provide information regarding hemispheric asymmetries. The rationale for Spatial Span is that it provides a test appropriate for persons with language deficits and also can measure possible differences in abilities in different modalities (auditory versus visual).

Letter Span (WISC-III PI Only)　　This span test employs the same span plus one paradigm used for the digit and spatial span subtests. In addition to the same error analyses described above, it also permits an examination of the effect of the phonemic characteristics of the letters to be repeated (e.g., "rhyming" consonants [V-P-Z-G] versus nonrhyming consonants [R-N-K-H]). It has been demonstrated (Shankweiler, Liberman, Mark, Fowler, & Fischer, 1979) that good readers who rely on phonological processing had greater recall problems for the phonemically similar trials. Poor readers, on the other hand, showed less difference between phonologically similar and dissimilar letters, presumably because they do not use phonological processing strategies. Thus, the three types of span subtests (digit, spatial, and letter) contrast modality of input and output, nature of errors, as well as stimulus parameters.

Comprehension

Knowledge of conventional standards of behavior*
Social maturity*

Practical knowledge*

Skills at evaluating past experience (proper screening, integration, and organization of relationships and facts)*

Abstract reasoning (later items only)*

Ability to judge social situations, common sense, social judgment

Alertness to everyday world, awareness of external reality

Everyday problem solving, social judgment, and interpretation of proverbs are required in this subtest, as are language comprehension, attention, remote memory, understanding of societal conventions, and ability to foresee the consequences of behavior. Since Comprehension requires judgment and opinion related to sometimes emotionally charged areas, it is probably the best subtest to note idiosyncratic responses that might lead to inferences regarding personality. In particular, evidence of concrete thinking or impulsivity can frequently be revealed. However, one should remember that some individuals with compromised neuropsychological status may be able to give adequate responses in the abstract, but that this will not necessarily translate into appropriate judgment or behavior in a naturalistic situation.

For patients with diffuse, bilateral, or lateralized right hemisphere damage, Comprehension can be a good indicator of premorbid functioning (Zillmer, Waechtler, Harris, & Kahn, 1992). In contrast, left hemisphere damage can lower performance on Comprehension. Decreasing performance has also been found to parallel the progression of Alzheimer's disease (Storandt, Botwinick, & Danziger, 1986) and multiple sclerosis (Filley, Heaton, & Thompson, 1990).

High scores suggest good judgment, capacity for social compliance, awareness of external reality, and use of information in an emotionally relevant manner. *Low scores* may indicate poor judgment (especially if Comprehension is four or more scaled score points lower than Vocabulary), hostility towards one's environment, impulsiveness, or concrete thinking. Psychiatric patients might do poorly on Comprehension due to bizarre associations, antisocial tendencies, idiosyncratic thoughts, or impaired perception.

WAIS-R NI Comprehension Proverb Multiple Choice Only   The following five scoring choices are presented for each of the three proverbs:

1. Correct abstract interpretation
2. Correct but concrete interpretation
3. Choice that focuses on only one element of the proverb
4. Choice that contains identical words from the proverb
5. Totally unrelated proverb.

Clinical experience suggests that concrete or literal choices tend to increase in the elderly, and are more characteristic of patients with right frontal system pathology.

Relevant error categories and their implications are summarized below:

- *Misunderstanding/simplified answer.* These errors can result from poor attention, memory-span constriction, or language impairments. Language impairments might suggest a general difficulty in understanding complex relationships or the context of the question.

- *Dysfluency, word finding difficulties, verbal perseveration.* Since Comprehension requires the most open ended answers of any subtest in the Wechsler intelligence scales, it allows for the expression of language impairments.

- *Poor judgment.* Poor judgment, especially impulsiveness, can sometimes be seen among psychiatric patients or those with frontal system involvement.

- *Concrete responses.* Concrete responses are most likely to occur on the proverbs questions. These responses are higher among elderly populations and patients with right (especially right frontal) impairment.

Letter-Number Sequencing (WAIS-III Only)

Facility with overlearned sequences*

Auditory short-term memory

Concentration and attention

Sequencing ability

Facility with numbers

Learning ability

This is a new WAIS-III subtest and forms part of the Working Memory Index, and, along with Digit Span, is also included as a subtest on the WMS-III. Random series of letter-number combinations must be held in a working memory "buffer" while the subject first recites the numbers in ascending numerical order, and then the letters alphabetically. The examinee must therefore pay close attention to the numbers and letters, retain them in working memory, manipulate them into a new order, and repeat them in the new sequence.

If a client has a *high score* on Letter-Number Sequencing, it suggests good attention, concentration, sequencing, and working memory. Conversely, a *low score* suggests possible difficulties in these areas.

Performance Scale

The Performance scales reflect a person's ability to integrate perceptual stimuli with appropriate motor responses, work in concrete situations, have appropriate contact with the environment, work quickly, and evaluate visuospatial information. In contrast to the verbal scales, the performance scales are much less affected by education. Since many of these subtests involve active manipulation of stimulus materials, patients with visual or motor problems are at an obvious disadvantage. If a visual field cut or neglect is present, it may be necessary to displace the stimulus material to the intact visual field, rather than placing stimuli directly in front of the patient. Problems in auditory comprehension and/or establishing a response set may make it necessary for the examiner to repeat and clarify instructions, sometimes even modeling or shaping the desired response. The fact that most of these subtests are timed makes it incumbent on the neuropsychologist to search for the relationship in a given patient between speed versus accuracy. Time limits must be observed for standard scoring, but allowing the patient who is actively engaged in problem solving to work past the time limit may reveal slowed but ultimately quite successful processing. A number of modifications in the WAIS-III updating reflect increased sensitivity to the ways in which sensory and motor issues affect task performance. Thus, some of the visual stimuli were redrawn, enlarged, and in color. There is also less emphasis on speed.

The following interpretive possibilities are suggested if the Performance IQ is significantly (9 points or more for the WAIS-III and 12 points or more for the WISC-III) higher than the Verbal IQ (P > V):

- Language deficit
- Difficulties with auditory conceptual/processing skills
- Excellent perceptual organizational abilities
- Lower socioeconomic background
- Lower academic achievement
- Good ability to work under time pressure
- Immediate problem-solving abilities are better than those that rely on accumulated knowledge

Research has investigated the extent to which P > V is associated with unilateral left hemisphere lesions. Whereas this association has been documented (see Kaufman, 1990), it is not as pronounced as the V > P difference associated with unilateral right hemisphere impairment. Specifically, the V > P difference for unilateral right hemisphere damaged patients is an average of 9 points versus only 4 points for the P > V among left hemisphere patients. There is also a complex relationship such that the P > V difference is most pronounced among adult males, from lower socioeconomic backgrounds who have posterior (versus frontal) lesions. An elaboration of each one of these variables follows (summarized from Kaufman, 1990, 1994):

- *Age.* Inferences regarding lateralization should be made only on adults since P > V with left lesions has not been found among children.
- *Gender.* Males show greater P > V differences with unilateral left hemisphere lesions (average of 6.2 points) when compared to females who show a very small average difference of 1.6 points.
- *Education.* Since individuals with less than a high school education already have a 2- to 3-point higher P > V, this is likely to exaggerate the P > V discrepancy following left hemisphere lesions.
- *Type/location of lesion.* Whereas P > V discrepancies are found with unilateral left posterior lesions, this effect is not found with frontal lesions. The discrepancy is most likely to be noticeable with left hemisphere strokes and, to a somewhat lesser extent, left temporal lobe epilepsy. Tumors and whether the lesion is acute or chronic does not seem to have much of an effect on the P > V discrepancy.

Picture Completion

Visual alertness*

Accuracy in differentiating essential from nonessential details

Visual recognition (long term visual memory)

Visual concentration

Ability to visually organize environmental information

The examinee must identify some important missing visual component in each of a series of pictures. It is not necessary to verbalize the answer; simply pointing to the location of the absent feature is acceptable, even in the standard administration. This task requires attention to detail and differentiation of essential from irrelevant or inessential details. Persistence in searching and evaluating the stimuli when the missing detail is not immediately detected is also required. Some items can be solved at a simple perceptual level, while others require previous exposure or experience with the item, and higher levels of inference and integration of knowledge. The larger, more realistic, colored picture format in the WAIS-III and WISC-III relative to previous smaller line-drawn versions is helpful in assessing individuals with diminished visual acuity; however, the clinician should be alert to basic perceptual problems which may lead to diminished perception or misidentification of the stimuli. Although it is perfectly creditable for the examinee to point to the location of the missing feature, a tendency to point instead of naming the feature should alert the clinician to the possibility of word finding problems.

Picture Completion is generally quite resistant to deterioration. Studies of patients with Alzheimer's disease, multiple sclerosis, and stroke patients have indicated that Picture Completion is usually the subtest with the highest score (Filley et al., 1990; Zillmer et al., 1992). Even with disease progression, Picture Completion generally remains unaffected. However, subcortical disease does tend to decrease Picture Completion performance (Huber & Bornstein, 1992).

High scores suggest good ability to differentiate relevant from irrelevant details, alertness, and excellent visual acuity. *Low scores* may indicate poor visual organization or poor concentration. However, persons with a quick, impulsive problem-solving style might do poorly on Picture Completion simply because they have failed to analyze the pictures in sufficient detail.

WAIS-R NI and WISC-III PI Picture Completion: Qualitative Features   There are no alternative administration procedures for Picture Completion. However, careful attention to qualitative responses can help to understand possible neuropsychological deficit. Pictures may be divided into those that require an appreciation of pattern violation versus those that assume previous experience with or knowledge of the item. In the WISC-III this dichotomy is equally represented throughout the subtest. An analysis of the following errors may provide lateralizing evidence of primary perceptual problems:

- *Inattention to details on the left side of the pictures.* Left-sided inattention suggests posterior right hemisphere lesions.
- *Visual field defects.* The quadrant having defects can have localizing significance: upper left (right temporal), lower left (right parietal), upper right (left temporal), lower right (left parietal).
- *Pointing responses.* A greater reliance on pointing responses and vague verbal responses (e.g., "the thingy") raise the question of a language disorder particularly word finding difficulties (i.e., anomia).

- *Errors on pattern/symmetry versus knowledge-based items.* A greater proportion of errors in pattern/symmetry-related items (i.e., clock, woman's face) suggests difficulties with visual spatial relationships. In contrast, a high proportion of missed items related to knowledge-based pictures (i.e., thermometer, umbrella) might indicate problems learning factual material (check performance on Information).

9. *Digit Symbol-Coding (WAIS-III)/Coding (WISC-III)*

Psychomotor speed*

Ability to follow directions*

Visual short-term memory*

Paper-pencil skills*

Clerical speed and accuracy*

Sequencing ability

Mental flexibility; ability to shift mental set

Ability to learn new visual material

Sustained effort, mental efficiency, concentration

Associative learning, ability to imitate newly learned visual material

This strictly timed paper-pencil task involves perceptually pairing symbols with corresponding digits followed by rapidly transcribing the symbols with the corresponding digits. The above long listing of abilities indicates that good performance involves a complex interaction. It requires combining the newly learned number/symbol pairs, accurate visual perception, appropriate eye-hand motor coordination, short-term memory, and ongoing focused attention. All this must be done under the pressure of time constraints. Because of the complexity of the task, it can be disrupted for a number of different reasons. This means that, in contrast to Vocabulary or Picture Completion, it is extremely sensitive to deterioration.

Patients who are depressed or brain damaged have a difficult time with Digit Symbol-Coding. Even examinees with subtle cognitive impairment often do quite poorly (Lezak, 1995; Reitan & Wolfson, 1993). Digit Symbol-Coding is sufficiently sensitive so that even in the early stages of dementia, the score is significantly lowered and can be used to monitor disease progression (Botwinick, Storandt, & Berg, 1986). Digit Symbol-Coding is also the subtest most sensitive to the effects of age and is likely to be the lowest subtest among chronic alcoholics (Miller & Saucedo, 1983). Learning disabled persons often have Digit Symbol-Coding as their lowest subtest score (Bannatyne, 1974; Groth-Marnat, in press; Kaufman, 1994). Rapid tumor growth is likely to lower scores significantly more than slow growth (Reitan & Wolfson, 1993). Patients with motor problems (e.g., hemiplegia of the dominant hand, or any condition that compromises speed or coordination) are particularly at risk for being penalized for slow motor output. The clinician may want to consider prorating the Performance IQ score without this subtest in such patients. However, it is an excellent neuropsychological task and should still be administered since it often reveals perseverative tendencies as well as the extent to which the patient is "pulled" to the perceptual features of the test stimuli.

The WAIS-III has incorporated the optional *incidental learning condition* introduced in the WAIS-R NI (Kaplan et al., 1991) in which the examinee is asked to recall and write down the appropriate symbol for as many digits as possible. An optional *symbol copying condition* has also been introduced, so that a more pure measure of motor speed can be evaluated separately from the cognitive demands of the coding task. These procedures help to isolate the degree to which memory versus speed has contributed to the patient's performance. For example, if the optional incidental learning condition (memory) is much higher than symbol copying (speed), then the client's memory is likely to be relatively intact but their performance might be reduced by slow psychomotor abilities (or an extremely reflective problem-solving style). Obviously, an examinee might achieve high or low scores on both conditions which would suggest that both memory and speed are good (or poor).

High scores suggest good capacity for rote learning, good short-term visual memory, rapid psychomotor reactions, excellent visual-motor abilities, and mental efficiency. In contrast, *low scores* may suggest poor mental alertness, poor short-term visual memory, difficulty with visual associative learning, or impaired visual motor functioning.

WAIS-R NI and WISC-III PI Coding Modifications   During the standard administration of this subtest, the examiner can more sensitively evaluate the effect of visual-motor speed by calculating the number of symbols correctly transcribed in successive 30-second intervals. The contribution of pure motor speed, however, is best evaluated by the symbol copy condition.

Performance speed over the 120 second period provides one measure of incidental learning (i.e., one may assume that performance accelerates as the digit-symbol pairs are learned and the examinee does not need to check the reference key). A more direct measure of incidental learning is the recall of the symbols that are paired with the digits in the absence of the reference key. A measure of procedural learning is obtained in the free recall symbol condition. In the WISC-III PI, an additional paired associate condition has been added by pairing a digit with its given symbol (rather than a symbol with its given digit). This reversed recall condition provides a measure of the depth of information processing. An error analysis of the symbols produced during the standard subtest condition, incidental recall in the paired associate conditions, free recall of the symbols alone condition, and the copy condition provide rich visuospatial processing and motor information.

The following summary outlines the main errors and meanings associated with these errors:

- *Problems with graphomotor production.* Graphomotor difficulties might include line tremor, overwriting (writing on top of symbols that have already been written), expansion of the symbol beyond the boxes, distortions, extremely light pencil line, or micrographia (tiny writing). These difficulties might reflect impaired coordination, weakness, or bradykinesia. A narrative writing sample can often help to obtain more informative samples of the examinee's writing difficulties.
- *Variations in speed.* A gradual increase in speed suggests that the examinee requires a warm-up phase before achieving optimal performance (often found in the elderly) or that there has been a gradual increase in incidental learning. A slowing

in performance suggests fatigue, possibly resulting from depression or a generalized deficit in activation or sustained attention.

- *Distortions of symbols.* Distorted symbols might reflect impaired visuoperceptual processes (check performance on and interpretations for Block Design and Object Assembly).
- *Poor scanning.* Inattention (visual neglect) can result in not responding to one side (usually the left) of the numbers. Difficulties with scanning might also be noted if the examinee takes a long time to find the correct place on the record form.
- *Loss of "set"/perseveration.* Sometimes examinees will simply lose track of the nature of the task and begin writing the symbols in the sequence they appear in the reference key. Similarly, perseverations may be reflected in the examinee copying symbols from previous digit-symbol pairs. Both of these types of errors can reflect poor executive functions resulting from frontal or diffuse impairment.
- *Skipping spaces.* The presence of spaces that have been skipped suggests difficulties with visual scanning or loss of set. Loss of set might also be indicated by the child simply copying the digits, writing the symbols in the order in which they are listed in the key, or writing symbols that are not in the key.
- *Rotations.* The presence of rotations might indicate visuoperceptual difficulties.
- *Significant number of overall errors.* A large number of errors suggests impulsivity, visuographic difficulties, or a lack of self-monitoring. Note, however, that 3 errors are not unusual.

Block Design

Spatial visualization*

Analysis of whole into component parts*

Visual-motor coordination in combination with perceptual organization

Nonverbal concept formation

Concentration; capacity for sustained effort

Visual-motor-spatial coordination; manipulative and perceptual speed

The examinee must organize a set of red and white blocks to match the patterns presented in a booklet. All designs conform to 2×2 or 3×3 matrices. This task requires pattern analysis into component parts, visuospatial organization, formulation and application of a coherent problem-solving strategy, as well as self-monitoring and self-correction of any transient errors. This is the subtest with the highest correlation with the Performance IQ score. Kaplan et al. (1991) have also pointed out that its lack of visual details that could be easily verbalized by the examinee strengthens its status as a measure of spatial analysis. This is consistent with it having a fairly low correlation with education and yet it correlates highly with general intelligence. Block Design has also been found to be moderately related to measures of everyday visuospatial abilities (Groth-Marnat & Teal, in press).

This task is very sensitive to right hemisphere damage, and yet individuals with damage to the left hemisphere have also been found to show selective impairments (Kaplan, 1988). These errors tend to differ qualitatively in that patients with right hemisphere damage tend to fail to appreciate the basic 2×2 or 3×3 design matrix so that their errors contain gross distortions of the overall gestalt. In contrast, persons with left hemisphere damage typically produce errors in which internal details of the design are incorrect but the overall matrix is intact. However, errors are much more frequent with right hemisphere damage than left. Sometimes inattention (neglect) can be detected by a failure to complete the left portion of the design. It has also been noted that errors at the upper visual fields of the design reflect temporal lobe involvement whereas lower field errors suggest problems in the parietal lobes (Kaplan et al., 1991). Constructional dyspraxia can occur if a patient accurately perceives what needs to be done, but cannot manipulate the blocks accordingly.

Block Design is often a difficult task for chronic alcoholics which suggests that they have visuospatial deficits (Miller & Saucedo, 1983). It is frequently one of the lowest subtests for patients with Alzheimer's disease; it is sensitive to both the early stages of the illness and can also be used to monitor its progression (LaRue & Jarvik, 1987). In contrast, patients having pseudo dementia due to depression do not usually have lowered Block Design scores. As a result, it can be used to assist in making this often difficult differential diagnosis. Correll et al. (1993) report that patients with acute head injuries, even if moderate to severe, perform well on Block Design (as well as Similarities) relative to other subtests.

High scores on Block Design suggest good nonverbal concept formation, excellent capacity for visuospatial organization, good concentration, and fast visual-motor speed. *Low scores* may suggest difficulties working with visuospatial materials (especially if Matrix Reasoning and Object Assembly are also lowered), problems with sustained effort, or poor perceptual abilities.

WAIS-R NI Block Design Modifications Administration procedures for the WAIS-R NI differ from the standard procedures for the WAIS-R and WAIS-III in the following ways: additional blocks are presented (9 for the 2×2 designs and 12 for the 3×3 designs). One of the clear advantages of Block Design is that it is easy to actually observe the patient's problem-solving style. For example, the ability to select the correct number of blocks indicates that the examinee appreciates the composition of the design. The WAIS-R NI manual details techniques for systems of notation to record an examinee's problem-solving strategies. These strategies include the starting position, selection of correct number of blocks, block placements, self-corrections, and varieties of breaks in the configuration (i.e., violations of the 2×2 and 3×3 matrices). Testing clinical limits may include allowing the examinee to continue to work on the design after the time limits have been exceeded so that slow but accurate solutions can be distinguished from unsuccessful solutions. In the case of failed items, the examinee should be asked whether he or she believes the response is correct. Finally, a grid may be superimposed on the target design, reducing the demands for spatial analysis, and enabling the examinee to focus on a block-by-block strategy.

A summary of error types and possible interpretations include:

- *Distortion of the global shape of design.* Unilateral right hemisphere patients (especially those with posterior lesions) often demonstrate gross distortions such as breaking the $2 \times 2/3 \times 3$ configuration, or distorting the pattern beyond recognition.

If asked if their design is correct, often they report that indeed it is, even when there are obvious errors.

- *Errors of internal details.* Unilateral left hemisphere patients are likely to misalign the internal details of the design, especially on the right side of the design (contralateral to the area of damage), while preserving the external configuration.
- *Initiation problems/long response latencies.* Some patients (i.e., early/middle stage Parkinson's and Huntington's disease) have preserved spatial abilities but have low scores due to slow responses to the stimuli. Testing the limits can often identify that spatial abilities are intact, since the designs are eventually reproduced accurately. Long delays can also occur with frontal lobe patients who have difficulties planning, initiating, and monitoring their behavior.

WISC-III PI Block Design Modifications   Performance on this multifactorial task can reflect impairments in many cognitive, perceptual, and motor abilities. The following modifications in administration and scoring are an attempt to parse these components: (1) in the standard WISC-III administration of Block Design noting breaks in configuration (described earlier) both en route to the final solution and in the final solution; partial-credit score based on the number of correctly placed blocks regardless of whether the final solution is correct or not; location of the starting position; and error analysis (e.g., rotation of single blocks or whole design).

WISC-III PI Block Design Subtest

1. *Unstructured condition.* Twelve blocks are provided (more than are needed for each design) for solving six new, highly patterned designs relatively lacking an implicit grid, administered and scored as above.
2. *Structured condition.* Failed designs are re-presented with a superimposed grid.
3. *Motor-free (multiple choice) Block Design.* Twenty designs with four response options each are individually presented to the examinee. This multiple-choice subtest eliminates the constructional (motor) component and more directly permits the evaluation of perceptual and integrative abilities.

The following WISC-III PI error categories can help to further understand a child's responses:

- *Breaks in configuration.* Breaking the $2 \times 2/3 \times 3$ configuration on the final response was uncommon among clinical groups in the standard administration of Block Design. When breaks do occur, it is most likely to be the result of immaturity (developmental delay). However, breaks in configuration *en route* to completing the task occurred more frequently among children who were language impaired, learning disabled, and those with generally low intellectual functioning. Adults who break configurations indicate right hemisphere involvement (Kaplan, 1988) but this inference cannot be made for children.
- *Higher partial credit than standard score.* Giving credit for correct placement of each block (partial credit scoring) provides a more detailed recording of the

accuracy of a child's responses. When the score for partial credit is significantly higher (see WISC-III PI norms) than for the standard score, it suggests that the child was able to work accurately through much of each of the designs, but might have been penalized due to working beyond the time limit (slowed performance). It might also suggest that the child is impulsive or has difficulties with blocks in particular parts of space.

• *Uses extra blocks.* The unstructured condition makes the Block Design task somewhat more difficult by providing the child with more blocks than required. Using more blocks than necessary might reflect impulsivity, poor self monitoring (consistent with poor executive abilities), or difficulties with visual perception.

• *Relatively high score on motor-free/multiple choice version.* Using the multiple choice format separates the perceptual from the motor aspect of Block Design. As a result, a significantly higher score (see WISC-III PI norms) on the multiple choice format suggests superior perceptual versus motor (including speed, planning and self-monitoring) abilities.

• *Rotations or substitutions of solid red/white blocks for half red-white blocks.* Rotations or substituting the wrong type of blocks suggests perceptual disturbances.

• *Overly simplified designs.* An overly simple design suggests that the child is overly stimulus bound and is neither monitoring their behavior nor using a systematic strategy. This is further reinforced if the child rarely looks at the design to check how they are performing.

Matrix Reasoning (WAIS-III Only)

Nonverbal problem solving with no time limit*

Analogic reasoning*

Spatial visualization

Figural evaluation

Differentiating relevant from irrelevant visual information

Holistic/simultaneous processing

Visuospatial reasoning

This task is new on the WAIS-III. Each item consists of a visual matrix from which a piece is missing; the task requires choosing from among alternatives, the piece that would best complete the design. (All items are printed on a page, so that no physical manipulation of the materials is necessary or possible). The easiest items require only simple perceptual discrimination, but the more difficult ones involve active mental manipulation of multiple stimulus dimensions as well as analogical reasoning. Insofar as this task is not timed and requires only pointing, it avoids some of the confounds of the other visuospatial subtests. In addition, the lack of time limits means that it does not penalize persons who have a cautious, reflective, problem-solving style. It is also useful to use with persons in older age groups who might otherwise do poorly on strictly timed subtests. Matrix Reasoning is conceptually similar to Standard Progressive Matrices.

In a neuropsychological assessment context, analysis of errors on Matrix Reasoning may reveal clinically important information. For example, visual neglect might be indicated by differential frequency of errors on items in a given sector of visual space. Perseveration might be suggested by a serial position response bias. Cognitive rigidity (or "pull" towards selected features) might be reflected in a tendency to impulsively choose a piece that matches the details of the stimulus rather than one that completes the overall pattern. Since the matrices are in different colors, the possibility of color blindness should be investigated as a reason for poor performance.

High scores may indicate good nonverbal abstract reasoning, a strength in simultaneous processing of information, and excellent visual information processing. *Low scores* may suggest low visual concept formation, poor or at least rigid visual reasoning, or poor concentration. Negativism might be indicated if the examinee seems unmotivated and produces responses such as "none of them match."

Picture Arrangement

    Anticipation of consequences*

    Time concepts and temporal sequencing*

    Planning ability (comprehending and evaluating situations)*

    Understanding nonverbal interpersonal situations

    Visual organization; ability to assess essential visual cues

    Speed of associating and planning information

    Skills at comprehending a situation and assessing its implications

    Appreciation of humor

Sets of cards depicting sequential, nonverbal interactions are presented out of order, and the examinee must rearrange the pieces so that they make a coherent story. Visual perception, tacit understanding of the rules that guide social interactions, sequencing, and integration of parts into a coherent whole are necessary for successful completion. It also requires that the examinee understand interpersonal relations within a given cultural (Western/American) context. As a result, performance from persons with divergent cultural backgrounds should be interpreted cautiously. Some items also require an appreciation of humor. Both Picture Arrangement and Block Design have some similarities in that they assess nonverbal concept formation. However, Block Design involves abstract designs whereas Picture Arrangement focuses more on actual objects and people. In addition, good performance on Block Design can be achieved by working on one piece of the design at a time. In contrast, Picture Arrangement requires the examinee to "size up" or grasp the whole situation and then arrange the pictures accordingly.

Standard administration specifies arrangement of the pictures from left to right, but in the case of patients having a visual field defect, it may be preferable to lay the cards out vertically. Testing the limits may be done after all items have been administered by going back and having the examinee explain each card sequence verbally. This will give the examiner useful information about whether errors are based on visual misperception, or on the examinee having missed the point of the series. This may be of particular interest on those items that contain an element of surprise or humor, to which some examinees are oblivious. Examinees with sequencing or attentional problems may achieve substantially correct solutions, with only a single item mis-sequenced. Individuals who have made inattentive errors and who have failed to self-monitor may sometimes detect and correct the error when they are subsequently asked to review their arrangement and tell the story.

Patients who have brain injuries that interfere with nonverbal social skills are likely to do poorly on Picture Arrangement. A Picture Arrangement score that is significantly low relative to other subtests is consistent with a static lesion to the right anterior temporal lobe (Reitan & Wolfson, 1993). Right hemisphere lesions that are larger (and involve more posterior areas) will lower not only Picture Arrangement, but also Block Design and Object Assembly (Russell, 1979). Walsh (1987) has noted that frontal lobe patients often do poorly on Picture Arrangement due to impulsiveness and difficulty assessing an entire situation.

High scores on Picture Arrangement may suggest that the examinee can anticipate the consequences of actions and has good nonverbal social intelligence. In contrast, *low scores* might indicate difficulty with planning, slow speed of information processing (check other speeded tests), a paucity of ideas, poor rapport, problems with interpersonal relationships, and a poor sense of humor.

WAIS-R NI AND WISC-III PI Picture Arrangement Scoring   Two methods of administration are suggested: (1) following the standard WAIS-R presentation of all card sequences the examinee is asked to tell the story about what was happening in the sequence, or (2) the verbal account follows each arrangement. Sequence scoring for the arrangement is based on the number of correct junctures in an arrangement. The advantages of Method 1 are that it is possible to obtain a standard scaled score and to preclude the influence of verbal encoding on what may have otherwise been a reliance on visuospatial processing. Generated stories are evaluated for a focus on details versus appreciation of the gist of the story.

Patterns of errors and possible meanings associated with these errors are:

- *Overlooking small details.* An examinee might verbally report a correct understanding of the story but make incorrect responses due to overlooking small details. This suggests the possibility of left hemisphere dysfunction.
- *Not appreciating the point of the story.* Typically patients with right hemisphere involvement have a difficult time appreciating the point of the story or understanding the underlying humor involved in it.
- *Passive approach.* A passive approach occurs when an examinee only moves the cards to a minimal extent. Often this will be associated with a verbal story that has little to do with the cards. Such responses may occur with right frontal damage.
- *Inattention to one (usually left) side.* This can reflect inattention associated with right parietal damage. Sometimes patients who are aware of this difficulty will arrange the cards vertically as a means of compensation.

In the WISC-III PI, Picture Arrangement is not administered, but a table of frequencies of given error arrangements by age is presented in the WISC-III PI manual so that the clinician can determine the relative frequency of a given incorrect arrangement at a given age. The most common errors that have been noted for the easier items are reversals of two adjacent cards, ordering on the basis of shared common perceptual features, and displacement of the initial card to the final position.

Sentence Arrangement (WAIS-R NI and WISC-III PI)   This new test was designed to be a verbal analogue to Picture Arrangement. The examinee is required to rearrange the cards with words into a meaningful sentence and then to read the arrangement aloud. To perform adequately, the examinee must be able to read the words, (in the WISC-III PI, the words are at the primer-level) comprehend their meaning, and appreciate the syntactic and semantic aspects of a sentence. Most importantly, the examinee must have mental flexibility to try different arrangements, to appreciate multiple meanings of a word, and avoid being "captured" by common word sequences (Kaplan et al., 1991; Shallice & Evans, 1982). Thus, this test is sensitive to both executive dysfunction and language and reading disorders.

The following qualitative errors can be useful in interpretation:

- *"Capture" errors.* Capture errors on Sentence Arrangement occur when words that have a high probability of co-occurring are grouped together even though they do not make sense in the final sentence. This is particularly common among frontal lobe patients who may not be able to appreciate the semantically incorrect sentence.
- *Read differently.* Sometimes a child will read the sentence in a different order from how the words appear on the arranged cards. These errors can include sentences that are read correctly (but the arrangement is incorrect), the sentence is grammatically correct but it is not one of the correct responses, or the child might read a sentence that is grammatically incorrect. These errors can indicate spoken or written language dysfunction.
- *Lack of active arranging.* If the child only places minimum effort into the task it might reflect passivity or an underlying impairment in the abilities required by the subtest.
- *Inability to separate two words having a high probability of occurring together.* Sometimes a child will cluster two words together such as *bus* and *stop* which are not a correct alignment of the cards but are nonetheless still clustered together. This suggests that the child might be too easily pulled by the stimulus value of the words. This might be consistent with a lack of cognitive flexibility resulting in difficulties deconstructing the phrases and developing alternative arrangements.

Symbol Search

　　Speed of visual search*
　　Speed of information processing
　　Visual acuity
　　Spatial visualization
　　Planning
　　Visual-motor coordination

New to the WAIS-III but familiar to users of the WISC-III, this task requires the subject to scan each line of symbols for the presence or absence of designated targets, which differ from line to line. The score is based on items completed correctly within the two-minute time limit. Since the subject must place a mark in boxes designated "yes" or "no" at the right end of each line, left handers with inverted writing postures must move their writing hand away each time so as not to cover up the line. As a result, they may be at a disadvantage on this task. A patient with a severe motor handicap could, however, complete this task in a nonstandard manner by scanning each line and then dictating "yes" or "no" to the examiner, although scores so obtained would not be comparable with the standard administration.

A *high score* indicates that the client can rapidly absorb and integrate new information as well as make appropriate responses to this information. It might also indicate good short-term visual memory, excellent visual-motor coordination, and a high level of attention and concentration. In contrast, *low scores* may suggest a slowing of mental processes, poor short-term memory, poor visual acuity, poor motivation, motor slowing, or a careful, reflective problem-solving style.

Object Assembly (Now Optional on the WAIS-III)

   Understanding the relationship between parts*

   Ability to benefit from visuomotor feedback*

   Simultaneous (holistic) processing

   Synthesis; arranging parts in a familiar configuration

   Visuomotor organization

   Skill at differentiating familiar objects

   Speed of perceiving how unknown puzzle pieces relate to each other

This subtest, while still a mainstay of the WISC-III Performance scale, is no longer required for calculating the WAIS-III IQ or Index scores. It consists of jigsaw-type puzzles, and requires visuoperceptual analysis and synthesis, appreciation of part/whole relationships, and sensorimotor processing speed. Maximum clinical information can be derived by keeping a flow chart of test progress and strategies. Encouraging the examinee to name the target object as soon as it can be identified will help the examiner judge whether he or she has made a mental manipulation and is planning constructional efforts accordingly, or is simply operating by trial and error which in some cases is quite aimless. It should be noted that sometimes subjects make "lucky" responses and therefore perform better than might be expected given their other subtest scores. As a result, some individuals with high IQs perform unexpectedly poorly on Object Assembly whereas others with lower IQs may do quite well. This is an important factor contributing to the subtest's generally low reliability and high SEM. It also has quite low subtest specificity. Despite these difficulties, an advantage of Object Assembly (along with Block Design and Picture Arrangement) is that it is possible to actually observe the client's problem-solving style.

Since Object Assembly is a speeded test, it is sensitive to the generalized effects of brain damage. However, it also has some localizing implications in that patients with posterior lesions tend to do poorly on Object Assembly, especially those with right parietal involvement. Whereas patients with right-sided lesions are more likely to match surface details, persons with left-sided lesions are more likely to join pieces by relying on edge contours (Kaplan et al., 1991).

A *high score* suggests good visuomotor organization, the ability to think flexibly, and good perceptual-motor coordination. A *low score* might indicate disorganized visuomotor processes, poor visual concept formation, and a concrete, rigid mental outlook. However, given Object Assembly's inadequate subtest specificity, low reliability, and high SEM, any interpretations should be made cautiously.

WAIS-R NI   Both the WAIS-R NI and the WAIS-III have introduced assemblies that examinees must solve by using either a configurational strategy based solely on available contour features (a "moon" and a "butterfly"), or a feature analysis (a "cow" and a "house"). The rationale behind this is to develop two kinds of object assembly tasks that rely on quite different strategies. Parsing these strategies can help with localizing the site of the lesion (right versus left hemisphere) as well as provide further depth into understanding the nature of an examinee's difficulties (poor visuospatial relations versus impaired ability to understand details). Many of these same interpretive principles are also relevant for Block Design.

If an examinee cannot complete an object assembly, even after the time limits have been extended, the clinician may further test limits by providing additional structure such as telling the examinee the name of the object that the pieces are supposed to become. The clinician can then observe the examinee to determine whether or not providing this information is helpful. However, patients with posterior right hemisphere lesions, and others with difficulty in visual imagery, are typically unable to profit from being given this kind of cue. The clinician may also work interactively with the patient, placing key puzzle pieces to see if the examinee can utilize this kind of priming. Of course these procedures violate the standard administration and preclude computing a scaled score.

An outline of major error categories and their possible meanings follow:

- *Poor edge alignment.* Patients with unilateral right hemisphere damage have difficulty perceiving the overall gestalt of the object and thus do a poor job of lining up the edges of the object. The resulting assembly typically does not look like the intended object that they are supposed to be assembling. However, they focus more on the internal lines of the puzzle pieces. In other words, they focus on details rather than the configuration.
- *Poor surface alignment.* Patients with left hemisphere damage can accurately perceive the overall gestalt but have difficulties with lining up smaller internal details of the object. Thus, the assembled object will generally look like the intended object but internal details might be incorrect.

Mazes (WISC-III Only; Optional)

Planning ability; foresight

Visuomotor coordination and speed

Perceptual organization

Nonverbal reasoning

A series of increasingly difficult Porteus-like printed mazes is presented, and the examinee must use a pencil to draw a path through the maze to a specified exit. Planning and inhibition of impulsive responses are required, and the score is based on time to completion, with entry into blind alleys penalized. Since Mazes correlates poorly with Full Scale IQ and is accordingly a poor measure of general intelligence, it is not used very frequently. However, it has the advantage of being a nonverbal measure of planning ability.

A *high score* suggests good planning abilities that involves both maintaining a flexible mental set and impulse control. In contrast, a *low score* indicates poor visuomotor coordination and impulsivity. Low scores may also reflect poor planning, sequencing, and monitoring behavior, that are often associated with frontal lobe impairment (see Chapter 13).

WISC-III PI Elithorn Mazes   These perceptual mazes (Benton, Elithorn, Fogel, & Kerr, 1963) have been substituted for the WISC-III Mazes. This subtest was added to the WISC-III PI to more closely evaluate executive functions such as planning behavior and impulse control. Here it is critical to note latencies or contemplation time before initiating a response. Each maze has a lattice shape with multiple paths on which there are nodes (dots). For each maze, a given number of nodes must be passed through before exiting at the top of the maze. Latencies and other evidence of planning (e.g., tracing the path with a finger), the ability to hold the correct solution in memory before executing the maze with a pencil, and an error analysis including evidence of impulsivity, rule violations, and motor-imprecision errors are very informative. Base rates of errors as well as the possibility of computing scaled scores makes this subtest sensitive to a number of clinical populations, particularly ADHD and math learning disabilities.

The following error categories provide potentially useful information related to a child's performance:

- *Motor planning.* This observation can be scored when the child used their pencil or finger to plan a solution to the task. Motor planning peaks around Age 10 or 11 since children at this age are likely to do more overt planning (older children are more likely to internalize their planning). Less motor planning was noted among children with math disabilities, closed head injury, and low intellectual functioning.

- *Motor imprecision.* Motor-imprecision is scored each time the child's line brushes or enters (without crossing completely over) the green (non-"path") portion of the maze. Such imprecision was noted more frequently among groups of children with math disabilities, learning disabilities, and combined writing, math, and reading disabilities.

- *Rule violation.* Rule violations occur when a child starts in the wrong place, cuts across one of the green (non-"path") sections, or draws the line in the opposite direction they are supposed to. These might reflect impulsivity and/or immaturity.

- *Latency (contemplation) time.* Latency time on Trial 1 was stable across all ages but increased on Trial one across Ages 10–16. This is because the older children were both given more of the difficult mazes and were more reflective. A short latency time combined with poor performance suggests impulsivity and poor planning abilities.

RECOMMENDED READING

Groth-Marnat, G. (1999). *Handbook of psychological assessment* (3rd ed. rev.). New York: Wiley.

Kaplan, E., Fein, D., Morris. R., & Delis, D. (1991). *The WAIS-R as a neuropsychological instrument.* San Antonio, TX: Psychological Corporation.

Kaplan, E., Fein, D., Morris, R., Kramer, J.H., & Delis, D.C. (1999). *The WISC-III as a process instrument.* San Antonio, TX: Psychological Corporation.

Kaufman, A.S. (1990). *Assessing adolescent and adult intelligence.* Boston: Allyn & Bacon.

Kaufman, A.S. (1994). *Intelligent testing with the WISC-III.* New York: Wiley.

Kaufman, A.S., & Lichtenberger, E.O. (1999). *Essentials of WAIS-III assessment.* New York: Wiley.

Milberg, W.P., Hebben, N., & Kaplan, E. (1996). The Boston process approach to neuropsychological assessment. In I. Grant & K.M. Adams (Eds.), *Neuropsychological assessment of neuropsychiatric disorders* (2nd ed.), pp. 58–80. New York: Oxford University Press.

Sattler, J.M., & Ryan, J.J. (1999). *Assessment of children, revised and updated third edition, WAIS-III supplement.* San Diego, CA: Jerome Sattler Publisher.

APPENDIX A

Directions for Completing Worksheet for Determining Magnitude of WISC-III Subtest Fluctuations*

The following directions allow examiners to determine whether subtests fluctuate at a statistically significant level from the full scale, verbal, or performance means. The four steps in this process are numbered to correspond to the numbered (1–4) sections of the worksheet.

1. Decide whether it is appropriate to use either the Full Scale mean (based on the 10–13 WISC-III subtests) or the verbal and/or performance subtest means. If there is a significant discrepancy between Verbal and Performance IQs (12 points or more to be significant at the .05 level), then calculate the mean subtest scores separately for the verbal and for the performance scales. If Verbal and Performance IQ scores are not significantly different (e.g., less than 12 points), then calculate the mean for all the subtests used to develop the Full Scale IQ.

2. Write down the relevant Verbal, Performance, or Full Scale mean(s) in the "Mean" column. Calculate the magnitude of any potentially discrepant subtests by noting the differences between the age-corrected subtest scores (Step 1) and the relevant means. Record the differences in the "Difference" column.

---

* Directions and tables adapted from Groth-Marnat (1999b).

Appendix A.1.   Worksheet for determining magnitude (.05) of WISC-III subtest fluctuations

Subtest	1. Subtest Scores			2. Mean	Difference	3. Score Required for Difference to Be Significant (0.5 level)*			4. Strength or Weakness
	Full Scale	V	P			Full Scale (12 Subtests; Excluding Mazes)	V	P (Excluding Mazes)	
I						3.4	3		
S						3.6	3.1		
A						3.9	3.3		
VB						3	2.7		
C						4	3.4		
DSp						3.3	2.9		
PC						3.9		3.5	
Coding						3.9		3.4	
PA						4		3.6	
BD						3.1		2.9	
OA						4.5		3.9	
SS						4		3.6	
Mean									

*Data are from Wechsler (1991).

3. To determine whether the difference is significant, note whether the magnitude of the difference is greater than the value indicated for a specific subtest. For example, if, upon initial appraisal, the WISC-III Information subtest looked as if it might be a significant strength, then it would first need to be decided whether the Full Scale mean or Verbal mean would be the most appropriate to use. Then Information would need to be greater than or equal to the Full Scale mean by a value of 3.4 points, or if the Verbal mean was calculated, then the difference would need to be greater than or equal to 3. However, be aware that these are average values calculated for all age groups across the standardization sample. Some age groups may require different values to achieve significance at the set values. This is especially important for the WISC-III where the youngest samples typically have a wider range of error and thus require greater values to achieve significance (see Wechsler, 1991, Table 5.2 for a greater precision across age groups).

4. All subtests that achieved significance should be indicated as either a strength ("S") or a weakness ("W"). If a subtest is neither a strength nor a weakness, then leave the section blank.

APPENDIX B

Guidelines for Hypothesizing Subtest Strengths and Weaknesses*

To complete Appendixes B.1, B.2, and B.3, you will need to determine values for examinee's subtests based on whether they are *significantly above, above, equal to, below,* or *significantly below* their relevant mean score. Which mean score to use (Full Scale, Verbal, Performance) and what the means are, have already been determined on the WAIS-III record form or, if using the WISC-III, on Appendix A. For Appendix B.1, use the verbal mean if there was a significant difference between Verbal and Performance IQ; otherwise use the mean for all the subtests administered. Similarly for Appendix B.2, use the Performance mean if there was a significant difference between Verbal and Performance IQs. For Appendix B.3, use Verbal means when determining values for Verbal subtests and Performance means when determining values for Performance subtests if there was a significant discrepancy between Verbal and Performance IQs. If there was not a significant difference between Verbal and Performance IQs, then use the mean for the total number of subtests administered.

To complete Appendixes B.1, B.2, and B.3, work through the following steps:

1. Designate the following values in the columns directly under the subtests:
   a. *Significantly Above.* Place a "++" in the ability-related boxes in the column(s) under each subtest abbreviation that has been determined to be a significant (.05) strength (see Level IIIa). For example, if someone had a significant

---

* Directions and tables adapted from Groth-Marnat (1999b).

Appendix B.1.   Guidelines for determining subtest strengths and weaknesses (verbal)

Ability	Verbal Subtests							Strength or Weakness
	V	S	A	DSp	I	C	LN-S (WAIS-III)	
Verbal Memory (with Little Verbal Expression)	▓	▓				▓	▓	
Verbal Conceptualization (Concept Formation)			▓	▓	▓		▓	
Fund of Information		▓						
Abstract Verbal Reasoning				▓	▓		▓	
Auditory Short-Term Memory	▓	▓			▓			
Auditory Sequencing	▓	▓					▓	
Verbal Comprehension			▓	▓			▓	
Acquired Knowledge		▓		▓		▓		
Retention	▓			▓		▓		
Language Development and Word Knowledge		▓	▓		▓	▓		
Computational and Numerical Skill	▓			▓	▓			
Long-Term Memory		▓		▓		▓		
Complex Verbal Expression	▓			▓			▓	
Simple Verbal Expression	▓	▓				▓	▓	
Practical Knowledge and Judgment Related to Conventional Standards of Behavior	▓	▓	▓	▓			▓	
Amount of Benefit from Old Learning or Schooling, Intellectual Curiosity, Range of Interests		▓		▓		▓		

Appendix B.2. Guidelines for determining subtest strengths and weaknesses (performance)

Ability	PC	DSy coding	BD	MR (WAIS-III)	PA	SS	OA	Mazes (WISC-III)	Strength or Weakness
				Performance					
Visual Organization									
Visual-Motor Coordination									
Visual Perception & Processing of Abstract Information									
Visual Perception & Processing of Meaningful Stimuli									
Nonverbal Reasoning									
Reproduction of Models									
Simultaneous Processing of Visual-Spatial Information									
Visual Sequencing									
Visual Closure									
Visual Memory									
Synthesis									
Trial and Error Learning									
Visual-Spatial Reasoning (Concept Formation)									
Perceptual Organization/Spatial Ability									
Speed of Processing Information									
Planning Ability and Anticipation of Consequences									
Analysis of Whole into Component Parts									
Anticipation of Relationships among Parts									
Clerical Speed and Accuracy									
Visual Short-Term Memory									
Spatial Visualization									
Speed of Visual Search									

Appendix B.3. Guidelines for determining subtest strengths and weaknesses using verbal and performance scales combined

Ability	Verbal							Performance								Strengths or Weaknesses
	V	S	A	DSp	I	C	L-NS (WAIS-III)	PC	DSy coding	BD	MR	PA	SS	OA	Mazes (WISC-III)	
General Ability																
Social Comprehension																
Abstract Reasoning																
Attention & Concentration																
Sequencing																
Fluid Intelligence																
Crystallized Intelligence																
Achievement																
Immediate Role Learning and Recall																
Alertness & Recognition of Relevant from Irrelevant Details																
Alertness to Day-to-Day World																
Ability to Evaluate Past Experience, Social Judgment																
Flexibility of Thinking																
Ability to Evaluate Information																
Short-Term Memory (Visual or Auditory)																

strength in Picture Arrangement, then all the boxes directly under Picture Arrangement should have ++ placed in them.

b. *Above.* Place a "+" in the ability-related boxes under each subtest that is greater than 1 scaled score above the relevant mean (but lower than the magnitude required to be significantly above the relevant subtest means).

c. *Equal to.* Place a "0" in each ability-related box with subtest scores between 1 subtest score above and 1 subtest score below the mean.

d. *Below.* Place a "−" in each ability-related box with subtest score 1 subscale score below the relevant mean (but not lower than the magnitude required to be significantly above the relevant mean).

e. *Significantly below.* Indicate significant weaknesses by placing a "− −" in the ability-related boxes under each subtest that has been determined to be a significant weakness (see Level IIIa).

2. The next step is to decide whether a hypothesized ability is actually a relative strength (or weakness). The basic strategy is that if a strength (or weakness) is to be accepted, then other subtests measuring the same ability should also be high (or low if weaknesses are being determined). However, this is made somewhat more complicated in that there are various numbers of ability boxes in the rows to the right of the ability descriptions. For example, in the first ability listing (Verbal Memory), there are three boxes in the row to the right. Similarly, there are three boxes in the next ability listing (Verbal Conceptualization). However, others have only one box to the right of the ability and others have up to eight. The number of these boxes needs to be taken into account when deciding whether to accept or reject a hypothesized strength or weakness. The following decision rules are recommended:

One box. In some cases, there are abilities that are specific to a certain subtest and therefore have only one ability related to them. If this ability is determined to be a significant strength (++), then the hypothesized ability is strengthened. For example, in the ability described as "Practical knowledge and judgment related to conventional standards of behavior," only the Comprehension subtest is indicated as being the subtest that measures this area. Thus, consideration of whether or not the other subtests were above, equal to, or below the mean is obviously not possible. However, *these subtest specific abilities* should be interpreted with caution with additional outside support provided whenever possible (behavioral observations, relevant history).

Two boxes. To accept a hypothesized strength comprised of a composite of two boxes, one box must be significantly (as determined in Level IIIa) above the mean (++) and the other must also be above the mean (+), although not necessarily significantly above the mean. To accept a hypothesized weakness, the opposite logic would apply in that one box would need to be significantly below the mean (− −) and the other would need to be below the mean (− or− −) and the other would need to be below the mean (− or− −).

Three to Four Boxes. To accept strengths comprised of composites of three or four subtests, one ability box must be designated as significantly above the relevant mean (++), another must be above the mean (+ or ++), and while it is *preferable* for the third and fourth to be above the mean, one or both are permitted to be at the mean (but none must be below the mean). Again, the opposite logic would be used to accept or reject relative weaknesses.

Five or more Boxes. To accept a hypothesized strength comprising five or more subtests, at least one of the ability boxes must be a significant strength (++). The rest of the boxes need to be designated as above (+ or ++) or equal (0) to the relevant mean with the exception that one can be below the mean (−) and it is even permissible for it to be significantly below the mean (− −) assuming that most of the other subtests are above the mean. The opposite logic would be used to accept or reject a relative weakness.

3. Examiners should indicate on the far right any strength that has been accepted by writing an "S": similarly a "W" should be written if it is a weakness. For example, a person who had a significantly high Picture Arrangement score would have had a "++" placed in the ability-related box for sequencing. If other subtests measuring sequencing (Arithmetic, Digit Span, Digit Symbol, Letter-Number Sequencing) also had average and/or above average scores (with one being permissible in the below average range), then this would support the hypothesis that good Sequencing was the (or at least one of the) relative cognitive strengths resulting in an elevated score on Picture Arrangement. The higher the corroborating scores from the other subtests also relating to sequencing, the stronger the support that sequencing is the relevant ability. However, note that in most cases abilities will be found to be neither strengths nor weaknesses and thus the box on the far right will need to be left blank.

4. Examiners should work through Steps 1 to 3 only for those abilities in subtests found to be either significantly high or significantly low based on calculations in Level IIIa.

REFERENCES

Adams, R.L., Smigielski, J., & Jenkins, R.L. (1984). Development of a Satz-Mogul short form of the WAIS-R. *Journal of Consulting and Clinical Psychology, 52,* 908.

Allen, S.R., & Thorndike, R.M. (1995). Stability of the WAIS-R and WISC-III factor structure using cross-validation of covariance structures. *Journal of Clinical Psychology, 51,* 648–657.

Anastopolous, A.D., Spisto, M.A., & Maher, M.C. (1994). The WISC-III freedom from distractibility factor: Its utility in identifying children with attention deficit hyperactivity disorder. *Psychological Assessment, 6,* 368–371.

Bannatyne, A. (1974). Diagnosis: A note on recategorization of WISC scaled scores. *Journal of Learning Disabilities, 7,* 272–273.

Batchelor, E.S., Sowles, G., Dean, R.S., & Fischer, W. (1991). Construct validity of the Halstead-Reitan Neuropsychological Battery for children with learning disorders. *Journal of Psychoeducational Assessment, 9,* 16–31.

Bar-On, R. (1998). *Bar-On Emotional Quotient Inventory (EQ-itm): Technical manual.* Toronto, Canada: Multi Health Systems.

Benton, A.L. (1974). *The Revised Visual Retention Test* (4th ed.). New York: Psychological Corporation.

Benton, A.L., Elithorn, Fogel, & Kerr, (1963). A perceptual maze test sensitive to brain damage. *Journal of Neurology, Neurosurgery, and Psychiatry, 26,* 540–544.

Benton, A.L., & Hamsher, K. (1989). *Multilingual aphasia examination.* Iowa City, IA: AJA Associates.

Botwinick, J., Storandt, M., & Berg, L. (1986). A longitudinal, behavioral study of senile dementia of the Alzheimer's type. *Archives of Neurology, 43,* 1124–1127.

Bracken, B.A., & McCallum, R.S. (Eds.). (1993). *Wechsler Intelligence Scale for Children–Third edition. Journal of psychoeducational assessment: Advances in psychoeducational assessment.* Brandon, VT: Clinical Psychology.

Butters, N., & Cermak, L.S. (1980). *Alcoholic Korsakoff's syndromes.* New York: Academic Press.

Campbell, J. (1998). Internal and external validity of seven Wechsler Intelligence Scale for Children–Third edition. Short forms in a sample of psychiatric inpatients. *Psychological Assessment, 10,* 431–434.

Canivez, G.L., & Watkins, M.W. (1998). Long-term stability of the Wechsler Intelligence Scale for Children. *Psychological Assessment, 10,* 285–291.

Carroll, J.B. (1993). *Human cognitive abilities: A survey of factor analytic studies.* New York: Cambridge University Press.

Carroll, J.B. (1997). Commentary on Keith and Witta's hierarchical and cross-age confirmatory factor analysis of the WISC-III. *School Psychology Quarterly, 12,* 108–109.

Caruso, J.C., & Cliff, N. (1999). The properties of equally and differentially weighted WAIS-III factor scores. *Psychological Assessment, 11,* 198–206.

Ceci, S.J., & Williams, W.M. (1997). Schooling, intelligence, and income. *American Psychologist, 52,* 1051–1058.

Correll, R.E., Brodginski, S.E., & Rokosz, S.F. (1993). WAIS performance during the acute recovery stage following closed-head injury. *Perceptual and Motor Skills, 76,* 99–109.

Cooper, S. (1995). *The clinical use and interpretation of the Wechsler Intelligence Scale for Children–Third edition.* Springfield, IL: Thomas.

Donders, J. (1996). Cluster subtypes in the WISC-III standardization sample: Analysis of factor index scores. *Psychological Assessment, 8,* 312–318.

Donders, J. (1997). Sensitivity of the WISC-III to injury severity in children with traumatic head injury. *Assessment, 4,* 107–109.

De Renzi, E., & Vignolo, L. (1962). The Token Test: A sensitive test to detect receptive disturbances of aphasia. *Brain, 85,* 665–678.

Edwards, R., & Edwards, J.L. (1993). The WISC-III: A practitioner perspective. In B.A. Bracken & S.R. McCallum (Eds.), *Journal of psychoeducational assessment: Advances in psychoeducational assessment* (pp. 144–150). Brandon, VT: Clinical Psychology.

Elliott, C.D. (1990). *Differential Abilities Scales: Introductory and technical handbook.* San Antonio, TX: Psychological Corporation.

Fantuzzo, J.W., Blakey, W.A., & Gorsuch, R.L. (1989). *WAIS-R: Administration and scoring training manual.* San Antonio, TX: Psychological Corporation.

Filley, C.M., Heaton, R.K., & Thompson, L.L. (1990). Effects of disease course on neuropsychological functioning. In S.M. Rao (Ed.), *Neurobehavioral aspects of multiple sclerosis.* New York: Oxford University Press.

Fletcher, J.M., Francis, D.J., Rourke, B.P., & Shaywitz, S.E. (1992). The validity of discrepancy-based definitions of reading disabilities. *Journal of Learning Disabilities, 25,* 555–561.

Flynn, J.R. (1999). Searching for justice: The discovery of IQ gains over time. *American Psychologist, 54,* 5–20.

Garb, H.N. (1998). *Studying the clinician.* Washington, DC: American Psychological Association.

Gardner, H. (1993). *Multiple intelligences: The theory in practice.* New York: Basic Books.

Glutting, J.J., McDermott, P.A., Watkins, M.M., Kush, J.C., & Konold, T.R. (1997). The base rate problem and its consequences for interpreting children's ability profiles. *School Psychology Quarterly, 26,* 176–188.

Glutting, J.J., Youngstrom, E.A., Ward, T., & Ward, S. (1997). Incremental efficacy of WISC-III factor scores in predicting achievement: What do they tell us? *Psychological Assessment, 9,* 295–301.

Goldberg, E., & Costa, L.D. (1981). Hemispheric differences in the acquisition and use of descriptive systems. *Brain and Language, 14,* 144–173.

Goodglass, H., & Kaplan, E. (1983). *The assessment of aphasia and related disorders* (2nd ed.). Philadelphia: Lea & Febiger.

Groth-Marnat, G. (1993). Neuropsychological effects of styrene exposure: A review of current literature. *Perceptual and Motor Skills, 77,* 1139–1149.

Groth-Marnat, G. (1999a). Financial efficacy of clinical assessment: Rational guidelines and issues for future research. *Journal of Clinical Psychology, 55,* 813–824.

Groth-Marnat, G. (1999b). *Handbook of psychological assessment* (3rd ed., rev.). New York: Wiley.

Groth-Marnat, G. (in press). Learning disabilities assessment with the Wechsler Intelligence Scales. In A.S. Kaufman & N.L. Kaufman (Eds.), *Learning disabilities: Psychological assessment and evaluation.* Cambridge, England: Cambridge University Press.

Groth-Marnat, G., & Teal, M. (in press). Block design as a measure of everyday spatial ability: A study of ecological validity. *Perceptual and Motor Skills.*

Hale, J.B. (1996). *Linking neuropsychological profiles to effective interventions.* Keynote address at the annual meeting of the New York Advocacy Consortium of College Educators, Rochester, NY.

Harrison, P.L., Flanagan, D.P., & Genshaft, J.L. (1997). An integration and synthesis of contemporary theories, tests, and issues in the field of intellectual assessment. In D.P. Flanagan, L.G. Genshaft, & P.L. Harrison (Eds.), *Contemporary intellectual assessment: Theories, tests, and issues* (pp. 533–561). New York: Guilford Press.

Horn, J.L. (1994). The theory of fluid and crystallized intelligence. In R.J. Sternberg (Ed.), *Encyclopedia of human intelligence* (pp. 443–451). New York: Macmillan.

Huber, S.J., & Bornstein, R.A. (1992). Neuropsychological evaluation of Parkinson's disease. In S.J. Huber & J.L. Cummings (Eds.), *Parkinson's disease: Neurobehavioral aspects.* New York: Oxford University Press.

Jones, D.R., & James, S. (1993). Best uses of the WISC-III. In H.B. Vance (Ed.), *Best practices in assessment for school and clinical settings* (pp. 231–269). Brandon, VT: Clinical Psychology.

Joreskog, K.G., & Sorbom, D. (1989). *LISREL 7: A guide to the program and applications* (2nd ed.). Chicago: SPSS.

Kamphaus, R.W., Benson, J., Hutchinson, S., & Platt, L.O. (1994). Identification of factor models for the WISC-III. *Educational and Psychological Measurement, 54,* 174–186.

Kaplan, E. (1988). A process approach to neuropsychological assessment. In T. Boll & B.K. Bryant (Eds.), *Clinical neuropsychology and brain function: Research, measurement, and practice* (pp. 125–167). Washington, DC: American Psychological Association.

Kaplan, E., Fein, D., Morris, R., & Delis, D. (1991). *The WAIS-R as a neuropsychological instrument.* San Antonio, TX: Psychological Corporation.

Kaplan, E., Fein, D., Morris, R., Kramer, J.H., & Delis, D.C. (1999). *The WISC-III as a process instrument.* San Antonio, TX: Psychological Corporation.

Kaplan, E., Gallagher, R., & Glosser, G. (1998). Aphasia-related disorders. In M. Sarno (Ed.), *Acquired aphasia* (3rd ed.). New York: Academic Press.

Kaplan, E., Goodglass, H., & Weintraub, S. (1983). *The Boston Naming Test.* Philadelphia: Lea & Febiger.

Kaufman, A.S. (1990). *Assessing adolescent and adult intelligence.* Boston: Allyn & Bacon.

Kaufman, A.S. (1993). King WISC the Third assumes the throne. *Journal of School Psychology, 31,* 345–354.

Kaufman, A.S. (1994). *Intelligent testing with the WISC-III.* New York: Wiley.

Kaufman, A.S., & Lichtenberger, E.O. (1999). *Essentials of WAIS-III assessment.* New York: Wiley.

Katz, L., Goldstein, G., Rudisin, S., & Bailey, D. (1993). A neuropsychological approach to the recategorization of the Wechsler intelligence scales. *Journal of Learning Disabilities, 26,* 65–72.

Kløve, H. (1963). Clinical neuropsychology. In F.M. Forster (Ed.), *The medical clinics of North America.* New York: Saunders.

Konold, T.R., Kush, J.C., & Canivez, G.L. (1997). Factor replication of the WISC-III in three independent samples of children receiving special education. *Journal of Psychoeducational Assessment, 15,* 123–137.

Kush, J.C. (1996). Factor structure of the WISC-III for students with learning disabilities. *Journal of Psychoeducational Assessment, 14,* 32–40.

LaRue, A., & Jarvik, L.R. (1987). Cognitive function and prediction of dementia in old age. *International Journal of Aging and Human Development, 25,* 78–89.

Lezak, M.D. (1988). IQ: RIP. *Journal of Experimental and Clinical Neuropsychology, 10,* 351–361.

Lezak, M.D. (1995). *Neuropsychological assessment* (2nd ed.). New York: Oxford University Press.

Little, S.G. (1992). The WISC-III: Everything old is new again. *School Psychology Quarterly, 7,* 148–154.

Luria, A.R. (1980). *Higher cortical functions in man* (2nd ed.). New York: Basic Books.

Macmann, G.M., & Barnett, D.W. (1994). Structural analysis of correlated factors: Lessons from the verbal-performance dichotomy of the Wechsler scales. *School Psychology Quarterly, 9,* 161–197.

Matarazzo, J.D. (1972). *Wechsler measurement and appraisal of adult intelligence* (5th ed.). Baltimore: Williams & Wilkins.

Matarazzo, J.D. (1990). Psychological assessment versus psychological testing: Validation from Binet to school, clinic, and courtroom. *American Psychologist, 45,* 999–1017.

Mattis, S. (1988). *Dementia Rating Scale (DRS).* Odessa, FL: Psychological Assessment Resources.

McDermott, F.A., Fantuzzo, J.W., & Glutting, J.L. (1990). Just say no to subtest analysis: A critique on Wechsler theory and practice. Conference on Intelligence: Theories and Practice (1990 Memphis, TN). *Journal of Psychoeducational Assessment, 8,* 290–302.

McFie, J. (1975). *Assessment of organic intellectual impairment.* London: Academic Press.

McGrew, K.S., & Wrightson, W. (1997). The calculation of new and improved WISC-III subtest reliability, uniqueness, and general factor characteristic information through the use of data smoothing procedures. *Psychology in the Schools, 34,* 181–195.

Messick, S. (1995). Validity of psychological assessment: Validation of inferences from persons' responses and performances as scientific inquiry into score meaning. *American Psychologist, 50,* 741–749.

Milberg, W.P., Hebben, N., & Kaplan, E. (1996). The Boston process approach to neuropsychological assessment. In I. Grant & K.M. Adams (Eds.), *Neuropsychological assessment of neuropsychiatric disorders* (2nd ed., pp. 58–80). New York: Oxford University Press.

Miller, W.R., & Saucedo, C.F. (1983). Assessment of neuropsychological impairment and brain damage in problem drinkers. In C.J. Golden, J.A. Moses, & J.A. Coffman (Eds.), *Clinical neuropsychology: Interface with neurologic and psychiatric disorders.* New York: Grune & Stratton.

Mitrushina, M., & Satz, P. (1995). Base rates of the WAIS-R intersubtest scatter and VIQ-PIQ discrepancy in normal elderly. *Journal of Clinical Psychology, 51,* 70–78.

Mittenberg, W., Hammeke, T.A., & Rao, S.M. (1989). Intrasubtest scatter on the WAIS-R as a pathognomonic sign of brain injury. *Psychological Assessment, 1,* 273–276.

Moon, G.W., Blakey, W.A., Gorsuch, R.L., & Fantuzzo, J.W. (1991). Frequent WAIS-R administration errors: An ignored source of inaccurate measurement. *Professional Psychology, 22,* 256–258.

Morrow, L.A., Furman, J.M.R., Ryan, C.M., & Hodgson, M.J. (1988). Neuropsychological deficits associated with verbatim abnormalities in solvent workers. *The Clinical Neuropsychologist, 2,* 272–273.

Naglieri, J.A. (1993). Pairwise and ipsative comparisons of WISC-III IQ and index scores. *Psychological Assessment, 5,* 113–116.

Neisser, U., Boodoo, G., Bouchard, T.J., Boykin, A.W., Brody, N., Ceci, S.J., Halpern, D.F., Loehlin, J.C., Perloff, R., Sternberg, R.J., & Urbina, S. (1996). Intelligence: Knowns and unknowns. *American Psychologist, 51,* 77–101.

Newby, R.F., Recht, D.R., Caldwell, J., & Schaefer, J. (1993). Comparison of the WISC-III and WISC-R IQ changes over a two year time span in a sample of children with dyslexia. In B.A. Bracken & R.S. McCallum (Eds.), *Journal of Psychoeducational Assessment monograph series, advances in psychoeducational assessment: Wechsler Intelligence Scale for Children* (pp. 87–93). Germantown, TN: Psychological Corporation.

Powell, D.H., Kaplan, E., Whitta, D., Weintraub, S., Catlin, R., & Funkenstein, H.H. (1993). *MicroCog: Assessment of cognitive functioning.* San Antonio, TX: Psychological Corporation.

Psychological Corporation. (1999). *Wechsler Abbreviated Scale of Intelligence.* San Antonio, TX: Author.

Raven, J.C. (1976). *Standard progressive matrices.* Oxford, England: Oxford Psychologists Press.

Reitan, R.M. (1956). The relationship of the Halstead Impairment Index and the Wechsler-Bellevue Total Weighted Score to chronological age. *Journal of Gerontology, 11,* 447.

Reitan, R.M., & Wolfson, D. (1992). *Neuropsychological education of older children.* South Tucson, AZ: Neuropsychology Press.

Reitan, R.M., & Wolfson, D. (1993). T*he Halstead Reitan Neuropsychological Test Battery: Theory and clinical interpretation.* South Tucson, AZ: Neuropsychology Press.

Reschly, D.J. (1997). Diagnostic and treatment utility of intelligence tests. In D.P. Flanagan, J.L. Genshaft, & P.L. Harrison (Eds.), *Contemporary intellectual assessment* (pp. 437–456). New York: Guilford Press.

Reynolds, C.R., Sanchez, S., & Willson, V.L. (1996). Normative tables for calculating the WISC-III Performance and Full Scale IQ's when symbol search is substituted for coding. *Psychological Assessment, 8,* 378–382.

Riccio, C.A., Cohen, M.J., Hall, J.R., & Ross, C.M. (1997). The third and fourth factors of the WISC-III: What they don't measure. *Journal of Psychoeducational Assessment, 15,* 27–39.

Roid, G.H., Prifitera, A., & Weiss, L.G. (1993). Replication of the WISC-III factor structure in an independent sample. In B.A. Bracken & R.S. McCallum (Eds.), *Journal of Psychoeducational Assessment monograph series, advances in psychoeducational assessment: Wechsler Intelligence Scale for Children* (pp. 6–21). Germantown, TN: Psychological Corporation.

Rudel, R.G., & Denckla, M.B. (1974). Relation of forward and backward digit repetition in neurological impairment in children with learning disability. *Neuropsychologia, 12,* 12, 109.

Russell, E.W. (1979). Three patterns of brain damage on the WAIS. *Journal of Clinical Psychology, 35,* 611–620.

Ryan, J.J., Lopez, S.J., & Werth, T.R. (1998). Administration estimates for WAIS-III subtests, scales, and short forms in a clinical sample. *Journal of Psychoeducational Assessment, 16,* 315–323.

Ryan, J.J., & Ward, L.C. (1999). Validity, reliability and standard errors of measurement for two seven-subtest short forms of the Wechsler Adult Intelligence Scale-III. *Psychological Assessment, 11,* 207–211.

Ryan, J.J., Paolo, A.M., & Smith, A.J. (1992). Wechsler Adult Intelligence Scale–Revised intersubtest scatter in brain damaged patients: A comparison with the standardization sample. *Psychological Assessment, 4,* 63–66.

Sattler, J.M. (1992). *Assessment of children* (3rd ed., rev.). San Diego, CA: Author.

Sattler, J.M., & Ryan, J.J. (1999). *Assessment of children, revised and updated third edition, WAIS-III supplement.* San Diego, CA: Jerome Sattler.

Satz, P., & Mogul, S. (1962). An abbreviation of the WAIS for clinical use. *Journal of Clinical Psychology, 18,* 77–79.

Sbordone, R.J., & Long, C.J. (1996). *Ecological validity of neuropsychological testing.* Delray Beach, FL: GR Press/St. Lucie Press.

Schwean, V.L., Saklofske, D.H., Yackulic, R.A., & Quinn, D. (1993). WISC-III performance of ADHD children. In B.A. Bracken & R.S. McCallum (Eds.), *Journal of Psychoeducational Assessment monograph series, advances in psychoeducational assessment: Wechsler Intelligence Scale for Children* (pp. 56–70). Germantown, TN: Psychological Corporation.

Shallice, T., & Evans, P. (1982). Specific impairment of planning. In D.E. Broadbent & L. Weiskrants (Eds.), *The neuropsychology of cognitive function* (pp. 199–209). London: The Royal Society.

Shankweiler, D., Liberman, I.Y., Mark, L.S., Fowler, C.A., & Fischer, F.W. (1979). The speech code and learning to read. *Journal of Experimental Psychology: Human Learning and Memory, 5,* 531–545.

Siegel, D.J., & Piotrowski, R.J. (1994). Reliability of WISC-III subtest composites. *Assessment, 1,* 249–253.

Slate, R.J. (1995). Two investigations of the validity of the WISC-III. *Psychological Reports, 76,* 299–306.

Slate, R.J., & Fawcett, J. (1995). Validity of the WISC-III for deaf and hard of hearing persons. *American Annals of the Deaf, 140,* 250–254.

Slate, R.J., Jones, C.H., & Murray, R.A. (1991). Teaching administration and scoring of the Wechsler Adult Intelligence Scale Revised: An empirical evaluation of practice administrations. *Professional Psychology, 22,* 375–379.

Springer, S.P., & Deutsch, G. (1998). *Left brain right brain: Perspectives from cognitive neuroscience* (5th ed.). New York: Freeman.

Sternberg, R.J., & Kaufman, J.C. (1998). Innovation and intelligence testing: The curious case of the dog that didn't bark. *European Journal of Psychological Assessment, 12,* 175–182.

Sternberg, R.J., Wagner, R.K., Williams, W.M., & Horvath, J.A. (1995). Testing common sense. *American Psychologist, 50,* 912–927.

Storandt, M., Botwinick, J., & Danziger, W.L. (1986). Longitudinal changes: Patients with mild SDAT and matched healthy controls. In L.W. Poon (Ed.), *Handbook of clinical memory assessment of older adults.* Washington, DC: American Psychological Association.

Sullivan, K., & Bowden, S.C. (1997). Which tests do neuropsychologists use? *Journal of Clinical Psychology, 53,* 657–661.

Sweeney, J.A., Meisel, L., Walsh, V.L., & Castrovinci, D. (1989). Assessment of cognitive dysfunction in poly-substance abusers. *Journal of Clinical Psychology, 45*, 346–351.

Sweet, J.J., Moberg, P.J., & Westergaard, C.K. (1996). *The Clinical Neuropsychologist, 10*, 202–221.

Swierchinsky, D. (1978). *Manual for the adult neuropsychological examination.* Springfield, IL: Thomas.

Tulsky, D.S., Zhu, J., & Prifitera, A. (in press). Assessing adult intelligence with the WAIS-III. In G. Goldstein (Ed.), *Handbook of psychological assessment.* Boston: Allyn & Bacon.

Tupa, D.J., Wright, M.O., & Fristad, M.A. (1997). Confirmatory factor analysis of the WISC-III with child psychiatric inpatients. *Psychological Assessment, 9*, 302–306.

Vance, B., & Fuller, G.B. (1995). Relation of scores on WISC-III and WRAT-3 for a sample of referred children and youth. P*sychological Reports, 76*, 371–374.

Walsh, K. (1987). *Neuropsychology* (2nd ed.). Edinburgh, England: Churchill-Livingstone.

Wechsler, D. (1939). *The measurement of adult intelligence.* Baltimore: Williams & Wilkins.

Wechsler, D. (1958). *The measurement and appraisal of adult intelligence* (4th ed.). Baltimore: Williams & Wilkins.

Wechsler, D. (1989). *Wechsler Preschool and Primary Scale of Intelligence–Revised.* San Antonio, TX: Psychological Corporation.

Wechsler, D. (1991). *Wechsler Intelligence Scale for Children–Third edition.* San Antonio, TX: Psychological Corporation.

Wechsler, D. (1992). *Wechsler Individual Achievement Test.* San Antonio, TX: Psychological Corporation.

Wechsler, D. (1997a). *WAIS-III Administration and scoring manual.* San Antonio, TX: Psychological Corporation.

Wechsler, D. (1997b). *WAIS-III/WMS-III technical manual.* San Antonio, TX: Psychological Corporation.

Weinberg, R.A. (1989). Intelligence and IQ: Landmark issues and great debates. *American Psychologist, 44*, 660–669.

Wilkinson, G.S. (1993). *WRAT3 Administration Manual.* Delaware: Wide Range.

Zillmer, E.A., Waechtler, C., Harris, B., & Kahn, A. (1992). The effects of unilateral and multifocal lesions on the WAIS-R: A factor analytic study of stroke patients. *Archives of Clinical Neuropsychology, 7*, 29–40.

Chapter 6

THE WECHSLER MEMORY SCALES

MICHAEL D. FRANZEN and GRANT L. IVERSON

In the early part of the 20th century, memory was frequently conceptualized as a unitary construct. This conceptualization was partly influenced by the ascendancy of the mass action and equipotentiality theories. Under these ideas, it was believed that the effects of brain damage were more highly related to the amount of brain mass lesioned than to the site of the damage. Accordingly, it was held that cognitive impairment could be detected by the use of a single instrument such as the Bender-Gestalt. Similarly, memory impairment could be detected by the use of a single technique such as word list learning. Currently, the conceptualization of memory is much more complex and more highly articulated. (See Chapter 9 in this volume for a more complete discussion of these issues.) Memory is now conceptualized as being differentiable into stages and modalities, and recall versus recognition. This means that the modern memory assessment instrument will need to take these aspects into account by assessing memory using more than one method.

WECHSLER MEMORY SCALE

The original Wechsler Memory Scale (WMS; Wechsler, 1945) was designed to be a method of evaluating memory by examining different components thought to be implicated in memorial processes. The procedures included memory for text, for simple visual designs, for paired words, and for number sequences. The advantages of a battery approach to the assessment of memory include the fact that a battery better reflects modern conceptualizations of memory as involving multiple relatively independent processes. Additionally, a battery approach allows clinicians to separate out relative strengths and weaknesses in memorial processes and to reduce the possibility of missing impairment in an aspect of memory simply because that aspect was not sampled in the single method chosen. For example, a word list procedure would be insensitive to deficits in visual memory. There were several limitations to the WMS, including unsophisticated methods of scoring and a simple algorithm of summing the subtests into a single Memory Quotient. There was an alternate form, but it was rarely used and had limited empirical data supporting it. Due to its relative brevity and componential structure, the WMS became an almost ubiquitous instrument in the assessment of memory.

WECHSLER MEMORY SCALE-REVISED

History and Development

The Wechsler Memory Scale-Revised (WMS-R; Wechsler, 1987) is the most frequently used instrument to evaluate memory processes in clinical practice. It is widely used by both clinical psychologists and clinical neuropsychologists. The wide usage is true whether the context is clinical (Guilmette, Faust, Hart, & Arkes, 1990) or forensic (Lees-Haley, Smith, Williams, & Dunn, 1996). As its name implies, the WMS-R is a revision of the original Wechsler Memory Scale (Wechsler, 1945). This revision, coming after nearly four decades of use of the original, was long overdue. The Wechsler Memory Scale-Third Edition (WMS-III) has recently been published, but data on this incarnation is largely limited to that contained in the manual. Therefore, a limited review will be provided at the end of the chapter.

The WMS-R has several intended improvements over the original WMS. The WMS-R has age-related norms for nine age groups: 16–17 years, 18–19 years (estimated), 20–24 years, 25–34 years (estimated), 35–44 years, 45–54 years (estimated), 55–64 years, 65–69 years, and 70–74 years. The interpolation procedure resulted in early criticism and in a suggestion to use the WMS in the age groups where interpolated scores were given in the manual (D'Elia, Satz, & Schretlen, 1989), although other authors suggested the continued use of the WMS-R based on other superiorities over the WMS (Bowden & Bell, 1992). Although the procedure of estimating standardized scores for some groups may seem reasonable because of the known monotonic decreasing relation between age and memory performance, there is some evidence to suggest that the statistical procedure used may not be entirely accurate. In a sample of 50 residents of Florida who otherwise matched the standardization sample criteria in the WMS-R manual, the differences between interpolated and actual standardized scores for the WMS-R indices were 2 points for Attention-Concentration (lower for the Florida sample) and less than one for Verbal Memory (lower for the Florida sample) and General Memory (higher for the Florida sample). However, for Visual Memory and Delayed Recall, the differences were 4 and 3 points; in both cases the Florida sample exhibited higher scores (Mittenberg, Burton, Darrow, & Thompson, 1992). Therefore caution should be applied when using scores derived from interpolated normative information.

Because of criticisms regarding the loss of information in using a single WMS memory quotient (MQ), the WMS-R has five composite scores: General Memory, Attention-Concentration, Verbal Memory, Visual Memory, and Delayed Recall. Each of these composite or index scores has a mean of 100 and a standard deviation of 15. There also were new subtests added in order to obtain nonverbal information (related to figural, spatial, and visual associative memory) analogous to the verbal information obtained on the original WMS. A delayed-recall procedure was added, and scoring procedures were revised in order to make them more reliable. The items related to Information and Orientation were deleted from the computation of index scores because of the controversy regarding whether they reflected memory. Administration time for the WMS-R varies according to the level of impairment of the patient but can average approximately 45 minutes. There are 12 scorable subtests of the WMS-R, and these are listed in Table 6.1 along with the Indexes to which these subtests belong.

Table 6.1. Subtests of the Wechsler Memory Scale-Revised

Subtest	Attention/ Concentration	Visual Memory	Verbal Memory	General Memory	Delayed Recall
Mental Control	X				
Digit Span	X				
Visual Memory Span	X				
Figural Memory		X		X	
Visual Paired Associates		X		X	
Visual Reproduction		X		X	
Logical Memory			X	X	
Verbal Paired Associates			X	X	
Verbal Paired Associates II					X
Visual Paired Associates II					X
Logical Memory II					X
Visual Reproduction II					X

The column header "Index" spans Attention/Concentration, Visual Memory, Verbal Memory, General Memory, and Delayed Recall.

The scores for the Digit Span and Visual Memory Span subtests can be converted to percentiles by age, separately for the forward and the backward procedures. Percentile equivalents are also available for the Logical Memory and the Visual Reproduction subtests separately by age for both the original administration and the delayed-recall procedures.

A nationally stratified sample of 316 individuals was used to standardize the scoring system. There were approximately 50 individuals in each of the six age groups mentioned earlier. The sample was approximately one half male and one half female. The racial composition of the sample was proportionate to information derived from the 1980 census. Subjects were stratified across four geographic regions according to the 1980 census data. Subjects were also stratified across three educational groups: 0 to 11 years, 12 years, and 13 or more years of education. The number of subjects in each educational group was proportional within age groups, based on 1980 census data. Each subject was administered all or a portion of the Wechsler Adult Intelligence Scale-Revised (WAIS-R) in order to help ensure that the distribution of IQ scores in subjects from each age group was equivalent to the distribution of IQ scores in the general population.

The developers of the WMS-R used a variety of sophisticated statistical methods to determine the best method of combining the scores into indices. The WMS-R subtests are weighted and combined during the scoring process. This weighting procedure was chosen by comparing the methods of simple unweighted combination, weighting the subtests proportional to the inverse of the standard deviation of each subtest, and weighting the subtests inversely proportional to the standard error of measurement of the subtests. The comparison was based on the criteria of optimal reliability and maximum discrimination between a normal sample and a clinical sample. The best overall method of combination was based on the third method (inverse proportion of the standard error of measurement). This is highly technical, but the final message is that the weighting method used to calculate index scores was chosen on the basis of psychometric characteristics.

The stratification and sampling strategy used by the test developers appears to have been successful in obtaining accurate normative information and transformation formulae. In one study, the use of the WMS-R tended to result in a lower proportion of clinical subjects being classified as impaired than did the use of the California Verbal Learning Test (CVLT). In addition, for normal individuals, the WMS-R standardized scores are more consistent with the scores expected on the basis of the education and the intellectual level of the subjects, whereas the CVLT scores are more likely to be in the impaired range for the control subjects (Randolph, Gold, Kozora, & Cullum, 1994).

There have been some additional data generated to provide a wider normative base for the WMS-R. Because the incidence of memory complaints increases with the age of the population, it is important to have normative information beyond that given in the manual because the standardization sample contained no people over the age of 74 years. Clinical neuropsychologists at the Mayo Clinic have published a series of studies involving data from healthy older individuals who were administered a variety of tests of cognitive function, including the WMS-R. These authors subsequently provided factor scores for the entire battery used (WAIS-R, WMS-R, and Rey Auditory Verbal Learning Test) and replicated the covariance structure in a clinical sample (Smith, Ivnik, Malec, & Tangalos, 1993). Smith, Wong, Ivnik, and Malec (1997) published information related to norms for the Logical Memory (I and II) stories based on a sample of 349 normal individuals aged from 56 to 93 years. Marcopulos, McLain, and Giuliano (1997) provided normative information for rural older people (over the age of 55) with fewer than 10 years of education. Lichtenberg and Christensen (1992) also provided information related to performance on the WMS-R by older people.

Psychometric Properties

The manual provides four-to-six-week test-retest reliability for the Mental Control subtest ($r = .51$), for both the initial ($r = .58$) and the delayed-recall ($r = .58$) procedures of the Visual Paired Associates subtest and for the initial ($r = .60$) and the delayed-recall ($r = .41$) procedures of the Verbal Paired Associates subtest. Internal consistency reliability estimates are provided for Figural Memory ($r = .44$), Logical Memory I ($r = .74$), Logical Memory II ($r = .75$), Visual Reproduction I ($r = .59$), Visual Reproduction II ($r = .46$), Digit Span ($r = .88$), and Visual Memory Span ($r = .81$). Bowden, Whelan, Long, and Clifford (1995) investigated the test-retest reliability of the WMS-R index scores in a sample of people with alcoholism with a somewhat longer intertest interval (4 months) than was used in the manual. They found slightly higher test-retest correlations for the index scores for people 20 to 24 years old and 55 to 64 years old than for those presented in the WMS-R manual, and comparable coefficients as compared to people 70 to 74 years old.

Because the scoring criteria for most of the subtests are objective and the scores are derived from simple computational procedures, interscorer reliability would be expected to be high. Interscorer reliability was computed and reported in the manual only for the Logical Memory and Visual Reproduction subtests because scoring these subtests requires some degree of clinical judgment. Two trained scorers rated a set of 60 protocols. The interscorer reliability coefficient was .99 for Logical Memory and .97 for Visual Reproduction. Sullivan (1996) corroborated the high reliability coefficients when undergraduate students scored the Logical Memory subtest. O'Carroll and Bade-noch (1994) reported similarly high interrater reliability coefficients for the Visual Re-production subtest (greater than .92), regardless of whether the protocols were scored by experienced psychologists or by relatively inexperienced trainees. Interrater reliability coefficients have been replicated in clinical samples for both the Logical Memory and Visual Reproduction subtests (Woloszyn, Murphy, Wetzel, & Fisher, 1993).

The standard errors of measurement (in standard scores), as reported in the manual, ranged from 4.86 for the Attention-Concentration Index to 8.47 for the Visual Memory Index. In addition, the standard error of difference for three pairwise comparisons were computed and reported in the manual. The standard error of difference for comparing General Memory with Attention-Concentration is 16.38. The standard error difference for comparing Verbal Memory with Visual Memory is 21.89. The standard error of difference for comparing General Memory with Delayed Memory is 19.75. These sug-gested values have been elaborated on and complemented by Atkinson (1991). Mitten-berg, Thompson, and Schwartz (1991) calculated and reported confidence intervals for intratest scale comparisons. There is no empirical evidence for interpreting the differ-ences, and they are best interpreted in terms of abnormality of the difference. Early re-ports suggested that laterality may be reflected in Visual-Verbal Memory Index comparisons (Chelune & Bornstein, 1988); however, Loring, Lee, Martin, and Meador (1989) demonstrated the difficulties in interpreting Visual-Verbal Memory Index scores as reflecting laterality of brain damage.

There are multiple reasons why there have been a number of factor analytic studies conducted on the WMS-R. Perhaps the most relevant reason is that the WMS-R is com-posed of subtests that are summed into subscale scores as well as a general score (the General Memory Index). The composition of the indices was determined on a concep-tual theoretical basis rather than from empirical research. The factor analytic studies can therefore help to evaluate whether the assignment of subscales to indices is correct, as well as to determine whether the indices are in fact separate, discriminable, and ap-propriate for independent interpretation.

The manual reports the results of a principal-components factor analysis con-ducted on the standardization sample in which two factors seemed to emerge: (1) a General Memory and Learning factor and (2) an Attention-Concentration factor. Principal-components factor analysis of a mixed clinical sample provided similar re-sults. Roid, Prifitera, and Ledbetter (1988) reported the results of a confirmatory factor analysis on the data from the normative sample, indicating that the two-factor solution provided the best fit to the data.

Bornstein and Chelune (1988) subsequently reported a series of principal-compo-nents factor analysis of data derived from 434 patients referred for neuropsychological evaluation. When the initial administration subtest scores were included, a two-factor solution similar to that obtained with the standardization sample was obtained. When WAIS-R Verbal IQ (VIQ) and Performance IQ (PIQ) were included in the analysis, the factor structure of the clinical sample remained unchanged; however, in the normal sam-ple, the two factors switched places, with the attentional factor being extracted first. When the delayed-recall subtests were included in the factor analysis along with the ini-tial administration subtests, a three-factor solution emerged: Verbal Memory, Nonverbal Memory, and Attention. When PIQ and VIQ were included in the analysis, they tended to load on the third factor. Apparently, the factor structure of the WMS-R differs slightly in a normal sample, as opposed to a clinical sample. Jurden, Franzen, Callahan, and Ledbetter (1996) found that although the factor structure of the WMS-R may vary across clinical samples, the index scores have relatively stable characteristics across clinical samples.

Contrasted groups designs were used to evaluate the validity of the WMS-R. There were significant differences between the standardization sample and the mixed clinical samples of patients with psychiatric disorder, schizophrenia, alcoholism, closed head injury, stroke, tumor, seizure disorder, multiple sclerosis, and neurotoxin exposure (Wechsler, 1987). Subsequent reports have focused on patients with Alzheimer's disease and Huntington's disease (Butters et al., 1988), patients with multiple sclerosis (Fischer, 1988) and alcoholism (Ryan & Lewis, 1988), and patients exposed to industrial solvents (Crosson & Wiens, 1988).

Reid and Kelly (1993) reported that the WMS-R indices discriminated between patients with closed head injury and matched control subjects. Additionally, all of the indexes were related to severity of everyday memory impairment, but only the Visual Memory Index correlated with severity of injury as measured by duration of posttraumatic amnesia. Gass and Apple (1997) demonstrated that performance on the Logical Memory subtest but not on the Visual Reproduction subtest was found to be significantly related to subjective complaints of memory disturbance in a sample of patients with closed head injury.

O'Mahony and Doherty (1993) demonstrated that patients with alcoholism show a pattern of nonspecific memory impairment on the WMS-R. In addition, the WMS-R has been used to study aspects of schizophrenia (Hawkins, Sullivan, & Choi, 1997) and the effects of aging on memory processes (Fastenau, Denburg, & Abeles, 1996).

Nestor and colleagues (1993) reported a positive correlation between magnetic resonance imaging (MRI) measures of temporal lobe volume and WMS-R verbal memory tasks, but not visual memory tasks, in a small sample of patients with schizophrenia. Gale, Johnson, Bigler, and Blatter (1995) reported that measures of brain atrophy, especially fornix atrophy, correlated with WMS-R performance in a sample of patients with closed head injury.

Chelune and Bornstein (1988) investigated WMS-R performance in patients with unilateral lesions. They found that although there was a significant multivariate difference *between* the two groups of patients, there was a significant univariate difference only for the Verbal Memory score. On the other hand, comparison among subtests in the *same individuals* indicated that patients with left hemisphere lesions performed better on the subtests of verbal memory than on the subtests of visual memory, and that patients with right hemisphere lesions performed better on the subtests of visual memory than on the subtests of verbal memory. Loring et al. (1989) reported similar inconsistent patterns of Visual-Verbal Memory Index score differences in patients with unilateral temporal lobectomy. Apparently, the distinction between the subtests that comprise the Visual Memory Index and the subtests that comprise the Verbal Memory Index may not reflect laterality.

The WMS-R has been compared to other tests as a means of investigating concurrent validity. The earliest concurrent validity study published investigated the relation between the WMS-R and the CVLT. This study (Delis, Cullum, Butters, & Cairns,

1988) indicated that there are significant correlations between the two tests. There were a total of 460 correlations computed, of which 341 were significant at the .01 level. The WMS-R has been recommended in combination with the Kaufman Adolescent Intelligence Test in order to evaluate the role of general memory functions when evaluating individuals with learning disabilities (McIntosh, Waldo, & Koller, 1997). The WMS-R was found to be similar to the Rivermead Behavioural Memory test in its relations to estimates of everyday memory function (Koltai, Bowler, & Shore, 1996). This point is especially interesting because the Rivermead has been promoted as an instrument with greater ecological validity than typical psychometric tests of memory. In contrast, the Memory Assessment Scales (MAS; Williams, 1991) produced lower standard scores than the WMS-R for the constructs of visual memory, verbal memory, general memory, attention, and delayed memory in a small sample of 30 adults. Even though the standard scores are generally lower for the MAS, there were still modest correlations between the standard scores derived from the two tests.

The construct validity of the Attention-Concentration Index has been investigated separately from the WMS-R memory indexes. The Attention-Concentration Index may not be independently related to other measures of attention, although it is related to other measures of memory (Johnstone, Erdal, & Stadler, 1995). Schmidt, Trueblood, Merwin, and Durham (1994) reported the results of a factor analysis of various measures purported to measure attention and found that although the Digit Span and Visual Span measures from the WMS-R seemed to form a separate factor interpreted as Visual-Auditory Spanning, this factor was weak and may not have been robust. On the other hand, when examining the *sensitivity* of the various instruments in the sample, it appeared that the Attention-Concentration Index was among the most sensitive of the measures in identifying cognitive impairment.

Assets and Limitations

Although the WMS-R is a vast improvement over its predecessor, the scale does have shortcomings. The minimum score available for the indices is 50; therefore, there is likely to be overestimation of memory function in individuals with severe memory deficits. Although the transformation of raw scores to standardized scores is stratified by age group, there are no actual normative data available for subjects in the age groups 18–19 years, 25–34 years, and 45–54 years. Instead, scores for these subjects are estimated. Loring (1989) criticized the WMS-R for not separating delayed memory into visual and verbal components. The most serious limitation of the WMS-R, as noted by Elwood (1991), is the low reliabilities of the subtests and the indices. These low reliabilities seriously limit measurement accuracy.

Another limitation involves the interpretation of the Index scores. The various factor analytic studies discussed previously in this chapter do not lend confidence in the ability to state which aspects of memory may be reflected in the scores, even though these scores may be generally sensitive to cognitive impairment and to diagnostic categories. Alternately, the interpretation of subtest scores may be more easily conducted because the subtests do not have the same degree of heterogeneity that is present in the Indexes. The factor analytic studies do support the distinction between visual memory and verbal memory, as well as the distinction between immediate recall and delayed recall. What is uncertain is whether the calculation procedures specified in the manual as well as the exact components of the constructs are related to these distinctions.

The main asset of the WMS-R is that it allows measurement of different aspects of memory in a single composite instrument. This feature is especially useful when comparisons of different forms of memory are necessary for diagnosis or for treatment planning. Another major asset of the WMS-R is the large number of empirical studies that have been conducted and that inform the clinical use of the test. The fact that it has been utilized in several different populations is another positive attribute. In a curious way, the various studies that determine the shortcomings of the WMS-R are also assets because these studies help define the proper applications of the instrument. Researchers have enhanced the clinical usefulness of the WMS-R by studying retention rates, by expanding the norms for older people, by developing procedures for partialling out the effects of constructional problems on Visual Reproduction, and by developing a recognition procedure for Logical Memory.

Interpretation

Some of the psychometric aspects of interpretation of the WMS-R have been presented previously in discussions of individual scales. It is also useful to have a general strategy or series of steps in approaching interpretation.

1. The first step would be examination of the basic Index scores, both in terms of absolute levels and in terms of relative values in comparing them among themselves. The manual gives values for minimum differences between pairs of Index scores in order to determine if the observed differences are reliable. The General Memory Index can be considered a reasonable index of overall performance on the WMS-R, but its limitations as a single index of memory functioning should be considered. The Delayed Memory Index should always be interpreted in light of the percent retention and in terms of its absolute level.

2. A second step in WMS-R interpretation would be to examine percentile scores for the subtests for which these scores are available (i.e., Digit Span Forward and Backward, Visual Memory Span Forward and Backward, Logical Memory, and Visual Reproduction).

3. Next the qualitative features of performance should be considered. In examining the Visual Reproduction subtests, the clinician would ask: Were there signs of visual spatial construction deficits? Are there signs of **perseveration** (repetition of information) or **intrusion** (information from one stimulus being inserted into another stimulus) in the protocol? What is the degree of scatter among the subtests?

4. Finally, the results of the WMS-R can be compared to the results of other test procedures in order to provide an integrated interpretation of the assessment overall.

Examination of Basic Index Scores

The general interpretive features of the Wechsler scales are well known by psychologists and neuropsychologists. Level of performance is described through qualitative descriptors, such as "superior" or "low average." These descriptors relate to ranges of standard scores (e.g., scaled scores, IQ scores, Index scores). Confidence intervals, based on score-distribution characteristics and reliability estimates, provide the margin-of-error for the obtained score(s).

The WMS-R Index scores can be interpreted as reflecting general abilities grossly analogous to their names. The Attention-Concentration Index consists of tasks requiring simple attention to complex attention (e.g., digit span forward vs. digit or spatial span backward). The Verbal Memory Index is better conceptualized as an Immediate Auditory Memory Index because it involves immediate recall of auditorily presented information. Persons who report significant memory impairment will probably be detected by this scale because the tasks on it (Logical Memory, Verbal Paired Associates) are the types of everyday memory tasks where impairment is noticeable to even the casual observer. The Visual Memory Index is appropriately named; but the content reflects immediate memory for visually presented information, and it is possible that some of this "visual" information can be verbally encoded. The General Memory Index also is appropriately named, provided that the clinician appreciates that this represents a global measure of immediate learning and memory for both auditory and visual information. Low scores here probably reflect a significant impairment in learning and recall of information, but a full interpretation would require examination of the various component processes and other index scores. The Delayed Recall Index represents what is generally considered to be *memory*—a person's ability to recall previously learned information.

A serious problem with the clinical interpretation of WMS-R scores is related to the low reliabilities of several of the subtests and the Index scores. This was elaborated by Elwood (1991) in his critique of the psychometric characteristics of the scale. Essentially, the reliabilities are so low that the confidence intervals for the obtained scores (or the estimated true scores) are very broad. For example, the 95% confidence interval for the General Memory Index is ±14 points. If a patient scores 87, then the confidence interval surrounding the obtained score ranges from borderline to average (i.e., from 73 to 101)! There is no doubt that assessing memory functioning with the WMS-R is less reliable than assessing intellectual functioning with the WAIS-R. In general, it is best to interpret the Index scores, as opposed to individual subtest scores. If the entire WMS-R is not administered, it is notable that the most reliable subtest scores are derived from Logical Memory, Digit Span, and Visual Memory Span (average coefficients for all ages ranging from .74 to .88). Although it is common practice among many neuropsychologists to administer only the Logical Memory and Visual Reproduction subtests, relatively little is known about the reliability and validity of this approach to memory assessment.

Examination of Subtest Percentile Scores

Examining the subtest percentile scores can help identify relative strengths and weaknesses as well as absolute strengths and weaknesses. For example, if performance on the Digit Span Forward is at the 99th percentile and performance on the Digit Span Backward is at the 5th percentile, simple verbal auditory attention for this patient might be a relative strength in comparison to mental concentration and manipulation of information. Additionally, Digit Span Forward would be an absolute strength (in comparison to the normative population) because of the high percentile score, and Digit Span Backward would be an absolute strength because of the low percentile score.

Examination of Qualitative Features

Consideration of the manner in which a patient approaches a task can be helpful in determining the diagnosis. If the patient recalls the Logical Memory information as disjointed details out of sequence and draws the Visual Reproduction stimuli as disconnected pieces of information, a clinical hypothesis would include the possibility of executive dysfunction. If there is perseveration in the Visual Reproduction designs, frontal dysfunction would need to be ruled out. If there is contamination of information and mixing of the designs in an older patient, a hypothesis of Alzheimer's dementia needs to be considered.

Comparison to Other Test Results

The WMS-R is often given in conjunction with the WAIS-R. It is presumed that many clinical conditions may differentially affect these cognitive abilities; for example, people with Korsakoff's disease may show major memory impairment with relatively preserved intellectual functioning (Parkin & Leng, 1993). Therefore, IQ-Memory discrepancy scores may be useful for understanding clinical conditions and for planning rehabilitation activities. Atkinson (1991b) used reliability data from the WAIS-R and the WMS-R manuals to calculate the standard error of differences between various IQ and Index scores. These standard errors of differences were multiplied by 1.96 to create a 95% confidence interval for the various difference scores. This provides the clinician with an *estimate* of measurement error for the IQ-Index difference scores. The statistically reliable difference scores ($p < .05$) between the Full Scale IQ (FSIQ) and the Indexes, on average for all age groups, were 11 points for Attention-Concentration, 15 points for Verbal Memory, 17 points for Visual Memory, 14 points for General Memory, and 15 points for Delayed Recall.

Bornstein, Chelune, and Prifitera (1989) computed the base rates of various IQ-Memory difference scores in normal controls from the standardization sample and in clinical patients. As a group, the patients demonstrated larger *FSIQ-Delayed Memory Index difference scores* than the normal control. These data are very helpful to the clinician. A difference score of *15 points* is unusual in the general population (i.e., experienced by 10% or less) and a difference score of *22 points* is rare (i.e., experienced by 5.5% or less of the general population). No patient in the general population had a difference score of *28 points* or more. The base rates of these difference scores in the clinical patients were 32.5% (22 points), 18.8% (28 points), and 11.5% (28 points).

Detecting Improvement or Decline

The WMS-R is often used in serial assessments for the purpose of detecting improvement or decline in functioning. Unfortunately, relatively limited data is available to assist the clinician in this matter. A few important considerations, however, are known. First, people from the general population and from some clinical groups are known to show practice effects, especially over relatively brief retest intervals (Bowden et al., 1995; Chelune, Naugle, Lüders, Sedlak, & Issam, 1993; Wechsler, 1987). Second, the stability coefficients for the Index scores, and for the subtest scores, are relatively low. Therefore, the reliable change difference scores are large. Calculation of reliable change difference scores is a method for estimating the probability that a given test-retest difference score is not within the probable range of measurement error. Reliable change difference scores are estimated from the standard error of difference (S_{diff}); the S_{diff} is an estimate of measurement error relating to both test and retest scores. The S_{diff} is derived from the standard error of measurement (SEM) from both the test and retest scores. Essentially, each SEM is squared, and these products are added together. The S_{diff} is equal to the square root of that sum. The S_{diff} is then multiplied by a z-score to provide a confidence interval for possible measurement error (e.g., $S_{\text{diff}} \times 1.64 = .90$, or $S_{\text{diff}} \times 1.28 = .80$). Jacobson and Truax (1991) advocated this approach for psychotherapy research, and Chelune and colleagues have applied this methodology to the evaluation of change following temporal lobectomies (Chelune et al., 1993; Sawrie, Chelune, Naugle, & Lüders, 1996). It is important to realize that previous researchers have used an estimated (i.e., prorated) S_{diff}, as opposed to the "obtained" S_{diff}; that is, their calculational formulas used the SEM from time one only, as opposed to separate SEMs for test and retest.

To assist the clinician with interpretation of retest scores on the WMS-R, reliable change difference scores, based on S_{diffs}, were calculated for several clinical samples (at each step in the calculations, all values were rounded to two decimal places). These S_{diffs}, along with 80% and 90% confidence intervals for measurement error, are provided in Table 6.2. The S_{diffs} for the first two samples (i.e., epilepsy and alcohol dependency) were calculated using the SEMs from both test and retest, whereas the remaining S_{diffs} were estimated using the SEM from time one only because these samples were only tested once (i.e., this is an estimated S_{diff}). *It is essential to remember that the WMS-R subtests and index scores are susceptible to significant practice effects.* Therefore, it usually is appropriate to correct these confidence intervals for known practice effects.

The data provided in Table 6.2 are useful for determining whether a patient's memory has improved or declined. Each standard error of difference was multiplied by a z-score of 1.28 or 1.64 to form the .80 and .90 confidence intervals, respectively. The clinician can use these values to interpret individual change scores. For example, if an older man is tested at baseline and obtains a Delayed Recall Index of 83, and then one year later he scores 72, the clinician can infer that the retest score is outside the range of measurement error (i.e., the 90% confidence interval for patients with Alzheimer's is 9 points). If a woman with a left hemisphere stroke obtains a General Memory Index score of 77 at baseline and then 88 at retest, the clinician would not interpret this change in performance as significant improvement because this change is not outside the range of probable measurement error (i.e., 13 points for people with left hemisphere lesions).

Retention Rates and Recognition Memory

One clear advancement in the use of the WMS-R subtest scores is the calculation of retention rates (i.e., savings scores). This issue, although rather obvious, may be neglected by rapid, routine interpretations of subtest performance. For example, suppose a 36-year-old man with a closed head injury recalls 9 bits of information on Logical Memory I and 8 bits of information on Logical Memory II. These raw scores correspond to the 3rd and 9th percentiles, respectively. The clinician may then suggest that the patient's immediate memory and delayed memory for stories is in the borderline range. However, the patient retained 89% of the originally recalled information, which

Table 6.2.   Reliable change difference scores for several clinical groups on the WMS-R

	Reliable Change Scores		
	S^{diff}	.80	.90
Alcohol Dependence[a]			
Attention-Concentration	10.37	13 points	17 points
Verbal Memory	8.49	11 points	14 points
Visual Memory	9.53	12 points	16 points
General Memory	8.15	10 points	13 points
Delayed Recall	7.99	10 points	13 points
Epilepsy[b]			
Attention-Concentration	13.11	17 points	22 points
Verbal Memory	10.35	13 points	17 points
Visual Memory	11.01	14 points	18 points
General Memory	10.87	14 points	18 points
Delayed Recall	13.01	17 points	21 points

	Estimated Reliable Change Scores		
	Est. Sdiff	.80	.90
Alzheimer's Disease[c]			
Attention-Concentration	6.82	9 points	11 points
Verbal Memory	5.61	7 points	9 points
Visual Memory	7.52	10 points	12 points
General Memory	4.44	6 points	7 points
Delayed Recall	5.44	7 points	9 points
Huntington's Disease[c]			
Attention-Concentration	10.15	13 points	17 points
Verbal Memory	9.59	12 points	16 points
Visual Memory	10.11	13 points	17 points
General Memory	9.18	12 points	15 points
Delayed Recall	9.42	12 points	15 points
Multiple Sclerosis[d]			
Attention-Concentration	9.74	12 points	16 points
Verbal Memory	8.26	11 points	14 points
Visual Memory	11.02	14 points	18 points
General Memory	9.79	13 points	16 points
Delayed Recall	10.30	13 points	17 points
Schizophrenia[e]			
Attention-Concentration	9.93	13 points	16 points
Verbal Memory	10.0	13 points	16 points
Visual Memory	13.05	17 points	21 points
General Memory	9.09	12 points	15 points
Delayed Recall	10.17	13 points	17 points
Right Hemisphere Lesions[f]			
Attention-Concentration	14.71	19 points	24 points
Verbal Memory	9.16	12 points	15 points
Visual Memory	14.13	18 points	23 points
General Memory	11.53	15 points	19 points
Delayed Recall	12.35	16 points	20 points
Left Hemisphere Lesions[f]			
Attention-Concentration	12.45	16 points	20 points
Verbal Memory	10.95	14 points	18 points
Visual Memory	10.10	13 points	17 points
General Memory	9.91	13 points	16 points

[a] Bowden etInblal. (1995); [b] Chelune etInblal. (1993); [c] Butters etInblal. (1988); [d] Fischer (1988); [e] Gold etInblal. (1992); [f] Chelune & Bornstein (1988)

is perfectly normal for his age. Thus, his problem is in the initial acquisition of the material, not in the encoding or later recall of that material (i.e., his "rate of forgetting was normal"). If this patient has problems with concentration, then the clinician would be inaccurate in concluding that his delayed memory was borderline. (See Chapter 9, Memory and Learning.)

Retention rates initially were studied on the WMS (e.g., Bornstein, 1982; Delaney, Rosen, Mattson, & Novelly, 1980; Russell, 1975). Unfortunately, they were not included in the WMS-R manual but were later presented at a conference (Prifitera & Ledbetter, 1992). Subsequently, researchers have reported retention rate information from multiple clinical populations, including patients with schizophrenia, traumatic brain injury, Alzheimer's disease, and Huntington's disease (Gass, 1995; Gold, Randolph, Carpenter, Goldberg, & Weinberger, 1992; Tröster et al., 1993). Interpretation of retention rates is strongly recommended because failure to consider these rates can result in misinterpretation of delayed-recall scores on Logical Memory and Visual Reproduction. Normative data on retention rates is available from M. Ledbetter at the Psychological Corporation.

One obvious limitation of the WMS-R is the lack of recognition memory subtests. All procedures relate to free recall, and these procedures are often too difficult for patients at a lower level of functioning. Gass (1995) has published multiple-choice recognition procedures to allow interpretation of results related to deficits in retrieval versus deficient storage. Most useful is his 21-item five-option multiple choice procedure for Logical Memory; this procedure is administered in paper-pencil format after Logical Memory II. He also employed a cueing procedure for the designs: The examiner slowly draws a portion of the "forgotten" design until the patient remembers, then the patient completes the drawing (in a different color pencil). The drawing is scored, according to the criteria in the manual, for only those parts completed independently by the patient. Gass reported that a sample of veterans with mixed psychiatric disorders performed better on the recognition procedures than a sample of veterans with either traumatic brain injuries or strokes.

Interpretation of Visual Reproduction

Performance on the Visual Reproduction subtests requires several component skills. Haut and colleagues (Haut, Weber, Wilhelm, Keefover, & Rankin, 1994) demonstrated empirically what is a clinical assumption: A person must be able to perceive and to draw geometric designs in order for the clinician to interpret Visual Reproduction subtest performance as reflective of memory. (See Chapter 12, Visuoconstructive Abilities.) These researchers have added tasks designed to assess perception (i.e., multiple choice matching task) and visual construction (i.e., straight copy of each design). Patients with Alzheimer's disease performed more poorly on both the copy and the matching tasks than did patients with frontal lobe lesions and older control subjects (Haut et al., 1994). In a second study, these researchers reported a scoring methodology for controlling the effects of constructional dysfunction on memory performance on the Visual Reproduction subtests (Haut, Weber, Demarest, Keefover, & Rankin, 1996). These studies illustrate that it is important to determine whether perceptual or constructional problems are adversely affecting visual memory performance.

Detecting Biased Responding

The WMS-R has also been used to evaluate patterns of performance related to biased responding and to attempts to malinger. Although the diagnosis of malingering requires much more than simply a pattern of test scores, it appears that the WMS-R often possesses a distinctive pattern associated with biased responding (Mittenberg, Azrin, Millsaps, & Heilbronner, 1993). The two most common findings in the literature relate to the Digit Span subtest and a particular pattern of index scores.

The Digit Span subtest of the WAIS-R and WMS-R has been used in several studies involving analog malingerers who, when asked to simulate cognitive impairment, significantly suppressed their performance on the Digit Span procedure (Bernard, 1990; Binder & Willis, 1991). Other studies have found that analog malingerers drawn from undergraduates, Federal prison inmates, and psychiatric inpatients performed much more poorly on Digit Span than did patients with acquired brain damage and documented memory impairment (Iverson & Franzen, 1994, 1996). As a marker for nonoptimal performance, the basic premise is that potential malingerers may not realize that Digit Span abilities often are relatively preserved in patients with brain impairment (Baddeley & Warrington, 1970; Black, 1986; Cermak & Butters, 1972, 1973; Drachman & Arbit, 1966; Warrington & Weiskrantz, 1973). Therefore, severely deficient performance may be indicative of exaggeration, especially when this performance is obtained from an individual with a mild head injury.

Mittenberg and colleagues used discriminant function analysis to develop a "malingering index" for the WMS-R (Mittenberg et al., 1993). These investigators found that experimental-malingerers had a pattern of WMS-R Index scores distinctly different from those of nonlitigating patients with head injuries. Subjects given instructions to malinger suppressed their Attention-Concentration Index relative to their General Memory Index ($M = 71$ versus 85, respectively). The patients with head injuries showed the opposite pattern (i.e., the mean Attention-Concentration Index was 96 and the mean General Memory Index was 85). A discriminant function analysis using the General Memory–Attention-Concentration (GM–A-C) difference score as the independent variable yielded an 83% correct classification rate, with 10% false positives and 23% false negatives. A table was developed reflecting the probability that a given difference score will be consistent with the performance of experimental-malingerers (Mittenberg et al., 1993, p. 37; their Table 4). Slick, Iverson, and Franzen (1996) examined the base rate of the GM–A-C difference score in a large sample of nonlitigating individuals from an inpatient substance abuse program ($N = 332$). Only a small percentage of patients showed large GM–A-C difference scores (i.e., 22 or more points). These results provide further support for the validity of this difference score as a marker for nonoptimal effort.

The GM–A-C difference score as an index of nonoptimal effort is supported on theoretical grounds. Because learning new information requires a certain degree of attentional functioning, a person with normal memory should not demonstrate significantly impaired attentional abilities. Therefore, it should be possible to have significantly impaired memory with relatively intact attention, but not the converse. This theoretical position, of course, is limited by the construct validity of the index scores. In other words, the theory is persuasive to the degree to which the Attention-Concentration Index is a valid measure of "attentional functioning."

CASE EXAMPLE—WMS-R

Alice Beam

Alice Beam is a 36-year-old Caucasian woman who experienced a closed head injury in a motor vehicle accident approximately 9 months prior to this evaluation. At the time of the injury, she reportedly had a one-hour loss of consciousness. Her period of post-traumatic amnesia extended for about 24 hours. She had obtained a bachelor's degree in marketing and was working in that field at the time of the accident. Examination of the scores in Table 6.3 indicate that her memory is generally impaired for both initial registration and delayed recall. There is not a reliable difference between her performance on the Verbal Memory Index and the Visual Memory Index. She showed relatively greater impairment on the Attention-Concentration Index, which may be responsible for the poor initial registration. Her percent of delayed recall indicates that the low Delayed Memory Index score is not an artifact of the low immediate-recall performance, but actually represents rapid forgetting.

Qualitatively, her Visual Reproduction protocol did not show evidence of intrusion, but there were signs of perseveration. Her construction skills appeared to be adequate to the task. Her low scores here were largely related to paucity of detail. Her recall of the narrative on the Logical Memory subtest was disorganized and not in the same temporal sequence as it had been presented. Her performance on the attention measures was inconsistent, in that she missed some trials at early levels before reaching the discontinuance criterion.

The results of IQ testing showed somewhat lower scores than would be expected from her age and education, but generally higher scores than her WMS-R Index

Table 6.3. Wechsler Memory Scale-Revised and Wechsler Adult Intelligence Scale-Revised results for Alice Beam

WMS-R			WAIS-R	
Index	Score		Index	Score
General Memory	80		VIQ	92
Verbal Memory	83		PIQ	86
Visual Memory	86		FSIQ	89
Attention-Concentration	74			
Delayed Recall	51			
Subtest	Percentile			
Digit Span Forward	1			
Digit Span Backward	42			
Visual Memory Span Forward	40			
Visual Memory Span Backward	26			
Logical Memory I	12			
Logical Memory II	6	Percent Retention—67%		
Visual Reproduction I	62			
Visual Reproduction II	4	Percent Retention—40%		

scores. Her memory was more significantly affected by the injury than her intellectual capacity. Testing on the Benton Visual Form Discrimination test underlined the memory impairment aspect of the Visual Reproduction performance as opposed to visual perceptual impairment.

WECHSLER MEMORY SCALE-THIRD EDITION

History and Development

The Wechsler Memory Scale-Third Edition (WMS-III; Wechsler, 1997a), as noted by Edith Kaplan in the foreword to the manual, is far more than a mere revision to the WMS-R; the WMS-III is meant to be a "state-of-the-art assessment instrument that comprehensively addresses the complexity of brain/behavior relationships involved in learning and memory" (page iii). The WMS-III consists of six primary and five optional subtests. According to the manual, the primary subtests can be administered in 30 to 35 minutes. The normative sample consists of 1,250 adults between the ages of 16 to 89. Thirteen age bands were used for the normative tables; the first 11 have 100 individuals each, and the last two have 75 individuals each. Information on the standardization sample and norms development is available in the technical manual (Wechsler, 1997a).

In the development of the WMS-III, there were substantial revisions of the WMS-R subtests, the administration and scoring procedures, and the index configurations. Specifically, new subtests were added, and stimulus materials were revised. Scoring procedures have become much more sophisticated. Subtests are now individually normed with, and presented as, scaled scores; and there are more specific index scores. Although extensive details of these revisions are provided in the manual (Wechsler, 1997a), some of the highlights will be reviewed in this chapter.

The changes in the WMS-III were made for various reasons. Some changes were brought about in response to criticism of the WMS-R. Some changes were meant to reflect current theories of memory as involving stages of processing, as being relatively independent in modalities, and as involving both retrieval and recognition aspects. The WMS-III is integrated with the WAIS-III with a sample of individuals in the standardization samples being shared across the two instruments. Two of the subtests, Digit Span and Letter-Number Span, are shared across the two instruments so that when both the WAIS-III and the WMS-III are given, those subtests only need be administered once.

Eight index scores are derived from age-adjusted scaled scores. The subtests that comprise each index are listed in Table 6.4. The indices have been named to more accurately represent how the information is presented and to more clearly identify the presumed underlying ability. For example, the Auditory Immediate Index is comprised of Logical Memory I and Verbal Paired Associates I, and the Visual Delayed Index is comprised of Faces II and Family Pictures II.

Psychometric Properties

In general, the reliability of the WMS-III is higher than the reliability of the WMS-R. This is true for estimates of both internal consistency and stability. The average

Table 6.4. WMS-III indexes, primary subtests, and optional subtests and procedures

Primary Subtests to Calculate Indexes

1. Auditory Immediate: Logical Memory I, Verbal Paired Associates I
2. Visual Immediate: Faces I, Family Pictures I
3. Immediate Memory: Logical Memory I, Verbal Paired Associates I, Faces I, Family Pictures I
4. Auditory Delayed: Logical Memory II, Verbal Paired Associates II
5. Visual Delayed: Faces II, Family Pictures II
6. Auditory Recognition: Logical Memory Recognition, Verbal Paired Associates Recognition
7. General Memory: Logical Memory II, Verbal Paired Associates II, Faces II, Family Pictures II, Auditory Recognition
8. Working Memory: Letter-Number Sequencing, Spatial Span

Optional Subtests and Procedures

Information and Orientation
1. Word Lists I and II
2. Visual Reproduction I and II
3. Mental Control
4. Digit Span

---

internal consistency coefficients for all age groups ranged from .74 to .93 for the primary subtest scores. All of the primary indices have average internal consistency estimates of .82 or greater, with the exception of the Auditory Recognition Delayed Index ($r = .74$). The average test-retest reliability coefficients, for all age groups, ranged from .62 to .82 for the primary subtest scores and from .75 to .88 for the primary indices (with the exception of the Auditory Delayed Recognition Index of .70).

The validity of the WMS-III was examined through special group studies. In these studies, independent researchers collected data on small groups of clinical patients. For a sample of 35 patients with mild Alzheimer's disease, most of the mean primary index scores fell in the range from 60 to 71, with the exception of Working Memory ($M = 80.4$). The lowest primary index scores for the sample of patients with traumatic brain injuries were Visual Immediate, Immediate Memory, Visual Delayed, and General Memory (i.e., 74.3 to 81.9). Results from small samples of patients with Huntington's disease, Parkinson's disease, multiple sclerosis, temporal lobe epilepsy, chronic alcohol abuse, Korsakoff's syndrome, schizophrenia, ADHD, and learning disabilities also were reported. In general, the clinical patients performed more poorly than did the standardization individuals. The next step would be to see if the pattern of performances on subtests matches theories regarding the specific types of memory impairment seen in these different diagnostic groups.

Assets and Limitations

The WMS-III shows great promise because of its greater theoretical underpinnings and standardization data. Perhaps its greatest contribution is the conorming with the WAIS-III. However, the promise of the WMS-III is in need of independent empirical evaluation. Lessons learned from experiences with the WMS-R include the fact that not all theoretical assumptions are eventually supported under the light of careful scrutiny. Furthermore, based on experience with the WMS-R, clinicians are likely to use only selected subtests of the WMS-III. Availability of percentile translations for subtests will facilitate this process but may also detract from use of the entire instrument. An area of research would then be the decision rules related to choice of subtest procedures and to interpretations possible when the entire battery is not given.

The length and complexity of the WMS-III can be seen as both an asset and a limitation. These two features of the WMS-III will allow a more finely grained examination of memory processes than would be possible with either the WMS-R or with most other memory assessment instruments. However, these two features may also discourage clinicians from using the instrument or may limit its appropriate use and interpretation.

Future research directions include examining the relation of WMS-III scores to everyday functioning. This is an important question not only for the WMS-III but also for memory instruments in general. However, given its relative stature, it is especially important that the WMS-III be evaluated. Furthermore, empirical investigations of the theoretical bases of the WMS-III and the interpretative strategies suggested in the manual are warranted. Viewing the explosion of studies following publication of the WMS-R, the possibility of these investigations can almost be guaranteed.

Interpretation

Interpretation of the WMS-III is complex. The scale, through careful inclusion of different aspects of the extant literature on human memory, can be used to describe numerous global and specific features of attention, learning, and memory. Many of the interpretive features of the WMS-III are presented in Table 6.5.

Interpretation of the WMS-III can be organized according to the following four sequential steps:

1. A general strategy would be to first examine the absolute level of the Index scores. Low scores on the Auditory Immediate index might indicate deficits in the ability to encode new verbal auditory information. Low scores on the Visual Immediate index might indicate deficits in the ability to learn and encode new visual information. Low scores on the Auditory Delayed index or the Visual Delayed index might indicate deficits in the capacity to retain new information, but this hypothesis should be checked against the percent retained from the immediate recall conditions. Low raw scores on delayed recall procedures that are identical to scores on immediate recall procedures would reflect the initial poor learning rather than rapid forgetting. Low scores on the Auditory Recognition Delayed index might reflect deficits in initial registration of the information rather than poor retrieval skills. Low scores on the General Memory index could reflect a variety of processes and should be checked against performance on the component scales. Low scores on the Working Memory index might reflect deficits in attentional skills, but more empirical information is needed before results on this index can be confidently interpreted in isolation.

2. Next, evaluate the reliability of the differences among the Index scores. In particular, the difference between the General Memory and the Working Memory can

Table 6.5.   Selected interpretive features of the WMS-III

Orientation: Orientation to person, place, date, and general information.

Simple Attention: Ability to comprehend and repeat a series of digits. Ability to repeat a series of sequential taps on a spatial form board. Specific procedures: Digit Span Forward and Spatial Span Forward.

Complex Attention: Ability to repeat digits backward. Ability to repeat a sequence of taps on a spatial form board backward. Ability to mentally hold and sequence a series of numbers and letters. Specific procedures: Digit Span Backward, Spatial Span Backward, and Letter-Number Sequencing.

Learning: Verbal associative learning and word list learning. Specific procedures: Verbal Paired Associates and Word Lists.

Memory: Immediate and delayed recall for stories. Percent retention (i.e., forgetting rates) and recognition memory for stories. Immediate and delayed recognition memory for faces. Immediate and delayed free recall of animated pictures. Immediate and delayed recall, and recognition memory for, geometric designs. Global measures of immediate and delayed recall for auditorily and visually presented information and for global measures of memory. Specific procedures: Seven of the eight primary index scores relate to different aspects of memory functioning. Specific subtests that may be interpreted singly are Logical Memory, Faces, and Visual Reproduction.

Visual Perception: Ability to visually discriminate and match geometric designs. Specific procedures: Visual Reproduction Discrimination.

Visual Construction: Ability to copy geometric designs. Specific procedures: Visual Reproduction Copy.

help define whether a primary memory deficit or an impairment in attention and the early stages of memory processing is present.

3. Examination of the composite scores is the next step, and this examination focuses on more finely tuned learning, that is, single trial issues versus learning slope issues and a more finely tuned examination of retrieval and retention. Individual subtest scores can be interpreted in terms of their percentile scores. However, caution is necessary here. The construct validity of the subtests has not been completely explicated in empirical terms. The interpretation of the subtests can be conducted in reference to theoretical considerations regarding the requisite skills; however, these interpretations should be viewed as preliminary and should be verified against other clinical information.

4. Finally, the interpretation of the WMS-III needs to be fitted into a consideration of performance on other tests in the context of the patient's characteristics.

Intelligence-Memory Discrepancy Analyses

Interpretation of IQ-memory discrepancies is much more accurate and sophisticated on the WMS-III, versus the WMS-R, given that the WAIS-III and WMS-III were conormed. As such, it is possible to determine if a given IQ-memory discrepancy is reliable, unusual, and/or abnormal. The magnitudes of reliable, unusual, and abnormal splits, on average for all age groups, are provided in Table 6.6. All splits are unidirectional; that is, the memory index is lower than the FSIQ. The reliable splits on the

Table 6.6.   Reliable, unusual, and abnormal differences between FSIQ and Index Scores averaged for all ages

	Reliable	Unusual ≤15%	Unusual ≤10%	Abnormal ≤5%
Auditory Immediate	8.8	14	17	23
Visual Immediate	13.1	18	22	29
Immediate Memory	9.7	15	17	23
Auditory Delayed	11.7	14	17	23
Visual Delayed	12.9	17	21	26
Auditory Recognition Delayed	15.7	16	20	25
General Memory	9.9	13	16	22
Working Memory	11.9	13	15	20

Derived from Table C.1 and C.4; p. 288 and 291 in the Technical Manual.

WMS-III (i.e., discrepancies that are not due to measurement error) range from 9 points on the Auditory Immediate Index to 16 points on the Auditory Recognition Delayed Index. On average for all ages, the clinician could conclude that a General Memory Index that is 10 points lower than the individual's FSIQ represents a reliable difference ($p < .15$), indicating that memory is a *relative weakness* for the person. However, a split of this magnitude is common in the general population, so it is not until the split reaches a magnitude of 13 to 16 points that the clinician should conclude that the difference is both reliable and "unusual" (i.e., the split occurs in less than 15% or 10% of the general population, respectively). A FSIQ-General Memory Index discrepancy score of 22 points occurs in 5% or less of the general population (i.e., a statistically "abnormal" split) and should be considered rare.

In interpreting the WMS-III results, impaired performance on the percent retention score is likely to be the result most sensitive to the types of everyday memory impairment subjectively reported by many individuals. This is likely to be true regardless of the etiology of the memory impairment. Poor performance on the Logical Memory subtest also has conceptual relations to subjective memory complaints because a frequent index of everyday memory is the ability to follow and to remember textual narratives spoken by other people.

Interpretation of Visual Reproduction

The Visual Reproduction subtest of the WMS-III is an optional subtest. There have been some concerns from colleagues regarding the length of the subtest and the complexity of the scoring, which may result in decreased use of this subtest in clinical practice. However, the subtest is now more sophisticated than ever before, allowing the neuropsychologist to make inferences regarding basic visual perception, visual-constructional, immediate and delayed recall, percent retention, and recognition memory for geometric designs. These refinements emerged out of the literature relating to percent retention, perception, and construction on the WMS-R (e.g., Haut et al., 1994; Tröster et al., 1993). For example, in order to remember the designs, the patient must accurately perceive them. The Discrimination procedure is a simple matching task in which the patient is asked to select the target design from a set of distracters. The vast majority of people in the standardization sample scored either 6/7 or 7/7 on this task. Scores of 5/7 or less occur in 5% or less of people under the age of 75 (thus, scores in this range may be indicative of a perceptual problem). Normative data also are available for straight copy of the designs. Scores range from 0 to 104, and scores falling in the very low 90s for people under the age of 65 *may* be a reflection of visual-constructional problems. It should be noted that other tests of visual construction and memory also have complex scoring and less sophisticated norms (e.g., Rey-Osterrieth Complex Figure, see Chapter 9), so the complexity of the scoring should not be a deciding factor on whether to include this subtest in a comprehensive neuropsychological evaluation.

CASE EXAMPLES—WMS-III

Two case examples are provided to illustrate basic clinical interpretation of WAIS-III/WMS-III performance. The first case illustrates that the new test battery has lower basal scores, making it more appropriate than the WAIS-R and the WMS-R for patients who function at a very low level. The second case illustrates the use of the WMS-III, in conjunction with the WAIS-III, to assist with a depression-dementia differential diagnosis.

Frank Smith

Frank Smith is a 44-year-old man with 12 years of education who sustained a severe anoxic episode in a suicide attempt by hanging. He was successfully employed for 20 years in automobile sales, and he has no history of learning disability or prior neurological problems. He has a history of modest alcohol use. The evaluation was conducted 4 years post–anoxic injury. He was living semiindependently in a residential placement and was admitted to an inpatient neuropsychiatric facility because of agitated behavior. Selected test results from the WAIS-III and the WMS-III are presented in Table 6.7.

Discussion of Neuropsychological Test Findings: Mr. Smith has no significant motor or sensory problems that interfere with his day-to-day functioning. His language abilities are sufficient for basic communication. He can understand directions within the hospital setting, and he can communicate his basic needs. However, he is disoriented to aspects of person, place, and time. Moreover, his global intellectual abilities are substantially declined from his estimated average-range premorbid level of functioning. Mr. Smith's FSIQ on the WAIS-III was 66, placing him in the impaired classification range. His performance was lower than more than 99% of his same-aged peers. His verbal and nonverbal intellectual abilities were roughly comparable.

Mr. Smith has serious memory impairment. This memory impairment is global in that he has deficits for information he hears and for information he sees. There is no difference in the magnitude of his verbal versus visual memory deficits. Mr. Smith's memory impairment is greater than would be predicted from his impaired intellectual functioning. Specifically, his general memory abilities were substantially worse than his global intellectual functioning (i.e., a FSIQ-General Memory Index discrepancy of 21 points). In other words, his acquired brain dysfunction

Table 6.7. Mr. Smith's WAIS-III and WMS-III test results

	Score	Classification Rating
Intellectual Functioning		
Full Scale IQ	66	Impaired
Global Verbal-Comprehension Skills (VCI)	72	Borderline
Global Perceptual-Organizational Skills (POI)	65	Impaired
Fund of Knowledge (Information)	5	Borderline
Verbal Reasoning (Similarities)	5	Borderline
Nonverbal Reasoning (Matrix Reasoning)	6	Borderline
Attention to Visual Details (Picture Completion)	2	Impaired
Simple Visual-Perception (Discrimination-WMS)	⅞	Average
Visual-Constructional of (VR Copy-WMS)	10	Average
Spatial-Motor Integration (Block Design)	4	Borderline
Processing Speed (visual-motor; PSI)	73	Borderline
Concentration and Working Memory		
Digit Span Forward (cumulative %)*	79.5	Low average
Digit Span Backward (cumulative %)*	86.5	Low average
Visual-Spatial Span Forward	8	Average
Visual-Spatial Span Backward	4	Borderline
Complex Attention (Letter-Number Sequencing)	4	Borderline
Working Memory (WMI)	73	Borderline
Learning and Memory		
Word List Learning (Recall Total Score)	2	Impaired
Delayed Recall of Words	5	Borderline
Retention Rate for Words	4	Borderline
Recognition Memory for Words	2	Impaired
Auditory Immediate Memory	50	Moderately Impaired
Visual Immediate Memory	49	Moderately Impaired
Global Immediate Memory	45	Moderately Impaired
Auditory Delayed Memory	52	Moderately Impaired
Visual Delayed Memory	53	Moderately Impaired
Global Delayed Memory	45	Moderately Impaired

*Lower cumulative percentages reflect higher span capacities as compared to the normative sample.

likely had even greater impact on his memory functioning than on his intellectual abilities.

It is obvious that Mr. Smith has experienced a major decline in his functioning. It is estimated that his intellectual abilities have declined from the average to the impaired classification range and that his memory abilities have declined even further. The results are consistent with acquired dysfunction of the anterior regions of his brain, including functional areas associated with both the frontal and the temporal lobes. His current level of functioning is consistent with dementia secondary to anoxia. All of his index scores are in the significantly impaired range with only small difference among them, indicating relatively uniform memory impairment across modalities and stages of processing.

Robert Miller

Robert Miller is a 56-year-old owner of a successful construction company. He has 13 years of education and no history of significant neurological problems, with the exception of one or two concussions while playing high school football. He is 6 months post-divorce, following 28 years of marriage. He was referred by his family physician due to the patient's concern that he may be developing Alzheimer's disease (possible family history in maternal grandmother, but not in parents).

Discussion of Neuropsychological Test Findings: On the WAIS-III, Mr. Miller's verbal comprehension and perceptual organizational abilities are in the average range. There is not a statistically reliable difference between his Verbal Comprehension Index and his Perceptual Organization Index scores, indicating that his verbal and nonverbal intellectual abilities are comparable (see Table 6.8). His processing speed, which is in the low average range, is a relative weakness for him, that is, he demonstrates statistically reliable differences between his Processing Speed Index and all three of the other indices on the WAIS-III (Verbal Comprehension, Perceptual-Organization, and Working Memory). Although processing speed is a relative weakness, these results are not rare or abnormal, as compared to his same-aged peers in the general population.

Mr. Miller demonstrated adequate sustained attention to be able to participate in long periods of neuropsychological testing. On a global measure of concentration and working memory, he scored in the average range (WMI = 102). His immediate and delayed memory index scores for both auditory and visual information were in the average range. However, a pattern emerged indicating that his delayed memory was a relative weakness for him. He demonstrated statistically reliable Auditory Immediate-Delayed and Visual Immediate-Delayed difference scores, and these differences are somewhat unusual in the general population (i.e., occurring in less than 15% and 10%, respectively). There were no statistically reliable differences between his memory for auditorily presented versus visually presented information, indicating that he does not have a relative strength in memory for one type of information versus another.

Table 6.8. Mr. Miller's WAIS-III and WMS-III Index Scores

WAIS-III		WMS-III	
Index	Score	Index	Score
Verbal Comprehension Index	101	Auditory Immediate Index	108
Perceptual Organization Index	109	Visual Immediate Index	106
Working Memory Index	102	Immediate Memory Index	108
Processing Speed Index	88	Auditory Delayed Index	97
VIQ	101	Visual Delayed Index	91
PIQ	105	Auditory Recognition Delayed Index	115
FSIQ	103	General Memory Index	98
		Working Memory Index	102

The WMS-III also allows comparisons between recall and recognition. *Recall* refers to the ability to spontaneously retrieve information from memory. *Recognition* refers to the ability to recognize the originally presented information from distracter information. There was a statistically reliable difference between his ability to recall versus recognize the auditorily presented information. His recognition was in the high average range, and his recall was in the average range. A difference of this magnitude occurs in less than 17% of the general population.

Comparisons between intelligence test scores and memory test scores can be helpful in determining whether a person is experiencing a decline in memory functioning. Mr. Miller demonstrates a very consistent pattern of scores, most of which are in the average range. There are no relative weaknesses in memory, as compared to his general level of intellectual functioning.

Mr. Miller's pattern of test results is consistent more with depression and stress than with early Alzheimer's disease. He has relative weakness in his processing speed and his delayed memory. However, his recognition memory is clearly better than his free recall, indicating that with cues he is able to remember previously forgotten information. Mr. Miller's memory test scores are in the average range and are consistent with his intelligence test scores. Therefore, given that he is experiencing numerous symptoms of stress and depression, such as insomnia, fatigue, irritability, poor concentration, lack of interest in activities, and poor appetite, it would be best to treat him for these psychiatric problems and determine whether he experiences concomitant improvement in his concentration and memory.

RECOMMENDED READING

Parkin, A.J. & Leng, N.R.C. (1993). *Neuropsychology of the Amnesic Syndrome.* Hillsdale, NJ: Lawrence Erlbaum Associates.

Squire, L.R. & Butters, N. (Eds.). (1992). *The Neuropsychology of Memory* (2nd ed.), New York: Guilford.

REFERENCES

Atkinson, L. (1991a). Concurrent use of the Wechsler memory scale–revised and the WAIS-R. *British Journal of Clinical Psychology, 30,* 87–90.

Atkinson, L. (1991b). Three standard errors of measurement and the Wechsler memory scale–revised. *Psychological Assessment, 3,* 136–138.

Baddeley, A.D., & Warrington, E.K. (1970). Amnesia and the distinction between long- and short-term memory. *Journal of Verbal Learning and Verbal Behavior, 9,* 176–189.

Bernard, L.C. (1990). Prospects for faking believable memory deficits on neuropsychological tests and the use of incentives in simulation research. *Journal of Clinical and Experimental Neuropsychology, 12,* 715–728.

Binder, L.M., & Willis, S.C. (1991). Assessment of motivation after financially compensable minor head trauma. *Psychological Assessment, 3,* 175–181.

Black, W.F. (1986). Digit repetition in brain-damaged adults: Clinical and theoretical implications. *Journal of Clinical Psychology, 42,* 770–782.

Bornstein, R.A. (1982). Effects of unilateral lesions on the Wechsler memory scale. *Journal of Clinical Psychology, 38,* 389–392.

Bornstein, R.A., & Chelune, G.J. (1988). Factor analysis of the Wechsler memory scale-revised. *Clinical Neuropsychologist, 2,* 107–115.

Bornstein, R.A., Chelune, G.J., & Prifitera, A. (1989). IQ-memory discrepancies in normal and clinical samples. *Psychological Assessment: A Journal of Consulting and Clinical Psychology, 1,* 203–206.

Bowden, S.C., & Bell, R.C (1992). Relative usefulness of the WMS and WMS-R: A comment on D'Elia et al. (1989). *Journal of Clinical and Experimental Neuropsychology, 14,* 34–346.

Bowden, S.C., Whelan, G., Long, C.M., & Clifford, C.C. (1995). Temporal stability of the WAIS-R and WMS-R in a heterogeneous sample of alcohol dependent clients. *Clinical Neuropsychologist, 9,* 194–197.

Butters, N., Salmon, D.P., Cullum, C.M., Cairns, P., Tröster, A.I., Jacobs, D., Moss, M., & Cermak, L.S. (1988). Differentiation of amnesic and demented patients with the Wechsler memory scale–revised. *Clinical Neuropsychologist, 2,* 133–148.

Cermak, L.S., & Butters, N. (1972). The role of interference and encoding in the short-term memory deficits of Korsakoff patients. *Neuropsychologia, 10,* 89–96.

Cermak, L.S., & Butters, N. (1973). Information processing deficits of alcoholic Korsakoff patients. *Quarterly Journal of Studies on Alcohol, 34,* 1110–1132.

Chelune, G.J., & Bornstein, R.A. (1988). WMS-R patterns among patients with unilateral brain lesions: Initial validity studies of the Wechsler memory scale–revised [Special issue]. *Clinical Neuropsychologist, 2,* 121–132.

Chelune, G.J., Naugle, R.I., Lüders, H.O., Sedlak, J., & Issam A.A. (1993). Individual change after epilepsy surgery: Practice effects and base-rate information. *Neuropsychology, 7,* 41–52.

Crosson, J.R., & Wiens, A.N. (1988). Wechsler memory scale-revised: Deficits in performance associated with neurotoxic solvent exposure. *Clinical Neuropsychologist, 2,* 181–187.

Delaney, R.C., Rosen, A.J., Mattson, R.H., & Novelly, R.A. (1980). Memory function in focal epilepsy: A comparison of non-surgical, unilateral temporal lobe and frontal lobe samples. *Cortex, 16,* 103–117.

D'Elia, L.F., Satz, P., & Schretlen, D. (1989). Wechsler memory scale: A critical appraisal of the normative studies. *Journal of Clinical and Experimental Neuropsychology, 11,* 551–568.

Delis, D.C., Cullum, C.M., Butters, N., & Cairns, P. (1988). Wechsler memory scale–revised and California verbal learning test: Convergence and divergence. *Clinical Neuropsychologist, 2,* 188–196.

Drachman, D.A., & Arbit, J. (1966). Memory and the hippocampal complex: II. *Archives of Neurology, 15,* 52–61.

Elwood, R.W. (1991). The Wechsler memory scale–revised: Psychometric characteristics and clinical application. *Neuropsychology Review, 2,* 179–201.

Fastenau, P.S., Denburg, N.L., & Abeles, N. (1996). Age differences in retrieval: Further support for the resource-reduction hypothesis. *Psychology and Aging, 11,* 140–146.

Fischer, J.S. (1988). Using the Wechsler memory scale–revised to detect and characterize memory deficits in multiple sclerosis. *Clinical Neuropsychologist, 2,* 149–172.

Gale, S.D., Johnson, S.C., Bigler, E.D., & Blatter, D.D. (1994). Traumatic brain injury and temporal horn enlargement: Correlates with tests of intelligence and memory. *Neuropsychiatry, Neuropsychology, and Behavioral Neurology, 7,* 160–165.

Gale, S.D., Johnson, S.C., Bigler, E.D., & Blatter, D.D. (1995). Nonspecific white matter degeneration following traumatic brain injury. *Journal of the International Neuropsychological Society, 1,* 17–28.

Gass, C.S. (1995). A procedure for assessing storage and retrieval on the Wechsler memory scale–revised. *Archives of Clinical Neuropsychology, 10,* 475–487.

Gass, C.S., & Apple, C. (1997). Cognitive complaints in closed-head injury: Relationship to memory test performance and emotional disturbance. *Journal of Clinical and Experimental Neuropsychology, 19,* 290–299.

Gold, J.M., Randolph, C., Carpenter, C.J., Goldberg, T.E., & Weinberger, D.R. (1992). The performance of patients with schizophrenia on the Wechsler memory scale–revised. *Clinical Neuropsychologist, 6,* 367–373.

Guilmette, T.J., Faust, D., Hart, K., & Arkes, H.R. (1990). A national survey of psychologists who offer neuropsychological services. *Archives of Clinical Neuropsychology, 5,* 373–392.

Haut, M.W., Weber, A.M., Demarest, D., Keefover, R.W., & Rankin, E.D. (1996). Controlling for constructional dysfunction with the visual reproduction subtest of the Wechsler memory scale–revised in Alzheimer's disease. *Clinical Neuropsychologist, 10,* 309–312.

Haut, M.W., Weber, A.M., Wilhelm, K.L., Keefover, R.W., & Rankin, E.D. (1994). The visual reproduction subtest as a measure of visual perceptual/constructional functioning in dementia of the Alzheimer's type. *Clinical Neuropsychologist, 8,* 187–192.

Hawkins, K.A., Sullivan, T.E., & Choi, E.J. (1997). Memory deficits in schizophrenia: Inadequate assimilation or true amnesia? Findings from the Wechsler memory scale–revised. *Journal of Psychiatry and Neuroscience, 22,* 169–179.

Iverson, G.L., & Franzen, M.D. (1994). The recognition memory test, digit span, and Knox cube test as markers of malingered memory impairment. *Assessment, 1,* 323–334.

Iverson, G.L., & Franzen, M.D. (1996). Using multiple objective memory procedures to detect simulated malingering. *Journal of Clinical and Experimental Neuropsychology, 18,* 38–51.

Jacobson, N.S., & Truax, P. (1991). Clinical significance: A statistical approach to defining meaningful change in psychotherapy research. *Journal of Consulting and Clinical Psychology, 59,* 12–19.

Johnstone, B., Erdal, K., & Stadler, M.A. (1995). The relationship between the Wechsler memory scale–revised (WMS-R) Attention index and putative measures of attention. *Journal of Clinical Psychology in Medical Settings, 2,* 195–204.

Jurden, F.H., Franzen, M.D., Callahan, T., & Ledbetter, M. (1996). Factorial equivalence of the Wechsler memory scale–revised across standardization and clinical samples. *Applied Neuropsychology, 3,* 65–74.

Koltai, D.C., Bowler, R.M., & Shore, M.D. (1996). The Rivermead behavioural memory test and Wechsler memory scale–revised: Relationship to everyday memory impairment. *Assessment, 3,* 443–448.

Lees-Haley, P.R., Smith, H.H., Williams, C.W., & Dunn, J.T. (1996). Forensic neuropsychological test usage: An empirical survey. *Archives of Clinical Neuropsychology, 11,* 45–51.

Lichtenberg, P.A., & Christensen, B. (1992). Extended normative data for the logical memory subtests of the Wechsler memory scale–revised: Responses from a sample of cognitively intact elderly medical patients. *Psychological Reports, 71,* 745–746.

Loring, D.W. (1989). The Wechsler memory scale–revised, or the Wechsler memory scale-revisited? *Clinical Neuropsychologist, 3,* 59–69.

Loring, D.W., Lee, G.P., Martin, R.C., & Meador, K.J. (1989). Verbal and visual memory index discrepancies from the Wechsler memory scale–revised: Cautions in interpretation. *Psychological Assessment: A Journal of Consulting and Clinical Psychology, 3,* 198–202.

Marcopulos, B.A., McLain, C.A., & Giuliano, A.J. (1997). Cognitive impairment or inadequate norms: A study of healthy, rural, older adults with limited education. *Clinical Neuropsychologist, 11,* 111–131.

McIntosh, D.E., Waldo, S.L., & Koller, J.R. (1997). Exploration of the underlying dimension and overlap between the Kaufman adolescent and adult intelligence test and the Wechsler memory test–revised. *Journal of Psychoeducational Assessment, 15,* 15–26.

Mittenberg, W., Azrin, R., Millsaps, C., & Heilbronner, R. (1993). Identification of malingered head injury on the Wechsler memory scale–revised. *Psychological Assessment, 5,* 34–40.

Mittenberg, W., Burton, D.B., Darrow, E., & Thompson, G.B. (1992). Normative data for the Wechsler memory scale–revised: 25- to 34-year-olds. *Psychological Assessment, 4,* 363–368.

Mittenberg, W., Thompson, G.B., & Schwartz, J.A. (1991). Abnormal and reliable differences among Wechsler memory scale–revised subtests. *Psychological Assessment: A Journal of Consulting and Clinical Psychology, 3,* 492–495.

Nestor, P.G., Shenton, M.E., McCarley, R.W., Haimson, J., Smith, R.S., O'Donnell, B., Kimble, M., Kikinis, R., & Jolesz, F.A. (1993). Neuropsychological correlates of MRI temporal lobe abnormalities. *American Journal of Psychiatry, 150,* 1849–1855.

O'Carroll, R.E., & Badenoch, L.D. (1994). The inter-rater reliability of the Wechsler memory scale–revised visual memory test. *British Journal of Clinical Psychology, 33,* 208–210.

O'Mahony, J.F., & Doherty, B. (1993). Patterns of intellectual performance among recently abstinent alcohol abusers on the WAIS-R and WMS-R subtests. *Archives of Clinical Neuropsychology, 8,* 373–380.

Parkin, A.J., & Leng, N.R.C. (Eds.). (1993). *Neuropsychology of the amnesic syndrome.* Hove, UK: Erlbaum.

Prifitera, A., & Ledbetter, M. (1992, November). *Normative delayed recall rates based on the Wechsler memory scale–revised standardization sample.* Paper presented at the 12th annual meeting of the National Academy of Neuropsychology, Pittsburgh.

Randolph, C., Gold, J.M., Kozora, E., & Cullum, C.M. (1994). Estimating memory function: Disparity of Wechsler memory scale–revised and California verbal learning test indices in clinical and normal samples.*Clinical Neuropsychologist, 8,* 99–108.

Reid, D.B., & Kelly, M.P. (1993). Wechsler memory scale–revised in closed head injury. *Journal of Clinical Psychology, 49,* 245–254.

Roid, G.H., Prifitera, A., & Ledbetter, M. (1988). Confirmatory analysis of the factor of the Wechsler memory scale–revised. *Clinical Neuropsychologist, 2,* 116–120.

Ross, T.P., & Lichtenberg, P.A. (1997). Effects of age and education on neuropsychological test performance: A comparison of normal vs. cognitively impaired geriatric medical patients. *Aging Neuropsychology and Cognition, 4,* 74–79.

Russell, E.W. (1975). A multiple scoring method for the assessment of complex memory functions. *Journal of Consulting and Clinical Psychology, 43,* 800–809.

Ryan, J.J., & Lewis, C.V. (1988). Comparison of normal controls and recently detoxified alcoholics on the Wechsler memory scale–revised. *Clinical Neuropsychologist, 2,* 173–180.

Sawrie, S.M., Chelune, G.J., Naugle, R.I., & Luders, H.O. (1996). Empirical methods for assessing meaningful neuropsychological change following epilepsy surgery. *Journal of the International Neuropsychological Society, 2,* 556–564.

Schmidt, M., Trueblood, W., Merwin, M., & Durham, R.L. (1994). How much do "attention" tests tell us? *Archives of Clinical Neuropsychology, 9,* 383–394.

Slick, D., Iverson, G.L., & Franzen, M. (1996, August). *Evaluation of Wechsler memory scale–revised savings scores in a sample of substance-abuse inpatients.* Paper presented at the 26th International Congress of Psychology, Montreal, Canada.

Smith, G.E., Ivnik, R.J., Malec, J.F., & Tangalos, E.G. (1993). Factor of the MOANS core battery: Replication in a clinical sample. *Psychological Assessment: A Journal of Consulting and Clinical Psychology, 5,* 121–124.

Smith, G.E., Wong, J.S., Ivnik, R.J., & Malec, J.F. (1997). Mayo's older American normative studies: Separate norms for WMS-R logical memory stories. *Assessment, 4,* 79–86.

Sullivan, K. (1996). Estimates of interrater reliability for the logical memory subtest of the Wechsler memory scale–revised. *Journal of Clinical and Experimental Neuropsychology, 18,* 707–712.

Tröster, A.I., Butters, N., Salmon, D.P., Cullum, C.M., Jacobs, D., Brandt, J., & White, R.F. (1993). The diagnostic utility of savings scores: Differentiating Alzheimer's and Huntington's diseases with the logical memory and visual reproduction tests. *Journal of Clinical and Experimental Neuropsychology, 15,* 773–788.

Warrington, E.K., & Weiskrantz, L. (1973). An analysis of short- and long-term memory defects in man. In J.A. Deutsch (Ed.), *The physiological basis of memory.* New York: Academic Press.

Wechsler, D. (1945). A standardized memory scale for clinical use. *Journal of Psychology, 19,* 87–95.

Wechsler, D. (1987). *Wechsler memory scale–revised manual.* San Antonio: The Psychological Corporation/Harcourt Brace Jovanovich.

Wechsler, D. (1997a). *WAIS-III/WMS-III technical manual.* San Antonio: The Psychological Corporation/Harcourt Brace & Company.

Wechsler, D. (1997b).*Wechsler memory scale-third edition: Administration and scoring manual.* San Antonio: Psychological Corporation/Harcourt Brace & Company.

Williams, J.M. (1991). *Memory assessment scales.* Odessa, FL: Psychological Assessment Resources.

Woloszyn, D.B., Murphy, S.G., Wetzel, L., & Fisher, W. (1993). Interrater agreement on the Wechsler memory scale–revised in a mixed clinical sample. *Clinical Neuropsychologist, 7,* 467–471.

Chapter 7

THE HALSTEAD-REITAN NEUROPSYCHOLOGICAL TEST BATTERY

Donna K. Broshek and Jeffrey T. Barth

The traditional Halstead-Reitan Neuropsychological Test Battery (HRB) is a fixed battery comprised of eight standardized and individually administered tests (Category Test, Tactual Performance Test, Speech Sounds Perception, Seashore Rhythm, Finger Oscillation, Trail Making Test, Aphasia Screening Examination, and Sensory-Perceptual Examination). The HRB assesses a variety of abilities that have been shown to be sensitive to cerebral dysfunction. The battery includes measures of auditory attention, cognitive processing speed and visual scanning, nonverbal abstract reasoning, psychomotor problem solving, incidental spatial memory, and motor and sensory perceptual functioning. The purpose of the HRB is to elucidate cognitive and behavioral strengths and weaknesses and to relate these processes to neurologic functions, to determine or confirm diagnoses and prognoses, and to assist in developing intervention strategies.

The interpretation of the HRB is based on four methods of inference that have a long history of clinical use but that had not been formally incorporated into neuropsychological assessment until the HRB (Reitan & Wolfson, 1993). The first method is the level of performance, which refers to how well or how poorly a patient performs on individual tests and the total battery. *Level of performance* data is derived from comparisons between groups, and clinical evaluation requires the comparison of a patient's performance with normative data (Boll, 1981). The second method examines patterns and *variations in performance* that might be indicative of cerebral dysfunction. Ralph Reitan's development of pattern analysis as a method of inference has been described as his most important contribution to neuropsychology (Russell, 1998). The third method of inference is that of identifying *pathognomonic signs,* which are specific deficits indicative of cerebral pathology and which rarely occur in normal individuals. The fourth method, *lateralization,* is typically based upon comparing the motor and the sensory-perceptual performances of each side of the body to make inferences regarding the functioning of the right and left cerebral hemispheres.

A neuropsychological evaluation that incorporates the HRB typically also involves the administration of the Wechsler Adult Intelligence Scale-Revised (WAIS-R) or the Wechsler Adult Intelligence Scale-Third Edition (WAIS-III) and the Minnesota Multiphasic Personality Inventory-2 (MMPI-2). Supplementary measures are often administered, including various memory tests, such as the Wechsler Memory Scale-III, the

California Verbal Learning Test, the Buschke Selective Reminding Test, the Rey Auditory Verbal Learning Test, or the Rey Complex Figure Test. These measures of memory are included because limited memory assessment is one of the weaknesses of the HRB. The Grooved Pegboard (Kløve, 1963) and Grip Strength Test (Reitan & Wolfson, 1993) are also frequently administered along with the Finger Tapping Test, as is the Lateral Dominance test. Reitan has also developed the Halstead Neuropsychological Test Battery for children ages 9 to 14 and the Reitan Indiana Neuropsychological Test Battery for children ages 5 to 8.

HISTORY AND DEVELOPMENT

After completing his doctoral degree in physiological psychology at Northwestern University in 1935, Ward Halstead developed a working relationship with neurosurgeons Percival Bailey and Paul Bucy, who encouraged Halstead to study their patients at the University of Chicago (Reitan & Wolfson, 1994, 1996). The collaboration between Halstead, Bailey, and Bucy in 1935 resulted in the first full-time laboratory for the study of human brain-behavior relationships (Reitan & Wolfson, 1996). Halstead studied the behavior of patients with neurologic impairment in their daily living environment and noted the wide range of deficits demonstrated by these patients. His naturalistic observations suggested that a single test would not be sufficient to identify the variety of deficits displayed by these patients. According to Reitan (1994), Halstead "had a strong notion that the brain, as the organ of basic adaptive abilities, should be evaluated behaviorally in terms of practical aspects of adjustment. He was less interested in the traditional psychometric measures of intelligence, which he felt centered largely around development of vocabulary skills, other verbal abilities, and academic success" (p. 52). Halstead also observed that patients with brain damage demonstrated deficits in complex problem solving and in drawing accurate conclusions from various situations they faced in their daily life (Reitan & Wolfson, 1994). He began experimenting with a variety of tests and eventually identified a battery of 10 tests that formed the basis for his theory of biological intelligence. Of these 10 tests, only 3 (Critical Flicker Frequency, Critical Flicker Fusion, and Time Sense Test) are not included in the Halstead-Reitan Neuropsychological Test Battery (HRB).

Halstead (1947) proposed a factor–analytically derived biological theory of intelligence based on his observations and standardized assessment of patients with brain lesions (Reitan, 1994). He proposed a Central Integrative Factor, which represented a general factor that included a person's background, experience, and memory; Abstraction, which represented complex reasoning ability; Power, which provided the energy for intelligence; and the Directional Factor, which was based on the receptive and express abilities of the brain. Although subsequent research failed to find support for Halstead's theory of intelligence, Halstead's work was admired and lauded by many leading neurologists of his day, including Bucy, Lashley, Kluver, and McCullough (Reitan, 1994; Reitan & Wolfson, 1993).

Reitan's first empirical investigation of the HRB compared the results of 50 patients with brain damage and 50 control individuals who had no known neurological disease and who were comparable in age and level of education (Reitan, 1955a). Seven of Halstead's measures showed differences in mean performance between the two groups that were statistically significant at greater than the .000000000001 level, with the Category Test demonstrating the greatest sensitivity to neurologic impairment (Reitan & Wolfson, 1993). According to Reitan, these findings were even more noteworthy because most studies conducted at that time relied upon intelligence tests to assess cognitive functioning and typically identified only minimal effects of brain damage. Reitan added the Wechsler-Bellevue Scale to more thoroughly assess intellectual ability and added tests to assess motor and sensory-perceptual functioning to evaluate the functional integrity of both sides of the body (Reitan, 1975). Noting the complexity of brain-behavior relationships, Reitan described the primary task facing neuropsychologists as identifying "the most systematic and efficient way to develop a set of measures that represent the behavioral manifestations of brain functions" (Reitan, 1975, p. 190). His elegant research demonstrated the strong relationship between lateralized findings and dysfunction in the contralateral cerebral hemisphere (Reitan & Fitzhugh, 1971).

Reitan and Wolfson (1986a, 1988a) have developed a theory of brain-behavior relationships that provides a conceptual framework for interpreting the HRB. This hierarchical model requires sensory input to the brain from the external environment. After the senses have relayed this information to the brain, the first step in central processing represents attention, concentration, and memory, which is identified as the "registration phase." Because these abilities underlie many neuropsychological functions, it is important to assess alertness and concentration as part of a neuropsychological evaluation. In the HRB, these abilities are assessed by the Seashore Rhythm Test and the Speech Sounds Perception Test. Once information has been registered, it is processed by the specialized functions of each hemisphere. In general, language skills are processed in the left hemisphere, and visuospatial information is processed in the right hemisphere. The integrity of the left hemisphere is assessed via the Aphasia Screening Examination and the verbal subtests of the WAIS-R. Right hemisphere functioning is examined by the drawings on the Aphasia Screening Examination, the WAIS-R performance subtests, and, partially, by the Trail Making Test. Additional information about each hemisphere is provided by motor and sensory-perceptual tasks and by the Tactual Performance Test. The highest level of central processing is abstract reasoning and concept formation, which provide information "relevant to the complexity of real-life situations" (Reitan & Wolfson, 1986a, p. 138). This level is assessed by the Category Test, the Trail Making Test, and the overall performance on the Tactual Performance Test (TPT). Finally, output functions are assessed. Although not fully evaluated in the HRB, assessment of motor functions provides information about the integrity of cerebral functioning and motor output.

In addition to extensive formal research on the HRB dating back to the 1950s, Reitan conducted over 8,000 blind interpretations of patient performance on the HRB in which he analyzed test results and wrote reports without knowledge of the patient's history or neurological findings (Reitan & Wolfson, 1996). His findings were later corroborated with information independently obtained by neurologists, neurosurgeons, or pathologists that provided additional information about the battery's validity in assessing brain-behavior relationships. The HRB has been described as having "perhaps the most widespread impact of any approach in clinical neuropsychology" and as the "primary force in stimulating clinical research and application in this country" (Meier, 1985).

Although the HRB validation was based upon differentiating between groups of individuals with no evidence of neurologic impairment and those with known neurologic disorders, the application of the HRB with individual patients is clinically based and requires a clinical orientation, an integrated assessment approach, and a focus on individual characteristics (Reitan & Wolfson, 1993). Although the HRB has been criticized for being an actuarial approach (see Lezak, 1995), Reitan actually espouses clinical assessment of the individual patient (Russell, 1998). According to Reitan, the "important point to mention . . . is that a coalescence of experimental and clinical approaches permit application of assessment procedures to individual subjects in describing the uniqueness of their higher-level brain functions" (Reitan, 1975, p. 193). Russell emphasizes that pattern analysis requires the use of a fixed battery, such as the HRB, to provide a constant background on which variations in individual performance can be discerned. He argues that flexible batteries do not provide the foundation for pattern analysis and that they fail to assess the patient in his or her entirety.

PSYCHOMETRIC PROPERTIES

The HRB has been more thoroughly investigated than any other neuropsychological battery (Reitan & Wolfson, 1986a, 1993). Although most of the research has focused on the validity of the HRB, data are available on the HRB's reliability. Test-retest reliability for each test, based on administration of the entire battery, ranged from .87 on Trail Making, Part B, to .59 on TPT Localization (Klonoff, Fibiger, & Hutton, 1970). Matarazzo and colleagues (Matarazzo, Matarazzo, Wiens, Gallo, & Klonoff, 1976; Matarazzo, Wiens, Matarazzo, & Goldstein, 1974) found a high degree of clinical reliability (i.e., correctly classifying subjects based on the Halstead Impairment Index) for healthy men and for patients with schizophrenia or cerebrovascular disease or who had undergone endarterectomy. Research has indicated that the Category Test, TPT Localization, and the Impairment Index are most influenced by practice effects (Dodrill & Troupin, 1975). Patients with mild to moderate impairment are most likely to demonstrate practice effects as compared to patients with no impairments or with severe impairments (Franzen & Robbins, 1989). The performance of individuals with no impairments is likely to be affected by ceiling effects, whereas patients with severe impairments are not typically able to learn the tests well enough to demonstrate practice effects. Few studies have assessed the internal consistency of the HRB (Franzen & Robbins, 1989). The Category Test demonstrated a split-half reliability of .98 (Shaw, 1966), whereas two combinations of items from the Seashore Rhythm Test had split-half reliabilities of .77 and .74 (Bornstein, 1983).

The HRB has been described as one of only two validated neuropsychological batteries (Russell, 1998). As previously noted, Reitan's (1955a) original validation study yielded a significance level of .000000000001 in differentiating patients with no impairments from those with brain damage. Reitan developed his research systematically to assess the validity of the HRB for general to specific brain-behavior relationships (Reitan & Wolfson, 1993). He first investigated the overall effects of heterogeneous cerebral lesions, then studied the effects of lateralized brain lesions, and then the effects of regional localization. This research was followed by an examination of chronic and/or static lesions with acute and/or rapidly progressive lesions. Finally, Reitan studied the interaction among all of these variables. A later validation study by Reitan (1964) thoroughly documented the clinical utility of the HRB. This complex and impressive study examined the HRB performance of 64 patients with right anterior, left anterior, right posterior, or left posterior cerebral lesions with equal numbers in each group diagnosed with extrinsic tumors, intrinsic tumors, focal traumatic lesions, or cerebrovascular lesions. An additional 48 patients with diffuse cerebral dysfunction secondary to cerebral arteriosclerosis, closed head injury, or multiple sclerosis were also included. Blind interpretations of the patients' HRB performance were made and judgments were made as to whether the lesions were due to cerebrovascular disease, tumor, head injury, or multiple sclerosis. Tumors were rated as extrinsic or intrinsic, and head trauma was classified as either penetrating or closed head injury. Using this method of blind interpretation, an impressive 88 of the 112 patients were correctly classified based on their HRB performance. According to Russell (1998), "no other study since then has so well demonstrated the clinical validity of any battery or approach" (p. 373). According to Boll (1981), the first major cross validation study was conducted by Vega and Parsons in 1967. These researchers were able to discriminate individuals with brain damage from those without brain damage based on their HRB performance, despite the overall poorer performance for both groups when compared to Reitan's normative sample. A recent review of the validity of the HRB found that diagnostic accuracy of indices ranged from 58% to 92% and that, after consideration of the quality of various studies, the accuracy of clinical judgment in combination with HRB results was approximately 85% (Russell, 1995). The ability of the HRB to detect structural and functional changes in cerebral functioning is well documented (see extensive reviews in Kane, 1991; Reitan & Wolfson, 1986a; Russell, 1995). Additional validity data will be included in this chapter's section regarding the interpretation of specific HRB tests.

ASSETS AND LIMITATIONS

The primary assets of the HRB are its psychometrically sound and well-validated comprehensive assessment of a wide variety of neuropsychological functions, including indicators of cerebral dysfunction that might not be apparent during a clinical interview (Smith, Barth, Diamond, & Giuliano, 1998). In fact, the validity of the HRB is based on a larger number of empirical studies than is the validity of any other neuropsychological test (Jarvis & Barth, 1994). Furthermore, large standardization samples have been employed, and both general and specific indicators of brain functioning, such as the level of performance and pathognomonic signs, are included in the HRB (Smith et al., 1998). The HRB has been extensively validated with a variety of neuropathological conditions, which increases the confidence with which one can make diagnostic inferences regarding lesion detection and localization (Reitan & Wolfson, 1996). In addition, the HRB provides a consistent set of procedures that form the basis for analyzing a patient's pattern of performance as an inferential method for detecting neuropsychological impairment (Russell, 1998). The diagnostic utility of the HRB has increased with the publication of demographic adjustments for age and education (Heaton, Grant, & Matthews, 1991). The HRB assets far outweigh its limitations.

The HRB is often criticized for its lengthy administration time, which can become even more burdensome when supplementary measures are added, such as intellectual assessment, memory, and personality tests (Smith et al., 1998). A related issue is the expense to the patient or insurance company of such a lengthy assessment and the expense to the practitioner of obtaining the HRB test materials. As a fixed battery, the HRB has been criticized for limited flexibility in tailoring the assessment to patient needs and to the referral question (Lezak, 1995). In addition, the HRB does not assess verbal memory, which is a crucial area of examination, particularly for individuals who have experienced a head injury (Smith et al., 1998). It has also been criticized for its emphasis on quantitative scores rather than on qualitative factors that might have affected the patient's performance. Furthermore, the HRB, along with many other neuropsychological test-batteries, does not fully address issues related to the typical daily functioning of patients (i.e., issues of ecological validity), and, although general statements can be made, there is little information about the relationship between performance on the HRB and treatment planning.

Research has indicated that there are differences in performance on the HRB due to age, education, and gender (see Heaton, Ryan, Grant, & Matthews, 1996 for a review) that are not taken into account by Reitan's originally recommended methods of interpretation. According to Heaton and his colleagues, using standard cutoff scores on the HRB resulted in the misclassification of less educated and older subjects as "brain damaged." They argue that "standard cutoffs are not appropriate as norms for most subjects over the age of 60 or, equally important, for most subjects with less than a high school education, regardless of their age" (p. 149). Fortunately, use of the Heaton norms corrects for these important demographic variables. Reitan and Wolfson (1995b) have argued that the HRB scores of patients with neurologic impairment should not be corrected for age and education because their research indicates that these adjustments affect General Neuropsychological Deficit Scale (GNDS) scores only in individuals who are neurologically intact. Their research and conclusions have been criticized, however, because they used an "extremely diverse range" (p. 206) of patients with neurological impairments, they did not match the severity of impairment level in the neurologic patients across age and education subgroups, and they neglected to match groups by education when examining the effects of age and by education when examining age (Shuttleworth-Jordan, 1997). It has also been noted that the original HRB normative group ranged in age from 14 to 50 years with a mean age of 28.3 (Franzen & Robbins, 1989). This restriction in range raises serious concerns about the interpretation of the HRB with a sample of older people, and, as a result, Reitan and Wolfson's findings have been questioned due to the possible confounding variables that might have affected their research. A study that essentially replicated Reitan and Wolfson's study (1995b) found that when the Heaton norms (Heaton et al., 1991) were used, age and education had similar effects on neuropsychological summary scores (GNDS, Halstead Impairment Index, and Average Impairment Rating) for people both with and without neurological impairments (Vanderploeg, Axelrod, Sherer, Scott, & Adams, 1997). Across both groups, younger people performed better than older people, more educated people performed better than less educated people, and people without brain damage performed better than people with brain damage, even though the correlations between age, education, and the summary scores were low. The research of

Vanderploeg and colleagues also demonstrated that the use of the Heaton norms improved diagnostic accuracy as compared to the use of nonadjusted scores.

As with most neuropsychological tests, there are little data available on the performance of various ethnic or racial groups on the HRB. As a result, caution should be used when interpreting the performance of individuals who are not Caucasian (Heaton et al., 1996). Recent research indicates that performance of Latinos on several tests of the HRB was affected by level of acculturation (Arnold, Montgomery, Castaneda, & Longoria, 1994). For additional information on assessing patients with English as a second language, consult *A Compendium of Tests* (Spreen & Strauss, 1998), *Handbook of Neuropsychology with Hispanic Populations* (Ponton & Leon-Carrion, 1999), and *Handbook of Normative Data for Neuropsychological Assessment* (Mitrushina, Boone, & D'Elia, 1998, www.normativedata.com.net).

ADMINISTRATION

Detailed and extensive administration instructions are provided by Reitan and Wolfson (1993). These administration instructions emphasize that the "principal effort is aimed at eliciting the best performance of which the subject is capable" (p. 120) without providing any actual assistance in completing the task. Every effort should be made to ensure that patients understand what they are expected to do on each task. Instructions may be repeated, restated, and/or clarified as necessary. Patients may be prompted only when it becomes clear that they would not respond otherwise, but patients should be encouraged to attempt all items. Patients should not be allowed to erase or to cross out errors because these provide important diagnostic information. In order to elicit the patient's best performance, the examiner must be sure to establish good rapport, to interact with the patient in a friendly manner, and to be flexible and encouraging. It is also recommended that examiners tell patients prior to testing that it is important for them to put forth their best effort and explain that the tests are sensitive to any deficits they might be experiencing, so it is not necessary for them to exaggerate their difficulties. We also explain that they will find some tests to be quite easy whereas others might be quite difficult for them. Presenting this information prior to testing helps enlist the cooperation of patients, helps ensure their motivation, and minimizes their distress when they encounter more difficult tasks.

According to Reitan and Wolfson (1993), most invalid responses on the Sensory-Perceptual Examination are due to administration and procedural errors. It is the examiner's responsibility to ensure that the patient is actively attentive. The examiner may need to slow the pace of the examination, to periodically redirect the patient's attention to the task, and to determine if the patient is correctly perceiving the stimuli but responding incorrectly. For example, the patient may correctly perceive the tactile stimulation during the finger agnosia test, but have confused the numbers assigned to each finger. Additional cautions and clarifications in the administration of the Sensory-Perceptual Examination are provided in Reitan and Wolfson.

Administration of the HRB requires a high level of skill and attention to detail. Ideally, training in the administration of the HRB should begin with observation of a skilled examiner. Preferably, trainees should observe multiple administrations with a variety of patients. Once the trainee has demonstrated familiarity with the administration instructions and procedures by practicing on volunteers, the trainee should be observed multiple times while administering the HRB to volunteers and patients. Only after the trainee has demonstrated competence in administration should he or she be permitted to administer the battery independently. Because errors are frequently made in scoring or recording information on the data sheet, these should be double checked by a skilled examiner.

Neuropsychologists frequently employ trained psychometricians to administer the HRB. In fact, Halstead pioneered the use of nonprofessional, trained technicians in administering neuropsychological tests (Russell, Neuringer, & Goldstein, 1970). The use of psychometricians has been likened to the use of EEG technicians by neurologists and is a well-accepted practice that has been sanctioned by the Division of Clinical Neuropsychology of the American Psychological Association (Bigler & Dodrill, 1997; Goldstein, 1997). Psychometricians ensure that tests are administered in a standardized and reliable manner; the test data are then interpreted by a qualified neuropsychologist, along with information obtained by the neuropsychologist during the clinical interview. Some people have criticized the use of technicians because of concerns that technicians might be less likely to modify test administration procedures when necessary (Levin, 1994), and a recent position paper on neuropsychology suggested that neurologists should determine whether their neuropsychology referral sources utilize technicians (Report of the Therapeutics and Technology Assessment Subcommittee of the American Academy of Neurology, 1996).

As previously noted, the HRB does not adequately assess memory. Many neuropsychologists typically add the Rey Auditory Verbal Learning Test (Lezak, 1983), subtests from the Wechsler Memory Scale-Revised or Wechsler Memory Scale-III (Wechsler, 1987, 1997a), or other standardized memory tests. The Paced Auditory Serial Addition Test (Gronwall, 1977; Gronwall & Sampson, 1974) can be helpful in identifying subtle deficits in rapid new problem solving. The Grooved Pegboard (Kløve, 1963) and Grip Strength (Reitan & Wolfson, 1993) are frequently administered along with the Finger Tapping Test from the HRB and are used to make lateralizing determinations. The MMPI or MMPI-2 (Hathaway & McKinley, 1942, 1989) provides information about the psychological functioning of patients. Examination of the validity scales can yield clues as to the patient's symptom presentation (e.g., tendency to exaggerate or minimize symptoms). The use of collateral tests can enrich the data provided by the HRB (and Wechsler intelligence scales), increase the diagnostic accuracy of the neuropsychological evaluation, and assist in the development of treatment recommendations.

INTERPRETATION OF INDIVIDUAL TESTS

Tests of the Halstead-Reitan Neuropsychological Test Battery

The individual tests comprising the Halstead-Reitan Neuropsychological Test Battery (and allied procedures that are suggested as adjunct measures and that will be marked with a "+") are described. Some of the most important interpretations or hypotheses related to deficient or intact performance are considered, and brief summaries of research findings pertinent to each individual test are noted. This method of hypotheses generation and evaluation was developed by Jarvis and Barth (1994). It draws on the research of Reitan and others to raise issues (hypotheses) relevant to the determination of presence or absence, severity, velocity, lateralization, localization, and specific processes of neuropathology. Hypotheses noted in this chapter are based on Jarvis and Barth's *The Halstead-Reitan Neuropsychological Battery: A Guide to Interpretation and Clinical Applications.*

Although Reitan and Wolfson argue that psychiatric illness should not affect the performance of patients on the HRB (Reitan & Wolfson, 1997), the possibility that psychiatric symptoms may be contributing to patients' poor performance should be considered as a hypothesis to be actively ruled out, particularly by the beginning clinician who needs to develop sensitivity to *all* factors that might contribute to a patient's poor performance. As a result, psychiatric symptoms that *might* contribute to poor performance on various tests will be listed for consideration. Similarly, other factors that might result in poor performance, such as deficits in motivation or peripheral injuries, will be noted.

Category Test

The Category Test assesses abstract reasoning and complex concept formation. Due to its format, which requires that patients develop concepts using only feedback that the item has been solved correctly or incorrectly, this can be one of the more frustrating tasks for patients. The examiner presents the patient with a pattern of geometric figures and designs on a screen and instructs him or her to press the key that is suggested by the picture. Keys are numbered 1, 2, 3, and 4. If the patient presses the correct key, a bell sounds; whereas if the patient responds incorrectly, a buzzer sounds. With the exception of the last subtest, only one principle or idea underlies each subtest. Once the patient identifies a principle and applies it consistently, the patient will correctly solve each problem. At the beginning of each new subtest, the examiner informs the patient that a new subtest is beginning and that the idea or principle might be the same or it might be different and that it is up to the patient to identify the principle. The sixth and last subtest contains items from the other subtests and is the only subtest to contain more than one idea. Because patients may become frustrated or discouraged and begin responding randomly, the examiner should repeat or elaborate instructions as necessary and should encourage patients to think about their answers and why they might be incorrect. Additional administration information is provided in Reitan and Wolfson (1993).

The Category Test has been found to be robust to variations in method of administration (Holtz, Gearhart, & Watson, 1996; Mercer, Harrell, Miller, Childs, & Rockers, 1997). Mercer and colleagues (1997) compared the traditional version of the Category Test (Reitan & Wolfson, 1985) to the Booklet Category Test (DeFilippis & McCampbell, 1979) and to a computerized version of the Category Test (Miller, 1993) with samples of healthy adults and samples of adults with brain injuries who did not differ significantly with respect to age, education, or gender. They found that although there were some minor differences in the results for some subtests, there were no statistically significant differences in total score across groups and that each version produced the same number of false negative and false positive classifications. Higher scores on the Category Test reflect greater impairment.

A high score may indicate:

- *Cerebral dysfunction.* The Category Test is second only to the Halstead Impairment Index (HII) as the most sensitive indicator of brain impairment (Reitan, 1959b).
- *A focal, static lesion of the anterior frontal lobes* if the Trails B performance is also poor and other tests are nearly normal (Reitan, 1959b). Interpret with caution, however, because the Category Test is not a test of frontal lobe functions (Reitan & Wolfson, 1995c).
- *Parkinson's disease.* Patients with Parkinson's disease typically have average intellectual ability with deficits on the Category Test, the Trail Making and motor tests, and a high HII (Reitan & Boll, 1971).
- *Alcoholism.* Patients with a history of alcoholism typically have overall intact intellectual ability but significant deficits on the Category Test, memory tests, and other HRB tests (Grant, 1987).

Low scores may indicate:

- *The absence of large cerebrovascular accidents (CVAs) or intracerebral tumors,* even if the HII is high and other HRB tests are impaired, but performance on the Category Test and the Seashore Rhythm Test is acceptable (Reitan, 1972; Reitan & Wolfson, 1993).
- *Good prognosis for recovery of language functions,* even in the presence of indicators of left hemisphere dysfunction, if the HII is low and the Category Test, the Speech Sounds Perception, and the Seashore Rhythm performance are within normal limits (Reitan, 1959b).
- *Multiple sclerosis* may be suggested by good performance on the Category Test in conjunction with poor performance on the TPT (Reitan & Wolfson, 1993).

The Category Test's sensitivity to the detection of cerebral dysfunction has been called "indisputable" (Choca, Laatsch, Wetzel, & Agresti, 1997). It is the *single test that is most sensitive to the detection of damage occurring anywhere in the brain* (Jarvis & Barth, 1994; Reitan, 1959b). Research indicates, however, that it lacks specificity and does not contribute to the localization of cognitive dysfunction (see Choca et al., 1997, for a review). Although it is commonly thought of as a test of frontal lobe functions, research indicates that scores on the Category Test do not discriminate between patients with frontal lesions and patients with nonfrontal lesions (Reitan & Wolfson, 1995a). Scores on the Category Test tend to be negatively correlated with measures of intellectual ability, particularly nonverbal intellectual ability (Cullum, Steinam, & Bigler, 1984). A factor analytic study, however, found that the Category Test measures two distinct reasoning processes, spatial reasoning and proportional reasoning, that are different from those abilities tapped by the WAIS-R (Johnstone, Holland, & Hewett, 1997). Principal components analysis revealed that the Category Test loads heavily on conceptual reasoning ability even after removing the variance due to WAIS-R Full Scale IQ scores, which also indicates that the Category Test is not merely a weak indication of general intellectual ability (O'Donnell, MacGregor, Dabrowski, Oestreicher, & Romero, 1994).

Seashore Rhythm Test

The Seashore Rhythm Test is based upon the Seashore Tests of Musical Ability (Jarvis & Barth, 1994). It assesses the ability to discriminate between pairs of nonverbal, rhythmic sounds, as well as sustained attention and concentration to auditory stimuli. The test requires adequate hearing ability and visual acuity that is sufficient for patients to appropriately mark the answer sheet. The test is administered by a tape recorder that has 30 pairs of rhythmic sounds. Patients are asked to write an "S" if the sounds are the same and a "D" if they are different in each of the three, 10-item subtests. The recording moves at a quick pace, and the pairs are not numbered on the recording. If patients become momentarily distracted, they may lose their place and have difficulty recovering until the beginning of the next subtest. The tape player should be placed directly in front of the patient, with the volume adjusted so that it can be easily heard by the patient. The first three items are played for the patient as samples and then readministered when the actual test begins. The number of correct responses is recorded on the answer sheet. Higher scores on the Seashore Rhythm Test indicate better performance, while lower scores reflect impaired performance.

Intact scores may indicate:

- A diminished likelihood of a rapidly progressive lesion (Reitan, 1959b; Reitan & Wolfson, 1993).
- Good post-trauma recovery (Reitan, 1959a, 1972; Reitan & Wolfson, 1993).

Impaired performance may indicate:

- General brain tissue destruction (Golden, 1978).
- A left temporal lesion if aphasic signs are also observed (Reitan & Wolfson, 1993).
- Attention deficits.
- Hearing loss.

The Seashore Rhythm Test has demonstrated sensitivity to the detection of brain damage, but it does not appear to contribute lateralizing information or to uniquely assess attention (Reitan & Wolfson, 1993; Sherer, Parsons, Nixon, & Adams, 1991). It has been recommended that the Seashore Rhythm Test not be used in isolation because there are concerns about its low reliability and because the items have been found to be "too easy" for the majority of patients (Charter & Webster, 1997).

Speech Sounds Perception Test

The Speech Sounds Perception test assesses sustained attention and perception of verbal stimuli (i.e., nonsense syllables). It is similar to the Seashore Rhythm Test in that it is administered by a tape recorder. In contrast, however, its answer sheet is numbered, the pace is slower, and the number of stimuli presented is twice as great as the Seashore Rhythm Test (Jarvis & Barth, 1994). Sixty nonsense syllables containing the "ee" sound are presented, and patients are asked to underline on an answer sheet the matching sound from a list of four nonsense syllable choices. It requires a longer period of sustained attention and concentration compared to the Seashore Rhythm Test, but the numbered items provide greater structure, which enables patients who are distracted to quickly find their place. The Speech Sounds Perception Test also requires adequate visual acuity and hearing ability. The number of errors is recorded on the scoring sheet.

Scores can be interpreted as follows:

- Higher scores reflect impaired performance, whereas lower scores indicate intact abilities.
- The interpretative considerations for the Seashore Rhythm Test also apply to Speech Sounds Perception: Impaired performance indicates general brain tissue destruction, left temporal lesion if aphasic signs are present, attention deficits, or hearing loss. Intact performance indicates diminished likelihood of a rapidly progressive lesion and good post-trauma recovery.

A review of the literature (Sherer et al., 1991) revealed that the Speech Sounds Perception Test is generally sensitive to the presence of brain damage, but its purported ability to aid in the detection of left hemisphere dysfunction has inconsistent research support. An empirical study conducted by Sherer and his colleagues found that the Speech Sounds Perception Test significantly discriminated between patients with brain-damage and "pseudoneurologic" symptoms, but it failed to distinguish among patients with right hemisphere, left hemisphere, or diffuse dysfunction. These authors also found that Speech Sounds Perception Test performance is not "uniquely" associated with attention and should not be considered a measure of attention.

Tactual Performance Test (TPT)

The Tactual Performance Test assesses psychomotor problem-solving ability and incidental spatial memory, all in the absence of visual cues. The patient is blindfolded prior to the exposure of the form board, and the form board should be taken from view prior to the removal of the blindfold. Patients should never see the form board to avoid compromising the integrity of the test. After the patient has been blindfolded, the examiner explains that the patient is to place large wooden blocks of different shapes into cutouts on a form board in front of them. The examiner moves the patient's hand across the blocks and around the outline of the form board to orient him or her. Once the trial begins, the patient is to pick up each block and place it into the appropriate space on the form board using only the dominant hand. The trial is repeated using only the nondominant hand, followed by a trial in which the patient is allowed to use both hands simultaneously. Occasionally the blindfold may slip or loosen, or patients may actively attempt to peek. The examiner should be vigilant and ensure that patients are not able to see the form board or blocks. In addition, it is common to find patients attempting to use the wrong hand. Such attempts must be caught and the patient redirected to use the appropriate hand. After the three trials are completed and the form board is removed from view, the examiner removes the blindfold and asks the patient to draw an outline of the form board and, in their proper location, as many shapes as can be recalled. Any misshapen drawings should be queried to determine if the patient accurately recalled a shape that was poorly drawn. The time to complete each trial and the total time for completing all three trials is recorded, along with the number of shapes recalled (i.e., TPT Memory) and the number of shapes recalled in their appropriate location (i.e., TPT Localization). The TPT requires the integration of various abilities for successful performance, including sensory ability, motor functions, problem-solving skills, and interhemispheric transfer of information. The traditional expectation was that the nonpreferred hand would perform 30 to 40% faster than the preferred hand in individuals without neurological impairment (due to learning and transfer of information from one cerebral hemisphere to the other through the corpus callosum) and that deviations from this pattern were indicative of cerebral dysfunction and lateralization (Golden, 1978). More recent research, however, has provided the following interpretative guidelines (hypotheses):

- A lesion in the contralateral hemisphere to the nonpreferred hand is possible if the nonpreferred hand fails to perform 20% faster than the preferred hand in patients 40 years old or younger and with more than nine years of education (Thompson, Heaton, Matthews, & Grant, 1987).

- A lesion in the contralateral hemisphere to the preferred hand is possible if the nonpreferred hand performs more than 30% faster than the preferred hand in patients 40 years old or younger and with more than nine years of education (Thompson et al., 1987).

- For patients with fewer than nine years of education or over 40 years of age, fluctuations from the previous two relationships are not necessarily clinically significant (Thompson et al., 1987).

- As previously noted, one deviation on motor tests from expected relationships between the preferred and nonpreferred hands is not necessarily clinically significant because the majority of non-impaired individuals have at least one discrepant finding (Thompson et al., 1987); three or more consistent findings on the TPT, Finger Tapping, Grip Strength, and Grooved Pegboard is very atypical and suggests cerebral dysfunction with possible lateralizing significance.

- When the third trial is slower than both the first and the second trials, it is an indication of severe impairment, such as an intracerebral neoplasm or other tissue destroying lesion (Jarvis & Barth, 1994); when the third trial is slower, it suggests that the impaired performance of one hand is interfering with the performance of the other hand.

- If performance steadily declines across all three trials, fatigue, poor motivation, resistance, or depression may be factors (Jarvis & Barth, 1994).

- Poor performance on the TPT might also be indicative of peripheral injuries; the patient should be queried as to any history of injury to the shoulders, the arms, or the hands.

- The TPT Localization score is the third most sensitive indicator of cerebral dysfunction (Reitan, 1959b).

- A contralateral posterior lesion (away from the motor strip) is suggested if the TPT performance is more impaired than the Finger Tapping score with the same hand; conversely, if the TPT performance is better than the Finger Tapping score, a contralateral anterior lesion is suggested (Reitan, 1959b).
- When right-hand TPT and Finger Tapping performance are within normal limits, but other indicators of left cerebral hemisphere dysfunction are present (e.g., lowered VIQ, dysphasia), a focal lesion that is situated away from the motor strip is suggested (Reitan, 1959b).
- There is no lateralizing significance for TPT Memory and Localization scores (Reitan & Wolfson, 1993).

A series of discriminant analyses revealed that the TPT Total Time and TPT Location were among the best predictors of impairment in a study that examined patients with verified brain disease and a pseudoneurologic control group (Mutchnick, Ross, & Long, 1991). Using an 18-variable combination, these authors found that TPT Total Time and TPT Memory were among the top five predictors of cerebral dysfunction. The TPT can also provide important qualitative information, as well as quantitative data (Heilbronner & Parsons, 1989).

Finger Tapping Test

The Finger Tapping Test, also known as the Finger Oscillation Test, assesses upper extremity gross motor speed and contributes to the Halstead Impairment Index. The test equipment consists of a small lever or telegraph-type key attached to a flat board with a mechanical counter. The examiner asks the patient to tap as rapidly as possible with his or her dominant hand index finger for five, 10-second trials. The procedure is then repeated with the patient's nondominant hand. Reitan suggests that patients should never be allowed to alternate trials between their dominant and nondominant hands. A brief, mandatory rest period is required after the third trial to minimize fatigue, and patients are encouraged to practice briefly before beginning the trials. The average number of taps per hand across trials is then computed. Examiners are cautioned to be careful to start the stopwatch when the patient makes the first tap rather than when the examiner says, "Go," because the test is not a measure of reaction time. The examiner must also be vigilant and observe the number on the counter when the 10 seconds are up. Patients often continue to tap a few extra times after the trial is over, and these taps must be subtracted from the score for the trial. Because patients often demonstrate variability in performance across trials, the examiner must obtain 5 consecutive trials that are within 5 taps of each other. Up to, but not more than, 10 trials may be administered in order to obtain relatively consistent performance across trials. If 10 trials are administered and no 5 are within 5 taps of each other, the highest and the lowest scores can be dropped and an average calculated for the remaining 8 trials (Jarvis & Barth, 1994). The examiner should also make sure that the patient uses only the index finger during this test, without large movements of the hand and arm, and keeps the heel of the hand on the board during tapping trials.

Higher scores on this test reflect a greater degree of fine motor speed, whereas lower scores are indicative of impaired performance. In patients who are right-hand dominant, the right-hand performance should be approximately 10% better than the left-hand performance. Patients with left-hand dominance might show more equal performance between their two hands or better left-hand performance.

Bilateral high scores may indicate:

- The absence of cerebral dysfunction.
- The absence of peripheral injury.

Bilateral low scores may indicate:

- Cerebral dysfunction.
- Peripheral injury.
- Fatigue, general weakness, and/or psychomotor retardation (e.g., systemic illness, depression).
- Poor effort or motivation.

Unilateral deficits may indicate:

- Cerebral dysfunction in the contralateral hemisphere.
- Anterior lesion near the motor strip if Finger Tapping and Grip Strength are impaired (Reitan, 1959b).
- Unilateral peripheral injury.
- Contralateral CVA if discrepancy between hands is significant (Reitan & Wolfson, 1993).
- Contralateral anterior lesion if TPT with the same hand is intact or less impaired (Reitan, 1959b).

Variations in performance are common with the majority of patients failing to demonstrate the "expected" 10% better performance with the dominant hand on one of the four motor tests (TPT, Finger Tapping, Grip Strength, Grooved Pegboard; Thompson et al., 1987). Discrepancies of more than one standard deviation in a consistent direction on three of the motor tests are highly unusual, however, as are two discrepancies of more than two standard deviations in the same direction (Thompson et al., 1987). Therefore, performance on motor tests should not be interpreted in isolation; instead, the pattern of performance across motor tests should be examined.

Trail Making Test, A and B

The Trail Making Test, Part A, assesses simple cognitive processing speed. Part B assesses complex cognitive processing speed and mental flexibility. Both parts require visual scanning skills and attention. The Trail Making Test is a two-part, timed, paper-and-pencil test. Both Parts A and B are preceded by samples to ensure that patients understand the directions. Part A consists of circles that are numbered from 1 to 25 and that are randomly distributed across a page. The examiner asks patients to draw a line from circle number 1 to circle number 2 to circle number 3, and so on, as fast as possible. The time to complete the task in seconds is noted. The examiner quickly points out any errors to patients and quickly redirects patients to their last correct circle. On Part

B, the circles contain both numbers and letters. The examiner asks patients to integrate and sequence the numbers and letters by drawing a line from 1 to A, A to 2, 2 to B, and so on, as quickly as possible. For both Parts A and B, the examiner quickly points out errors to patients, quickly redirects them to their last correct point, and asks them to continue. Errors are noted but are not deducted from the time to completion because errors contribute to a slower overall performance. On the Trail Making Test, higher scores reflect poorer performance, while lower scores are indicative of better performance.

Higher scores (slower times) may indicate:

- Cerebral dysfunction; Trails B is the fourth most sensitive score in the HRB battery, behind the HII, Category Test, and TPT Localization (Reitan, 1959b).
- A static or focal lesion of the anterior frontal lobes if performance on the Category Test is also poor and other tests are within normal limits or nearly so (Reitan, 1959b); however, this should be interpreted with caution because these tests are not measures of frontal lobe functioning (Reitan & Wolfson, 1995a).
- Slow cognitive processing speed.
- Visual scanning deficits due to central or peripheral dysfunction (e.g., macular degeneration).
- Depression with psychomotor retardation.
- Lack of motivation or effort.

Lower scores (better) may indicate:

- Absence of cerebral dysfunction.
- Absence of visual scanning deficits.

Early studies revealed that the Trail Making Test was able to discriminate between patients with and patients without neurologic impairment (Reitan, 1955c, 1958). Although the Trail Making Test is remarkably sensitive to brain dysfunction, it is not able to discriminate between patients with frontal lesions and patients with nonfrontal lesions (Reitan & Wolfson, 1995a). Therefore, it should not be thought of as a "frontal lobe" test. Principal components analysis revealed that Part B of the Trail Making Test loads on both visual scanning, attention, and conceptual reasoning (O'Donnell et al., 1994). In fact, the correlations between Part B and conceptual reasoning measures (Category Test and Wisconsin Card Sorting Test) were almost as strong as the association between Part B and measures of attention (Visual Search and Attention Test and Paced Auditory Serial Addition Test). These relationships persisted even after WAIS-R Full Scale IQ was partialled out. Other research indicated that Trails B had a greater loading on visuospatial intelligence than on attention and information processing; however, measures of perceptual motor speed were not included, which might have altered these findings (Larrabee & Curtiss, 1995). There is also evidence to suggest that Trails B is more difficult than Trails A not only because it demands greater cognitive skills, but also because it requires greater motor speed and visual search skills (Gaudino, Geisler, & Squires, 1995). Overall, Trails B appears to be a complex measure of multiple cognitive functions (Gaudino et al., 1995; Larrabee & Curtiss, 1995).

Reitan-Indiana Aphasia Screening Test

The Aphasia Screening Test consists of a variety of simple tasks that are easy for most non-impaired adults, but that can identify pathognomonic signs in individuals with specific cognitive dysfunction. The instructions to patients note that many of the tasks are quite simple, but that it is important for patients to complete each item carefully and to put forth their best effort. It is important for this point to be communicated to ensure that patients do not make careless errors or respond hastily to these apparently easy tasks.

The Aphasia Screening Test begins with the examiner asking patients to draw a square (shown to them in a booklet) without lifting their pencil from the paper. The examiner then asks patients to name the square and to spell the word *square.* This procedure is repeated with a cross and a triangle (i.e., draw it, name it, spell it). An example of a possible pathognomonic error (i.e., possible dysnomia) is the patient's naming the cross as a "Red Cross sign" (Reitan & Wolfson, 1993). The examiner asks patients to name drawings of a baby and of a fork and to write the name of a clock depicted in a drawing without saying the name out loud. Next, the examiner asks patients to read material of increasing length (e.g., "M G W"; "See the black dog"; "He is a friendly animal, a famous winner of dog shows"). Articulation is assessed by having patients repeat words stated by the examiner. These items are "triangle," "Massachusetts," and "Methodist Episcopal." The examiner then asks the patient to copy the word *square,* which is printed in the stimulus booklet, onto his or her paper. If the patient prints it, he or she is asked to write it in cursive. Next, the examiner asks patients to read the word *seven* printed in the stimulus booklet and to repeat the word *seven* as spoken by the examiner. After patients repeat the phrase "He shouted the warning," the examiner tells them to explain the meaning of that sentence in their own words and then to write the sentence on their paper. This is followed by two simple arithmetic problems. For one problem, the use of paper and pencil is encouraged, whereas the other one must be done without paper and pencil. The examiner then asks patients to name a key shown in the booklet, to demonstrate its use, and to draw a reasonable facsimile on their paper. The final items assess left-right orientation (e.g., "Place left hand to right ear"; Place left hand to right ear") and subtle confusion of body parts ("Put your left hand to your left elbow").

Reitan and Wolfson (1993) provide detailed scoring criteria with excellent examples. They recommend that the Aphasia Screening Test not be evaluated in a pass-fail manner, but that it should be used to identify specific deficits or pathognomonic signs that are indicative of specific cerebral dysfunction. Tables 7.1 and 7.2 present descriptions of the technical terms for various types of errors on the Aphasia Screening Test and their correspondence with left, right, and diffuse cerebral dysfunction. The Aphasia Screening Test aids in the identification of pathognomonic signs. If signs of aphasia are observed, a more thorough aphasia evaluation may be indicated. Test errors and their possible implications (hypotheses) are described as follows:

- Aphasia signs are frequently indicative of left cerebral hemisphere dysfunction (Reitan, 1959a; Reitan & Wolfson, 1993).
- Left cerebral hemisphere impairment is suggested by dysnomia, dyslexia, dysgraphia, spelling dyspraxia, and dyscalculia (Reitan, 1959b). Other indicators

Table 7.1.   Deficits identified by the Reitan-Indiana aphasia screening test

Term	Definition
Auditory Verbal Dysgnosia	A deficit in the ability to comprehend verbal communication through the auditory avenue.
Body Dysgnosia	Inability to identify or errors in identifying body parts.
Central Dysarthria	Omission, addition, or transposing of syllables in enunciating multi-syllabic words; as contrasted with slurring or unclear enunciation of the sounds involved.
Constructional Dyspraxia	A deficit in constructing (drawing) simple spatial configurations, with distortion of spatial relationships.
Dyscalculia	An inadequate ability to perform simple arithmetical calculations because of impaired understanding of the procedures involved or of quantitative relationships.
Dysgraphia	A deficit in the ability to write letters and words legibly, characterized by improper construction of the spatial configuration of letters.
Dyslexia	A deficit in the ability to read words and sentences.
Dysnomia	A deficit in the ability to name common objects.
Right/Left Confusion	Incorrect identification of the right and left sides of the subjects own body.
Spelling Dyspraxia	A deficit in spelling of the kind associated with cerebral damage.
Visual Letter Dysgnosia	A deficit in recognizing and correctly identifying individual letters of the alphabet.
Visual Number Dysgnosia	A deficit in recognizing and correctly identifying individual numbers or number combinations.

Reprinted by special permission: From Reitan, R.M., & Wolfson, D. (1995). *Advanced workshop in neurological inferences of underlying brain disorder.* Tucson, AZ: Neuropsychology Press, pp. 1–316.

include drawing the clock instead of writing the word (Reitan & Wolfson, 1993), central dysarthria, and reading "7 SIX 2" as "7-S-I-X-2" (Reitan, 1972).

- Left anterior impairment is suggested by signs of expressive aphasia, such as dysnomia, dysgraphia, and spelling dyspraxia (Reitan, 1959b).
- Left posterior impairment is suggested by signs of receptive aphasia, auditory verbal agnosia, visual letter agnosia, visual form agnosia, and auditory number agnosia (Reitan, 1959b).
- Right hemisphere impairment is suggested by constructional dyspraxia; but 15 to 20% of patients with this pathognomonic sign have only left hemisphere dysfunction, so interpret with caution (Reitan, 1959b).
- Right parietal impairment is suggested by neglecting the left side of a stimulus (e.g., reading the stimulus "M-G-W" as "G-W") or by constructional dyspraxia with a Block Design score that is much lower than Picture Arrangement (Golden, 1978).

Sensory-Perceptual Examination

The Sensory-Perceptual Examination is a simple series of tests that require skill, experience, and attention to detail by the examiner. Until the examiner has gained sufficient

Table 7.2.   Percentage of each criterion group showing a positive sign for each variable in the Reitan-Indiana Aphasia Screening Test

Left and right indicators are separated and listed by rank-order of deficits in each group. (These data are based on groups of adult subjects who had the advantage of normal brains with which to develop their neuropsychological abilities, even though 3 of the 4 groups sustained or developed brain lesions after physical maturation.)

Test Variable: Left Indicator	Criterion Groups			
	Left	Right	Diffuse	Control
Dyscalculia	55.32	14.04	20.37	00.00
Central dysarthria	55.32	10.53	37.04	08.65
Dysnomia	53.19	00.00	16.67	00.96
Dysgraphia	51.06	01.75	25.93	00.00
Spelling dyspraxia	48.94	05.26	16.67	06.73
Dyslexia	46.81	00.00	20.37	00.00
Right-left disorientation	42.55	05.26	29.63	09.62
Right finger agnosia	36.17	01.75	25.93	00.96
Right dysstereognosis	29.79	01.75	09.26	00.00
Visual letter dysgnosia	25.53	00.00	07.41	00.00
Right tactile imperception	14.89	00.00	18.52	00.00
Auditory verbal dysgnosia	12.77	00.00	07.41	00.00
Visual number dysgnosia	10.64	00.00	01.85	00.00

Test Variable: Right Indicator	Left	Right	Diffuse	Control
Constructional dyspraxia	14.89	61.40	44.44	07.69
Left dysstereognosis	02.13	29.82	11.11	00.00
Left finger dysgnosia	00.00	28.07	16.67	02.88
Left tactile imperception	02.13	21.05	14.81	00.00
Left visual imperception	02.13	15.79	07.41	00.00
Left auditory imperception	02.13	14.04	18.52	00.00

*Reprinted with permission. From Wheeler, I., & Reitan, R.M. (1962). Presence and laterality of brain damage predicted from responses to a short aphasia screening test. *Perceptual and Motor Skills, 15,* 783–799.

experience, it is recommended that he or she record immediately any patient errors because of their important diagnostic significance. With experience, examiners are better able to recall errors correctly and to record them during natural breaks in testing (Reitan & Wolfson, 1993). Tactile, auditory, and visual modalities are first assessed with stimulation to one side of the body (known as unilateral stimulation). Unilateral stimulation is used in order to determine that patients can respond to stimulation on both sides of the body and to identify the minimal stimulation necessary to elicit a correct response. It should also be noted that errors in unilateral stimulation, especially tactile perception, may have lateralizing significance, although errors in auditory unilateral stimulation may be indicative of unilateral peripheral hearing loss (Reitan & Wolfson,

1993). **Sensory-suppression** refers to the inability to perceive a stimulus on one side of the body when both sides are stimulated simultaneously. **Bilateral simultaneous sensory stimulation** assesses the receptive abilities of the brain and the possibility of cortical suppressions. Therefore, examiners should be alert to any signs of confusion by the patient. If left-right confusion is noted in patient responses, the following procedures may be modified so that patients point to the side that has been stimulated (Reitan & Wolfson, 1993).

Because there are many commonalities in interpreting sensory results across modalities, a few general rules will be noted. First, suppression errors typically do not occur in neurologically intact individuals (Golden, 1978; Heaton et al., 1991). Patients who are inattentive, however, may occasionally make errors. Again, it is important for examiners to continually redirect patients' attention during sensory testing to ensure their maximum effort. Intact performance on suppression testing indicates that an acutely destructive, posterior-space-occupying lesion is not likely (Reitan, 1959b). Conversely, severe, unilateral, sensory perceptual deficits may indicate either an acute cerebrovascular disorder or a rapidly progressive intracerebral neoplasm (Reitan, 1959b, 1972). The following are the subtests of the Sensory-Perceptual Examination:

Sensory-Imperception Examination-Tactile   The examiner asks patients to place their hands palm down on a table and to close their eyes. The examiner then *lightly* touches the back of the patient's hand and asks the patient to say "right" if the right hand has been touched and "left" if the left hand has been touched. After determining the lightest stimulation that can be perceived by the patient, the examiner then touches the patient's right hand, left hand, and both hands simultaneously in random order for a total of 12 stimulations. The examiner should not tell the patient that both hands will be touched simultaneously and should not give bilateral stimulation on consecutive trials (Reitan & Wolfson, 1993). After completing the trials with both hands, a similar procedure is followed in which either the patient's right hand, the left side of the face, or both are touched, followed by the left hand, the right side of the face, or both. If patients have difficulty keeping their eyes closed, the examiner may blindfold them.

Tactile suppressions may indicate:

- Parietal lobe dysfunction (Golden, Osman, Moses, & Berg, 1981).
- Vascular lesions.

Sensory-Imperception Examination-Auditory   During auditory stimulation, the examiner stands behind the seated patient and makes a barely perceptible sound by rubbing the thumb and another finger across each other near each ear. It is important not to touch the ear or the patient's hair to avoid giving tactile cues. Older individuals and others with hearing loss may require increased stimulation (i.e., a louder sound) in order to perceive it. Once it has been determined that a patient can hear the unilateral stimulation, additional unilateral and bilateral stimulation is administered in random order.

Auditory suppressions may indicate:

- A lesion in the contralateral temporal lobe (Reitan, 1959b).

Sensory-Imperception Examination-Visual   The examiner should be seated approximately 4 feet away from and facing the seated patient during visual stimulation. The examiner's arms are extended to approximately 24 inches on each side and about 1 foot above eye level. Stimulation is administered by moving the index finger of each hand. The examiner instructs the patient to focus on the examiner's nose and to indicate whether the stimulation has occurred on the patient's left side or right side. Stimulation is presented unilaterally and simultaneously to both sides in random fashion. The examiner repeats this procedure with his or her hands at eye level and then at approximately 1 foot below eye level. It should be noted that this test can be very confusing for the beginning examiner because patients are instructed to identify stimulation on their right side or left side, which is the opposite side for the examiner. Extreme care must be taken to accurately record the side of the patient's error.

Visual suppressions may indicate:

- Dysfunction in the contralateral cerebral hemisphere (Golden, 1978; Golden et al., 1981).

Visual field defects may indicate:

- Temporal or parietal dysfunction, particularly due to a CVA or to intracerebral neoplasm (Reitan & Wolfson, 1993).
- The presence of tissue-destroying lesions (Reitan & Wolfson, 1993).
- Damage anterior to the optic chiasm, such as a peripheral lesion of the eye or an extracerebral neoplasm if there is complete loss of vision in one eye (Jarvis & Barth, 1994).
- A lesion near the optic chiasm such as that seen in pituitary tumors if there is complete loss of vision in one eye and loss of vision in half of the other visual field (Reitan, 1972).

Tactile Finger Recognition Test   The Tactile Finger Recognition Test assesses the inability to localize tactile finger stimulation, known as finger **agnosia.** As with the other sensory tests, the examiner uses only very light stimulation, and the patient's eyes are closed. The examiner asks the patient to place his or her hand palm down on the table and then touches each finger and gives it a number. For instance, the thumb is identified as number one, the index finger as number two, and so on. Once the fingers have been so identified, the examiner touches the patient's fingers in random order and asks the patient to identify the touched finger by number. This test is first carried out with the dominant hand and then the nondominant hand.

Errors may indicate:

- Parietal lobe dysfunction (Golden et al., 1981).
- Peripheral neuropathy.
- Cerebrovascular lesions.
- Inattention.

Finger-Tip Number Writing Perception Test This test assesses dysgraphesthesia, which is the patient's ability to discern numbers written on their finger tips. The examiner asks the patient to place his or her hands palm up on a table and then writes the numbers 3, 4, 5, and 6 on the palm with a stylus using a "form that might resemble 'first grade instruction'" (Reitan & Wolfson, 1993, p. 257). In contrast to the other tactile tests, this test requires the use of steady pressure in writing the numbers. Once the examiner demonstrates the numbers on the patient's palm, he or she writes the numbers on the patient's finger tips, first on the dominant hand and then on the nondominant hand, in a specified sequence and asks the patient to verbally identify the number. The sequence in which numbers are presented is listed on the Sensory-Perceptual Examination recording sheet. The examiner may need to remind patients to keep their eyes closed during this test. Beginning examiners should note that the first box on the recording form (i.e., furthest left) lists the numbers to be written on the thumb for trials one through four with each hand, the second box contains the numbers to be written on the index finger for all four trials, and so on. It may help the examiner to write the name of the finger above each box to aid in careful documentation of patient responses.

Errors may indicate:

- Parietal lobe dysfunction (Golden et al., 1981).
- Peripheral neuropathy.
- Vascular lesions.
- Inattention or confusion.

Tactile Form Recognition Test The Tactile Form Recognition Test assesses patients' ability to discriminate shapes with their hands, also known as **stereognosis.** The patient's right hand, regardless of handedness, is visually screened by a form board that has four small shapes (triangle, circle, cross, and square) across the top. The examiner places one of the shapes in the patient's hand on the other side of the form board and asks the patient to point to the matching shape on the form board. The examiner records the number of seconds that it took for the patient to identify the shape, as well as any errors in identification. The procedure is repeated with the left hand, and another trial is administered with the right hand followed by the left hand. Misidentification of the circle has the greatest pathognomonic significance (Jarvis & Barth, 1994).

Errors may indicate:

- Parietal lobe dysfunction (Golden et al., 1981).
- Vascular lesions.

Grip Strength Test (+)

The Grip Strength Test assesses upper extremity motor strength. One of the quickest and easiest tests to administer, it requires that patients squeeze a hand dynamometer as hard as possible. The examiner adjusts the dynamometer to fit the hands of the patient and asks the patient to stand with his or her arm straight down and the dynamometer pointing toward the floor. The examiner administers two trials for each hand with the trials alternating between dominant and nondominant hands. If the second trial for either hand is not within 5 kilograms, however, the examiner conducts additional trials until two trials are obtained within 5 kilograms.

Higher scores on this test reflect greater upper extremity motor strength; lower scores are indicative of less strength. Performance on this test provides information related to lateralization of cerebral dysfunction. It is particularly important to consider gender, age, and extent of physical activity (e.g., laborer vs. sedentary job) in interpreting Grip Strength. It is interesting that the average difference in Grip Strength between hands in neurologically intact individuals is only 7.7%, and significant variability in performance between both hands is often observed (Thompson et al., 1987).

Interpretation of scores:

- See the hypotheses listed for the Finger Tapping Test.

Grooved Pegboard Test (+)

The Grooved Pegboard Test provides information about manual dexterity and eye-hand coordination. The examiner instructs the patient to pick up small, key-shaped, metal pegs with the dominant hand and to insert them into matching keyholes. The keyholes are arrayed in five rows with five holes per row. The examiner records the amount of time it takes the patient to insert all of the pegs and the number of pegs that are dropped. The task is then repeated with the nondominant hand. Patients frequently must be reminded to use only the hand being assessed.

Higher scores on this test reflect impaired performance; lower scores indicate intact functioning. The caveats noted for Grip Strength also apply to Grooved Pegboard with even greater variability in performance between hands likely for the latter (Thompson et al., 1987). As a result, extreme caution should be used in interpreting laterality based on Grooved Pegboard performance.

Interpretation of scores:

- See the hypotheses for the Finger Tapping Test.

Lateral Dominance Examination (+)

The Lateral Dominance Examination is designed to aid in the determination of patients' dominant hands, feet, and eyes. The examiner asks patients to perform or to pantomime a variety of tasks (e.g., throwing a ball, turning a door knob, using scissors, and kicking a football) and to write their name. The hand used spontaneously is considered to be the preferred, or dominant, hand. The examiner records the amount of time that the patient requires to write his or her name and then repeats the procedure with the nonpreferred hand. This test is typically administered first in order to determine hand dominance for other tests, such as the TPT or motor tests.

Halstead Impairment Index

The Halstead Impairment Index (HII) is comprised of the seven tests originally included in the HRB by Ward Halstead: Category Test, TPT Total Time, TPT Memory, TPT Localization, Seashore Rhythm, Speech Sounds Perception, and dominant hand Finger Tapping. Test scores that fall in the impaired range based on cutoff points are considered impaired. The cutoff points are listed in Table 7.3. To calculate the Halstead Impairment Index, one decides the number of scores that are in the impaired range and divides that number by the total number of tests given that contribute to the Halstead Impairment Index (maximum 7). This results in a decimal value between 0.0 and 1.0. If none of the scores were in the impaired range, the Impairment Index would be 0.0. If all of the scores were in the impaired range (7 divided by 7, 6 divided by 6, etc.), the Impairment Index would be 1.0 (Jarvis & Barta, 1994). According to Reitan and Wolfson (1993), the HII cutoff scores are based upon Halstead's (1947) original work and "do not correspond perfectly with more recent findings" (p. 311). Therefore, HII scores should be considered a gross indication of overall level of impairment.

An HII score of 0.0 to 0.2 indicates normal functioning; 0.3 to 0.4, mild impairment; 0.5 to 0.7, moderate impairment; and 0.8 to 1.0, severe impairment.

Research has indicated that the HII is quite sensitive to the detection of cerebral dysfunction (Reitan, 1959a). In fact, Reitan (1994) reported that the HII has "never failed" to discriminate between patients with cerebral lesions and normal controls in any empirical investigation.

General Neuropsychological Deficit Scale (GNDS)

The GNDS was designed to provide an indication of a patient's overall level of neuropsychological functioning (Reitan & Wolfson, 1996). It consists of 42 variables from the HRB for adults and is divided into the four areas based on the methods of inference: Level of Performance, Dysphasia and Related Variables (Pathognomonic Signs), Patterns and Relationships, and Right-Left Differences (Reitan & Wolfson, 1993). Scores of 0, 1, 2, or 3 are assigned to each variable, with scores of 0 representing normal performance; 1 indicates normal but less than ideal performance; 2 indicates mild to moderate impairment; and 3 indicates severe impairment. Scores between 1 and 2

Table 7.3.   Halstead Cutoff Scores suggesting brain damage

Tests	Halstead Cutoff Scores
Category Test	51 or more errors
TPT Total Time	15.7 minutes or more
TPT Memory	5 or fewer correct
TPT Localization	4 or fewer correct
Seashore Rhythm	25 or fewer correct
Speech Sounds Perception	8 or more errors*
Finger Tapping—Dominant Hand	50 or fewer taps in 10 seconds
Impairment Index	5 or above

(From Reitan, 1955-1959; and based on Halstead, 1947).

* Reitan and Wolfson (1985) suggest a cutoff score of 11 or more errors on Speech-Sounds Perception Test based on analysis of more recent data.

Reproduced by special permission of Psychological Assessment Resources, Inc., from *The Halstead-Reitan Neuropsychological Test Battery: A Guide to Interpretation and Clinical Application* by Paul Jarvis, Ph.D., and Jeffrey Barth, Ph.D. Copyright 1994. Further reproduction is prohibited without permission from PAR, Inc.

represent the dividing line between normal and impaired performance. Scores from each of the four areas are summed to produce a total GNDS score. Detailed scoring information, including rules and charts for determining the score assigned to each variable, are provided in Reitan and Wolfson (1993). A computer scoring program for the GNDS is available for purchase from the Reitan Neuropsychology Laboratory.

A GNDS score of 0 to 25 indicates normal functioning; 26 to 40, mild impairment; 41 to 67, moderate impairment; and greater than 68, severe impairment.

Validation studies produced by Reitan and his colleagues found highly significant differences in GNDS total and subtest scores between a heterogeneous group with brain damage and a control group with no brain damage (Reitan & Wolfson, 1993). They also found that the GNDS total score reflected similar levels of impairment for groups of patients with either generalized or lateralized cerebral dysfunction across three categories of neuropathology: heterogeneous cerebral dysfunction, cerebrovascular damage, or traumatic injury. Reitan and Wolfson (1988b) found that the GNDS had a 96% accuracy rate in discriminating between patients with documented brain damage and controls with no brain damage. Although the GNDS was found to discriminate between patients with pseudoneurologic symptoms and patients with brain damage, the GNDS was not more sensitive than the HII in this regard (Sherer & Adams, 1993). A later study by Reitan and Wolfson (1995b) found that a GNDS cutoff score of 28 to 29 resulted in a better classification rate compared to an earlier study (Reitan & Wolfson, 1988b) that used a cutoff score of 25 to 26. They noted that the control group used by Sherer and Adams (1993) had an unusually high mean GNDS score of 26.56. Reitan and Wolfson (1995b) noted that determination of the most appropriate cutoff is dependent on the desire to avoid false negatives or false positives, but that scores falling between 26 and 29 fall into a grey area requiring clinical judgment. The GNDS was found to discriminate between groups of patients with head injury or learning disabilities and controls with no impairments, all of whom were matched for FSIQ (Oestreicher & O'Donnell, 1995). The patients with head injury had a mean GNDS score of 44.5 (SD = 13.2); the patients with learning disabilities had a mean GNDS score of 28.7 (SD = 10.6); and individuals in the control group had a mean GNDS score of 18.53 (SD = 4.1). Additionally, Oestreicher and O'Donnell found the GNDS to be 45% more effective in discriminating among these three groups as compared to the HII.

SEQUENTIAL STEPS TO INTERPRETATION

Determining Presence, Severity, and Location of Lesion Through Hypothesis Generation

Identifying the Presence and/or Severity of Impairment

The first step in examining patient data is a determination of overall level of impairment. This can be accomplished by calculating the HII or the GNDS. Prior to the advent of the GNDS, the HII was demonstrated to be the most significant indicator of brain dysfunction (Reitan, 1959b; Wheeler, Burke, & Reitan, 1963). Scores that fall into the impaired range suggest the presence of cerebral dysfunction. GNDS or HII scores that fall into the nonimpaired range suggest the possibility that impaired performance on individual tests might be acceptable variations of normal performance. Higher scores represent more severe cerebral dysfunction. Keep in mind that Reitan and Wolfson's suggested cutoff scores might overestimate cerebral dysfunction in older individuals or those with less formal education.

Examination of Cutoff Scores Suggestive of Brain Damage

In addition to examining the HII or GNDS, the patient's performance on each test that contributes to the HII should be examined to identify the nature of the impairment. This provides useful information that can be used in the interpretive steps to follow. (Refer to Table 7.3 for a list of cutoff scores.) The following tests should be examined individually to determine whether they fall above or below the cutoff scores: Category Test, TPT Total Time, TPT Memory, TPT Localization, Seashore Rhythm, Speech Sounds Perception, Finger Oscillation, Trail Making Test (although not included in the original HII, cutoff scores for both parts of the Trail Making Test have been established: Part A—40 seconds or more; Part B—91 seconds or more).

Calculating T-Scores

Using the raw scores from the HRB, *T*-scores should be calculated using the Heaton norms (Heaton et al., 1991). Either the manual or the computer scoring version may be used. If the manual is used, a data summary sheet should be used on which the raw scores and Heaton derived *T*-scores can be listed. Once the *T*-scores have been obtained, each should be examined and classified based on level of performance. Suggested classifications of *T*-scores have been made by Heaton et al. (1991, p. 16) and are listed in Table 7.4.

Table 7.4.   Tentative clinical classification of
**   *T* Scores**

Classification	*T* Score
Above average	55+
Average	45–54
Below average/Borderline	40–44
Mild impairment	35–39
Mild-to-moderate impairment	30–34
Moderate impairment	25–29
Moderate-to-severe impairment	20–25
Severe impairment	1–19

Reproduced by special permission from the Publisher, Psychological Assessment Resources, Inc., 16204 North Florida Avenue, Lutz, Florida 33549, from the Comprehensive Norms for an Expanded Halstead-Reitan Battery: Demographic Corrections, Research Findings and Clinical Applications by R.K. Heaton, I. Grant, and C.G. Matthews, Copyright 1991 by PAR, Inc. Further reproduction is prohibited without permission of PAR, Inc.

Determining the Severity of the Impairment

Determinations regarding the severity of impairment are based on the HII and/or GNDS and *T*-scores for each test. Such determinations, however, must take into account such hypotheses and variables as the following:

- HII scores increase with age beginning at ages 45 to 50. Thus, they are less clinically significant; the Heaton norms (Heaton et al., 1991) can be useful for controlling for the normal effects of aging.
- Category Test scores are negatively correlated with intellectual ability (Cullum et al., 1984); therefore, individuals with low premorbid intellectual ability would be expected to demonstrate poorer performance.
- The most concerning error on the Tactile Form Recognition Test is failure to correctly identify the circle (Jarvis & Barth, 1994).
- Visual field defects and sensory suppression errors suggest the possibility of a tissue destroying lesion (Reitan & Wolfson, 1993).
- Patients who have been institutionalized due to schizophrenia are more likely to demonstrate a greater level of impairment (Jarvis & Barth, 1994).
- Psychiatric disorders may also adversely affect patients' general level of performance (Jarvis & Barth, 1994). In such cases, one should place emphasis on multiple methods of inference and not rely solely on level of performance (Golden et al., 1981). Whenever possible, testing should be deferred until patients have been stabilized on psychotropic medication to minimize medication effects on test performance (Heaton & Crowley, 1981), and patients should be observed closely to determine whether they might be responding to internal stimuli during testing (Golden et al., 1981). Evidence of the latter might invalidate the assessment.

Determining the Velocity of the Impairment

The *velocity* of neuropsychological impairment refers to the determination of whether a lesion is static or progressive, based on neuropsychological test data (Jarvis & Barth, 1994).

The following are possible indicators (hypotheses) of a static or slowly progressive lesion (Jarvis & Barth, 1994):

- IQ scores are generally intact, but there is strong evidence of cerebral impairment (Reitan, 1959b).
- Verbal and Performance IQ scores are not significantly different (Reitan, 1959b).
- A focal, static lesion in the anterior frontal lobes is suggested by nearly normal performance on the Category Test and Trails B (Reitan, 1959b).

The following are possible indicators of a rapidly progressive lesion:

- Impaired performance on the Category Test, Trails B, and Speech Sounds Perception Test may suggest an acute destructive lesion (Reitan & Wolfson, 1993).
- Impaired performance on the Speech Sounds Perception Test and Seashore Rhythm Test indicates severely impaired attention and concentration are almost

always observed in patients with rapidly destructive lesions (Jarvis & Barth, 1994; Reitan, 1959b, 1972; Reitan & Wolfson, 1993). There are many other reasons, however, why such deficits might be observed, and a careful observation of patient behavior is necessary to accurately interpret such findings.

Determining Whether Impairment Is Diffuse

Diffuse impairment is most often due to neuropathological processes such as primary neuronal degeneration, general infections, or cerebrovascular disease (Jarvis & Barth, 1994). Other forms of neurotrauma, such as closed head injury, may result in diffuse impairment with some focal findings at the sites of impact and contre coup areas. An important differential diagnosis is that between diffuse impairment and impairment with bilateral, multiple localizing signs. Diffuse impairment tends to result in generalized impairment across tests, whereas multiple localizing deficits result in a profile with significant weaknesses among areas of intact functioning.

Indicators of diffuse impairment include:

- The lack of lateralizing findings (Golden, 1978).
- The absence of a significant difference between VIQ and PIQ scores (Reitan, 1959b).
- Significantly impaired performance on Speech Sounds Perception and Seashore Rhythm (Golden, 1978).

Diffuse impairment may indicate:

- Cortical atrophy, general cerebral arteriosclerosis, and infectious processes (Golden, 1978).
- Chronic alcoholism, especially if focal memory deficits are also observed (Golden, 1978).

Determining Lateralization

The most significant indicators of lateralized cerebral dysfunction are the evaluations of motor and sensory-perceptual functioning and deficits observed on the Aphasia Screening Examination. Pathognomonic signs, such as visual field defects, have the greatest significance in determining lateralization (Jarvis & Barth, 1994). Tumors and CVAs often produce clear lateralizing signs, although they may also produce diffuse impairment. Localizing or lateralizing signs in the presence of intact FSIQ and the lack of a significant difference between VIQ and PIQ scores indicate that an intracerebral tumor or a vascular disorder is unlikely (Golden et al., 1981).

Indicators of right cerebral hemisphere dysfunction include:

- A PIQ that is 20 points or more lower than VIQ (Reitan, 1955a). It is important to keep in mind, however, that cerebral lesions are more likely to affect PIQ performance because the PIQ has timed components and measures new learning; verbal subtests are least likely to be affected by cerebral dysfunction (Reitan, 1959b).

- Constructional dyspraxia, although 15 to 20% of patients with only left hemisphere dysfunction will also demonstrate constructional dyspraxia (Golden, 1978).
- Auditory suppressions in the left ear.
- Left-sided neglect (e.g., reading "G-W" for "M-G-W"; Golden, 1978).

Possible indicators of left cerebral hemisphere dysfunction include:

- Significantly impaired performance on Similarities (Reitan, 1959b); an intact Similarities score does not indicate the absence of such dysfunction.
- Significantly impaired Speech Sounds Perception and signs of aphasia may indicate a left temporal lobe lesion although Speech Sounds Perception is not in and of itself a test of lateralization (Long & Hunter, 1981).
- Attempting to draw the clock on the Aphasia Screening Examination rather than writing "clock" (Reitan & Wolfson, 1993).
- Adding 85 and 27, rather than subtracting, on the Aphasia Exam in patients with an average level of education (Reitan & Wolfson, 1993).
- Reading the stimulus "7 SIX 2" as "7-S-I-X-2" (Reitan & Wolfson, 1993).

Determining Localization

One of the first steps in determining localizing signs is examining sensory and motor performance to determine whether lesions are anterior or posterior (Jarvis & Barth, 1994). Sensory functions are posterior to the central sulcus, and motor functions are anterior; keeping this bit of neuroanatomy in mind aids in localization.

The following indicators (hypotheses) aid in determining the anterior (versus posterior) location of lesions:

- Depressed motor performance, such as on Finger Tapping and Grip Strength, suggest the presence of a lesion near the motor strip (Reitan, 1959b).
- An anterior lesion in the contralateral hemisphere is suggested if Finger Tapping is more impaired than TPT performance with the same hand; conversely, a posterior lesion in the contralateral hemisphere is suggested if the TPT performance is more impaired than Finger Tapping (Reitan, 1959b).
- Involvement of the sensory strip may be indicated when Finger Tapping is normal and TPT scores are impaired and/or sensory deficits are noted (Reitan, 1959b).

Although frontal lobe lesions are difficult to detect with the HRB, particularly if they are well removed from the motor strip (Jarvis & Barth, 1994), the following are indicators or hypotheses related to frontal lobe dysfunction:

- Impaired performance on the Category Test and Trails B with generally intact performance on the other HRB tests suggests the possibility of a focal, static lesion of the anterior frontal lobes (Reitan, 1959b); however, more recent research indicates that the Category Test and Trail Making Test do not discriminate between patients with frontal lesions and patients with nonfrontal lesions (Reitan & Wolfson, 1995a).

- Signs of expressive aphasia, such as **dysgraphia, dysnomia,** and **spelling dyspraxia** are indicative of left anterior impairment (Reitan, 1959b).

Temporal lobe dysfunction may present a complex diagnostic picture. To fully assess the integrity of the temporal lobes, supplemental memory measures are recommended. The following are indicators of, or hypotheses related to, temporal lobe dysfunction:

- Impaired performance on Similarities suggests left temporal lobe dysfunction; intact performance does not rule out such a lesion (Reitan, 1959b).
- If Picture Arrangement is significantly lower than Block Design, a right anterior temporal lobe lesion may be indicated (Reitan, 1959b).
- A right temporal-parietal lesion is suggested if performance on both Picture Arrangement and Block Design is impaired (Reitan, 1959b).
- Signs of aphasia and impaired Speech Sounds Perception may be associated with left temporal dysfunction (Long & Hunter, 1981).
- Left posterior temporal lobe dysfunction is suggested by signs of receptive aphasia, such as visual form agnosia, dyslexia, auditory verbal agnosia, visual letter agnosia, and auditory number agnosia (Reitan, 1959b).
- Visual field defects may indicate temporal or parietal lobe dysfunction (Reitan & Wolfson, 1993).
- Auditory suppression errors indicate dysfunction in the contralateral temporal lobe (Reitan, 1959b).
- **Dysgraphesthesia** may be associated with temporal lobe dysfunction (Long & Hunter, 1981).

Parietal lobe dysfunction is typically identified through deficits in tactual perceptual ability and motor tasks that require sensory feedback. The following may indicate parietal lobe dysfunction:

- A right parietal-occipital lesion is suggested by a Block Design score that is significantly lower than Picture Arrangement (Reitan, 1959b).
- A right temporal-parietal lesion is suggested if both Picture Arrangement and Block Design scores are impaired (Reitan, 1959b).
- A right parietal lesion is suggested if Block Design is impaired relative to Picture Arrangement and constructional dyspraxia is present (Reitan, 1959b).
- A right parietal lesion is suggested if patients demonstrate left side neglect of stimuli (e.g., reading "G-W" instead of "M-G-W"; Golden, 1978).
- Visual field defects indicate possible temporal or parietal lobe dysfunction (Reitan & Wolfson, 1993).
- Impaired performance on Fingertip Number Writing, Finger Agnosia, and Tactual Form Recognition are suggestive of parietal lobe lesions (Jarvis & Barth, 1994).

Occipital lobe dysfunction may be suggested by the following:

- Visual suppression errors suggest dysfunction posterior to the optic chiasm in the contralateral cerebral hemisphere (Golden, 1978).
- A right parietal-occipital lesion is suggested by a significantly impaired Block Design score relative to Picture Arrangement performance (Reitan, 1959b).

Pathognomonic Signs

Pathognomonic signs are typically found in the Aphasia Screening Examination. Responses should be examined carefully for unusual properties, false starts, or failures. Detailed information about scoring and interpreting pathognomonic signs are presented in Reitan and Wolfson (1993). Because pathognomonic signs were included as indicators of lateralization and localization, they will not be repeated here. Refer also to Tables 7.1 and 7.2 for descriptions and information about lateralizing significance.

WAIS-R and WAIS-III Performance

Examination of the FSIQ, VIQ, PIQ, and subtest scores is an important part of interpreting the HRB. The WAIS-R Freedom from Distractibility Index (similar, but not identical to, the WAIS-III Working Memory factor) has been shown to add significant predictive ability to the HRB and, in fact, accounted for the most variance of all WAIS-R IQ and factor scores when used with HRB scores (Scott, Sherer, & Adams, 1995). Particular patterns with lateralizing-localizing significance were detailed earlier and will not be repeated here. For detailed information on the neuropsychological interpretation of WAIS-R–WAIS-III scores, please refer to the Wechsler chapter in this book (Chapter 5).

HYPOTHESES BASED ON NEUROPATHOLOGICAL CONDITION

Neuropathological Findings on the HRB

Although full descriptions of various neuropathological conditions are beyond the scope of this chapter, selected hypotheses suggestive of various conditions will be described. The reader is referred to Reitan and Wolfson (1993) and to Jarvis and Barth (1994) for additional information.

Head Injury

Neuropsychological hypotheses include the following:

- A closed head injury typically presents as static velocity, especially if a significant amount of time has elapsed since the injury (Jarvis & Barth, 1994).
- Mild diffuse damage is suggestive of closed head injury; severe impairment and pathognomonic signs are typically absent, and the FSIQ is likely to be intact (Binder, 1986).
- The HII is likely to be higher with penetrating head injuries and lower with mild to moderate closed head injuries (Golden, 1978).

- A penetrating head injury may result in significantly discrepant Finger Tapping scores (Reitan & Wolfson, 1993).

Neoplasms

Neuropsychological hypotheses include the following:

- If sensory suppression errors are absent, an acute destructive posterior lesion is unlikely (Reitan, 1959b).
- Extracerebral tumors are typically not associated with a significant difference between VIQ and PIQ (Reitan, 1972).
- Intact Finger Tapping along with other severe impairment may indicate an extracerebral neoplasm (Reitan & Wolfson, 1993).
- Lower scores on the HII are associated with extracerebral neoplasms, whereas higher HII scores may indicate intracerebral neoplasms.
- Intracerebral tumors tend to cause global dysfunction and affect PIQ; an intact FSIQ with no significant VIQ-PIQ difference and the presence of localizing-lateralizing signs indicates that an intracerebral tumor is not likely (Golden et al., 1981; Reitan, 1959b).
- Intracerebral lesions, regardless of location, typically affect abstract reasoning; therefore, intact performance on the Category Test suggests the absence of an intracerebral lesion (Reitan, 1972; Reitan & Wolfson, 1993).
- A rapidly progressive intracerebral lesion may present with prominent unilateral sensory and motor deficits, although this pattern is more typical of an acute CVA (Reitan, 1959b, 1972).
- Left side visual neglect may indicate a right parietal lobe lesion (Golden, 1978).
- Multiple focal deficits in the presence of significantly impaired overall performance are suggestive of metastatic carcinomas (Golden, 1978).

Cerebrovascular Disorders

Neuropsychological hypotheses include the following:

- Massive CVAs tend to cause global dysfunction and to affect PIQ; an intact FSIQ with no significant VIQ-PIQ difference and the presence of localizing-lateralizing signs indicates that a massive CVA is not likely (Golden et al., 1981; Reitan, 1959b).
- Massive CVAs, regardless of location, typically affect abstract reasoning; therefore, intact performance on the Category Test suggests the absence of a massive CVA (Reitan, 1972; Reitan & Wolfson, 1993).
- An acute CVA may present with prominent unilateral sensory and motor deficits (Reitan, 1959b, 1972).
- A CVA may be present if Finger Tapping scores are very discrepant (Reitan & Wolfson, 1993).
- Left side visual neglect may indicate a right parietal lobe CVA (Golden, 1978).

Degenerative Diseases

Primary Degenerative Dementia

Also known as senile dementia Alzheimer's type (SDAT), this form of dementia can present with the following findings on neuropsychological assessment:

- Diffuse impairment and the absence of lateralizing or localizing signs (Barth & Macciocchi, 1986).
- Impaired recent memory and intact remote memory in mild SDAT (Barth & Macciocchi, 1986).
- Greater impairment in PIQ than in VIQ in mild SDAT (Jarvis & Barth, 1994).
- Often, difficulty in comprehension of task instructions (Jarvis & Barth, 1994).
- Often, dysnomia, dyscalculia, constructional dyspraxia, and auditory verbal agnosia (Hom, 1992).
- Aphasia (American Psychiatric Association [APA], 1994).

Parkinson's Disease

Neuropsychological hypotheses include:

- Impaired performance on motor tests, Category Test, and Trailmaking Test, high HII, and generally intact FSIQ (Reitan & Boll, 1971).
- Micrographia and tremor on the Aphasia Screening Examination (Reitan, 1959b).

Multiple Sclerosis

Neuropsychological hypotheses include:
- Scattered sensory and motor deficits and impaired TPT performance, along with a generally intact Category Test score (Reitan & Wolfson, 1993).
- Relatively normal FSIQ with deficits observed on Picture Arrangement and Digit Symbol (Reitan & Wolfson, 1993).

Alcoholism

Neuropsychological deficits include:

- Relatively intact IQ scores and severely impaired Category Test (Reitan & Wolfson, 1993).
- Significant impairment on the most sensitive indicators of cerebral dysfunction: GNDS, HII, Category Test, Trails B, and TPT Localization (Reitan & Wolfson, 1993).
- Memory deficits and confabulation (Jarvis & Barth, 1994).

Anoxia

Typical neuropsychological findings include the following:

- Diffuse static impairment with significant memory deficits are typical (Jarvis & Barth, 1994).

- An attempted hanging may result in lateralized deficits if only one carotid artery was occluded (Jarvis & Barth, 1994).
- Chronic obstructive pulmonary disease (COPD) may produce mild impairment in abstraction, memory, and performance speed (Prigatano, Parsons, Wright, Levin, & Hawryluk, 1983).

TREATMENT PLANNING

Although there are varying degrees of empirical support for using tests in the HRB for treatment planning, a variety of hypotheses can be presented (Jarvis & Barth, 1994). In the area of activities of daily living, sensory or motor deficits may indicate that a patient will have difficulty with grooming, dressing, or driving. A patient with sensory or motor deficits would benefit from referral for physical and occupational therapy and/or further assessment of driving skills via a computerized driving simulator. Depending on their professions, patients with sensory or motor impairment may have difficulty returning to work, thus requiring vocational counseling and job retraining. Constructional dyspraxia is also an indicator that a patient might have difficulty with grooming or dressing (Baum & Hall, 1981).

Deficits in executive functioning (e.g., impaired Trails B and/or Category Test) may signal deficits in initiation that affect self-care skills, as well as impaired inhibition of behavior, self-monitoring, sequencing, or flexibility, with implications for most aspects of daily functioning (Jarvis & Barth, 1994). Behavioral interventions, including coaching, prompting, and supervision, are helpful in managing such executive function deficits. Memory deficits are likely to cause difficulties in all areas of functioning. Helpful interventions include the use of appointment books, tape recorders, visual prompts such as charts or schedules, and wristwatch alarms. Severe memory deficits have implications for the ability of patients to return to independent living and to manage their own affairs. Impaired arithmetic skills on the WAIS-III might predict difficulty in managing a checkbook or in making purchases. Further assessment of such practical skills by the neuropsychologist or referral to occupational therapy is recommended as part of treatment planning.

Addressing the ability of patients to manage their own affairs, to return to school or work, or to live independently are a crucial aspect of treatment planning. Information relevant to these areas can be gleaned from the HRB (Jarvis & Barth, 1994). Significant deficits on the Category Test indicate that patients might have difficulty with solving problems in their life or making nonroutine decisions (Heaton & Pendleton, 1981). Impairments in new problem solving, in ability to attend to two stimuli simultaneously (i.e., Trails B), in cognitive processing speed, or in memory are indicators that a person might have difficulty adapting to new situations at work, learning new skills, or completing multiple tasks (Jarvis & Barth, 1994). Treatment planning for such individuals should focus on breaking new skills into small steps, encouraging repetition of new behavior, and providing coaching and reinforcement until the new skill has been acquired. Global, more severe neuropsychological impairment (an HII greater than .5) is associated with the increased likelihood of unemployment (Heaton, Smith, Lehman, & Vogt, 1978). Such pervasive impairment is also indicative of a patient's greater need for supervision, a structured living situation, and/or assistance with activities of daily living. For additional information pertinent to the use of the HRB in treatment planning, please see Jarvis and Barth (1994). Information regarding the ecological validity of neuropsychological assessment can be found in *Ecological Validity of Neuropsychological Testing* (Sbordone & Long, 1996).

CAVEATS

This chapter was designed to aid the beginning student in neuropsychology by providing an overview of the HRB and basic interpretive steps. Due to the complexity of neuropsychological assessment, however, trainees should interpret data from the HRB under the supervision of an experienced neuropsychologist. For example, focal lesions may cause more diffuse impairment by disrupting fiber tracts or vascular flow or by causing increased pressure on other areas of the brain (Jarvis & Barth, 1994). Furthermore, individuals often present with multiple pathologies, such as a patient with a history of learning disability, alcohol abuse, closed head injury, and schizophrenia. Such complex symptom presentations complicate the interpretation of neuropsychological data and are different from the patients with relatively clean neurological impairments studied by Reitan and others in the early development of the HRB. Therefore, the information contained in this chapter should be used to develop tentative hypotheses for further consideration. Because only a small percentage of the hypotheses and interpretive statements typically used in the analysis of the HRB are listed in this chapter, the reader is encouraged to refer to original sources cited in this chapter.

RECOMMENDED READING

Jarvis, P.E., & Barth, J.T. (1994). *The Halstead-Reitan Neuropsychological Test Battery: A Guide to Interpretation and Clinical Applications.* Odessa, FL: Psychological Assessment Resources.

Reitan, R.M., & Wolfson, D. (1988). *Traumatic brain injury: Vol. II. Recovery and rehabilitation.* Tucson, AZ: Neuropsychology Press.

Reitan, R.M., & Wolfson, D. (1993). *The Halstead-Reitan Neuropsychological Test Battery: Theory and Clinical Interpretation.* Tucson, AZ: Neuropsychology Press.

Russell, E.W. (1998). In defense of the Halstead-Reitan Battery: A critique of Lezak's review. *Archives of Clinical Neuropsychology, 13,* 365–381.

REFERENCES

American Psychiatric Association. (1994). *Diagnostic and statistical manual of mental disorders* (4th ed.). Washington, DC: Author.

Arnold, B.R., Montgomery, G.T., Castaneda, I., & Longoria, R. (1994). Acculturation and performance of Hispanics on selected Halstead-Reitan neuropsychological tests. *Assessment, 1,* 239–248.

Barth, J.T., & Macciocchi, S.N. (1986). Dementia: Implications for clinical practice and research. In S.B. Filskov & T.J. Boll (Eds.), *Handbook of clinical neuropsychology* (Vol. 2, pp. 398–425). New York: Wiley.

Baum, B., & Hall, K.M. (1981). Relationship between constructional praxis and dressing in the head injured adult. *American Journal of Occupational Therapy, 35,* 438–442.

Bigler, E.D., & Dodrill, C.B. (1997). Assessment of neuropsychological testing [Letter to the editor]. *Neurology, 49,* 1180–1182.

Binder, L.M. (1986). Persisting symptoms after mild head injury: A review of the postconcussive syndrome. *Journal of Clinical and Experimental Neuropsychology, 8,* 323–346.

Boll, T.J. (1981). The Halstead-Reitan neuropsychological test battery. In S.B. Filskov & T.J. Boll (Eds.), *Handbook of clinical neuropsychology* (pp. 577–607). New York: Wiley.

Bornstein, R.A. (1983). Verbal IQ-performance IQ discrepancies on the Wechsler adult intelligence scale-revised: Inpatients with unilateral or bilateral cerebral dysfunction. *Journal of Consulting and Clinical Psychology, 51,* 779–780.

Charter, R.A., & Webster, J.S. (1997). Psychometric structure of the Seashore rhythm test. *Clinical Neuropsychologist, 11,* 167–173.

Choca, J.P., Laatsch, L., Wetzel, L., & Agresti, A. (1997). The Halstead category test: A fifty year perspective. *Neuropsychology Review, 7,* 61–75.

Cullum, C.M., Steinam, D.R., & Bigler, E.D. (1984). Relationship between fluid and crystallized cognitive functions using category test and WAIS scores. *International Journal of Clinical Neuropsychology, 1,* 172–174.

DeFilippis, N.A., & McCampbell, E. (1979). *The booklet category test: Research and clinical form (Manual).* Odessa, FL: Psychological Assessment Resources.

Dodrill, C.B., & Troupin, A.S. (1975). Effects of repeated administrations of a comprehensive neuropsychological battery among chronic epileptics. *Journal of Nervous and Mental Disease, 161,* 185–190.

Franzen, M.D., & Robbins, D.E. (1989). The Halstead-Reitan neuropsychological battery. In M. Franzen (Ed.), *Reliability and validity in neuropsychological assessment.* New York: Plenum Press.

Gaudino, E.A., Geisler, M.W., & Squires, N.K. (1995). Construct validity in the trail making test: What makes Part B harder? *Journal of Clinical and Experimental Neuropsychology, 17,* 529–535.

Golden, C.J. (1978). *Diagnosis and rehabilitation in neuropsychology.* Springfield, IL: Thomas.

Golden, C.J., Osman, D.C., Moses, J.A., & Berg, R.A. (1981). *Interpretation of the Halstead-Reitan neuropsychological battery.* New York: Grune & Stratton.

Goldstein, G. (1997). Assessment of neuropsychological testing [Letter to the editor]. *Neurology, 49,* 1179–1180.

Grant, I. (1987). Alcohol and the brain: Neuropsychological correlates. *Journal of Consulting and Clinical Psychology, 55,* 310–324.

Gronwall, D. (1977). Paced serial auditory serial-addition task: A measure of recovery from concussion. *Perceptual and Motor Skills, 44,* 367–373.

Gronwall, D., & Sampson, H. (1974). *The psychological effects of concussion.* Auckland, New Zealand: Oxford University.

Halstead, W. (1947). *Brain and intelligence: A quantitative study of the frontal lobes.* Chicago: University of Chicago Press.

Hathaway, S.R., & McKinley, J.C. (1942). *Minnesota multiphasic personality inventory.* Minneapolis: University of Minnesota Press.

Hathaway, S.R., & McKinley, J.C. (1989). *Minnesota multiphasic personality inventory-2.* Minneapolis: University of Minnesota Press.

Heaton, R.K., & Crowley, T.J. (1981). Effects of psychiatric disorders and their somatic treatments on neuropsychological test results. In S.B. Filskov & T.J. Boll (Eds.), *Handbook of clinical neuropsychology* (pp. 481–524). New York: Wiley.

Heaton, R.K., Grant, I., & Matthews, C.G. (1991). *Comprehensive norms for an expanded Halstead-Reitan battery.* Odessa, FL: Psychological Assessment Resources.

Heaton, R.K., & Pendleton, M.G. (1981). Use of neuropsychological tests to predict adult patients' everyday functioning. *Journal of Consulting and Clinical Psychology, 49,* 807–821.

Heaton, R.K., Ryan, L., Grant, I., & Matthews, C.G. (1996). Demographic influences on neuropsychological test performance. In I. Grant & K.M. Adams (Eds.), *Neuropsychological assessment of neuropsychiatric disorders* (pp. 141–163). New York: Oxford University Press.

Heaton, R.K., Smith, H.H., Lehman, R.A., & Vogt, A.T. (1978). Prospects for faking believable deficits on neuropsychological testing. *Journal of Consulting and Clinical Psychology, 46,* 892–900.

Heilbronner, R.L., & Parsons, O.A. (1989). The clinical utility of the tactual performance test (TPT): Issues of lateralization and cognitive style. *Clinical Neuropsychologist, 3,* 250–264.

Holtz, J.L., Gearhart, L.P., & Watson, C.G. (1996). Comparability of scores on projector- and booklet-administered forms of the category test in brain-impaired veterans and controls. *Neuropsychology, 10,* 194–196.

Hom, J. (1992). General and specific cognitive dysfunctions in patients with Alzheimer's disease. *Archives of Clinical Neuropsychology, 4,* 249–268.

Jarvis, P.E., & Barth, J.T. (1994). *The Halstead-Reitan neuropsychological battery: A guide to interpretation and clinical applications.* Odessa, FL: Psychological Assessment Resources.

Johnstone, B., Holland, D., & Hewett, J.E. (1997). The construct validity of the category test: Is it a measure of reasoning or intelligence? *Psychological Assessment, 9,* 28–33.

Kane, R.L. (1991). Standardized and flexible batteries in neuropsychology: An assessment update. *Neuropsychology Review, 2,* 281–339.

Klonoff, H., Fibiger, C.H., & Hutton, G. (1970). Neuropsychological patterns in chronic schizophrenia. *Journal of Nervous and Mental Diseases, 150,* 291–300.

Kløve, H. (1963). Clinical neuropsychology. In F.M. Forster (Ed.), *The medical clinics of North America.* New York: Saunders.

Larrabee, G.J., & Curtiss, G. (1995). Construct validity of various verbal and visual memory tests. *Journal of Clinical and Experimental Neuropsychology, 17,* 536–547.

Levin, H.S. (1994). A guide to clinical neuropsychological testing. *Archives of Neurology, 51,* 854–859.

Lezak, M.D. (1983). *Neuropsychological assessment* (2nd ed.). New York: Oxford University Press.

Lezak, M.D. (1995). *Neuropsychological assessment* (3rd ed.). New York: Oxford University Press.

Long, C.J., & Hunter, S.E. (1981). Analysis of temporal cortex dysfunction by neuropsychological techniques. *Clinical Neuropsychology, 3,* 16–23.

Matarazzo, J.D., Matarazzo, R.G., Wiens, A.N., Gallo, A.E., & Klonoff, H. (1976). Retest reliability of the Halstead impairment index in a normal, schizophrenic, and two samples of organic patients. *Journal of Clinical Psychology, 32,* 338–349.

Matarazzo, J.D., Wiens, A.N., Matarazzo, R.G., & Goldstein, S. (1974). Psychometric and test-retest reliability of the Halstead-Reitan impairment index in a sample of healthy, young, normal men. *Journal of Nervous and Mental Disease, 158,* 37–49.

Meier, M.J. (1985). Review of the Halstead-Reitan neuropsychological test battery. In J.V. Mitchell (Ed.), *The ninth mental measurements yearbook* (pp. 646–649). Highland Park, NJ: Gryphon Press.

Mercer, W.N., Harrell, E.H., Miller, D.C., Childs, H.W., & Rockers, D.M. (1997). Performance of brain-injured versus healthy adults on three versions of the category test. *Clinical Neuropsychologist, 11,* 174–179.

Miller, D.C. (1993). *Computerized version of the category test for the Macintosh personal computer: Adult form.* Denton, TX: Author.

Mitrushina, M., Boone, K., & D'Elia, L.F. (1998). *Handbook of normative data for neuropsychological assessment.* New York: Oxford University Press.

Mutchnick, M.G., Ross, L.K., & Long, C. (1991). Decision strategies for cerebral dysfunction: IV. Determination of cerebral dysfunction. *Archives of Clinical Neuropsychology, 6,* 259–270.

O'Donnell, J.P., MacGregor, L.A., Dabrowski, J.J., Oestreicher, J.M., & Romero, J.J. (1994). Construct validity of neuropsychological tests of conceptual and attentional abilities. *Journal of Clinical Psychology, 50,* 596–600.

Oestreicher, J.M., & O'Donnell, J.P. (1995). Validation of the general neuropsychological deficit scale with nondisabled, learning-disabled, and head-injured young adults. *Archives of Clinical Neuropsychology, 10,* 185–191.

Ponton, M.O., & Leon-Carrion, J. (1999). *Handbook of neuropsychology with Hispanic populations.* Mahwah, NJ: Erlbaum.

Prigatano, G.P., Parsons, O., Wright, E., Levin, D.C., & Hawryluk, G. (1983). Neuropsychological test performance in mildly hypoxic patients with chronic obstructive pulmonary disease. *Journal of Consulting and Clinical Psychology, 51,* 108–116.

Reitan, R.M. (1955a). Certain differential effects of left and right cerebral lesions in human adults. *Journal of Comparative and Physiological Psychology, 48,* 474–477.

Reitan, R.M. (1955b). An investigation of the validity of Halstead's measures of biological intelligence. *Archives of Neurology and Psychiatry, 73,* 28–35.

Reitan, R.M. (1955c). The relation of the trail making test to organic brain damage. *Journal of Consulting and Clinical Psychology, 19,* 393–394.

Reitan, R.M. (1958). The validity of the trail making test as an indicator of organic brain damage. *Perceptual and Motor Skills, 8,* 271–276.

Reitan, R.M. (1959a). The comparative effects of brain damage on the Halstead impairment index and the Wechsler-Bellevue scale. *Journal of Clinical Psychology, 15,* 281–285.

Reitan, R.M. (1959b). *The effects of brain lesions on adaptive abilities in human beings.* Seattle: University of Washington.

Reitan, R.M. (1964). Psychological deficits resulting from cerebral lesions in men. In J.M. Warren & K. Aken (Eds.), *The frontal granular cortex and behavior* (pp. 295–312). New York: McGraw-Hill.

Reitan, R.M. (1972). *Neuropsychological interpretations of underlying neurological disorders.* Seattle: University of Washington.

Reitan, R.M. (1975). Assessment of brain-behavior relationships. In P. McReynolds (Ed.), *Advances in psychological assessment* (Vol. 3, pp. 186–242). San Francisco: Jossey-Bass.

Reitan, R.M. (1994). Ward Halstead's contributions to neuropsychology and the Halstead-Reitan neuropsychological test battery. *Journal of Clinical Psychology, 50,* 47–70.

Reitan, R.M., & Boll, T.J. (1971). Intellectual and cognitive functions in Parkinson's disease. *Journal of Consulting and Clinical Psychology, 37,* 364–369.

Reitan, R.M., & Fitzhugh, K.B. (1971). Behavioral deficits in groups with cerebral vascular lesions. *Journal of Consulting and Clinical Psychology, 37,* 215–223.

Reitan, R.M., & Wolfson, D. (1985). *The Halstead-Reitan neuropsychological test battery: Theory and clinical interpretation.* Tucson, AZ: Neuropsychology Press.

Reitan, R.M., & Wolfson, D. (1986a). The Halstead-Reitan neuropsychological test battery. In D. Wedding, A.M. Horton, Jr., & J. Webster (Eds.), *The neuropsychology handbook: Behavioral and clinical perspectives* (pp. 134–160). New York: Springer.

Reitan, R.M., & Wolfson, D. (1986b). *Traumatic brain injury: Vol. II. Recovery and rehabilitation.* Tucson, AZ: Neuropsychology Press.

Reitan, R.M., & Wolfson, D. (1988a). The Halstead-Reitan neuropsychological test battery and REHABIT: A model for integrating evaluation and remediation of cognitive impairment. *Cognitive Rehabilitation, 6,* 10–17.

Reitan, R.M., & Wolfson, D. (1988b). *Traumatic brain injury* (Vol. 2). Tucson, AZ: Neuropsychology Press.

Reitan, R.M., & Wolfson, D. (1993). *The Halstead-Reitan neuropsychological test battery: Theory and clinical interpretation* (2nd ed.). Tucson, AZ: Neuropsychology Press.

Reitan, R.M., & Wolfson, D. (1994). *Workshop in clinical neuropsychology.* Tucson, AZ: Neuropsychology Press.

Reitan, R.M., & Wolfson, D. (1995a). Category test and trail making test as measures of frontal lobe functions. *Clinical Neuropsychologist, 9,* 50–56.

Reitan, R.M., & Wolfson, D. (1995b). Cross-validation of the general neuropsychological deficit scale (GNDS). *Archives of Clinical Neuropsychology, 10,* 125–131.

Reitan, R.M., & Wolfson, D. (1995c). Influence of age and education on neuropsychological test results. *Clinical Neuropsychologist, 9,* 151–158.

Reitan, R.M., & Wolfson, D. (1996). Theoretical, methodological, and validational bases of the Halstead-Reitan neuropsychological test battery. In I. Grant & K.M. Adams (Eds.), *Neuropsychological assessment of neuropsychiatric disorders.* New York: Oxford University Press.

Reitan, R.M., & Wolfson, D. (1997). Emotional disturbances and their interaction with neuropsychological deficits. *Neuropsychology Review, 7,* 3–19.

Report of the Therapeutics and Technology Assessment Subcommittee of the American Academy of Neurology. (1996). Assessment: Neuropsychological testing of adults. *Neurology, 47,* 592–599.

Russell, E.W. (1995). The accuracy of automated and clinical detection of brain damage and lateralization in neuropsychology. *Neuropsychology Review, 5,* 1–68.

Russell, E.W. (1998). In defense of the Halstead-Reitan battery: A critique of Lezak's review. *Archives of Clinical Neuropsychology, 13,* 365–381.

Russell, E.W., Neuringer, C., & Goldstein, G. (1970). *Assessment of brain damage: A neuropsychological key approach.* New York: Wiley-Interscience.

Sbordone, R.J., & Long, C.J. (1996). *Ecological validity of neuropsychological testing.* Delray Beach, FL: St. Lucie Press.

Scott, J.G., Sherer, M., & Adams, R.L. (1995). Clinical utility of WAIS-R factor-derived standard scores in assessing brain injury. *Clinical Neuropsychologist, 9,* 93–97.

Shaw, D.J. (1966). The reliability and validity of the Halstead category test. *Journal of Clinical Psychology, 21,* 405–408.

Sherer, M., & Adams, R.L. (1993). Cross-validation of Reitan and Wolfson's neuropsychological deficit scales. *Archives of Clinical Neuropsychologist, 8,* 429–435.

Sherer, M., Parsons, O.A., Nixon, S.J., & Adams, R.L. (1991). Clinical validity of the speech-sounds perception test and the Seashore rhythm test. *Journal of Clinical and Experimental Neuropsychology, 13,* 741–751.

Shuttleworth-Jordan, A.B. (1997). Age and education effects on brain-damaged subjects: 'Negative' findings revisited. *Clinical Neuropsychologist, 11,* 205–209.

Smith, R.J., Barth, J.T., Diamond, R., & Giuliano, A.J. (1998). Evaluation of head trauma. In G. Goldstein, P.D. Nussbaum, & S.R. Beers (Eds.), *Neuropsychology* (pp. 135–170). New York: Plenum Press.

Spreen, O., & Strauss, E. (1998). *A compendium of neuropsychological tests: Administration, norms, and commentary* (2nd ed.). New York: Oxford University Press.

Thompson, L.L., Heaton, R.J., Matthews, C.G., & Grant, I. (1987). Comparison of preferred and nonpreferred hand performance on four neuropsychological tests. *Clinical Neuropsychologist, 1,* 324–334.

Vanderploeg, R.D., Axelrod, B.N., Sherer, M., Scott, J., & Adams, R.L. (1997). The importance of demographic adjustments on neuropsychological test performance: A response to Reitan and Wolfson (1995). *Clinical Neuropsychologist, 11,* 210–217.

Vega, A., & Parsons, O. (1967). Cross-validation of the Halstead-Reitan tests for brain damage. *Journal of Consulting Psychology, 31,* 619–625.

Wechsler, D. (1981). *WAIS-R manual: Wechsler adult intelligence scale–revised.* San Antonio, TX: The Psychological Corporation.

Wechsler, D. (1987). *WMS-R manual: Wechsler memory scale–revised.* New York: The Psychological Corporation.

Wechsler, D. (1997a). *WMS-III administration and scoring manual.* San Antonio, TX: The Psychological Corporation.

Wechsler, D. (1997b). *WAIS-III manual.* San Antonio, TX: The Psychological Corporation.

Wheeler, L., Burke, C.J., & Reitan, R.M. (1963). An application of discriminant functions to the problem of predicting brain damage using behavioral variables. *Perceptual and Motor Skills, 16,* 417.

Chapter 8

THE LURIA NEBRASKA NEUROPSYCHOLOGICAL BATTERY

CHARLES J. GOLDEN, SHAWNA M. FRESHWATER, and JYOTHI VAYALAKKARA

The Luria-Nebraska Neuropsychological Battery (LNNB) is a testing method that integrates the qualitative information generated by the techniques of A.R. Luria with that gleaned from traditional American psychometric procedures. This hybrid approach takes elements from both significant traditions. The test has been found to have a strong psychometric base and to provide the clinician with the opportunity to make numerous and valuable qualitative observations and discriminations of highly specific problems in clients that cannot be easily made with traditional psychometric instruments. The test battery itself provides a brief but comprehensive evaluation in less than 3 hours, which makes it practical to use in situations of limited time and with patients whose ability to be tested over long time periods is limited.

The test consists of 12 scales derived from the work of Luria, based on his descriptions in Luria (1980) and on the excellent work of Christensen (1975). Each of these scales consists of items within a given theme area (such as receptive language), but each scale tests a different qualitative aspect of performance within the theme area. A scale such as the LNNB Receptive Speech scale consists of items requiring phonemic recognition, the writing of phonemes, simple commands, complex commands, vocabulary, abstractions, grammatical inversions, and so on, with each scale item focusing on a different aspect of these areas. This allows the clinician to use variations in item presentation and content to quickly survey the wide range of problems possible in the area of receptive language. A more traditional test like Block Design would have a scale for each of these areas and would consist of items that are very similar except for difficulty level. This is a practice that is consistent with more common tests, but one that is very time consuming. In the end, many additional specific areas are not evaluated. This is consistent with Luria's emphasis on the very specific details of the client's deficits rather than on more generalized and less specific information generated from other tests. Although this battery time is time limited, it still possesses psychometric reliability and validity. A traditional exam that evaluated all of the areas contained in the LNNB would likely take up to 2 days to administer to a client.

HISTORY AND DEVELOPMENT

Traditionally, the major goal of neuropsychological tests has been the identification of individuals as having brain damage or not. Extensive literature throughout the twentieth century has attempted to validate individual tests or batteries of tests for the purpose of this basic identification. Although this designation remains a goal of neuropsychological testing, its importance has diminished with the introduction of computerized tomography (CT), magnetic resonance imaging (MRI), and measures of brain metabolism, including regional cerebral blood flow (rCBF), positron emission tomography (PET), and single photon excitement computed tomography (SPECT). These neuroradiological techniques have increased the accuracy of diagnosing the presence of brain injury, although certain disorders still manage to evade detection by these techniques. As neuroradiological techniques have improved, neuropsychological testing has increasingly focused on the sequelae of brain injuries rather than on the presence of a brain injury. Such description can range from localizing an injury to detailed descriptions of the strengths and weaknesses of the client.

Luria's qualitative procedures were ideally suited for a detailed evaluation of the client's strengths and weaknesses. However, their application to clients was difficult because the examination lacked consistently employed content, was devoid of a scoring system other than the examiner's impressions, and lacked a systematic interpretive strategy that could be evaluated for its accuracy and usefulness in different populations. On the other hand, traditional neuropsychological techniques were psychometrically sound but lacked the ability to provide the rich clinical interpretive information that could be gained from Luria's work.

Whereas Golden was trained in the strong psychometric tradition of the Halstead-Reitan Neuropsychological Test Battery (HRB), it was clear to this author that the HRB was restricted in terms of the fine detail it generated (although the HRB and the LNNB cover essentially the same overall field of functions). Originally, attempts were made to shorten aspects of the HRB (e.g., Golden, 1976a; Golden & Anderson, 1977) to allow time for the introduction of other tests (Golden, 1976b). This approach, while useful, still failed to produce an adequately comprehensive and time-limited procedure that collected the information necessary to make a Lurian time analysis.

The publication of Christensen's (1975) version of Luria's battery gave much more detail on the actual procedures employed than were then available in Luria's own seminal works (Luria, 1966, 1973). With this information, it appeared possible to adapt the information in Christensen so as to produce a quantitative and qualitative hybrid of her purely qualitative presentation.

Working with a group of graduate students at the University of South Dakota, Golden developed an initial adaptation of Christensen (1975) and Luria (1966) that attempted to cover everything presented in both works. This led to a battery with over 1,000 procedures that took 18 hours or so to administer to people with no impairments. From this extremely comprehensive battery, items were statistically deleted based on their redundancy and on this failure to produce reliable scores or to measure what was intended. Other items were eliminated clinically because of their length or because they did not return enough useful information. This allowed the battery to be cut down to slightly over 3 hours. Additional data was collected, and some additional items were eliminated because of lack of reliability or because of inability to identify clients with brain injuries.

The battery, labeled the Luria-South Dakota, was first presented in a symposium chaired by Golden at the 1977 American Psychological Association (APA) convention in Montreal. The test was immediately very popular despite the fact that there had been relatively little research to date, largely because it seemed to tap a strong area of interest both in Luria's work and in the need for briefer, more focused instruments. The test was initially simply copied and distributed to individuals interested in the battery, leading to more research as well as to increased demand. The battery was revised one last time to produce the Luria-Nebraska Neuropsychological Battery (Golden, Purisch, & Hammeke, 1985), which was published by Western Psychological Services. Initial publication of the LNNB data was published in the *Journal of Consulting and Clinical Psychology* (Golden, Hammeke, & Purisch, 1978; Purisch, Golden, & Hammeke, 1978) as well as in the *International Journal of Neuroscience* (Hammeke, Golden, & Purisch, 1978), which exposed the battery to an even larger stage.

After the introduction of the LNNB, work began immediately on an alternate form (Form II) of the test, both to provide a parallel form and to improve on the battery. The major changes on Form II were adding a Delayed Memory scale, as well as providing a new set of stimulus items that were more modern and appropriate for some populations. These changes were also intended to make the battery more widely available, especially because the Christensen (1975) materials on which Form I was based were frequently unavailable due to printing issues. Form II of the test was published in 1985, along with a newly expanded and more extensive test manual for both forms of the test (Golden et al., 1985).

The LNNB provides a framework for Luria's evaluative style by adding an objective scoring system and standard administration procedures. This structuring provides a foundation of items that can be given to all clients, scored in an objective and reliable manner, and evaluated for systematic effectiveness across different populations. At the same time, Luria's qualitative and flexible administration is retained around this framework, yielding an instrument that can be (1) studied psychometrically and, at the same time, (2) used in a purely clinical and impressionistic manner.

In order to reach these two goals, it was necessary to carefully modify the administration so that it was reproducible but also accounted for the client's individuality and allowed the clinician adequate flexibility to investigate qualitative behavior of the client. To achieve this adaptability, a number of techniques were adopted for the test administration. First, instructions for items were made flexible so that the clinician could be assured that the client understood the instructions. In the case of many standardized instructions, clients make errors because they do not understand the task requirements. The LNNB allows paraphrasing and repeating instructions, answering client questions, and offering examples to ensure that the client understands what is required. Simultaneously, the process of client information is garnered in this communicative process. For example, if the client learns only from examples or rapidly forgets instructions and needs frequent repetition, information directly relevant to the client's condition and learning style is gained. Attention to this communicative process throughout the test can assist in making an accurate diagnosis and description of the client.

Second, testing of the limit procedures are encouraged throughout the evaluation. Although such procedures are built into the items themselves, the test organization allows the clinician to add these procedures without affecting the validity of the standard scores. An important aspect of this flexibility is the emphasis on identifying the client's underlying mechanism of performance. Any item on any test, regardless of the simplicity, can be missed for a variety of reasons. A full understanding of the client's condition can be achieved only with comprehension of the client's failure.

Further, qualitative observations are encouraged throughout the test. These observations not only focus on the question of why an item was missed, but on behavior between items throughout the test. For example, a person with attentional problems who is otherwise intact may receive normal scores on the test if sufficiently redirected to the questions. The need and nature of such redirection, while not scored in any item, becomes a significant part of the evaluation. In traditional tests, client errors are often misinterpreted in terms of item content rather than in terms of the attentional process. Through clinician involvement in the testing process, the LNNB separates the content issues of the items from such conditions as arousal, attention, concentration, emotionality, frustration, motivation, and fatigue.

Finally, the emphasis of the LNNB is on obtaining optimal client performance. Many traditional tests encourage suboptimal performance in clients with brain injuries through minimal feedback, excessive testing times, misunderstood instructions, and other similar features. Such procedures maximize differences between those clients with brain injuries and those without, increasing hit rates but decreasing individual differences among clients with brain injuries. Many of these tests may end up maximizing the manifestations of client impairment.

The LNNB attempts to have clients with a specific deficit in an area miss only specific related items by seeking to optimize performance throughout the test. It is believed that optimal performance tells clinicians more about how the brain functions, although the individual may not perform at such levels in real life due to various psychiatric and environmental reasons. By understanding what arises from brain injury and what arises from other sources, clinicians can achieve the best understanding of the individual. For example, on motor speed items on any test, clients may become distracted, forget what they are doing, lose interest, or perform at an inappropriate rate, resulting in performance less than their capability. The LNNB accounts for this problem qualitatively and diagnostically, allowing variations in administration or readministered so that the final standard score is not affected by these extraneous factors. This method has the effect of making individual items and scales less sensitive to brain injury but better able to specify the underlying cause of impaired performance.

The LNNB, Form II, consists of 279 items organized into 12 basic scales (Golden et al., 1985). Because many of the items have more than one subpart, the actual number of procedures in the test is approximately 1,000. The LNNB scales are nontraditional because the same procedure or question is not asked repeatedly at different levels of difficulty. The purpose of the LNNB is not to stratify individuals as "average" or "superior" but rather to address basic functions, which underlie all complex behavior. Each scale is organized to test different aspects of behavior within each area evaluated. Although the items differ from one another in a variety of ways, they all have a common theme, such as memory functions or language functions.

The content of the LNNB scales differs within each scale around a single theme as has been discussed. A more detailed description of the content of each scale follows. The content for the two forms of the test is identical except for the addition of the Intermediate Memory Scale to Form II.

Motor (C1)

The 51-item motor scale begins with 4 items measuring motor speed of the left hand and the right hand. Speed is measured on one simple item (opening and closing a hand) and one complex item (touching each finger in sequence with the thumb). This is followed by 4 items that examine the role of muscle feedback when performing simple motor behaviors and 10 items examining the ability to perform simple bilateral motor movements by imitation. Two items examine the ability to perform simple items by command. Three items examine bilateral speeded coordination. Perseverative and fine motor skills are examined in an item that requires copying a repetitive figure (alternating the letter *m* with the letter *n*).

The ability to perform complex motor movements by verbal instruction and without props is measured by four items such as, "Show me how you would open up a can with a can opener." This evaluation is followed by 9 items evaluating the ability to perform simple and speeded oral motor movements and 13 items looking at the speed and quality of simple drawings by command and from copying. The final 4 items request contradictory behavior under verbal control, such as, "If I tap once, you tap twice." These latter items examine the ability of the client to inhibit imitation and to control behavior through inner speech.

Rhythm (C2)

The 12-item Rhythm scale evaluates the ability to hear rhythmic patterns and musical tones, to evaluate these stimuli, and to reproduce them. Items range from identifying similarity of patterns or tones and to reproducing patterns, tones, and musical sequences.

Tactile (C3)

This 22-item scale uses a series of 11 measures on both the right and the left sides of the body independently. These tasks include indicating where the person is touched, whether a touch is hard or soft, whether a touch is sharp or dull, how many points are touching the person, the direction of movement of a touch, which letters or numbers are written on the wrist, copying gross motor movements by muscle feedback, and identifying simple objects placed in the hand.

Visual (C4)

The 14-item Visual scale examines visual and visual-spatial skills that do not require motor movements. Although some of the items involve verbal feedback, clients do not need to name objects accurately but must indicate that they recognize the object's purpose or use. The items include simple identification, identification when parts of the item are missing, and identification of overlapping items. Spatial items include completing visual patterns (similar to Raven's Matrices), telling time on an analog clock, identifying directions, imagining items in three dimensions, and rotating items into new configurations.

Receptive Language (C5)

The 33-item Receptive Language scale evaluates speech comprehension, including basic phonemes and complex sentences. Eight items examine phonemic comprehension. Six items examine word comprehension, and the rest evaluate the comprehension of sentences at various levels of complexity.

Expressive Language (C6)

The 42-item Expressive Language scale evaluates speech utilizing simple sounds and complex sentences under a variety of conditions. The first 10 items look at repetition of sounds and words, and the next 11 involve reading similar sounds and words (with the diagnostic emphasis on the fluency of pronunciation rather than on accuracy of reading). Three items involve repetition of sentences. Three items examine naming skills. Five items evaluate automatic naming (such as counting or the days of the week). The remainder of the items concern complex and less structured speech, such as responding to a question, describing a picture, speaking about the weather, using specific words in a sentence, and reorganizing words into a sentence.

Writing (C7)

This 12-item scale scores both for motor writing errors (the motor performance of forming letters and words) and for spelling. The items range from single letters to sentences. One composition sample is included as well. The scale measures basic writing and spelling skills up to a seventh-grade level.

Reading (C8)

The 13-item Reading scale involves the reading of items ranging from single letters to paragraphs. Two items look at the ability to hear letters and to articulate them into sounds and words. Unlike the reading items on the Expressive Language scale, the items are scored for reading accuracy, not expressive fluency. As with the Writing scale, the test measures basic abilities up to a seventh-grade level.

Arithmetic (C9)

This 22-item scale evaluates the reading and writing of numbers and simple computational skills. Nine items examine number recognition and writing at various levels of complexity. Two items involve simple number comparison. Nine items look at basic computational skills up through a seventh-grade level. The final 2 items involve serial sevens and serial thirteens. Items are designed to examine the spatial nature of numbers as well as more basic number recognition.

Memory (C10)

The 13-item Memory scale evaluates verbal and nonverbal immediate memory with and without interference. The scale begins with the learning of a seven-item word list, followed by picture memory with and without delays. Immediate rhythmic and tactile-visual memory are assessed, as is verbal-visual memory. These appraisals are followed by simple list learning with interference and sentence learning with interference. One item involves recall of a paragraph. The last item examines visually cued verbal memory using a 7-item paired list.

Intelligence (C11)

The 34-item Intelligence scale yields an estimate of general IQ by employing many types of items traditionally used in intelligence evaluations. Four items involve picture interpretations, and 2 items involve picture sequencing. Verbal items include interpretations of stories and proverbs, vocabulary, similarity items, difference items, the ability to generalize from the specific to the general, the ability to make deductions from general rules to specific instances, and categorization skills. The final 12 items involve simple mathematical word problems.

Delayed Memory (C12)

This scale tests delayed memory of items that initially required memory (from the Memory scale) as well as recognition and retention of material in the remainder of the test. This procedure usually involves delays ranging from 30 minutes to 2 hours. Both verbal and nonverbal items are included.

PSYCHOMETRIC PROPERTIES

Reliability

The reliability of the LNNB has been examined from a number of perspectives, including interrater agreement, internal consistency, and test-retest reliability. A study by Golden et al. (1978), examined 1,345 comparisons resulting from the battery administration to five separate clients by five independent pairs of examiners. A high level of interrater agreement was obtained, based on 95% of identical comparisons. This was further corroborated by a follow-up study by Bach, Harowski, Kirby, Peterson, and Schulein (1981).

The internal consistency estimates (alpha) ranged from .82 on C2 to .94 on C1, for the 14 clinical-summary scales on 146 clients with brain damage and 74 control clients (Mikula, 1981). A more recent study examined this in a mixed sample of clients with brain damage and without ($n = 559$), along with separate groups of clients with brain impairment ($n = 451$) and with schizophrenia ($n = 414$), a mixed group of psychiatric patients ($n = 128$), and a normative sample with 108 participants (Maruish, Sawicki, Franzen, & Golden, 1984). The correlations for all the groups except the normative sample were quite high, ranging from .81 to .93.

The test-retest reliabilities of the clinical scales ranged from .78 on C3 to a high of .96 on C9 (Golden, Berg, & Graber, 1982). Another study by Plaisted and Golden (1982) analyzed the test-retest reliability for the 14 original scales, for localization scales, and for the factor scales. For the 14 original scales, the reliability ranged from .83 to .96. For the eight localization scales, the range was between .78 and .95. However, the widest range was for the original factor scales, where the reliability ranged from .01 to .96, with an overall mean of .81. Those scores with lower reliabilities were eliminated from the test to yield a sample of 30 scales.

Validity

A number of empirical studies have estimated the criterion-related, concurrent, and construct validity of the LNNB. One study by Golden et al. (1978) tested the diagnostic efficiency of items in discriminating between individuals with brain damage and without (the controls). They found the two groups to significantly differ with regard to education, but not to age and gender (t (98) $= 3.51$ $p < .01$). Covariance was used to control for the effect of education. Significant differences were found between the performance of the two groups on all 14 original scales ($p < .001$). Hit rates for these scales ranged from 74% for C6 to 96% for C10 in the control group and from 58% for C2 to 86% for C6 in the group with brain damage. Discriminant analysis was able to correctly classify all 50 of the controls and 43 out of 50 individuals with brain damage, for an overall hit rate of 93%. Cross-validation of this study was conducted by Moses and Golden (1979) comparing a neurological sample and control sample, using Form I of the LNNB. The neurological diagnoses included cerebral trauma, cerebrovascular accidents (CVAs), epilepsy, neoplasms, and metabolic or toxic disorders. Here, the results obtained were almost identical to Golden et al. (1978).

Noting the paucity of research in assessing the neuropsychological functioning in an elderly population, MacInnes et al. (1983) compared results of a sample of "healthy" older people (mean age of 72 years) and a sample of older people with brain damage (mean age of 68 years). Multivariate analysis of variance suggested significant differences ($p < .001$) between the two groups on 11 clinical scales, using age, sex, and education as covariates. The hit rates using the classification rules were 92% for the healthy group, 86% for the group with brain damage, and 88% for the total sample.

The most ambitious studies identifying the usefulness of the LNNB in localizing and lateralizing brain injuries were completed by Lewis et al. (1979) and Osmon, Golden, Purisch, Hammeke, and Blume (1979). These studies demonstrated that the Left and Right Hemisphere scales alone were able to lateralize more than 80% of cases with clear lateralized disorders, and the test as a whole showed a 74% accuracy in discriminating among eight groups of localized injuries (compared to an expected finding of 12.5%) by chance).

ASSETS AND LIMITATIONS

Assets

The major assets of the LNNB lie in several areas. The test is relatively brief yet allows an investigation of many neuropsychological functions. In cases where time is limited, the clinician can efficiently gather a wide range of data that can be interpreted both qualitatively and quantitatively. In cases where more time is available, the LNNB can effectively identify areas where further investigation may profitably reveal the most useful information. Second, the test offers an interface that allows for flexibility in administering the test to clients with serious impairments. This flexibility allows the user to better tease out which deficits are basic and which are only a secondary result of other deficits.

The ability to determine basic underlying deficits makes the LNNB more useful in a rehabilitation setting. Although rehabilitation can be more general, it is usually more efficient when focused on specific problems. Another advantage is the simple interface of the items that makes them easier to translate across cultures as well as across languages. The simpler tests have a cleaner relationship to basic brain functions, which are less effected by culture and language and which have a more understandable relationship to functions of specific systems of the brain. For examples of this, see Marwaha-Sonali and Barnes (1991); Xun, Gong, and Matthews (1987); and Kang (1992).

Limitations

The limitations of the test are rooted in its strengths. Although the LNNB is very useful for assessing complex neuropsychological functions, the simple nature of the items preclude observations of very complex functions, which are a sum of these basic skills. In some cases of injury, especially in high-functioning people, the major deficits lie in the integration of these basic functions rather than in the functions itself. It should be noted, however, that such deficits are not always the result of brain injury but may arise from emotional problems and environmental issues. In the experience of the senior author using the LNNB with other test batteries in a wide variety of medical and forensic settings, the LNNB is much more likely to underdiagnose brain injury compared to other tests and will rarely overdiagnose problems that turn out to be related to nonneurological factors. As with most other tests, relevant history, detailed clinical observations, and special medical diagnostic procedures should be used to supplement, corroborate, and investigate the test results.

There are certain client characteristics required for the administration of the LNNB. Hence, these tests are inappropriate for clients who are overtly hostile and uncommunicative or for clients with extremely disorganized thinking processes. In addition, individuals with low verbal ability will have difficulty in completing this test battery.

For individuals who wish to rely on quantitative information alone, the reliance of the LNNB on qualitative information generally causes some distress. In contrast, for individuals who believe in only qualitative data, the imposition of a standardized, quantitative framework may be seen as inappropriate. It was felt in putting the test together that the integration of the two along with the need for a briefer exam created an ideal compromise that offers features of both approaches.

Perhaps the largest limitation of this approach is the demands on the user. This test requires an understanding of the theoretical underpinnings of the test and of neuropsychology in order to be used in the most effective manner. Although the test can be used based on basic rules (see the test manual and the interpretation section), this approach uses only a tiny part of the information generated by the test. As a result, mastering the test is a complex process, which demands more of the user but also delivers more when done properly.

ADMINISTRATION

Scoring the LNNB occurs on several different levels, including scoring of specific items, scoring of the scales, and qualitative scoring.

Item Scoring

All items on the LNNB are scored as 0 (indicating normal performance), 1 (borderline performance), or 2 (impaired performance). For items that are only scorable as right or wrong, 0 represents right, and 2 represents wrong. For those items (such as motor speed items) that involve counting of responses, the raw score is translated into a score of 0, 1, or 2 by using norms given on the test form. The use of this common scoring procedure allows for statistical and clinical interitem comparisons.

Scale Scoring

Each scale is scored by adding up the 0, 1, and 2 scores from each of the items. A total raw score is generated, which is converted into a T-score using the table in the test form. The T-scores have a mean of 50 and a standard deviation of 10. High scores reflect poorer performance. These scores are classified as normal or impaired by reference to a cutoff score, which is individually determined by the client's age and education using a table in the test form. Scores above the cutoff are considered impaired. The average cutoff is 60, but may vary from 50 to over 70, depending on the age and the education of the client.

In addition to these basic scales, the LNNB items may be rearranged into scales for specific purposes. Three of these scales are used frequently. (1) The Left Hemisphere scale consists of all items related to the right side of the body. (2) The Right Hemisphere scale consists of all items related to the left side of the body. (3) The Pathognomonic scale consists of a series of items that are sensitive to the severity and the acuity of the cognitive dysfunction. Additional scales also include the factor scales, which represent factors extracted from individual scales as well as the overall test. All of these additional scales are scored just as the original scales, adding up the scale scores on each item. These scales represent such subfactors as motor speed, drawing, basic language, spatial skills, repetition, verbal memory, verbal arithmetic, general intelligence, simple tactile, complex tactile, naming, verbal-spatial skills, phonemic skills, complex expressive language, basic reading, and so on. Other scales have been developed for specific uses. There is no limit to the range and the type of scales that can be developed from the basic data. An example of a basic profile is seen in Figure 8.1.

Qualitative Scoring

In addition to item scoring and scale scoring, the LNNB includes 60 qualitative scoring categories, which can be scored at any time during the test, including in between items. A review of these indices is not within the scope of this chapter, but a sample can be discussed to show their usefulness.

In general, qualitative indices represent recording of observations by the tester during the course of the examination. These reports generally fall into the categories of (1) problems that relate to inadequate client comprehension of procedures; (2) observations that explain why the client is missing an item; (3) unusual behaviors between items that impact the testing; and (4) problems that manifest during an item performance but that are not related to the objective scoring of the test.

Problematic client comprehension generally involves confusion, insufficient vocabulary, attention deficits, arousal problems, fatigue, and motivation.

Observations during the item that clarify errors differ depending on the scale, but they will include paralysis, motor slowness, motor awkwardness, hearing difficulties, attentional problems, tactile sensation loss, visual difficulties, visual agnosia, inability to comprehend speech, naming problems, slowness in comprehension, inability to attend to the left side of stimuli, dysarthria, slowness of speech, word substitutions in speech,

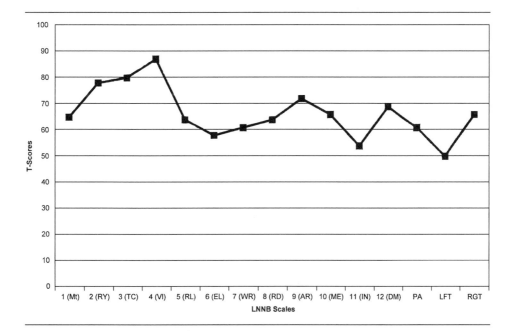

Figure 8.1.   LNNB profile for case example (EF)

sound substitutions in speech, syllable substitution in words, inability to progress from one sound to another, perseveration, concreteness, dyslexia, failure to recognize letters, failure to recognize sounds, failure to recognize number, visual-motor problems, memory problems, and fatigue.

Unusual behaviors may include distractibility, inability to recall instructions, inappropriate emotional reactions, excessive fatigue, hyperactivity, lack of cooperation, poor arousal, seizures, and other related problems.

The final category can include any problems seen when the *person responds correctly but still shows a problem,* for example, an individual may correctly describe an object but fail to name it correctly, thus demonstrating dysnomia. An individual may be literate but only in a dysfluent manner, suggesting expressive speech problems such as dysarthria.

The qualitative indices are not limited to those discussed here and in the test manual but rather reflect any behaviors that help further understand the client: any observations of behavior that do not make sense or that otherwise seem unusual, even if the examiner does not know what they mean or their etiology.

INTERPRETATION

With the LNNB, there are many levels of client classification, ranging from normal-abnormal to sophisticated analysis of the precise deficits and precise neurological causes of a given deficit (see Table 8.1). The first and most basic level of classification concerns quantifying profiles as normal or abnormal. The second level involves a more detailed pattern analysis using the quantitative scores. The third level involves a detailed item analysis yielding a description of what the client can and cannot do without any inferences about neurological causes. The fourth level involves an analysis of the qualitative data and its integration with the quantitative data. The fifth level examines the role of the client history in the analysis. This final level involves the integration of psychometric, qualitative, historical, and medical findings to form a definitive picture of the client's problems (their causes and their interaction with the environment), the role of the client's personal and medical history, and the implications of this data for rehabilitation and prognosis in general.

Table 8.1. Levels of interpretation for the LNNB

Level I. Identifying the presence of brain damage from quantitative scores.

Level II. Detailed pattern analysis of quantitative scores to identify specific deficits.

Level III. Detailed quantitative item analysis looking at patterns of item errors.

Level IV. Qualitative item analysis and integration with quantitative results.

Level V. Integration of client history, medical findings, and all other sources of information with the quantitative and qualitative results.

Level I: Identifying Brain Damage

The LNNB provides several independent methods to identify the possible presence of a brain injury. The first involves a comparison of the 12 basic skills along with the Pathognomonic Scale to the critical level (CL) discussed in the scoring section. More than three scores above the critical level is indicative of brain injury. The probability of this occurrence in an individual without brain injury is less than 1 in 100. If no scale or one scale is elevated, the profile is considered to be normal. If two scales are elevated (which is likely to happen in 1 of 25), the profile is a borderline case.

Because the CL is dependent on age and education, the accuracy of this rule depends on the accuracy of the information. Age is rarely misstated in a significant fashion, but education is much more difficult to calculate. For example, the CL will overestimate the premorbid abilities of a client who physically attended school for 12 years but was impaired due to retardation or brain injury. In such a case, the choice of a specific level of education for the formula often depends on the question being asked. If a clinician simply wishes to know how the person is performing in relation to other people with 12 years of educational opportunity, then using 12 is appropriate. If a clinician wishes to know if the person had a recent brain injury (since the end of school), then using the client's actual achievement level may be more appropriate. Furthermore, the test manual includes a formula for calculating the critical level from premorbid IQ levels.

A second method for identifying brain injury is noting the difference between the lowest and the highest T-scores. Individuals with no brain injuries typically show less than a 20-point spread between the lowest and the highest scores, with a few individuals showing up to a 25-point spread (with the highest scores often being on Arithmetic or Writing, because of spelling, in such cases). Clients with brain injuries typically show greater variability. Using this information, score differences exceeding 30 points are considered clearly indicative of brain dysfunction. Spreads between the highest and the lowest scores of less than 30 but more than 20 are considered borderline; spreads of 20 and under are considered normal. It should be emphasized that the absence of a wide spread does not itself make a profile normal.

Level II: Pattern Analysis Using the Quantitative Scores

The basic quantitative scales of the LNNB yield profiles much like those of the Minnesota Multiphasic Personality Inventory (MMPI) and other similar tests. These profiles suggest which scales represent the highest elevations and are most likely to show the general areas where the client has the most difficulty. Two-point codes (the highest two scales) and three-point codes (the highest three scales) can be determined to generate statistical descriptions of the client's most likely problems. This information can be generated without reference to the full complexity of the profile, often yielding a valuable starting point for profile classification.

Most work has been done on the interpretation of the two-point profiles with some work on three-point profiles. Before interpretation, a distant profile classification must be determined. A clear-cut, two-point profile is one in which both of the two highest scales are at least 10 points higher than the third highest scale among the 12 basic scales plus the Pathognomonic, Right Hemisphere, and Left Hemisphere scales or one in which the two scales are the only scores elevated over the critical level. A clear-cut, three-point profile is one in which all three of the three highest scales are at least ten points higher than the fourth highest scale or where the three scales are the only scales higher than the critical level. Four-point and five-point code types may be defined in a similar manner. A scale is generally not included in a high point profile if it does not exceed the critical level. Interpretive suggestions given in research or in the test manual are generally more accurate when the profile is "clear-cut."

While the test manual provides more extensive descriptions of the many possible high point codes, several common two point examples which are given here to clarify the process. The following interpretations are abstracted from Golden, Purisch, and Hammeke (1985).

Motor-Tactile

This combination is often seen in clients where there is lateralized impairment, often caused by a cerebral vascular accident of some kind. In general, these occurrences are cortical strokes, whose side can be reliably determined by the comparison of the Left and Right Hemisphere scales. These strokes are generally accompanied by severe cognitive deficits, the nature of which depends on lateralization of injury. In general, the scales representing those cognitive areas (e.g., Expressive Language) will show secondary elevations.

Motor-Visual

This two-point profile is most often associated with anterior right hemisphere injuries. The client shows intact basic visual skills but has trouble with more abstractive and visual reasoning tasks. Motor impairment is generally greatest on the left side of the body. Impairment elevations on the Rhythm scale may be seen as well, producing a Motor-Visual-Rhythm three-point code. When the two-point code is Motor-Rhythm, the lesion is generally more anterior than when the two-point code is Motor-Visual. The Motor-Rhythm combination is generally associated with attentional problems, difficulties in emotional control or emotional recognition, poor insight, poor social skills (especially if the lesion is long-standing), and difficulties in following the relationships between sequences of events. This profile may also be seen in many subcortical injuries, including mild to moderate head injury.

Motor-Receptive Language

This combination is rare and occurs most often in individuals with anterior left hemisphere and subcortical left hemisphere injuries. Such individuals generally have problems with bilateral coordination and have difficulty following complex verbal commands, especially those that require an action that is inconsistent with what the individuals are seeing, such as, "When I tap once, you tap twice." However, their basic verbal communications and understanding are usually intact.

Motor-Expressive

This combination is seen in individuals with anterior left hemisphere injuries, usually arising from a relatively serious problem such as a stroke or a fast growing tumor. Such clients have dysfluent speech. They may slur their words, speak haltingly, repeat sounds, and substitute sounds that makes the client unintelligible. In extreme cases, they may be mute or unable to communicate verbally at any level, although nonverbal communication (reading and writing) may be intact. Naming problems are frequently present and may be consistent with Expressive Aphasia, also called Broca's Aphasia.

Motor-Writing

This two-point code is seen primarily in disorders in which the dominant hand is dysfunctional. This result can be seen in lateralized subcortical disorders but can also indicate a peripheral disorder in which the function of the arm is disrupted by spinal-cord or nerve injuries or fractures. When the disorder is in the brain, there are usually secondary attentional or arousal problems, which will be noted in the testing process. When the injuries are peripheral, the deficits are generally limited to items that tap motor speed and coordination and tactile sensitivity. Thus, drawing is often disrupted as well as writing and the speeded items. Secondary elevations may be seen on the Tactile, the Right Hemisphere, or the Left Hemisphere scales.

Motor-Reading

The Motor-Reading combination is rarely present in a normal person who has had a brain injury, but does occur in people who have a learning disorder (dyslexia) prior to a brain injury. This situation is most often seen in teenagers and young adults who have had a head injury and who also have a history of school problems. The occasional exception to this tendency is seen in individuals with multiple strokes who may develop an acquired dyslexia from a small stroke along with more general motor problems. This condition is usually a precursor to a more fully developed multi-infarct dementia.

Motor-Arithmetic

The Motor-Arithmetic code is seen in individuals with primarily subcortical lesions who have motor and attentional problems. It is also seen in many individuals with preexisting arithmetic disorders, which occur in up to 30% of normal controls on the LNNB. In cases where there is a premorbid arithmetic difficulty, it is best to ignore this scale and to look for the two-point code without Arithmetic included. This discrimination usually provides a more accurate picture of the impact of a current lesion, although the premorbid Arithmetic elevation may reflect a learning disability and early brain injury in some cases.

Motor-Memory

The Motor-Memory combination is nearly always seen in subcortical injuries. This deficit is common after mild to moderate head injuries. The clients have generally mild but pervasive motor problems as well as difficulty retaining information, especially with interference. They perform better with simple memorization tasks. They generally have little insight into their condition or the impact of their memory problems. Emotional liability and irritability is also common.

Motor-Intermediate Memory

This two-point code has a similar interpretation as for Motor-Memory, but the condition tends to be somewhat milder than when Motor-Memory is the two-point code, although both may have serious consequences for day-to-day functioning.

Motor-Intelligence

As in the case of Motor-Reading, the Motor-Intelligence code type is rarely seen. It may represent preexisting problems or may reflect a multi-infarct or similar process (such as multiple tumors). It is very important with this and similar codes to discriminate what was preexisting, particularly if the testing is administered to assess the effects of an injury, although this concern is less important when the test is used simply to determine the degree of a client's deficit. If this finding represents a new disorder, such as a multi-infarct process, it generally represents a more advanced dementing process than does the Motor-Reading code. However, these codes are very rare and will not likely be seen by most clinicians.

Rhythm-Visual

This two-point code is associated with defects in nonverbal processing. In mild elevations, this profile is associated with subcortical injuries, which may affect the processing of items demanding attention or detail, whereas with more severe elevations, it is usually associated with lesions in the temporal-parietal areas of the right hemisphere where such processing is interrupted by the inability to analyze novel or less overlearned material.

Rhythm-Receptive

The Rhythm-Receptive code is associated with problems in auditory processing. This code can be caused by poor hearing abilities, so peripheral hearing loss must be ruled out as a possible cause. In the absence of a peripheral hearing loss, a bilateral central hearing loss must also be investigated. In the presence of adequate hearing, the deficit is most often associated with damage to the left temporal area, but it can also be seen in bilateral temporal injuries. When elevations are over 70, this may represent a stroke or an open head trauma, but it can also be seen in a variety of degenerative processes.

Rhythm-Memory

This code is generally associated with subcortical injuries to either hemisphere, depending on the analysis of the exact deficits shown on the scales. This is rarely seen in purely cortical injuries but often follows closed head traumas and other diffuse processes.

Tactile-Reading

This combination is often seen in left parietal injuries, which may be long-standing (as seen in learning disabilities) or may be more recent injuries, generally along the lines of a stroke, open head injury, abscess, hemorrhage, or other condition that destroys brain tissue. These latter injuries are usually associated with other substantial problems as well, although this may be seen as residual many years after an event.

Visual-Receptive, Visual-Arithmetic and Visual-Memory

These high-point codes are often associated with right hemisphere problems, usually in the posterior areas. Such deficits can reflect an inability to do spatial processing and to visualize material, although the person may function well in terms of verbal skills (depending of course on the elevation of the entire profile). It is important that when any

Arithmetic deficit is considered, one establish that the deficit is not a preexisting condition but is the result of some type of more recent cerebral event. This issue is highlighted in that arithmetic difficulties, along with poor spelling skills (on the Writing scale) (even the simple ones measured on the LNNB) are the deficits most commonly seen in people in the United States who are otherwise free of deficits.

Receptive-Expressive

A high-point code, comprised of Receptive and Expressive, may represent a breakdown of speech processes in general. This is most often seen in patients with strokes and other disorders that destroy brain tissue, with lesser elevations reflecting residual deficits. These deficits are often associated with very high profiles because these basic skills are necessary to understand the test instructions. Such a profile may also be seen in severe dementing processes as well.

Receptive-Intelligence

This combination (with elevations on one or more of the achievement scales) reflects a more posterior injury than the Receptive-Expressive combination. This may be seen as the result of an adult-onset injury or may reflect long-standing learning disabilities or mental retardation. Such profiles are usually associated with substantial disabilities that affect day-to-day life.

The previous two-point combinations provide a wide range of possible interpretations. A full consideration of the power of this technique would involve all possible two-point codes, as well as the common three- and four-point codes. A similar process may be used with the major factor scales. The reader is referred to the test manual for a more detailed consideration of these codes.

Level III: Item Analysis

The next level of interpretation involves the pattern of errors. Each scale can be divided into groups of items, which explore a specific aspect of the overall scale area. Item analysis involves focusing on these specific item groupings to evaluate contributions to the overall scale elevations. Consequently, more specific hypotheses of the underlying deficits are generated. This information can be used to modify the more statistically based interpretations generated from the high-point codes and can provide more precise details of the specific problems.

The item analysis is conducted scale by scale and begins with the highest (most impaired) T-score. In general, as the scale elevations decrease, the contribution of these scales to the item analysis also decreases. In many cases, the deficits seen on the more normal scales reflect the impact of the client's major deficits. For example, some items on the Intelligence scale may be missed not because of a lack of intelligence, but because of visual or visual-spatial problems. Thus, if the Visual scale is poorly performed and Intelligence is relatively better except in this one area, such deficits are better explained on the basis of the deficits on the Visual scale.

By analyzing the more impaired scale first, we are able to avoid overdiagnosing such secondary deficits, which may otherwise appear to be additional problem areas. In making an analysis, one always attempts to identify the fewest number of problems that can account for the full range of the client's errors. This distillation yields a more parsimonious description of the client and leads to more accurate diagnoses and better targeted treatment suggestions.

The analysis of any case will differ considerably depending on the exact items missed, but the general analysis follows the item subtypes listed earlier. For example, if the Receptive Language scale is the most impaired, the client's ability to discriminate phonemes is examined in the first section of the test. Half of the items require writing the letter of the phoneme, while the other half requires repeating the sound. If the client can do either half, then phonemic hearing is likely to be intact, and the problem is attributed to pronunciation, writing, or sound-letter conversions. If the client is unable to do both types of problems, he or she may be confused as to the task or maybe unable to discriminate phonemes. A finer analysis can be made to see if the client can understand phonemes when presented singly or if he or she has problems only when the phonemes are presented in groups, such as two or three sounds at a time. A client's ability to hear phonemes singly may reflect a very basic phonemic discrimination deficit, whereas an inability to hear them only in groups may suggest a milder discrimination problem.

These scenarios can be compared with the next set of items, which require the client to follow simple commands. If the client can complete these items but not the phonemes, he or she may be unable to discriminate sounds in isolation but able to do so in context or with well-learned words. In such cases, the client is likely to have problems both with single phonemes and with unfamiliar words. Such clients may appear to understand more than they do in reality because they follow the simple or common elements of communication.

However, if the client can manage phonemes but not simple commands, this deficit would suggest an inability to comprehend the meaning of sentences and words. The items may be analyzed to evaluate the complexity level at which the client fails: single concrete words, abstract words, similar sounding words, simple sentences, or complex sentences. The higher the level the person can achieve, the milder the impact of the injury as well as differences in the probable location of the injury. If the client cannot perform any of these items, he or she may be confused or may have dementia or a severe receptive language deficit (seen most often in people with infarcts, bleeding aneurysms, or some forms of open head injury).

The last group consists of the more complex verbal-visual items. If the client has had no problem up until this point, errors in this group often reflect injuries in the right hemisphere or anterior areas of the brain. Such deficits may reflect difficulty in understanding the relationship or spatial nature of some words or in following the sequential learning required by such items. Individuals with these deficits appear to have intact receptive speech but develop misunderstandings when sentences become multipart and require retention and analysis. This limitation may be due to memory or to a direct verbal-spatial problem. Errors in these items after failure to process simple commands, however, are most likely due to an inability to follow speech. In cases where phonemes are impaired, where simple items are intact, and where these verbal-spatial items are impaired, a language problem may exist that spares well-practiced or automatic language, but not other forms of receptive language.

By combining this analysis with a similar analysis on each of the other scales along with the scale patterns, a reasonably detailed description of what areas affect the client can be developed and etiologic hypotheses may be formed. The accuracy of the analysis depends heavily on attentiveness to precise item patterns and to recognition of the differential emphasis of each item.

Level IV: Qualitative Data

At this point, addition of the qualitative data enables the examiner to focus on the etiology of the client's deficits. This data is more descriptive and relies heavily on the observations and the recognition of the examiner. Familiarity with the range of client behavior permits more insights relevant to the neuropsychological diagnosis. Developing these skills requires experience and appropriate supervisory instruction to avoid the oversight of subtle aspects. The LNNB, through its qualitative scales, expedites this process by alerting the user to the general categories and the specific types of qualitative information that have been useful in understanding neuropsychological deficits. However, observations should not be limited to these categories because more information may explain the client's behavior and enlighten the examiner.

The interpretation of the qualitative information can occur at two levels. The first level is purely descriptive. Statements such as "The client needed frequent redirection to attend to each item" or "Motor behavior was marked by severe tremors that occurred only when the client's hands were at rest" help to clarify a client's performance. The rule of thumb should be that any deviant or extraordinary behavior or activity that necessitated a change in the testing procedures should be recorded and presented.

The second level is more complex and requires a working knowledge of how different brain injuries affect behavior. The goal at this level requires recognition of the neurological and neuropsychological implications of the observed behavior. To reach this level successfully, the user needs a wide range of knowledge in the areas of neurophysiology, neuroanatomy, neuropathology, and recognized neuropsychological syndromes. This experience cannot be accomplished through the simple administration of the test, it requires study within these distinct areas. This preparation is the essence of Luria's original evaluation approach. It is arguably the most difficult to master.

Level V: Integration of Psychometric, Qualitative, Historical, and Medical Findings

At one time, neuropsychology emphasized "blind analysis," which transpired in the absence of any client information except age, education, gender, handedness, and test scores. Client history is now recognized an integral part of any neuropsychological evaluation or testing. Thus, in addition to generating the data, neuropsychologists must also become familiar with the client and the client's past. This background helps characterize the symptoms as they relate to such variables as rate of onset, age of onset, duration, severity, complicating factors, and potential etiologies. In addition, issues such as nonneurological psychiatric problems, which could alter the test results, must also be examined. However, the patient history is not received without scrutiny. For example, prior head injury does not necessarily explain the patient's current complaint or neuropsychological status. There must be integration with the test data to demonstrate that the history itself is reliable and related to the test results. In cases where forensic issues are involved, multiple methods of ascertaining the accuracy of history are advocated when possible.

The final and most complex step is the integration of these different sources of data. In some cases, this may be relatively simple if the lesion is localized, the data consistent, the history simple, and the quantitative and qualitative data concur. In many other cases, however, clients will be inconsistent due to varying levels of motivation and arousal, the impact of their injuries, secondary emotional issues, preexisting problems, ethnic and cultural variations, variable learning and educational experiences, and different premorbid strengths and weaknesses. Although in research the differences among lesions may appear to be straightforward, such research eliminates individuals with many of the complicating problems that are faced in real practice.

As a result, this final process is highly dependent on knowledge, experience, and a rigorous examination of all of the data for patterns and inconsistencies that focus on the client as an individual rather than as a diagnosis (such as "left hemisphere injury"). This procedure is primarily a clinical process for which there is no consistent or unambiguous rules, yet it represents the apex of neuropsychological training. Ultimately this analysis-assessment reflects the capability of the clinician. This previously described diagnostic process is best illustrated by a detailed case example.

Case Example

MR. EF

Mr. EF was injured in an automobile accident 3 years ago. Mr. EF, a 42-year-old man with 12 years of formal education, was a pedestrian who was hit by a drunk driver who went through a red light. The client was initially unconscious and was taken to a local hospital. A magnetic resonance imaging (MRI) revealed hemorrhage in the right parietal area of the brain and clinical evidence of severe concussion. A small hematoma was detected over the left frontal-parietal area. This was initially treated conservatively, but the hematoma continued to expand. Several hours later, burr holes were drilled in the skull in order to drain the hematoma.

The client was unresponsive for approximately 48 hours. Subsequently, he reacted only to loud sounds and to his name. He did not respond with any language until 4 days after the accident when he requested water. One week after the injury, he was able to reliably recognize his family and staff members, but he tended to confuse people with similar features and was unsure of names. Subsequently, he had brief periods of agitation, but he eventually progressed to self-care tasks.

Mr. EF showed bilateral weaknesses, which were worse on the left side. As time progressed, his hand strength improved bilaterally but was clumsy and awkward with his left hand. Initially, he had some difficulty dressing, but he overcame this within a week. He was discharged from the hospital and rehabilitation 5 weeks after his injury. The current testing occurred approximately 7 months post-injury as part of an evaluation related to settlement of an insurance claim. Mr. EF is a salesman and has reported more problems achieving his sales goals since his return to work 4 months before the evaluation.

HISTORY

The client's referring history has already been detailed, but in the course of the evaluation, several salient additional points were uncovered. Although Mr. EF graduated from high school, he did poorly in school, barely graduating with a low "C average." He was never interested in school and made little effort. He worked from an early age, even while attending school, and he stated that this was always his focus. He was not in Special Education at any level. He had not received any standard IQ tests as a child or as an adult, but he remembered his scores on standardized school tests as low and could offer no more specific information.

There was no history of head injuries or any other neurological disorder. To Mr. EF's knowledge, he achieved normal developmental milestones and had no illnesses beyond the normal childhood maladies. He was never hospitalized, but he was once seen in an emergency room for an uncomplicated fractured upper arm resulting from a "jungle gym" fall as a child. He did not hit his head in that accident and had not been unconscious. He consumes beer occasionally but denies heavy drinking or ever having passed out from drinking, although there were episodes when he got sick, especially as a teenager. He denied current use of drugs, but admitted to experimenting on a small scale as an adolescent. He denied drug abuse and stated he had never been treated for any alcohol or drug problems.

PRESENCE OF BRAIN DAMAGE

Mr. EF's scores on the basic scales of the LNNB are listed in Table 8.2 (and are reproduced earlier in the chapter in Figure 8.1). His critical level is 60 as calculated

Table 8.2. Scores on the basic scales of the LNNB for Mr. EF

Scale	T-Score
Motor	65
Rhythm	78
Tactile	80
Visual	87
Receptive Language	64
Expressive Language	58
Writing	61
Reading	64
Arithmetic	72
Memory	66
Intelligence	54
Delayed Memory	69
Pathognomonic	61
Left Hemisphere	50
Right Hemisphere	66

from his age and education, so nearly all the scales of the test are elevated, and the profile can be considered abnormal. Furthermore, the range of scores from high to low is 37 points, also well into the range of brain damage.

SCALE PATTERN

The highest scores are Visual (87) and Tactile (80), although this is not a clear-cut code. There is a clear-cut three-point high code of Visual, Tactile, and Rhythm (78). This three-point code is almost exclusively associated with right hemisphere injuries, usually in the posterior areas of the hemisphere. Such clients typically have substantial difficulty with spatial relationships, nonverbal communication, complex pictures, overlapping pictures, left-sided tactile sensation, left-sided motor awkwardness and slowness, bilateral coordination, and visual memory. Clients with more severe impairments, may neglect the left side of objects and written material, and they may have difficulty drawing complex figures and many simple figures. Drawing, even when intact, may be slow. Some clients have difficulty with some everyday tasks like dressing. They may show confusion over tasks that require sequences of behaviors, as well as verbal materials that involve spatial or logical relationships. They may have difficulty doing some mathematical processes that involve sequencing and doing mental arithmetic and such processes as borrowing. They may exhibit emotional liability, as well as problems understanding their own emotions and those of others.

ITEM PATTERN

The items within the highest scales are evaluated first. On the Visual Scale, Mr. EF was able to identify real objects and simple representations of real objects (line drawings). However, when the item was obscured (as in a blurry photograph) or when part of it was missing, he was unable to recognize the objects. When item drawings overlapped one another, he was unable to separate most of the objects out of the picture. Items requiring the completion of spatial patterns were poorly performed, although he was able to complete one item in which logical verbal analysis could be substituted for spatial analysis. He was unable to tell time on analog clocks or to draw the hands of the clock at a specific time. He was unable to visualize objects in three dimensions or to rotate objects in two dimensions in his head.

On the Tactile Scale, he could perceive basic touch on both sides of the body. On the left side, however, he had difficulty identifying where he was touched, how hard he was touched, or the sharpness or direction of the touch. On these items, he performed well above chance but did poorly when compared to normal controls. He had bilateral difficulty with identifying objects drawn on his wrist, but he could recognize letters and numbers drawn in the same manner on his right side but not those drawn on his left side. He was very slow to recognize objects by touch alone with the left hand compared to normal performance with the right hand.

On the Rhythm scale, he could discriminate basic sounds but had difficulty distinguishing patterns. Thus, if he were presented with two rhythmic patterns, he would have difficulty identifying and comparing them. This was evident both when he had to judge similarity of patterns or when he needed to reproduce the patterns. He was able to sing and to recognize whether tones were high or low pitched. He was also able to count the number of beats or tones in a pattern without difficulty.

On the Arithmetic scale, he was able to recognize Arabic and Roman numbers. He could write and read numbers without failure. He was able to complete simple computations, but he could not do computations in his head that required borrowing or carrying. He was unable to do serial sevens and serial thirteens. He was able to compare numbers without difficulty, and he understood how numbers in different places within the number had different values.

On Delayed Memory, Mr. EF showed much stronger performance on the verbal items as compared to the visual items. Although he could remember words memorized during the test and describe procedures, he had difficulty remembering what pictures he had seen throughout the test and had difficulty remembering how words and pictures had been associated on the Memory scale. Verbal memory with and without interference was intact. The pattern of errors on the Memory scale was very similar, with visual items performed more poorly than verbal items.

On the Motor scale, his speeded movements with his left hand were somewhat slow, although right-hand items were performed at a normal speed. Bilateral coordination was clearly impaired and slow. He had several errors imitating hand positions by sight alone. He would make spatial distortions, and he would mirror image the examiner by using his left hand instead of his right and vice versa. His drawings of simple figures (such as a square or circle) were intact, but they were drawn slowly. However, his drawing of the more complex Greek cross was poor, and he was very slow drawing alternating *m*s and *n*s. He was able to perform motor movements on command, to show how to carry out actions, and to follow conflicting verbal commands without error. Oral-motor items were intact as well.

On Receptive Language, Mr. EF was able to understand phonemes and simple statements and commands without error. However, he had difficulty with items involving spatial relationships ("Draw a circle to the right of a cross") and verbal relationships ("Mary is taller than Beth, and Amy is shorter than Beth. Who is the tallest?"). There were no problems of routine communication for him.

On the Reading scale, he had difficulty reading complex words, but basic reading was intact, as were letter-sound combinations. Writing was also generally intact except for a slightly higher than normal level of spelling errors. Expressive Language was performed well, except he had difficulty with the days of the week backward, picture interpretation, and sequencing mixed-up words into a sentence.

QUALITATIVE OBSERVATIONS

Whereas the preceding could be generated from simply looking at Mr. EF's scores, the qualitative observations permit analysis of individual and comprehensive scale performance. Throughout test administration, Mr. EF maintained adequate arousal and concentration and was not fatigued by the process. He did not become frustrated by failure. He appeared unaware of poor performance. There was no evidence of the neglect of the left side of words, sentences, or visual stimuli.

Any item that required visual-spatial transformations or analysis without external aids were performed very poorly. His basic drawings were adequate, but complex drawings were severely spatially distorted. Use of the left side of his body showed rigidity and awkwardness. He could perform speeded tasks while watching his hands and fingers, but "testing the limits" found that he slowed considerably when he was asked to do such tasks with his eyes closed. He showed great confusion when he needed to use any kinesthetic or proprioceptive feedback from the left side. Although bilateral coordination was slowed, this was due entirely to interference from the left hand.

His difficulties with language occurred when visual interpretation, visual-spatial, or relationship concepts were required. When describing pictures that were not overlapping or obscured, he could focus on concrete details but failed to observe the interrelationships of the pieces. This was evident across several scales including Receptive, Expressive, and Intelligence. Verbal processes were preserved. His problems with arithmetic involved carrying and borrowing, especially when he had to do them in his head. Problems on Writing and Arithmetic were greater than expected, given his age and education, and consisted of difficulty with more complex words. His reading and spelling levels appeared to be below sixth grade, but he did understand basic phonemic relationships to letters. He was able to integrate sounds to produce approximations of words and was able to spell phonetically, although not necessarily correctly. His expressive speech was fluent.

He did not show any difficulty with failure (primarily because he seemed not to notice it), but he did show some emotional reactivity when he desired a rest or when the testing was accidentally interrupted. He regained composure easily, but his initial reactions were greater than expected.

INTEGRATION

This is a reasonably consistent case, which appears to follow a rational pattern. The worst of Mr. EF's injuries, per his medical records, were in the right posterior area. This is consistent with his visual-spatial problems and with his left-sided tactile-kinesthetic-proprioceptive problems. The absence of any left-sided motor problems that cannot be attributed to his sensory problems indicate that the lesion is relatively posterior and spares the more anterior motor areas of the brain. The absence of any visual-field loss and the absence of left-sided neglect suggests that the lesion is circumscribed and does not extend over wide areas of the brain. The occipital areas appear intact.

His poor verbal performance on some of the scales raises the question of the role of his left hemisphere hematoma. Most of his verbal problems, however, can be easily attributed to the spatial problems in the right hemisphere. Dysfluency was not evident. Verbal intellectual processes are intact. Several lines of evidence suggest that his reading and writing problems may be preexisting. First, there are his own reports of performing poorly in school. Second, the data itself suggests that the brain-based basic processes required for achievement, such as phonemic discrimination, letter-sound matching, decoding, phonemic integration, and the like, are all intact. His inability to analyze more complex words appears to be more related to a lack of schooling and practice rather than to a deficit in any underlying neuropsychological skill. Finally, there are none of the qualitative findings that would be expected with a left hemisphere injury.

All of these lines of evidence suggest that the impact of the hematoma was minimal and is currently so minor as to not be identifiable. This is consistent with the type of hematoma he had because it was treated properly, and there was no bleeding or significant bruising in the same area. His memory problems are restricted to nonverbal material, another indicator of a relatively focal right hemisphere injury. He clearly had difficulty with both immediate and delayed memory in these areas. Typically, victims of head injury on the LNNB show much worse Delayed as opposed to Immediate Memory problems. The exception occurs in cases similar to this where there is actual destruction of brain tissue in a focal area, which may produce the current pattern rather than the more diffuse pattern seen in many head injuries.

There was no qualitative or quantitative evidence in the test of frontal problems. His logical processes and problem-solving abilities were intact, as were his attention, concentration, and behavioral control. Perseveration and inflexibility were not present. Although there was some unawareness of his deficits, such unawareness is often seen in right parietal injuries. Some believe that such deficits imply a frontal disorder, but this author has seen this in other cases with clear focal injuries of this type. There were no right-sided motor problems or evidence of any dysfluency or other Expressive Language problem.

Overall, Mr. EF clearly suffered a substantial brain injury the residual impact of which is seen in the posterior right hemisphere. He has retained many intact skills, especially in verbal areas, but shows deficits in visual memory, visual-spatial skills, left side somatosensory (tactile) functions, and nonverbal problem solving. He shows mild emotional lability, which he is generally able to control. These deficits are serious enough to affect many major functions, including driving. Although driving itself may be overlearned and his dominant motor skills are normal, his ability to judge relative speeds and traffic patterns may be impaired. In heavy or complex traffic situations, he is likely to have a much higher chance of making errors.

His salesmanship skills would also be affected. His verbal skills are well preserved, but his memory for faces and for other nonverbal stimuli is impaired. As a result, he may not be able to relate to customers as well as he once did, which may interfere with his performance. He also may have difficulty understanding nonverbal communications from customers, a skill integral to salesmanship. These deficits would be consistent with the drop-off in his performance since the accident. Although he can continue to work, his job requirements need to be reviewed or the expectations for his achievement lowered.

The evaluation does not reveal anything that should interfere with basic living skills, but such clients will have other social difficulties. They also can be very irritating to others because of their lack of awareness of their impact on others. It is important for those close to him to receive some feedback and perhaps therapy to understand why this is happening and the appropriate responses for them to take. Without such intervention, there is a high likelihood of social disruption or marital problems.

RECOMMENDED READING

Golden, C. (1980). *Item interpretation of the Luria-Nebraska Neuropsychological Battery*. Lincoln, NE: University of Nebraska.

Golden, C., Purish, A., & Hammeke, T. (1985) *Manual for the Luria-Nebraska Neuropsychological Battery*. Los Angeles: Western Psychological Services.

Golden, C., Zillmer, E., & Spiers, M. (1992) *Intervention and diagnosis in clinical neuropsychology.* Springfield, IL: Charles C. Thomas, Publisher.

Luria, A.R. (1973) *The Working brain.* New York: Oxford.

Luria, A.R. (1980) *Higher cortical functions in man.* New York: Plenum.

Reynolds, C.R., & Fletcher-Jantzen, E. (1997). *Handbook of clinical-child psychology.* New York: Plenum.

REFERENCES

Bach, P.J., Harowski, K., Kirby, K., Peterson, P., & Schulein, M. (1981). The interrater reliability of the Luria-Nebraska neuropsychological battery. *Clinical Neuropsychology, 3*(3), 19–21.

Christensen, A.L. (1975). *Luria's neuropsychological investigation.* New York: Spectrum.

Golden, C.J. (1976a).The identification of brain damage by an abbreviated form of the Halstead-Reitan neuropsychological battery. *Journal of Clinical Psychology, 32,* 821–826.

Golden, C.J. (1976b). Identification of brain disorders by the Stroop Color and Word Test. *Journal of Clinical Psychology, 32,* 654–658.

Golden, C.J., & Anderson, S.M. (1977). Short form of the Speech Sounds Perception Test. *Perceptual and Motor Skills, 45,* 485–486.

Golden, C.J., Berg, R.A., & Graber, B. (1982). Test-retest reliability of the Luria-Nebraska neuropsychological battery in stable, chronically impaired patients. *Journal of Consulting and Clinical Psychology, 50,* 452–454.

Golden, C.J., Hammeke, T.A., & Purisch, A.D. (1978). Diagnostic validity of a standardized neuropsychological battery derived from Luria's neuropsychological tests. *Journal of Consulting and Clinical Psychology, 46,* 1258–1265.

Golden, C.J., Purisch, A.D., & Hammeke, T.A. (1985). *Manual for the Luria-Nebraska neuropsychological battery.* Los Angeles: Western Psychological Services.

Hammeke, T.A., Golden, C.J., & Purisch, A.D. (1978). A standardized, short, and comprehensive neuropsychological test battery based on the Luria neuropsychological evaluation. *International Journal of Neuroscience, 8,* 135–141.

Kang, Y. (1992). A preliminary study for a Korean version of the Luria-Nebraska neuropsychological battery–children's revision. *Korean Journal of Child Studies, 13,* 203–216.

Lewis, G., Golden, C.J., Moses, J.A., Jr., Osmon, D.C., Purisch, A.D., & Hammeke, T.A. (1979). Localization of cerebral dysfunction with a standardized version of Luria's neuropsychological battery. *Journal of Consulting and Clinical Psychology, 47,* 1001–1019.

Luria, A.R. (1966). *Higher cognitive functions in man.* New York: Basic Books.

Luria, A.R. (1973). *The working brain.* New York: Basic Books.

Luria, A.R. (1980). *Higher cognitive functions in man* (2nd ed.). New York: Plenum Press.

MacInnes, W.D., Gillen, R.W., Golden, C.J., Graber, B., Cole, J.K., Uhl, H.S., & Greenhouse, A.H. (1983). Aging and performance on the Luria-Nebraska neuropsychological battery. *International Journal of Neuroscience, 19,* 179–190.

Maruish, M.E., Sawicki, R.F. Franzen, M.D., & Golden, C.J. (1984). Alpha coefficient reliabilities for the Luria-Nebraska neuropsychological battery summary and localization scales by diagnostic category. *International Journal of Clinical Neuropsychology, 7,* 10–12.

Marwaha-Sonali, B., & Barnes, B.L. (1991). Application of the Luria-Nebraska neuropsychological battery (Form I) to the Indian population. *Indian Journal of Clinical Psychology, 18*(1), 19–23.

Mikula, J.A. (1981). The development of a short form of the standardized version of Luria's neuropsychological assessment (Doctoral dissertation, Southern Illinois University, Carbondale, 1979). *Dissertation Abstracts International, 41,* 3189B.

Moses, J.A., & Golden, C.J. (1979). Cross validation of the discriminative effectiveness of the standardized Luria neuropsychological battery. *International Journal of Neuroscience, 9,* 149–155.

Osmon, D.C., Golden, C.J., Purisch, A.D., Hammeke, T.A., & Blume, H.G. (1979). The use of a standardized battery of Luria's test in the diagnosis of lateralized cerebral dysfunction. *International Journal of Neuroscience, 9,* 1–9.

Plaisted, J.R., & Golden, C.J. (1982). Test-retest reliability of the clinical, factor, and localization scales of the Luria-Nebraska neuropsychological battery. *International Journal of Neuroscience, 17,* 163–167.

Purisch, A.D., Golden, C.J., & Hammeke, T.A. (1978). Discrimination of schizophrenic and brain damaged patients by a standardized version of Luria's neuropsychological tests. *Journal of Consulting and Clinical Psychology, 34,* 661–663.

Xun, Y., Gong, Y.X., & Matthews, J.R. (1987). The Luria-Nebraska neuropsychological battery revised for China. *International Journal of Neuropsychology, 9,* 97–101.

PART THREE

Frequently Used Tests According to Functional Domains

Chapter 9

LEARNING AND MEMORY

EDWARD HELMES

Disorders of memory are among the more common complaints of cognitive problems that individuals may bring to a psychologist or a physician. Causes of these disorders range widely from genetic disorders through neurologic and metabolic dysfunctions to emotional and psychological disturbances. At times, a preliminary assessment of learning and memory can determine that what is perceived to be a problem by the client is in fact not an indication of true dysfunction but more an indication of the expectations and evaluations that an individual may place on these cognitive processes. At other times, the screening assessment may confirm serious problems that may then require more detailed medical and neuropsychological evaluation by specialists.

Although the concepts of learning and memory are intrinsically intertwined, the demand for assessment often arises at opposite ends of the age spectrum. Learning and learning disabilities are the focus of concern for school-age children and adolescents, whereas memory complaints are more the concern of older people. Brain disease and trauma can be causative factors at any age, but even here, learning difficulties are more apt to be the identified problem if the affected person is in a formal educational program. The issue of education leads to additional relevant factors, namely age and intelligence. Age becomes relevant because of developmental changes as children grow and also because of apparent age-related changes of people in their seventh and later decades. Age effects are often confounded with differences in education as well because of the tendency of older cohorts of the general population to have fewer years of formal education than younger cohorts. At the level of the individual to be assessed, age, formal education, and intelligence would all be relevant factors to be considered in the interpretation of test scores related to learning and memory. These factors will be discussed explicitly prior to the sections on the interpretation of the tests under discussion in this chapter, that is, two of the measures of learning and memory developed by Andre Rey—the Complex Figure Test and the Auditory Verbal Learning Test (RAVLT). Both tests are widely used in practice. In a survey of 500 members of the International Neuropsychological Society, Butler, Retzlaff, and Vanderploeg (1991) found that the Complex Figure was used by 60% of the respondents, with 55% using the delayed recall trial. The Auditory Verbal Learning Test (RAVLT) was less widely used, with 46% of the survey respondents reporting its use. Before proceeding with how to work with the RAVLT and the Complex Figure Test, there are some other issues that need to be considered.

It should be stressed that this chapter does not attempt to provide a comprehensive review of measures of learning and memory. That project is of much greater scope than can be accommodated here, especially given the range of material that could be included. If educational achievement assessment is regarded as requiring the assessment of learning, then the scope increases even more. For a partial review of some of the issues and some of the major tests of educational achievement, see Chapter 10 (this volume). As the present situation stands, a recent volume on memory disorders alone runs to over 600 pages (Baddeley, Wilson, & Watts, 1995).

Both learning and memory can be regarded as major topics of the advances in studies of cognitive psychology in the past three decades. The currently dominant models are variations of the original information-processing model developed by Atkinson and Schiffrin (1968) that proposed the basic distinction between short-term memory and long-term memory (sometimes referred to as primary memory store and secondary memory store, respectively). Although there have been alternative models proposed, there is still substantial empirical and theoretical support for the Atkinson-Schiffrin model of memory (Healy & McNamara, 1996). The concept of working memory was described by Baddeley (1992) as a set of processes including an executive and an attentional system with a limited capacity. This accounts for several phenomena not handled well by the primary and secondary memory models and has attracted substantial experimental and clinical interest.

Another distinction among types of learning and associated memory has been the distinction between procedural or implicit memory and declarative, episodic, or explicit memory (Tulving, 1985). Different theorists have used different terms, but the basic distinction has remained between memory that is conscious and reflected in verbal reports of events, facts, or experiences and memory that is unconscious and assessed implicitly by changes in performance. Typical measures of procedural memory are increases in speed of learning or shifts in choice bias.

Fruitful experimental analyses and theoretical debates on models of human memory continue. One of the strengths of current models of memory is that they are largely consistent both with findings from the experimental studies of cognitive processes and with clinical experience with individuals with various forms of memory deficits (e.g., Stringer, 1996). Another strength is that there are increasing numbers of specific models that link neuroanatomical structures to memory processes (Eichenbaum, 1997).

GENERAL ISSUES

Conducting a good initial interview and obtaining a personal and a medical history from the client are a matter of standard good clinical practice. There are many guides available on the content of such interviews, and Sbordone (this volume, Chapter 4) provides a good summary of issues relevant to neuropsychological assessment. If at all possible, reports about the client from specialized investigations, such as electroencephalograms (EEGs), computerized tomography (CT), and magnetic resonance imaging (MRI) scans, should be obtained, as well as reports from family members and other significant parties. Although self-report is of major importance in evaluating the importance of a client's difficulties, confirmation of problems by others becomes highly relevant in some circumstances.

One such circumstance arises in those evaluations in which compensation or litigation are involved. For many years, neuropsychological assessment has been conducted on the basis that the clients' reports were accurate and their motivation to do well on the tests was natural and automatic. It has now become evident that not only are some people motivated to distort their responses to neuropsychological tests, but that they do so. Adults (Binder & Willis, 1991; W. Miller & Miller, 1992), adolescents (Faust, Hart, Guilmette, & Arkes, 1988), and children (Faust, Hart, & Guilmette, 1988) have all been implicated. Incentives to distort responses in order to appear impaired are substantial. In financial terms, the sums of money involved in litigation over injury, malpractice, and negligence can amount to the equivalent of several years' wages. Disability pensions to compensate for loss of wages over a working life can also amount to substantial sums. The degree to which an individual's self-esteem and self-image become invested in being disabled may result in further strengthening a client's need to appear impaired on neuropsychological tests. With increasing interest on the topic, various methods of evaluating the likelihood of a person feigning impairment have been developed. Several strategies exist, including floor effects, performance curves, magnitude of errors, symptom validity, atypical presentation, psychophysiological measures (Allen, Iacono, & Danielson, 1992), and psychological sequelae (Rogers, Harrell, & Liff, 1993); and some have demonstrated effectiveness with malingering in nonlaboratory settings (Binder, 1992; Rogers et al., 1993).

There has been some research on the ability of the two Rey tests under discussion here to detect malingering. Binder, Villanueva, Howieson, and Moore (1993) reported that the RAVLT recognition trial performance of a group with substantive evidence of motivation to fake deficits was significantly poorer than that of groups with confirmed brain damage or head trauma but with no evidence of poor motivation. Bernard and his colleagues (Bernard, 1990, 1991; Bernard, Houston, & Natoli, 1993) used the primacy and recency effects on the RAVLT to distinguish students instructed to malinger from people with true closed head injuries. Few studies on malingering have been done with the Complex Figure, but Bernard developed a discriminant function that showed promise of distinguishing malingered responses from accurate reports (Bernard et al., 1993). This work does not appear to have been cross-validated or replicated in other groups since the original research. Meyers and Meyers (1995b) reported on the utility of Atypical Recognition Errors and Recognition Failure Errors on the recognition trial they developed to identify simulated malingering by normal volunteers. A Recognition Failure Error consists of occurrences of correctly identifying an element of the Figure during delayed recall but then failing to identify it during recognition. Such errors were only made by simulators. Atypical Recognition Errors consist of elements that are very rarely incorrectly answered by individuals both with and without brain damage. The simulators made such errors much more commonly than did the group with true brain damage. The unimpaired group in the study cited by Meyers and Meyers did not make either type of error, and clients with brain damage made relatively few Atypical Recognition Errors and no Recognition Failure Errors. This is the only report to date of the use of such indices with simulated malingering, and results are promising in suggesting that such indices may be valid indicators of malingered impairment. Further work is needed to confirm the utility of the suggested cutoff points of two or more of either error type or one of each type as suggestive of questionable motivation.

A basic assumption implicit in the assessment of learning and memory is that the client has accurately perceived the stimulus material to be learned and that the client is motivated to absorb and to later recall the information. In the case of malingering just discussed, the latter is certainly suspect, but malingering is far from the only context in which questions might be raised as to the accuracy of the assumption that material read to or placed before a client is actually absorbed. This is of course critical for measures of learning and memory.

Ponsford (this volume, Chapter 11) deals with attention and input cognitive activities in more detail. These matters can be analyzed at several levels, given the broad nature of the topic, from levels of arousal to awareness of the body and its position in space to the more complex forms of attention that are evaluated by tests like Digit Span and the Trail Making Test.

On one level, close observation of the client can help determine if materials are being attended to. Direction of gaze, posture, and facial expression can help determine if the client is at least oriented toward absorbing information. Observations of behavior can also provide information as to the consistency of a client's reported problems with actual behavior. For example, clients may claim that they are unable to concentrate on anything for more than a few seconds, yet they draw the Complex Figure or perform other tasks that require sustained concentration with no obvious difficulty. The history can also provide useful information, including such symptoms as absence attacks, transient changes in vision or sensation, headache, and reading disorders or significant medical illnesses, such as diabetes or multiple sclerosis. Finally, formal assessment of vigilance and concentration can be performed (see Chapter 11 for details). Procedures such as Digit Span from the Wechsler tests (Groth-Marnat, Gallagher, Hale, & Kaplan, Chapter 5, this volume) evaluate short-term, or primary, memory capacity, a function that is theoretically distinct from attention. Similarly, coding tasks such as the Wechsler Digit Symbol-Coding and the Symbol Digit Modalities Test (A. Smith, 1982) are classed as measures of *complex attention* by Lezak (1995). These tests involve both motor speed, because they are timed, and visual coordination, because of the nature of the stimulus material. The speed factor and the need for complex coordination of visual input with fine motor control make such tests sensitive to a wide variety of brain damage but not very specific for any particular disorder. If a client is suspected of having attention problems, simpler types of tests should be used.

Age

With increasing numbers of older people in most industrialized countries, age differences in learning and memory are becoming increasingly important in interpreting test results. Modest declines of 1 to 3 points in copy and in immediate and delayed recall on the Complex Figure in healthy normal adults after the age of 70 were noted by Chiulli, Haalund, LaRue, and Garry (1995). Rosselli and Ardila (1991) reported larger differences for copy and immediate recall conditions from age 56 to over age 75 in 346 normal older adults. Boone, Lesser, Hill-Gutierrez, and Berman (1993) and Berry, Allen, and Schmitt (1991) reported similar degrees of lower scores from the age of 45. Rapport, Charter, Dutra, Farchione, and Kingsley (1997) reported moderate correlations (−.28 to −.48) with age for the Complex Figure.

Normal adults over the age of 60 recalled an average of two to six words fewer than younger adults on Trials 3, 4, and 5 of the AVLT (Savage & Gouvier, 1992). Delayed recall was also poorer for older adults in this study. Scores also decline by an average of 1 to 2 points from age 65 to age 90 (Tuokko & Woodward, 1996).

Education

Education also influences the level of performance on measures of learning and memory. Berry et al. (1991) reported correlations with years of education of .33 and .25 with immediate and delayed recall administrations of the Complex Figure. Rosselli and Ardila (1991) reported similar correlations of .43 and .37 with copy and immediate recall conditions. Rapport et al. (1997) found correlations of .30 and .17 for the same administration procedures. However, Boone et al. (1993) did not find any correlation of education with Complex Figure scores in their group of middle aged to older healthy adults. This is probably due to the use by Boone et al. of stepwise multiple regression in which IQ was also used. IQ may have drawn the significant variance that education may have accounted for in other studies in which IQ was not used.

There have been relatively fewer studies of the influence of demographic factors on performance on other instruments for measuring learning and memory. Selnes, Jacobson, Machado, and Becker (1991) reported correlations of .02 to .16 of various AVLT indices with years of education. Recognition had the lowest correlation, whereas the total of Trials 1 to 5 had the highest correlation. With the exception of the total of Trials 1 to 5, most changes in the level of performance on the indices from the AVLT with increasing education were modest at best, being less than one word on average. More substantial differences (on the order of two words or more) were noted by Tuokko and Woodward (1996) in association with increasing education across all recall trials of the AVLT.

Level of Intelligence

Separating the effects of individual differences in intelligence beyond the effects of age and years of education has rarely been attempted in neuropsychological assessment in any formal way. Obviously, it is a factor to be taken into consideration in interpreting the results of many tests, and most practitioners will do so as a matter of course. Use of the Wechsler instruments for assessing intelligence is widespread and is dealt with by Groth-Marnat et al. (this volume, Chapter 5). Given the need for large samples in order to distinguish the effects of education and intelligence, it is perhaps not surprising that there are very few such studies in this area. Using stepwise multiple regression, Boone et al. (1993) found that Full Scale IQ accounted for a significant proportion of the variance in both copy and immediate recall scores of the Complex Figure, whereas sex and education did not show such an influence. Simple Pearson correlations reported by Meyers and Meyers (1995b) of Wechsler Full Scale IQ are all statistically significant with copy accuracy, delayed recall, and recognition, except for time to copy and Recognition False Negatives measures.

There has been some research on the influence of formal education on performance on the RAVLT in addition to the effects of age beyond that already discussed. Geffen, Moar, O'Hanlan, Clark, and Geffen (1990) used stepwise regression to investigate the relative contributions of age, gender, IQ (estimated by scores on the National Adult Reading Test [NART]; Nelson, 1983), and education to performance on the RAVLT. IQ was associated with initial learning on Trial 1 and with delayed recall and recognition.

Despite the reduction in variance by other relevant factors, most notably IQ, education still accounted for significant variance on initial learning on Trials 2 to 5. Uchiyama et al. (1995) showed higher scores on most RAVLT indices increasing with more years of education.

IQ was also correlated with scores on recognition in studies by Query and Berger (1980) and by Query and Megran (1983) in adults, and all trials *except* recognition were significantly correlated with IQ in the study by Wiens, McMinn, and Crossen (1988). In children, results are more mixed, with moderate (.22 to .36) correlations reported with both learning and delayed recall and recognition scores (Bishop, Knights, & Stoddart, 1990).

Within neuropsychology, a debate has recently arisen on the advisability of conducting adjustments to test scores for age and education. Reitan and Wolfson (1996) originally strongly argued against making such corrections, although later arguments and data favored such corrections (Shuttleworth-Jordan, 1997; Vanderploeg, Axelrod, Sherer, Scott, & Adams, 1997). Vanderploeg et al. concluded "that such adjustments are necessary for all neuropsychological measures in order to minimize error variance in test interpretation" (p. 217). Indeed, Marcopulos, McLain, and Giuliano (1997) showed that standard cutoffs on several screening tests would result in conclusions of mild to moderate impairment among rural older people with limited formal education and with no impairments.

Language and Culture

Issues of language and culture are increasingly important as migration of individuals and families has become more common. Both voluntary migrants and refugees may have difficulties adapting to new environments and may experience illness or injury that may bring them for psychological assessment. Such individuals may have little or no experience with standardized testing in their native language and so will require special considerations when they are assessed. Translators may be required if the psychologist is not fluent in the language of the client. The use of translators brings additional problems (Artiola i Fortuny & Mullany, 1998; Shah, 1997), particularly if the translator is a family member or someone not well educated or not conversant with the language and psychological jargon that often creep into history taking. There are at least three aims that must be balanced in the assessment of learning and memory in individuals who are not fluent in English. These are, first, to obtain as accurate information about the nature of the perceived problem as possible while, second, maintaining good rapport and putting the client at ease and, third, ensuring that questions and test instructions are fully understood by the client. If the psychologist is not fully fluent, then the best course may be to refer the client to someone who is fluent in that language (Artiola i Fortuny & Mullany, 1998).

COMPLEX FIGURE TEST

Since its introduction by Rey in 1941 (Corwin & Bylsma, 1993; Rey, 1964), the Complex Figure has enjoyed wide use in neuropsychological assessment for the evaluation of visual perception, drawing, constructional praxis, and visual memory (Moye, 1997).

The evaluation of visuospatial perception and related processes are discussed by Lacks (this volume, Chapter 12). This section will concentrate on the uses of the Complex Figure for the evaluation of memory. Learning is implicitly evaluated in the recall of the figure after the copy trial, but the emphasis is generally not on learning in the common sense of examining performance over repeated trials with the same material. It should be noted that the distinction between learning and memory is easier to make in theory than in practice. Certainly, impairments in either visual memory or visuoperceptual or visuoconstructional abilities will lead to poor performance on the Complex Figure (Janowsky & Thomas-Thrapp, 1993). The Rey Figure is not a "pure" measure of visual memory, if such an entity even exists (Heilbronner, 1992), and how well it functions as a measure of visual memory is reviewed here.

Among other developments in the area of assessing nonverbal or visual memory are two instruments newer than the Complex Figure that do explicitly assess the learning of visuospatial material: (1) the Continuous Visual Memory Test (CVMT; Trahan & Larrabee, 1988) and (2) the Visual Object Learning Test (VOLT) (Glahn, Gur, Ragland, Censits, & Gur, 1997). The CVMT involves three tasks: Visual Discrimination, Acquisition, and Delayed Recognition. Visual Discrimination allows for distinction between deficits in visual perception and deficits in visual memory. Acquisition is a recognition task in which the client identifies repeated visual designs in an ongoing series of 112 designs. Delayed Recognition is administered 30 minutes after the Acquisition Task. Split-half reliabilities ranged from .80 to .98, with test-retest reliability over a 7-day delay of .76 to .85. The CVMT offers distinct advantages in assessing visual memory in its use of the Visual Discrimination Task and the less threatening and less demanding approach of using only recognition memory. Additional research with the CVMT will determine if it offers advantages in practice over tests such as the Rey Complex Figure. The VOLT is an object-list learning task administered on a computer, with four learning trials, a distracter trial, and immediate and delayed recall trials. Glahn et al. reported that the internal consistency was over .90 and that the VOLT was sensitive to lower scores with increasing age. It illustrates some of the benefits that can be gained through computer-based test administration, but it also requires additional validation and clinical use to determine its utility in practice.

These two tests are among the possible alternatives to the Rey and the Taylor Complex Figures for the assessment of visual learning and memory. With additional research on these two instruments, a better understanding of their relationship to the neuropsychological factors involved in visuospatial functions should emerge.

Psychometric Properties

Parallel Forms

An alternate form for the original figure was developed by L. Taylor (1979) and is often used as a parallel form on occasions in which an individual is being retested. Scores from the copy trials of the two Complex Figures are generally reported to be equivalent in both normal and patient groups (Duley et al., 1993; Kuehn & Snow, 1992; Pierson & Jansen, 1997; Spreen & Strauss, 1998; Strauss & Spreen, 1990; Tombaugh & Hubley, 1991). The Taylor Figure is more easily recalled (i.e., it gives higher recall score) than is the original Rey Figure in over 80% of an adult sample (Tombaugh, Faulkner, &

Hubley, 1992), perhaps because it is more amenable to verbal mediation (Delaney et al., 1992; Duley et al., 1993; Strauss & Spreen, 1990; Tombaugh & Hubley, 1991). Correlations between the Rey and the Taylor Complex Figures for the copy, immediate recall, and delayed recall administrations were .50, .76, and .69, respectively, for 54 older people (Berry et al., 1991), with test-retest stabilities of the Rey Figure over one year of .47 and .59 for immediate and delayed recall trials, and .18 for the copy trial (Berry et al., 1991). Lower correlations for the copy trial are not surprising, given the limited range of scores that generally results for the copy of either figure with normal populations.

The fact that the Taylor Figure is easier to recall than the Rey Figure makes its use as a parallel form for retesting more difficult. Differences in recall can be in the neighborhood of 5 points between the Rey and the Taylor versions (Strauss & Spreen, 1990). Thus individuals with no memory problems would be expected to score better at Time 2 with the administration of the Taylor Figure than with the initial administration of the Rey Figure. Someone with the same scores for recall trials under these circumstances would likely have a mild memory problem because the more accurate expectation than that of equal scores in this case is for higher recall scores for the Taylor Figure.

Tombaugh, Schmidt, and Faulkner (1992) described an interesting variation for the Taylor Figure that provides an index of learning for visual material. Thus, it is one of the very few tests to offer this useful information. Clients are told that they will have to learn a design and will have to draw it from memory. They are then given four trials in which they observe the Taylor Complex Figure for 30 seconds and have 2 minutes to make their copy, and then have a 15-minute delayed recall trial. This procedure provides a learning curve, and the normative sample consists of over 400 people. Unfortunately, this variation has not attracted much independent use that has been published.

Scorer Reliability

Intraclass correlations for four scorers of the Complex Figure under copy and delayed recall conditions by a group of 95 individuals diagnosed with dementia ranged from .93 to .96 (Tupler, Welsh, Asare-Aboagye, & Dawson, 1995). The maximum differences in raw scores between two independent scorers were 5 points in several studies (Carr & Lincoln, 1988; Duley et al., 1993; Liberman, Stewart, Seines, & Gordon, 1994), with about 90% of the differences lying within 2 points for both copy and delayed recall trials in the study of Duley et al. (1993). Even higher figures of .95 to .99 were reported for copy and recall trials by Rapport et al. (1997), and a figure of .99 was reported by Carr and Lincoln (1988) for the copy administration. Berry et al. (1991) reported scorer correlations of .80, .93, and .96 for copy, immediate recall, and delayed recall, respectively, in 87 normal older people with a mean age of 65 years, with most differences in scores within 1 point. Liberman et al. reported that 14 of the 18 commonly scored units received identical scores more than 80% of the time. The exceptions to this were units 1, 5, 6, and 10 (the cross in the upper left corner, the vertical midline of the major rectangle, the small rectangle inside the major rectangle on the left side, and the small vertical line to the right of the midline). These should be given special attention for scoring accuracy.

Berry et al. (1991) reported scorer reliabilities of .84, .97, and .93 for copy, immediate recall, and delayed recall of the Taylor Complex Figure. Less is known about which units of the Taylor Figure may be more prone to disagreements among scorers than for the Rey Figure. The limited evidence available suggests that the Taylor Figure can be scored with reliabilities in the acceptable range, although figures may be slightly lower than for the Rey Figure.

For most clinical purposes, in which other tests would also be administered to assess the same cognitive functions, the scorer reliability of the Complex Figure is acceptable. For more stringent and critical applications, the use of two scorers with final interpretations based upon the average of their scores could be the solution (Liberman et al., 1994).

Internal Consistency

The units of the scoring system can be regarded as items, and internal consistency reliability can be computed as for any test. Rapport et al. (1997) reported coefficient alpha for the copy using the Lezak scoring system of .94 and .90 for the immediate recall trial. These figures reflect the common nature of the content and the psychological processes used in completing the drawings and by the most commonly used scoring system and are psychometrically quite acceptable.

Test-Retest Reliability

The expectations for test-retest reliability for a memory test are less well defined than for most other tests. There is inherently an expectation of change over the delay interval that may interact with individual differences to produce what would be unacceptable figures in another test. If the stimulus materials are not repeated after the delay interval, then a normal decrement in recall is expected. If the stimulus materials are repeated, performance is expected to be at a higher level than on the initial presentation. Both of these conditions are at variance with the normal assumption in test-retest studies that the characteristic in question is stable over time. Many of the studies cited earlier in the section on parallel forms do, in fact, include delay intervals and report modest correlations over time across forms, a condition that includes elements of both test-retest and parallel form reliability. For a memory test, the shorter the delay, the higher the likely correlation. Indeed, the intraclass correlations of the Complex Figure from copy to a delayed recall condition of 3 to 5 minutes by a group of 95 individuals diagnosed with dementia ranged from .94 to .95 (Tupler et al., 1995). Spreen and Strauss (1998) reported unpublished data to support the existence of practice effects for both the Rey and the Taylor Complex Figures of about 10% improvement in percent recall after a one-month interval. The use of correlations to evaluate stability over time is limited by the fact that copy and recognition trials are apt to show ceiling effects that limit the range of possible scores. Despite this, Meyers and Meyers (1995b) reported moderate to high correlations of .76 for immediate recall and .89 for delayed recall over a six-month interval in a small group of 12 healthy adults. Berry et al. (1991) reported lower figures of .47 for immediate recall and .59 for delayed recall over a one-year interval in a group of 41 older adults. Berry et al. noted that these figures were likely to be underestimates. The figure of .18 that Berry et al. (1991) gave for the one-year test-retest is of little value because of the limitations for copy trials in normal samples noted earlier.

A test such as the Complex Figure can be used for many different purposes. Its validity thus depends on the particular situation. The question of the validity of the

Complex Figure for various purposes is better taken up in the section on Interpretation later in the chapter.

Assets and Limitations

The ease of administration and the low cost of materials for the Complex Figure are considerable advantages in times of budget restrictions and escalating test costs. The Figure has also demonstrated sensitivity to unilateral brain damage in the right hemisphere (see Lezak, 1995, and Spreen & Strauss, 1998, for summaries). The qualitative scoring systems provide information about planning and organizational skills, as well as visuoconstructive and motor functions. Furthermore, memory functions are evaluated in cases in which deficits are not due to any of the additional factors. The commercial availability of a manual, materials, and a recognition trial should help improve the use in practice of the Complex Figure.

The complexity of completing the task for the client and interpreting it for the psychologist is one of the major weaknesses of the Complex Figure. Various other cognitive functions must be evaluated before a poor score on the Complex Figure can be properly interpreted. As such, its utility as a measure of visual memory is weakened. Its sensitivity as a measure of memory has been demonstrated, but its value as a measure of specific visual memory deficits is equivocal (Meyers & Meyers, 1995b; Moye, 1997).

In addition, the number of administrative procedures and scoring systems together with the lack of widespread, representative population norms constitute a real limitation for the test. Spreen and Strauss (1998) described four different administrative systems for which normative samples of moderate size are available. Unfortunately, the lack of large, representative normative samples and the use of different administrative procedures are common for many neuropsychological tests, not just the Complex Figure. This condition is also one that is not likely to be remedied soon. The manual by Meyers and Meyers (1995b) does assist in pulling together information from diverse sources and in establishing some common ground. The availability of such a manual may be a deciding factor in opting for using the Meyers approach over adopting the traditional approach.

Materials

The user of the Complex Figure must make a basic decision as to the source of materials and procedures to be used. One option is to purchase the Rey Complex Figure Test and Recognition Trial available commercially from Psychological Assessment Resources (Meyers & Meyers, 1995b). By doing so, a standard procedure and set of materials that includes a recognition trial is immediately at hand. This option may be preferred by those who have less experience with the Complex Figure or who will be using it only occasionally and would not be rapidly acquiring familiarity with the Figure through frequent use.

The other option may be preferable to those with some familiarity with the Rey (1964) and the L. Taylor (1979) Complex Figures or to those who will be using it frequently and who will need to develop local norms or to use specialized norms that are available in the literature. In this case, the user will need to obtain the necessary copy of the Complex Figure itself from the reproduction in Lezak (1995) or other sources, such as Spreen and Strauss (1991, 1998) and Liberman et al. (1994), and to assemble a set of norms and useful procedures from the literature. This chapter will provide enough information and references that this can be done. Figure 9.1 reproduces the Rey Figure, and Figure 9.2 is the Taylor Complex Figure. Table 9.1 provides the Taylor variation of the scoring criteria for the Rey Complex Figure, and Table 9.2 contains the scoring criteria for the Taylor Figure.

One drawback of this approach is the variation in the original drawings of the Figure. Given the long period of time in which the Figure was not commercially available, an unknown number of independently produced copies exist, many of which are of different sizes. Using Lezak (1995, pp. 570–571) as the authority, the major rectangle of the Rey Complex Figure measures 82 mm along the horizontal axis by 58 mm along the vertical axis. The major square in the L. Taylor (1979) figure is 75 mm square. Tombaugh and Hubley (1991) addressed the issue of different sizes of figures and did not find any notable differences in results for figures that varied by 13 sq cm^2 in area. (Note that the copy of the Taylor Figure in Lezak is rotated 180 degrees: the arrow at the tip of the triangle should be on the left and point upward.)

Other materials that are needed are quite basic. These include sheets of standard white paper and either a pencil or a set of colored pens, pencils, or felt-tip markers, together with some type of stopwatch or other timer in order to record the time taken to complete the Figure.

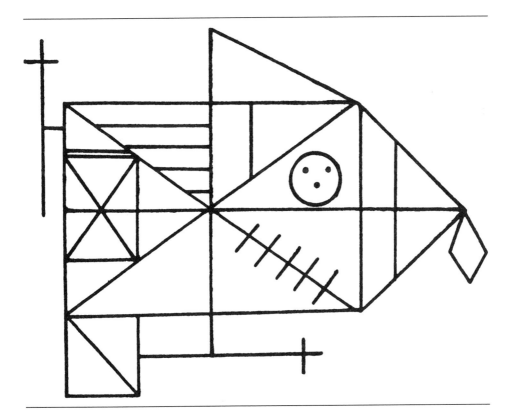

Figure 9.1.   Rey complex figure

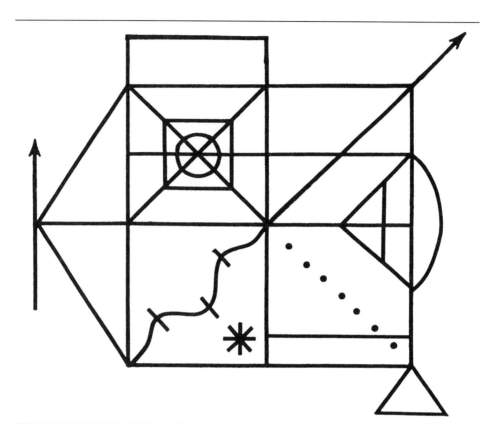

Figure 9.2.   Taylor complex figure

The use of a set of colored pencils was originally recommended by Osterrieth (Corwin & Bylsma, 1993) in order to determine the sequence in which the client completed elements of the Figure. Other methods of recording the sequence in which elements of the Figure are drawn are also used, most of which allow the client to use a single pencil or pen (see Lezak, 1995, pp. 569–570). Meyers and Meyers (1995b) recommended the use of a single pencil in order to minimize disruption for clients with impairments and because there are no validated guidelines for determining the optimal points at which to change colors. Troyer and Wishart (1997) noted that no qualitative information need be lost if colored pencils are not used. The major advantage of the use of the colored pencils is the documentation of the order in which elements are completed. The standard scoring system does not use this order, but the more sophisticated scoring systems can require additional details of such things as whether lines are completed in one step or two. Such systems require alternative recording systems, and some of these are described later in the chapter.

Administration

One of the merits of the Complex Figure is its comparative ease of administration. The examiner provides the client with the Figure, a pencil or pencils or other type of writing

Table 9.1.   Taylor variation of the scoring criteria for the Rey Complex Figure

1. Cross at upper left corner, outside the main rectangle

    The cross must descend to the horizontal midline of the rectangle and must extend above the rectangle. The line that joins the cross to the rectangle must be approximately in the middle of the cross and must come between Number 7 and the top of the rectangle.

2. Large rectangle

    The horizontal dimensions of the rectangle must not be greater than twice the vertical dimension of the rectangle, nor must the rectangle resemble a square. Give a score of ½ point if the rectangle is incomplete or distorted in any way.

3. Diagonal cross

    The large diagonal cross must touch each of the four corners of the large rectangle and intersect in the middle of the rectangle.

4. Horizontal midline

    The horizontal midline must go clearly across from the midpoint of the left side of the rectangle to the midpoint of the right side of the rectangle in one unbroken line.

5. Vertical midline

    The vertical midline must start at the midpoint of the bottom of the rectangle and go through in an unbroken line to the midpoint at the top of the rectangle. In scoring for position of 4, 5, and 6, these lines should intersect at the midpoint of the rectangle. If they do not, usually only one line is scored as incorrect for position. Seldom are all three scored as incorrect for position.

6. Small rectangle at left of large rectangle

    The small rectangle must be within the large rectangle and to the left side of it. The boundaries are defined by the top of the rectangle falling between lines 2 and 3 of the parallel lines that make up Number 8, and the width of the small rectangle must be approximately one quarter the width of the large rectangle; that is, it should come to the midpoint between the left side of the large rectangle and the vertical midpoint of the rectangle. The cross within Number 6 must come from the four corners of the small rectangle and should intersect at the midpoint of the rectangle (i.e., intersect on Number 4).

7. Straight line above small rectangle

    This short line must be shorter than the horizontal aspect of Number 6 and must fall between the top of Number 6 and the second line of Number 8.

8. Four parallel lines in upper left of large rectangle

    The four parallel lines in the upper left corner of the large rectangle should have the spaces between them approximately equal. If the lines are unduly slanted or, of course, if there are more or less than four of them, then the scoring is penalized.

9. Triangle above the large rectangle

    The height of this triangle is less than the base.

10. Vertical line within the large rectangle below Number 9

    The small vertical line in the upper right corner of the large rectangle should be clearly shifted to the left within the upper right quadrant of the large rectangle.

11. Circle with three dots

    The circle with three dots must be in the lower right half of the upper right quadrant. It must not touch any of the three sides of the triangular area in which it is placed, and the positioning of the dots must be such that there are two dots above and one dot below, such that it resembles a face.

(continued)

Table 9.1. *(Continued)*

12. Five parallel lines in lower right quadrant

The five parallel lines that cross the lower right aspect of Number 3 must all be within the lower right quadrant. They must not touch any sides of the quadrangle, and they should be approximately equidistant from one another.

13. Triangle at right side of large rectangle

The height of the triangle must not be greater than half of the horizontal midline of the rectangle, and the slope of the sides of the triangle must not be a continuation of the slope of Number 9.

14. Diamond at the end of Number 13

The diamond must be appropriately shaped and attached to the end of Number 13. It must not extend below the bottom of the large rectangle, Number 2.

15. Vertical line within triangle on right

The vertical line within the triangle of Number 13 must be parallel to the right vertical side of the large rectangle, and it must be shifted to the left with Number 13.

16. Horizontal line within Number 13

The horizontal line within the triangle of Number 13 is a continuation of Number 4 to the right. It must come from the midpoint of the right side of the large rectangle and extend to the right apex of Number 13. If Number 13 is slightly askew, or if Number 4 does not meet the midpoint of the right side of the rectangle, Number 16 should still be scored as a full 2 points if it extends from the midpoint of the right side of the rectangle to the apex of the triangle on the right.

17. Cross below the large rectangle

The right side of the cross below the large rectangle must be clearly longer than the left side of the cross, but it must not extend beyond the right end of the large rectangle. At its left end, the cross should also commence at the midpoint of the right side of the square, Number 18.

18. Square at lower left of large rectangle

The lower left figure outside the large rectangle must clearly be a square, and its sides should be the same size as the vertical aspect of Number 6, extending halfway between the left edge of the large rectangle and the vertical midline of the rectangle.

Note: For each of the 18 components of the Figure, score 2 points if correct and properly placed, 1 point if correct and poorly positioned or if distorted or incomplete and properly placed, ½ point if distorted but recognizable and poorly placed, and 0 points if absent or not recognizable. Maximum total score is 36 points.

Table 9.2. **Scoring criteria for the Taylor Complex Figure**

1. Vertical arrow at the left

The vertical arrow at the left edge of the Figure extends above and below the midpoints of the upper and lower quadrants of the large square, but not extending beyond the upper or the lower limits of the square, and with its midpoint meeting Number 4.

2. Triangle at the left

The triangle has its base as the left side of the large square, with the altitude of the triangle less than half the width of the large square.

3. Large square

The large square is the basic element of the Figure. It must look like a square and not a rectangle.

Table 9.2. *(Continued)*

---

4. Horizontal midline

   The horizontal midline of the large square extends beyond the square on the left through Number 2 to the midpoint of Number 1.

5. Vertical midline of the large square

6. Horizontal line bisecting the top half of the large square

7. Diagonal lines

   The diagonal lines bisect the small upper left quadrant of the large square, and begin and end in the corners.

8. Small square in upper left quadrant

   The small square is positioned in the center of the top left quadrant and is one quarter the size of the quadrant, with the corners of the squares located on the diagonals.

9. Circle in upper left quadrant

   Circle is in the center of Number 8 in the upper left quadrant.

10. Rectangle above upper left quadrant

    The height of the rectangle is less than one quarter of the height of the large square.

11. Arrow at upper right

    The arrow extends from the center of the large square through the top right corner of the right upper quadrant, with not more than one third of its length outside the large square.

12. Semicircle on the right

    The semicircle at the right side of the Figure extends from the horizontal bisector of the top half of the base square (Number 6) to the equivalent point in the lower half of the base square.

13. Triangle within square on the right

    This triangle has as its base the same section of the right side of the large square as the semicircle (Number 13). Its altitude is one quarter the width of the large square.

14. Seven dots

    The row of seven dots (not circles) is evenly spaced in a straight line from the center of the large square to the lower right corner of the quadrant.

15. Horizontal line in lower right quadrant

    The horizontal line in the lower right quadrant lies between the sixth and seventh dots of Number 14.

16. Triangle at bottom right

    The equilateral triangle has its apex at the lower right corner of the large square; its height is not more than one quarter of the height of the large square.

17. Curved line in bottom left quadrant

    The curved line has a cross-bar at the center of each of three sinusoids in the lower left quadrant, and it extends from the bottom left corner to the top right corner of the quadrant.

18. Star

    The star comprises eight lines radiating from a central point, and it is placed in the lower left quadrant, near its lower right corner.

Note: For each of the 18 components of the Figure, score 2 points if correct and properly placed, 1 point if correct and poorly positioned or if distorted or incomplete and properly placed, ½ point if distorted but recognizable and poorly placed, and 0 points if absent or not recognizable. Maximum total score is 36 points.

tool, and a blank piece of paper and then asks the client to copy the Figure. Additional sheets of paper are needed for recall trials. Care should be taken to ensure that the stimulus Figure and paper are aligned in parallel in order to make any rotation errors made in reproducing the Figure clearly evident. One administrative variant has been to reproduce the Figure in the upper half of a sheet of paper and to ask the client to copy the Figure in the space below. It is not known how this method compares to the traditional method (using a separate card for the Figure) in terms of rotation errors or errors of omission. It may thus be a somewhat less desirable procedure than the more common use of a separate stimulus card.

The normal administration procedure for the evaluation of memory with the Complex Figure (Figure 9.1) from its introduction has been the use of a recall trial 3 minutes later, as initially described by Osterrieth (Corwin & Bylsma, 1993). The verbatim instructions given by Spreen and Strauss (1991) and Corwin and Bylsma provide for a delayed recall trial about 30 minutes later instead of the immediate recall trial. Spreen and Strauss (1998) provide instructions for both immediate and delayed recall administrations. Both variations of a copy and one recall trial are used in practice, along with the use of all three administrations: copy, immediate recall, and delayed recall. Regardless of the number of administrations used, the instructions used should always be standardized in order to maintain consistency and wide applicability of norms.

The examiner gives the following instructions for the copy administration (from Meyers & Meyers 1995b):

> Look at this figure. [Point to the blank sheet of paper.] I would like you to copy that figure onto this sheet of paper. [Point back to the card.] Copy it so that I would know that this is the figure you drew. Do a good job.

The examiner starts timing when he or she has finished speaking. There is no formal time limit to any phase of the Complex Figure, nor are norms published for completion times. The main purpose is to document any unusually short or long times for completing the drawing. Most adults who are without impairments take 2 to 3 minutes, and rarely does anyone take more than 5 minutes. Instructions vary in terms of allowing the client to erase mistakes. The instructions provided by Spreen and Strauss (1991, 1998) forbid erasures; those of Meyers and Meyers (1995b) allow them. No published instructions permit the use of a straight edge, ruler, or other type of guide.

Once the copy has been made, there are variations on the procedures used to evaluate memory in terms of using either the immediate recall trial, the delayed recall trial, or both. If the short 3-to-5-minute delay is used, this time can be filled with conversation or some other brief test, preferably one that does not require visual memory or stimulus material that resembles the Figure in any way.

Once 3 to 5 minutes have elapsed, the examiner gives the client a pencil and a new blank sheet of paper. One set of instructions (from Meyers & Meyers, 1995b) is:

> A short time ago, I had you copy a figure. I would like you to draw that figure again, but this time from memory. Draw that figure here. [Point to the blank piece of paper.]

If a delayed recall trial is used, the examiner should use 30 minutes for other tasks that do not involve visuospatial perception and then give the person a blank sheet of paper and say (from Meyers & Meyers, 1995b):

A short time ago, I had you copy a figure. I would like you to draw that figure again, but this time from memory. Draw that figure here. [Point to the blank sheet of paper.]

Delayed recall trials are commonly used with delays ranging from 20 to 45 minutes (Lezak, 1995) or up to 60 minutes (Spreen & Strauss, 1998). Delayed recall is likely to be better if an immediate recall trial is used than if only the copy trial is administered (Meyers & Meyers, 1995b; Loring, Martin, Meador, & Lee, 1990). Delays from 15 minutes to 60 minutes do not appear to provide any different results in healthy older adults (Berry & Carpenter, 1992), although delays over 1 hour may result in lower recall scores.

It should be noted that the traditional method of administration recommended by Spreen and Strauss (1991) and by Corwin and Bylsma (1993) does not incorporate the immediate recall trial. The procedure used by Meyers and Meyers (1995b) and by Spreen and Strauss (1998) follows Osterrieth in using an immediate delayed recall trial. In selecting the procedure to be used, it is important to consider which set of norms is appropriate because some norms use the procedure with two trials and other norms are based on the administration of three trials.

The procedure suggested here is to use both the immediate recall trial and a 30-minute delayed recall trial. This allows for a comparison of short- and long-term retention relative to the original copy.

If the client cannot make an adequate copy of the Figure, then it is likely that either a perceptual difficulty is distorting the image for the client or that a motor problem is limiting the client's ability to reproduce the Figure accurately. Often the likelihood of this happening can be determined from the medical history, and use of the Complex Figure avoided. Nevertheless, at times, an individual who may have no obvious a priori reason will produce a very poor copy of the Figure. In such a case, Lezak (1995, p. 475) recommends that there is little point to administering a recall trial. Even if the copy is poor, however, a comparison can be made between copy and recall trials to determine if the same general approach was used and if the same elements are present in both reproductions, and some estimate can be made of savings in the recall.

Recognition trials require special materials, such as those developed by Fastenau (1996) and Meyers and Meyers (1995a, 1995b). Fastenau's recognition trial involves 30 multiple-choice items in which the options reflect the major elements of the Figure and common errors made in reproducing the Figure. There are subscales for Global (7 items) and Details (23 items), subdivided into Left Details (9 items) and Right Details (11 items). Coefficients alpha range from .59 to .84 for the subscales. Preliminary results are promising, although no further research on Fastenau's scale has emerged at the time of this writing. The recognition scale developed by Meyers and Lange (1994) has been available for a longer period of time and is incorporated into the published version (Meyers & Meyers, 1995b). This trial uses a different format from that of Fastenau. Twenty-four drawings are reproduced in the test booklet, and the client is instructed to circle those designs that were part of the Figure that he or she drew. Half of the designs were from the Figure, and the recognition test is scored for True and False Positives and for True and False Negatives. Test-retest reliability over 6 months was .87 for the recognition trial. Use of the recognition trial increased by almost 17% (Meyers & Meyers, 1995b) the correct classification by discriminant functions of groups of patients with no impairments and with brain damage or psychiatric disorders. The benefits of the use of the recognition trial appear to be significant, and the commercial availability of the recognition materials should help increase the research needed to develop the knowledge base about this application with the Complex Figure.

Scoring

There are several scoring systems available for the Complex Figure, but the original system of Osterrieth based upon 18 major elements or units in the Figure is probably the most widely used, and it forms the core of most systems. Scoring details are provided by both Lezak (1995) and by Spreen and Strauss (1991, 1998) and are used by Meyers and Meyers (1995b) as well. The system reported in Spreen and Strauss (1991, 1998) includes some additional guidelines from Taylor and provides the additional clarity that can be particularly useful for those who are just learning to use the Complex Figure (Table 9.1). Hamby, Wilkins, and Barry (1993) provided additional details for scoring the organizational quality of the Figure, while Duley et al. (1993) provided more explicit and detailed instructions for scoring the elements of the basic scoring system. Loring et al. (1990) described a system that resembles that of the original but differs in some details, with more explicit scoring instructions.

Denman's system (1984) divided the Figure into 24 "designs" that are scored for accuracy on a 0-to-3-point scale. Although scoring is complex and requires the use of a ruler and protractor, it is internally consistent, and it has excellent interscorer reliability (Rapport et al., 1997). Visser's (1973) system required the use of a registration sheet on which the examiner records the order in which elements are completed as well as interruptions of lines and omissions of elements. Bennett-Levy's (1984) system scored for the Gestalt principles of symmetry, strategy, and continuation (completing a line in one movement instead of two or more). The Boston Qualitative System (Stern et al., 1994) provided scores for such features as distortion, perseveration, rotation, and neatness. The preliminary report indicates that it is reliable (intraclass correlations over .90 for 5 of 6 Summary Scores). This system has been used to analyze developmental trends in visuospatial functions (Akshoomoff & Stiles, 1995a, 1995b). Waber and Bernstein (Bernstein & Waber, 1996; Waber & Bernstein, 1995; Waber & Holmes, 1985, 1986) devised a developmental scoring system for the Complex Figure that quantifies accuracy, errors, style, and organization. This system has shown sensitivity to age from 5 up to 14 years for both copy and delayed recall trials (Waber & Bernstein, 1985, 1986). Shorr, Delis, and Massman (1992) described a somewhat simpler system of scoring perceptual clustering that is also reliable in its initial report based on patients with neuropsychiatric impairments, and that has the potential for providing additional information over the more common scoring system that captures accuracy of the copy.

Other systems of varying complexity exist as well (see Lezak, 1995, for references and other information). Whether any of these offer substantial advances over the standard system is not clear, given the paucity of empirical comparisons. The general tendency with the scoring systems is that the more complex ones require more detailed records of the exact procedures that the client uses during the process of copying and recall. In the absence of strong evidence to suggest the superiority of another system, the common method based upon Osterrieth's original 18-point system has definite advantages in terms of standardization and the availability of norms. For clarity and consistency in scoring, Taylor's guidelines that are reproduced in Spreen and Strauss (1991, pp. 162–163, 1998, p. 350) and in Table 9.1 should be used for most purposes. Those interested in the qualitative features of the Complex Figure should investigate the various systems cited in more detail before selecting one for use. It should be noted at this point that norms for all the qualitative systems are limited.

Each element of one of the Figures receives from 0 to 2 points according to the accuracy of the drawing. Two points are given for an element that is in the correct place and correctly oriented and that is approximately the same size as in the original. One point is given if the element is the correct size and shape but is in an inappropriate place. Examples of 1 point scores would be placing the cross in the upper left (Detail 1) *at* the midline instead of above it or placing the vertical line (Detail 15) to the left or to the right of center. One point is also given if the element is in the correct place but is drawn poorly such that the figure is significantly distorted or has parts of it missing. Examples of the second type of 1 point scores would be having an incorrect number of lines for Detail 8, the four parallel lines in the upper left quadrant, or for Detail 12, the five parallel lines in the lower right quadrant. Other examples of 1 point scores would be having other than three dots in the circle in the upper right quadrant or having the dots in a different orientation (Detail 11). If the reproduction of an element meets the criteria for 1 point in terms of poor reproduction, but it is also incorrectly placed, then only a half point (.5) is given. An example of a half-point score would be a drawing of Detail 1 with a long cross arm, placed at the midline of the large rectangle. Finally, if an element is omitted or if the drawing bears little resemblance to the original, then no points are given for that element.

There has been surprisingly little empirical research comparing the different scoring systems. Chervinsky, Mitrushina, and Satz (1992) reported that the Denman accuracy scoring system was the only one to show age differences in the copy condition across four age groups of people from age 57 to age 85 years, but that no scoring system showed differences on the recall trial. Only one study examined differences in scores between the Denman and traditional systems, and it did not report notable discrepancies in outpatients with psychiatric disorders (Knight, Miller, Forsyth, & McWilliams, 1993). Troyer and Wishart (1997) compared several qualitative systems, including several that are not mentioned here. They reported that the Bennett-Levy (1984) system and one described by Bylsma and colleagues (cited in Troyer & Wishart, 1997) showed the most utility in having a wide range of scores and in assessing multiple aspects of performance.

Interpretation

Norms

The interpretation of scores and performance on the Complex Figure requires some knowledge of what constitutes "normal" performance. All evidence suggests that individuals with no known neurological or neuropsychological deficits copy the Figure with few if any errors. Normative performance of individuals from adolescence to old age (into the early 90s) is to score at least 30 points out of 36 for a copy of the Figure (Boone et al., 1993; Chiulli et al., 1995; Mitrushina & Satz, 1989; Poulton & Moffitt, 1995). Children below the age of 12 make more errors, with 6-year-olds obtaining scores of about 17, ranging up to 28 by the age of 11 (see Spreen & Strauss, 1998). Copy trial scores for children over the age of 12 fall in the same ranges as those of adults.

Immediate recall of the Figure after a short 3-to-5-minute delay is naturally poorer than for the copy, with older adults scoring from 13 points (by those over 80) to 17 points (for those from 70 to 74 years of age) in one study (Chiulli et al., 1995) and scoring from 13 points (at age 57 to 65) to 11 points (at age 76 to 85) in another study (Mitrushina & Satz, 1989). Recall by younger people is comparable to older age groups, with both adults 45 to 59 years of age and 13-year-olds obtaining scores of 19 on average (Boone et al., 1993; Poulton & Moffitt, 1995).

A longer delay of 30 minutes or so results in scores approximately the same as for shorter delays for older adults, but with somewhat higher scores at younger ages, ranging from 23 to 26 points for people from 12 to 30 years of age (Chiulli et al., 1995; Spreen & Strauss, 1991, 1998).

The figures for normative performance given in the preceding paragraphs are approximate means and are derived from several sources. There is no comprehensive collection of normative figures for either of the Complex Figures. There are several sources of norms for the Rey Figure, the best of which are probably in Spreen and Strauss (1998) and in Meyers and Meyers (1995b). Mitrushina, Boone, and D'Elia (1999) include further normative data. There is a Web site that can be consulted for information about normative data and interpretive and scoring programs (http://www.normativedata.com). Note that the norms in Spreen and Strauss (1991) do not use an immediate recall trial, whereas those in Meyers and Meyers (1995b) and Spreen and Strauss (1998) do.

The original norms of Osterrieth that are reproduced in Lezak (1995) should not be used for delayed recall because they are for the 3-minute delay. Osterrieth did not use a longer period for delayed recall. Furthermore, the individuals in the sample were fairly well educated, and there may be additional differences in either cohort or culture that make conclusions drawn from the 1944 norms for copy and immediate recall trials questionable. In general, copy trials are the best standardized, and comparisons across studies are straightforward if the same scoring system has been used. The major variations in normative studies have been in the use of an immediate recall trial and in the variability in time before the delayed recall trial. Because the use of immediate recall results in higher delayed recall scores, it is imperative that the norms used to interpret the scores are based on the same administrative procedures. There are few norms available for qualitative systems beyond those provided by the developers, except where noted earlier. Other available norms are briefly mentioned here.

The Complex Figure has been used with some success (Waber & Bernstein, 1995), with children as young as 5 years of age, and some norms are available for children of that age and older (Spreen & Strauss, 1998). Poulton and Moffitt (1995) reported norms for 740 New Zealand 13-year-olds for copy and immediate recall conditions, with delays of about 3 to 5 minutes between the two trials. Norms for Denman's (1984) system include 432 people aged 10 to 89 years in 11 age groups.

Performance of adults with no known impairment on the copy trial is generally very good. Scores of 32 or over were obtained by 85% of the normative sample aged 59 or lower on the copy trial. Eighty-five percent of those in the normative sample aged 60 to 89 scored above 27 on the copy trial. Table 9.3 reports normative performance figures

Table 9.3.   Normative performance on immediate and delayed recall trials of the Rey Complex Figure at different age levels

	Percentile									
	90		70		50		30		10	
Age	Immed.	Delay	Immed.	Delay	Immed.	Delay	Immed	Delay	Immed	Delay
18–19	30.5	31	27	27.5	25	25.5	23	23.5	20	20
20–24	30.5	31	27	27	25	25	22.5	23	19.5	19.5
25–29	30	30	26.5	26.5	24	24.5	22	22	18.5	18.5
30–34	29.5	29.5	25.5	26	23.5	23.5	21	21	17.5	17.5
35–39	28.5	28.5	25	25	22.5	22.5	20	20.5	16.5	17
40–44	28	27.5	24	24	21.5	21.5	19	19	15.5	15.5
45–49	27	26.5	23	23	20.5	20.5	18	18	14.5	14.5
50–54	25.5	25.5	21.5	21.5	19	19.5	17	17	13	13.5
55–59	24	24	20.5	20	18	18	15.5	15.5	11.5	12
60–64	23	22.5	19	19	16.5	16.5	14	14.5	10.5	11
65–69	21	20.5	17	17	14.5	14.5	12.5	12.5	9	9.5
70–74	19.5	19	15.5	15.5	13.5	13.5	11	11.5	7.5	8
75–79	17.5	17	14	14	11.5	12	9.5	9.5	6	6.5
80–89	14	14	11	11	9	9	6.5	6.5	3.5	4.5

Note: Adapted from Meyers and Meyers (1995b).

for a U.S. census-matched sample. Figures are given for 90th, 70th, 50th, 30th, and 10th percentiles for immediate and delayed recall trials. Table 9.3 does not report percentiles for the copy trial because of the high level of performance. More detailed figures and full percentiles and T-score equivalents are given by Meyers and Meyers (1995b), who also report cutoff scores at the 16th percentile for poor performance on the copy trial. They also reported data on the frequency of very low scores in the normative group. Spreen and Strauss (1998) reported means and standard deviations for copy and 30-minute delayed recall trials for children aged 6 to 15 years. Comparable data for the Taylor Complex Figure do not exist at present, so interpretations of scores on it will require the exercise of appropriate skills and judgment.

Functional Interpretation

One of the uses of the Complex Figure is simply to describe performance in copying visuospatial material. Another use involves going beyond the descriptive level to inferences from this performance to the nature of functioning of the brain. Such inferences can be made in terms of left and right hemisphere functioning or at the level of different lobes of the cerebral hemispheres.

There are no studies that suggest firm and cross-validated cutoff points for discriminating normal from abnormal performance on the copy trial, although Meyers and Meyers (1995b) used the 16th percentile of their normative sample. One reason for the absence of recommended cutoff points is that interpretation of Complex Figure scores must incorporate knowledge of the client's performance on other measures. Successful copying of the Figure requires intact fine-motor control and visuospatial perception. In addition, planning and organizational skills must be sufficiently intact to allow the copy to be made. A poorly executed copy that took a long time to complete could certainly be regarded as evidence of poor planning and organizational skills, other things being equal. Certainly the process of copying the figure requires sufficient attention and concentration and provides an opportunity for the examiner to evaluate the client's behavior in those domains.

The most basic inference from the copy trial relates to hemispheric functioning. In most individuals with no known impairments, language functions are concentrated in the left hemisphere, which also has functional involvement in sensory and motor systems related to the right side of the body. The right hand is normally dominant for strength and fine-motor control in the great majority of right-handed people. In inferring lateralized hemispheric dysfunction, the interpretation of the Complex Figure includes the expectation that the qualitative features of gross distortion, omission or neglect, and perseveration suggest pathology of the right hemisphere, which is specialized for visuospatial functions in most people (Lezak, 1995, pp. 58–61; Stringer, 1996; Tranel & Damasio, 1995). These characteristics would be better captured by the qualitative scoring systems for the Complex Figure than by the simple accuracy score.

Both Binder (1982) and Piguet, Saling, O'Shea, and Berkovic (1994) reported that distortion scores in the copy trial were sensitive to right hemisphere dysfunction. Binder (1982) noted that groups of people with both left and right hemisphere damage differed in the nature of common distortions. Rapport and her colleagues (Rapport, Dutra, Webster, Charter, & Morrill, 1995; Rapport, Farchione, Dutra, Webster, & Charter, 1996) reported that measures of omission are more sensitive to the neglect that can accompany right hemisphere damage, whereas accuracy scores are not so sensitive. These results suggest that low accuracy scores on the copy trial may suggest either left hemisphere, right hemisphere, or bilateral dysfunction, whereas the qualitative errors such as omission and distortion are more sensitive to right hemisphere dysfunction.

Inferences can also be made to areas within hemispheres, given the evidence to implicate the temporal lobes and the hippocampus in memory functions (Tranel & Damasio, 1995). Given the nature of specialized functions of the hemispheres, poor visual memory could be used to infer right temporal lobe damage or additional involvement of the parietal lobe if copying of the Figure was also relatively poor.

Interpretation of the Complex Figure as a measure of memory implicitly involves a comparison with both normative levels of performance for the person's age and education and with the score obtained on the copy trial. Some practitioners use an arithmetic ratio of immediate recall score to copy score as an index of percent savings (recall score/copy score × 100) or of forgetting by including delayed recall scores ([immediate recall score − delayed recall score]/immediate recall score × 100; see the discussion in Lezak, 1995, p. 479). These should be viewed with caution in cases in which the copy itself is defective because this imposes a limit on how low the recall scores can be. Such ratios provide a distorted picture of actual recall in such cases. Individuals with right temporal lobe damage tend to perform more poorly on delayed recall (L. Taylor, 1979) than do those with left temporal lobe damage, but the results are far from consistent (Spreen & Strauss, 1998). Lee, Loring, and Thompson (1989) reported that neither the Complex Figure score nor the Form Sequence Learning Test score changed after surgical removal of the right temporal lobe for epilepsy, including scores on delayed recall. This was in contrast to the reductions in scores on measures of verbal learning after left temporal lobectomy. Lee et al. (1989) suggested that visual memory tests would be more likely to be sensitive to right temporal lobe damage if they consisted of "unfamiliar, complex, and difficult-to-verbalize visual stimuli" (p. 196). This suggestion had been noted earlier with less closely localized cortical dysfunction by King (1981). At the same time, it may be that the conventional quantitative systems do not record the nature of the errors made by those with right temporal lobe dysfunction.

Qualitative errors on the delayed recall trial were able to differentiate right temporal lobe dysfunction in epilepsy; accuracy scores were not (Loring, Lee, & Meador, 1988). They found that the quantitative scores did not differentiate those with right temporal lobe epileptic foci from those with left temporal lobe dysfunction, but that the qualitative scores that they used did discriminate. Such results suggest that the use of a qualitative scoring system will increase the utility of the Complex Figure both in differentiating right hemisphere from left hemisphere dysfunction, and also in more selective localization of the dysfunction to the temporal lobes when the qualitative measures are used on the delayed recall trial.

Interpretation of poor Complex Figure scores in other populations is mixed. One application involving people with bilateral cortical and subcortical dysfunction was reported by Brouwers, Cox, Martin, Chase, and Fedio (1984), in which the Rey Complex Figure showed the ability to discriminate people with Huntington's dementia from people with Alzheimer's dementia. Both copy and recall trials were able to discriminate people with Parkinson's disease from controls (Ogden, Growden, & Corkin, 1990). However, the Figure appears not to be sensitive to the deficits associated with mild closed head injuries (Zappala & Trexler, 1992).

Given the increased utility that qualitative scores appear to provide over the more widely used quantitative approach, it is unfortunate that such systems are so little reported in the literature on the Complex Figure. Thus, it is not possible to give strong recommendations on which scoring systems to use, although the systems of Bennett-Levy (1984) and Stern et al. (1994) appear to be among the most promising.

REY AUDITORY VERBAL LEARNING TEST

Tasks involving learning a list of words have a very long history in psychology, and a great deal is known about learning and recall of such material. Although techniques in cognitive psychology have moved away from such comparatively simple procedures, learning and later recalling a list of words remains almost prototypic of a memory task.

The Rey Auditory Verbal Learning Test (RAVLT) is a supraspan word-list learning task first described by Rey in the 1940s. The RAVLT consists of lists of 15 words that are read one at a time to the client over a series of at least five trials. The words used are short, with the longest word on List B having eight letters, widely used in English, and concrete (high imagery), in that all are nouns for different objects. After each trial, the client is requested to recall as many words as possible. Several variations have been developed over the intervening years, including translations into several languages and alternate forms, but only recently has a formal handbook been developed

(Schmidt, 1996). For many years, few research reports appeared in the literature, and the review of the RAVLT by Peaker and Stewart (1989) noted that most of the research had appeared in the 1980s. Since then, there has been a substantial increase in the number of publications that report its use, perhaps due in part to the increasing recognition of the utility of the information obtained over that provided by the Wechsler Memory Scale (WMS).

Memory tests such as the Wechsler Memory Scales (Wechsler, 1987, 1997; Wechsler & Stone, 1945) that have been widely used in neuropsychology have not typically incorporated list learning tasks (see Chapter 6). Only in the most recent edition of the Wechsler scales—the Wechsler Memory Scale, Third Edition (WMS-III)—has such material been included. The WMS-III Word List subtest comprises 12 words repeated on four trials and may be administered as an option (Wechsler, 1997). Other recent comprehensive batteries do have list learning tasks, such as the Memory Assessment Scales (MAS; Williams, 1991).

The California Verbal Learning Test (CVLT; Delis, Kramer, Kaplan, & Ober, 1987) is probably the most widely available alternative to the RAVLT. It benefits from certain developments from cognitive psychology that have emerged since the initial translation of the RAVLT into English (E. Taylor, 1959), and it has a form specifically developed for use with children (Delis, Kramer, Kaplan, & Ober, 1994). For example, its 16 words can be semantically clustered into four classes of objects; the RAVLT words cannot be clustered. Similarly, the 12 words on the MAS word-list task can be semantically clustered into four classes. Use of these clusters provides additional information on the cognitive processes used by the individual being tested, and this option is not available for the RAVLT. The other difference between the RAVLT and the CVLT lies in the nature of the words and in the context in which the words are presented to the client. With the RAVLT, the words have nothing in common and are presented simply as words to be learned. With the CVLT, the words are all items available in stores, and the context that is used is one of a shopping list of items to be purchased. This is intended to provide greater acceptability to clients, particularly older clients who may otherwise resist completing the test. There are few data to support this belief of greater acceptability among clients, but there are data to suggest that the RAVLT may be less acceptable among older clients than some other tests. Tuokko, Kristjansson, and Miller (1995) reported that the RAVLT had the highest frequency of problems in administration in a national community sample of older adults, and it also had the highest rates of refusal and of missing data for other reasons as compared to the other neuropsychological tests that were used.

Empirical comparisons between the RAVLT and the CVLT have found little difference after adjusting for the differences in the length of the word lists that are used in the two tests in a group of people with no impairments (Crossen & Wiens, 1994). However, the same was not the case for a group of people with moderate to severe closed head injuries (Stallings, Boake, & Sherer, 1995). Stallings et al. found that their group did more poorly on the CVLT than expected and also that clinical decisions were highly dependent on which sets of norms were used for both tests. This issue will be taken up in more detail in the section on interpretation, but until the compilation of the metanorms by Schmidt (1996), it was clear that the unified norms for the CVLT gave it a definite advantage over the RAVLT for the novice user who did not have extensive experience with the test or with the reference material in which normative information on the RAVLT resided.

On the level of practical usage, one benefit for users of the CVLT is the commercial availability of a computer scoring program that scores the various indices and provides comparisons for the CVLT norms. To balance this, Geffen, Geffen, Smyth, and Manning (1996) described a scoring program that provides similar information for their administrative procedure for the RAVLT. The Psychological Corporation provides scoring software for the RAVLT that uses the Mayo norms for people from 56 to 97 years of age. Thus, although the computer scoring system for the CVLT is based upon the largest set of norms available for it, the computerized scoring systems for the RAVLT force the user into using the set of norms for the programs, neither of which is the most commonly used administrative system.

From the perspective of the client, there is unlikely to be much difference among the word list tests. The shopping-list format of the CVLT may have been intended to make it more acceptable to clients than the RAVLT, but no studies actually confirm this. The difficulty of both tests is apparent to the client once the number of items to be recalled is revealed in the first trial, and the additional clinical literature on the RAVLT and the breadth of normative studies provide definite benefits over the CVLT.

Psychometric Properties

Parallel Forms

Uchiyama et al. (1995) reported that List A and List C gave similar, parallel results in a large group of controls in the Multicenter AIDS Cohort Study when List C was used as the parallel form for List A. One-year test-retest alternate-form reliabilities ranged from a low of .39 for Delayed Recognition up to a moderately good reliability of .81 for Delayed Recall.

If List C is used as an alternate for List B as the distracter trial, the differences in word frequency between List B and C become relevant (Crawford, Stewart, & Moore, 1989). Fuller, Gouvier, and Savage (1997) reported better recall of the interference trial and better discrimination of List A words in the recognition trial if List C was used rather than List B.

Lezak (1995) reproduced the two word lists generated by Crawford et al. (1989) that were matched for frequency and word length. Crawford et al. found the new lists to be good parallel equivalents to the original lists. They noted a substantial practice effect when retesting used the same form. This did not occur with the parallel lists. Shapiro and Harrison (1990) used word frequency and also imagery value to develop two new pairs of word lists. These yielded mean scores equivalent to the original lists, with a mean correlation of .80 across forms.

Geffen, Butterworth, and Geffen (1994) described a new alternative form of the RAVLT (Form 4). The new Lists A and B are matched to the original Lists A and B for word length and frequency of occurrence, with additional materials for a recognition trial. Intraclass correlations across forms ranged from .31 to .78 (Pearson's *r* ranged from .25 to .78) across the various measures in the RAVLT. Practice effects were somewhat less on average than one word for test-retest and were not statistically significant.

Vakil and Blachstein (1994) used an additional trial after a recognition memory trial in which clients are given a list based on List A in which the words have been re-ordered. They are then asked to place the words into the original order of administration. This provides an index of the client's judgment of temporal order.

Test-Retest Reliability

Correlations of List A trial scores with scores from parallel trials of List C ranged from .61 to .86 for Trials 1 to 5, and from .51 to .72 for recall trials (Delaney et al., 1992). Test-retest correlations over 6 to 14 days were equivalent to the parallel form reliabilities reported earlier for Geffen et al. (1994). Uchiyama et al. (1995) reported retest reliabilities from 6 months to 3 years that range from .30 for Trial 1 at 1 year to .78 for Delayed Recall at 3 years. Excluding the Intrusion Errors measure, the median test-retest reliability reported was a moderate .53.

Assets and Limitations

Once again, one definite advantage to the use of the RAVLT over certain other measures of verbal learning and memory is its modest cost. The word lists and administration instructions can be obtained from several sources. The test is also reliable and of demonstrated validity in documenting learning and recall processes and in differentiating among relevant clinical groups. Neuropsychologists have rated it as one of the most useful diagnostic tests for dementia (Tuokko et al., 1995).

The various measures and indices that have been developed for the RAVLT provide a great deal of information about learning and recall in a relatively short period of time. Its utility compares well to some tests, such as the Wechsler Memory Scale, Revised (WMS-R), in this regard. Such efficiency is desirable in a test in the current environment in which the time of both the client and the examiner is limited.

On the other side of the picture, there are again several alternative administrative procedures that complicate the administrative and interpretive processes. In this case, the handbook of Schmidt (1996) does integrate much of the available normative information for one recommended administrative procedure and summarizes what is known about the others. The RAVLT is also less sophisticated than newer variants of word-list learning tasks found on the CVLT and MAS in that it does not have measures of clustering and is more daunting to clients than perhaps it needs to be. At the same time, the absence of obvious organizational cues means that it probably has a higher ceiling than the other tests and is better suited for more highly educated populations.

Materials

The standard word lists for the RAVLT are reproduced in Groth-Marnat (1999), Lezak (1995), Schmidt (1996), and Spreen and Strauss (1991, 1998) and in several of the articles on the RAVLT. There are three standard 15-word lists: List A is commonly used for the five learning trials and for immediate recall and as the base for recognition trials; List B is usually used for the distracter trial and in some variants of recognition trials; List C is intended to be used to replace either List A or List B when necessary. These lists are reproduced in Table 9.4, along with alternate lists generated by Crawford et al.

Table 9.4.   Word lists used in the Rey Auditory Verbal Learning Test

List A	List B	List C	Crawford et al., A	Crawford et al., B
DRUM	DESK	BOOK	DOLL	DISH
CURTAIN	RANGER	FLOWER	MIRROR	JESTER
BELL	BIRD	TRAIN	NAIL	HILL
COFFEE	SHOE	RUG	SAILOR	COAT
SCHOOL	STOVE	MEADOW	HEART	TOOL
PARENT	MOUNTAIN	HARP	DESERT	FOREST
MOON	GLASSES	SALT	FACE	WATER
GARDEN	TOWEL	FINGER	LETTER	LADDER
HAT	CLOUD	APPLE	BED	GIRL
FARMER	BOAT	CHIMNEY	MACHINE	FOOT
NOSE	LAMB	BUTTON	MILK	SHIELD
TURKEY	GUN	LOG	HELMET	PIE
COLOR	PENCIL	KEY	MUSIC	INSECT
HOUSE	CHURCH	RATTLE	HORSE	BALL
RIVER	FISH	GOLD	ROAD	CAR

(1989) for use on repeated trials as alternative forms. As mentioned earlier, these forms should be used on those occasions when it is necessary to repeat the administration of the RAVLT. Table 9.5 gives a 50-word recognition trial, and Crawford et al. provide a recognition list for the alternative words in Table 9.4.

Administration

With the several variations on administration, as well as the availability of different word lists for the RAVLT, it is important to decide on a standard administration procedure. Spreen and Strauss (1991, 1998) and Lezak (1995) provide sets of standardized instructions that are based on those originally provided by E. Taylor (1959) in her translation of the French version. These instructions are widely used, but they differ from Rey's initial set in providing for the administration of a second list of words after the completion of the first five trials with the initial word list. Rey had used a recognition trial. Following the administration of the second word list, the Taylor administration includes a final request for the recall of the words from the first list.

Since its introduction into English, different variations in administration have been developed, along with alternative word lists. Schmidt (1996) provides a good summary of 19 variations that have been used and published, together with directions for the various alternatives. Only the standard administration procedure will be dealt with here and readers are referred to Schmidt for other details. The administrative procedure used here is one that has been frequently used in research and in clinical practice.

The following administration instructions have been taken from Groth-Marnat (1999), Lezak (1995), and Schmidt (1996). The basic instructions are the same in several sources for the basic administration. If used with a 30-minute delayed recall trial, these instructions comprise the standard administration for which a wide variety of norms exist, as outlined later in the section on Interpretation of the RAVLT.

Table 9.5. 50-word Recognition Memory Trial and Scoring Key for RAVLT Lists A and B

Bell—A	Coffee—A	Farmer—A
Window—SA	Mouse—PA	Rose—SPA
Hat—A	River—A	Cloud—B
Barn—SA	Towel—B	House—A
Ranger—B	Curtain—A	Stranger—PB
Nose—A	Flower—SA	Garden—A
Weather—SB	Color—A	Glasses—B
School—A	Desk—B	Stocking—SB
Hand—PA	Gun—B	Shoe—B
Pencil—B	Crayon—SASB	Teacher—SA
Home—SA	Church—B	Stove—B
Fish—B	Turkey—A	Nest—SPB
Moon—A	Fountain—PB	Children—SA
Tree—PA	Boat—B	Drum—A
Balloon—PA	Hot—PASB	Toffee—PA
Bird—B	Parent—A	Lamb—B
Mountain—B	Water—SA	

A—List A
B—List B
SA—Semantic foil for List A
SB—Semantic foil for List B
PA—Phonetic foil for List A
PB—Phonetic foil for List B

> I am going to read a list of words. Listen carefully, for when I stop, you are to say back as many as you can remember. It doesn't matter in what order you repeat them. Just try to remember as many as you can.

The examiner reads the words on the first list at a rate of one per second and writes down the client's responses in the order in which they are recalled. The examiner should take care to record the words recalled by the client in the exact order in which they are recalled. If desired, information on repeated words and queried responses can also be recorded (Lezak, 1995). When no further words can be remembered, the examiner administers the second trial:

> Now I'm going to read the same list again, and once again when I stop, I want you to tell me as many words as you can remember, including words you said the first time. It doesn't matter in what order you say them, just say as many words as you can remember, whether or not you said them before.

The examiner repeats the preceding instructions for the third, fourth, and fifth trials. After the fifth trial with the first list, the examiner presents the second list:

> Now I'm going to read a second list of words. This time, again, you are to say back as many words of this second list as you can remember. Again, the order in which you say the words does not matter. Just try to remember as many as you can.

After completion of the second, distracter list, the examiner administers the last recall trial but does NOT read the words from the first list again:

Now tell me all the words you remember from the first list.

If a delayed recall trial is to be used, the examiner fills the delay period with other tasks that do not involve similar word recall tasks, such as vocabulary tests. After the completion of the 30-minute delay period, the examiner administers the following instructions:

A short while ago, I read a list of words to you several times, and you were trying to learn these words. Tell me the words from this list again.

The examiner should clarify that he or she is asking for words from the first list, if necessary.

If a recognition trial is to be used (as in the standard administration), the instructions appropriate for the particular method should be used. Recognition trials offer sufficient useful information that using one is justified.

Lezak (1995) provides materials for a 50-word recognition trial that can be administered in written or oral form (also reproduced in Groth-Marnat, 1999, and in Spreen & Strauss, 1998). It contains both semantic and phonemic foils. Lezak suggests that it not be used if the client has recalled 13 or more words on the delayed recall trial. This list is reproduced in Table 9.5. Spreen and Strauss (1991, 1998) provide norms for this version. Recognition scores below 13 are rare in normal adults (Bleecker, Bolla Wilson, Agnew, & Meyers, 1988; Geffen et al., 1990; Ivnik et al., 1990; Selnes et al., 1991). There are two variants of instructions for this version, one of which asks the client to identify whether the recognized word comes from List A or List B. The following administration instructions for recognition trials are taken from Schmidt (1996). For the written administration of the first variation, the examiner says:

This list contains the words from the first list I read to you, the one I read several times. Look the words over carefully and check off the words from the list.

For the oral administration, the examiner says:

I am going to read a list of words to you, one at a time. If the word was on the first list, say "Yes," and if it wasn't, say "No."

For the modified variation in which the list of origin is identified, the examiner says:

I am going to give you some words now. Tell me if the word was one of the ones I read to you before. If it was one of the words you heard before, then tell me if it was on the first list or the second list.

The recognition trial can also be administered in the form of a story that contains the words from List A. The story and the administration instructions are given in Appendix A of Schmidt (1996). Other variations exist as well. Bishop et al. (1990) described a multiple-choice version of the first type of recognition trial, and Ivnik et al. (1992) used a 30-word list. There do not appear to be any empirical data as to whether the story format is more acceptable to clients or whether it results in higher recognition scores.

A common form of administration thus consists of five Trials of initial learning, a sixth distracter Trial, and a seventh Trial consisting of recall of the first list. In addition, 30 minutes later, an eighth delayed recall Trial and a ninth recognition memory Trial are also recommended.

Scoring

The normal scores that are used in interpreting RAVLT results are the total number of words correctly recalled on Trials 1 to 5, the distracter trial (6), and the immediate recall (7) and delayed recall trials (8) and the number(s) correctly identified on the recognition trial (9). Repetitions in free recall trials are not counted toward the total score of number correct, but some practitioners do note the total frequency of both repetitions and of intrusions from either List B or those arising from the unique characteristics of the client. Scores from recognition trials vary according to the nature of that task. Various additional indices of aspects of memory can be derived as well.

The various RAVLT scores and indices can be interpreted in terms of concepts derived from the common information processing models of memory. Thus, Trial 1 can be regarded as a measure of initial acquisition, along with Trial 6, the distracter trial. These are measures of immediate, or primary, memory. A comparison of these two trials, the distracter trial compared to Trial 1, is an index of proactive interference, a process operative during acquisition. The exact index used here is the ratio of the distracter trial to initial learning (Trial 6 ÷ Trial 1), due to Geffen et al. (1990). Ivnik et al. (1990) and Wiens et al. (1988) reported other data for such an index multiplied by 100 to give a percentage figure. Another acquisition measure, learning rate, can be evaluated as the difference score between Trial 5 and Trial 1 (Vakil & Blachstein, 1993; Wiens et al., 1988).

Other measures derived from the RAVLT can be regarded as reflecting memory retrieval processes. Trial 5 is normally the maximal, or best, learning (but only in the event that it actually is the highest score in Trials 1 to 5; in the case in which Trial 3 or 4 is the highest, that score is used). The sum of Trials 1 to 5 gives an index of total learning (Vakil & Blachstein, 1993; Wiens et al., 1988). A comparison of Trial 5 with the recall trial that follows the distracter trial is a measure of retroactive interference (Trial 7 ÷ Trial 5; Geffen et al., 1990). A plot of the scores on Trials 1 to 5 gives a learning curve. Recall of List A after a delay period compared to Trial 5 is an index of forgetting (Trial 8 ÷ Trial 5; Geffen et al., 1990).

Primacy and recency effects can be measured for a group by a plot of the likelihood of recall of the particular word by the serial position of the words in the list and, more simply for an individual, by dividing the list into the first five items (primacy), middle five items, and the last five items (recency; Bigler, Rosa, Schultz, Hall, & Harris, 1989). O'Donnell, Radtke, Leicht, and Caesar (1988) provided some data on serial position effects using blocks of three items.

Normally, the recognition trial is seen as a measure of long-term storage, apart from the more complex retrieval processes associated with free recall trials. Recognition trials can provide information not only on retrieval efficiency, but also on decision-making processes when a signal detection approach is used to analyze the results. The use of signal detection theory goes beyond the scope of this section, but norms for the hit rates and false positive rates that are needed for signal detection analysis are given by Forrester and Geffen (1991) and by Geffen et al. (1990). These norms are also reproduced in Schmidt (1996).

Interpretation

Norms

There are several sets of norms available for the RAVLT, some based on substantial numbers of people, and the total available normative sets cover a wide age range. The major difficulty in interpreting norms is the need to ensure that the administration procedures for the norms match the procedure used with the client, as noted earlier. The original norms provided by Rey (reproduced in Schmidt, 1996, p. 24) for the RAVLT should not be used because some words were altered from the original French in the initial translation and because there were procedural variations as well (Wiens et al., 1988). Schmidt (1996) provides a set of age-stratified metanorms for the RAVLT for people aged 13 to 89 years. The metanorms are based on a synthesis and a pooling of existing sets of norms into one set from those studies that used the standard administration procedure. Schmidt (1996) also summarized 19 existing normative studies done up to 1995. Tuokko and Woodward (1996) provided additional demographic-corrected norms for 215 people aged 65 to 90. The book of normative information by Mitrushina et al. (1999) again has a section that is relevant to the RAVLT, and it can be consulted for further notes on normative data.

There are more normative data available for the standard RAVLT administration described previously than for any of the alternative administrative procedures. This makes the use of this procedure more compelling and may outweigh other considerations, such as the computer scoring program for the RAVLT that uses norms derived for Geffen's administrative procedures (Procedure 3 in Schmidt, 1996, p. 9). This is close to the standard administration, differing in using a 20-minute delayed recall and in administering the recognition Trial after Trial 6. A set of norms based on the standard administration is provided in Table 9.6. Tables 9.7 and 9.8 report norms derived from Forrester and Geffen (1991) and Geffen et al. (1990) for selected supplementary

Table 9.6.   Norms for the standard administration of the RAVLT

											Trial									
	1		2		3		4		5		Sum 1–5		6		7		Delayed Recall		Recognition	
Age	M	SD	M	SD	M	SD	M	SD	M	SD	M	SD	M	SD	M	SD	M	SD	M	SD
13	6.8	1.9	9.4	2.1	11.4	1.9	12.1	1.7	13.1	1.3	52.8	7.0	6.2	2.1	11.8	2.0	12.0	2.1	14.1	1.3
14–15	6.7	1.6	9.5	1.8	11.4	1.9	12.2	1.9	12.9	1.7	52.7	7.0	6.1	1.6	11.6	2.2	11.8	2.4	14.4	1.0
16–19	6.8	1.6	9.2	2.0	11.4	1.7	12.3	1.4	12.8	1.4	53.9	6.7	6.5	1.7	11.4	2.4	11.7	2.2	14.2	1.2
20–29	7.0	1.8	9.9	1.8	11.5	2.1	12.4	1.9	12.9	1.8	56.1	7.3	6.7	2.0	11.5	2.3	11.3	2.3	14.3	1.1
30–39	6.7	1.8	9.9	2.2	11.4	2.2	12.2	2.0	12.7	1.9	53.6	8.3	6.5	2.0	11.2	2.7	11.1	2.8	14.2	1.2
40–49	6.6	1.7	9.3	1.9	10.8	2.1	11.7	2.1	12.3	1.9	51.1	8.6	6.1	1.9	10.4	2.8	10.2	2.8	14.0	1.4
50–59	6.2	1.6	9.0	1.9	10.5	1.9	11.4	1.9	12.1	2.1	47.6	8.1	5.7	2.2	9.9	2.8	9.9	3.2	13.9	1.4
60–69	5.9	1.6	8.4	2.0	9.8	2.3	10.9	2.3	11.3	2.3	43.4	7.7	5.1	1.3	9.3	2.9	8.8	3.0	13.5	1.3
70–79	5.5	1.6	7.7	2.1	8.8	2.1	9.8	2.4	10.3	2.4	37.1	7.5	3.9	1.6	8.1	3.0	7.0	2.4	13.3	1.5

Note: Adapted from Schmidt (1996).

Table 9.7. **Norms for supplementary measures of the RAVLT for men**

	Measure																
	Intrusions		Repeats		Proactive Interference		Retroactive Interference		Forgetting		List A Recognition		List B		Misassignments A to B		B to A
Age	M	SD	M	SD	M	SD	M	SD	M	SD	M	SD	M	SD	M	SD	M	SD
7–8	1.3	2.0	—	—	1.1	0.8	0.8	0	1.1	0.3	14.5	0.7	6.1	2.2	1.2	2.1	0.5	0.7
9–10	1.1	1.6	—	—	1.0	0.3	0.8	0.2	1.1	0.2	14.2	1.2	7.5	1.9	1.0	0.9	0.4	0.5
11–12	0.3	0.5	—	—	1.0	0.3	0.8	0.2	1.0	0.2	14.5	0.8	7.2	2.2	0.8	0.8	0.3	0.6
14–15	1.2	2.1	—	—	1.0	0.4	0.8	0.1	1.0	0.1	14.3	0.9	7.3	1.8	1.2	1.1	0.1	0.3
16–19	0.4	0.6	5.9	5.6	1.0	0.2	0.9	0.1	1.0	0.1	14.4	0.9	8.4	2.8	0.8	1.0	0.1	0.3
20–29	0.7	1.2	8.0	4.6	0.8	0.2	0.9	0.1	1.0	0.1	14.2	0.8	8.2	2.7	1.0	0.9	0.4	0.8
30–39	1.2	3.1	3.0	3.6	0.9	0.2	0.9	0.1	1.1	0.1	13.5	1.5	4.4	2.0	0.7	1.2	0.6	0.7
40–49	0.6	0.8	4.1	2.9	1.0	0.2	0.9	0.2	1.1	0.2	14.2	1.2	6.9	2.6	1.2	1.3	0.2	0.6
50–59	0.7	1.2	7.3	7.5	0.8	0.2	0.8	0.2	1.1	0.1	13.9	0.9	4.7	2.9	1.2	1.5	0.3	0.6
60–69	0.3	0.7	5.0	3.6	1.0	0.4	0.8	0.2	0.9	0.4	12.4	2.8	4.9	2.7	2.2	1.3	1.4	1.8
70+	0.9	1.7	5.1	8.6	1.0	0.3	0.8	0.3	0.8	0.3	11.5	2.6	3.0	2.5	0.8	1.0	1.0	1.2

Note: Adapted from Forrester and Geffen (1991), Geffen et al. (1990). Figures for ages 7 to 15 are for both genders.

indices. The norms for the supplementary indices should be regarded with caution because of the small numbers of individuals at each age level. There is the additional factor that the reliability of calculated indices tends to be lower than that of the component scores from which they are derived, and the literature on the interpretation of these indices is often scant. Taken together, these factors suggest that the interpretation of the supplementary indices in Tables 9.7 and 9.8 should be suggestive only and that inferences about individuals should be made with appropriate caution.

Functional Interpretation

Tables 9.7 and 9.8 organize the supplementary indices into acquisition and recall measures. The extent to which the various indices can be interpreted as distinct and different

Table 9.8. **Norms for supplementary measures of the RAVLT for women**

	Measure																
	Intrusions		Repeats		Proactive Interference		Retroactive Interference		Forgetting		List A Recognition		List B		Misassignments A to B		B to A
Age	M	SD	M	SD	M	SD	M	SD	M	SD	M	SD	M	SD	M	SD	M	SD
7–8	1.3	2.0	—	—	1.1	0.8	0.8	0.3	1.1	0.3	14.5	0.7	6.1	2.2	1.2	2.1	0.5	0.7
9–10	1.1	1.6	—	—	1.0	0.3	0.8	0.2	1.1	0.2	14.2	1.2	7.5	1.9	1.0	0.9	0.4	0.5
11–12	0.3	0.5	—	—	1.0	0.3	0.8	0.2	1.0	0.2	14.5	0.8	7.2	2.2	0.8	0.8	0.3	0.6
14–15	1.2	2.1	—	—	1.0	0.4	0.8	0.1	1.0	0.1	14.3	0.9	7.3	1.8	1.2	1.1	0.1	0.3
16–19	0.9	1.4	5.5	6.5	1.0	0.4	0.9	0.2	1.0	0.1	13.8	2.0	7.8	3.1	0.5	0.5	0.2	0.4
20–29	1.2	1.4	10.6	14.3	1.0	0.3	0.9	0.1	1.0	0.1	14.4	0.8	8.0	2.9	0.4	1.0	0.3	0.5
30–39	1.2	1.7	5.0	5.8	0.8	0.2	1.0	0.1	1.0	0.2	14.2	1.7	8.9	4.1	0.3	0.6	0.0	0.0
40–49	0.8	1.2	8.0	4.8	0.8	0.2	0.9	0.1	1.0	0.1	14.4	0.8	7.4	2.8	1.2	1.6	0.2	0.6
50–59	0.8	1.3	4.9	3.7	0.7	0.2	0.9	0.4	1.0	0.2	13.7	1.1	5.7	2.4	1.6	1.9	0.3	0.7
60–69	0.7	1.1	4.8	2.8	1.0	0.5	0.8	0.1	1.0	0.2	13.8	1.1	7.5	3.6	1.4	1.4	0.6	0.7
70+	0.5	1.0	3.5	4.8	0.8	0.5	0.8	0.2	1.1	0.1	13.6	2.0	7.5	3.7	0.9	1.4	1.1	0.9

Note: Adapted from Forrester and Geffen (1991), Geffen et al. (1990). Figures for ages 7 to 15 are for both genders.

components of memory can be evaluated empirically. Vakil and Blachstein (1993) analyzed various combinations of the preceding indices and found that either two or three factors emerged that they identified as reflecting storage (recognition measures), acquisition (immediate memory and proactive interference), and retrieval from long-term storage (best learning, delayed recall, retroactive interference). Learning rate was distinct from total learning and aligned itself with the immediate retrieval factor. Total learning and the temporal order index (Vakil & Blachstein, 1994) were both associated with the retrieval factor. G. Smith, Malec, and Ivnik (1992) reported that the RAVLT delayed recall index was associated with other measures of long-term retention, such as the Paired Associates and Logical Memory subtests from the WMS-R. These findings support Craik's (1977) suggestion that both primary (immediate) and secondary (long-term) memory are distinct processes, both of which are involved in supraspan learning tasks such as the RAVLT.

Measures of immediate recall and proactive interference are generally seen as measures of acquisition under this general model. Most individuals from the age of 13 through the age of 70 years, of average ability levels and with no pathology, will recall 6 or 7 words on the first recall trial (Uchiyama et al., 1995). Note that this is the average range for Digit Span and within G. Miller's (1956) famous range of 7 ± 2. Younger children of ages 7 and 8 may recall only 4 or 5 words, with the number recalled on the first trial increasing to adult levels by about the age of 11 or 12 years (Forrester & Geffen, 1991). Most people will also recall the same number or more on the successive trials, leading to the expected learning curve. Normative figures show that the number of words recalled increases up to 12 to 14 words through about the mid-70s, with normal performance dropping off after that age, although older data sometimes show lower levels of performance than this (Query & Megran, 1983). The relationship between learning measures on the RAVLT and age thus appears to be nonlinear (Vakil & Blachstein, 1997). Performance on the learning trials that is below 1.5 to 2 standard deviations for age and education normative levels can be seen as suggestive of retrieval problems.

Proactive inhibition can be measured by the relative performance on Trial 1 compared to the distracter trial list (Trial 6). In normal samples, the difference in the number of words recalled on these trials rarely exceeds three words, or the 0.8 level for the ratio index reported in Tables 9.7 and 9.8. Individuals with relatively poor learning ability will tend to show only recency effects, that is, will recall mostly words from the last part of the list. In contrast, individuals with no disabilities also show a primacy effect in having better recall of words from the beginning of the list than of the ones in the middle.

Although there are no normative figures that describe learning curves, certainly the vast majority of people show a positive learning curve over Trials 1 to 5. An absence of a learning curve is characteristic of the memory problems associated with Alzheimer's disease (Bigler et al., 1989). The highest score obtained on a learning trial is often also taken as a measure of acquisition (Vakil & Blachstein, 1993).

Retrieval of information after a delay is often taken as the primary measure of retrieval processes. Generally, scores on the delayed recall trial (Trial 8) of the RAVLT are very similar to those on the trial after the distracter trial (Trial 7) in normal groups. This difference in scores obtained after a 30-minute delay is a useful index of forgetting, whether taken as the difference in raw scores or as a weighted ratio (Forrester &

Geffen, 1991; Geffen et al., 1990; Mungas, 1983). The latter index is reported in Tables 9.7 and 9.8. People with amnesia and those with brain injuries may have scores on the delayed recall trial that are three or more words lower than on the immediate recall trial (Mungas, 1983), with ratio index values of 0.75 or less.

Retroactive interference is one of the other indices related to retrieval processes. It is generally assessed by the relative performance on the immediate recall trial and on the last learning trial. Immediate recall after the distracter trial (Trial 7) is usually lower than Trial 5 by one or two words in normal groups (Lezak, 1995; Mungas, 1983). The ratio index of retroactive inhibition reported in Tables 9.7 and 9.8 are thus usually above 0.8 in normal individuals.

Recently, Geffen, Geffen, Bishop, and Manning (1997) provided information on long-term delayed recall trials. Recall of the List A words after one day had dropped by about one word, with one additional word lost after a 7-day delay. The delayed recall information was obtained by telephone interview. Retention by the group of men in this study was lower than same-aged women by about one word on 30-minute, 1-day, and 7-day recall trials.

The recognition trial is taken to reflect minimal demands on memory and on information processing resources. Therefore, it is generally accepted that if recognition delayed recall is better than conventional delayed free recall, then the memory problem is likely to be one of retrieval. Normally, of course, best learning and performance on the recognition trial are very similar. If performance is equally poor on both types of recall, then the memory problem is a generalized one. One example of the utility of a recognition trial is given by Bleecker et al. (1988), who reported that the recognition trial was the only RAVLT measure studied that was not influenced by age, gender, or vocabulary knowledge.

One important point to consider in interpreting some of these indices, particularly the position indices such as primacy and recency, is that these measures are also influenced by the total number of words recalled (Schmidt, 1997). However, one example of their potential use was noted by Crockett, Hadjistavropoulos, and Hurwitz (1992), who found that groups with either anterior or posterior brain damage did not differ from a psychiatric control group of patients with psychiatric disorders, but without brain damage in terms of primacy and recency effects. Schmidt noted that other indices may be preferable to the simple counts that are often used to assess position effects and gave examples of these.

In general, the empirical evidence supports the use of the RAVLT as a measure of verbal learning and memory (Lezak, 1995). For example, Rosenberg, Ryan, and Prifiteria (1984) reported that a group of people independently diagnosed as memory-impaired scored lower than a control group on all RAVLT measures; and Powell, Cripe, and Dodrill (1991) showed that the number of words recalled on Trial 5 performed better than the Halstead Impairment Index (see Barth & Broshek, Chapter 7, this volume) in differentiating a series of people with confirmed brain injuries from gender-, age-, and education-matched controls. In a comparison of a group of 16 people with mild brain injuries to controls matched for age, gender, and education, the RAVLT had overall accuracy rates of about 70%, with modest sensitivity (ranging from 38% for Trial 5 score to 75% for the Sum of Trials 1 to 5) and good specificity (69% to 100%; Guilmette & Rasile, 1995). These results replicate earlier reports that also gave a figure of about 70% for overall accuracy in classification of similar groups (Powell et al., 1991). Recall after the distracter list has been shown to be sensitive to the severity of head injury, as indexed by the length of post-traumatic amnesia (Geffen, Butterworth, Forrester, & Geffen, 1994). Similarly, the RAVLT differentiated controls from a group of young adults with specific language impairments (Records, Tomblin, & Buckwalter, 1995).

Individuals with progressive neurological disorders tend to show distinctive patterns. For example, people with Alzheimer's disease have low initial recall on Trial 1 and show a modest learning increment, if any, by Trial 5 (Bigler et al., 1989; Mitrushina, Satz, & van Gorp, 1989). They also tend to have more intrusion errors than do older people with no known impairments (Bigler et al., 1989; Burt, Zembar, & Niederehe, 1995).

RECOMMENDED READING

Lezak, M.D. (1995). *Neuropsychological assessment* (3rd ed.). Oxford: Oxford University Press.

Meyers, J.E., & Meyers, K.R. (1995a). *Rey Complex Figure Test and recognition trial.* Odessa, FL: Psychological Assessment Resources.

Schmidt, M. (1996). *Rey Auditory and Verbal Learning Test: A handbook.* Los Angeles: Western Psychological Services.

Schmidt, M. (1997). Cautions on interpreting qualitative indices for word-list learning tests. *The Clinical Neuropsychologist, 11*(1), 81–86.

Spreen, O., & Strauss, E. (1998). *A compendium of neuropsychological tests: Administration, norms, and commentary* (2nd ed.). New York: Oxford University Press.

REFERENCES

Akshoomoff, N.A., & Stiles, J. (1995a). Developmental trends in visuospatial analysis and planning: I. Copying a complex figure. *Neuropsychology, 9,* 364–377.

Akshoomoff, N.A., & Stiles, J. (1995b). Developmental trends in visuospatial analysis and planning: II. Memory for a complex figure. *Neuropsychology, 9,* 378–389.

Allen, J.J., Iacono, W.G., & Danielson, K.D. (1992). The identification of concealed memories using event-related potential and implicit behavioral measures: A methodology for prediction in the face of individual differences. *Psychophysiology, 29,* 504–522.

Artiola i Fortuny, L., & Mullany, H.A. (1998). Assessing patients whose language you do not know: Can the absurd be ethical? *Clinical Neuropsychologist, 12,* 113–126.

Atkinson, R.C., & Schiffrin, R.M. (1968). Human memory: A proposed system and its control processes. In K.W. Spence & J.T. Spence (Eds.), *The psychology of learning and motivation: Advances in research and theory* (pp. 89–105). New York: Academic Press.

Baddeley, A.D. (1992). Is working memory working? The fifteenth Bartlett lecture. *Quarterly Journal of Experimental Psychology, 44A,* 1–31.

Baddeley, A.D., Wilson, B.A., & Watts, F.N. (1995). *Handbook of memory disorders.* Chichester, England: Wiley.

Bennett-Levy, J. (1984). Determinants of performance on the Rey-Osterrieth complex figure test: An analysis and a new technique for single-case assessment. *British Journal of Clinical Psychology, 23,* 209–119.

Bernard, L.C. (1990). Prospects for faking believable memory deficits on neuropsychological tests and the use of incentives in simulation research. *Journal of Clinical and Experimental Neuropsychology, 12,* 715–728.

Bernard, L.C. (1991). The detection of faked deficits on the Rey auditory verbal learning test: The effect of serial position. *Archives of Clinical Neuropsychology, 6,* 81–88.

Bernard, L.C., Houston, W., & Natoli, L. (1993). Malingering on neuropsychological memory tests: Potential objective indicators. *Journal of Consulting Psychology, 49,* 45–53.

Bernstein, J.H., & Waber, D. (1996). *Developmental scoring system for the Rey-Osterrieth complex figure (DSS-ROCF).* Odessa, FL: Psychological Assessment Resources.

Berry, D.T., Allen, R.S., & Schmitt, F.A. (1991). Rey-Osterrieth complex figure: Psychometric characteristics in a geriatric sample. *Clinical Neuropsychologist, 5,* 143–153.

Berry, D.T., & Carpenter, G.S. (1992). Effect of four different delay periods on recall of the Rey-Osterrieth complex figure by older persons. *Clinical Neuropsychologist, 6,* 80–84.

Bigler, E.D., Rosa, L., Schultz, F., Hall, S., & Harris, J. (1989). Rey auditory verbal learning and Rey-Osterrieth complex figure design performance in Alzheimer's disease and closed head injury. *Journal of Clinical Psychology, 49,* 277–280.

Binder, L.M. (1982). Constructional strategies on complex figure drawings after unilateral brain damage. *Journal of Clinical Neuropsychology, 4,* 51–58.

Binder, L.M. (1992). Malingering detected by forced choice testing of memory and tactile sensation: A case report. *Archives of Clinical Neuropsychology, 7,* 155–163.

Binder, L.M., Villanueva, M.R., Howieson, D., & Moore, R.T. (1993). The Rey AVLT recognition memory task measures motivational impairment after mild head trauma. *Archives of Clinical Neuropsychology, 8,* 137–147.

Binder, L.M., & Willis, S.C. (1991). Assessment of motivation after financially compensable minor head trauma. *Psychological Assessment: A Journal of Consulting and Clinical Psychology, 3,* 175–181.

Bishop, J., Knights, R.M., & Stoddart, C. (1990). Rey auditory verbal learning test: Performance of English and French children aged 5 to 16. *Clinical Neuropsychologist, 4,* 133–140.

Bleecker, M.L., Bolla Wilson, K., Agnew, J., & Meyers, D.A. (1988). Age-related sex differences in verbal memory. *Journal of Clinical Psychology, 44,* 403–411.

Boone, K.B., Lesser, I.M., Hill-Gutierrez, E., & Berman, N.G. (1993). Rey-Osterrieth complex figure performance in healthy, older adults: Relationship to age, education, sex, and IQ. *Clinical Neuropsychologist, 7,* 22–28.

Brouwers, P., Cox, C., Martin, A., Chase, T., & Fedio, P. (1984). Differential perceptual-spatial impairment in Huntington's and Alzheimer's dementias. *Archives of Neurology, 41,* 1073–1076.

Burt, D.B., Zembar, M.J., & Niederehe, G. (1995). Depression and memory impairment: A meta-analysis of the association, its pattern, and specificity. *Psychological Bulletin, 117,* 285–305.

Butler, M., Retzlaff, P., & Vanderploeg, R. (1991). Neuropsychological test usage. *Professional Psychology: Research and Practice, 22,* 510–512.

Carr, E.K., & Lincoln, N.B. (1988). Inter-rater reliability of the Rey figure copying test. *British Journal of Clinical Psychology, 27,* 267–268.

Chervinsky, A.B., Mitrushina, A.M., & Satz, P. (1992). Comparison of four methods of scoring the Rey-Osterrieth complex figure drawing test on four age groups of normal elderly. *Brain Dysfunction, 5,* 267–287.

Chiulli, S.J., Haalund, K.Y., LaRue, A., & Garry, P.J. (1995). Impact of age on drawing the Rey-Osterrieth figure. *Clinical Neuropsychologist, 9,* 219–224.

Corwin, J., & Bylsma, F.W. (1993). Translations of excerpts from Andre Rey's psychological examination of traumatic encephalopathy and P.A. Osterrieth's the complex figure test. *Clinical Neuropsychologist, 7,* 3–21.

Craik, F.I.M. (1977). Age differences in human memory. In J.E. Birren & K.W. Schaie (Eds.), *Handbook of the psychology of aging.* New York: Van Nostrand-Reinhold.

Crawford, J.R., Stewart, L.R., & Moore, J.W. (1989). Demonstration of savings on the AVLT and development of a parallel form. *Journal of Clinical and Experimental Neuropsychology, 11,* 975–981.

Crockett, D.J., Hadjistavropoulos, T., & Hurwitz, T. (1992). Primacy and recency effects in the assessment of memory using the Rey auditory verbal learning test. *Archives of Clinical Neuropsychology, 7,* 97–107.

Crossen, J.R., & Wiens, A.N. (1994). Comparison of the auditory-verbal learning test (AVLT) and California verbal learning test (CVLT) in a sample of normal subjects. *Journal of Clinical and Experimental Neuropsychology, 16,* 190–194.

Delaney, R.C., Prevey, M.L., Cramer, J., Mattson, R.H., & VA Epilepsy Cooperative Study #264 Research Group. (1992). Test-retest comparability and control subject data for the Rey-auditory verbal learning test and Rey-Osterrieth/Taylor complex figures. *Archives of Clinical Neuropsychology, 7,* 523–528.

Delis, D.C., Kramer, J.H., Kaplan, E., & Ober, B.A. (1987). *California verbal learning test manual. Research edition.* San Antonio, TX: Psychological Corporation.

Delis, D.C., Kramer, J.H., Kaplan, E., & Ober, B.A. (1994). *CVLT-C: California verbal learning test, children's version manual.* San Antonio, TX: Psychological Corporation.

Denman, S.B. (1984). *Manual for the Denman memory battery.* Charleston, SC: Author.

Duley, J.F., Wilkins, J.W., Hamby, S.L., Hopkins, D.G., Burwell, R.D., & Barry, N.S. (1993). Explicit scoring criteria for the Rey-Osterrieth and Taylor complex figures. *Clinical Neuropsychologist, 7,* 29–38.

Eichenbaum, H. (1997). Declarative memory: Insights from cognitive neurobiology. *Annual Review of Psychology, 48,* 547–572.

Fastenau, P.S. (1996). Development and preliminary standardization of the "extended complex figure test" (ECFT). *Journal of Clinical and Experimental Neuropsychology, 18,* 63–76.

Faust, D., Hart, K., & Guilmette, T.J. (1988). Pediatric malingering: The capacity of children to fake believable deficits on neuropsychological testing. *Journal of Consulting and Clinical Psychology, 56,* 578–582.

Faust, D., Hart, K., Guilmette, T.J., & Arkes, H.R. (1988). Neuropsychologists' capacity to detect adolescent malingerers. *Professional Psychology: Research and Practice, 19,* 508–515.

Forrester, G., & Geffen, G. (1991). Performance measures of 7- to 15-year-old children on the Rey auditory verbal learning test. *Clinical Neuropsychologist, 5,* 345–359.

Fuller, K.H., Gouvier, W.D., & Savage, R.M. (1997). Comparison of list B and list C of the Rey auditory verbal learning test. *Clinical Neuropsychologist, 11,* 201–204.

Geffen, G.M., Butterworth, P., Forrester, G.M., & Geffen, L.B. (1994). Auditory verbal learning test components as measures of the severity of closed-head injury. *Brain Injury, 8,* 405–411.

Geffen, G.M., Butterworth, P., & Geffen, L.B. (1994). Test-retest reliability of a new form of the auditory verbal learning test (AVLT). *Archives of Clinical Neuropsychology, 9,* 303–316.

Geffen, G.M., Geffen, L.B., Bishop, K., & Manning, L. (1997). Extended delayed recall of AVLT word lists: Effects of age and sex on adult performance. *Australian Journal of Psychology, 49,* 78–84.

Geffen, G.M., Geffen, L.B., Smyth, D., & Manning, L.M. (1996). *Auditory verbal learning test manual, including a computerized scoring program (MS-DOS and Windows).* University of Queensland. Cognitive Psychophysiology Laboratory, Technical Report No. 7.

Geffen, G.M., Moar, K.J., O'Hanlan, A.P., Clark, C.R., & Geffen, L.B. (1990). Performance measures of 16- to 86-year-old males and females on the auditory verbal learning test. *Clinical Neuropsychologist, 4,* 45–63.

Glahn, D.C., Gur, R.C., Ragland, J.D., Censits, D.M., & Gur, R.E. (1997). Reliability, performance characteristics, construct validity, and an initial clinical application of a visual object learning test (VOLT). *Neuropsychology, 11,* 602–612.

Groth-Marnat, G. (1999). *Handbook of psychological assessment* (3rd ed. rev.). New York: Wiley.

Guilmette, T.J., & Rasile, D. (1995). Sensitivity, specificity, and diagnostic accuracy of three verbal memory measures in the assessment of mild brain injury. *Neuropsychology, 9,* 338–344.

Hamby, S.L., Wilkins, J.W., & Barry, N.S. (1993). Organizational quality on the Rey-Osterrieth and Taylor complex figures: A new scoring system. *Psychological Assessment: A Journal of Consulting and Clinical Psychology, 5,* 27–33.

Healy, A.F., & McNamara, D.S. (1996). Verbal learning and memory: Does the modal model still work? *Annual Review of Psychology, 47,* 143–172.

Heilbronner, R.L. (1992). The search for a "pure" visual memory test: Pursuit of perfection? *Clinical Neuropsychologist, 6,* 105–112.

Ivnik, R.J., Malec, J.F., Smith, G.E., Tangalos, E.G., Petersen, R.C., Kokmen, E., & Kurland, K.T. (1992). Mayo's older American normative studies: Updated AVLT norms for ages 56 to 97. *Clinical Neuropsychologist, 6*(Suppl.), 83–104.

Ivnik, R.J., Malec, J.F., Tangalos, E.G., Petersen, R.C., Kokmen, E., & Kurland, L.T. (1990). The auditory-verbal learning test (AVLT): Norms for ages 55 years and older. *Psychological Assessment: A Journal of Consulting and Clinical Psychology, 2,* 304–312.

Janowsky, J.S., & Thomas-Thrapp, L.J. (1993). Complex figure recall in the elderly: A deficit in memory or constructional strategy? *Journal of Clinical and Experimental Neuropsychology, 15,* 159–169.

King, M.C. (1981). Effects of non-focal brain dysfunction on visual memory. *Journal of Clinical Psychology, 37,* 638–643.

Knight, J.A., Miller, S.A., Forsyth, J.P., & McWilliams, J. (1993). *Comparison of the equivalence of two scoring systems for the Rey-complex figure.* Paper presented at the annual meeting of the American Psychological Association, Toronto.

Kuehn, S.M., & Snow, W.G. (1992). Are the Rey and Taylor figures equivalent? *Archives of Clinical Neuropsychology, 7,* 445–448.

Lee, G.P., Loring, D.W., & Thompson, J.L. (1989). Construct validity of material-specific unilateral temporal lobe ablations. *Psychological Assessment: A Journal of Consulting and Clinical Psychology, 1,* 192–197.

Lezak, M.D. (1995). *Neuropsychological assessment* (3rd ed.). Oxford, England: Oxford University Press.

Liberman, J., Stewart, W., Seines, O., & Gordon, B. (1994). Rater agreement for the Rey-Osterrieth complex figure test. *Journal of Clinical Psychology, 50,* 615.

Loring, D.W., Lee, G.P., & Meador, K.J. (1988). Revising the Rey-Osterrieth: Rating right hemisphere recall. *Archives of Clinical Neuropsychology, 3,* 239–247.

Loring, D.W., Martin, R.C., Meador, K.J., & Lee, G.P. (1990). Psychometric construction of the Rey-Osterrieth complex figure: Methodological considerations and interrater reliability. *Archives of Clinical Neuropsychology, 5,* 1–14.

Marcopulos, B.A., McLain, C.A., & Giuliano, A.J. (1997). Cognitive impairment or inadequate norms? A study of healthy, rural, older adults with limited education. *Clinical Neuropsychologist, 11,* 111–130.

Meyers, J.E., & Lange, D. (1994). Recognition subtest for the complex figure. *Clinical Neuropsychologist, 8,* 153–166.

Meyers, J.E., & Meyers, K.R. (1995a). Rey complex figure test under four different administration procedures. *Clinical Neuropsychologist, 9,* 63–67.

Meyers, J.E., & Meyers, K.R. (1995b). *Rey complex figure test and recognition trial.* Odessa, FL: Psychological Assessment Resources.

Miller, G.A. (1956). The magical number seven, plus or minus two: Some limits on our capacity for processing information. *Psychological Review, 63,* 81–97.

Miller, W.G., & Miller, E.S. (1992). Malingering and neuropsychological assessment. *Physical Medicine and Rehabilitation: State of the Art Reviews, 6,* 547–563.

Mitrushina, M., Boone, K., & D'Elia, L.G. (1999). *Handbook of normative data for neuropsychological assessment.* New York: Oxford University Press.

Mitrushina, M., & Satz, P. (1989). Differential decline of specific memory components in normal aging. *Brain Dysfunction, 2,* 330–335.

Mitrushina, M., Satz, P., & van Gorp, W. (1989). Some putative cognitive precursors in subjects hypothesized to be at-risk for dementia. *Archives of Clinical Neuropsychology, 4,* 70–78.

Moye, J. (1997). Nonverbal memory assessment with designs: Construct validity and clinical utility. *Neuropsychology Review, 7,* 157–170.

Mungas, D. (1983). Differential clinical sensitivity of specific parameters of the Rey auditory-verbal learning test. *Journal of Consulting and Clinical Psychology, 51,* 848–855.

Nelson, H.E. (1983). *The national adult reading test (NART) test manual.* Windsor, England: NFER-Nelson.

O'Donnell, J.P., Radtke, R.C., Leicht, D.J., & Caesar, R. (1988). Encoding and retrieval processes in learning-disabled, head-injured, and nondisabled young adults. *Journal of General Psychology, 115,* 355–368.

Ogden, J.A., Growden, J.H., & Corkin, S. (1990). Deficits on visuospatial tests involving forward planning in high-functioning Parkinsonians. *Neuropsychiatry, Neuropsychology, and Behavioral Neurology, 3,* 125–139.

Peaker, A., & Stewart, L.E. (1989). Rey's auditory verbal learning test—A review. In J.R. Crawford & D.M. Parker (Eds.), *Developments in clinical and experimental neuropsychology* (pp. 219–236). New York: Plenum Press.

Pierson, A.R., & Jansen, P. (1997). Comparability of the Rey-Osterrieth and Taylor forms of the complex figure test. *Clinical Neuropsychologist, 11,* 244–248.

Piguet, O., Saling, M.M., O'Shea, M.F., & Berkovic, S.F. (1994). Rey figure distortions reflect nonverbal recall differences between right and left foci in unilateral temporal lobe epilepsy. *Archives of Clinical Neuropsychology, 9,* 451–460.

Poulton, R.G., & Moffitt, T.E. (1995). The Rey-Osterrieth complex figure test: Norms for young adolescents and an examination of validity. *Archives of Clinical Neuropsychology, 10,* 47–56.

Powell, J.B., Cripe, L.I., & Dodrill, C.B. (1991). Assessment of brain impairment with the Rey auditory verbal learning test: A comparison with other neuropsychological measures. *Archives of Clinical Neuropsychology, 6,* 241–249.

Query, W.T., & Berger, R.A. (1980). AVLT memory scores as a function of age among general medical, neurologic and alcoholic patients. *Journal of Clinical Psychology, 36,* 1009–1012.

Query, W.T., & Megran, J. (1983). Age-related norms for AVLT in a male patient population. *Journal of Clinical Psychology, 39,* 136–138.

Rapport, L.J., Charter, R.A., Dutra, R.L., Farchione, T.J., & Kingsley, J.J. (1997). Psychometric properties of the Rey-Osterrieth complex figure: Lezak-Osterrieth versus Denman scoring systems. *Clinical Neuropsychologist, 11,* 46–53.

Rapport, L.J., Dutra, R.L., Webster, J.S., Charter, R., & Morrill, B. (1995). Hemispatial deficits on the Rey-Osterrieth complex figure drawing. *Clinical Neuropsychologist, 9,* 169–179.

Rapport, L.J., Farchione, T.J., Dutra, R.L., Webster, J.S., & Charter, R.A. (1996). Measures of hemi-inattention on the Rey figure copy for the Lezak-Osterrieth scoring method. *Clinical Neuropsychologist, 10,* 450–454.

Records, N.L., Tomblin, J.B., & Buckwalter, P.R. (1995). Auditory verbal learning and memory in young adults with specific language impairment. *Clinical Neuropsychologist, 9,* 187–193.

Reitan, R.M., & Wolfson, D. (1996). Relationships of age and education to Wechsler adult intelligence scale IQ values in brain-damaged and non-brain-damaged groups. *Clinical Neuropsychologist, 10,* 293–304.

Rey, A. (1964). *L'examen clinique en psychologie* (2nd ed.). Paris: Presses universitaires de France.

Rogers, R., Harrell, E.H., & Liff, C.D. (1993). Feigning neuropsychological impairment: A critical review of methodological and clinical considerations. *Clinical Psychology Review, 13,* 255–274.

Rosenberg, S.J., Ryan, J.J., & Prifiteria, A. (1984). Rey auditory-verbal learning test performance of patients with and without memory impairment. *Journal of Clinical Psychology, 40,* 785–787.

Rosselli, M., & Ardila, A. (1991). Effects of age, education, and gender on the Rey-Osterrieth complex figure. *Clinical Neuropsychologist, 5,* 370–376.

Savage, R.M., & Gouvier, W.D. (1992). Rey auditory verbal learning test: The effects of age and gender, and norms for delayed recall and story recognition trials. *Archives of Clinical Neuropsychology, 7,* 407–414.

Schmidt, M. (1996). *Rey auditory and verbal learning test: A handbook.* Los Angeles: Western Psychological Services.

Schmidt, M. (1997). Cautions on interpreting qualitative indices for word-list learning tests. *Clinical Neuropsychologist, 11,* 81–86.

Selnes, O.A., Jacobson, L., Machado, A.M., & Becker, J.T. (1991). Normative data for a brief neuropsychological screening battery. *Perceptual and Motor Skills, 73,* 539–550.

Shah, A.K. (1997). Interviewing mentally ill ethnic elders with interpreters. *Australian Journal on Ageing, 16,* 220–221.

Shapiro, D.M., & Harrison, D.W. (1990). Alternate forms of the AVLT: A procedure and test of form equivalency. *Archives of Clinical Neuropsychology, 5,* 405–410.

Shorr, J.S., Delis, D.C., & Massman, P.J. (1992). Memory for the Rey-Osterrieth figure: Perceptual clustering, encoding, and storage. *Neuropsychology, 6,* 43–50.

Shuttleworth-Jordan, A.B. (1997). Age and education effects on brain-damaged subjects: 'Negative' findings revisited. *Clinical Neuropsychologist, 11,* 205–209.

Smith, A. (1982). *Symbol digit modalities test (SDMT) manual* (Rev. ed.). Los Angeles: Western Psychological Services.

Smith, G.E., Malec, J.F., & Ivnik, R.J. (1992). Validity of the construct of nonverbal memory: A factor analytic study in a normal elderly sample. *Journal of Clinical and Experimental Neuropsychology, 14,* 211–221.

Spreen, O., & Strauss, E. (1991). *A compendium of neuropsychological tests: Administration, norms, and commentary.* New York: Oxford University Press.

Spreen, O., & Strauss, E. (1998). *A compendium of neuropsychological tests: Administration, norms, and commentary* (2nd ed). New York: Oxford University Press.

Stallings, G.A., Boake, C., & Sherer, M. (1995). Comparison of the California verbal learning test and the Rey auditory verbal learning test in head-injured patients. *Journal of Clinical and Experimental Neuropsychology, 17,* 706–712.

Stern, R.A., Singer, E.A., Duke, L.M., Singer, N.G., Morey, C.E., Daughtrey, E.W., & Kaplan, E. (1994). The Boston qualitative scoring system for the Rey-Osterrieth complex figure: Description and interrater reliability. *Clinical Neuropsychologist, 8,* 309–322.

Strauss, E., & Spreen, O. (1990). A comparison of the Rey and Taylor figures. *Archives of Clinical Neuropsychology, 5,* 417–420.

Stringer, A.Y. (1996). *A guide to adult neuropsychological diagnosis.* Philadelphia: Davis.

Taylor, E.M. (1959). *Psychological appraisal of children with cerebral defects.* Cambridge, MA: Harvard University Press.

Taylor, L.B. (1979). Psychological assessment of neurological patients. In T. Rasmussen & R. Marino (Eds.), *Functional neurosurgery.* New York: Raven Press.

Tombaugh, T.N., Faulkner, P., & Hubley, A.M. (1992). Effects of age on the Rey-Osterrieth and Taylor complex figures: Test-retest data using an intentional learning paradigm. *Journal of Clinical and Experimental Neuropsychology, 14,* 647–661.

Tombaugh, T.N., & Hubley, A.M. (1991). Four studies comparing the Rey-Osterrieth and Taylor complex figures. *Journal of Clinical and Experimental Neuropsychology, 13,* 587–599.

Tombaugh, T.N., Schmidt, J.P., & Faulkner, P. (1992). A new procedure of administering the Taylor complex figure: Normative data over a 60-year age span. *Clinical Neuropsychologist, 6,* 63–79.

Trahan, D.E., & Larrabee, G.J. (1988). *Continuous visual memory test. Professional manual.* Odessa, FL: Psychological Assessment Resources.

Tranel, D., & Damasio, A.R. (1995). Neurobiological foundations of human memory. In A.D. Baddeley, B.A. Wilson, & F.N. Watts (Eds.), *Handbook of memory disorders* (pp. 27–50). Chichester, England: Wiley.

Troyer, A.K., & Wishart, H.A. (1997). A comparison of qualitative scoring systems for the Rey-Osterrieth complex figure test. *Clinical Neuropsychologist, 11,* 381–390.

Tulving, E. (1985). How many memory systems are there? *American Psychologist, 40,* 385–398.

Tuokko, H., Kristjansson, E., & Miller, J. (1995). Neuropsychological detection of dementia: An overview of the neuropsychological component of the Canadian study of health and aging. *Journal of Clinical and Experimental Neuropsychology, 17,* 352–373.

Tuokko, H., & Woodward, T.S. (1996). Development and validation of a demographic correction system for neuropsychological measures used in the Canadian study of health and aging. *Journal of Clinical and Experimental Neuropsychology, 18,* 479–616.

Tupler, L.A., Welsh, K.A., Asare-Aboagye, Y., & Dawson, D.V. (1995). Reliability of the Rey-Osterrieth complex figure in use with memory-impaired patients. *Journal of Clinical and Experimental Neuropsychology, 17,* 566–579.

Uchiyama, C.L., D'Elia, L.F., Dellinger, A.M., Becker, J.T., Selnes, O.A., Wesch, J.E., Chen, B.B., Satz, P., van Gorp, W., & Miller, E.N. (1995). Alternate forms of the auditory-verbal learning test: Issues of test comparability, longitudinal reliability, and moderating demographic variables. *Archives of Clinical Neuropsychology, 10,* 133–145.

Vakil, E., & Blachstein, H. (1993). Rey auditory-verbal learning test: Structure analysis. *Journal of Clinical Psychology, 49,* 883–890.

Vakil, E., & Blachstein, H. (1994). A supplementary measure in the Rey AVLT for assessing incidental learning of temporal order. *Journal of Clinical Psychology, 50,* 240–245.

Vakil, E., & Blachstein, H. (1997). Rey AVLT: Developmental norms for adults and the sensitivity of different memory measures to age. *Clinical Neuropsychologist, 11,* 356–369.

Vanderploeg, R.D., Axelrod, B.N., Sherer, M., Scott, J., & Adams, R.L. (1997). The importance of demographic adjustments on neuropsychological test performance: A response to Reitan and Wolfson (1995). *Clinical Neuropsychologist, 11,* 210–217.

Visser, R.S.H. (1973). *Manual of the complex figure test.* Amsterdam, The Netherlands: Swets & Zeitlinger.

Waber, D.P., & Bernstein, J.H. (1995). Performance of learning-disabled and non-learning-disabled children on the Rey-Osterrieth complex figure: Validation of the developmental scoring system. *Developmental Neuropsychology, 11,* 237–252.

Waber, D.P., & Holmes, J.M. (1985). Assessing children's copy productions of the Rey-Osterrieth complex figure. *Journal of Clinical and Experimental Neuropsychology, 7,* 264–280.

Waber, D.P., & Holmes, J.M. (1986). Assessing children's memory productions of the Rey-Osterrieth complex figure. *Journal of Clinical and Experimental Neuropsychology, 8,* 563–580.

Wechsler, D. (1987). *Wechsler memory scale–revised manual.* San Antonio, TX: Psychological Corporation.

Wechsler, D. (1997). *WMS-III—Wechsler memory scale–third edition. Administration and scoring manual.* San Antonio, TX: Psychological Corporation.

Wechsler, D., & Stone, C.P. (1945). *Wechsler memory scale manual.* New York: Psychological Corporation.

Wiens, A.N., McMinn, M.R., & Crossen, J.R. (1988). Rey auditory-verbal learning test: Development of norms for healthy young adults. *Clinical Neuropsychologist, 2,* 67–87.

Williams, J.M. (1991). *Memory assessment scales manual.* Odessa, FL: Psychological Assessment Resources.

Zappala, G., & Trexler, L.E. (1992). Quantitative and qualitative aspects of memory performance after minor head injury. *Archives of Clinical Neuropsychology, 7,* 145–154.

Chapter 10

LANGUAGE AND ACADEMIC ABILITIES

Brick Johnstone, Daniel Holland, and Carmen Larimore

As part of the neuropsychological evaluation, the assessment of language functions and academic skills is accomplished through both direct and indirect measurement, including objective testing and behavioral observation. The assessment of language functions and academic skills is often driven by the use of the most popular assessment tools, as well as by a need to briefly screen for deficits in these domains. Even though comprehensive batteries exist for the evaluation of both language functions (i.e., Boston Diagnostic Aphasia Examination) and academic skills (i.e., Woodcock-Johnson Psycho-Educational Test Battery-Revised), because of increasingly restricted time constraints in both academic and health care settings, these batteries are not frequently used as a standard component of a typical neuropsychological evaluation and are reserved for those patients who have been clearly identified as requiring a specific and thorough assessment of the particular functional domain. Therefore, neuropsychologists need to have a clear understanding of the information that can be drawn from general measures of language abilities and academic skills that are an inherent part of virtually any neuropsychological evaluation. The clinician will then be able to utilize these general measures as screening tools to: (1) assist with diagnostic considerations (e.g., identify language deficits suggestive of dominant hemisphere impairment); (2) identify relative strengths and weaknesses, which can assist in providing functional recommendations; and (3) determine which individuals would benefit from more thorough and specific evaluations (e.g., an individual demonstrating paraphasias on language screening measures clearly warrants a comprehensive speech-language evaluation).

Language functions and academic skills are partially overlapping constructs with both shared and independent aspects. It is critical to decide whether deficits are related to acute events (e.g., stroke, brain injury) or to long-standing developmental weaknesses (e.g., learning disabilities or developmental language disorders). If it is determined that language or academic deficits are due to long-standing weaknesses, it must then be further determined whether these weaknesses stem from environmental factors (e.g., lack of formal education, cultural differences) or from innate cognitive limitations (e.g., learning disability, developmental disorder). This differentiation can rarely be made from considering the results of a single measure. Rather, it comes from analyzing the pattern of comprehensive tests that are consistent with specific organic etiologies. Therefore, the clinician must be familiar with individual measures of language and academic abilities, as well as with the pattern of language and academic abilities associated with different cognitive and academic disorders. Although there are numerous tests that can briefly assess these basic areas, tests or subtests that are already core components of most standard batteries are usually sufficient for screening purposes.

The following sections review the most common language and academic disorders, as well as the tests most commonly used to assess them in neuropsychological evaluations. It is essential to note that for each of the following tests, it is important to determine both their diagnostic and functional uses.

LANGUAGE DISORDERS

This section focuses on specific aphasic disorders that are best assessed by specific language tests. General verbal abilities (i.e., the ability to verbally express ideas and facts) are also frequently evaluated as part of a comprehensive language evaluation, with the Wechsler Adult Intelligence Scale-III (WAIS-III) Verbal Intelligence subtests (i.e., Vocabulary, Information, Comprehension, etc.) used most frequently to evaluate general verbal skills (see Chapter 5 for a more thorough description of the WAIS-III verbal subtests). Although this section focuses on the evaluation of language disorders by neuropsychologists, the most comprehensive speech-language evaluations are often best conducted by speech pathologists. Although several noted psychologists are well trained in the assessment of language disorders, most psychologists are not adequately trained to diagnose specific language disorders. More important, training guidelines in health-related psychological specialties (i.e., neuropsychology, rehabilitation psychology, health psychology) do not provide any specific suggestions for either the diagnosis or the treatment of specific language disorders. Therefore, it is essential for neuropsychologists to work collaboratively with speech-language pathologists to provide the best coordinated care for individuals with neuropsychological and language impairments.

In order to best assess language abilities, it is necessary for neuropsychologists to have a conceptual framework for those language abilities that need to be evaluated in a neuropsychological evaluation. Holland, Hogg, and Farmer (1997), based on interdisciplinary team interactions, suggested the following as a guideline for assessing language abilities. Note that the emphasis is on language skills, with a deemphasis on assessment measures:

1. Expressive Language
   - *Semantics:* the accurate use of words and word meanings.
   - *Syntax:* the ability to form grammatically correct sentences.
   - *Pragmatics:* the ability to employ language in a goal-directed manner.
   - *Discourse:* the ability to understand and demonstrate mastery over the subtle rules, flow, and context of conversation.
   - *Written language:* any written expressive ability, from the most basic symbol-letter recognition to the completion of written ideas in sentence form.
2. Receptive Language
   - *Reading comprehension:* the ability to understand any written form.
   - *Auditory comprehension:* the ability to understand information and the emotional content of what is said.

In addition to following a conceptual framework when evaluating language abilities, psychologists should be knowledgeable regarding language impairments indicative of pathognomic brain dysfunction. When a person's brain is injured or diseased, the dysfunction may be readily apparent in his or her daily conversations, although it is important to determine the specific nature and the severity of the impairment. Disruptions in language occur along a very broad spectrum, ranging from difficulties with basic units of language, such as sounding phonemes or manipulating simple written language symbols, to difficulty processing higher order language skills or conversational competence. The basic pathognomic signs of language dysfunction include deficits in naming, fluency, repetition, writing, and/or comprehension. The basic aphasic syndromes and their characteristics include:

- *Broca's aphasia:* nonfluent, halting speech; reduced speech length; impaired prosody; awkward articulation.
- *Wernicke's aphasia:* fluent verbal output with marked auditory comprehension deficits resulting in paraphasic errors.
- *Transcortical motor aphasia:* paucity of speech with early mutism; nonfluent verbal output with relatively spared verbal repetition ability.
- *Transcortical sensory aphasia:* severely impaired auditory comprehension with intact repetition abilities; fluent paraphasic speech.
- *Conduction aphasia:* marked verbal repetition deficit despite good auditory comprehension and fluent although paraphasic speech.
- *Global aphasia:* severely impaired across all abilities; nonfluent.

These basic aphasic symptoms may be reliably identified by aphasia screening tests like the Reitan Aphasia Screen Test (see Chapter 7), although language deficits in higher order language skills, like discourse or semantics, may escape detection by a brief screening measure not specifically targeting such constructs. A screening test aimed at identifying or ruling out specific aphasic symptoms should not be perceived as a comprehensive language assessment. Rather, the test is useful for the identification of speech-language deficits that have diagnostic implications and functional relevance for performance on other tests in the battery. Once language deficits of any kind are detected, a comprehensive language assessment, usually conducted by a speech-language pathologist, is required for clarifying diagnostic issues and treatment planning. Following are descriptions of some language tests frequently used by neuropsychologists.

BOSTON NAMING TEST

History and Development

The Boston Naming Test (BNT) is one of the most commonly used measures of gross language skills currently used by psychologists (Kaplan, Goodglass, & Weintraub, 1983). It was originally published by Kaplan et al. in 1978 but was revised and shortened in 1983 into the version that is in use today. The BNT is used as a brief screening for expressive language abilities (i.e., ability to name pictures) and is made up of 60 pictures ranging from common and easily identifiable objects (e.g., comb) to less frequently used items (e.g., abacus). Individuals are asked to spontaneously identify each picture within 20 seconds. If an individual is unable to spontaneously name the object, they are provided with a stimulus cue (i.e., description of the object) and then a phonemic cue (i.e., initial sound of the object) if necessary.

Psychometric Properties

The psychometric properties of the BNT have not been thoroughly documented until the past decade. Test-retest reliability has been shown to be as high as .94 for individuals with epilepsy (Sawrie, Chelune, Naugle, & Lüders, 1996), and various split-half correlations have been shown to range between .81 and .97, depending on the sample (Huff, Collins, Corkin, & Rosen, 1986).

Construct validity studies have generally shown the BNT to be a measure of word knowledge and general verbal skills. For example, Halperin, Healy, Zeitschick, Ludman, and Weinstein (1989) indicated that the BNT loaded on a word knowledge-vocabulary factor with the Peabody Picture Vocabulary Test, with low loadings on a verbal fluency-memory factor. Similarly, Hawkins et al. (1993) reported correlations between .74 and .87 between the BNT and the Gates-McGinite Reading Vocabulary Test for adults with no known impairments. However, the BNT has also been shown to be related to general, nonspecific factors of intelligence, including verbal comprehension, perceptual organization, and freedom from distractibility (Axelrod, Ricker, & Cherry, 1994).

Diagnostic utility of the BNT has been found to be variable. Jordan, Cannon, and Murdoch (1992) found no differences between children with and without traumatic brain injury on the BNT, and Weyandt and Willis (1994) found that the BNT did not differ between children with and without attention deficit hyperactivity disorder (ADHD). However, others (LaBarge, Balota, Storandt, & Smith, 1992; Zec, Vicari, Kocis, & Reynolds, 1992) found the BNT to discriminate between those with and without mild Alzheimer's, as well as between those with Alzheimer's versus vascular dementia (Barr, Benedict, Tune, & Brandt, 1992).

Assets and Limitations

The primary strengths of the BNT are its brevity, ease of administration, relative accuracy as a simple screening measure for gross language skills, and wide spread use by psychologists. The BNT can be used to quantify gross language problems that can then be more adequately evaluated by other more specific measures of expressive language functions. Identification of naming deficits on the BNT may be amenable to some remediation strategies currently in use (German, 1993).

The primary weakness of the BNT involves the continued questionable use of data from non-normal distributions to make inferences about picture-naming abilities. A fundamental assumption in interpreting data is that the data is evenly distributed among low, average, and high scores. Interpretation based on negatively and positively skewed data will likely lead to over- and underestimation of deficits, respectively.

Another acknowledged weakness of the BNT is that it measures only one of many aphasic deficits, the ability to name objects. The BNT is commonly reported as a measure of several global, imprecise abilities, such as expressive language, word naming, picture naming, and so forth. However, as previously stated, individuals with expressive language disorders can experience deficits in numerous and specific areas such as semantics, syntax, pragmatics, discourse, and written language. Furthermore, different types of aphasias (e.g., Broca's, Wernicke's, transcortical motor, etc.) lead to specific language deficits (e.g., problems in fluency, repetition, naming), only some of which involve deficits in naming. Therefore, the BNT may identify some individuals with aphasias but miss others.

Finally, a relative weakness with the BNT is that identification of naming deficits does not lead to any standard, commonly used treatment recommendations. Given psychologists' limited training in specific speech-language disorders and, particularly, relevant treatments, it is difficult to provide specific recommendations based solely on the BNT, other than that an individual may benefit from semantic or phonemic cues or that they should be referred to speech-language pathologists for more specific evaluation and treatment.

Administration

Children begin the test at item 1, while adults begin at item 30 unless they miss that item. If adults miss item 30, they are presented with the previous items until they accurately identify eight items in a row. Administration is discontinued after six successive failures. The BNT typically takes 15 to 30 minutes to administer and score. Five scores are reported for the test: (1) the number of items correctly identified without cues; (2) the number of stimulus cues given; (3) the number of items correctly identified following stimulus cues; (4) the number of phonemic cues given; and (5) the number of items successfully identified following phonemic cues. The total score is derived by adding the first score (the total number of correct items spontaneously given) and the third score (the total number of correct items given following stimulus cues), including the total number of items that preceded the starting point of the test.

Interpretation

The BNT has only limited normative data available for interpretation, with the norms accompanying the test appropriate for individuals ages 18 to 59. Frequently used normative data for the BNT have been published by Heaton, Grant, and Matthews (1991), with other normative data available on the World Wide Web (e.g., www.normative-data.com.net). Appropriate normative data for populations of older people have been published by Mitrushina and Satz (1989) and by Ivnik, Malec, and Smith (1996). Interpretation of the test must take demographic variables into account because several studies suggest that age and education effects are expected on the BNT (Ivnik et al., 1996; Tombaugh & Hubley, 1997). See Table 10.1 for normative data for the BNT commonly used for adult (non-geriatric) populations.

Relative performance on the BNT can also be determined by comparing individual test scores to mean scores reported for groups with differing aphasia severity. For example, the BNT test manual reports mean scores for six different groups differing in terms of severity level (ranging from 0 to 5), as determined by performance on the Boston Diagnostic Aphasia Examination. Others use cutoff scores to determine

Table 10.1.   Boston Naming Test: norms
for adults

Age	n	M	SD
25–34	22	55.9	2.8
35–44	28	55.5	3.9
45–54	33	54.8	4.1
55–59	24	55.2	3.6

Source: From Tombaugh and Hubley, 1997.

relative performance for differing groups depending on age and/or level of education (Heaton et al., 1991; Ross & Lichtenberg, 1997; Ross, Lichtenberg, & Christensen, 1995).

A problem that exists with BNT interpretation involves the use of "normative" data. However, in order to use "normative" data, it is necessary that the data be normally distributed, that is, 68% of the population falling within 1 standard deviation (SD) of the mean (M), 95% falling within 2 standard deviations of the mean, and 99% of the population falling within 3 standard deviations of the mean. The majority of currently published normative data for the BNT are negatively skewed with the mean number of correct scores near the possible total number of correct items (60). For example, Van Gorp, Satz, Kiersch, and Henry (1986) reported mean scores (and standard deviations) for older individuals to range from 51.5 (7.0) for 80- to 85-year-olds to 56.7 (3.0) for 60- to 64-year-olds. These data indicate that very few individuals can be rated as being above average (greater than 1 standard deviation above the mean), but that many individuals can be determined to have below-average naming abilities (greater than 1 standard deviation below the mean). Making interpretative inferences regarding the BNT using means and standard deviations has obvious limitations given these psychometric limitations of the test.

In contrast, more appropriate normative data for the BNT appear to be available for children (see Table 10.2). Halperin et al. (1989) provided normative data for children ages 6 through 12, with means (and standard deviations) ranging from 34.00 (6.0) for 6-year-olds to 47.90 (4.1) for 12-year-olds. These data appear to be more "normal," allowing for better interpretive statements to be formulated. Caution should also be used in interpreting the BNT because several studies have also demonstrated that the BNT is affected by age, education, and gender (Kindlon & Garrison, 1984; LaBarge, Edwards, & Knesevich, 1986; Montgomery & Costa, 1983; Taussig, Henderson, & Mack, 1988).

CONTROLLED ORAL WORD ASSOCIATION TEST

History and Development

The Controlled Oral Word Association Test (COWAT; Benton, Hamsher, & Sivan, 1994) is also known as the Word Fluency Test and the FAS-Test. It is a general measure of a person's ability to spontaneously state words that begin with a certain letter or that are of a given categorical class (e.g., animals) within a limited time frame. It has been argued that the label "word fluency" is a misnomer because the test does not

Table 10.2. Norms for normal school children on the Boston Naming Test

	Men			Women		
Age	*n*	*M*	*SD*	*n*	*M*	*SD*
5						
6	16	35.69	6.1	18	32.50	5.6
7	18	39.94	4.9	22	37.91	6.7
8	23	41.17	3.0	15	39.93	4.1
9	20	43.20	4.7	25	42.92	5.2
10	16	45.56	5.9	22	46.41	4.4
11	16	46.44	3.5	20	46.90	5.2
12	2	51.50	3.5	8	47.00	3.9
13						

Source: From Halperin, Healy, Zeitschick, Ludman, and Weinstein, 1989.

measure true fluency, that is, the ability to produce continuous speech free from error (Marshall, 1986).

The examiner administers the COWAT by asking the individual to state as quickly as possible, as many words as he or she can think of that begin with a certain letter. Proper nouns, such as names of individuals (e.g., Frank, Francis), are not permitted (or scored), nor are variations of the same words (e.g., kind, kindly). The examiner first asks the individual to state as many words as he or she can that begin with the letter *F* for one minute, and then for the letters *A* and *S*. Other variations of the test are available, including ones that use the letters *C, F,* and *L* and *P, R,* and *W.* For younger children who may not be aware of how to spell, alternative forms of the test have been developed that require them to state *animals, foods, things in the kitchen,* or *things in a store.*

Psychometric Properties

Test-retest reliability of the COWAT has been demonstrated to be .88 for adults after 19 to 42 days (desRosiers & Kavanaugh, 1987) and .70 for older adults after one year (Snow, Tierney, Zorzitto, Fisher, & Reid, 1988). COWAT performance has been negatively correlated with age (−0.19) and positively correlated with education (0.32; Yeudall, Fromm, Reddon, & Stefanyk, 1986). Construct validity has not been clearly demonstrated, because the COWAT had stronger correlations with the WAIS PIQ than with the VIQ (Yeudall et al., 1986). In a similar way, factor analytic studies have reported that the COWAT loads on many different factors of unclear relation to "verbal fluency," such as verbal knowledge, reading-writing, and abstract mental operations (Crockett, 1974; desRosiers & Kavanaugh, 1987; Groth-Marnat, 1999; Snow et al., 1988).

In general, numerous studies have indicated that individuals with brain dysfunction perform more poorly on the COWAT than controls do and that individuals with frontal lobe damage (and particularly left frontal damage) score more poorly than unimpaired individuals on this measure (Parks et al., 1988; Ruff, Allen, Farrow, Niemann, & Wylie, 1994). Results vary for individuals with dementia, however, with some studies suggesting that diminished word fluency is not related to progressive dementia (Ober, Dronkers, Koss, Delis, & Friedland, 1986) and others suggesting that it is (Murdoch, Chenery, Wilks, & Boyle, 1987).

Assets and Limitations

The strengths of the COWAT include its brevity, ease of administration, and use as a gross measure of expressive language dysfunction. However, its weaknesses include such facts as that it is unclear what exact construct it measures, that it appears to be of questionable diagnostic utility, and that it is unclear how this test can lead to specific functional recommendations. Caution should also be exercised when using alternative forms of the COWAT because different letters have different frequency occurrences in the alphabet (e.g., *C* versus *Y*).

Administration

Instructions for the examiner to use in administration of the COWAT are published in Spreen and Strauss (1998), and are as follows:

> I will say a letter of the alphabet. Then I want you to give me as many words that begin with that letter as quickly as you can. For instance, if I say "B," you might give me "bad, battle, bed." I do not want you to use words which are proper names, such as "Boston, Bob, or Buick (Brylcreem)." Also, do not use the same word again with a different ending, such as "eat" and "eating." Any questions? (Pause) Begin when I say the letter. The first letter is *F.* Go ahead.

The examiner begins timing and allows 1 minute for each letter (*F, A,* and *S*). If the individual discontinues before time is up, the examiner encourages them to continue. If there is a silence of greater than 15 seconds, the examiner repeats the basic instructions and the letter. The examiner should write down the words in the order in which they are stated or make plus signs if production is too rapid for verbatim recording. If repetitions occur that may be accepted if an alternate meaning was intended by the individual (e.g., "four" and "for," "son" and "sun"), then the examiner should ask what was meant by the words at the end of the one-minute period (i.e., determine if the words are homonyms). The COWAT takes approximately 5 minutes to administer and score, and it is scored by adding the total number of allowable words generated over the three trials.

Interpretation

Adequate normative data for the COWAT has been limited until recently, because normative groups were relatively young (Yeudall et al., 1986) or uneducated (Spreen & Benton, 1969/1977). However, more appropriate norms are now available that allow for corrections for older individuals (Tombaugh, Kozak, & Rees, 1996). Age-corrected norms are essential because several studies have indicated that a decrease in word fluency is expected with advancing age, beginning as early as the fifties (Benton, Eslinger,

Table 10.3.   Norms for school-age children (FAS)

Age	Women			Men			Total		
	n	*M*	*SD*	*n*	*M*	*SD*	*n*	*M*	*SD*
6	30	4.6	5.0	22	4.1	4.1	52	4.4	4.6
7	24	16.0	7.3	27	14.1	6.5	51	15.0	6.9
8	23	23.1	5.7	25	22.5	7.7	48	22.8	6.8
9	30	25.0	7.3	23	22.6	6.4	53	24.0	6.9
10	25	27.4	7.1	25	23.8	8.2	50	25.6	7.8
11	22	31.1	6.8	22	28.2	8.1	44	29.7	7.6
12	13	32.0	6.8	13	29.4	8.1	26	30.7	7.4
13	12	37.3	5.8	17	28.8	8.3	29	32.3	8.4

Source: Gaddes and Crockett, 1975.

& Damasio, 1981; Schaie & Parham, 1977). See Table 10.3 for FAS normative data for children (Gaddes & Crockett, 1975) and Table 10.4 for COWAT norms for adults, which are reported according to gender and education (Ruff, Light, & Parker, 1996).

ACADEMIC DISORDERS

The assessment of academic disorders involves the measurement of abilities that are generally learned (e.g., based on language symbols) versus those that are innate (e.g., memory skills). Tests of academic abilities can be used to diagnose specific learning disabilities, as well as to direct academic interventions or to assist in vocational planning.

The most commonly evaluated academic disorders are specific learning disabilities. The *Diagnostic and Statistical Manual of Mental Disorders-Fourth Edition* (DSM-IV) lists three types of learning disabilities, each of which represents a discrepancy between intellectual functioning and academic achievement.

Table 10.4.   Controlled Oral Word Association Test (Form CFL) in adults ages 16 to 70 years by education level

Education	Men (*n* = 180)		Women (*n* = 180)		Both Genders (*n* = 360)	
	M	*SD*	*M*	*SD*	*M*	*SD*
12 years or less	36.9	9.8	35.9	9.6	36.5	9.9
13 to 15 years	40.5	9.4	39.4	10.1	40.0	9.7
16 years or more	41.0	9.3	46.5	11.2	43.8	10.6
All education levels	39.5	9.8	40.6	11.2	40.1	10.5

Source: Ruff, Light, and Parker, 1996, with permission of the authors and the National Academy of Neuropsychology.

- Disorders of Reading.
- Disorders of Written Expression.
- Disorders of Mathematics.

Learning disabilities are typically diagnosed when there is a weakness in a specific academic ability, usually indicated by a significant difference (i.e., at least a 1.0 standard deviation difference) between academic and intelligence tests. It is important to note that different states and educational systems have different diagnostic criteria for learning disabilities, with most states recognizing learning disabilities in these specific areas: reading recognition, reading comprehension, oral expression, written expression,

**Table 10.5. Missouri State Department of Education LD
Determination Guidelines**

The following table utilizes a regression analysis procedure and a 1.50 Standard Deviation criterion level to establish a significant discrepancy between ability and achievement. The standard score measure of ability used to develop this table was the WISC-R (Full Scale IQ). Evaluators utilizing other standard score measurements of ability should investigate the correlation between the WISC-R Full Scale and their instrument prior to applying the tables. As with all standardized assessment procedures, caution must be exercised to assure that the instrument is appropriate for the student to be evaluated and that the diagnostic team takes into account the standard error of measurement for the instrument used when applying the criterion level.

IQ	Criterion Level	IQ	Criterion Level	IQ	Criterion Level
70	64	91	76	111	88
71	64	92	77	112	89
72	65	93	77	113	89
73	65	94	78	114	90
74	66	95	79	115	91
75	67	96	79	116	91
76	67	97	80	117	92
77	68	98	80	118	92
78	68	99	81	119	93
79	69	100	82	120	94
80	70	101	83	121	94
81	70	102	83	122	95
82	71	103	83	123	95
83	71	104	84	124	96
84	72	105	85	125	97
85	73	106	85	126	97
86	73	107	86	127	98
87	74	108	86	128	98
88	74	109	87	129	99
89	75	110	88	130	100
90	76				

and mathematical computations. For example, the state of Missouri Department of Education uses the following cutoff scores, based on IQ scores, to determine if a child qualifies for special education services (see Table 10.5).

It is also important to note that some academic disorders (e.g., inability to read, inability to write) can be related to central nervous system disorder or injury, including severe traumatic brain injury, thalamic injury, or specific injuries associated with association areas in the dominant hemisphere (Crosson, 1992).

In addition to diagnosing long-standing learning disabilities or an academic disorder related to an acute event or disease process, it is also essential to use academic tests to provide functional recommendations related to academic and vocational pursuits. Academic testing can assist in:

1. Identifying specific remediation strategies to help compensate for relative weaknesses in reading, written expression, and/or mathematical abilities in education settings.
2. Determining if an individual has the requisite skills to be trained for or to hold specific vocational positions. For example, an individual with a weakness in written expression may not be appropriate for a secretarial position, or an individual with a learning disability in math may not be able to major in engineering or to be a bookkeeper.

The following section describes two of the most commonly used measures of academic abilities. The Woodcock Johnson-Revised (WJ-R) was included because it is one of the most comprehensive measures of academic abilities, including the evaluation of both broad academic skills (e.g., reading, writing, math) and specific academic skills (e.g., reading comprehension, dictation, applied math problems). The Wide Range Achievement Test-3 (WRAT-3) was included because it is one of the most frequently used screening measures of academic abilities, and neuropsychologists frequently use the WRAT-3 Reading subtest as a measure of premorbid functioning. When choosing any measure of academic functioning, it is important to select tests that evaluate a broad spectrum of abilities, that are psychometrically sound, and that have been normed on large, diverse samples.

WOODCOCK-JOHNSON PSYCHO-EDUCATIONAL BATTERY-REVISED: TESTS OF ACADEMIC ACHIEVEMENT

History and Development

The Woodcock Johnson Psycho-Educational Battery-Revised (WJ-R; Woodcock & Johnson, 1989) is one of the most popular tests of academic achievement administered as part of neuropsychological evaluations, primarily because it is arguably the most comprehensive academic battery in current use. The original Woodcock Johnson was published in 1977 and revised in 1990. The WJ-R is made up of both Standard and Supplemental batteries and provides numerous Cluster scores that provide indices of performance in diverse academic domains. It takes approximately 80 to 90 minutes to administer the test and 30 to 40 minutes to score and interpret it.

The WJ-R Tests of Achievement are designed to evaluate competencies in four basic academic areas: reading, mathematics, written language, and knowledge. The test is appropriate for use with individuals from the age of 2 to 90 and is administered in flip-page easel books. The books contain instructions for each subtest, and manuals are provided for information about scoring, administration, and interpretation. Most of the subtests are untimed and have ceiling and basal levels.

WJ-R Standard Battery

The WJ-R Standard Battery is comprised of the following nine individual subtests, which take a total of 50 to 60 minutes to administer:

1. *Letter-Word Identification:* a basic test of the ability to recognize letters and words.
2. *Passage Comprehension:* a measure of the ability to comprehend passages that are read by the individual taking the test.
3. *Calculation:* a test of the ability to perform various mathematical calculations, including addition, subtraction, trigonometry, geometry, calculus, and logarithmic functions. The specific mathematical procedures are provided, and no applications need to be determined.
4. *Applied Problems:* a test of the ability to solve practical mathematical problems that are presented visually or that are read to the individual. The individual must identify the correct mathematical procedure to use, must use the appropriate data, and must perform relatively simple mathematical calculations.
5. *Dictation:* a measure of ability to respond in writing to simple questions, with scoring dependent on punctuation, capitalization, spelling, and word usage.
6. *Writing Samples:* tests of the ability to write responses to a variety of demands, with scoring emphasis placed on basic quality of expression, with minimal concern for spelling or punctuation demands.
7. *Science:* test of general knowledge in basic biological and physical sciences.
8. *Social Studies:* test of general knowledge of geography, government, and economics.
9. *Humanities:* measure of general knowledge of the arts, music, and literature.

WJ-R Supplemental Battery

The WJ-R Supplemental Battery is used to assess more specific areas of academic functioning. It consists of the following five tests, which take approximately 30 minutes to administer:

1. *Word Attack:* measures the ability to phonologically and structurally analyze reading skills by having the individual read nonsense words.
2. *Reading Vocabulary:* measures the ability to read and apply appropriate meanings to words. This subtest requires the individual to state synonyms and antonyms for presented words.
3. *Quantitative Concepts:* assesses general knowledge of mathematical concepts and vocabulary, without performance of any calculations.

4. *Proofing:* tests the ability to identify and correct an error in a written passage. The error may be in punctuation, capitalization, spelling, or usage.

5. *Writing Fluency:* evaluates the ability to formulate and write simple sentences. Individuals are shown a picture and then given three words that they must use in describing the picture within a 7-minute time frame.

Cluster Scores

The WJ-R provides numerous Cluster scores to represent the most general (broad) academic skills. The WJ-R Cluster scores calculated from the Standard Battery subtests are the most commonly used and they represent the following five basic curriculum areas:

1. *Broad Reading:* derived from the Letter-Word Identification and Passage Comprehension tests.

2. *Broad Mathematics:* derived from the Calculation and Applied Problems tests.

3. *Broad Written Language:* made up of the Dictation and Writing Samples tests.

4. *Broad Knowledge:* calculated from the Science, Social Studies, and Humanities tests.

5. *Skills:* derived from the Letter-Word Identification, Applied Problems, and Dictation tests.

Six additional Cluster scores, representing more specific academic areas, can be calculated from combinations of both the Standard and the Supplemental Batteries and include:

1. *Basic Reading Skills:* calculated using the Letter-Word Identification and Word Attack subtests.

2. *Reading Comprehension:* derived from the Passage Comprehension and Reading Vocabulary subtests.

3. *Basic Mathematics Skills:* calculated from the Calculation and Quantitative Concepts subtests.

4. *Mathematics Reasoning:* comprised of only the Applied Problems subtest.

5. *Basic Writing Skills:* made up of the Dictation and Proofing subtests.

6. *Written Expression:* made up of the Writing Samples and Writing Fluency subtests.

Furthermore, elements from all 14 of the Standard and Supplemental Battery subtests are used to calculate global scores in Punctuation and Capitalization (P), Spelling (S), Usage (U), and Handwriting (H).

Psychometric Properties

The WJ-R was normed on 6,359 individuals in over a hundred geographic locations (Woodcock & Mather, 1989). The individuals in the normative sample ranged in age from 2 to 95 and included pre-, elementary, high school, and college-university students and other adults not in school. Communities were selected to be included in the normative sample based on 13 socioeconomic variables. Split-half reliability coefficients are reported to be in the .80 to .90 range, with test-retest reliability (.76) reported only for the Writing Fluency test (Mather, Vogel, Spodak, & McGrew, 1991). Spreen and Strauss (1998) indicated that, as expected, those tests that are within a given curriculum area are correlated more highly with one another than with those in other curriculum domains.

Content validity was reportedly established using item validity studies and expert opinion. Construct validity, determined by calculating correlations among subtest scores, appears to have been appropriately established. For example, the test manual reports studies of concurrent validity to range from .50 to .70, using several other similar academic tests (e.g., Kaufman Assessment Battery for Children, Peabody Picture Vocabulary Test, Peabody Individual Achievement Test, Wide Range Achievement Test-Revised, Test of Written Language).

Assets and Limitations

One of the major strengths of the WJ-R is its general acceptance and use across school, hospital, and university settings. In addition, it was developed using a large normative sample based on a diverse population. The results provide a thorough evaluation of a broad range of both basic and specific academic functions. Evaluation of general academic abilities (e.g., broad reading, broad math, broad written language) can assist in diagnostic determination of specific learning abilities, and evaluation of more specific abilities (e.g., letter-word attack, passage comprehension, calculation, applied problems) can assist in developing specific remediation plans.

A major weaknesses of the WJ-R is that it takes a significant amount of time to administer and score the complete WJ-R Tests of Achievement (80 to 90 minutes to administer, 30 to 40 minutes to score and interpret). Furthermore, the calculation of the numerous subtest and Cluster scores can be confusing. The sheer number of calculations also increases the possibility of making clerical errors that could potentially lead to incorrect inferences.

Administration

Specific guidelines for administering and scoring the test are included in the test manual. The testing materials and the listing of basal and ceiling levels make for easy administration and scoring. The subtests can be administered in any order, and not all subtests must be administered. Scoring is relatively simple because the administration books provide examples of correct and incorrect items. A number of performance indices can be calculated, including age equivalents, grade equivalents, percentile ranks, standard scores, T-scores, and stanines. Numerous tables are provided to calculate the various subtest and Cluster scores. The test can be scored by both age and grade (i.e., last grade completed, with 12th grade as highest range). Determination of all standard and derived scores can be complicated, given the numerous scores and tables used to calculate them. However, computer scoring programs simplify scoring procedures and greatly reduce the risk of making errors.

Interpretation

The WJ-R Scoring Manual provides numerous indices of performance, including age equivalents, grade equivalents, percentile ranks, standard scores, T-scores, and stanines. Relative Mastery Indexes can also be calculated, which describe qualitative aspects of performance (i.e., an individual's expected level of performance compared to similar ones).

Calculation of standard scores and percentile rank profiles allow psychologists to determine relative strengths and weaknesses in individual academic areas. Different tables in the scoring manual then allow for the determination of significant differences between subtest and Cluster scores, including differences between actual and predicted scores. Determination of the presence of specific learning disabilities can be made by comparing the academic scores to indices of intellectual functioning.

WIDE RANGE ACHIEVEMENT TEST-3

History and Development

The Wide Range Achievement Test-3 (WRAT-3; Wilkenson, 1993) is one of the oldest and most commonly used measures of academic abilities (Sullivan & Bowden, 1997; Sweet, Moberg, & Westergaard, 1996). The original WRAT was published in 1936 and was developed to compliment the Wechsler-Bellevue Intelligence Scales by measuring basic word recognition, spelling, and mathematical computations. The WRAT-R was published in 1984 with updated, expanded, and improved normative data. The latest version, the WRAT-3, was published in 1993 and provides two alternative forms (i.e., BLUE and TAN) that measure basic reading, spelling, and arithmetic abilities. Both the BLUE and the TAN forms can be used in the same evaluation and are referred to as the COMBINED form. The WRAT-3 differs minimally from the WRAT-R, although the time limit for the Arithmetic test was extended from 10 to 15 minutes. The total time for administration and scoring is approximately 20 to 35 minutes. The WRAT-3 was normed on 4,433 individuals who were selected to be representative of a normal sample. Variables taken into account included age, region of residence, gender, ethnicity, and socioeconomic level. The age range of the normative sample was 5 years to 74 years, 11 months.

The three subtests that make up the WRAT-3 include:

1. *Reading:* assesses the ability to recognize and name letters and to pronounce words out of context. Individuals are asked to name up to 15 letters of the alphabet and to read up to 42 words.
2. *Spelling:* assesses the ability to write one's name and to write dictated letters and words. Depending on age and ability levels, individuals may be asked to spell 15 items on the Name-Letter Writing section and up to 40 words on the Word Spelling section.
3. *Arithmetic:* measures basic arithmetic skills, including counting, reading number symbols, solving oral problems, and performing written computations.

Children younger than 7 years old begin with the Oral Arithmetic section, while individuals 8 and older begin with the Written Arithmetic section and are awarded the 15 points from the Oral section. Fifteen minutes are provided for the Arithmetic subtest, which includes problems evaluating the following mathematical skills: addition, subtraction, multiplication, and division, as well as knowledge of fractions, algebra, and logarithmic functions.

It takes significantly less time to administer and score the WRAT-3 than the WJ-R, making it a more efficient screening measure of gross academic abilities. The WRAT-R Reading subtest has been shown to be an appropriate estimate of premorbid abilities, whereas the WJ-R Reading subtest has not. In contrast, the WRAT-3 does not assess specific academic abilities as thoroughly as the WJ-R, and as a result it is less appropriate to use to make treatment recommendations.

Psychometric Properties

The test manual indicates that measures of internal consistency of the WRAT-3 range from .92 to .95 (Wilkenson, 1993). The average correlations between the two WRAT-3 alternative forms were .98 for the Reading subtests, .98 for the Spelling subtests, and .98 for the Arithmetic subtests. Test-retest reliability for the WRAT-3 subtests ranged from .91 to .98 for a sample of 142 individuals ages 6 through 16 (Wilkenson, 1993).

The WRAT-3 manual states that there is "strong evidence" of content validity of each of the WRAT-3 subtests. Construct validity was determined by calculating correlations with the California Test of Basic Skills - 4th Edition ($r = .60$ to $.80$), California Achievement Test Form E ($r = .41$ to $.77$), and the Stanford Achievement Test ($r = .72$ to $.87$ (Wilkenson, 1993)). Scores on the WRAT-3 have been shown to range between .50 and .60 with the Wechsler Intelligence Scale for Children-III Full Scale IQ, with higher correlations with the Verbal than with Performance IQ scales (WISC-III; Wechsler, 1991). WRAT-3 subtest scores are reported to correlate between .54 and .91 with one another and between .79 and .99 with the WRAT-R subtests.

Several researchers have demonstrated that the WRAT-R Reading subtest is an accurate estimate of premorbid abilities (Johnstone, Callahan, Kapila, & Bouman, 1996; Kareken, Gur, & Saykin, 1995), with correlations with the WAIS-R FIQ ranging between .45 and .62. However, the utility of the WRAT-3 Reading subtest as an estimate of premorbid abilities has been only minimally researched to date, although it appears to show promise (Johnstone & Wilhelm, 1996).

Assets and Limitations

The primary strengths of the WRAT-3 are its simplicity, relatively brief administration time, and ability to evaluate gross academic abilities. Psychologists can quickly determine an individual's academic strengths and weaknesses, as well as the possible presence of a specific learning disability. The WRAT-3 has also been demonstrated to be an accurate estimate of premorbid abilities for those who show cognitive decline (e.g., traumatic brain injury, dementia), and to be better at predicting premorbid intelligence than other estimates of premorbid functioning (Johnstone et al., 1996; Johnstone & Wilhelm, 1996).

The primary weakness of the WRAT-3 is that it does not thoroughly evaluate specific academic abilities and, thus, does not allow for specific academic recommendations to be formulated. For example, most state departments of education make distinctions between learning disabilities in reading and those in reading comprehension. Specific functional recommendations are necessary for each specific learning disability. Unfortunately, the WRAT-3 does not allow for the determination of such specific disabilities. Furthermore, most school systems provide special educational services for learning disabilities in written expression. However, the WRAT-3 does not allow for detailed treatment planning because it only provides a brief measure of the ability to spell single words and does not assess such skills as sentence dictation, written fluency, punctuation, and grammar. Such specific written language abilities may be better evaluated by the specific subtests that constitute the WJ-R Written Expression Cluster score.

Administration

The WRAT-3 has a 15-minute time limit for the Arithmetic subtest and no time limit for the Reading and Spelling subtests. It provides several indices of academic abilities, including raw scores, absolute scores, standard scores, grade equivalents, and percentiles. For children age 8 and older, the preliminary section is not administered if the individual is able to correctly answer 5 or more of the formal Spelling or Reading items. All individuals younger than 8 are administered all of the preliminary sections. Any individual who does not correctly answer 5 of the formal items is administered all of the respective preliminary items. The Reading and Spelling subtests are discontinued after the individual incorrectly responds to 10 items in a row.

Interpretation

For each of the subtests, the test manual provides standard scores, percentiles, and grade equivalents for age groups ranging from 5 years to 74 years, 11 months. Scores can be calculated to compare individuals to others of the same age range or grade equivalent. Of note, scores on the WRAT-3 are typically lower than those on the WRAT-R because of the fewer number of items on the WRAT-3 subtests. Performance on the WRAT-3 can be compared to other intelligence measures to determine the presence of gross learning disabilities, depending on diagnostic criteria used by individual states or by organizations to diagnose learning disabilities.

RECOMMENDED READING

Holland, D., Hogg, J., & Farmer, J. (1997). Fostering effective team cooperation and communication: Developing community standards within interdisciplinary cognitive rehabilitation settings. *NeuroRehabilitation, 1,*21–29.

Lezak, M.D. (1995). *Neuropsychological Assessment* (3rd ed.). New York: Oxford University Press.

Spreen, O., & Strauss, E. (1998). *A Compendium of Neuropsychological Tests* (2nd ed.). New York: Oxford University Press.

Wilkenson, G.S. (1993). *WRAT-3 Administration Manual.* Delaware: Wide Range.

Woodcock, R.W., & Johnson, M.B. (1989, 1990). *Woodcock-Johnson Psycho-Educational Battery-Revised.* Itasca, IL: Riverside.

Woodcock, R.W., & Mather, N. (1989,1990). *WJ-R Tests of Achievement: Examiner's Manual.* In R.W. Woodcock & M.B. Johnson, Woodcock-Johnson Psycho-Educational Battery-Revised. Itasca, IL: Riverside.

REFERENCES

Axelrod, B.N., Ricker, J.H., & Cherry, S.A. (1994). Concurrent validity of the MAE visual naming test. *Archives of Clinical Neuropsychology, 9,*317–321.

Barr, A., Benedict, R., Tune, L., & Brandt, J. (1992). Neuropsychological differentiation of Alzheimer's disease from vascular dementia. *International Journal of Geriatric Psychiatry, 7,* 621–627.

Benton, A.L., Eslinger, P.J., & Damasio, A.R. (1981). Normative observations on neuropsychological test performances in old age. *Journal of Clinical Neuropsychology, 3,* 33–42.

Benton, A.L., Hamsher, K., & Sivan, A.B. (1994). *Multilingual Aphasia examination* (3rd ed.). Iowa City: AJA Associates.

Crockett, D.J. (1974). Component analysis of within correlations of language-skill tests in normal children. *Journal of Special Education, 8,* 361–375.

Crosson, B. (1992). *Subcortical functions in language and memory.* New York: Guilford Press.

desRosiers, G., & Kavanaugh, D. (1987). Cognitive assessment in closed head injury: Stability, validity and parallel forms for two neuropsychological measures of recovery. *International Journal of Clinical Neuropsychology, 9,* 162–173.

Gaddes, W.H., & Crockett, D.J. (1975). The Spreen-Benton aphasia tests, normative data, as a measure of normal language development. *Brain and Language, 2,* 257–280.

German, D. (1993). *Word finding intervention program.* Itasca, IL: Riverside.

Groth-Marnat, G. (1999). *Handbook of psychological assessment* (3rd ed. rev.). New York: Wiley.

Halperin, J.M., Healy, J.M., Zeitschick, E., Ludman, W.L., & Weinstein, L. (1989). Developmental aspects of linguistic and amnestic abilities in normal children. *Journal of Clinical and Experimental Neuropsychology, 11,* 518–528.

Hawkins, K.A., Sledge, W.H., Orleans, J.F., Quinland, D.M., Rakfeldt, J., & Hoffman, R.E. (1993). Normative implications of the relationship between reading vocabulary and Boston naming test performance. *Archives of Clinical Neuropsychology, 8,* 525–537.

Heaton, R.K., Grant, I., & Matthews, C.G. (1991). *Comprehensive norms for an expanded halstead-reitan battery: Demographic corrections, research findings, and clinical applications.* Odessa, FL: Psychological Assessment Resources.

Holland, D., Hogg, J., & Farmer, J. (1997). Fostering effective team cooperation and communication: Developing community standards within interdisciplinary cognitive rehabilitation settings. *NeuroRehabilitation, 1,*21–29.

Huff, F.J., Collins, C., Corkin, S., & Rosen, T.J. (1986). Equivalent forms of the Boston naming test. *Journal of Clinical and Experimental Neuropsychology, 8,* 556–562.

Ivnik, R.J., Malec, J.F., & Smith, G.E. (1996). Neuropsychological test norms above age 55: COWAT, MAE token, WRAT-R reading, AM-NART, Stroop, TMT, and JLO. *Clinical Neuropsychologist, 10,* 262–278.

Johnstone, B., Callahan, C.D., Kapila, C.J., & Bouman, D.E. (1996). The comparability of the WRAT-R reading test and NAART as estimates of premorbid intelligence in neurologically impaired patients. *Archives of Clinical Neuropsychology, 11,* 513–519.

Johnstone, B., & Wilhelm, K.L. (1996). The longitudinal stability of the WRAT-R reading subtest: Is it an appropriate estimate of premorbid intelligence? *Journal of the International Neuropsychology Society, 2,* 282–285.

Jordan, F.M., Cannon, A., & Murdoch, B.E. (1992). Language abilities of mildly closed head injured (CHI) children 10 years post-injury. *Brain Injury, 6,* 39–44.

Kaplan, E.F., Goodglass, H., & Weintraub, S. (1983). *The Boston naming test* (2nd ed.). Philadelphia: Lea & Febiger.

Kareken, D.A., Gur, R.C., & Saykin, A.J. (1995). Reading on the wide range achievement test-revised and parental education as predictors of IQ: Comparison with the Barona formula. *Archives of Clinical Neuropsychology, 10,* 147–157.

Kindlon, D., & Garrison, W. (1984). The Boston naming test: Normative data and cue utilization in a sample of normal 6- and 7-year-old children. *Brain and Language, 21,* 255–259.

LaBarge, E., Balota, D.A., Storandt, M., & Smith, D. (1992). An analysis of confrontation naming errors in senile dementia of the Alzheimer type. *Neuropsychology, 6,* 77–95.

LaBarge, E., Edwards, D., & Knesevich, J.W. (1986). Performance of normal elderly on the Boston naming test. *Brain and Language, 27,* 380–384.

Marshall, J.C. (1986). The description and interpretation of aphasic language disorder. *Neuropsychologia, 24,* 5–24.

Mather, N., Vogel, S.A., Spodak, R.B., & McGrew, K.S. (1991). Use of the Woodcock-Johnson-revised writing tests with students with learning disabilities. *Journal of Psychoeducational Assessment, 9,* 296–307.

Mitrushina, A.M., & Satz, P. (1989). Differential decline of specific memory components in normal aging. *Brain Dysfunction, 2,* 330–335.

Montgomery, K., & Costa, L. (1983). *Neuropsychological test performance of a normal elderly sample.* Paper presented at the meeting of the International Neuropsychological Society, Mexico City.

Murdoch, B.E., Chenery, H.J., Wilks, V., & Boyle, R.S. (1987). Language disorders in dementia of the Alzheimer type. *Brain and Language, 31,* 122–137.

Ober, B.A., Dronkers, N.F., Koss, E., Delis, D.C., & Friedland, R.P. (1986). Retrieval from semantic memory in Alzheimer-type dementia. *Journal of Clinical and Experimental Neuropsychology, 8,* 75–92.

Parks, R.W., Loewenstein, D.A., Dodrill, K.L., Barker, W.W., Yoshii, F., Chang, J.Y., Emran, A., Apicella, A., Sheramata, W.A., & Duara, R. (1988). Cerebral metabolic effect of a verbal fluency test: A PET scan study. *Journal of Clinical and Experimental Neuropsychology, 10,* 565–575.

Ross, R.P., & Lichtenberg, P.A. (1997). *Expanded normative data for the Boston naming test in an urban medical sample of elderly adults.* Paper presented at the meeting of the International Neuropsychology Society, Orlando, FL.

Ross, R.P., Lichtenberg, P.A., & Christensen, K. (1995). Normative data on the Boston naming test for elderly adults in a demographically diverse medical sample. *Clinical Neuropsychologist, 9,* 321–325.

Ruff, R.M., Allen, C.C., Farrow, C.E., Niemann, H., & Wylie, T. (1994). Figural fluency: Differential impairment in patients with left versus right frontal lobe lesions. *Archives of Clinical Neuropsychology, 9,* 41–55.

Ruff, R.M., Light, R.H., & Parker, S.B. (1996). Benton controlled word association test: Reliability and updated norms. *Archives of Clinical Neuropsychology, 11,* 329–338.

Sawrie, S.M., Chelune, G.J., Naugle, R.I., & Lüders, H.O. (1996). Empirical methods for assessing meaningful change following epilepsy surgery. *Journal of the International Neuropsychological Association, 2,* 556–564.

Schaie, K.W., & Parham, I.A. (1977). Cohort-sequential analyses of adult intellectual development. *Developmental Psychology, 13,* 649–653.

Snow, W.G., Tierney, M.C., Zorzitto, M.L., Fisher, R.H., & Reid, D.W. (1988). *One-year test-retest reliability of selected tests in older adults.* Paper presented at the meeting of the International Neuropsychological Society, New Orleans.

Spreen, O., & Benton, A.L. (1977). *Neurosensory center comprehensive examination for aphasia* (NCCEA). Victoria: University of Victoria Neuropsychology Laboratory. (Original work published 1969)

Spreen,O., & Strauss, E. (1998). *A compendium of neuropsychological tests* (2nd ed.). New York: Oxford University Press.

Sullivan, K., & Bowden, S.C. (1997). Which tests do neuropsychologists use? *Journal of Clinical Psychology, 53,* 657–661.

Sweet, J.J., Moberg, P.J., & Westergaard, C.K. (1996). Five-year follow-up survey of practices and beliefs of clinical neuropsychologists. *Clinical Neuropsychologist, 10,* 202–221.

Taussig, I.M., Henderson, V.W., & Mack, W. (1988). *Spanish translation and validation of a neuropsychological battery: Performance of Spanish- and English-speaking Alzheimer's disease patients and normal comparison subjects.* Paper presented at the meeting of the Gerontological Society of America, San Francisco.

Tombaugh, T.N., & Hubley, A.M. (1997). The 60-item Boston naming test: Norms for cognitively intact adults aged 25- to 88-years. *Journal of Clinical and Experimental Neuropsychology, 19,* 922–932.

Van Gorp, W.G., Satz, P., Kiersch, M.E., & Henry, R. (1986). Normative data on the Boston naming test for a group of normal older adults. *Journal of Clinical and Experimental Neuropsychology, 8,* 702–705.

Wechsler, D. (1991). *Wechsler intelligence scale for children* (3rd ed.). San Antonio: The Psychological Corporation.

Weyandt, L.L., & Willis, W.G. (1994). Executive functions in school children: Potential efficacy of tasks in discriminating clinical groups. *Developmental Neuropsychology, 10,* 27–38.

Wilkenson, G.S. (1993). *WRAT3 administration manual.* Delaware: Wide Range.

Woodcock, R.W., & Johnson, M.B. (1989). *Woodcock-Johnson psychoeducational battery–revised.* Itasca, IL: Riverside.

Woodcock, R.W., & Mather, N. (1989). WJ-R tests of achievement: Examiner's manual. In R.W. Woodcock & M.B. Johnson (Eds.), *Woodcock-Johnson psycho-educational battery–revised.* Itasca, IL: Riverside.

Yeudall, L.T., Fromm, D., Reddon, J.R., & Stefanyk, W.O. (1986). Normative data stratified by age and sex for 12 neuropsychological tests. *Journal of Clinical Psychology, 42,* 918–946.

Zec, R.F., Vicari, S., Kocis, M., & Reynolds, T. (1992). Sensitivity of different neuropsychological tests to very mild DAT [Abstract]. *Clinical Neuropsychologist, 6,* 327.

Chapter 11

ATTENTION

JENNIE L. PONSFORD

Attentional difficulties are associated with most forms of brain injury and disease, congenital learning disabilities, and emotional or psychiatric disorders. As a consequence, complaints of difficulty concentrating or sustaining attention to tasks, distractibility, inattention to detail, mental slowness, and/or difficulty in doing more than one thing at once confront psychologists within a broad range of contexts.

The assessment of attention following TBI is not a straightforward task. There is little agreement as to definitions of attention and there are few established criteria for measurement. It is important to acknowledge that attention is a multidimensional concept, requiring a number of mental operations performed by diverse brain areas. Before discussing specific aspects of attention and relevant tests, some important general assessment issues will be addressed.

IMPORTANT ISSUES IN ASSESSING ATTENTION

The importance of taking a thorough history prior to the neuropsychological assessment cannot be over emphasized (see Chapter 4). This is particularly so in the case of attentional difficulties, given the number of factors that potentially impact upon attention. Those pertinent to performance on attentional measures include developmental history, specifically the presence of learning difficulties, intellectual strengths and weaknesses, educational background, visual or auditory problems, current and previous use of alcohol and drugs, current use of medications, history of neurological or psychiatric problems, current emotional state, and the presence of other stressors. It is also essential to consider fatigue, pain levels, and motivation to perform in the assessment situation, all of which may significantly affect attentional behavior.

During the assessment, qualitative as well as quantitative observations should be made of relevant attentional behaviors, such as the person's speed of performance, ability to focus attention, avoid distraction, divide attention across more than one task or aspect of a task, attend to visual and auditory detail and sustain attention over time. It is particularly important to monitor fatigue levels over the course of the assessment.

The person's level of intelligence and other cognitive abilities will need to be established as a background against which to interpret test performances. Practice effects, effects related to age, education, and other premorbid factors (e.g., substance abuse, psychiatric history, learning difficulties). Motor impairments and the impact of emotional factors on test performance may also confound interpretation of findings. Tests vary in terms of their vulnerability to these effects. It is therefore important to understand the specific impact of each of these factors on the various attentional measures. These are discussed in the next section and in the later sections pertaining to the Paced Auditory Serial Addition Task and the Stroop.

Practice Effects

Feinstein, Brown, and Ron (1994) investigated practice effects on a range of tests of attention in 10 healthy volunteers, aged 25 to 57 years. These subjects were assessed at two to four week intervals, over eight test sessions. There are statistically, significant linear improvements in performance on the Purdue Pegboard, the Color Naming and Interference conditions of the Stroop, the Paced Auditory Serial Addition task (PASAT), the Paced Visual Serial Addition Task, and a Choice Reaction Time task with a warning signal. There was a nonsignificant trend toward improvement on the Symbol Digit Modalities Test. However, there was no improvement on a Simple Reaction Time task. Younger subjects improved more with practice than older subjects. Stuss, Stethem, and Poirier (1987) reported significant practice effects on retesting one week after initial assessment on both parts of the Trail Making Test and the PASAT.

Relationship of Test with Ability Levels

Attention cannot be studied in isolation from other abilities, particularly those of memory, executive function, and the integrity of processes within the specific modality being studied, such as visual scanning, search abilities, and auditory discrimination. As van Zomeren and Brouwer (1994) pointed out, the symbolic stimulus material used in tests of speed of information processing might involve visual search, mental arithmetic, mental rotation, sentence comprehension, or any other cognitive activity. Performance on such tasks may therefore be affected by abilities in the domains of perception, intelligence, education, or semantic memory.

There appears to be little relationship between simple reaction time and education. The more complex the task becomes, the more likely it is that performance will be related to ability levels in the domain being tested, education, and intelligence. This is exemplified by the demonstrated associations of performance on the PASAT with arithmetic ability, education, and intelligence to be discussed later. Scores on Part B of the Trail Making Test have been shown to be strongly associated with the level of education and intelligence of the subject (Bornstein, 1985; Heaton, Grant, & Matthews, 1986; Warner, Ernst, Townes, Peel, & Preston, 1987). Intellectual level may contribute to performances on the Stroop (Comalli, Wapner, & Werner, 1962; Regard, 1981). IQ and education influence performance on the Symbol Digit Modalities Test (Richardson & Marottoli, 1996; Uchiyama et al., 1994).

Age-Related Effects

There is clear evidence of age-related effects on many of the tests used to assess aspects of attention. Stuss et al. (1987) and Stuss, Stethem, and Pelchat (1988) found that with age there was a gradual decline in performance on the Trail Making Test, but not on the PASAT. However, as will be discussed later, Brittain, LaMarche, Reeder, Roth, and Boll (1991) and Crawford, Obonsawin, and Allan (1998) did show a reduction in PASAT performance with age, particularly over age 50. Evidence of slowing in color naming and an increase in the Stroop interference effect with age will be presented in a later section. Performance on the SDMT is affected by advancing age (Emmerson, Dustman, Shearer, & Turner, 1990; Gilmore, Royer, & Gruhn, 1983; Richardson & Marottoli, 1996). There is also evidence that reaction times are faster in younger age groups (Feinstein et al., 1994). It is therefore very important to utilize age-appropriate normative data in evaluating test performances.

Motor Impairments

Reaction time studies by Gronwall and Sampson (1974), and van Zomeren (1981) indicated no significant prolongation of movement time in head-injured subjects. However, Stuss et al. (1985) found that they performed significantly poorer than controls on a finger-tapping task. This finding has been replicated more recently by Haaland, Temkin, Randahl, and Dikmen (1994). They studied a group of 40 patients with head injuries, predominantly mild to moderately severe, who did not have peripheral injuries. This head-injured group was impaired on measures of grip strength and finger-tapping speed at one month relative to a matched control group. Residual impairment was still evident on the finger-tapping task, but not grip strength one year after injury. These findings suggest the possibility that motor impairments may contribute to slowness in performing visuomotor tasks used in the assessment of attention, such as Digit Symbol-Coding and the Trail Making Test. It is, therefore, important to assess for motor impairments and take these into account when interpreting test performances. When using reaction time tasks, it is wise to separate movement time from decision time.

Differentiating Organic from Non-Organic Impairments

Attention tests have been shown to be vulnerable to the impact of emotional disturbances, such as depression and anxiety. In a study of teachers suffering from mixed anxiety and depression associated with chronic stress, Walters, Anderson, Creamer, and Hosking (1995) found significant impairment on the PASAT, Digit Span forward and backward, and recall of prose passages. These findings confirmed the results of previous studies, demonstrating impairment of speed of information processing (Brand & Jolles, 1987; Calvo & Alamo, 1987), mental control as measured on the Wechsler Memory Scale (Breslow, Kocsis, & Belkin, 1980; Stromgren, 1977), Digit Span (Abas, Sahakian, & Levy, 1990; Colby & Gotlib, 1988; Gass & Russell, 1986), and long-term memory encoding (Watts & Cooper, 1989) in individuals with anxiety and/or depression.

Clinicians also need to consider the possibility that patients, particularly those assessed within a litigation context, may attempt to fake poor performances. Strauss, Spellacy, Hunter, and Berry (1994) demonstrated that people attempting to feign the effects of brain injury performed more poorly than nonmalingerers on a simple auditory reaction time task and the PASAT. The reaction time task proved particularly effective at detecting simulated performances, these being manifested as exaggerated slow reaction times. On the PASAT, malingerers tended not to show the normal pattern of decline in performance with increasing task difficulty.

Test Selection

In view of all these issues, the importance of gathering historical information from a range of sources cannot be over emphasized. Qualitative observations of behavior will significantly contribute to the assessment process, but particularly with regard to attentional behavior. The tests selected will, to some extent, need to be determined by the stage of recovery and/or severity of cognitive impairment, and particularly the person's level of arousal. In the early stages of recovery from traumatic brain injury, for example, the focus will be on assessing alertness and awareness of the environment and incoming stimuli, using measures such as the Glasgow Coma Scale (Teasdale & Jennett, 1976), and scales for assessing orientation and the ability to retain events in patients in post-traumatic amnesia (PTA). These might include the Westmead PTA Scale (Shores, Marosszeky, Sandanam, & Batchelor, 1986) or the Galveston Orientation and Amnesia Test (GOAT) (Levin, O'Donnell, & Grossman, 1979). Assessment of the person who has just emerged from PTA may be limited by low levels of alertness, rapid fatigue, extreme slowness, inability to cope with more than one thing at once, and, in some patients, distractibility. At this level of functioning any of the tasks described will elicit impairments. This will also be the case for those who remain very severely cognitively impaired.

As patients recover, or present with a higher level of functioning, it is necessary to administer a broader range of attentional tasks. Many of the tests sensitive to impairments in those functioning at higher levels may be too overwhelming for some very severely injured individuals. Tests that have been shown to be more sensitive following mild traumatic brain injury, for example, are the more complex tests of speed of information processing, such as Digit Symbol, the PASAT, or tests involving a significant distracting load, such as the modified version of the Stroop used by Bohnen, Jolles, and Twijnstra (1992). Difficulties with goal-directed allocation of attentional resources and cognitive flexibility may also be more apparent on complex tasks.

There is no doubt that, particularly at higher levels, many tests of attention fail to elicit the attentional difficulties, which are observed in the everyday behaviors of brain-injured patients. Test scores may also fail to capture qualitative aspects of performance, which enhance the clinician's understanding of attentional difficulties in individual cases. Tests are generally administered within a quiet and highly structured situation, which may maximize the patient's performance in a way that everyday environments do not. Many individuals appear to be able to put in the effort to maintain the level of their performance under such circumstances, but may not be able to within the context of daily life. Some attentional difficulties may be manifested only in more complex environments or over longer periods of time than exist in the structured test situation. The neuropsychologist can only speculate as to the ways in which the impairments evident on assessment affect the person's performance of daily activities. It seems clear that no structured experimental or neuropsychological assessment situation can capture the full extent and variety of attentional difficulties experienced by cognitively impaired individuals in their daily lives. Therefore, it is very important to use every possible means of obtaining information about the patient's attentional behavior as it is manifested in performance of daily activities. Methods of doing this will be discussed further in a later section.

ASPECTS OF ATTENTION

Attentional operations involve diverse regions of the brain, including the frontal, temporal, parietal, and occipital lobes, as well as thalamic, tegmental, and basal ganglia structures. These areas are linked by neural networks or functional systems. Over the past 25 years, investigators have identified and operationalized a large number of components or constructs of attention. These are by no means mutually exclusive or exhaustive, and there are wide variations in the use of technology. Aspects of attention include:

- *Visuo-spatial orienting and shifting of attention* (Posner & Petersen, 1990). These aspects of attention are considered to represent the activity of the posterior attentional network, involving the superior colliculus, lateral pulvinar nucleus of the posterolateral thalamus, and the posterior parietal lobe. This network performs operations to bring attention to a specific location in space and generates awareness. Disorders are manifested as object recognition difficulties and unilateral spatial neglect. (See Chapter 12 for a more elaborate discussion of visuo-spatial abilities.)

- *Alertness, vigilance, or sustained attention.* The ability to prepare and sustain alertness to process high priority signals over extended periods of time (Posner & Petersen, 1990). Alertness is thought to be mediated by the reticular activating system. Posner and Rothbart (1992) postulated a relationship between sustained attention and locus coeruleus norepinephrine input to the cortex and have argued for a significant role of the right hemisphere.

- *Selective or focused attention.* Posner and Petersen (1990) define this aspect of attention as the detection or selection of signals for conscious processing (target detection), and the ability to maintain attention in the presence of distraction or conflicting response tendencies. Selective attention is linked with awareness, and voluntary or conscious control over information processing. Anterior or frontal structures appear to be important in the processes of selection and focusing of attention and the ability to inhibit responses to irrelevant information. This system involves the anterior cingulate gyrus, midprefrontal cortex, and the basal ganglia (Posner & Rothbart, 1992). Conscious or controlled processing has a limited capacity and rate. *Divided attention* difficulties arise from limitations in the speed of consciously controlled processing. They occur whenever controlled processing fails to deal with all the information that should be processed for optimal task performance. Thus, capacity and speed of information processing are critical factors in determining the efficiency of divided attention.

    Norman and Shallice (1980) proposed that the *Supervisory Attentional System* (SAS), is responsible for supervising the focusing and dividing of attention on non-routine tasks, for optimally distributing the limited conscious processing capacity over various tasks as necessary, in a goal-directed fashion, using plans and strategies. This function is thought to be impaired as a result of frontal lobe dysfunction.

- *Working Memory* (Baddeley, 1993). This provides a means of temporary storage and manipulation during information processing. It incorporates a Central Executive, which is analogous to Shallice's SAS (Baddeley, 1986).

From this overview, it is clear that the assessment of attention in clinical settings is not a simple process. First, there is no single test of attention. The assessment requires examination of a broad range of abilities, as outlined above, across different sensory modalities. Most of the tests available are multifactorial and do not necessarily correspond closely to specific constructs of attention. There are wide variations in terminology used to describe them. For some constructs, there are no clinically available validated tests.

Factor analytic studies have shed some further light upon constructs of attention as measured neuropsychologically. In an investigation of the construct validity of eight tests of attention (Letter Cancellation, Serial Subtraction, Digit Span, Digit Symbol, Stroop Color-Word, Trail Making, Symbol Digit Modality, and Knox Cubes), Shum, McFarland, and Bain (1990) found that 13 measures from these tests loaded on three factors in separate groups of normal and head-injured subjects. The first component was defined by time taken on Letter Cancellation, scores obtained on Digit Symbol and the Symbol Digit Modalities Test, and time taken to complete the Trail Making Test. This component was labelled *visual scanning*. However, it should be noted that all tasks involve speed. The second component comprised Serial 7s, Serial 13s and the Stroop Interference Score. These tasks required an ability to sustain ongoing mental processes and select features for processing. This was labeled *sustained selective processing*. The third component was defined by tasks requiring immediate attention span, namely Digit Span and Knox Cubes. This was labelled *visual/auditory spanning*.

O'Donnell, MacGregor, Dabrowski, Oestreicher, and Romero (1994), in a study of 117 community-living persons, found that a letter cancellation task, namely the Visual Search and Attention Test (Trenerry, Crosson, DeBoe, & Leber, 1990), the Trail Making Test Part B and scores on the PASAT, loaded together on a factor identified as measuring mental processing, psychomotor speed, and focused attention. Mirsky (1989) obtained a comparable factor using the Trail-Making Test Part B, WAIS Digit Symbol, a letter cancellation task and the Stroop.

Wechsler Adult Intelligence Scale, Third Edition (WAIS-III) factor analytic studies have resulted in two factors associated with aspects of attention, labeled Working Memory and Processing Speed, respectively (Wechsler, 1997). Tests loading on the Working Memory factor are the Arithmetic, Digit Span, and Letter-Number Sequencing sub-tests. Those loading on the Processing Speed factor are Digit Symbol-Coding and Symbol Search. Furthermore, a Working Memory Index may be derived from the WMS-III Letter-Number Sequencing and Spatial Span subtests.

Most existing clinically available, validated tests fall under the rubric of selective, focused or divided attention, and/or working memory. This chapter will focus on the more commonly used of these neuropsychological measures of aspects of attention, excluding visuo-spatial aspects of attention. It is not possible to provide a detailed review of all tests of attention. Moreover, numerous attentional measures referred to here have been comprehensively described in other chapters, and will therefore be discussed only very briefly. Detailed discussions of the use of the PASAT and the Stroop Color-Word

Test are included in this chapter, since these are commonly used tasks, which are not discussed elsewhere in this text. However, it is important to understand that neither of these tests, nor any other test, constitutes a comprehensive measure of attention.

TESTS OF ASPECTS OF ATTENTION

Measures of Sustained Attention or Vigilance

Due to the generally stressful nature of vigilance tasks which elicit impairments, and a lack of normative data, there are few clinically available tests of aspects of alertness or sustained attention. Robertson, Ward, Ridgeway, and Nimmo-Smith (1994) published the only comprehensive battery of attentional tasks known as the Test of Everyday Attention (TEA). According to the authors, the development of this test was based largely upon Posner and Petersen's (1990) model of attention. In order to enhance the real-life relevance of the task, the test is based on an imaginary scenario of a vacation trip to Philadelphia. Materials used include maps and telephone directories. The TEA has eight subtests and three parallel versions. Performance on the TEA is affected by age, and norms are available for four age bands.

A number of subtests from the Test of Everyday Attention are described as tests of sustained attention. These include Elevator Counting, Telephone Search while Counting, and the Lottery Task. The Elevator Counting task, requires the subject to count seven strings of tones, presented at a variable rate of one tone every 2 to 5 seconds. It is more a measure of *level* of vigilance/alertness than of decline in performance over time, as the strings are quite short. The Telephone Search while Counting task requires the subject to search a telephone directory for key symbols, but also simultaneously count strings of tones presented on an answering machine. The Lottery Task requires the subject to listen to tape-recorded strings of letters and numbers, and to write down the two letters preceding all numbers ending at 55. There are ten target items presented over ten minutes. The last two tasks have been shown to differentiate traumatically brain-injured subjects from controls in terms of the level of vigilance performance (Robertson et al., 1994). There are no data regarding decline in performance over time.

Tests of Selective or Focused Attention

Assessment of selective or focused attention involves measurement of a person's ability to focus on one aspect of a task and screen out distractions or competing response tendencies. There are a number of different types of tasks which fall into this category. These include letter cancellation and visual search tasks, such as the Concentration Endurance (d2) test (Brickenkamp, 1981), the Ruff 2 and 7 Attention Test (Ruff, Neimann, Allen, Farrow, & Wylie, 1992), the Visual Search and Attention Test (Trenerry et al., 1990), and the Map Search and Telephone Search subtests of the Test of Everyday Attention (Robertson et al., 1994). Map Search is a timed task involving searching for symbols on a map over a 2-minute period. Telephone Search involves searching for symbols in a telephone directory. The TEA also has three *auditory* selective attention tasks: (1) Elevator Counting, (2) Elevator Counting with Distraction, each requiring selective attention to particular tones on an audiotape, and (3) the

Lottery task. However, these tasks do not require the subject to suppress conflicting response tendencies. The most commonly used task in this category is the Stroop Color Word Test (Stroop, 1935). A detailed discussion of this test follows later.

The ability to divide attention selectively is determined by the efficiency of a number of different cognitive processes. Arguably the most important of these are the speed and capacity of information processing, as well as the ability to switch attention between tasks. Numerous studies have indicated that impaired speed of information processing is one of the most consistent neuropsychological indices of any form of impairment, be it neurological, developmental, or psychiatric. Moreover, some of these measures will be used almost invariably within the context of neuropsychological assessment.

Simple and choice reaction time tasks are commonly used to assess speed of response (Ponsford & Kinsella, 1992; Stuss et al., 1989; van Zomeren, 1981). Other tests involving a significant speed of processing component, include the WAIS-III Digit Symbol-Coding and Symbol Search subtests (see Chapter 5), the Symbol Digit Modalities Test (Smith, 1991), color naming and word-reading scores from the Stroop Color-Word test, and the Trail Making Test from the Halstead-Reitan Neuropsychological Battery (Reitan & Wolfson, 1993) (see Chapter 7). The Stroop and the Trail Making Tests also assess mental flexibility or the ability to voluntarily shift attention from one aspect of a stimulus or task to another.

The Symbol Digit Modalities Test (SDMT; see Lezak, 1995; Spreen & Strauss, 1998) monitors psychomotor speed, as well as visual scanning and tracking. It is similar to the Digit-Symbol subtest from the Wechsler Intelligence Scales, but the format is altered such that nine meaningless symbols are presented in the top row, each associated with a number on the bottom row of the key. Instead of being required to substitute the symbols, the subject is required to reproduce the number associated with each symbol (see Figure 11.1). The test has written and oral formats. In the written format, the subject writes the number in a box beneath each symbol, in the oral format, the subject states each number aloud to the examiner, who marks it on another sheet. As for the WAIS Digit Symbol subtest, the score represents the number of correct substitutions in 90 seconds. The Oral format lends itself for use in cases where motor impairment interferes

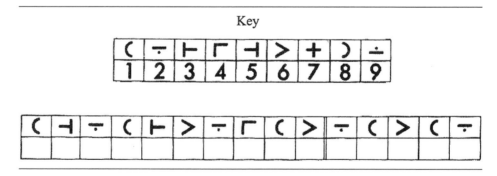

Figure 11.1.   Material from the *Symbol Digit Modalities Test* © 1973 by Western Psychological Services

with manual task performance. When both versions are administered, the written format should be given first.

Spreen and Strauss (1998) report that in normal adults the written and oral formats of the SDMT correlate above .78 with each other. Smith (1991) reports test-retest correlations of .80 for the written version and .76 for the oral version. Scores increased an average of four points on each version on retest. Hinton-Bayre, Geffen, and McFarland (1997) developed three alternate forms of the SDMT. Morgan and Wheelock (1992) found that the written form of the SDMT correlated .91 with the WAIS Digit Symbol subtest, but noted that the SDMT scores were lower than Digit Symbol scores. Glosser, Butters, and Kaplan (1977) argued, on the other hand, that the SDMT is more difficult because there are no cues for spatial location in the key. The SDMT is particularly sensitive to impairments in speed of processing associated with traumatic brain injury (Ponsford & Kinsella, 1992). Impaired performances are evident in a broad range of conditions (see Lezak, 1995; Spreen & Strauss, 1998). Performance on the SDMT is affected by advancing age (Emmerson et al., 1990; Gilmore et al., 1983; Richardson & Marottoli, 1996), moreover, IQ and education have shown to influence performance levels (Richardson & Marottoli, 1996; Uchiyama et al., 1994). Smith (1991) provides comprehensive norms for both children and adults. Richardson and Marottoli (1996) have published norms for adults over 75 years.

Dual-task paradigms are arguably more sensitive measures of divided attention, given the additional demands they place upon the conscious processing system. Of the few validated dual-tasks available, the Telephone Search while Counting subtest from the Test of Everyday Attention (Robertson et al., 1994), involves searching a telephone directory and simultaneously counting strings of digits. Robertson et al. demonstrated significant impairment in brain-injured individuals on this task. Whether or not the ability to *divide* attention between tasks is impaired in addition to speed of processing is a matter of debate (van Zomeren & Brouwer, 1994). By virtue of the load they place on the attentional system, dual tasks are more likely to elicit impairments than are single channel tasks, particularly in individuals with mild TBI.

Another test used to demonstrate mental slowness is the Paced Auditory Serial Addition Test, or PASAT (Gronwall, 1977; Gronwall & Sampson, 1974). This test will be discussed in detail in a separate section.

Shallice (1982, 1988) developed the Tower of London Task as a measure of Supervisory Attentional Control, that is, the ability to allocate attentional resources in a goal-directed fashion. This task requires the subject to manipulate three beads of different colors, one by one, from a starting configuration on three sticks of unequal length to a target position within a designated number of moves, and according to certain rules. Shallice and Burgess (1991) developed the Six Elements Test as a measure of the ability to efficiently allocate attention across several tasks in order to complete them within a specific time frame. These are tests of executive function (see Chapter 13).

Tests of Working Memory

Another group of attentional tasks used clinically are tests of immediate span of recall of verbal and nonverbal material. In the former category the most commonly used are the Digit Span subtests from the Wechsler intelligence scale and the Wechsler Memory

Scale (see Chapters 5 and 6). This subtest comprises two separate tasks: Digits Forward and Digits Backward, and the scores for these tests are combined for the purpose of deriving standardized scores. However, as Lezak (1995) points out, it is important to consider performance on these tasks separately because each involve different cognitive activities and is affected by different forms of brain damage.

Letter-Number Sequencing is another task which, together with Digit Span and Arithmetic, loads on the Working Memory factor from the WAIS-III. In this, more demanding task, the subject is presented with a string of alternating letters and numbers (e.g., 7-Y-3-R), and is asked to repeat them, with numbers first in ascending order and letters next in alphabetical order. Together with Spatial Span, Letter-Number-Sequencing also forms the WMS-III Working Memory Index. The Spatial Span task requires the subject to imitate a sequence of tapping by the examiner and therefore measure immediate visuo-spatial attention span. It is similar to the Spatial Span subtest from the WAIS-R NI (Kaplan, Fein, Morris, & Delis, 1991). The WAIS-III and WMS-III Working Memory Indices show significant correlations with scores on Part B of the Trail Making test (Wechsler, 1997).

Finally, there are a number of tasks, which require sustained manipulation of material mentally and thereby tap attentional resources. These include the optional Mental Control subtest from the WMS-III, which has increased in complexity from that in the WMS-R, serial addition/subtraction tasks, and the WAIS-III Arithmetic subtest (see Chapters 5 and 6). Table 11.1 summarizes the tests of different aspects of attention.

PACED AUDITORY SERIAL ADDITION TASK

History and Development

The Paced Auditory Serial Addition Task (PASAT) was developed as a measure of information processing capacity and rate. It is based upon a visual paced serial addition task developed by Sampson (1956). A series of single digit numbers was presented on a screen and the subject was required to add each number of the preceding number. Effects of stimulus duration and frequency of presentation were examined. This task was adapted by Dorothy Gronwall and her colleagues (Gronwall, 1977; Gronwall & Sampson, 1974; Gronwall & Wrightson, 1974, 1975) to study the recovery of rate of information processing following concussion. They converted it to an auditory task. The task requires subjects to listen to a tape recording of 61 single-digit numbers, presented at four different rates 2.4, 2.0, 1.6, and 1.2 seconds in the same sequence on each trial. Subjects must add each new digit to the number immediately preceding it and give the response before the presentation of the next stimulus. For example, if the numbers 3, 4, 2, and 8 were presented, the correct responses would be 7, 6, and 10, respectively. Thus attention must be divided across a number of mental processes, namely processing each stimulus, remembering the number preceding it, performing the addition and making the response, all at an externally paced rate.

There have been several modifications of the original PASAT. Levin et al. (1987) used a version in which a different set of 50 single digits was presented for each of the four trials. This was designed to minimize practice effects. Several normative studies have used this version (Brittain et al., 1991; Levin et al., 1987; Roman, Edwall, Buchanan, &

Table 11.1.   Test of aspects of attention

Sustained Attention or Vigilance

Test of Everyday Attention (TEA) subtests (Robertson et al., 1994)
- TEA Elevator Counting
- TEA Telephone Search while Counting
- TEA Lottery Task

Selective or Focused Attention

Cancellation/Search Tasks
- Concentration Search Tasks
- Ruff 2 and 7 Attention Test
- Visual Search and Attention Test

Stroop Color Word Test

Tests of Divided Attention and Speed
- Choice Reaction Time
- Symbol Digit Modalities Test
- TEA Telephone Search while Counting
- Paced Auditory Serial Addition Task

Tests of Supervisory Attentional Control
- Tower of London
- Six Elements Test

Tests of Attention Span and Mental Control

Digit Span—Forward and Backward (WAIS-III & WMS-III)

Letter—Number Sequencing (WAIS-III & WMS-III)

Spatial Span (WMS-III)

Mental Control (WMS-III)

Arithmetic (WAIS-III)

Serial Addition/Subtraction Tasks

Patton, 1991). Some studies have used different trial pacings. For example, Egan (1988) and Deary, Langan, Hepburn, and Frier (1991) used only 2-second and 4-second pacings. Sherman, Strauss, and Spellacy (1997) used only the 2- and 1.6-second pacings.

A children's version of the PASAT, known as the CHIPASAT, has also been published (Dyche & Johnson, 1991; Johnson, Roethig-Johnston, & Middleton, 1988). This uses the digits 1–5 only. For example, the digits 1, 3, 2, 5 may be presented. The correct responses by the child would be to add 1 + 3 to respond 4, then add 3 + 2 to respond 5, and 2 + 5 to respond 7. The order of digits is structured so that no answer exceeds 10. The task begins with a 2.8 second pacing trial, followed by 2.4, 2.0, 1.6, and 1.2-second pacings. The CHIPASAT is not recommended for children under the age of 9 years and 6 months. Johnson et al. provide normative data for children aged 8–14.6 years. Dyche and Johnson reported a test-retest reliability co-efficient of 0.90, with gains of approximately 19.7% on re-testing after a four-week interval. Correlations of 0.38 with WISC-R Arithmetic and 0.35 with Digit Span scores were also reported by Dyche and Johnson. Performance is related to age and information processing capacity.

Psychometric Properties

Reliability and Effects of Practice

Egan (1988) reported a split-half reliability of .96, using a version with 2- and 4-second pacings. Mean percentage accuracy and standard deviation remained the same across four subtest epochs, implying high internal consistency. Crawford et al. (1998) obtained a Cronbach's alpha of .90, using the original Gronwall (1977) version. There are also high correlations between performances across each trial. Ponsford (1989) found these correlations ranged from .72 to .86.

There are *significant* practice effects on the PASAT (Gronwall, 1977). Stuss et al. (1987) found an average increase of six points when normal subjects were given the PASAT on two occasions a week apart. Gronwall noted that practice effects are minimal after the second presentation. However, Feinstein et al. (1994) found linear decreases in the number of errors made on the 2-second pacing of the PASAT over the first five of eight presentations at 2- to 4-weekly intervals in normal subjects. The Levin et al. (1987) version of the PASAT was designed to reduce practice effects by changing the order of digits from one presentation to the next, but Feinstein et al. also used four different sets of digits and still found significant practice effects. Therefore, in using this task, it would seem to be crucial to pay attention to the possibility of practice effects and control for these wherever possible.

Validity

Gronwall and her colleagues (Gronwall & Sampson, 1974; Gronwall & Wrightson, 1974, 1975) found the PASAT to be sensitive to speed of information processing impairments following mild head injury. Gronwall and Wrightson (1974) found that impairment of performance on the PASAT was related to the presence of post-concussional symptoms, and Gronwall (1976) reported that scores on the PASAT improved as the symptoms resolved. The PASAT has since been used to demonstrate impaired speed of processing in numerous studies of the effects of mild, moderate, and severe head injury (O'Shaughnessy, Fowler, & Reid, 1984; Ponsford & Kinsella, 1992; Stuss et al., 1988). Roman et al. (1991) have postulated that it is more sensitive to diffuse white matter damage caused by acceleration/deceleration, rather than more static injuries, such as assaults.

PASAT performance has also been shown to differentiate malingerers from those with organic impairments. Strauss et al. (1994) found that malingerers did not exhibit the normal decline in performance with increasing speed of presentation of digits.

Significant correlations have been demonstrated between PASAT performance and scores on attentional measures from the WAIS-R, such as Digit Symbol (.38–.39) and Digit Span (.29–.35) (Deary et al., 1991; Dyche & Johnson, 1991; Sherman et al., 1997) and the Freedom from Distractibility factor (.46) (Deary et al., 1991; Sherman, Strauss, Spellacy, & Hunter, 1995). Crawford et al. (1998) found that the PASAT loaded highly (.75) on the attention/concentration factor of the WAIS-R.

Significant correlations have also been obtained between PASAT performance and other measures of processing speed, namely inspection time on a two-choice discrimination test ($r = .35$), decision time on a four-choice reaction time task ($r = .53$), Stroop subtest scores ($r = .51$–.56), scores on the written and oral versions of the Symbol Digit Modalities Test ($r = .56$–.60), and a Cancellation Test ($r = .47$) (Deary et al.,

1991; Ponsford, 1989; Sherman et al., 1997). Correlations were generally higher for the fastest (1.2 second) pacing. In a study of severely head-injured patients by Haslam, Batchelor, Fearnside, Haslam, and Hawkins (1995), the PASAT loaded on the same factor as the Symbol Digit Modalities test. O'Donnell et al. (1994) found that PASAT performances loaded highly (.83) on the same factor as the Visual Search and Attention Test (Trenerry et al., 1990) and the Trail Making Test Part B, a factor they identified as measuring mental processing, psychomotor speed and focused attention.

The PASAT, like many other attentional tests, also involves a number of other cognitive processes. As such, performance may be determined by factors other than processing speed. In Deary et al.'s (1991) study, 4-second PASAT scores correlated at highly significant levels with all Rey Auditory-Verbal Learning Test indices, except recall of List B, with correlations ranging from .27 to .49. Correlations for the 2-second pacing were much lower. Gronwall and Sampson (1974) reported that the task had only modest correlations with general intelligence (.28) and with arithmetic ability (.24). However, these findings were based upon the performances of a group of service personnel, who do not necessarily represent the broader population. More significant correlations have since been reported between PASAT performance and measures of intelligence (Brittain et al., 1991; Crawford et al., 1998; Deary et al., 1991; Egan, 1988; Roman et al., 1991; Wiens, Fuller, & Crossen, 1997). Crawford et al. found that the PASAT's loading on general intelligence was .72. However, it also loaded significantly on attention/concentration (.75), and .44 when permitted to load simultaneously on intelligence. Stuss et al. (1988) and Ponsford and Kinsella (1992) have noted a statistically significant association between PASAT scores and years of education.

Recent studies have demonstrated that PASAT performance is significantly related to mathematical ability (Bruins, van Niewenhuizen, & Brouwer, 1990; Chronicle & MacGregor, 1998; Crawford et al., 1998; Sherman et al., 1997). For example, Crawford et al. found a correlation of .63 between PASAT performance and WAIS-R Arithmetic performance. There is also a significant but modest linear decline in PASAT performance with age (Brittain et al., 1991; Crawford et al., 1998; Roman et al., 1991; Wiens et al., 1997). It is recommended that all of these factors are taken into account when interpreting PASAT performances.

Assets and Limitations

The PASAT's major advantage is its apparent sensitivity to relatively subtle impairments of speed of information processing, which may not be evident on other measures. It is particularly useful for individuals of above average ability, who may continue to perform at a high level on many tasks despite reporting subjective experience of attentional and information processing difficulties. Recent studies have provided fairly comprehensive norms so that it is possible to make corrections for IQ, arithmetic ability, and age. As there is no published manual, it is important to refer to these norms, and ensure that the method of administration used is consistent with that used to gather the normative data. The instructions provided here and in Spreen and Strauss (1998) relate to the original version, the best norms for which have been published by Crawford et al. (1998).

Due to the fairly significant level of demands placed on the subject, the PASAT is better suited for assessment of those with a relatively high level of functioning, those with mild or moderate injuries, or those with severe injuries in the later stages of re-covery. It is not suitable for individuals of limited intelligence or arithmetic ability. Arithmetic ability should be checked prior to attempting the task. Roman et al. (1991) also caution against using the PASAT with those who are very anxious.

One other potential problem in the use of the PASAT, noted by Spreen and Strauss (1998), concerns its reliance on rapid verbal responses. This renders it unsuitable for use with dysarthric patients or those with other impairments of speech or language. The test is also clearly unsuitable for subjects who do not have sufficient hearing to comfortably listen to the tape. This should be checked. The requirement for a tape recorder, no background noise or distraction, and the time taken for administration can also present difficulties in certain assessment situations.

Administration

The PASAT takes approximately 15 to 20 minutes to administer. Materials comprise an audiotape and record form. The volume on the tape-recorder should be adjusted so that it is comfortably audible to the subject. Instructions for the task are recorded on the tape, but it may be necessary to present the instructions in the manner set out in Spreen and Strauss (1998). These instructions have been reprinted with the authors' permis-sion below:

Oral and Written Demonstration

I am going to ask you to add together pairs of single-digit numbers. You will hear a tape-recorded list of numbers read one after the other. I will ask you to add the numbers in pairs and give your answers out loud.

Although this is really a concentration task, and not a test to see how well you can add, it might help to do a little adding before I explain the task in more detail. Please add the following pairs of numbers together as fast as you can and give your answers out loud: 3,8(11); 4,9(13); 7,8(15); 8,6(14); 8,9(17); 5,7(12); 6,5(11); 6,9(15); 4,7(11); 7,6(13).

Good.

The task that I want you to do involves adding together pairs of numbers, just like you have done, except that the numbers will be read as a list, one after the other. Let me give you an example with a short, easy list. Suppose I gave you the following: 1, 2, 3, 4. This is what you would do. After hearing the first two number on the list, which were 1, 2 you would add these together and give your answer, 1 + 2 = 3. The next number on the list is 3, so when you heard it, you would add this number to the number right before it on the list, which was 2, and give your answer, 2 + 3 = 5. Are you following so far? The last number you heard was 4 (remember the list is 1, 2, 3, 4), so you would add 4 to the num-ber right before it, which was 3, and give your answer, 3 + 4 = 7. The important thing to remember is that you must add each number on the list to the number right before it on the list, and not to the answer you have just given. You can forget your answers as soon as you have said them. All you have to remember is the last digit that you have heard and add it to the next digit that you hear. O.K.? Let's try that short list again, only this time you say the answers. Ready? 1, 2, (3), 3, (5), 4(7). Now let's try another, longer practice list of numbers. This time the numbers on the list won't be in any particular order. Ready? 4, 6(10), 1, (7), 8(9), 8, (16), 4, (12), 3, (7), 8, (11), 2, (10), 7(9).

Good.

If the subject has difficulty understanding the oral instruction, then provide a written demonstration. Say:

That sounds complicated. Let me show you what I mean. Write down a list of five numbers: 5, 3, 7, 4. You see, you add the 5 and the 3 together, and say 8, then you have to forget the 8 and remember the 3. When the 7 comes along you add it to the 3, and say 10, and you have to remember the 7. All right, what do you say after 4?

Continue until the subject understands what he or she is to do. Say:

It's very easy when all the numbers are written down for you. Try it with me saying some numbers to you.

See above list. Discontinue if the subject is unable to get at least the first three answers from the un-paced practice list correct, after two trials.

Paced Practice

Remember I said the numbers would be tape-recorded? The task is not easy and no one is expected to get all of the answers right. The hard part is keeping up with the speed of the recording. However, if you can't answer in time, don't worry; just wait until you hear two more numbers, add them together and go on from there, O.K.? Any questions? I'll play a practice list of numbers and get you to give the answers.

Play to the end of the first practice list.

Test Trials

You see what I meant about the task measuring how well you can concentrate? It doesn't have anything to do with how smart you are. Now we'll try the first real trial. This trial is just the same as the practice trial you've just done, except that it is six times as long, so it goes on for almost two and a half minutes. Don't worry if you make adding mistakes or miss some answers. This is a difficult task. I want to see not only how long you can keep going without stopping, but also how quickly you can pick up again if you do stop. No one is expected to get all the answers. After this trial, we will take a break and then do another trial at a faster speed.

It is very important that the subject understands the task, so the examiner should repeat the instructions orally and/or provide a written demonstration until he or she has understood. As recommended by Spreen and Strauss (1998), the subject should be given several unpaced practice trials. The task should be discontinued if the subject cannot provide correct answers on these unpaced, practice lists after several trials. Unpaced practice is followed by a paced practice list. Once it is clear that the subject fully understands the task, begin the first trial. The first trial is played at a rate of 2.4 seconds. The second trial is played at a rate of 2.0 seconds, the third at 1.6 seconds and the fourth at 1.2 seconds. There should be a break of at least 60 seconds between each trial. The subject also needs to be warned that each trial will be faster than the previous one. Some subjects find this task very difficult and stressful. Spreen and Strauss recommend administering the 1.6 and 1.2 second pacings only if the subject has scored more than 40 on the first trial. Gronwall (personal communication) also suggests that the task should be discontinued if the subject has significant difficulty with the first two trials. She does not believe task performance should be interpreted on the basis of performance of only one or two subtests.

Scoring   A sample scoring sheet is provided in Figure 11.2. The examiner must record each response as it is made for each trial. As such, the task is somewhat demanding of the examiner, and should not be administered without extensive practice beforehand. Numerous methods of scoring have been used. The most common method is to record the total number of items and percentage correct for each trial/pacing speed. The Crawford et al. (1998) norms are computed on the basis of the total number of items correct summed across the four trials. These scores can, in turn, be converted to the mean time per correct response to allow for direct comparison of tests where a different number of trials was given. The total trial time is divided by the number correct for each of the pacing rates. The results are averaged to give a composite score. Gronwall (1977) recommends that in circumstances where one result is abnormally high, as may occur when there is an interruption, results can be discarded for any trial which is more than 0.6 seconds slower than the other pacing rates, provided the subject scores over 24 correct at the slowest speed.

PASAT

| Name | | Date | | Tested by | |

	2.4"	2.0"	1.6"	1.2"		2.4"	2.0"	1.6"	1.2"		2.4"	2.0"	1.6"	1.2"
7 (9)					8 (12)					5 (13)				
5 (12)					7 (15)					4 (19)				
1 (6)					1 (8)					8 (12)				
4 (5)					6 (7)					2 (10)				
9 (13)					3 (9)					1 (3)				
6 (15)					5 (8)					7 (8)				
5 (11)					9 (14)					5 (12)				
3 (8)					2 (11)					9 (14)				
8 (11)					7 (9)					1 (10)				
4 (12)					5 (12)					3 (4)				
3 (7)					3 (8)					6 (9)				
2 (5)					4 (7)					2 (8)				
6 (8)					7 (11)					9 (11)				
9 (15)					1 (8)					7 (16)				
3 (12)					5 (6)					8 (15)				
4 (7)					8 (13)					2 (10)				
5 (9)					3 (11)					4 (6)				
8 (13)					4 (7)					7 (11)				
6 (14)					6 (10)					6 (13)				
4 (10)					8 (14)					3 (9)				

	Total Correct	z	%ile	Time/Resp	z	%ile
2.4" pacing						
2.0" pacing						
1.6" pacing						
1.2" pacing						

Figure 11.2.   PASAT scoring form

From *A Compendium of Neuropsychological Tests, Second Edition.* Administration, norms and commentary by Otfried Spreen and Esther Strauss. Copyright © 1998 by Oxford University Press, Inc. Used by permission of Oxford University Press, Inc.

Table 11.2.   Normative data derived from Stuss, D.T., Stethem, L.L., and Pelchat, G. (1998)

| Presentation Rate (in sec) | Age in Years | | | | | |
| | 16–29 (n = 30) | | 30–49 (n = 30) | | 50–69 (n = 30) | |
	M	SD	M	SD	M	SD
2.4	47.4	10.1	43.4	10.2	43.5	13.6
1.6	36.0	13.0	33.1	12.2	30.8	15.9
1.2	27.4	9.9	24.6	10.6	21.2	14.4

"Three tests of attention and rapid information processing: An extension," *The Clinical Neuropsychologist, 2,* 246–250. From *A Compendium of Neuropsychological Tests, Second Edition.* Administration, norms and commentary by Otfried Spreen and Esther Strauss. Copyright © 1998 by Oxford University Press, Inc. Used by permission of Oxford University Press, Inc.

Norms

Stuss et al. (1988) published norms for three age groups (16–29 years, 30–49 years, 50–69 years) for the original version of the PASAT. These are reproduced in Table 11.2. Stuss et al.'s sample had a relatively high level of education. Crawford et al. (1998) have presented normative data on a larger sample, also using the original version of the PASAT. These are based upon a U.K. sample of 152 adults, for three age bands: 16–29, 30–49, and 50–74 years. Scores represent the total correct responses across all four trials, out of a total of 240. Crawford et al.'s (1998) normative data are reproduced in Table 11.3. These scores are somewhat higher than those obtained by Stuss et al. However the advantage of the Crawford et al. norms is that they have also built regression equations to permit quantitative comparison of obtained PASAT scores and predicted PASAT scores, based upon NART and age, and with scores based upon WAIS-R IQ and age (Table 11.4). They recommend using the regression equations to make individualized comparison standards, in addition to the use of conventional normative data, when

Table 11.3.   Normative data for Gronwall and Sampson's (1974) version of PASAT for three age bands

| | Age Bands in Years | | |
	16–29	30–49	50–74
n	38	78	36
Mean age (SD)	25(3.27)	38.1(5.67)	60.7(7.41)
Mean PASAT (SD)	169.2(30.12)	149.8(40.29)	136.9(43.79)
PASAT SEM	9.38	12.54	13.63

From Crawford, J.R., Obonsawain, M.C., & Allan, K.M. (1998), "PASAT and components of WAIS-R performance: Convergent and discriminant validity," *Neuropsychological Rehabilitation, 8,* 255–272. Reprinted by permission of Psychology Press Ltd.

Table 11.4.   Results from regression analyses predicting PASAT scores from NART plus age and WAIS-R FSIQ plus age

Predictors	Regression Equations	Multiple R	SEest	Discrepancy Required to Exceed Given Percentage of Health Sample*		
				85%	90%	95%
NART errors, age	$215.74 - (1.85 \times NART) - (.77 \times Age)$	.52	34.87	35.9	44.6	57.2
WAIS-R FSIQ, age	$12.87 + (1.65 \times FSIQ) - (.87 \times Age)$	.66	30.66	31.6	39.3	50.3

*The Values are one-tailed.

From Crawford, J.R., Obonsawin, M.C., & Allan, K.M. (1998), "PASAT and components of WAIS-R performance: Convergent and discriminant validity," *Neuropsychological Rehabilitation, 8,* 255–272. Reprinted by permission of Psychology Press, Ltd.

interpreting PASAT performance in clinical practice. Crawford et al. have written a computer program to make the necessary calculations. This can be downloaded from the author's website at: *http://www.psyc/abdn.ac.uk/homedir/jcrawford/jcrawford.htm.*

Using the Levin modification of the PASAT, Brittain et al. (1991) have published comprehensive normative data, based upon 526 healthy U.S. adults aged 17 to 88. Brittain et al.'s norms for mean time per correct response and errors are presented for each trial and for all trials for four different age groups and three different intelligence levels. Wiens et al. (1997) have also published norms for the Levin version of the PASAT, based upon a sample of 821 adults, stratified for three age-bands: 20–29, 30–39, and 40–49 years, and six levels of IQ. Roman et al.'s (1991) norms for this version are based upon a more restricted sample. Normative data for the children's version of the PASAT, the CHIPASAT, for children aged 8 to 14.6 years, are provided by Johnson et al. (1988) and reproduced in Spreen and Strauss (1998).

Interpretation

The PASAT has been used almost exclusively in studies of patients with traumatic brain injury. Those with mild head injury or concussion tend to show impaired performances within the first week after injury, but most recover quite quickly thereafter. The majority have recovered fully within 1 to 3 months of injury, although a subgroup may exhibit ongoing difficulties (Gronwall & Wrightson, 1981; Leininger, Gramling, & Farrell, 1990; Ponsford et al., 1996). Those with more severe head injuries tend to exhibit more lasting impairments on the PASAT (Ponsford & Kinsella, 1992). Performance in terms of percent correct and mean time per correct response generally declines progressively as each pacing becomes more rapid.

In view of the findings presented earlier, it is clear that individual PASAT results need to be interpreted in relation to the subject's intelligence level, and arithmetic ability. Wherever possible, use the relevant corrections, such as those recommended by Crawford et al. (1998). There may also be a general effect of trauma and hospitalization. Ponsford (1989) found lower normative scores in a group of 30 young adults (24 males, 6 females) hospitalized with traumatic orthopaedic injuries, aged 16 to 42 years (M = 25.4, SD = 5.9), but with no history of loss of consciousness, neurological or psychiatric disturbance. They had an average of 11.4 years of education (SD = 1.5 years), which is lower than that in Crawford et al.'s sample, but was demographically matched with a head-injured sample. Mean PASAT scores for this group, expressed in terms of percent correct, were 64.7 (SD = 21.4) for the 2.4-second pacing, 62.5 (SD = 16.6) for the 2.0-second pacing, 55.3 (SD = 16.6) for the 1.6-second pacing, and 39.8 (SD = 12.7) for the 1.2-second pacing. The mean time per correct response was 3.5 (SD = 1.1) and the error rate 7.6 (SD = 7.4).

Performance on the PASAT declines significantly with age, so it is essential to use normative data for the relevant age group. Crawford et al.'s (1998) norms suggest mean total correct scores of 169.2 for the age group 16 to 29 years, declining to 149.8 in the 30 to 49-year age group, and 136.9 in the 50 to 74 year age group. Given the evidence of practice effects on the PASAT, great care needs to be taken in interpreting results from repeated administrations, particularly at short intervals. Stuss et al. (1988) have published mean scores obtained by three age groups on both the first and the second PASAT administration one week later. These provide a useful basis from which to separate practice effects from recovery. They suggest an average increase of six points at the second administration. The findings of Feinstein et al. (1994) suggest that improvements due to practice may continue over up to five serial assessments spaced 2 to 4 weeks apart. On each testing occasion, it may be advisable to give one full practice trial before the test administration. It is not uncommon for the subject to perform at around the same level on the second trial (2.0 sec pacing) as on the first trial, the effect of faster pacing being counterbalanced by the familiarity with the task

Anxiety may also affect performance on the PASAT to a very marked degree. As such, the task is not very useful where one is attempting to discriminate between the presence of post traumatic stress disorder and mild head injury. Indeed, the PASAT is such a stressful task that it is best kept for those situations where other tasks fail to elicit information processing deficits. If a patient has been obviously stressed during task performance, results should be interpreted with great caution.

THE STROOP COLOR-WORD TEST

History and Development

The Stroop Color Word Test is one of the most commonly used tests of selective or focused attention. Following earlier findings that reading color names could be accomplished more quickly than naming of colors, Stroop (1935) conducted three experiments. The materials used were three cards, on which were printed 10 rows of 10 items. Stroop found that color names (red, blue, green, brown, purple) printed in nonmatching colored ink could be read as quickly as when they were printed in black ink. Results of a second experiment showed that naming the colors of square patches was accomplished much more quickly than naming the color of the ink of nonmatching color names. In a third experiment, Stroop demonstrated improvement in speed of color naming on this latter task following daily practice sessions. The procedure, used particularly in Stroop's second experiment, has since been used widely both in research and clinical settings. Close to 1000 articles pertaining to Stroop's work have been published (see reviews by Dyer, 1973; Jensen & Rohwer, 1966; and MacLeod, 1991).

There are many different versions of this test, which incorporate up to four sub-tests: (1) reading printed color names printed in black ink (BCNb, or W); (2) reading color names printed in incongruent colored ink (RCNd); (3) naming the colors of patches, blocks of Xs or dots, (NC or C); and (4) naming the color in which words are printed, these words themselves being non-matching color names (naming colors of words or NCWd or CW). Graf, Uttl, and Tuokko (1995) include an additional card with color names printed in congruent colors.

Studies have consistently demonstrated that speed of reading color names is invariably faster than the naming of colored blocks, which is in turn, significantly faster than the naming of the ink color of words that are themselves incongruent color names. It is thought that performance on this third subtest is slower because it provokes conflicting response tendencies, the more automatic response being to read the printed word. This interference effect has become known as the Stroop effect.

According to Shiffrin and Schneider (1977), the Stroop effect represents an example of a focused attention error, which arises when automatic attention responses interfere with the task at hand. Shum et al. (1990, p. 159) have referred to this test as one of selective processing of "only one visual feature while continuously blocking out the processing of others." Others have referred to the task as a measure of response inhibition, selective attention, the ability to ward off distractions, or cognitive flexibility (Dyer, 1973; Lezak, 1995; Spreen & Strauss, 1998; Zajano & Gorman, 1986). Stroop (1935) concluded that the relatively greater speed in reading words over naming of colors was due to greater training or practice in the former activity. Reading words was thus thought to be more automatic, faster, and therefore, created stronger interference than color naming.

Earlier theories of Stroop interference were based upon linear processing models of attention. However, MacLeod (1991) concluded that the Stroop effect was most successfully explained by the theory of parallel processing of relevant and irrelevant information (Cohen, Dunbar, & McClelland, 1990). According to this so-called parallel distributed processing model, processing occurs through activation moving along pathways of different strength. The strength of a processing pathway increases with training. "If two pathways are active simultaneously and produce conflicting activation at their intersection, interference results; if they produce coinciding activation, facilitation results. Attention tunes or modulates, the operation of processing units in a pathway." (MacLeod, 1991, p. 192). Although the adequacy of this model has also been questioned (Kanne, Balota, Spieler, & Faust, 1998; Mewhort, Braun, & Heathcote, 1992), it remains the most strongly favored theory advanced to date.

A number of analogous tasks to the Stroop have also been developed. One version involves the use of line drawings of common objects with matching or mismatching words embedded inside. Subjects are required to name the pictures (Hentschel, 1973; Rosinski, Golinkoff, & Kukish, 1975). Another version uses sets of numerals presented in a matching or mismatching number of items (e.g., the digit 4 printed 8 times) (Shor, 1971; Windes, 1968). All tasks involve performing a relatively automatic function, such as naming of colors or pictures or reading of words, as opposed to performing the same task in the presence of incongruent or conflicting stimuli. The interference score is represented by the difference between the incongruent and the neutral condition. MacLeod (1991) concluded from his review of relevant studies, that the amount of interference experienced was influenced by the strength of association between conflicting stimuli and the subject's familiarity with the stimuli to be ignored, and attended to.

Graf et al. (1995) examined the hypothesis that Stroop interference is a general, rather than a test-specific measure of cognitive flexibility by comparing performance on a color-word Stroop task and a picture-word Stroop test in 129 healthy older adults. Data analyses indicated differential age effects, present only on the picture-word task, and different factor loadings for the color- and picture-word tasks. Graf et al. concluded that the tests measure different cognitive functions, at least in old age.

Published Versions of the Stroop

Although Jensen and Rohwer (1966) strongly recommended the adoption of a standard Stroop task produced and distributed by a single supplier, this has not eventuated. Different versions of the Stroop Test have been published by Comalli et al. (1962), later adapted by Edith Kaplan, Dodrill (1978), Golden (1976, 1978), Graf et al. (1995), Regard (1981), and Trenerry, Crosson, DeBoe, and Leber (1989). These versions use between three and five colors. There are significant differences between each of these versions, which in turn do not all correspond closely to the original Stroop experiments. Each will be examined with regard to its procedures and the aspects of attention measured. The Golden (1978) and Comalli et al. (1962)/Kaplan versions will be discussed in more detail. Of the published versions, they most closely resemble the original Stroop task, since their formats allow for proper evaluation of the interference effect. The Golden version has a published manual. Its variations from the original task have been validated. Although the original Golden norms appear to have been adapted from other studies, a number of other normative data sets have subsequently been developed. Comprehensive normative studies have also been conducted using the Comalli et al. (1962)/Kaplan versions.

Group versions of the color-word test have been developed by Kipnis and Glickman (1962, cited in MacLeod, 1991), Golden (1975a), and Harbeson, Kennedy, and Bittner (1981). However, as MacLeod (p. 166) notes in his review, the use of group tests has been "infrequent and the results not very compelling." Their equivalence with individual versions has never been clearly established. Computerized versions of the Stroop have also been used both experimentally and clinically (e.g., Henik, Singh, Beckley, & Rafal, 1993; Hepp, Maier, Hermle, & Spitzer, 1996; Lemelin, Baruch, Vincent, Everett, & Vincent, 1997; Osimani, Alon, Berger, & Abarbanel, 1997; Renaud & Blondin, 1997; Siegrist, 1995; Thomas, Raoux, Everett, Dantchev, & Widl'ocher, 1997). However, to the author's knowledge none of these has been made available commercially with accompanying norms.

Stroop Color and Word Test (Golden, 1978)

The Golden (1978) version involves three subtests. The first requires the subject to read color words (red, green, blue) printed in black ink on a single sheet in 5 columns of 20 words, as many as possible in 45 seconds (W). The second subtest involves naming as many colors of blocks of XXXXs, printed in red, green, or blue, as possible in 45 seconds. In the third subtest the words from page 1 are printed in the colors from page 2, but none of the words are printed in congruent colors (C). The subject is asked to name the color of the ink in which the word is printed (as many as possible in 45 seconds), rather than read the word (CW).

Golden (1975a) had previously found that the use of three, four, or five colors made no difference to performance. The Xs were used instead of color patches, so that the color values and size would closely resemble those on the color-word page. Five rows of 20 items were used in preference to 10 rows of 10 items in order to minimize the number and difficulty of changes in spatial orientation. Administration and scoring guidelines for the Golden (1978) version of the Stroop are set out in a later section.

The Comalli et al. (1962) and Kaplan Stroop

Comalli et al. (1962) used three white cards, $9\frac{1}{4} \times 9\frac{1}{4}$, with 100 stimuli arranged in a 10 × 10 grid, and an additional row of 10 practice items at the top. The first (word-reading) card consists of color words (red, blue, green) printed in black ink. The second (color naming) card consists of rectangles of the same colors. The third (interference) card comprises color names printed in incongruent colored ink. Each line is scanned from left to right. Time to complete 100 items and number of errors made on each card are recorded.

The Kaplan version of Comalli et al.'s (1962) Stroop uses the same card layout. The only difference is that the order of administration of the cards is altered. The color-naming card is administered first, followed by the word-reading task, immediately before the interference subtest. This change was made in order to maximize the interference from the word-reading task.

The Victoria Version (Regard, 1981)

As outlined in Spreen and Strauss (1998), the Victoria version of the Stroop was developed by Marianne Regard (1981), and based upon the format used by Perret (1974) in a study demonstrating the sensitivity of the Stroop to frontal lobe lesions. Neutral conditions are included in order to allow for separate evaluation of speed and interference effects. The Victoria version has three subtests, always administered in the same sequence (see Spreen & Strauss, 1998). The first part, Part D, requires the subject to name the colors of 24 dots, printed in blue, green, red, or yellow in a pseudo-random order, each color being used six times. The second subtest, Part W, contains common words, such as *when, hard,* and *over* printed in lower case letters in the same colors. The subject must name the colors of the words. In the third subtest, Part C, color names are printed in lower case in blue, green, red, or yellow, the ink color being incongruent with the color name. Administration and scoring guidelines and normative data are set out in Spreen and Strauss. The scores are expressed in terms of mean reading time and errors for the 24-item card for each part of the test. Interference may be calculated as the difference required for the interference card (Part C) versus the color card (Part D). According to the recommendation of Graf et al. (1995), it is preferable to use a ratio index of interference (i.e., Part C/Part D).

Dodrill (1978) and Trenerry et al. Versions

Dodrill (1978) and Trenerry et al. (1989) omit the card with color-words printed in black, using only sheets with columns of color names printed in red, orange/tan, green, or blue. The first subtest (Part I) requires the subject to read the words, which are color names printed in incongruent colors. The second subtest (Part II) requires the subject to name the color of the ink in which the color names are printed. Graf et al. (1995) include an additional card with color names printed in congruent colors.

The Dodrill (1978) modification was developed as a part of his Neuropsychological Battery for Epilepsy as a test of concentration. It uses the same sheet of 176 words (11 across, 16 down) for each sub-test (Parts I and II). The times taken to complete the readings are recorded halfway through and at the end. According to Lezak (1995), it is felt that this allows the examiner to establish whether familiarity with the task and practice affect performance rate, or set maintenance or attentional factors. The time taken to complete Part I is recorded and subtracted from the time taken to complete Part II. This represents the Stroop score. Sacks, Clark, Pols, and Geffen (1991) developed five equivalent forms of the Dodrill-Stroop Color-Word Test. Sacks et al. found a significant slowing of color naming time in the second half of each trial, but not of word reading time. This was interpreted as being due to fatigue.

The Trenerry et al. (1989) version, known as the Stroop Neuropsychological Screening Test, has two separate sheets, each containing 112 color words (4 across, 28 down). The Color-Word score is the primary score used for interpretation. This represents the number of correct responses in 120 seconds. Percentiles and probability values for Color-Word scores for adults in the 18 to 49 and 50+ age ranges are provided in the test manual, based upon a normative sample of 156 adults in the 18 to 79 age range, screened to rule out histories of neurological disorder, major psychiatric illness, or physical handicaps which might affect performance.

Psychometric Properties of the Stroop

Reliability and Effects of Practice

Golden (1975b) reported reliabilities of .85, .82, and .73 for the individual version of the task, with reliabilities of the interference score being .70. Graf et al. (1995) reported reliable test-retest reliabilities for raw scores from each Color-Word subtest, ranging from .74 to .85. However the derived scores for measuring interference effects $(C - W, IC - C, C \div W, IC \div C)$ showed lower and at best marginal reliability, ranging from .50 to .71. The estimated reliabilities for the mean of two trials per card were all respectable for the raw and derived scores from the Color-Word test, ranging from .67 to .92.

Practice effects have been consistently demonstrated on the Stroop task. In his third experiment, Stroop (1935) examined the effects of daily practice at naming the ink colors of incompatible words for 8 days. Color-naming times decreased, suggesting that interference from incompatible words decreased with practice. Stroop also examined the impact of practice over the same period in naming colors of words printed in incongruent colors upon word reading. This resulted in increased interference, with longer reading times, but this effect had disappeared by the second post-test. Stroop concluded that differential practice accounted for the interference patterns obtained. Stroop made an equivalent form of the test by printing each card in reverse order. Other investigators have simply re-used the same set of cards for repeated testing.

Using Golden's (1978) version of the Stroop Color-Word test, Connor, Franzen, and Sharp (1988) examined the effects of type of practice (massed versus distributed), sex, and additional instructions upon performance of each Stroop subtest. They found no significant differences according to sex, type of practice, or type of instructions. No practice effects were evident on the word-reading or color-naming subtests. However there were significant practice effects evident on each of the subtests in terms of number completed in 45 seconds. Connor et al. did not, however, examine the interference effect directly. They concluded that experience with the Stroop will affect scores on each of the subtests to a fairly equal degree. Feinstein et al. (1994), on the other hand, found significant practice effects on the color-naming and interference trials, but not on the word-reading trial. Dulaney and Rogers (1994) found significant practice effects on the Stroop interference subtest.

In reviewing research studies examining the impact of practice or exposure in numerous forms of Stroop tasks, MacLeod (1991, p. 182) concluded that "Degree of practice in processing each of the dimensions of a multidimensional stimulus is influential in determining the extent of interference from one dimension on another. The greater the practice in processing a dimension, the more capable that dimension is of influencing the processing of another dimension." According to Reisberg, Baron, and Kemler (1980), this improvement in performance may be the result of active learning to suppress distraction or habituation of competing responses.

Validity   Jensen (1965) extracted three factors from all Stroop scores where C represents color naming, W represents word reading, and CW represents naming colors of words (interference task). The first was labeled a color difficulty factor, represented equally by scores C/W, W/C, C + W, (C − W)(C + W), and (C − W)/W. The second factor was identified as the interference factor, measured by CW − C. The third factor was labeled a speed factor, measured by the basic time on the word reading card (W).

Shum et al. (1990) found that the Stroop interference subtest score loaded on the same factor as Serial 7s and 13s, labeling this factor as "the ability to sustain ongoing mental processes and select features for processing." Graf et al. (1995) found that Stroop performance loaded on four factors. Word-reading and color naming loaded on the first factor, thought to reflect speed of automatic processing. Digit Span also loaded on this factor. The second factor, upon which all Color-Word subtests loaded, was associated with slowness in cued or prompted naming. Tasks loading on the third factor were the picture and congruent picture cards from the Picture-Word Task, as well as animal naming. None of the Color-Word subtests loaded on this factor, which was labelled strategic search of semantic memory. The Stroop Color-Word interference subtest loaded negatively on Factor 4 along with positive loadings for WAIS Block Design, Similarities and Digit Symbol. This was thought to reflect visuospatial-perceptual and conceptual abilities or cognitive flexibility.

Hanes, Andrewes, Smith, and Pantelis (1996) demonstrated relatively strong associations between Stroop performance, as measured by the time taken to name colors subtracted from the time taken to read words, and performances on a range of other executive control measures, namely a Category Fluency task ($r = .58$) and a modified version of the Tower of London ($r = .65$). Rossi et al. (1997) found a close association between Stroop performance and scores on the Wisconsin Card Sorting Test in schizophrenic subjects. On the other hand, Aloia, Weed, and Marx (1997) obtained a closer association between their modified Stroop task and Part B of the Trail Making Test, than they did with the Wisconsin Card Sorting Test.

Positron emission tomography has been used to measure changes in regional cerebral blood flow in normal volunteers while performing the Stroop task. A number of studies have found that performance of the Stroop interference task was associated with increased activation of the right anterior cingulate gyrus, which was less apparent on the congruent task (Bench et al., 1993; Carter, Mintun, & Cohen, 1995; Pardo, Pardo, Janer, & Raichle, 1990). Carter, Mintun, Nichols, and Cohen (1997) demonstrated that patients with schizophrenia fail to activate the anterior cingulate gyrus during Stroop interference task performance, relative to controls. It has been hypothesized that these anterior structures play a crucial role in the process of selecting the desired response and suppressing habitual response tendencies. However, Taylor, Kornblum, Lauber, Minoshima, and Koeppe (1997) questioned the involvement of the anterior cingulate gyrus in overcoming Stroop interference. They found that activation in the left inferior frontal gyrus reflected processing specific to the Stroop task.

Certainly there is evidence of frontal involvement in Stroop performance, although there have been differential findings regarding laterality. Perret (1974), Regard (1981), and Holst and Vilkki (1988) found that patients with left frontal lobe lesions were more susceptible to the interference effect on the third subtest. On the other hand, Vendrell et al. (1995) showed that lesions in the right prefrontal lateral cortex were most related to errors on the Stroop.

The Stroop procedure/task has been used to study a wide range of conditions. A number of studies have examined the performance of traumatically brain-injured subjects on the Stroop. In his study of head-injured children at one and four months post-injury, Chadwick, Rutter, Brown, Shaffer, and Traub (1981) found that the children performed more slowly than orthopedic controls on all three subtests, but there was no evidence of a significantly greater interference effect on the third subtest. Similar findings were reported in adults with moderate to severe injuries by Ponsford and Kinsella (1992). Stuss et al. (1985) found slower performances only on the color-naming subtest in mild to very severely head injured subjects tested an average of 2.6 years post-injury.

There has been some evidence of increased sensitivity to the interference effect in head-injured individuals when an additional distracting load is added to the Stroop test (Bohnen, Jolles, et al., 1992; Elting, van Zomeren, & Brouwer, 1989). In Elting et al.'s study, response interference was increased by means of delayed feedback of the subject's voice heard via earphones. Bohnen, Jolles, et al. modified the third inference subtest by requiring subjects to shift to reading some rectangularly designated color-word items as words, whilst naming the colors of most items. This task elicited greater interference in subjects with mild TBI, who did not display a susceptibility to the interference effect on the usual interference task. Bohnen, Twijnstra, and Jolles (1992) found that mild TBI subjects who continued to report post-concussional symptoms at three months post-injury exhibited significantly greater interference effects on both the traditional and the more complex, modified interference tasks than did mild TBI subjects without continuing symptoms. Batchelor, Harvey, and Bryant (1995) also used this modification to study individuals with mild TBI. Although slowness was evident in mild TBI subjects relative to controls on all subtests, including the modified interference subtest, there was no greater interference effect on either the original or the modified interference measure.

Aloia et al. (1997) further modified the Bohnen, Jolles, et al. (1992) task to increase its set-shifting demands, by requiring the subjects to change response set whenever they reached one of a number of lines placed on the stimulus card. This task increased the correlation with Part B of the Trail Making test, another test of mental flexibility. However there was still little construct overlap with performance on the Wisconsin Card Sorting Test. Aloia et al. questioned the sensitivity of the Bohnen, Jolles, et al. (1992a) modification, concluding that it did not increases set-shifting demands. They argued the necessity of more significant modifications to increase its clinical sensitivity.

In patients with Alzheimer's disease, Koss, Ober, Delis, and Friedland (1984) found significant slowing on all three subtests, which was proportionate to the severity of dementia. Those with mild Alzheimer's disease showed a relatively stronger interference effect than moderately impaired cases. The authors concluded this was the result of increased slowness in color naming, changing linguistic impairment, and attitudes to errors. Those with milder dementia were perhaps more aware of their errors and were therefore relatively slower and more cautious in responding. A progressive decline in performance on the Stroop interference task has been associated with progression of the disease over a period of three years (Grady et al., 1988). Spieler, Balota, and Faust (1996) found that Dementia Alzheimer Type individuals showed interference proportionate to older adults, but a disproportionate increase in facilitation for congruent color-word trials, and an increased intrusion of word naming on incongruent color naming trials. They concluded that Alzheimer's disease was associated with an accelerated breakdown in inhibition. Fisher, Freed, and Corkin (1990) suggest that the Stroop should be used with caution in Alzheimer's disease patients due to a relatively high incidence of color confusion.

Studies of individuals with Parkinson's disease showed slower performances on all three Stroop subtests, but susceptibility to interference was not specifically examined (Hietanen & Teravainen, 1986; Portin & Rinne, 1980). Other studies revealed no significant impairment on the interference task relative to controls (Cools, Van den Bercken, Horstink, Van Spaendonck, & Berger 1984; Richards, Cote, & Stern, 1993). Henik et al. (1993) and Hanes et al. (1996) did, on the other hand, demonstrate significantly greater interference in Parkinson's disease patients, using the formula of CW − C to calculate interference. In a subsequent paper, Henik (1996) questioned the use of this formula. Hanes et al. also found a greater interference in patients with Huntington's disease and schizophrenia. Numerous studies in addition to that of Hanes et al. have demonstrated increased Stroop interference in schizophrenic subjects (Baxter & Liddle, 1998; Carter et al., 1997; Golden, 1976; Hepp et al., 1996; McGrath, Scheldt, Welham, & Clair, 1997; Purdon, 1998; Rossi et al., 1997).

Batchelor et al. (1995) noted that performance on the Stroop was affected by the presence of anxiety in subjects with mild TBI, but level of anxiety did not entirely account for group differences. Significant slowing and interference effects on the Stroop have also been demonstrated in patients with depression (Lemelin et al., 1997; Raskin, Friedman, & DiMascio, 1982; Thomas et al., 1997; Trichard, et al., 1995). Thomas et al.

found that the interference effect was diminished significantly with anti-depressant drug treatment.

Effects of Intelligence and Education   Using a version similar to that of Comalli et al. (1962), Pati and Dash (1990a, 1990b), Rush, Panek, and Russell (1990), and Klein, Ponds, Houx, and Jolles (1997), among others, have reported that intelligence may influence Stroop performance. The more intelligent the subject, the shorter the time taken to complete the color-word interference task (Klein et al., 1997). Boone (1999) reported that age and Full Scale IQ accounted for 15 percent and 13 percent, respectively of test score variance on the Comalli Stroop, but education did not contribute significantly. Using the Golden version of the Stroop, Ivnik, Malec, Smith, Tangalos, and Peterson (1996) found less than 8 percent shared variance between performances on Stroop subtests and education in subjects over 55 years of age, correlations for the word-reading, color naming, and interference subtests being .28, .18, and .15, respectively.

Reading Proficiency   Reading proficiency is an essential ingredient in producing the Stroop Interference effect. Cox et al. (1997) emphasized that single-word reading capacity must be fully automatized before the interference effect will fully manifest itself. They used the Golden (1978) version of the Stroop in a study of 306 parents of learning-disabled children, investigating the genetic bases of learning disabilities. They found that a word-reading score greater than or equal to the individual's Full Scale IQ, was a better indicator of reading automaticity than was a standard word-reading score within normal limits. Stroop Interference scores in those subjects satisfying this criterion correlated significantly with other measures of response inhibition, but not in those who did not satisfy this criterion.

Sex Differences   Stroop (1935) and others have found that girls/women are consistently faster at color naming (subtest 1) than boys/men. However, there is no consistent evidence of sex differences at any age on the Stroop Interference task (subtest 3) (Connor et al., 1988; Ivnik et al., 1996; Klein et al., 1997; MacLeod, 1991).

Age Effects   Comalli et al. (1962) conducted one of the more comprehensive studies of performance on all three Stroop tasks across the life-span, in subjects aged between 7 and 80 years. The interference effect becomes evident early in the school years and is at its highest around Grades 2 to 3, as reading skill develops. Interference steadily declines through the adult years with increased reading proficiency. At around age 60, it begins to steadily increase again. Color Naming and Word Reading times were significantly shorter than times for the interference task, Word Reading times being shortest. Time to perform both these tasks also declined steadily up to the age of 19, when they tend to plateau out. Performance on these tasks appeared to decline to only a very small degree with aging.

As Graf et al. (1995) point out, the adults in Comalli et al.'s (1962) study were not screened for health problems. Cohn, Dustman, and Bradford (1984) and Houx, Jolles, and Vreeling (1993) did screen subjects for health problems, and found that color naming slowed significantly with age and the interference effect increased to an even greater degree. Graf et al. attempted to discriminate whether these age-related effects were due to general slowing or more specific processing deficits, by computing the Stroop interference effect as a ratio of CW/C, or Color Word Naming/Color Naming, rather than a difference score. Much smaller differences were evident between age groups. They concluded that Stroop interference may index age-related slowing. This was confirmed in their own study of 129 healthy older adults aged between 65 and 95.

Results of a more recent study by Uttl and Graf (1997), using a broader age range, indicated a small age-related decline in performance on the interference task, but the authors again concluded that this reflected age-related slowing. A similar conclusion was reached by Verhaeghen and DeMeersman (1998) on the basis of a meta-analysis of 20 studies comparing younger and older adults on the Stroop interference effect. West and Baylis (1998), on the other hand, noted from their experiments that factors other than speed of processing contributed to the greater interference they observed in older adults. They found that older adults had difficulty maintaining a color-naming strategy to guide task performance.

Using a version similar to that of Comalli et al. (1962), Klein et al. (1997) studied 429 subjects aged between 25 and 80 years. Consistent with other studies, they demonstrated small effects of age on speed of word reading and color naming and significant effects upon naming colors of incongruent color names, particularly over the age of 55. They also examined effects of test-duration. Younger adults aged 25 to 35 years were relatively fast on the first half of the 100-item interference task, but slower on the second half, whereas older adults aged 70 to 80 years showed the reverse effect. It is suggested that the older adults may be more cautious and take longer to develop or adapt automatic processes on such tasks, beginning slowly and gradually speeding up, whereas younger adults are processing information efficiently and optimally from the beginning, but have difficulty in sustaining this. Klein et al. (1997) recommended that an abridged version of the task may be at least as sensitive as a longer version.

Rush et al. (1990) found that responses on the same version of the Stroop in older adults were related to several factors including age, level of cautiousness, and verbal intelligence. They emphasized the fact that performance on the Stroop is multidimensional, with different components of performance being related to separate factors. Individual variation in the performances of elderly people on the Stroop needs to be recognized and understood in the light of this.

Assets and Limitations

The Stroop is relatively quick and easy to administer and requires simple materials. One of its greatest assets is the fact that its use has been so widely researched. Almost every possible facet of the Stroop effect has been examined. The Stroop has been shown to be sensitive to attentional impairments associated with a broad range of neurological disorders, including head injury, Alzheimer's disease, Parkinson's disease, Huntington's disease, and psychiatric disorders, including schizophrenia, depression, and anxiety. A substantial amount of normative data are available for certain versions, particularly the Golden (1978) and Comalli/Kaplan versions. With appropriate scoring, the test allows for differentiation of impairments of speed of processing from those of selective or focused attention.

The breadth of the Stroop's use is also, however, a limitation. There has been a remarkable lack of uniformity in the manner in which the task is administered and scored. A relative paucity of studies has examined the interference effect properly, and this also appears to be the case in its clinical usage. There is also a lack of normative data pertaining to the interference effect. Like many other complex attentional measures, performance on the Stroop is sensitive to age, so that it is essential to make reference to age-relevant norms. It is unsuitable for use in the presence of significant visual acuity, or color vision problems, or reading difficulties. Results for those for whom the language of administration is not their native language have to be interpreted with caution. Allowances need to be made for practice effects with repeated administrations of the task.

Administration (Golden, 1978)

Administration guidelines for the Golden (1978) version of the Stroop Color and Word test are set out here. The three pages are placed on a flat surface in front of the subject, who is not allowed to lift or rotate the sheets more than 45 degrees. Instructions detailed in the manual (Golden, 1978) are set out below.

This is a test of how fast you can read the words on this page. After I say begin, you are to read down the columns starting with the first one [*point to the leftmost column*] and then continue without stopping down the remaining columns in order [*run your hand down the second column, then the third, fourth, and fifth columns*]. If you finish all the columns before I say "Stop," then return to the first column and begin again [*point to the first column*]. Remember, do not stop reading until I say "Stop" and read out loud as quickly as you can. If you make a mistake, I will say "No" to you. Correct your error and continue without stopping. Are there any questions? [*Instructions may be repeated or paraphrased as often as necessary so that the subject understands what is to be done. Then continue.*] Ready? . . . Then begin. [*As the subject starts, begin the stopwatch. After 45 seconds, say:*] Stop. Circle the item you are on. If you finish the entire page and begin again, put a one by your circle. Turn the page.

[*The instructions for the second page are identical. Except the first sentence reads:*] This is a test of how fast you can name the colors on this page. [*If the subject is largely intact, the remaining instructions can be given briefly.*] You will complete this page just as you did the previous page, starting with this first column. Remember to name the colors out loud as quickly as you can. [*If the subject has had any trouble following the instructions, they should be repeated in their entirety. As with the first page, the subject should be allowed 45 seconds. At the beginning of the third page, the following instructions should be used:*] This page is like the page you just finished. I want you to name the color of the ink the words are printed in, ignoring the word that is printed in each item. For example, [*point to the first item of the first column*] this is the first item: what would you say? [*If the subject is correct, go on with the instructions. If incorrect, say:*] No, that is the word that is spelled there. I want you to say the color of the ink the word is printed in. Now [*pointing to the same item*] what would the response be to this item? That's correct, [*point to the second item*] what would the response be to this item? [*If correct, proceed: if incorrect, repeat above as many times as necessary until the subject understands or it becomes clear that it is impossible to go on.*] Good. You will do this page just like the others, starting with the first column [*pointing*] and then going on to as many columns as you can. Remember, if you make a mistake, just correct it and go on. Are there any questions? [*As with the other two pages, the instructions can be repeated or paraphrased as* *often as necessary.*] Then begin. [*Time for 45 seconds, then say:*] Stop. Circle the item you are on.*

Instructions for a group administration are also included, substituting the words "by yourself" for "out loud." However, this version is not recommended for severely impaired individuals, such as brain-damaged or chronic schizophrenic populations.

The score on this version represents the number of items from each of the three pages completed in 45 seconds. Time to complete 100 items was also employed originally. The results of the two scoring methods were shown to be identical in normal subjects. Given the additional demands placed upon the subject in the 100-item version, the 45-second version was selected. Errors are not counted, but they result in a lower score as the subject is asked to repeat them.

Golden (1978) recommended that "pure" interference corrected for speed factors should be measured by CW − C or CW − predicted CW, the latter remaining more stable in an impaired population. Predicted CW is calculated as $(C \times W)/(C + W)$. C represents Color Naming, W represents Word Reading, and CW represents the Color-Word interference task. However, more recent studies have suggested the need to measure the interference effect in terms of the ratio of CW/C (Chen, 1996, 1997; Graf et al., 1995).

Norms   Normative data are included in the test manual, with means for younger subjects (15–45) and older subjects (46–64) (Golden, 1978). However the size, demographic, and IQ details of these normative samples are not specified. Other normative scores included in the manual have been derived from the previous studies of Stroop (1935), Jensen (1965), and Comalli et al. (1962) by calculating how many items would have been completed had the test been discontinued after 45 seconds. Golden recommends that all Stroop scores can be converted into T-scores. Age corrections are supplied for subjects older than 45 (45–65 and 65–85) and younger than 17, although it is acknowledged that these are purely experimental. Normal limits are *t*-scores 35–65. Overall the normative data published in the Golden manual should be interpreted with caution.

Ivnik et al. (1996) have published the most comprehensive set of norms using the Golden (1978) version of the Stroop. Scaled scores corrected for age > 55 and education for the three Stroop subtests. These are published along with norms for seven other neuropsychological tests: the Controlled Oral Word Association Test, Boston Naming Test, Token Test, Wide Range Achievement Test–Revised Reading subtest, the American version of the National Adult Reading Test, the Trail-Making Test, and Judgment of Line Orientation. These norms were simultaneously collected from the same group of 750 older caucasian adults, aged 56 to 94 years, who participated in Mayo's Older Americans' Normative Studies. As such, they provide a basis for comparing Stroop performance with performance on other cognitive measures. Ivnik et al. have assigned standard scores with a mean of 10 and standard deviation of 3 to raw scores on the basis of percentile ranks. They provide age-corrected norms for discrete age groups, which have been condensed by Mitrushina, Boone, and D'Elia (1999) and reproduced in Table 11.5. Using the table that corresponds to the subject's age, raw

---

*Reproduced by permission of the copyright owner: © Copyright 1978, Stoelting Co., Wood Dale, IL, USA.

Table 11.5.   Age-corrected norms for Stroop performance in each age group

Scaled Scores	Age Group in Years 56–62 Word	Color	C/W	63–65 Word	Color	C/W	66–68 Word	Color	C/W	Percentile
2	<60	<41	<17	<58	<39	<16	<58	<32	<16	<1
3	60–63	41–42	17–18	58	39–40	16	58	32–40	16	1
4	64–65	43–44	19–20	59	41–43	17	59	41–42	17	2
5	66–72	42–50	21–23	60–68	44–48	18–21	60–68	43–47	18–21	3–5
6	73–77	51–54	24–25	69–76	49–53	22–23	69–74	48–51	22	6–10
7	78–82	55–59	26–28	77–81	54–58	24–26	75–80	52–57	23–26	11–18
8	83–88	60–64	29–30	82–86	59–61	27–29	81–85	58–59	27–29	19–28
9	89–93	65–66	31–34	87–91	62–64	39–32	86–91	60–63	29–31	29–40
10	94–101	67–71	35–38	92–98	65–70	33–36	92–97	64–69	32–35	41–59
11	102–107	72–75	39–40	99–103	71–73	37–39	98–103	70–72	39–38	60–71
12	108–111	76–81	41–43	104–109	74–80	49–42	104–109	73–78	39–42	72–81
13	112–116	82–85	44–47	110–115	81–82	43–45	109–115	79–81	43–44	82–89
14	117–122	86–88	48–49	116–122	83–86	46–48	116–122	82–85	45–47	90–94
15	123–125	89–91	50–55	123–125	87–89	49–51	123–125	86–87	48–50	95–97
16	126–129	92–93	56–57	126–127	99–92	52–54	126–127	88–90	51–52	98
17	130–139	94–104	58–62	128–132	93–104	55–62	128–131	91–104	53–60	99
18	>139	>104	>62	>132	>104	>62	>131	>104	>60	>99
N	160	160	160	206	206	206	152	152	152	

Scaled Scores	Age Group in Years 69–71 Word	Color	C/W	72–74 Word	Color	C/W	75–77 Word	Color	C/W	Percentile
2	<44	<24	<16	<42	<24	<4	<42	<23	<4	<1
3	44–46	24–30	16	42–45	24–30	4–6	42–45	23	4–6	1
4	47–50	31–41	17	46–48	31–39	7–15	46–48	24–26	7–13	2
5	51–59	42–45	18–19	49–56	40–41	16–17	49–54	27–29	14–15	3–5
6	60–71	46–48	20–21	57–63	42–44	18–20	55–63	39–43	16–17	6–10
7	72–79	49–52	22–24	64–76	45–49	21–22	64–72	44–48	18–21	11–18
8	80–83	53–57	25–27	77–81	50–53	23–26	73–80	49–51	22–25	19–28
9	84–87	58–60	28–29	82–85	54–58	27–28	81–84	52–55	26–27	29–40
10	88–94	61–65	30–32	86–93	59–63	29–31	85–91	56–60	28–30	41–49
11	95–98	66–71	33–35	94–96	64–67	32–33	92–96	61–65	31–32	69–71
12	99–103	72–76	36–39	97–100	68–71	34–36	97–98	66–70	33–34	72–81
13	104–111	77–81	40–44	101–105	72–74	37–40	99–105	71–73	35–38	82–89
14	112–120	82–85	45	106–111	75–80	41–44	106–110	74–80	39–42	99–94
15	121–125	86–87	46–50	112–115	81	45	111–115	81	43–45	95–97
16	126–127	88–90	51–52	116–122	82–84	46–49	116–122	82–84	—	98
17	128–131	91–104	53–60	123–130	85–90	50–52	123–130	85–90	46	99
18	>131	>104	>60	>130	>90	>52	>130	>90	>46	>99
N	134	134	134	124	124	124	111	111	111	

(continued)

Table 11.5. *(Continued)*

	Age Group in Years									
Scaled Scores	78–80			81–83			84–86			Percentile
	Word	Color	C/W	Word	Color	C/W	Word	Color	C/W	
2	<41	<23	<4	<41	<23	<4	<41	<23	<4	<1
3	41–44	23	4–	41–44	23	4	41–44	23	4	1
4	45–48	24–26	7–13	45–47	24–25	5–6	45–47	24–25	5–6	2
5	49–52	27–39	14	48–52	26–30	7–10	48–52	26–30	7–10	3–5
6	53–63	40–41	15	53–63	31–39	11–15	53–63	31–39	11–15	6–10
7	64–70	42–45	16–20	64–69	40–42	16	64–69	40–42	16	11–18
8	71–76	46–48	21–22	70–74	43–45	17–19	70–74	43–45	17–19	19–28
9	77–82	49–51	23–25	75–80	46–49	20–22	75–80	46–49	20–22	29–40
10	83–88	52–57	26–28	81–86	50–53	23–25	81–86	50–53	23–25	41–59
11	89–93	58–60	29	87–91	54–56	26–28	87–91	54–56	26–28	60–71
12	94–96	61–65	30–32	92–96	57–59	29–30	92–96	57–59	29–30	72–81
13	97–98	66–71	33–36	97–98	60–64	31–32	97–98	60–64	31–32	82–89
14	99–104	72–75	37–39	99–104	65–71	33–38	99–104	65–71	33–38	90–94
15	105	76–80	40–43	105	72–78	39–40	105	72–78	39–40	95–97
16	106–109	81	44	106–109	79–80	41–43	106–109	79–80	41–43	98
17	110–114	82	45	110–114	81	44	110–114	81	44	99
18	>114	>82	>45	>114	>81	>44	>114	>81	>44	>99
N	88	88	88	79	79	79	79	79	79	

	Age Group in Years						
Scaled Scores	87–89			90–97			Percentile
	Word	Color	C/W	Word	Color	C/W	
2	<41	<23	<4	<41	<23	<4	<1
3	41–44	23	4	41–44	23	4	1
4	45–47	24–25	56	45–47	24–25	56	2
5	48–52	26–30	7–10	48–62	26–30	7–10	3–5
6	53–63	31–39	11–15	53–63	31–39	11–15	6–10
7	64–69	40–42	16	64–69	40–42	16	11–18
8	70–74	43–45	7–19	70–74	43–45	17–19	19–28
9	75–80	46–49	20–22	75–80	46–49	20–22	29–40
10	81–86	50–53	23–25	81–86	50–53	23–25	41–59
11	87–91	54–56	26–28	87–91	54–56	26–28	60–71
12	92–96	57–59	29–30	92–96	57–59	29–30	72–81
13	97–98	60–64	31–32	97–98	60–64	31–32	82–89
14	99–104	65–71	33–38	99–104	65–71	33–38	90–94
15	105	72–78	39–40	105	72–78	39–40	95–97
16	106–109	79–80	41–43	106–109	79–80	41–43	98
17	110–114	81	44	110–114	81	44	99
18	>114	>81	>44	>114	>81	>44	>99
N	79	79	79	79	79	79	

Age-Corrected Norms for Stroop Performance in each Age Group, adapted by Mitrushina, Boone & D'Elia (1999) from Ivnik, R.J., Malec, J.F., Smith, G.E., Tangalos, E.G., & Peterson, R.C. (1996). Neuropsychological tests' norms above age 55: COWAT, BNT, MAE Token, WRAT-R Reading, AMNART, STROOP, TMT, and JLO. *The Clinical Neuropsychologist, 10,* 262–278, © Swets & Zeitlinger. Used with permission.

scores may be converted into Age-Corrected Scaled Scores in the left-hand column. Percentile ranges for each score are presented in the right-hand column.

Four other studies report control data for the Golden (1978) version (Connor et al., 1988; Daigneault, Braun, & Whitaker, 1992; Fisher et al. 1990; Ponsford, 1989). Ponsford obtained control data from a group of 30 orthopeadically injured motor accident rehabilitation patients (24 males, 6 females), aged 16 to 42 years (M = 25.4, SD = 5.9), a mean of 11.4 years of education, with no history of neurological or psychiatric disturbance. Scores obtained by this group are set out in Table 11.6. These norms are useful if one is assessing head-injured patients and wanting to control for the nonspecific effects of trauma and hospitalization. Connor et al. obtained control data from 40 college student volunteers, aged 18 to 32. Daigneault et al. studied 128 French-speaking Canadian control subjects aged 20 to 35 years and 45 to 65 years. Information regarding gender, educational level, occupation, and geographic area is provided, but scores for the color interference subtest only are reported. Fisher et al. studied Golden Stroop performances in 36 older controls, with a mean age of 72.9 +/− 8.3.

Fairly comprehensive normative studies have also been carried out for the Comalli et al. (1962) and Kaplan versions of the Stroop. Six studies provide control data for the Comalli version (Boone, 1999; Boone, Ananath, Philpott, Kaur, & Dienderediians, 1991; Boone, Miller, Lesser, Hill, & D'Elia, 1990; Comalli et al., 1962; Stuss et al., 1985) and two for the Kaplan version (Demick & Harkins, 1997; Strickland, D'Elia, James, & Stein, 1997). For further information regarding these norms, see Mitrushina et al., (1999).

Interpretation

Speed of Information Processing

The Stroop has been shown to be sensitive to deficits in speed of information processing in a broad range of conditions and age groups, including children and adults

Table 11.6.   Mean scores obtained by orthopaedically-injured controls (n = 30), aged 16–42, on the three subtests of the Golden version of the Stroop Color and Word test, from Ponsford, J.L. (1989)

Stroop Subtests	Mean (SD)
Word Reading	
Scores	102.7 (15.5)
Errors	0.5 (0.9)
Color Naming	
Scores	73.7 (12.3)
Errors	0.4 (1.4)
Naming Colors of Words	
Scores	46.2 (10.0)
Errors	1.6 (1.5)

Assessment and rehabilitation of attentional deficits following closed head injury. PhD Thesis, LaTrobe University, Bundoora, Victoria, Australia.

with traumatic brain injury (Chadwick et al., 1981; Ponsford & Kinsella, 1992; Stuss et al., 1985), Alzheimer's disease (Koss et al., 1984), Parkinson's disease (Hanes et al., 1996; Heitanen & Teravainen, 1986; Henik et al., 1993; Portin & Rinne, 1980), Huntington's disease (Hanes et al., 1996), schizophrenia (Hanes et al., 1996), depression (Lemelin et al., 1997; Raskin et al., 1982; Trichard et al., 1995), and anxiety (Batchelor et al., 1995).

A measure of speed of information processing can be obtained by simply comparing the scores obtained on each of the subtests with age-matched normative data. Color naming is generally slower than word reading, and appears to be more vulnerable to the effects of neurological injury of any kind, as well as being lowered by increasing age. The multiplicative effects of slowed information processing may result in more marked slowing on the third, interference subtest.

It is important to note that speed of processing may be slowed for reasons other than the presence of organic brain injury. Slower processing may be evident in those with depression, with obsessive-compulsive disorder, or those who have a more careful problem-solving style, valuing accuracy more than speed. Klein et al. (1997) and Rush et al. (1990) have suggested that older individuals may be more cautious in their approach to the task, at least in the first half. As noted earlier, motor speed should always be taken into account when interpreting test performances.

Measuring Interference Effects

Once speed of information processing has been examined, one of the more important issues regarding test interpretation is measuring the interference effect. The Stroop is a particularly suitable measure of selective attention, or specifically the ability to selectively attend to the relevant color and suppress processing of the word. When the test is used for this purpose, it is the size of the interference effect, which is of interest. According to Stroop's original experiment, the important comparison is between neutral conditions, such as naming colors of blocks of XXXXs or patches, and incongruent conditions, where the subject is required to name the ink color of incongruent color names.

Many studies have simply compared the scores obtained by experimental and control groups on each subtest (i.e., word-reading, color naming, naming colors of incongruent words). However, the presence of significant differences between groups on each condition is indicative of slowed information processing in the patient groups. It does not provide an assessment of the presence of interference effects and thus the status of selective attention in these conditions. This necessitates comparison of performances on neutral and incongruent conditions.

Numerous methods have been used to calculate Stroop interference. The most commonly used method has been that of subtracting the neutral score from the incongruent condition (CW − C). However, Henik (1996) recommends running a two-way ANOVA, in which one factor is group (patient vs control) and the other factor is Stroop condition (neutral vs incongruent). He has argued that apparently significant effects calculated using the simple difference formula were not significant when examined using a two-way ANOVA. Graf et al. (1995) have noted that the difference score lacks sensitivity to slowing associated with advancing age. They recommend using a ratio index of interference (incongruent/congruent, or CW/C). On the basis of examination of regression functions for facilitation and interference effects, Chen (1996, 1997) also concluded that these are the consequence of multiplicative processes, and that the appropriate measure of the Stroop effect should be a ratio measure of the congruent (for facilitation) or conflicting (for interference) naming time over the neutral naming time.

The Dodrill (1978) and Trenerry et al. (1989) versions do not employ any strictly neutral conditions and hence do not properly assess the Stroop interference effect. The first subtest of both these versions requires the subject to read color words, which are printed in incongruent colors, rather than to name the colors of blocks. As Henik (1996) points out, this comparison confounds two different types of interference and two different tasks, reading and naming. It is not possible to differentiate whether poor performance on the second subtest reflects a difference between reading and color naming, or the interference of words with colors, or both. The score derived has been recommended as that which best differentiates brain-damaged subjects from controls, but this does not necessarily mean that they are differentiated on the basis of the presence of the interference effect. It may simply mean they are differentiated on the basis of speed of information processing. A neutral condition is necessary in order to separate general speed of responding from the interference effect.

The Golden (1978), Comalli et al. (1962)/Kaplan and Victoria versions of the Stroop do employ the neutral and incongruent conditions from Stroop's second experiment. These versions may therefore be used to examine resistance to interference by employing the methods recommended above—that is, dividing the score for the incongruent condition by that for the neutral color naming condition. If analyzing group data a one-way ANOVA could be employed, as recommended by Henik (1996).

Reading Proficiency

Following from the findings of Cox et al. (1997), it is also important to evaluate reading proficiency. The subject's word-reading score should be greater than or equal to Full Scale IQ in order to elicit the interference effect. According to Golden (1978), subjects with dyslexia typically obtain word scores below 50, alongside normal color scores and above normal color-word scores

On reviewing the findings of numerous studies of the Stroop effect in bilinguals, MacLeod (1991) concluded that, "Interference between two languages of a bilingual, although not as great as that within either one of the languages, is very robust: between-language interference typically is about 75 percent of within language interference. Furthermore, a dominant language has more potential for interfering than does a nondominant one." Certain languages, such as Chinese, appear to be more vulnerable to interference than others (Biederman & Tsao, 1979, cited in MacLeod, 1991). In bilinguals for whom the language of Stroop administration is not the first language, it is therefore also necessary to consider this factor when interpreting the strength of interference effects.

Visual Acuity/Color Vision

It is important to assess the subject's visual acuity and color vision prior to administering this task. Dyer (1973) found that degrading the word image, as may occur in cases of blurred vision or impaired visual acuity, diminishes the interference effect on the incongruent naming task. Color-blindness will obviously interfere with color naming. Patients with visuospatial neglect and other visual scanning difficulties are also likely to have great difficulty in scanning the columns and rows.

Effects of Medication

A number of medications are known to affect performance on cognitive tasks. Call-away and Stone (1960, cited in Golden, 1978) found that stimulant drugs (methamphet-amine) resulted in a decrease in Stroop interference effects and an increase in other subtest scores, whereas depressant medication (amoarbitol) caused a decline in performance on all Stroop subtests. Miller, Drew, and Kiplinger (1972) failed to find any effects on the Stroop from administration of marijuana to naïve subjects. In view of the known effects of many medications upon speed of processing and other aspects of attention, it is important to take the effects of medication into account when interpreting test performance, and preferably to assess the person when they are as free as possible of the effects of medication.

Practice Effects

In the light of the evidence of practice effects even when alternate forms of the Stroop are used, it is recommended to give the subject at least one practice trial, and to control for practice effects in group studies

Malingering

Osimani et al. (1997) used a computerized version of the Stroop test to examine its sensitivity in detection of malingering. Controls and brain-damaged subjects showed a clear Stroop effect, whilst simulators had significantly longer reaction times, increased error percentage but an inverted or absent Stroop interference effect. This pattern is identified as characteristic of feigning, independently of knowledge of the test.

Patterns of Test Performance

Brain-injured patients with diffuse injuries typically exhibit generalized slowing on all subtests. Patients with focal frontal lesions will perform the Stroop more slowly. They are also more likely to exhibit relatively greater interference effects, although the examiner needs to be careful to discriminate interference from general slowing using the methods recommended earlier. Normal Stroop scores do not rule out the presence of brain injury. For example, the Stroop will not necessarily be sensitive to the effects of mild traumatic brain injury. Moreover, given that Stroop performance may also be impaired in patients with a range of psychiatric diagnoses, it is always important to consider the influence of the person's psychiatric state upon test performance. Following from Osimani et al.'s (1997) findings, an absent or inverted Stroop interference effect in the presence of an increased error percentage and longer reaction times, is suggestive of feigning poor performance on the task. Effects of medication upon speed of performance should also be considered.

ASSESSING ATTENTION IN REAL WORLD CONTEXTS

Although some tasks, such as the Test of Everyday Attention, attempt to use materials and a context which have real-world significance to those being assessed, it must be recognized that this does not establish it as an ecologically valid test of attention in everyday life. It is still conducted within a quiet and structured assessment setting, in isolation from the real world. In a group of stroke patients, Robertson et al. (1994) have demonstrated modest correlations between some of the TEA subtests (Map Search and Elevator Counting) with scores on measures of ADL competence, the Barthel Index, and the Extended Activities of Daily Living Scale, as well as scores on a Rating Scale of Attentional Behavior (Ponsford & Kinsella, 1991). Numerous other studies have demonstrated significant associations between performance on attentional measures including reaction time, Digit Symbol-Coding, and the Trail Making Test and present or future independence in activities of daily living, employment, and social role performance (Fraser, Dikmen, McLean, & Temkin, 1988; Klonoff, Costa, & Snow, 1986; van Zomeren, 1981). However, it seems clear that, no matter how complex the task, no structured experimental or neuropsychological assessment situation can capture the full extent and variety of attentional difficulties experienced by TBI individuals in their daily lives. To date, there has been relatively little research assessing attentional behavior in everyday contexts.

Whyte et al. (1996) have attempted to measure distractibility in behavioral terms. Subjects were seated in a room with a research assistant. They were given a range of tasks to perform (e.g., shape sorting, jig saw) over a 45-minute period. "Naturalistic" distractions, such as the research assistant dropping a book or making a telephone call were introduced in a carefully controlled fashion. Inattentive behavior was defined by direction of head and/or eyes away from the task materials, or conversation. These behaviors occurred in response to the distractions with significantly higher frequency in severe TBI subjects than they did in controls. Although this setting was highly controlled, and thus far from the real world, this study does represent a useful first step toward measuring attentional behavior in objective and observable terms.

Another means of assessing attentional behavior is via the use of behavior rating scales or checklists. Ponsford and Kinsella (1991) developed a Rating Scale of Attentional Behavior for use in rehabilitation settings. Items reflected a broad range of observable clinical behaviors, also linked conceptually with aspects of attention, including alertness, selective attention, and sustained attention. Ratings on the items were made by therapists on the basis of observation of TBI patients' behavior in the context of different therapy settings.

The scale showed some validity as a measure of attentional behavior. It showed modest, but statistically significant correlations with neuropsychological measures of attention, including the Stroop, choice reaction time, Symbol Digit Modalities Test and PASAT ($r = .35–.55$) and a high level of internal consistency (Alpha = .91–.95). Reliability of ratings made by the same therapist three days apart was also very good, all correlation coefficients being above .91. However the correlations between ratings made by different raters in different contexts, although statistically significant, were lower (.50–.56). There is a significant influence of context and the frame of reference of the rater upon such ratings. These need to be taken into consideration when interpreting the results obtained on such scales.

In spite of this, the pattern of ratings of a group of 50 severe TBI patients' behavior was very similar across therapists. In all instances, the highest rating was given for the item rating the head-injured patients' slowness in performing mental tasks. Other items which were rated consistently higher (more impaired) than others included "being able to pay attention to more than one thing at once," "making mistakes because he/she wasn't paying attention properly," and "missing important details in what he/she was doing." The items rated lowest overall related to "staring into space for long periods" and "being restless."

There is a need for further work in developing measures of this nature that capture the perspective of therapists, family members, and others spending time with the injured person in a broader range of contexts. While the subjective nature of such measures limits their reliability, the observations of others should contribute to a balanced assessment of attentional abilities. For a more detailed discussion of methods of assessment of attentional behavior as it impacts upon performance of activities of daily living and the overall lifestyle of the injured person, the reader is referred to Sloan and Ponsford (1995).

RECOMMENDED READING

Golden, C.J. (1978). *Stroop color and word test.* Chicago: Stoelting.

Lezak, M.D. (1995). *Neuropsychological assessment* (3rd ed.). New York: Oxford University Press.

MacLeod, C.M. (1991). Half a century of research on the Stroop effect: An integrative review. *Psychological Bulletin, 109,* 163–203.

Mitrushina, M.N., Boone, K.B., & D'Elia, L.F. (1999). *Handbook of normative data for neuropsychological assessment.* New York: Oxford University Press.

Spreen, O., & Strauss, E. (1998). *A compendium of neuropsychological tests* (2nd ed.). New York: Oxford University Press.

Trenerry, M.R., Crosson, B., DeBoe, J., & Leber, W.R. (1989). *Stroop neuropsychological screening test.* Odessa, FL: Psychological Assessment Resources.

REFERENCES

Abas, M.A., Sahakian, B.J., & Levy, R. (1990). Neuropsychological deficits and CT scan changes in early depressives. *Psychological Medicine, 20,* 507–520.

Aloia, M.S., Weed, N.C., & Marx, B. (1997). Some construct network effects of modifying the Stroop Color and Word Test. *The Clinical Neuropsychologist, 11,* 54–58.

Baddeley, A.D. (1986). *Working memory.* London: Oxford University Press.

Baddeley, A.D. (1993). Working memory or working attention? In A.D. Baddeley & L. Weiskrantz (Eds.), *Attention: Selection, awareness and control. A tribute to Donald Broadbent.* Oxford, England: Oxford University Press.

Batchelor, J., Harvey, A.G., & Bryant, R.A. (1995). Stroop colour word test as a measure of attentional deficit following mild head injury. *The Clinical Neuropsychologist, 9,* 180–186.

Baxter, R.D., & Liddle, P.F. (1998). Neuropsychological deficits associated with schizophrenic syndromes. *Schizophrenia Research, 30,* 239–249.

Bench, C.J., Frith, C.D., Grasby, P.M., Friston, K.J., Paulesu, E., Frackowiak, R.S.J., & Dolan, R.J. (1993). Investigations of the functional anatomy of attention using the Stroop test. *Neuropsychologia, 31,* 907–922.

Bohnen, N., Jolles, J., & Twijnstra, A. (1992). Modification of the Stroop color word test improves differentiation between patients with mild head injury and matched controls. *The Clinical Neuropsychologist, 6,* 178–184.

Bohnen, N., Twijnstra, A., & Jolles, J. (1992). Performance in the Stroop color word test in relationship to the persistence of symptoms following mild head injury. *Acta Neurologica Scandinavica, 85,* 116–121.

Boone, K.B. (1999). Clinical neuropsychological assessment of executive functions: Impact of age, education, gender, intellectual level, and vascular status on executive test scores. In B.L. Miller & J. Cummings (Eds.), *The frontal lobes* (pp. 247–260). New York: Guilford Press.

Boone, K.B., Ananth, J., Philpott, L., Kaur, A., & Djenderedjian, A. (1991). Neuropsychological characteristics of nondepressed adults with obsessive-compulsive disorder. *Neuropsychiatry, Neuropsychology, and Behavioral Neurology, 4,* 96–109.

Boone, K.B., Miller, B.L., Lesser, I.M., Hill, E., & D'Elia, L. (1990). Performance on frontal lobe tests in healthy older individuals. *Developmental Neuropsychology, 6,* 215–223.

Bornstein, R.A. (1985). Normative data on selected neuropsychological measures from a nonclinical sample. *Journal of Clinical Psychology, 41,* 651–659.

Brand, N., & Jolles, J. (1987). Information processing in depression and anxiety. *Psychological Medicine, 17,* 145–153.

Breslow, R., Kocsis, J., & Belkin, B. (1980). Memory deficits in depression: Evidence utilizing the Wechsler Memory Scale. *Perceptual and Motor Skills, 51,* 541–542.

Brickenkamp, R. (1981). *Test d-2, Aufmerksamkeits-Belastungstet.* Goetingen, Germany: Hogrefe-Verlag.

Brittain, J.L., LaMarche, J.A., Reeder, K.P., Roth, D.L., & Boll, T.J. (1991). Effects of age and IQ on Paced Auditory Serial Addition Task (PASAT) performance. *The Clinical Neuropsychologist, 5,* 163–175.

Bruins, R., van Niewenhuizen, C.H., & Brouwer, W.H. (1990). *PASAT is PVSAT?* Unpublished manuscript, State University Groningen, Department of Neuropsychology, The Netherlands.

Calvo, M.G., & Alamo, L. (1987). Test anxiety and motor performance: The role of muscular and attentional demands. *International Journal of Psychology, 22,* 165–178.

Carter, C.S., Mintun, M., & Cohen, J.D. (1995). Interference and facilitation effects during selective attention: An H2150 PET study of Stroop task performance. *Neuroimage, 2,* 264–272.

Carter, C.S., Mintun, M., Nichols, T., & Cohen, J.D. (1997). Anterior cingulate gyrus dysfunction and selective attention deficits in schizophrenia: [150]H20 PET study during single-trial Stroop task performance. *American Journal of Psychiatry, 154,* 1670–1675.

Chadwick, O., Rutter, M., Brown, G., Shaffer, D., & Traub, M. (1981). A prospective study of children with head injuries: II. Cognitive sequelae. *Psychological Medicine, 11,* 49–61.

Chen, J.Y. (1996). A problem in measuring the Stroop facilitation and interference effects: Implications for measuring performance change in general. *Perceptual and Motor Skills, 83,* 1059–1070.

Chen, J.Y. (1997). How should the Stroop interference effect be measured? Further evidence from alternative versions of the Stroop task. *Perceptual and Motor Skills, 84,* 1123–1133.

Chronicle, E.P., & MacGregor, N.A. (1998). Are PASAT scores related to mathematical ability? *Neuropsychological Rehabilitation, 8,* 273–282.

Cohen, J.D., Dunbar, K., & McClelland, J.L. (1990). On the control of automatic processes: A parallel distributed processing account of the Stroop effect. *Psychological Review, 97,* 332–361.

Cohn, N.B., Dustman, R.E., & Bradford, D.C. (1984). Age-related decrements in Stroop color test performance. *Journal of Clinical Psychology, 40,* 1244–1250.

Colby, C.A., & Gotlib, I.H. (1988). Memory deficits in depression. *Cognitive Therapy and Research, 12,* 611–627.

Comalli, P.E. Jr., Wapner, S., & Werner, H. (1962). Interference effects of Stroop color-word test in childhood, adulthood, and aging. *Journal of Genetic Psychology, 100,* 47–53.

Connor, A., Franzen, M., & Sharp, B. (1988). Effects of practice and differential instructions on Stroop performance. *International Journal of Clinical Neuropsychology, 10,* 1–4.

Cools, A.R., Van den Bercken, J.H.L., Horstink, M.W.I., Van Spaendonck, K.P.M., & Berger, H.J.C. (1984). Cognitive and motor shifting aptitude disorder in Parkinson's disease. *Journal of Neurology, Neurosurgery and Psychiatry, 47,* 443–453.

Cox, C.S., Chee, E., Chase, G.A., Baumgardner, T.L., Scherholz, L.J., Reader, M.J., Mohr, J., & Denckla, M.B. (1997). Reading proficiency affects the construct validity of the Stroop test interference score. *The Clinical Neuropsychologist, 11,* 105–110.

Crawford, J.R., Obonsawin, M.C., & Allan, K.M. (1998). PASAT and components of WAIS-R performance: Convergent and discriminant validity. *Neuropsychological Rehabilitation, 8,* 255–272.

Daigneault, S., Braun, C.M.J., & Whitaker, H.A. (1992). Early effects of normal aging on perseverative and non-perseverative prefrontal measures. *Developmental Neuropsychology, 8,* 99–114.

Deary, I.J., Langan, S.J., Hepburn, D.A., & Frier, B.M. (1991). Which abilities does the PASAT test? *Personality and Individual Differences, 12,* 983–987.

Demick, J., & Harkins, D. (1997). *Role of cognitive style in the driving skills of young, middle-aged and older adults.* American association of retired persons (AARP) Andrus Foundation final grant report, Washington, DC.

Dodrill, C.B. (1978). A neuropsychological battery for epilepsy. *Epilepsia, 19,* 611–623.

Dulaney, C.L., & Rogers, W.A. (1994). Mechanisms underlying reduction in Stroop interference with practice in young and old adults. *Journal of Experimental Psychology: Learning, Memory, and Cognition, 20,* 470–484.

Dyche, G.M., & Johnson, D.A. (1991). Development and evaluation of CHIPASAT, an attention test for children: II. Test-retest reliability and practice effect for a normal sample. *Perceptual and Motor Skills, 72,* 563–572.

Dyer, F.N. (1973). The Stroop phenomenon and its use in the study of perceptual, cognitive and response processes. *Memory and Cognition, 1,* 106–120.

Egan, V. (1988). PASAT: Observed correlations with IQ. *Personality and Individual Differences, 9,* 179–180.

Elting, R., van Zomeren, A.H., & Brouwer, W.H. (1989). Flexibility of attention after severe head injury. *Journal of Clinical and Experimental Neuropsychology, 11,* 370.

Emmerson, R.Y., Dustman, R.E., Shearer, D.E., & Turner, C.W. (1990). P3 latency and symbol digit performance correlations in aging. *Experimental Aging Research, 15,* 151–159.

Feinstein, A., Brown, R., & Ron, M. (1994). Effects of practice on serial tests of attention in healthy subjects. *Journal of Clinical and Experimental Neuropsychology, 16,* 436–447.

Fisher, L.M., Freed, D.M., & Corkin, S. (1990). Stroop color-word test performance in Alzheimer's disease. *Journal of Clinical and Experimental Neuropsychology, 12,* 745–758.

Fraser, R., Dikmen, S., McLean, A., & Temkin, N. (1988). Employability of head injury survivors: First year post injury. *Rehabilitation Counselling Bulletin, 31,* 276–288.

Gass, C.S., & Russell, E.W. (1986). Differential impact of brain damage and depression on memory test performance. *Journal of Consulting and Clinical Psychology, 54,* 261–263.

Gilmore, G.C., Royer, F.L., & Gruhn, J.J. (1983). Age differences in symbol-digit substitution task performance. *Journal of Clinical Psychology, 39,* 114–124.

Glosser, G., Butters, N., & Kaplan, E. (1977). Visuoperceptual processes in brain-damaged patients on the Digit Symbol Substitution task. *International Journal of Neuroscience, 7,* 59–66.

Golden, C.J. (1975a). A group version of the Stroop color and word test. *Journal of Personality Assessment, 39,* 386–388.

Golden, C.J. (1975b). The measurement of creativity by the Stroop color and word test. *Journal of Personality Assessment, 39,* 502–506.

Golden, C.J. (1976). Identification of brain disorders by the Stroop color and word test. *Journal of Clinical Psychology, 32,* 654–658.

Golden, C.J. (1978). *Stroop color and word test.* Chicago: Stoelting.

Grady, C.L., Haxby, J.V., Horwitz, B., Sundaram, M., Berg, G., Schapiro, M., Friedland, R.P., & Rapoport, S.I. (1988). Longitudinal study of the early neuropsychological and cerebral metabolic changes in dementia of the Alzheimer type. *Journal of Clinical and Experimental Neuropsychology, 10,* 576–596.

Graf, P., Uttl, B., & Tuokko, H. (1995). Color- and picture-word Stroop tests: Performance changes in old age. *Journal of Clinical and Experimental Neuropsychology, 17,* 390–415.

Gronwall, D.M.A. (1976). Performance changes during recovery from closed head injury. *Proceedings of the Australian Association of Neurologists, 13,* 143–147.

Gronwall, D.M.A. (1977). Paced auditory serial-addition task: A measure of recovery from concussion. *Perceptual and Motor Skills, 44,* 367–373.

Gronwall, D.M.A., & Sampson, H. (1974). *The psychological effects of concussion.* Auckland: Auckland University Press.

Gronwall, D.M.A., & Wrightson, P. (1974). Delayed recovery of intellectual function after minor head injury. *The Lancet, 2,* 605–609.

Gronwall, D.M.A., & Wrightson, P. (1975). Cumulative effect of concussion. *The Lancet, 2,* 995–997.

Gronwall, D.M.A., & Wrightson, P. (1981). Memory and information processing capacity after closed head injury. *Journal of Neurology, Neurosurgery and Psychiatry, 44,* 889–895.

Haaland, K.Y., Temkin, N., Randahl, G., & Dikmen, S. (1994). Recovery of simple motor skills after head injury. *Journal of Clinical and Experimental Neuropsychology, 16,* 448–456.

Hanes, K.R., Andrewes, D.G., Smith, D.J., & Pantelis, C. (1996). A brief assessment of executive control dysfunction: Discriminant validity and homogeneity of planning, set shift, and fluency measures. *Archives of Clinical Neuropsychology, 11,* 185–191.

Harbeson, M.M., Kennedy, R.S., & Bittner, A.C. (1981). A comparison of the Stroop to other tasks for studies of environmental stress. *US Naval Biodynamics Laboratory* 80R008, 20–28. (From *Psychological Abstracts,* 1983, 69, Abstract no 7060.)

Haslam, C., Batchelor, J., Fearnside, M.R., Haslam, A.S., & Hawkins, S. (1995). Further examination of post-traumatic amnesia and post-coma disturbance as non-linear predictors of outcome after head injury. *Neuropsychology, 9,* 599–605.

Heaton, R.K., Grant, I., & Matthews, C.G. (1986). Differences in neuropsychological test performance associated with age, education, and sex. In I. Grant & K.M. Adams (Eds.), *Neuropsychological assessment of neuropsychiatric disorders.* New York: Oxford University Press.

Henik, A. (1996). Paying attention to the Stroop effect? *Journal of the International Neuropsychological Society, 2,* 467–470.

Henik, A., Singh, J., Beckley, D.J., & Rafal, R.D. (1993). Disinhibition of automatic word reading in Parkinson's disease. *Cortex, 29,* 589–599.

Hentschel, U. (1973). Two new interference tests compared to the Stroop color-word test. *Psychological Research Bulletin, Lund University, 13,* 1–24.

Hepp, H.H., Maier, S., Hermle, L., & Spitzer, M. (1996). The Stroop effect in schizophrenic patients. *Schizophrenia Research, 22,* 187–195.

Hietanen, M., & Teravainen, H. (1986). Cognitive performance in early Parkinson's disease. *Acta Neurologica Scandinavica, 73,* 151–159.

Hinton-Bayre, A.D., Geffen, G., & McFarland, K. (1997). Mild head injury and speed of information processing: A prospective study of professional rugby league players. *Journal of Clinical and Experimental Neuropsychology, 19,* 275–289.

Holst, P., & Vilkki, J. (1988). Effect of frontomedial lesions on performance on the Stroop test and word fluency tasks [Abstract]. *Journal of Clinical and Experimental Neuropsychology, 10,* 79.

Houx, P.J., Jolles, J., & Vreeling, F.W. (1993). Stroop interference: Aging effects assessed with the Stroop color-word test. *Experimental Aging Research, 19,* 209–224.

Ivnik, R.J., Malec, J.F., Smith, G.E., Tangalos, E.G., & Peterson, R.C. (1996). Neuropsychological tests' norms above age 55: COWAT, BNT, MAE Token, WRAT-R Reading, AMNART, STROOP, TMT, and JLO. *The Clinical Neuropsychologist, 10,* 262–278.

Jensen, A.R. (1965). Scoring the Stroop test. *Acta Psychologica, 24,* 398–408.

Jensen, A.R., & Rohwer, W.D. (1966). The Stroop color-word test: A review. *Acta Psychologica, 25,* 36–93.

Johnson, D.A., Roethig-Johnston, K., & Middleton, J. (1988). Development and evaluation of an attentional test for head injured children: I. Information processing capacity in a normal sample. *Journal of Child Psychology and Psychiatry and Allied Disciplines, 29,* 199–208.

Kanne, S.M., Balota, D.A., Spieler, & Faust, M.E. (1998). Explorations of Cohen, Dunbar, and McClelland's (1990) connectionist model of Stroop performance. *Psychological Review, 105,* 174–187.

Kaplan, E., Fein, D., Morris, R., & Delis, D.C. (1991). *WAIS-R as a neuropsychological instrument.* San Antonio, TX: The Psychological Corporation.

Klein, M., Ponds, R.W.H.M., Houx, P.J., & Jolles, J. (1997). Effect of test duration on age-related differences in Stroop interference. *Journal of Clinical and Experimental Neuropsychology, 19,* 77–82.

Klonoff, P.S., Costa, L.D., & Snow, W.G. (1986). Predictors and indicators of quality of life in patients with closed head injury. *Journal of Clinical and Experimental Neuropsychology, 8,* 469–485.

Koss, E., Ober, B.A., Delis, D.C., & Friedland, R.P. (1984). The Stroop color-word test: Indicator of dementia severity. *International Journal of Neuroscience, 24,* 53–61.

Leininger, B., Gramling, S., & Farrell, A. (1990). Neuropsychological deficits in symptomatic minor head injury patients after concussion and mild concussion. *Journal of Neurology, Neurosurgery and Psychiatry, 53,* 293–296.

Lemelin, S., Baruch, P., Vincent, A., Everett, J., & Vincent, P. (1997). Distractibility and processing resource deficit in major depression. Evidence for two deficient processing models. *Journal of Nervous and Mental Diseases, 185,* 542–548.

Levin, H.S., Mattis, S., Ruff, R.M., Eisenberg, H.M., Marshall, L.F., Tabbador, K., High, W.M., Jr., & Frankowski, R.F. (1987) Neurobehavioral outcome following minor head injury: A three-center study. *Journal of Neurosurgery, 66,* 234–243..

Levin, H.S., O'Donnell, V.M., & Grossman, R.G. (1979). The Galveston Orientation and Amnesia Test. *Journal of Nervous and Mental Disease, 167,* 675–684.

Lezak, M.D. (1995). *Neuropsychological assessment* (3rd ed.). New York: Oxford University Press.

MacLeod, C.M. (1991). Half a century of research on the Stroop effect: An integrative review. *Psychological Bulletin, 109,* 163–203.

McGrath, J., Scheldt, S., Welham, J., & Clair, A. (1997). Performance on tests sensitive to impaired executive ability in schizophrenia, mania and well controls: Acute and subacute phases. *Schizophrenia Research, 26,* 127–137.

Mewhort, D.J., Braun, J.G., & Heathcote, A. (1992). Response time distributions and the Stroop task: A test of the Cohen, Dunbar and McClelland (1990) model. *Journal of Experimental Psychology: Human Perception and Performance, 18,* 872–882.

Miller, L., Drew, W.G., & Kiplinger, G. (1972). Effects of marijuana on recall of narrative material and stroop color word performance. *Nature, 237,* 172–173.

Mirsky, A.F. (1989). The neuropsychology of attention: Elements of a complex behaviour. In E. Perecman (Ed.), *Integrating theory and practice in neuropsychology* (pp. 75–91). Hillsdale, NJ: Erlbaum.

Mitrushina, M.N., Boone, K.B., & D'Elia, L.F. (1999). *Handbook of normative data for neuropsychological assessment.* New York: Oxford University Press.

Morgan, S.F., & Wheelock, J. (1992). Digit Symbol and Symbol Digit Modalities Tests: Are they directly interchangeable? *Neuropsychology, 6,* 327–330.

Norman, D.A., & Shallice, T. (1980). Attention to action: Willed and automatic control of behaviour. *Center for Human Information Processing Technical Report no. 99.*

O'Donnell, J.P., MacGregor, L.A., Dabrowski, J.J., Oestreicher, J.M., & Romero, J.J. (1994). Construct validity of neuropsychological tests of conceptual and attentional abilities. *Journal of Clinical Psychology, 50,* 596–600.

O'Shaughnessy, E.J., Fowler, R.S., & Reid, V. (1984). Sequelae of mild closed head injuries. *Journal of Family Practice, 18,* 391–394.

Osimani, A., Alon, A., Berger, A., & Abarbanel, J.M. (1997). Use of the Stroop phenomenon as a diagnostic tool for malingering. *Journal of Neurology, Neurosurgery and Psychiatry, 62,* 617–621.

Pardo, J.V., Pardo, P.J., Janer, K.W., & Raichle, M.E. (1990). The anterior cingulate cortex mediates processing selection in the Stroop attentional conflict paradigm. *Proceedings of the National Academy of Science USA, 87,* 256–259.

Pati, P., & Dash, A.S. (1990a). Effects of grade, sex and achievement levels on intelligence, incidental memory and Stroop scores. *Psychological Studies, 35,* 36–40.

Pati, P., & Dash, A.S. (1990b). Interrelationships between incidental memory, non-verbal intelligence and Stroop scores. *Psycho Lingua, 20,* 27–31.

Perret, E. (1974). The left frontal lobe of man and the suppression of habitual responses in verbal categorical behaviour. *Neuropsychologia, 12,* 323–330.

Ponsford, J.L. (1989). *Assessment and rehabilitation of attentional deficits following closed head injury.* PhD Thesis, LaTrobe University, Bundoora, Victoria, Australia.

Ponsford, J.L., & Kinsella, G. (1991). The use of a rating scale of attentional behaviour. *Neuropsychological Rehabilitation, 1,* 241–257.

Ponsford, J.L., & Kinsella, G. (1992). Attentional deficits following closed-head injury. *Journal of Clinical and Experimental Neuropsychology, 14,* 822–838.

Ponsford, J.L., Willmott, Rothwell, A., Cameron, P., Kelly, A., Nelms, R., & Curran, C. (1996). Outcome following mild traumatic brain injury in adults [Abstract]. *Journal of the International Neuropsychological Society, 4,* 75.

Portin, R., & Rinne, U.K. (1980). Neuropsychological responses of Parkinsonian patients to long-term levodopa treatment. In U.K. Rinne, M. Klinger, & G. Stamm (Eds.), *Parkinson's disease: Current progress, problems and management* (pp. 271–304). Amsterdam, The Netherlands: Elsevier/North Holland.

Posner, M.I., & Petersen, S.E. (1990). The attention system of the human brain. *Annual Review of Neurosciences, 13,* 25–42.

Posner, M.I., & Rothbart, M.K. (1992). Attentional mechanisms and conscious experience. In A.D. Milner & M.D. Rugg (Eds.), *The neuropsychology of consciousness.* London: Academic Press.

Purdon, S.E. (1998). Olfactory identification and Stroop interference converge in schizophrenia. *Journal of Psychiatry and Neuroscience, 23,* 163–171.

Raskin, A., Friedman, A.S., & DiMascio, A. (1982). Cognitive and performance deficits in depression. *Psychopharmacology Bulletin, 18,* 196–202.

Regard, M. (1981). *Cognitive rigidity and flexibility: A neuropsychological study.* Unpublished Ph.D. dissertation, University of Victoria.

Reisberg, D., Baron, J., & Kemler, D.G. (1980). Overcoming Stroop interference: The effects of practice on distractor potency. *Journal of Experimental Psychology: Human Perception and Performance, 6,* 140–150.

Reitan, R.M., & Wolfson, D. (1993). *The Halstead Reitan Neuropsychological Test Battery: Theory and clinical interpretation.* Tucson, AZ: Neuropsychology Press.

Renaud, P., & Blondin, J.P. (1997). The stress of Stroop performance: Physiological and emotional response to color-word interference task pacing, and pacing speed. *International Journal of Psychophysiology, 27,* 87–97.

Richards, M., Cote, L.J., & Stern, Y. (1993). Executive function in Parkinson's disease: Set-shifting or set-maintenance? *Journal of Clinical and Experimental Neuropsychology, 15,* 266–279.

Richardson, E.D., & Marottoli, R.A. (1996). Education-specific normative data on common neuropsychological indices for individuals older than 75 years. *The Clinical Neuropsychologist, 10,* 375–381.

Robertson, I.H., Ward, T., Ridgeway, V., & Nimmo-Smith, I. (1994). *The test of everyday attention.* Bury St. Edmunds: Thames Valley Test Company.

Roman, D.D., Edwall, G.E., Buchanan, R.J., & Patton, J.H. (1991). Extended norms for the paced auditory serial addition task. *The Clinical Neuropsychologist, 5,* 33–40.

Rosinski, R.R., Golinkoff, R.M., & Kukish, K.S. (1975). Automatic semantic processing in a picture-word interference task. *Child Development, 46,* 247–253.

Rossi, A., Daneluzzo, E., Mattei, P., Bustini, M., Casacchia, M., & Stratta, P. (1997). Wisconsin card sorting test and Stroop test performance in schizophrenia: A shared construct. *Neuroscience Letters, 226,* 87–90.

Ruff, R.M., Niemann, H., Allen, C.C., Farrow, C.E., & Wylie, T. (1992). The Ruff 2 and 7 Selective Attention test: A neuropsychological application. *Perceptual and Motor Skills, 75,* 1311–1319.

Rush, M.C., Panek, P.E., & Russell, J.E. (1990). Analysis of individual variability among older adults on the Stroop color word interference test. *International Journal of Aging and Human Development, 30,* 225–236.

Sacks, T.L., Clark, C.R., Pols, R.G., & Geffen, L.B. (1991). Comparability and stability of performance of six alternate forms of the Dodrill-Stroop colour-word test. *The Clinical Neuropsychologist, 5,* 220–225.

Sampson, H. (1956). Pacing and performance on a serial addition task. *Canadian Journal of Psychology, 10,* 219–225.

Shallice, T. (1982). Specific impairments of planning. In D.E. Broadbent & L. Weiskrantz (Eds.), *The neuropsychology of cognitive function* (pp. 199–209). London: The Royal Society.

Shallice, T. (1988). *From neuropsychology to mental structure.* Cambridge, England: Cambridge University Press.

Shallice, T., & Burgess, P.W. (1991) Deficits in strategy application following frontal lobe damage in man. *Brain, 114,* 727–741.

Sherman, E.M.S., Strauss, E., & Spellacy, F. (1997). Validity of the Paced Auditory Serial Addition Test (PASAT) in adults referred for neuropsychological assessment after head injury. *The Clinical Neuropsychologist, 11,* 34–45.

Sherman, E.M.S., Strauss, E., Spellacy, F., & Hunter, M. (1995). Construct validity of WAIS-R factors: Neuropsychological test correlates in adults referred for possible head injury. *Psychological Assessment, 7,* 440–444.

Shiffrin, R.M., & Schneider, W. (1977). Controlled and automatic human information processing: II. Perceptual learning, automatic attending and a general theory. *Psychological Review, 84,* 127–190.

Shor, R.E. (1971). Symbol processing speed differences and symbol interference effects in a variety of concept domains. *Journal of General Psychology, 85,* 187–205.

Shores, E.A., Marosszeky, J.E., Sandanam, J., & Batchelor, J. (1986). Preliminary validation of a scale for measuring the duration of post-traumatic amnesia. *Medical Journal of Australia, 144,* 569–572.

Shum, D.H.K., McFarland, K.A., & Bain, J.D. (1990). Construct validity of eight tests of attention: Comparison of normal and closed head injured samples. *The Clinical Neuropsychologist, 4,* 141–162.

Siegrist, M. (1995). Reliability of the stroop test with single stimulus presentation. *Perceptual and Motor Skills, 81,* 1295–1298.

Sloan, S., & Ponsford, J.L. (1995). Assessment of cognitive difficulties. In J. Ponsford, S. Sloan, & P. Snow (Eds.), *Traumatic brain injury: Rehabilitation for everyday adaptive living* (pp. 65–101).

Smith, A. (1991). *Symbol digit modalities test.* Los Angeles: Western Psychological Services.

Spieler, D.H., Balota, D.A., & Faust, (1996). Stroop performance in healthy younger and older adults and in individuals with dementia of the Alzheimer's type. *Journal of Experimental Psychology: Human Perception and Performance, 22,* 461–479.

Spreen, O., & Strauss, E. (1998). *A compendium of neuropsychological tests* (2nd ed.). New York: Oxford University Press.

Strauss, E., Spellacy, F., Hunter, M., & Berry, T. (1994). Assessing believable deficits on measures of attention and information processing capacity. *Archives of Clinical Neuropsychology, 9,* 483–490.

Strickland, T., D'Elia, L., James, R., & Stein, R. (1997). Stroop color-word performance of African Americans. *The Clinical Neuropsychologist, 11,* 87–90.

Stromgren, L.S. (1977). The influence of depression on memory. *Acta Psychiatrica Scandinavica, 56,* 109–128.

Stroop, J.R. (1935). Studies of interference in serial verbal reactions. *Journal of Experimental Psychology, 18,* 643–662.

Stuss, D.T., Ely, P., Hugenholtz, H., Richard, M.T., Larochelle, S., Poirier, C.A., & Bell, I. (1985). Subtle neuropsychological deficits in patients with good recovery after closed head injury. *Neurosurgery, 17,* 41–47.

Stuss, D.T., Stethem, L.L., Hugenholtz, H., Picton, T., Pivik, J., & Richard, M.T. (1989). Reaction time after head injury: Fatigue, divided and focused attention, and consistency of performance. *Journal of Neurology, Neurosurgery, and Psychiatry, 52,* 742–748.

Stuss, D.T., Stethem, L.L., & Pelchat, G. (1988). Three tests of attention and rapid information processing: An extension. *The Clinical Neuropsychologist, 2,* 246–250.

Stuss, D.T., Stethem, L.L., & Poirier, C.A. (1987). Comparison of three tests of attention and rapid information processing across six age groups. *The Clinical Neuropsychologist, 1,* 139–152.

Taylor, S.F., Kornblum, S., Lauber, E.J., Minoshima, S., & Koeppe, R.A. (1997). Isolation of specific interference processing in the Stroop task: PET activation studies. *Neuroimage, 6,* 81–92.

Teasdale, G., & Jennett, B. (1976). Assessment and prognosis of coma after head injury. *Acta Neurochirurgica, 34,* 45–55.

Thomas, J., Raoux, N., Everett, J., Dantchev, N., & Widl'ocher, D. (1997). Deficit in selective attention and its evolution in depression. *Encephale, 23,* 108–112.

Trenerry, M.R., Crosson, B., DeBoe, J., & Leber, W.R. (1989). *Stroop neuropsychological screening test.* Odessa, FL: Psychological Assessment Resources.

Trenerry, M.R., Crosson, B., DeBoe, J., & Leber, W.R. (1990). *Visual search and attention test.* Odessa, FL: Psychological Assessment Resources.

Trichard, C., Martinot, J.L., Alagille, M., Masure, M.C., Hardy, P., Ginestet, D., & F'eline, A. (1995). Time course of prefrontal lobe dysfunction in severely depressed in-patients: A longitudinal neuropsychological study. *Psychological Medicine, 25,* 79–85.

Uchiyama, C.L., D'Elia, L.F., Dellinger, A.M., Selnes, O.A., Becker, J.T., Wesch, J.E., Chen, B.B., Satz, P., Van Gorp, W., & Miller, E.N. (1994). Longitudinal comparison of alternate versions of the Symbol digit modalities test: Issues of form comparability and moderating demographic variables. *The Clinical Neuropsychologist, 8,* 209–218.

Uttl, B., & Graf, P. (1997). Color-word Stroop test performance across the adult life span. *Journal of Clinical and Experimental Neuropsychology, 19,* 405–420.

van Zomeren, A.H. (1981). *Reaction time and attention after closed head injury.* Lisse, The Netherlands: Swets

van Zomeren, A.H., & Brouwer, W.H. (1994). *Clinical neuropsychology of attention.* New York: Oxford University Press.

Vendrell, P., Junqu'e, C., Pujol, J., Jurado, M.A., Molet, J., & Grafman, J. (1995). The role of prefrontal regions in the Stroop task. *Neuropsychologia, 33,* 341–352.

Verhaeghen, P., & DeMeersman, L. (1998). Aging and the Stroop effect: A meta-analysis. *Psychol Aging, 13,* 120–126

Walters, I., Anderson, V., Creamer, M., & Hosking, S. (1995). Memory and processing speed in depression and anxiety. In J. Fourez & N. Page (Eds.), *Treatment issues and long term outcomes* (Proceedings of the 18th Annual Brain Impairment Conference, Hobart, Australia, 1994). Bowen Hills, QLD: Australian Academic Press.

Warner, M.H., Ernst, J., Townes, B.D., Peel, J., & Preston, M. (1987). Relationship between IQ and neuropsychological measures in neuropsychiatric populations: Within-laboratory and cross-cultural replications using WAIS and WAIS-R. *Journal of Clinical and Experimental Neuropsychology, 9,* 545–562.

Watts, F.N., & Cooper, Z. (1989). The effects of depression on structured aspects of the recall of prose. *Journal of Abnormal Psychology, 98,* 150–153.

Wechsler, D. (1997). *Wechsler adult intelligence scale—third edition.* San Antonio, TX: The Psychological Corporation.

West, R., & Baylis, G.C. (1998). Effects of increased response dominance and contextual disintegration on the Stroop interference effect in older adults. *Psychol Aging, 13,* 206–217.

Whyte, J., Polansky, M., Cavallucci, C., Fleming, M., Lhulier, J., & Coslett, H.B. (1996). Inattentive behaviour after traumatic brain injury. *Journal of the International Neuropsychological Society, 2,* 274–281.

Wiens, A.N., Fuller, K.H., & Crossen, J.R. (1997). Paced auditory serial addition test: Adult norms and moderator variables. *Journal of Clinical and Experimental Neuropsychology, 19,* 473–483.

Windes, J.D. (1968). Reaction time for numerical coding and naming of numerals. *Journal of Experimental Psychology, 78,* 318–322.

Zajano, M.J., & Gorman, A. (1986). Stroop interference as a function of percentage of congruent items. *Perceptual and Motor Skills, 63,* 1087–1096.

Chapter 12

VISUOCONSTRUCTIVE ABILITIES

Patricia Lacks

The functional domain of perceptual-motor or visual-spatial skills was one of the earliest to be formally measured (e.g., Bender, 1938). The most recent term for this domain is *visuoconstructive abilities,* which combine perceptual skill with motor response in the context of a spatial task. This cognitive domain involves putting parts together to form a single object. The person must accurately perceive the spatial relationships among the component parts of the stimulus, must be able to organize those parts into a whole, and must use motor skills to reproduce it (Benton & Tranel, 1993). Disability can occur in any one or more of these functions. The history of neuropsychology shows early use of visuoconstructive tasks to diagnose general brain impairment and specific deficits. Because these construction measures require many brain functions to complete the task, poor performance can serve as a marker for dysfunction in many areas of the brain and from many etiologies. However, construction defects may not necessarily isolate the source of the patient's problem. This lack of test specificity necessitates careful observations of patient history and behavior as well as the results from other tests to distinguish among possible causes of any visuoconstruction deficits.

For many years, diverse tasks have been used to investigate visuoconstructive ability. Today, most comprehensive neuropsychological evaluations include at least one task from this cognitive domain. Traditionally, these tasks are divided into the two broad categories of *drawing,* both copying a model and freehand, and *building* or *assembly.* Drawing and assembly do not measure exactly the same brain functions. However, a high percentage of patients with brain damage show performance deficits on one or another form of construction tasks (Benton & Tranel, 1993). Some individuals do poorly on both types of tasks; others show deficits on only one or the other type. Although patients with unilateral lesions to either the right or the left hemisphere can have difficulty with construction tests, they tend to make different types of errors. In general, individuals with right hemisphere damage, especially to the posterior parietal lobe, take a more fragmented approach in which they lose the overall gestalt of the task. They also may not benefit much from a model. In contrast, those with left side lesions may maintain the overall gestalt of the model, but they tend to make errors on the details (Lezak, 1995). Patients with damage to the left hemisphere are more often able to improve their work with practice as compared to those with right hemisphere impairment.

DRAWING TESTS

Drawing tests have long been used in neuropsychological assessment because they are sensitive to many different kinds of brain dysfunction, that is, they measure a broad band of abilities. The two types of drawing tests are (1) copying from a model and (2) freehand drawing.

Copy Tests

The most widely used drawing procedure is the Bender Gestalt Test (BGT). Because it is also the most studied and discussed measure of visuoconstructive skills, it will be covered in detail later in this chapter. Several other copy tests are described briefly here.

Rey-Osterrieth Complex Figure Test (CFT)

In 1941, Rey designed a task that entailed copying one complex figure. Drawing this figure requires a variety of skills, including perception, planning, organization, and visual memory. Osterrieth (1944) standardized the procedure and developed the first norms. The examiner asks the person being evaluated to use different-colored pencils to copy separate elements of the design. This method allows the examiner to construct a flow chart of the process or strategy used in making the drawing. Three minutes (or another amount of time up to 1 hour) after completion of the copy phase, the examiner asks the person to draw the same design from memory. Because this test has both copy and memory components, it is covered in Chapter 9 and only briefly described here. Lezak (1995) and Spreen and Strauss (1998) also discuss this test in detail.

Scoring of the CFT evaluates both the *process* of copying (e.g., fragmented or confused sequence) as well as the end *product* (looking at 18 scorable elements). More recent normative data have been compiled by Meyers and Meyers (1995). Scores are related to both age and IQ, although older adults can continue to do well on the test with advancing age (Chiulli, Haaland, LaRue, & Garry, 1995). Research shows that the copy and recall phases have value in identifying patients with brain dysfunction and in specifying which functions are impaired (Lezak, 1995; Spreen & Strauss, 1998).

The Benton Visual Retention Test

Another visuoconstructive test with a memory component is the Benton Visual Retention Test (BVRT) devised by Arthur Benton (1974) and updated by Sivan (1992). However, the BVRT has higher correlations with other copy tests than it does with measures of memory. The test consists of three alternate forms, each with 10 stimulus cards containing geometric figures. Eight of the cards contain three figures, two large ones and one smaller peripheral one. The standard administration is a 10-second exposure with immediate copying from memory. The other two forms of the test can be used for various other formats of administration.

Scoring consists of the number of errors made (omission, distortion, perseveration, rotation, misplacement, and size) and the number of figures correctly drawn. The manual has precise descriptions and detailed scoring examples leading to high interscorer agreement. Normative data include corrections for age and IQ. The number of correct drawings, the number of errors, and the specific pattern of errors may aid in understanding whether the person has primarily attention, perception, or memory deficits (Lezak, 1995). Several researchers have provided additional norms (e.g., with a focus on individuals with higher education; Youngjohn, Larrabee, & Crook, 1993). Overall, the BVRT is sensitive to many kinds of brain damage because it taps diverse abilities, including the left brain verbal conceptualizations needed to describe and to commit the complex test stimuli to memory (Heaton, Baade, & Johnson, 1978). However, Brilliant and Gynther (1963) found that the attention requirements of the 10-second exposure made the BVRT (especially the error score) less useful than the copy-only Bender Gestalt Test for discriminating between psychiatric inpatients with and without brain damage. The BVRT combined score was 98% accurate for those cases it labeled as not having brain damage. This test also appears very sensitive to the cognitive deterioration found in early Alzheimer's disease (Storandt, Botwinick, & Danziger,1986).

Hooper Visual Organization Test

Another test, which might more strictly be classified as a perceptual-organizational rather than a visuoconstructive measure, is the Hooper Visual Organization Test (HVOT; Hooper, 1983). It consists of 30 cards, each containing a drawing of a common object (e.g., fish, table, lighthouse), displayed in different views or fragmented into several parts that are arranged illogically. The person being tested must name each object verbally or in writing. The score is the sum of correct identifications, with half credit given for some partially correct answers. Normative data can be found in D'Elia, Boone, and Mitrushina (1999) and other studies listed in Spreen and Strauss (1998). Test results appear to be unaffected by gender, education, IQ, or age, except for the very old (Lezak, 1995).

More than 11 errors on the HVOT may indicate some kind of brain impairment; false positive diagnoses are rare. However, Wetzel and Murphy (1991) reported that many patients with brain impairment can perform well on this test. Spreen and Strauss (1998) reviewed the research literature and recommended that the test be used to explore deficits in perceptual organization rather than to screen for brain damage. Comparison of results on the HVOT with those of other visuoconstructive measures may allow the clinician to tease out the differences between perceptual and visuoconstructive performance deficits. Errors are associated with impairment in various parts of the brain (e.g., Wetzel & Murphy, 1991) rather than in just the right posterior region.

Freehand Drawing Tasks

In the less structured, freehand drawing tasks, the person being evaluated does not have to attend to a stimulus and then reproduce it; instead, he or she calls to mind a visual stimulus and then draws it. Freehand drawings have been used for many years as an instrument of personality assessment, where the artwork is thought to be a symbolic representation of the unconscious (Handler, 1996). In 1926, Florence Goodenough developed a maturity of intelligence scale for children based on ratings of quality and detail in the drawing of a person. Others have extended her work. For example, Koppitz (1968) standardized a system for analyzing the human figure drawings of children ages 5 to 12 for mental maturity and for "interpersonal attitudes and concerns." For adults, freehand drawings of such objects as a person, a house, a bicycle, a Greek cross, and a clock are often used as part of a mental status examination. See Lezak (1995) for formal evaluative criteria for several of these drawn objects.

Examples of signs of brain impairment for the human figure drawing are asymmetry of parts, emptiness of facial expression, lack of details, omission of parts, and absence of clothing (Safran, 1997). In their handbook for human figure drawings, Mitchell, Trent, and McArthur (1993) include a general Impairment Scale with 74 scorable signs of general cognitive deficiency. Higher scores are associated with brain damage and mental retardation.

Clock Drawing Test (CDT)

Although drawing a clock appears to be a simple task, this freehand procedure samples multiple cognitive functions organized in diverse cerebral regions. Some of these functions are: *auditory language skills* to comprehend the instructions, *memory* to store the instructions for a certain time setting, ability to form a visuospatial representation of a clock, *perceptual-motor facility* to translate the representation into a drawing, *linguistic skills* to draw the numbers, and *executive functions* for planning and organization. The number and the nature of the errors made on the CDT can vary greatly depending on the type and the location of the impairment; specific types of errors can aid in localization of the deficits (Freedman et al., 1994).

The CDT is nonthreatening, brief, and simple to administer. It can even be given at the patient's bedside. For the standard administration, or drawing on *command*, the examiner provides the person with a blank letter-size (8.5-by-11-inch) piece of paper and asks him or her to draw a clock with all the numbers on it and the hands set to a specific time that varies among administrators: "20 to 4" or "10 after 11" are commonly used settings (see Freedman et al., 1994, for discussion of the merits of each time setting and for descriptions of other administration formats). Some psychologists follow this drawing procedure with a request to *copy* a model of a clock face. There is no time limit, although time to complete the task is recorded. Generally, the ability to draw the clock correctly is established by age 8 and to indicate the time by age 9 (Edmonds, Cohen, & Riccio, 1994). There are a number of different quantitative scales that gauge general accuracy of the drawing, specify types of errors (e.g., omission, perseveration, rotation), and note behaviors such as tremulousness. Examples of scoring systems are Freedman et al. (1994); Tuokko, Hadjistavropoulos, Miller, and Beattie (1992); and Rouleau, Salmon, Butters, Kennedy, and McGuire (1992). Because the CDT offers ease of administration, objective scoring procedures, and recent research providing empirical support, this test will be discussed in more detail than some of the other measures.

Visuoconstructive deficits are often seen early in dementia. As a result, recent research focuses on the CDT as a screening measure for this disorder. A good deal of research has been done to establish norms for older adults with and without dementia. For example, Tuokko et al. (1992) found that with their scoring system a group of nonpatient older adults averaged 1.48 ($SD = 3.65$) errors, and those with Alzheimer's disease averaged 8.26 ($SD = 7.28$) errors; an optimal cutoff score of 3 or more errors correctly classified 86% of those with Alzheimer's disease and 92% of the nonpatient older adults. Two types of errors were especially diagnostic: omissions and misplacements. Brodaty and Moore (1997) used samples of patients with mild and moderate Alzheimer's disease and age- and sex-matched controls to compare three different scoring methods. A 6-point classification method developed by Shulman, Gold, Cohen, and Zucchero (1993) performed best, identifying 86% of the patients with dementia (versus a 71% rate with the Mini Mental Status Exam).

Libon, Malamut, Swenson, Sands, and Cloud (1996) found that they could differentiate between Alzheimer's patients and those with ischaemic vascular dementia using two scales. The first one rates the adequacy of the drawing on the 10-point scale shown in Table 12.1. Examples of clocks drawn at each of the 10 levels are presented in Figure 12.1. A second scale analyzes 10 specific errors grouped into the three subscales of graphomotor functioning, hand/number placement, or executive control. Libon et al. (1996) found that the CDT scores on the first scale improved from the command to the copy condition for those patients with Alzheimer's disease but not for those with ischaemic vascular dementia. The pattern of specific errors suggested that failure to improve performance on the copy task was due to deficits in executive control. Rouleau et al. (1992) found the same pattern of results comparing patients with Alzheimer's disease to those with Huntington's disease. Spreen and Strauss (1998) and Safran (1997) reviewed many other recent studies on the CDT. The test also correlates with other lengthier cognitive screening measures (e.g., Brodaty & Moore, 1997) and appears to have low influence from IQ, education, and ethnicity (Shulman et al., 1993).

Table 12.1. Criteria for evaluating clock drawing

Scores 10–6: Circle and hands are basically intact, some impairment in hand placement.

Score	
10	Hands, numbers, and circle are totally intact.
9	Slight error(s) in hand/number placement; hands of equal length; any self-correction.
8	More noticeable errors in hand/number placement; hand length correct but shifted to one side or top/bottom.
7	Significant errors in hand placement; hand placement intact with some numbers deleted; minor preservation in number placement.
6	Inappropriate use of clock hands, i.e., digital display; circling numbers to indicate hand placement; connecting the numbers 10 and 11 or 11 and 2.

Scores 5–1: Circle, numbers, and/or hand placement are grossly impaired.

Score	
5	Crowding numbers to one side; numbers reversed; significant perseveration of numbers within circle boundary.
4	Loss of clock face integrity, numbers outside circle boundary, further distortion of number placement.
3	Numbers and clock face no longer connected.
2	Vague representations of a clock; clock face absent but numbers present.
1	Either no attempt or response is made; scattered bits or fragments are produced.

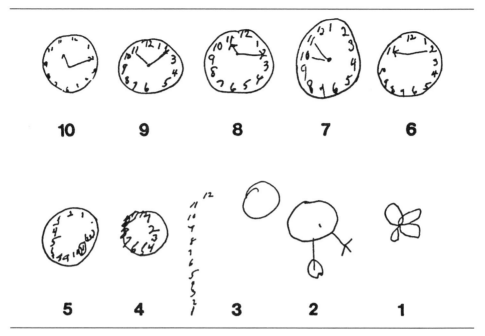

Figure 12.1.   Representative examples of clock drawing
Note: From "Further analyses of clock drawings among demented and nondemented older subjects," by D.J. Libon, B.L. Malamut, R. Swenson, L.P. Sands, and B.S. Cloud, 1996, *Archives of Clinical Neuropsychology, 11,* p. 409.

ASSEMBLY TESTS

The second broad category of visuoconstructive tests permits evaluation of the multiple skills necessary to build with or to assemble materials such as blocks, sticks, and puzzle parts. Some of the requisite skills for assembly are complex spatial and conceptual perception, logic, abstraction, motor construction, manipulative speed, concentration, and frustration tolerance. Two subtests of the Wechsler intelligence scales, Block Design and Object Assembly, are the most often used assembly measures (see also Chapter 5). Tests of cube construction tap three-dimensional building skills.

Block Design

This timed test requires the person to reproduce increasingly more complex displayed patterns using either four or nine red-and-white patterned blocks. The person has to problem solve nonverbally by breaking the model into its component parts and then conceptually reformulating these bits of information into a gestalt constructed with the blocks. Research reflects a high connection between scores on this test and general mental ability. The evaluator can obtain valuable diagnostic hints about which component abilities may be impaired by carefully observing the test performance (e.g., patient takes a trial-and-error rather than a conceptual approach).

Although there are no strong effects attributed to gender, ethnicity, or education, Block Design results are strongly tied to age, perhaps due largely to its timed format.

Declines in performance are especially steep after age 74. Age-stratified normative data are available in the Wechsler Adult Intelligence Scale-III (WAIS-III) manual and in other sources such as D'Elia et al. (1999). A detailed review of other research on this test can be found in Lezak (1995) and in Chapter 5.

Block Design scores are lower for persons with any kind of brain damage. Lesion size appears less important than its location. Each hemisphere appears to contribute different skills toward completing the assembly task. Performance deficits tend to be most pronounced with right posterior parietal lesions and least serious with left hemisphere, nonparietal impairment (e.g., Black & Bernard, 1984). According to Lezak (1995), patients with left hemisphere damage (especially parietal) tend to be confused and to approach the task in a simple and concrete manner. They work slowly, often taking more than the allowed time, but are able to preserve the pattern gestalt. If given no time limits, many of these patients can achieve average scores on Block Design. Chronic alcoholics tend to perform much as those with left-sided damage do.

Patients with right-sided damage, however, often demonstrate strong perceptual misperceptions and distortions of the patterns, even omitting sections of the designs. Being given extra time is less likely to improve test scores for these patients. Patients with frontal lobe damage may have lower performance due to impulsive and careless behavior and concrete thinking. Individuals with Alzheimer's disease show rapid deterioration on this test, with Block Design often being their lowest WAIS-R subtest (e.g., Storandt et al., 1986). As such, it can be used for early identification of the disease and for differentiation between it and other disorders, such as depression.

Object Assembly

Another form of assembly test requires putting together four puzzles of familiar objects, such as a hand or an elephant. Object Assembly is also a timed test, resulting in diminished performance with increasing age. Other demographic variables show similar effects as for Block Design. In fact, these two assembly tasks correlate more highly with each other than any other two WAIS subtests. However, unlike Block Design, this test requires little abstract thinking and is not strongly related to general mental ability. Speed of visual organization and motor response are essential to doing well on this test. Patients of any diagnosis who work too slowly or obsessively will receive time penalties. Results generally show the same pattern of relationship to left hemisphere versus right hemisphere damage as is found with Block Design. However, the test is not particularly sensitive to Alzheimer's disease. More caution should be used in interpreting this test because it has relatively low levels of test specificity and retest reliability.

BENDER GESTALT TEST

History and Development

The most frequently used visuoconstructive measure is the Bender Gestalt Test (BGT). Surveys over the past 30 years have shown that the BGT is part of an identifiable core of assessment tools most often used, across various work settings, by the majority of clinical psychologists (e.g., Watkins, Campbell, Nieberding, & Hallmark,

1995). Surveys of neuropsychologists have similarly indicated that the BGT is consistently ranked as one of the most frequently used tests for neuropsychological assessment (e.g., Butler, Retzlaff, & Vanderploeg, 1991).

The BGT is a copying task. It consists of nine designs (see Figure 12.2), mostly familiar geometric shapes, that are presented one at a time. The examiner asks the person being evaluated to copy these figures as accurately as possible on one or more blank sheets of paper. There is no time limit. The examiner inspects the finished product for accuracy of reproduction using one of several available scoring systems. The test is simple to administer even by a technician, brief (average of 6 minutes), nonthreatening, and applicable to ages 4 through 100.

Psychologists who employ this test have used it for a wide array of purposes: to measure children's school or reading readiness or to identify learning disabilities; to estimate nonverbal IQ; to assess personality or emotional adjustment; and to provide an innocuous warmup procedure at the beginning of a battery of tests. However, the widest use of the BGT is as a *screening* test of brain dysfunction, administered within a general battery of tests that usually includes the Wechsler intelligence scales. When the BGT or any of the tests in the battery suggest brain dysfunction, the psychologist can perform additional evaluation or make a referral for a comprehensive neuropsychological assessment (for further discussion of screening tests for brain impairment, see Berg, Franzen, & Wedding, 1994; Gregory, 1987; Groth-Marnat, 1999). Within the newer subspecialty of neuropsychology, the BGT is often used within a battery of neuropsychological tests to assess the specific cognitive domain of visuoconstructive skills.

This test was first introduced in 1938 by Lauretta Bender to study the relationship of perception to psychopathology. Her designs were adapted from ones used by Wertheimer (1923) for his research on visual perception. Bender was a child psychiatrist whose interest in the test was primarily maturational or developmental. During the 1940s, Max Hutt emphasized the BGT as a nonverbal, projective personality test, an approach that is most recently described in his 1985 book.

In the period from 1950 to 1980, psychologists recognized the need for some kind of reliable, objective evaluative method for this test. The introduction of the first formal scoring system (Pascal & Suttell, 1951) ushered in the psychometric approach to the BGT. The test became used more often as a screening procedure for brain impairment in psychiatric settings, and a number of other methods to score it were devised. During this period, most BGT research attempted to establish validity, reliability, norms, and diagnostic accuracy for these scoring systems (for a review, see Lacks, 1984, 1999; Tolor & Brannigan, 1980).

More recent attention is on the BGT's potential to identify older adults at high risk for cognitive decline (e.g., Storandt, 1990), on its application to adolescents (McIntosh, Belter, Saylor, Finch, & Edwards, 1988), and on its place within a comprehensive neuropsychological battery (e.g., James & Selz, 1997).

Psychometric Properties

What Does the BGT Measure?

It is desirable to have pure psychological tests that are very specific in what they assess, that is, that measure only one function or ability at a time. In reality, most tests

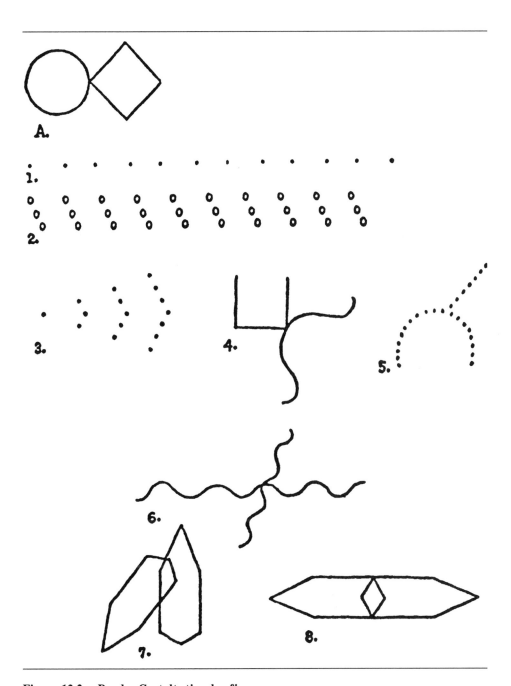

Figure 12.2.   Bender Gestalt stimulus figures
Reprinted with permission from *A Visual Motor Gestalt Test and its clinical uses* by Lauretta Bender. Published by the American Orthopsychiatric Association. Copyright © 1938, renewed 1965, by Lauretta Bender and the American Orthopsychiatric Association, Inc.

tap multiple, complex abilities. Neuropsychological tests in particular show low levels of specificity. For example, successful completion of the apparently simple BGT requires a wide variety of skills using many areas of the brain. Some of the identified determinants of BGT performance include intact vision, attention and concentration, perception of the design, recognition of spatial relations, verbal intelligence, memory, motor skills, perceptual-motor integration, and "executive" abilities, such as planning and drive or motivation.

It is obvious from this disparate list of abilities that more than one location of the brain operates for successful completion of the BGT. Because this test is considered primarily a perceptual-motor measure, psychologists usually ascribe BGT performance to the right parietal lobe. However, Benton and Tranel (1993) reported negligible differences in visuoconstructive test performance for persons with right hemisphere versus left hemisphere lesions. Black and Bernard (1984) studied 52 men who all had shrapnel wounds in one of four quadrants of the brain. Patients with damage to the right hemisphere did more poorly on the BGT than those with damage to the left hemisphere. Percentages of patients with poorly done BGTs were 6% of those with damage to the left anterior part of the brain, 25% to right anterior, 20% to left posterior, and 46% to right posterior. Lesion size had only a minor effect on test outcome. The researchers concluded that constructional deficits can occur with a lesion in any quadrant, though more frequently when damage is to the right posterior region. The perceptual-motor aspect of the BGT does make demands on the right hemisphere; however, other necessary skills such as deliberation and sustained attention may be linked to the left hemisphere. Executive functions such as planning are considered driven more by the frontal lobes.

In a meta-analysis of neuropsychological assessment research, Garb and Schramke (1996) found that neurological impairment is rarely limited to one small area of the brain. Many patients with structural lesions in one hemisphere may have diffuse consequences to the brain. Head injury, stroke, and tumors can affect the whole brain in addition to producing localized disruptions. As a result of the multiple skills required to reproduce the nine simple BGT designs, multiple functions from several different parts of the brain are probably being measured. Therefore, the BGT casts a broad net. This means that the test is sensitive to impairment from many areas of the brain and can serve as a marker of brain dysfunction. Individuals with diffuse brain damage (e.g., alcoholism, dementia from Alzheimer's disease, HIV infection, Parkinsonism, and Huntington's disease) do poorly on this test, as do those with damage to the right parietal area and to other areas as well.

Administration

To ensure reliable and valid results, the standardized administration for the Bender Gestalt Test should be followed meticulously. Child psychologists will find directions for this particular client group in Koppitz (1975). Materials necessary for administration include a supply of 8.5-by-11-inch white unlined paper, several number-2 pencils with erasers, a smooth writing surface, and the nine stimulus cards. The latter are 4-by-6-inch white cards, printed with geometric designs and numbered A and 1 through 8. The designs may be either the original ones developed by Lauretta Bender (1938), which are presented in Figure 12.2, or the slightly modified ones used by Hutt (1985). Before administering the test, the examiner should *always* check to make sure that the cards are face down in a stack, placed in the proper sequence and orientation.

The following instructions are for the standard or copy phase administration. As testing begins, without comment, the examiner places in front of the person one sheet of paper in the vertical (usual writing) position, places the extra pencils and remaining paper to the side, and then gives the following instructions (Hutt, 1985, p. 44):

> I am going to show you these cards, one at a time. Each card has a simple drawing on it. I would like you to copy the drawing on the paper, as well as you can. Work in any way that is best for you. This is not a test of artistic ability, but try to copy the drawings as accurately as possible. Work as fast or as slowly as you wish.

It may be wise, with some individuals, for the examiner to check that they understood and, if not, to repeat all or part of the instructions. Because the directions are so simple and straightforward, the examiner generally does not need to explain what is meant. Most clients or patients will be able to proceed. A few may be anxious because they believe they are not artistic or because they fear that they will be required to work quickly. Brief reassurance is usually enough to allay their fears.

The examiner should allow the person to adjust the paper (though still maintaining it in the vertical orientation) to suit drawing comfort and should then place the first card so that it is aligned with the top of the paper. As the person completes each drawing, the examiner removes the card and supplies the next one. Most people will draw all nine figures on one sheet of paper. Generally there is no limit on the number of sheets that may be used. However, it may be better if the person is restricted to the use of only one or two sheets. He or she might reveal aspects of planning and organizational ability that may be useful in the determination of cognitive skills. These two approaches have not yet been empirically contrasted; the standard approach is to use the extra pile of paper. The examiner begins timing inconspicuously when the first card is turned over; a wristwatch gives an accurate enough estimate.

The person being tested may move the card closer or may pick it up to get a better look. However, if he or she reorients the stimulus card, the examiner can indicate nonverbally the correct placement by returning the card to its original position. If someone insists on changing the card's orientation, allow him or her to do so. Immediately, at the end of the test, the examiner indicates the top of such a figure with an arrow on the protocol itself. The same arrow marks should be used to mark the top of the paper if the person placed the page in an unusual position. The examiner should not trust this important step to memory or he or she will have difficulty later in scoring the test.

Most individuals do not ask questions, and the test proceeds nonverbally. However, the examiner should answer the occasional queries with indirect replies (e.g., "Do it the way you think best" or "Do the best job you can") or by repeating or paraphrasing the instructions. Typical questions concern the need to count design elements, permission to erase or turn the paper, and how exact the reproductions need to be. Sketching (using a series of pencil strokes rather than drawing with one firm line) is not allowed because it renders the protocol unscorable.

For many clinicians, this ends the BGT. Some evaluators may wish to proceed with the variations of administration described later in this chapter, such as the recall or background interference procedures. The BGT shows little practice effect and can be repeated with confidence in the results.

Diagnostic Significance of Behavioral Observations

The Lacks adapted scoring method used in this chapter consists of 12 errors or *essential discriminators.* In general, the presence of any 5 of these errors is taken to indicate brain impairment or dysfunction. The effectiveness of this cutoff score has been verified in many studies. However, all of these errors can also be made by clients or patients who do not put forth their best efforts because of behaviors or attitudes such as minimal interest in the task, impulsivity, hostility toward the examiner, carelessness, fatigue, malingering, hearing or vision problems, and so on. Therefore, it is very important to attend to the *process* of the patient's drawing. The examiner must determine whether errors were made because of true perceptual-motor difficulties or because of other factors. Only in the former case should an error be scored. For example, suppose a man being tested reproduced figure 1 with only four dots. Also suppose he showed hostility toward being tested, barely glanced at the stimulus card before copying it, made some comment about there being too many dots to copy, and completed the test in only 2 minutes. He also showed this attitude in drawing the remainder of the designs. It is unlikely that this man is suffering from brain impairment; more likely he is just refusing to cooperate. Without having personally observed this performance or been told of it by the actual examiner, the clinician might easily find 5 errors and erroneously diagnose a cognitive disorder.

At the opposite extreme, a person with brain damage may be able to produce an adequate record (or one with 4 errors) through extreme effort, taking a great deal of time (maybe even 20 to 30 minutes), and making many erasures. As with the previous case, the behavioral observations are crucial if the clinician is to make the correct diagnosis. The average time to copy the nine figures for individuals who are not brain impaired generally falls below 6 minutes. If an individual takes more than 15 minutes to complete the test, it is usually another strong diagnostic sign, especially if the patient commits 4 errors.

A list of relevant behavioral observations can be seen in Figure 12.3. The list is divided into two parts: The first part shows *general test-taking attitudes,* such as motivation and cooperation, that are relevant to the analysis of most psychological tests. The second half of the list contains behaviors more specific to a visuoconstructive measure such as the Bender Gestalt Test. A few items on this second half are even necessary to score some of the errors (e.g., repeated unsuccessful attempts to correct errors). For convenience, the examiner may wish to reproduce this sheet.

Older adults are at a higher risk for decline in visual and hearing acuity. Therefore, when testing older adults, the examiner should systematically check these functions before beginning testing. (For additional details on examining special populations and maximizing performance level, see Lezak, 1995, p. 131.)

Variations in Administration

Since the introduction of the BGT in 1938, several variants of the standard procedure have been devised; all show promise of increased testing efficiency or better success in difficult diagnostic decisions. The most common alterations are group administration,

Name _____   Age _____   Education _____

Gender _____   Ethnicity _____   Date of Testing _____

General Test-Taking Attitudes

Takes test in serious manner -- Takes test lightly

Cooperative, compliant -- Uncooperative, resistant

Methodical, deliberate -- Careless

Persistent in difficult situations -- Gives up easily

Attentive, concentrating -- Distracted

Motivated to do well -- Unmotivated

Calm, relaxed -- Anxious, agitated

Good rapport with examiner -- Poor rapport

Specific Behavioral Observations

___ Rotation of drawing on figures _____   ___ Insufficient attention to test designs

___ Drawing difficulty due to physical disability   ___ Difficulty seeing figures

___ Considerable care and deliberation   ___ Evidence of fatigue

___ Trouble understanding instructions due to: ___ Low IQ   ___ Language difficulty   ___ Hearing

___ Expression of dissatisfaction with poorly executed drawings on figures _____

___ Repeated unsuccessful attempts to correct errors on figures _____

___ Motor incoordination or hand tremor: ___ Mild   ___ Moderate   ___ Severe

Minutes to complete test: _____

___ Other Behaviors _____

Figure 12.3.   Behavioral observations for the Bender Gestalt Test
Note: Developed by Patricia Lacks. Adapted and reproduced by special permission of the Publisher, Psychological Assessment Resources, Inc., Odessa, FL 33556, from the *Bender Gestalt Screening Software for Windows (V. 1),* copyright © 1996.

recall condition, and the Canter Background Interference Procedure. The latter two are not useful with children.

Because one of the primary uses of the BGT is as a screening test, in some situations it would be helpful to administer the test to more than one person at a time. *Group testing* has been used primarily with school children, mostly to screen large numbers inexpensively to predict school performance and reading achievement. However, the method could just as well be adapted for adults. Groups have been tested with enlarged stimulus cards at the front of the room, with individual booklets that have a stimulus figure at the top of each page and room to copy below, with individual decks of BGT cards that the child turns over, or with the image projected on a screen. These methods allow evaluation of 5 to 15 individuals at a time in 15 to 30 minutes. The adequacy of these techniques has been verified empirically; however, in most clinical situations, there would be no need to sacrifice important observations of process by using a group-testing method.

Another BGT variant is the *recall phase* for which individuals are asked to reproduce as many of the original designs as they can remember after they have completed the copy phase. The score used for this method is generally the number of figures correctly recalled, although sometimes the quality of the recalled designs is also assessed.

The recall method was originally developed to increase detection of the effects of brain impairment, especially when trying to differentiate this deficit from that due to schizophrenia. Armstrong (1965) compared the copy and recall scores of 80 psychiatric inpatients divided into five diagnostic groups. Her results showed that the patients with brain damage copied the designs more poorly, recalled fewer designs, and made more errors in their recalled designs than each of the four other psychiatric groups including patients with schizophrenia. Those with a diagnosed cognitive disorder recalled an average of 3.85 BGT figures, and the other four psychiatric groups recalled, on the average, 5.57 to 6.09 figures. The patients with brain damage showed a great deal of variability in copying but were consistently poor in recalling. Using an optimal cutoff score, there was little overlap on recall scores between the group with brain impairment and the other four patient groups, yielding about 80% accuracy for the correct diagnosis of impaired brain function.

One problem with the recall method is that it is not clear how accurate the drawing must be for it to be considered correctly recalled or how long an interval should pass after the copy phase before recall is requested. Until these important matters are settled, clinicians cannot use the recall method with much confidence. However, the research does suggest potential usefulness warranting further study. At this time, few psychologists use the BGT recall procedure.

Perhaps the most promising of the BGT variants and the one that has attracted the most attention is Canter's (1966) *Background Interference Procedure* (BIP). This method uses an individual's own performance on the standard administration as a baseline for comparison with a second performance drawn on paper previously marked with wavy lines. It was developed to reduce diagnostic inaccuracy caused by psychiatric patients' defective performance on the BGT. Canter (1971) found that 94% of a group of patients with brain damage did *worse* on the BIP phase compared to 24% of the long-term hospitalized patients with schizophrenia, 13% of the short-term hospitalized patients with schizophrenia, and 13% of the patients with neither brain damage nor schizophrenia. Most patients without brain damage *improved* their BIP performance, but no patient with brain injury showed improved performance on the BIP. The additional demands of the BIP appear to disrupt the cognitive integration of patients with brain dysfunction.

Early research with this modification reported very promising diagnostic hit rates; however, later studies produced less consistent success (e.g., Boake & Adams, 1982). Although the Canter BIP generated a good deal of research, it does not seem to be widely used clinically, perhaps because of inconsistent research findings, increased time demands from having to administer the test twice, and use of a time-consuming scoring method.

Scoring Systems

Originally, there were no formal procedures for quantifying BGT results. When Lauretta Bender first published her test stimuli and instructions for their use, she provided only a chart of test responses showing maturational progression from age 4 through 11. The first objective scoring system was published in 1951 by Pascal and Suttell. Although their system was the impetus for a great deal of research, it did not have an equal influence on clinical practice. Instead, BGT clinical protocols were often evaluated by means of clinical judgment. After Meehl's (1954) work on the general disadvantages of clinical prediction, psychologists became more interested in finding a brief, objective, and empirically based scoring system for this test. Now several scoring systems are available.

Numerous types of errors and distortions are possible when drawing the BGT figures. Each of the following scoring systems focuses on different potential errors, although there is some overlap. There are at least eight different published scoring systems for the standard administration with adults. At least three additional systems are available for work with children. The system developed by Koppitz (1963, 1975), called the Developmental Bender Test Scoring System, is the preferred procedure of scoring for children. For adults, the most popular systems in research reports have been the Pascal-Suttell, the Hain, and the Lacks adaptation of the Hutt-Briskin method. Interscorer reliabilities are generally acceptable for all these scoring approaches ($r = .79$ to 1.00). Test-retest reliability ranges from .63 to .92 depending on the degree of pathology of the patients and on the retest interval (ranging from 24 hours to 18 months). Published overall diagnostic accuracies range from 55% to 88%.

One of the earliest and most well-known scoring systems was developed by Pascal and Suttell (1951). It is a complex procedure of measuring the degree of psychopathology through 105 possible deviations in reproducing the figures. Each design is inspected for from 10 to 13 possible errors (weighted from 2 to 8). For example, figure 1 is assessed for 10 possible deviations such as wavy line of dots, dashes for dots, circles for dots, second attempt, and so on. The overall production is then examined for seven more configuration scores. Although it has been used frequently in published research, the Pascal-Suttell approach does not enjoy wide clinical application. It is cumbersome to use and very time-consuming (up to 20 minutes per protocol). Also, the range of this system is restricted because its use is confined to individuals aged 15 to 50 with more than 9 years of education.

Taking a different approach, Hain (1964) developed a system that consists of 15 signs, each with a weight ranging from 1 to 4. This approach looks at the BGT as a whole, rather than scoring each figure separately. Each sign is scored only once per record. It takes 3 minutes or fewer to score.

Taking an approach similar to Hain's, Hutt and Briskin (1960) suggested the use of 12 "essential discriminators of intracranial damage," a list that has been modified several times in subsequent publications (Hutt, 1985). Results using different versions of this system have been published by Lownsdale, Rogers, and McCall (1989). With the original Hutt-Briskin system, each protocol is evaluated for the presence or absence of the 12 signs; a score of 5 or more errors indicates brain impairment. An error may be scored only once per protocol so that scores range from 0 to 12. Because Hutt was most interested in the projective use of the BGT, he did not provide much detail nor empirical validation of these signs. However, Lacks (1984), taking a psychometric stance, devised a detailed scoring manual of Hutt and Briskin's procedures. Her system will be referred to as the Lacks adaptation of the Hutt-Briskin scoring system or simply as the Lacks method. This system has the advantage of taking fewer than 3 minutes per protocol to score.

One other scoring method, the Pauker Quick-Scoring System (1976), takes only about 1 minute per protocol. Reasons for its brevity are that no physical measurements are necessary and differential decisions are deemphasized. Each of the nine figures is rated on a 0-to-4 scale of amount of deviation from the original stimulus. Unlike the other systems, this one can be used with both adults and children. Only one study has been published on the diagnostic accuracy of this method (Lacks & Newport, 1980). Using an optimal cutoff score of 9 and above for a sample of 50 adult, mixed, psychiatric inpatients (cognitive disorder base rate of 34%), three scorers produced diagnostic accuracies of 78%, 78%, and 82%. These results, although promising, still await cross-validation.

It is difficult to make statements about the relative worth of these different systems because they are usually evaluated one system at a time. Also, almost all published evaluations are of the BGT as a screening test used within a psychiatric setting. One study (Lacks & Newport, 1980), however, did compare the usefulness of four brief scoring approaches to the BGT on the same sample of 50 mixed, psychiatric inpatients with a brain dysfunction base rate of 34%. Using the criteria of relative ease of application, availability, and frequency of recent use in the literature, the following systems were chosen for comparison: Hain (1964), Lacks adaptation of Hutt-Briskin (1999), and Pauker Quick-Scoring (1976). Each of these approaches requires fewer than 3 minutes per protocol.

Twelve scorers were used, three for each system. Scorers using the Lacks adaptation of the Hutt-Briskin system, with a standard cutoff score of 5 of the 12 possible errors, achieved the highest levels of diagnostic accuracy (84%). The Pauker system achieved 79% overall accuracy. Marsico and Wagner (1990) compared the Pascal-Suttell system to the Lacks method on a sample of 80 outpatients referred for psychological testing: 31 with brain damage and 49 with other psychiatric disorders. Using standard cutoff scores, the Lacks method correctly classified 65% of the patients with brain damage and 88% of the nonimpaired; respective results for the Pascal-Suttell system were 58% and 96%. Overall diagnostic accuracies were 79% for the Lacks method and 81% for the Pascal-Suttell procedures. Both scoring systems had a much higher number of missed cases than false positive outcomes. Because the two systems were highly correlated ($r = .83$), the researchers suggested using the Lacks method because of its relative ease of scoring and broader scope of application.

In the past, many psychologists did not use an objective scoring system to evaluate the BGTs of adults, probably because there was no system that was readily available and easy to use and that required a short amount of time to learn and apply. Instead, large numbers of psychologists relied on their subjective clinical acumen to arrive at diagnostic decisions with the BGT, a practice that has been repudiated by several research studies. Research on this topic indicates that psychologists can increase their diagnostic accuracy considerably (on the average by 10% to 15%) if they use a brief, easily learned, objective scoring system (Robiner, 1978).

This need to use objective methods to evaluate the BGT applies to psychologists of all levels of experience. Using 12 scorers representing three levels of expertise (expert, typical, and novice), Lacks and Newport (1980) found a maximum of 4% difference in diagnostic accuracy among the three levels for each of the three scoring systems plus number of rotations alone. High levels of accuracy were achieved with the Lacks and Pauker systems after very short training periods, even by individuals with no previous experience with tests for brain dysfunction. Robiner (1978) also found no differences in subjective diagnostic acumen between experienced clinicians and graduate students. In fact, for a range of experience from 1 to 30 years, the correlation between diagnostic accuracy and experience for his 10 judges was .07. This means that the scoring of BGT protocols can probably be entrusted in many situations to a capable psychometrician who has been trained to use a proven scoring system.

Description of the Lacks Scoring Method

The method of scoring advocated by Lacks (1984, 1999) originated with a list of 12 "essential discriminators of intracranial damage" first briefly described in the work of Hutt and Briskin in 1960. These 12 errors (see Table 12.2) are described in more detail here. Also, some of the errors are demonstrated in the clinical case presented in Figure 12.4. Note that these descriptions alone are not adequate to score a BGT protocol accurately. Lacks provides detailed scoring instructions with many examples in her book (Lacks, 1984, 1999).

1. *Rotation: Severe.* This error is scored when there is a change in the orientation of the major axis of the whole design of from 80 to 180 degrees. Mirror imaging is a form of this error. Rotation is not to be confused with turning of the stimulus card or of

Table 12.2.   Hutt-Briskin's twelve essential discriminators of Organic Brain Dysfunction

1. Rotation: severe
2. Overlapping difficulty
3. Simplification
4. Fragmentation
5. Retrogression
6. Perseveration
7. Collision or collision tendency
8. Impotence
9. Closure difficulty: marked and persistent
10. Motor incoordination
11. Angulation difficulty: severe
12. Cohesion

Source: Hutt and Briskin (1960).

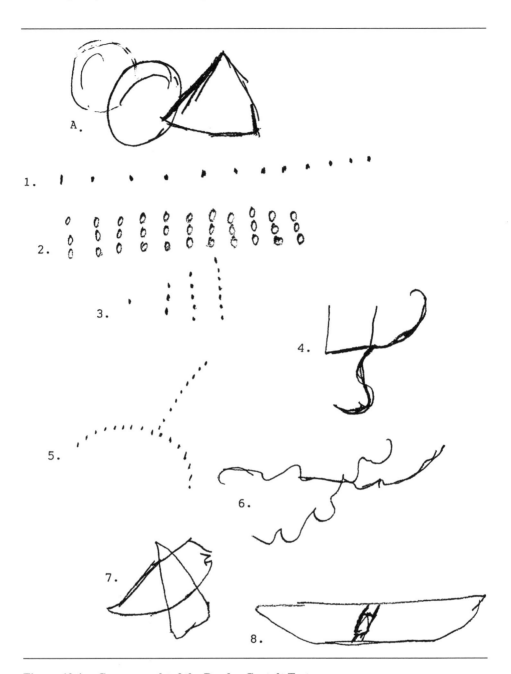

Figure 12.4.   Case example of the Bender Gestalt Test

the drawing paper and then drawing the figure accurately. Figure 12.4 does not contain any rotations.

2. *Overlapping Difficulty.* This error consists of difficulty in drawing those parts of figures that should overlap (only on designs 6, 7). Such difficulty can take many forms, such as failing to draw those portions of the figure that should overlap, simplifying either figure at the point of overlap, sketching or redrawing the figures at the

point of overlap, or distorting the figures where they overlap. See Figure 12.4 for an example of this error. On design 7, the two hexagons overlap at the wrong place. Design 6 is almost close enough to earn this error.

3. *Simplification.* Part or all of the design is replaced with a different and more simplified form that is not more primitive in terms of maturation. If it were more maturationally primitive, it would be scored Retrogression. Examples of simplification would be figure A drawn with an adjacent rather than a touching circle and square or design 5 drawn with a solid line instead of dots. This person did not produce any simplifications.

4. *Fragmentation.* This error is scored when there is destruction of the gestalt of a figure by incomplete reproduction (e.g., drawing fewer than 6 dots on design 1, or drawing two rows of circles instead of three on design 2). Another version of this error is breaking up the figure in such a way as to destroy the gestalt (e.g., drawing design 2 as one long line of 33 circles rather than 11 columns of 3 circles). No instances of fragmented designs appear in Figure 12.4.

5. *Retrogression.* This error requires the substitution of a maturationally more primitive figure for the design on the stimulus card (e.g., loops for circles, persistent and extreme dashes for dots, a triangle for a diamond or hexagon). There must be evidence that the person being tested is capable of drawing the more mature forms. In Figure 12.4, a triangle was substituted for a more complex form (diamond or hexagon) on designs A, 7, and 8.

6. *Perseveration. Type A* perseveration consists of the persistent and inaccurate substitution of the elements of a previous figure, such as continuing to use the dots of design 1 in design 2 or the circles of design 2 in designs 3 or 5.

Type B refers to the continued drawing of the elements of a figure beyond the limits called for by that stimulus. In design 1, this would mean drawing 14 or more dots (instead of 12), and in design 2, drawing 13 or more rows of circles (instead of 11).

A less common version of this error is the drawing of an additional row of circles on design 2 or dots on design 3. No examples of either form of this error can be seen in the sample case.

7. *Collision or Collision Tendency.* The error of Collision occurs when figures are drawn so close that they overlap or collide. Collision Tendency occurs when a figure is drawn too close to another figure (within 1/4 inch). Designs 2 and 3 in Figure 12.4 are drawn close enough together to indicate the error of Collision Tendency.

8. *Impotence.* When a person draws a figure incorrectly, seems to recognize this fact, but is unable to correct the error or makes repeated but unsuccessful attempts to improve the reproduction, that is an example of Impotence. Other examples are making many erasures but just repeating the errors, or expressions of frustration and inability to correct the errors. The patient who made the drawings in Figure 12.4 tried several times to draw the shapes of designs A and 8 to get them to meet the other part of the designs. However, she was unable to correct her errors and showed the classical reaction of perplexity that is commonly a part of the clinical picture of impotence.

9. *Closure Difficulty.* This error is scored when the person shows continuing difficulty in getting parts of figures to join that should join, for instance, closing circles and hexagons, or joining the circle and square of design A. The difficulty may manifest itself in small gaps, erasures, increased pressure, and overworking the lines at the points

where figures join. Larger gaps between parts of figures are scored Simplification. Closure Difficulty is scored only for designs A, 4, 7, and 8. The sample case committed this error on all four of these designs. In almost every place where parts of the designs join, this patient either missed the closing or reworked the drawing several times to accomplish the closing.

10. *Motor Incoordination.* Figures are drawn with irregular rather than smooth-flowing lines, indicating tremulousness. The sample case does not contain any illustrations of this problem.

11. *Angulation Difficulty.* Difficulty in producing the angles of designs 2 and 3 is shown through either increasing or decreasing the required angulation, showing variability of angulation, or angling the whole figure by rotating it fewer than 80 degrees. In Figure 12.4, problems with angulation are present in both designs 2 and 3, which are drawn with little or no angulation.

12. *Cohesion.* This term refers to an isolated increase or decrease in the size of a figure in relation to the other figures in the protocol (e.g., design A versus 3 in Figure 12.4). The increase or decrease in size may also be to only part of a figure in relation to the other parts of the same figure. The size must be decreased by more than one third of the dimensions used in the rest of the figure or by more than one third of the dimensions of some other figure in the protocol.

Validity

Many factors contribute to the validity of a psychological test such as the BGT. Normative data, diagnostic accuracy, comparison with other tests, and strength of influence from other variables are factors that clinicians use to judge the worth of an assessment tool.

Norms

Essential to the decision-making process is information about how various groups typically perform on the BGT. For this test, most of the available normative data for the Lacks scoring method are from neuropsychiatric patients. This group is the most important one for comparison purposes because the majority of BGT decisions are made in this context. Lacks (1984, 1999) collected normative data from 535 nonpatient adults, 334 nonpatient older adults, and 349 adult psychiatric inpatients. Tests were scored by the author without knowledge of the diagnosis. These samples are described more fully and their test results presented in detail in the Lacks book on the BGT (1984, 1999). In 1988, McIntosh et al. showed that this scoring system also has merit in the evaluation of adolescents ages 12 through 16 ($N = 337$). Space restrictions of this chapter allow only a brief overview of the normative data.

The *nonpatient* data show that during childhood and adolescence, there is a gradual improvement in visuoconstructive skill. With increasing age, there begins a slow decline in these abilities; individuals' mean BGT scores increase from a low of 1.47 errors for people ages 17 to 24 to a high of 2.62 errors for ages 55 to 59. Similarly, as education advances from less than 9 years to 16 or more, the mean BGT scores decrease from 3.20 errors to 1.02 errors. Only 5% of the entire sample of 495 nonpatient adults earned scores in the range of brain impairment (5 or more errors). Most of the nonpatient scores of 5 or more errors were made by individuals aged 45 or older with less than 9 years of education.

The *neuropsychiatric inpatients* were taken from an urban acute-treatment center and a Veterans Administration (VA) hospital (Brilliant & Gynther, 1963; Lacks, Colbert, Harrow, & Levine, 1970). They were assigned to three broad diagnostic groups (personality disorder including chronic alcoholism, psychosis including 70% schizophrenia, and brain dysfunction) based on the final hospital discharge diagnosis. Diagnostic decisions were made by senior staff training psychiatrists from the faculty of a large affiliated medical school, usually after at least several weeks of observation, interviews, assessment of response to treatment, interdisciplinary staff conferences, and physical and neurological exams and tests. Almost all patients were given an EEG. Patients with brain impairment represented a diverse spectrum of etiologies such as head trauma, chronic substance abuse, encephalitis, and dementia (e.g., Alzheimer's, vascular, Huntington's). No patient was included whose diagnosis was based in any part upon psychological tests.

In each sample, the mean *(M)* scores for the two groups of inpatients with no brain impairment ($M = 3.59$ and 3.38 errors) are significantly lower than those for the patients with brain impairment ($M = 5.87$). The scores for the inpatients with personality disorder versus psychosis are not significantly different from each other. For patients with a diagnosis of personality disorder, the percentage with scores of 5 or more averaged 24%; for those diagnosed as psychotic, the average was 27%; for those with diagnoses of brain dysfunction, the average was 82%. Table 12.3 displays the percentile

Table 12.3.   Percentile distributions of BGT total scores for various comparison groups

Number of Errors	Nonpatient Adults ($n = 495$)	Nonpatient Older Adults ($n = 334$)	Nonimpaired Psychiatric Inpatients ($n = 264$)	Brain-Damaged Psychiatric Inpatients ($n = 85$)
0	20	5	3	0
1	51	17	10	0
2	75	35	31	4
3	87	52	55	9
4	96	74	74	18
5	98	85	85	51
6	99	92	93	71
7	100	96	96	80
8		99	99	87
9		99	100	95
10		100		99
11				100
12				

Note: The cutoff score for brain dysfunction is 5 or more errors. This table is from Lacks, P. (in press). *Bender Gestalt screening for brain dysfunction* (2nd ed.). Copyright by John Wiley & Sons.

distributions of total number of errors for several comparison groups. As you can see, between 74% and 96% of the three groups without brain damage had BGT scores in the nonimpaired range but only 18% of those with brain damage had such high scores.

Diagnostic Accuracy

The normative data for psychiatric patients show clear group differences between patients with brain dysfunction and those with no known impairment. However, this information alone is not sufficient to assess the discriminative power of the BGT. A number of studies have investigated the *diagnostic accuracy* of the Lacks scoring method with neuropsychiatric inpatients. As an example, Lacks and Newport (1980) selected 50 patients from a larger sample of 194 consecutive admissions to an acute psychiatric treatment center. The subsample was chosen to match hospital base rates and to match groups on ethnicity, gender, age, education, and IQ. Three scorers of varying levels of experience who were blind as to diagnosis independently scored the test protocols. The combined mean BGT score for all three judges for the 17 patients with brain damage was 5.80 (*SD* = 2.37), with 71% earning scores of 5 and above. The 33 individuals with no brain damage had mean error scores of 2.58 (*SD* = 1.55), with 10% earning scores of 5 and above.

In six other published studies evaluating the validity of the BGT using this scoring method, scores were consistently found to be significantly higher for individuals with brain dysfunction when compared to psychiatric patients with no known cognitive disorders, including psychiatric patients with severe disturbances. More important, however, are the diagnostic accuracies for the correct diagnosis of the presence and the absence of brain impairment. For correct diagnosis of all cases, the BGT hit rate across the seven studies ranges from 70% to 86% when comparing neuropsychiatric inpatients with and without brain impairment. The mean accuracy overall was 80%; the median was 82%. These hit rates compare very favorably to prediction from base rates alone (about 65% to 70% for no impairments) and to the median hit rates reported by Heaton et al. (1978) for the five most used neuropsychological tests: 68% to 84%, across all tests; 76% for eight studies of the standard BGT.

This accuracy also matches the results of a meta-analysis of 11 studies using the Halstead-Reitan Battery (HRB) combined with the WAIS-R (Garb & Schramke, 1996). All of these studies used neuropsychologists as judges. In terms of detection of brain impairment, for 2,383 ratings, these researchers found an overall hit rate of 84% (compared to an average brain-damage base rate of 65%, going as high as 80% in one setting). Accuracy varied considerably across the 11 studies. For 1,682 ratings, the correct prediction of no impairment was 79%; the correct prediction of presence of impairment was 86%.

The results of the BGT studies reported in this chapter are especially impressive when compared to the 11 HRB/WAIS studies reported by Garb and Schramke (1996) because the HRB/WAIS evaluations consisted of very large amounts of neuropsychological data requiring many hours per patient. Also, none of the HRB/WAIS studies attempted the very difficult task of discriminating between patients with brain damage and those with diagnoses of severe psychiatric disorders such as Bipolar Disorders or Schizophrenia. In fact, some of these comparisons were made between neurological cases and nonpatient controls recruited for research. Diagnostic accuracy varies greatly depending on the difficulty of the comparison being made.

The results of the BGT studies also are particularly strong because the diagnostic accuracies are consistent across different scorers and across different patient populations (although the brain-dysfunction base rate was approximately the same: 30% to 35% for all but one of the neuropsychiatric samples. It appears that the BGT can be a useful screening tool to aid in discrimination of neuropsychiatric and neurological patients with and without neurological impairment.

It is also important to remember that these rates of diagnostic accuracy represent *minimal* success rates because they are based on an artificial situation, that is, blind prediction based on a *single* test. In real practice, the psychologist would deliver diagnostic decisions based on a *battery* of tests combined with at least demographic information, clinical observations, and a history.

Comparison with Other Tests for Brain Impairment

In their 1978 review of studies of neuropsychological tests, Heaton et al. found the median diagnostic accuracy in 36 studies of the five most frequently used tests to range from 68% for the Graham-Kendall Memory for Designs Test to 76% for the standard BGT to 84% for the BGT given with the Background Interference Procedure. Most of these studies investigated only a single test, so there is little basis to judge them against each other.

Two studies used the Lacks scoring method and also evaluated concurrently more than one neuropsychological test. In the first study, Brilliant and Gynther (1963) gave the BGT, the Benton Visual Retention Test (BVRT), and the Graham-Kendall Memory for Designs (MFD) test to 109 neuropsychiatric inpatients who were classified as having brain damage or not, based on the hospital discharge diagnosis by experienced psychiatrists. For correct diagnosis of all cases, the BGT appears to be the best single measure, with 82% accuracy overall. The BVRT error score was least adequate, with only 66% of the total number of cases correctly classified.

The second study compared the BGT with Lacks scoring to five of the eight tests from the HRB (Category, Tactual Performance, Seashore Rhythm, Speech Perception, and Tapping; Lacks et al., 1970). The participants were 63 White, male, VA patients (19 with brain damage, 27 with schizophrenia, and 17 with general medical conditions). Using Reitan's cutoff scores, the percentage of patients with correctly diagnosed brain damage ranged from 44% for the Memory score of Tactual Performance to 84% for the composite Impairment Index. The percentage of patients correctly diagnosed with no impairment ranged from 44% for the Category test to 86% for the Memory score of Tactual Performance. The prorated composite Impairment Index correctly diagnosed 64% of the patients with no impairments. These findings contrast with the BGT's ability to identify correctly those patients with (74%) and without (91%) brain dysfunction.

The findings of Lacks et al. (1970) suggest that use of the HRB will lead to a high percentage of correct classification of those patients with some cognitive disorder. However, use of this battery in a setting with large numbers of patients with schizophrenia will also lead to very frequent misclassification of this category of patient. Because this battery of tests requires 3 to 4 hours to administer, the results are especially disappointing when compared to the diagnostic accuracy of the 5-minute BGT. Of course, the multiple tests of the HRB provide much more extensive information about the patients' abilities in various domains.

Relationship to Demographic Variables

Research has shown that the BGT can be applied with confidence to men and women, African Americans and Whites, knowing that gender and ethnicity do not seem to have a large influence on BGT scores, especially for psychiatric patients. However, there is little available knowledge about ethnic groups other than African Americans. As with other cognitive or information-processing tests, the variables of age, IQ, and education are related to the BGT scores of both nonpatients and patients. This relationship is most strong at the extreme ranges of these three variables. Demographic effects are also stronger with individuals who do not have brain dysfunction in comparison to those with brain impairment. With such individuals, the clinician should interpret the BGT scores with additional caution. Norms by gender, ethnicity, age, and education are available for the BGT (Lacks, 1984, 1999).

Reliability

Two types of reliability are especially appropriate for a test such as the BGT: (1) temporal stability, or test-retest reliability, and (2) agreement among scorers, or interscorer reliability.

Temporal stability refers to the consistency of results when the test is repeated over time, due to multiple hospitalizations or for monitoring deterioration. Measures of stability, however, are problematic with a test such as the BGT; many of the patients given this test have some kind of deteriorating brain condition so that their scores are expected to decline over time. Differences in test results then are often the result of real changes, not test instability. The longer the retest interval, the less the agreement between repeated measures. Tolor and Brannigan (1980) reported satisfactory BGT test-retest reliabilities using various scoring systems and scorers with diverse experience. However, clinicians should rely on total scores or on test diagnosis rather than on specific individual errors that have lower reliabilities.

For the Lacks scoring method, the author investigated the reliability of BGT scores in a sample of 40 mixed psychiatric patients retested an average of 10 days later. Mean number of errors was 2.30 ($SD = 1.40$) and 2.05 ($SD = 1.65$) for the two times of testing. The test-retest correlation for total errors was .79. There was also 86% agreement on exact errors and 93% agreement on test diagnosis (brain damaged vs. not damaged) between the two testings. As would be expected, retesting nonpatient older adults and those with mild Alzheimer's disease resulted in lower agreement. The first group consisted of 57 nonpatient older adults who were given extensive neurological evaluations and were found to be free of brain dysfunction. When they were retested after 12 months, mean BGT errors increased from 2.26 to 2.55. Retest reliability of total scores was .58; agreement on exact signs was 81% and on specific diagnosis was 93%. For 25 outpatients with mild Alzheimer's disease, respective means were 4.52 and 5.67; correlation of total scores was .66. Agreement of exact scores was 63% and of diagnosis was 72%.

A second type of reliability measures the consistency among raters. Most of the BGT scoring systems have enjoyed satisfactory *agreement among scorers* (see Hutt, 1985). As for the Lacks adapted method, Lacks and Newport (1980) examined the scoring consistency of three raters (representing three levels of BGT experience) who evaluated the BGT protocols of 50 mixed psychiatric inpatients. Interscorer reliability ranged from .87 to .90. Agreement on exact scoring ranged from 77% to 86% for any two scorers and was 72% for all three taken together. The agreement for test diagnosis ranged from 86% to 94% for any two scorers and was 84% among all three together. Friedt and Gouvier (1989) obtained very similar results for two scorers working in a forensic setting. Agreement for the total score was 88%.

This brief review of BGT reliability shows that the Lacks scoring procedures demonstrate adequate test-retest reliability that is comparable with other scoring systems for the BGT and for other neuropsychological tests. Agreement over time on the test diagnosis is especially consistent. Furthermore, there is a high degree of interrater concurrence among users of this scoring system, even when the scorers differ greatly in level of experience with this test. A novice scorer who received about 2 hours of training (reading a scoring manual, scoring 10 practice cases, obtaining feedback) was able to match the results of a highly experienced scorer.

Special Populations

In the past 10 years, increased interest in the assessment of special populations has produced new information about evaluation of these groups. For the BGT, three special populations have been of particular interest: older adults, children, and adolescents. This section provides a brief overview for using the BGT with each of these groups.

Older Adults

Improved quality of and access to health care have resulted in an elongated life span and in increasing numbers of older adults in the population. More and more, psychologists are called upon to evaluate the cognitive functioning of members of this age group, to assess their ability to live independently, and to periodically monitor mental deterioration especially from dementia (for BGT results comparing different degrees of dementia, see Storandt, 1990). Much of the early research on neuropsychological tests systematically omitted individuals over age 55 (Lezak, 1987). Researchers now know that advancing age does not lead to an inevitable decline of all physical and mental abilities. Declines are not uniform across all functions and some abilities can be retained until late in life. Areas most affected are timed tasks and those that require memory and active problem solving. For visuoconstructive tasks, there is evidence of retention of the ability to recognize and process perceptual stimuli if the stimuli are familiar ones. Attention does not decline until well into older age unless the task is complex and demanding. Many more details about normal cognitive changes of older people can be found in Lezak (1995) and Franzen and Martin (1996).

The complete effect of aging on a multidimensional visuoconstructive task such as the BGT is not fully known. However, healthy seniors maintain their performance on this test well into their seventies and eighties—it is not a timed task, the stimuli are familiar and simple, it does not require active problem solving, and memory is not involved. Mittenberg, Seidenberg, O'Leary, and DiGiulio (1989) found that parietal-occipital lobe operations (often considered a primary source of visuoconstructive integration) are spared the effects of normal aging.

Norms for nonpatient adults living independently (Lacks & Storandt, 1982) show only a gradual decrease in BGT performance across the age span. From the sixth through the eighth decade, the mean number of BGT errors (using the Lacks scoring procedures) increased from 3.00 to 4.33, still below the brain-impairment cutoff score of 5 errors. Scores of 5 errors or more were seen in 21% of the youngest group of older adults and ranged to 39% of the oldest participants, those over age 80. This means that even into the ninth decade, 61% did not earn scores that would suggest visuoconstructive deficits. These findings argue against age-corrected norms for older adults. Because these norms were obtained from an unscreened sample, it is likely that some of the participants had undetected brain dysfunction, perhaps in its early stages. Making the norms more liberal might lead to missed cases of brain impairment. It may be more beneficial to keep the norms as they are and to further evaluate any person who makes 5 or more errors. As long as precautions are taken to ensure that a physical disability such as poor eyesight, poor hearing, or advanced arthritis does not compromise comprehension of instructions or execution of the task, the BGT appears to be an excellent choice to measure visuoconstructive impairment with the older population.

Children

The BGT is one of the most popular tools for evaluating children and in fact was first developed for use with this age group. Lauretta Bender was a child psychiatrist who became interested in the sidewalk chalk drawings of children in New York City; she believed that the variations in drawings by different-aged children helped explain aspects of child development. These observations led her to study the process of maturation of children's visual-motor function. Her original book contains many BGT case examples at different levels of maturation (Bender, 1938). According to Bender, this maturational process is essentially complete by age 11, unless something interferes with the process.

In 1963, Elizabeth Koppitz published the first widely accepted, formal scoring system for the BGTs of children ages 5 to 10, the Developmental Bender Test Scoring System (usually referred to as the Koppitz system). In 1975, she published a second volume that detailed the validity and reliability research on her methods. Much of the earlier work concerned the test's usefulness in evaluating learning difficulties and school readiness. More recently, there has been a rapid growth of the subspecialty of child neuropsychological assessment. Even though many other measures have been developed for use with children, the BGT is still utilized by many child and school psychologists.

Administration of the BGT to children entails the same minimal instructions and noncommittal replies to questions as it does with adults. Observations of the *process* of taking the test greatly facilitate analysis of the *product*. Children also have been successfully tested in groups. More details are available in Sattler (1992).

The Koppitz scoring system requires the examination of each of the nine BGT designs for four types of errors: *distortion* of the shape; *rotation* of at least 45 degrees; *failure to integrate* the parts of the design; and *perseveration* or repetition of the elements of some designs. A detailed and easily followed scoring manual assists the examiner to check for the presence of 30 possible errors (2 to 4 errors for each design). Interscorer agreement using the Koppitz system is high (e.g., Neale & McKay, 1985). Norms in 6-month increments for the years from ages 5 to 10 are provided from over 2,000 children.

Recent surveys indicate that cases of learning disability are rapidly increasing in the school population. However, research does not support the use of the BGT as an inexpensive general test of school readiness or achievement. Learning disability is so complex that its detection requires a variety of measures that tap various functions of the brain. However, this test does appear to have merit in identifying children with difficulties in visual-spatial processing that render them vulnerable to certain subtypes of learning disability. Because perceptual-motor function appears to play a role in a number of subtypes of learning disability, a measure of this function should be included in an assessment battery (James & Selz, 1997). However, Sattler (1992) cautions that poor performance on the BGT can be due to "maturational delay, limited intellectual stimulation, unfamiliarity with testing situations, or neurological impairment" (p. 361). Ability to recognize errors but inability to correct them may signal output deficits; inability to see errors may mean faulty input. Visuoconstructive difficulties on this test have to be integrated with many other sources of information about the child to arrive at an accurate diagnosis. Excellent child case examples demonstrating this integrative process have been provided by Sattler (1992).

The BGT also has worth as a measure of a specific function within a group of tests for comprehensive evaluation of brain dysfunction (D'Amato, Rothlisberg, & Rhodes, 1997). As such, it has been useful in research on topics such as drug treatment of "minimal brain dysfunction," the long-term effects of having alcoholic parents, and in utero exposure to the mother's chronic use of narcotics.

Most of the same variables that influence the BGT scores of adults also affect the performance of children. For example, Sattler and Gwynne (1982) found that White and Hispanic children performed about the same at various age levels, whereas African American children made about twice as many errors at every age level. Puente, Mora, and Munoz-Cespedes (1997) explore the impact of cultural environments on skill development, especially in Spanish-speaking children.

Although the focus of Koppitz's work was the development of visual-spatial skills, she also included a list of 12 indicators of emotional disturbance (e.g., small size of drawing, use of two or more sheets of paper). The amount, type, and results of research on these indicators does not inspire confidence in their use.

Adolescents

There has always been a dilemma in using the BGT with adolescents. Koppitz believes that the visuoconstructive skills of developmentally normal children are fully mature by age 10. Norms for her scoring system show children of ages 10 to 11 averaging fewer than 2 errors out of a possible 30. Norms for adult scoring systems generally begin at age 18. This situation throws adolescents into a kind of BGT limbo with nowhere for the psychologist to turn for the patient in the 12-to-17 age span. Clinicians have sometimes been advised to use the Koppitz norms for younger adolescents and the adult norms for those adolescents in the older age range. Fortunately, in 1988, McIntosh et al. investigated the validity of using the Koppitz and the Lacks scoring methods with nonpatient adolescents and with those adolescents who were psychiatric and neurological inpatients. They found both systems to be useful with this age group. Contrary to Koppitz's beliefs, individuals in this age group continued to show improved performance with increasing age when her scoring system was used. Mean errors at age 12 for nonpatients were 3.50 (out of a possible 30) and at age 16 were 1.67. The age effect was not as strong with the Lacks method; from ages 12 to 16, average errors decreased from 2.67 (out of a possible 12) to 2.17.

With both systems, there was a strong effect for diagnosis: those adolescents with mental retardation or neurological impairment did significantly worse on the BGT than either nonpatients or those with psychiatric disorders who were not different from each other. This same pattern for diagnosis was evident for the Koppitz Emotional Indicators (Belter, McIntosh, Finch, Williams, & Edwards, 1989). Two other studies showed results remarkably congruent with those of McIntosh et al. (1988) for the Koppitz system. For now, it appears that psychologists may use either of these scoring systems to evaluate the BGT performance of adolescents. However, more research needs to be done before psychologists can have high levels of confidence in their use with this age group.

Assets and Limitations

Since its development 50 years ago, the BGT remains one of the most popular psychological tests, both for clinical practice and for research. It is simple, brief, and easily learned, and it can be administered by a trained technician. A reliable and well-validated scoring system can be learned in a few hours. Because it is nonthreatening to most people, the BGT can be used as a warm-up to some of the more difficult or anxiety-arousing measures. It is a test that can be useful across the age span for a variety of purposes. There is also a very large volume of research on its psychometric properties and diagnostic efficacy, although not all of it is well done.

In spite of all these many assets, over recent years, the BGT has been the subject of a fair amount of criticism, especially among neuropsychologists. Many neuropsychologists believe that clinical psychologists misuse this test by relying on it as a single test for detecting brain damage or "organicity." Such use is naive and oversimplifies the reality of brain dysfunction. It is doubtful that such a practice was ever widespread, and, if so, it was not justified. Most psychologists, however, use this test within a battery of psychological measures that usually includes the Wechsler intelligence scales. More recent evidence supports a general-effect view of brain dysfunction in which even focal damage can often result in widespread effects on the brain. Research also shows that many skills, involving multiple areas of the brain, are necessary to do well on this simple test. Therefore, the BGT can serve as a marker of many different types of brain damage, especially from diffuse or right parietal brain impairment.

Psychologists who work in *psychiatric* settings are often called on to discriminate between patients with cognitive impairments (e.g., dementia, chronic alcoholism) and those with psychotic disturbances. These two groups frequently appear quite similar (e.g., confusion, mental deterioration, attention deficits). The base rates for both groups are high in these settings, and the treatments are very different. If a battery of tests including one or more screening measures for brain damage indicates possible brain impairment, the patient can be further evaluated or referred for more extensive neuropsychological assessment. The needs of neuropsychologists are generally quite different from those of clinical psychologists. Neuropsychologists often work in general hospitals or neurology services where the base rate of schizophrenia is very low and the incidence of focal lesions relatively high. They do not need a screening test for brain damage. In this setting, the BGT can be used within a battery of neuropsychological tests as a specific measure of the cognitive domain of visuoconstructive skills.

A serious limitation of BGT practice is the stubborn refusal of some psychologists to learn a quantitative scoring system for this test. These practitioners rely instead on their clinical judgment—it "looks good" or it "looks bad." This unacceptable approach also often relies on unsubstantiated clinical lore. For example, many psychologists believe that rotations are strongly indicative of brain damage, whereas the research shows otherwise. The same psychologists would never take such a casual approach to other tests such as the WAIS or MMPI. Perhaps it is because Lauretta Bender did not use a formal evaluation of her test. The first true scoring system for the BGT was published in 1951 (Pascal & Suttell). Furthermore, when the test is purchased, it does not include scoring instructions such as most tests do. A number of different methods of evaluation are available, however, and the clinician has to seek one out and learn it. Unfortunately, there are eight objective systems available for adult populations and three for children, so research efforts have been scattered, and few scoring methods have been compared to each other.

Of the available scoring systems, it is no longer acceptable to use the Pascal-Suttell method. Its norms from 1951 do not extend above or below the narrow age range of 15 to 50 years or below 9 years of education. It is also too time consuming to learn and use. Psychologists should select a method that is clear and easy to apply, quick to learn, and that has respectable reliability, validity, and diagnostic accuracy.

Sometimes research on the BGT appears contradictory. However, a closer examination shows that much of the inconsistency in research findings is due to methodological shortcomings and the use of different populations and scoring methods. The findings with different evaluative techniques are generally not equivalent. Early BGT research did not allow for the successful identification of individuals. Many of the studies had major flaws, such as small groups, unreliable diagnosis, and comparison of patients with brain damage to nonpatients rather than to those with psychiatric diagnoses. More recent research corrects most of these errors and includes blind test evaluation, consideration of base rates, and sophisticated diagnostic practices. *Norms* are now available for all ages, including the rapidly increasing group of older adults (e.g., Koppitz, 1975; Lacks, 1984, 1999; McIntosh et al., 1988; Storandt, 1990). The norms for adolescents are relatively new and need additional verification.

There is considerable evidence for the *clinical utility* of the BGT, especially when used with the Lacks adaptation of the Hutt-Briskin scoring system (Lacks, 1984, 1999). Clear differences exist among group scores of nonpatients, patients with no brain impairment, and those with documented neuropathology. In addition, a number of studies show the Lacks adaptation to have high accuracy in the diagnosis of individuals. Cross-validated overall hit rates, using the standard cutoff score, range from 80% to 85% accuracy across various populations and scorers (compared to about 70% accuracy from base-rate prediction alone). As with other cognitive tests, there are well-documented effects on BGT scores from the *demographic variables* of age, education, and IQ. However, any impact of these variables occurs mainly in the extreme upper and lower ranges of these variables. Future research needs to address more fully the effects of ethnicity on BGT scores.

Interpretation of BGT Results

A number of steps can be taken to interpret the results of the BGT test. However, clinicians should remember that interpretation provides only a *test diagnosis;* the results are meaningless until integrated with patient history and with the findings from other tests. This score is useful in deciding on a diagnosis of brain damage or in describing a person's visuoconstructive abilities. It is always best to use this test conservatively; clinicians should look for multiple confirmations of any conclusions they draw.

Interpretation Strategies for the BGT

Clinicians should consider eight pieces of information before drawing conclusions about the test results. Each will be explained briefly here; more details are available in Lacks (1999).

1. Decide if the patient's effort resulted in a *valid and reliable* product. Are the errors evidence of true visuoconstructive disability, or are they due to other factors, such as low motivation, poor visual acuity, malingering, or high anxiety. Be especially wary if the patient took a very short or overly long amount of time to complete the test. For example, a very short time to draw the figures resulting in 5 or more errors probably represents an overestimation of the true number of errors. An especially long time resulting in 4 errors is probably an underestimation.

2. *Compare the number of errors to the norms* for the appropriate normative group. Did the patient make more or fewer errors than someone of similar age and IQ?

3. *Classify the patient's score* into the categories of brain dysfunction or no brain dysfunction. Generally, 3 or fewer errors indicates an *absence* of visuoconstructive deficits or brain impairment; 4 errors is a *borderline* score; and 5 or 6 errors provide *some evidence* for brain impairment. The greater the number of errors, the greater the evidence for some type of brain impairment: *strong evidence* with 7 or 8 errors and *very strong evidence* with 9 to 12 errors.

4. You may use the percentile distributions of BGT scores in Table 12.3 to take an *actuarial approach* to interpretation, that is, to estimate the risks of a missed case or a false positive outcome. For example, note that no inpatients with known brain damage made as few as 0 or 1 error; therefore, the chances of missing brain damage in a person with this low a BGT score is very low. Note also that 4% with a score of 2, 9% with a score of 3 or fewer errors, and 18% with a score of 4 or fewer errors were misclassified as not having brain damage. In contrast, look at the column labeled "Non-Brain-Damaged Inpatients." Here we can see that 74% were correctly classified by earning a BGT score of 4 or fewer errors. However, 26% earned scores of 5 or more, resulting in a false positive diagnosis. Keep in mind that a low BGT score can not entirely rule out brain damage. The BGT can miss conditions such as mild cognitive deficits, language disorder, or a focal lesion. The younger the patient and the higher the IQ, the higher is the risk of a missed case. False positive cases tend to be those with lower IQs, greater age, or a diagnosis of chronic schizophrenia. For a person with a borderline score of 4 errors, consider the behavioral observations, results of other tests, the pattern of symptoms, and the patient's history.

5. Other diagnostic clues can be found in the patient's *specific errors.* Remember that the validity and the reliability of specific errors is lower than that of the total score. However, certain scores have been shown to appear with more frequency in the protocols of those with brain damage and are therefore more suggestive of impairment. Lacks (1984, 1999), Hutt (1985), and Friedt and Gouvier (1989) have all found similar error patterns. If any error can be considered a pathognomic sign of brain damage, it is Impotence, which occurs with eight times the frequency in inpatients with brain damage as it does with other psychiatric inpatients. Fragmentation and Motor Incoordination appear about three times as often in patients with impairments. In contrast, the following 5 errors appear as commonly in the drawings of persons with no brain dysfunction as they do in the BGTs of patients with brain impairment: Collision, Cohesion, Closure Difficulty, Overlapping Difficulty, and Perseveration. The remaining errors, including Rotation, are seen about twice as often in the inpatients with brain impairment and so may be considered somewhat suggestive of brain dysfunction. Looking at specific errors in another way, patients with schizophrenia sometimes also draw particular distortions though they tend to be ones that are not scored in the Lacks method. Examples of these errors are drawing symbols (e.g., stars for dots, making figure 3 into a Christmas tree) and including elaborations, embellishments, or doodles on the paper (Hutt, 1985). Although none of the evidence concerning specific errors is strong enough to confirm a diagnosis, it may be used as one more cumulative piece of information to rule brain damage in or out.

6. Many *variables can influence BGT performance,* thus complicating the test diagnosis and lowering confidence in the results. Examples of such variables are: lower education or IQ, ethnicity other than White, chronic schizophrenia, a situation that could encourage faking, older age, and a history of abuse of alcohol or other substances. Extra care should be taken in drawing conclusions about the BGT results of any person with these variables, especially if the person made 4 or more errors. A higher score for a person with any of these variables may be a case of accurate diagnosis, or it may be a false positive diagnosis. The clinician should *be familiar with the scientific research* dealing with these complicating variables.

7. The clinician should be sure to *apply scientific or actuarial decision-making rules* in the interpretation of test data (Wedding & Faust, 1989). A few of these rules are: Use a formal scoring method instead of clinical judgment; know the diagnostic base rates in your work setting; take into account regression toward the mean when you repeat testing; avoid hindsight bias such as acquiescing to diagnostic consensus among the team members.

8. Finally, remember that the BGT is one test providing only one source of information about the patient. No recommendations about diagnosis or treatment should be based solely on one test. The BGT alone, or for that matter any other single test, is not sufficient for making a diagnosis of brain dysfunction or for fully describing visuoconstructive abilities. "Only a collection of tests can hope to be effective in diagnosing impairment in so complex an organ as the human brain" (Gregory, 1987, p. 202). The results of the BGT should instead be integrated with the findings of other measures as well as mental status, observed behaviors, and history. If results are unclear, you may want to seek further clarification by administering other neuropsychological measures or by

referring the patient for a comprehensive neuropsychological evaluation or a neurological examination. To formulate a treatment or rehabilitation plan, much more information is needed than the BGT can provide, such as the type and location of damage to the brain, the specific impaired functions, the severity of the impairment, and the type and amount of the patient's strengths.

Computer-Assisted BGT Interpretation

Recently, psychologists have begun to rely on computers for help with administration, scoring, interpretation, and reporting aspects of psychological assessment (Piotrowski & Keller, 1989). Software is now available to assist with these tasks for many psychological tests such as the WAIS and the Rorschach. The reader is referred to Groth-Marnat's (1999) section on this topic for additional details.

As a drawing task, the BGT does not lend itself to electronic assistance with administration or scoring. However, electronic interpretation and report writing are feasible and have recently become available for the Lacks scoring method (Lacks, 1996). In this software, the psychologist enters demographic data, behavioral observations, background information, and the test scores into the computer. The computer program assesses the data for the various interpretive steps. Within minutes, the program then displays a detailed report on the BGT findings that can also be customized by the psychologist. This two- to three-page report is for the psychologist's use only, to aid in thoroughly analyzing the BGT findings before integrating the results with those of other tests into the overall psychological report. The following paragraph is a sample of the summary section only of a computer-assisted report. It summarizes the BGT results of the case presented in Figure 12.4.

> This patient made a BGT score of 7 reproduction errors out of a possible 12. Using the standard cutoff score of 5 errors, the results indicate strong evidence for brain pathology. For this number of errors, the risk of misclassifying someone as brain impaired is quite low. Also, the patient's test-taking behaviors and attitudes promote confidence in the validity and reliability of these BGT findings. Certain background information complicates the diagnostic picture in this case, such as the patient's ethnic/racial group and a low education or IQ. Because the BGT is only a brief screening test, a diagnosis of brain pathology should never be based on such an instrument used alone. Recommendations were made for additional assessment to make a more definitive diagnosis, specify the source and degree of impairment, and provide details to plan for treatment and rehabilitation.

RECOMMENDED READING

Hutt, M.L. (1985). *The Hutt adaptation of the Bender-Gestalt Test* (4th ed.). New York: Grune & Stratton.

Koppitz, E.M. (1975). *The Bender Gestalt Test for young children. Volume 2: Research and application. 1963–1973.* New York: Grune & Stratton.

Lacks, P. (1999). *Bender Gestalt screening for brain dysfunction* (2nd edition) New York: Wiley.

McIntosh, J.A., Belter, R.W., Saylor, C.F., & Finch, A.J., & Edwards, G.L. (1988). The Bender-Gestalt with adolescents: Comparison of two scoring systems. *Journal of Clinical Psychology, 44,* 226–230.

Sattler, J.M. (1992). *Assessment of children*. (3rd ed.). San Diego: Author.

Wedding, D., & Faust, D. (1989). Clinical judgment and decision making in neuropsychology. *Archives of Clinical Neuropsychology, 4,* 233–265.

REFERENCES

Armstrong, R.G. (1965). A reevaluation of copied and recalled Bender-Gestalt reproductions. *Journal of Projective Techniques and Personality Assessment, 29,* 134–139.

Belter, R.W., McIntosh, J.A., Finch, A.J., Williams, L.D., & Edwards, G.L. (1989). The Bender-Gestalt as a method of personality assessment with adolescents. *Journal of Clinical Psychology, 45,* 414–422.

Bender, L. (1938). *A visual motor gestalt test and its clinical use.* New York: American Orthopsychiatric Association.

Benton, A.L. (1974). *Revised visual retention test* (4th ed.). San Antonio, TX: The Psychological Corporation.

Benton, A.L., & Tranel, D. (1993). Visuoperceptual, visuospatial, and visuoconstructive disorders. In K.M. Heilman & E. Valenstein (Eds.), *Clinical neuropsychology* (pp. 165–213). New York: Oxford University Press.

Berg, R.A., Franzen, M., & Wedding, D. (1994). *Screening for brain impairment: A manual for mental health practice.* New York: Springer.

Black, F.W., & Bernard, B.A. (1984). Constructional apraxia as a function of lesion locus and size in patients with focal brain damage. *Cortex, 20,* 111–120.

Boake, C., & Adams, R.L. (1982). Clinical utility of the background interference procedure for the Bender-Gestalt test. *Journal of Clinical Psychology, 38,* 627–631.

Brilliant, P., & Gynther, M.D. (1963). Relationships between performance on three tests for organicity and selected patient variables. *Journal of Consulting Psychology, 27,* 474–479.

Brodaty, H., & Moore, C.M. (1997). The clock drawing test for dementia of the Alzheimer's type: A comparison of three scoring methods in a memory disorders clinic. *International Journal of Geriatric Psychiatry, 12,* 619–627.

Butler, M., Retzlaff, P., & Vanderploeg, R. (1991). Neuropsychological test usage. *Professional Psychology: Research and Practice, 22,* 510–512.

Canter, A. (1966). A background interference procedure to increase sensitivity of the Bender-Gestalt test to organic brain disorder. *Journal of Consulting Psychology, 30,* 91–97.

Canter, A. (1971). A comparison of the background interference procedure effect in schizophrenic, nonschizophrenic, and organic patients. *Journal of Clinical Psychology, 27,* 473–474.

Chiulli, S.J., Haaland, K.Y., LaRue, A., & Garry, P.J. (1995). Impact of age on drawing the Rey-Osterrieth figure. *Clinical Neuropsychologist, 9,* 219–224.

D'Amato, R.C., Rothlisberg, B.A., & Rhodes, R.L. (1997). Utilizing a neuropsychological paradigm for understanding common educational and psychological tests. In C.R. Reynolds & E. Fletcher-Janzen (Eds.), *Handbook of clinical child neuropsychology* (2nd ed., pp. 270–295). New York: Plenum Press.

D'Elia, L.F., Boone, K.B., & Mitrushina, A.M. (1999). *Handbook of normative data for neuropsychological assessment.* New York: Oxford University Press.

Edmonds, J.E., Cohen, M.J., & Riccio, C.A. (1994). The development of clock face drawing in normal children. *Archives of Clinical Neuropsychology, 9,* 125.

Franzen, M.D., & Martin, R.C. (1996). Screening for neuropsychological impairment. In L.L. Carstensen, B.A. Edelstein, & L. Dornbrand (Eds.), *The practical handbook of clinical gerontology* (pp. 188–216). Thousand Oaks, CA: Sage.

Freedman, M., Leach, L., Kaplan, E., Winocur, G., Shulman, K.I., & Delis, D.C. (1994). *Clock drawing: A neuropsychological analysis.* New York: Oxford University Press.

Friedt, L.R., & Gouvier, W.D. (1989). Bender-Gestalt screening for brain dysfunction in a forensic population. *Criminal Justice and Behavior, 16,* 455–464.

Garb, H.N., & Schramke, C.J. (1996). Judgment research and neuropsychological assessment: A narrative review and meta-analyses. *Psychological Bulletin, 120,* 140–153.

Goodenough, F. (1926). *Measurement of intelligence by drawings.* New York: World Book.

Gregory, R.J. (1987). *Adult intellectual assessment.* Boston: Allyn & Bacon.

Groth-Marnat, G. (1999). *Handbook of psychological assessment* (3rd ed. rev.). New York: Wiley.

Hain, J.D. (1964). The Bender-Gestalt test: A scoring method for identifying brain damage. *Journal of Consulting Psychology, 28,* 34–40.

Handler, L. (1996). The clinical use of drawings. In C.S. Newmark (Ed.), *Major psychological assessment instruments* (pp. 206–293). Boston: Allyn & Bacon.

Heaton, R.K., Baade, L.E., & Johnson, K.L. (1978). Neuropsychological test results associated with psychiatric disorders in adults. *Psychological Bulletin, 85,* 141–162.

Hooper, H.E. (1983). *Hooper visual organization test (VOT).* Los Angeles: Western Psychological Services.

Hutt, M.L. (1985). *The Hutt adaptation of the Bender-Gestalt test* (4th ed.). New York: Grune & Stratton.

Hutt, M.L., & Briskin, G.J. (1960). *The clinical use of the revised Bender-Gestalt test.* New York: Grune & Stratton.

James, E.M., & Selz, M. (1997). Neuropsychological bases of common learning and behavior problems in children. In C.R. Reynolds & E. Fletcher-Janzen (Eds.), *Handbook of clinical child neuropsychology* (2nd ed., pp. 157–179). New York: Plenum Press.

Koppitz, E.M. (1963). *The Bender-Gestalt test for young children.* New York: Grune & Stratton.

Koppitz, E.M. (1968). *Psychological evaluation of children's human figure drawings.* New York: Grune & Stratton.

Koppitz, E.M. (1975). *The Bender-Gestalt test for young children: Vol. 2. Research and application. 1963–1973.* New York: Grune & Stratton.

Lacks, P. (1984). *Bender-Gestalt screening for brain dysfunction.* New York: Wiley.

Lacks, P. (1996). *Bender-Gestalt screening software for Windows.* Odessa, FL: Psychological Assessment Resources.

Lacks, P. (1999). *Bender-Gestalt screening for brain dysfunction* (2nd ed.). New York: Wiley.

Lacks, P., Colbert, J., Harrow, M., & Levine, J. (1970). Further evidence concerning the diagnostic accuracy of the Halstead organic test battery. *Journal of Clinical Psychology, 26,* 480–481.

Lacks, P., & Newport, K. (1980). A comparison of scoring systems and level of scorer experience on the Bender-Gestalt test. *Journal of Personality Assessment, 44,* 351–357.

Lacks, P., & Storandt, M. (1982). Bender-Gestalt performance of normal older adults. *Journal of Clinical Psychology, 38,* 624–627.

Lezak, M.D. (1987). Norms for growing older. *Developmental Neuropsychology, 3,* 1–12.

Lezak, M.D. (1995). *Neuropsychological assessment.* New York: Oxford University Press.

Libon, D.J., Malamut, B.L., Swenson, R., Sands, L.P., & Cloud, B.S. (1996). Further analyses of clock drawings among demented and nondemented older subjects. *Archives of Clinical Neuropsychology, 11,* 193–205.

Lownsdale, W.S., Rogers, B.J., & McCall, J.N. (1989). Concurrent validation of Hutt's Bender-Gestalt screening method for schizophrenia, depression, and brain damage. *Journal of Personality Assessment, 53,* 832–836.

Marsico, D.S., & Wagner, E.E. (1990). A comparison of the Lacks and Pascal-Suttell Bender-Gestalt scoring methods for diagnosing brain damage in an outpatient sample. *Journal of Clinical Psychology, 46,* 868–877.

McIntosh, J.A., Belter, R.W., Saylor, C.F., Finch, A.J., & Edwards, G.L. (1988). The Bender-Gestalt with adolescents: Comparison of two scoring systems. *Journal of Clinical Psychology, 44,* 226–230.

Meehl, P.E. (1954). *Clinical versus statistical prediction.* Minneapolis: University of Minnesota Press.

Meyers, J.E., & Meyers, K.R. (1995). *The Meyers scoring system for the Rey complex figure and the recognition trial: Professional manual.* Odessa, FL: Psychological Assessment Resources.

Mitchell, J., Trent, R., & McArthur, M. (1993). *Human figure drawing test.* Los Angeles: Western Psychological Services.

Mittenberg, W., Seidenberg, M., O'Leary, D.S., & DiGiulio, D.V. (1989). Changes in cerebral functioning associated with normal aging. *Journal of Clinical and Experimental Neuropsychology, 11,* 918–932.

Neale, M.D., & McKay, M.F. (1985). Scoring the Bender-Gestalt test using the Koppitz developmental system: Interrater reliability, item difficulty, and scoring implications. *Perceptual and Motor Skills, 60,* 627–636.

Osterrieth, P.A. (1944). Le test de copie d'une figure complex: Contribution a l'etude de la perception et de la memoire. *Archives de Psychologie, 30,* 286–356.

Pascal, G.R., & Suttell, B.J. (1951). *The Bender-Gestalt test.* New York: Grune & Stratton.

Pauker, J.D. (1976). A quick-scoring system for the Bender-Gestalt: Interrater reliability and scoring validity. *Journal of Clinical Psychology, 32,* 86–89.

Piotrowski, C., & Keller, J.W. (1989). Psychological testing in outpatient mental health facilities: A national study. *Professional Psychology: Research and Practice, 20,* 423–425.

Puente, A.E., Mora, M.S., & Munoz-Cespedes, J.M. (1997). Neuropsychological assessment of Spanish-speaking children and youth. In C.R. Reynolds & E. Fletcher-Janzen (Eds.), *Handbook of clinical child neuropsychology* (2nd ed., pp. 371–383). New York: Plenum Press.

Rey, A. (1941). L'examen psychologique dans les cas d'encephalopathie traumatique. *Archives de Psychologie, 28,* 286–340.

Robiner, W. (1978). *An analysis of some of the variables influencing clinical use of the Bender-Gestalt.* Unpublished masters thesis, Washington University in St. Louis.

Rouleau, I., Salmon, D.P., Butters, N., Kennedy, C., & McGuire, K. (1992). Quantitative and qualitative analyses of clock drawings in Alzheimer's disease and Huntington's disease. *Brain and Cognition, 18,* 70–87.

Safran, S. (1997). Neuropsychological deficits in the interpretation of projective drawing: Drawings as a neuropsychological screen for visuospatial deficits in cognitive function. *Projective Drawing, 2,* 15–27.

Sattler, J.M. (1992). *Assessment of children* (3rd ed.). San Diego: Author.

Sattler, J.M., & Gwynne, J. (1982). Ethnicity and Bender visual motor Gestalt test performance. *Journal of School Psychology, 20,* 69–71.

Shulman, K.I., Gold, D.P., Cohen, C.A., & Zucchero, C.A. (1993). Clock drawing and dementia in the community: A longitudinal study. *International Journal of Geriatric Psychiatry, 8,* 487–496.

Sivan, A.B. (1992). *Benton visual retention test* (5th ed.). San Antonio, TX: The Psychological Corporation.

Spreen, O., & Strauss, E. (1998). *A compendium of neuropsychological tests: Administration, norms, and commentary* (2nd ed.). New York: Oxford University Press.

Storandt, M. (1990). Bender-Gestalt test performance in senile dementia of the Alzheimer type. *Psychology and Aging, 5,* 604–606.

Storandt, M., Botwinick, J., & Danziger, W.L. (1986). Longitudinal changes: Patients with mild SDAT and matched healthy controls. In L.W. Poon (Ed.), *Handbook for clinical memory assessment of older adults.* Washington, DC: American Psychological Association.

Tolor, A., & Brannigan, G.G. (1980). *Research and clinical applications of the Bender-Gestalt test.* Springfield, IL.: Thomas.

Tuokko, H., Hadjistavropoulos, T., Miller, J.A., & Beattie, B.L. (1992). The clock test: A sensitive measure to differentiate normal elderly from those with Alzheimer's disease. *Journal of the American Geriatrics Society, 40,* 579–584.

Watkins, C.E., Campbell, V.L., Nieberding, R., & Hallmark, R. (1995). Contemporary practice of psychological assessment by clinical psychologists. *Professional Psychology: Research and Practice, 26,* 54–60.

Wedding, D., & Faust, D. (1989). Clinical judgment and decision making in neuropsychology. *Archives of Clinical Neuropsychology, 4,* 233–265.

Wertheimer, M. (1923). Studies in the theory of Gestalt psychology. *Psychologische Forschung, 4,* 301–350.

Wetzel, L., & Murphy, S.G. (1991). Validity of the use of a discontinue rule and evaluation of discriminability of the Hooper visual organization test. *Neuropsychology, 5,* 119–122.

Youngjohn, J.R., Larrabee, G.J., & Crook, T.H. (1993). New adult age-and-education-correction norms for the Benton visual retention test. *Clinical Neuropsychologist, 7,* 155–160.

Chapter 13 ———————————————————

THE EXECUTIVE FUNCTIONS
OF THE BRAIN

ROBERT J. SBORDONE

The *executive functions* of the brain can be defined as the complex process by which an individual goes about performing a novel problem-solving task from its inception to its completion. This process includes the awareness that a particular problem exists, an evaluation of the particular problem, an analysis of the conditions of the problem, the formulation of specific goals (e.g., solve this problem), the development of a set of plans that determine which actions are needed to solve the problem, the evaluation of the potential effectiveness of these plans, the selection and initiation of a particular plan to solve the problem, evaluation of any progress made toward solving the problem, modification of the plan if it has not been effective, disregarding ineffective plans and replacing them with more effective plans, comparing the results achieved by the new plan with the conditions of the problem, terminating the plan when the conditions of the problem have been satisfied, storing the plan, and retrieving it later if the same or a similar problem appears.

Anatomy

Cummings (1995) has formulated a complex model of frontal-subcortical circuits that argues that the executive functions can become impaired when a circuit or a loop is broken. Thus, patients may exhibit what has been commonly termed a "frontal lobe syndrome," even though their frontal lobes may be neurologically intact, as a result of a lesion in the circuit or an alteration of the metabolic activity of the neural structures that form the circuit. For example, damage to the dorsolateral prefrontal cortex has been reported to produce a neurobehavioral syndrome characterized by an inability to maintain set, disassociation between verbal and motor behavior, deficits in complex or programmed motor activities, concrete thinking, poor mental control, and stimulus-bound behavior (Cummings, 1985, 1995). Somewhat similarly, lesions in the parietal, temporal, and occipital association areas and dorsal caudate nucleus may also produce neurobehavioral symptoms. This is because the dorsolateral prefrontal cortex has reciprocal connections with cortical and subcortical regions of the brain. Specifically, the dorsolateral prefrontal cortex receives information from the orbitofrontal cortex, parietal association cortex, auditory association cortex, cingulate gyrus, retrosplenial cortex, parahippocampal gyrus and presubiculum via the superior longitudinal fasciculus, inferior longitudinal fasciculus, and the inferior occipitofrontal bundle. The dorsofrontal cortex also modulates the activity of these structures and creates a conduit through which information from multiple cortical areas is projected to the dorsal caudate, which receives inputs from the parietal cortex, temporal cortex, occipital cortex, substantia nigra, and the medial dorsal nucleus of the thalamus. After these inputs are processed by the dorsal caudate, they are projected back to the dorsolateral prefrontal cortex (G. Alexander & Crutcher, 1990; Nieuwenhuys, Voogd, & van Huijzen, 1988; Yeterian & Pandya, 1993), thus creating a dorsolateral prefrontal-subcortical circuit (Cummings, 1995).

Damage to the orbitofrontal cortex has been reported to produce a neurobehavioral syndrome characterized by a lack of social tact, the use of crude or coarse language, inability to regulate one's behavior or emotions (disinhibition), emotional lability, insensitivity to the needs and welfare of others, and antisocial acts (Blumer & Benson, 1975; Cummings, 1985; Stuss & Benson, 1986). Similar behaviors can be produced by lesions in nonfrontal cortical and subcortical structures. For example, the orbitofrontal cortex receives inputs from the dorsolateral prefrontal regions, temporal pole, and amygdala. The amygdala receives information from the medial dorsal and central anterior nuclei of the thalamus. Because the orbitofrontal cortex also regulates the activity of the dorsolateral prefrontal cortex, temporal pole, and amygdala, it forms an orbitofrontal-subcortical circuit (Cummings, 1995).

Although damage to the medial frontal cortex has been shown to produce a neurobehavioral syndrome characterized by apathy, diminished motivation and interest, psychomotor retardation, diminished social involvement, and reduced communication (Cummings, 1995), damage to a variety of nonfrontal cortical and subcortical structures may produce similar behaviors. For example, the anterior cingulate cortex forms a medial frontal-subcortical circuit with the nucleus accumbens and with the amygdala. These structures receive information from the ventral tegmental area, substantia nigra, dorsal raphe nucleus, and the mediodorsal nucleus of the thalamus. The nucleus accumbens also receives information from the anterior insular cortex, anteroventral temporal region, cingulate gyrus, hypothalamus, amygdala, raphe nuclei, and the lateral habenula.

The dorsolateral prefrontal cortex receives information about the external environment, the internal milieu, and the emotional state of the organism and serves as the principal organ for integrating information from these three circuits. These circuits essentially provide the organism with the ability to guide its behavior through mental representations of the perceived world (e.g., working memory) and thus free it from its dependency on the environment (Bromfield et al., 1992).

Relationship to Psychiatric Disorders

Various psychiatric disorders impair the executive functions as a result of either lesions in the frontal-subcortical circuits or alterations of the metabolic activity of the circuits. For example, psychiatric disorders such as Alzheimer's disease (Chen, Sultzer, Hinkin, Mahler, & Cummings, 1998), alcoholism (Moscovich, 1982), AIDS dementia complex (Maruff et al., 1994), attention deficit disorder (Barkley, Grodzinsky, & DuPaul, 1992), depression (Cummings, 1992), head trauma (Mattson & Levin, 1990; Stuss, 1987), mania (Cummings & Mendez, 1984), obsessive-compulsive disorder (Baxter et al., 1987), Pick's disease (Gustafson, Risberg, Johanson, & Brun, 1984), psychosis (Cummings, Gosenfeld, Houlihan, & McCaffrey, 1983), and schizophrenia (Morris, Rushe, Woodruff, & Murray, 1995) have been reported to produce significant alterations in the executive functions.

Relationship to Subcortical Disorders

Impaired executive functions have been reported to be associated with a variety of subcortical disorders such as Parkinson's disease (Cools, Van den Bercken, Horstink, Van Spaendonck, & Berger, 1984; Flowers & Robertson, 1985; Lees & Smith, 1983; Taylor, Saint-Cye, Lang, & Kenny, 1986), progressive supranuclear palsy (Albert, Feldman, & Willis, 1974; Grafman, Litvan, Gomez, & Chase, 1990; Maher, Smith, & Lees, 1985), Huntington's disease (M. Alexander, Benson, & Stuss, 1989; Butters, Sax, Montgomery, & Tarlow, 1978; Fedio, Cox, Neophytides, Canal-Frederick, & Chase, 1979; Josiassen, Curry, & Mancall, 1983; Potegal, 1971), Korsakoff's syndrome (Lezak, 1995), and dementia caused by inhalation of organic solvents (Arlien-Soberg, Bruhn, Gyldensted, & Melgaard, 1979; Hawkins, 1990; Tsushima & Towne, 1977).

NEUROPSYCHOLOGICAL ASSESSMENT

Clinical Interview

The clinical interview provides the psychologist with an opportunity to gather data about the patient's presenting problems and background and to formulate hypotheses about the patient's underlying cognitive and emotional difficulties. Unfortunately, assessing patients with impaired executive functions is difficult via the clinical interview process because these patients will typically deny any cognitive or emotional difficulties and may appear relatively normal. However, the manner in which questions are posed to the patient may be helpful in identifying patients with executive dysfunction. For example, the interviewer might ask open-ended questions such as "What are your plans for the future?" or "How would you go about putting on a birthday party for a close friend?" rather than questions such as "What kind of work do you do?" or "What kind of neighborhood do you live in?" Open-ended questions require the patient to analyze the conditions of the question, to structure and organize his or her thoughts, to evaluate various alternative responses, and to engage in planning and abstract thinking.

Many psychologists utilize checklists or questionnaires to inquire about the patient's complaints and symptoms that are suggestive of underlying brain dysfunction or other organic conditions. Although these instruments are usually filled out by the patient while sitting in the waiting room, they may compensate for the patient's impaired executive functions by providing the patient with sufficient structure and organization to complete them (Sbordone, 1996). Furthermore, if the patient fails to complete these instruments, the examiner will usually ask the patient specific questions to obtain the missing information, thus further compensating for the patient's impaired executive functions. The observations of family members and/or significant others (particularly those who live or work with the patient) can often shed considerable light on the patient's executive functions (Sbordone, Seyranian, & Ruff, 1998), but psychologists often fail to conduct interviews with family members and/or significant others to determine what changes they have observed in the patient's cognitive, emotional, or behavioral functioning since his or her brain insult.

Neuropsychological Testing

The executive functions of the brain are poorly understood by the vast majority of psychologists. One of the many reasons for this is that training in professional psychology has strongly emphasized the administration, scoring, and interpretation of standardized neuropsychological tests and/or batteries utilizing statistical comparisons to age and educationally corrected norms. In contrast, training should also emphasize trying to understand the complex alterations of the patient's cognitive, behavioral, and emotional functioning following a brain insult. Thus, the understanding of a patient's executive functions is often based on the particular neuropsychological tests that are administered to the patient rather than on an understanding of the neurobehavioral consequences of an insult to the complex neural circuits and feedback loops that connect the frontal lobes with cortical and subcortical structures. This situation is similar to the story about a man coming home at 2 A.M. who noticed a stranger crawling on all fours in the middle of the street. The man asked the stranger, "Did you lose something?" The stranger replied, "Yes, my car keys." The man then asked, "Where did you lose them?" The stranger replied, "About a block away." The man, puzzled by the stranger's response, then asked, "Why are you looking here for your car keys, when they're a block away?" "Because the light is better here," replied the stranger.

Psychologists have frequently relied on the use of one or more of the following neuropsychological tests to assess the frontal lobes or executive functions of the brain: The Wisconsin Card Sorting Test (WISC), Halstead Category Test, Verbal Concept Attainment Test, Controlled Oral Word Association Test (COWAT), Thurstone Word Fluency Test, Design Fluency, Ruff Figural Fluency Test, Austin Maze, Porteus Maze Test, Tinker Toy Test, Stroop Test, Trail Making Test, and Rey Complex Figure Test and various motor tests such as the Finger Tapping, Purdue Pegboard, and Grooved Pegboard tests. Although these tests may have some sensitivity to the frontal lobes or executive functions, a patient's performance on these tests may not provide accurate information about whether their executive functions are intact because these tests may only assess one or two of the many steps that are involved in the complex process of the executive functions of the brain and ignore the remaining steps (Cripe, 1996). By analogy, the use of these tests is comparable to writing a review of the movie *Titanic* after watching only 10 minutes of the middle of the film. Ten minutes of the movie would not be sufficient time for comprehending the complexity, richness, and drama of this movie. Someone wishing to write a review would have to watch the entire movie from start to finish.

The executive functions are a complex process of integrated cognitive activities that cannot be easily categorized or quantified by traditional psychological tests or measures. Still, some formal executive function procedures may be helpful in predicting a patient's executive functions in a variety of everyday settings and will be discussed later in this chapter.

Bigler (1988) has stressed that damage to the frontal lobes and the regions connected to the frontal lobes can create complex alterations in cognitive processes, behavior, or executive functions such that no current battery of neuropsychological tests would be uniformly sensitive to them. He stressed the importance of careful observations of the patient's behavior and detailed interviews of family members and significant others to assess the alterations of the patient's executive functions. This is crucial because traditional psychological tests and measures are generally insensitive to such alterations and the patients themselves lack awareness that such alterations have occurred.

Mesulam (1986) has emphasized that the behavioral changes associated with frontal lobe damage introduce additional difficulties because they tend to be exceedingly complex, variable, difficult to define in technical terms, and almost impossible to quantify through current neuropsychological tests. In a similar vein, Damasio (1985) stressed that standardized neuropsychological tests are inadequate to assess the symptoms of frontal lobe dysfunction or the executive functions of the brain. For example, he described a 42-year-old patient whose computerized tomography (CT) scan showed clear evidence of bilateral damage to the frontal lobes and revealed that the orbital frontal surface and frontal polar cortex of both hemispheres were almost entirely missing as a consequence of an extensive ablation secondary to removal of a brain tumor. Although the patient's neuropsychological test scores were almost completely normal, this patient demonstrated a lack of awareness of his numerous cognitive and behavioral deficits, which included diminished sexual and exploratory behavior, an inability to focus his attention, marked confabulation, a loss of originality and creativity, inappropriate social and emotional behavior, and an inability to organize his thoughts or behavior and to engage in planning for the future.

COMPONENTS OF THE EXECUTIVE FUNCTIONS

Lezak (1995) has conceptualized the executive functions into four distinct components: (1) volition, (2) planning, (3) purposive action, and (4) effective performance. Figure 13.1 presents a flow chart of the role played by the executive functions of the brain based on these four components.

Manifestations of Deficits in Volition

Patients with significant volitional problems are likely to exhibit the following symptoms:

1. Apathy or indifference.
2. Deterioration in personal grooming and hygiene.
3. Loss of curiosity.
4. Loss of self-awareness.
5. Poor awareness of their cognitive and behavioral problems.
6. Loss of interest in previously enjoyed activities.
7. Loss of social awareness.

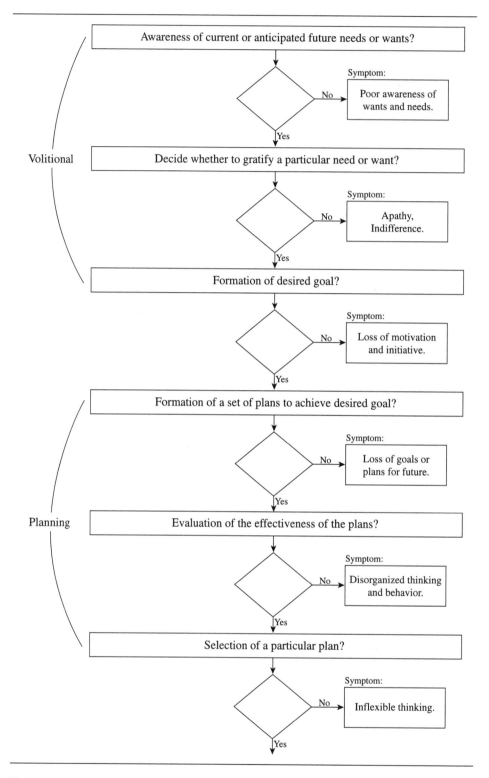

Figure 13.1.   Role of the executive functions of the brain

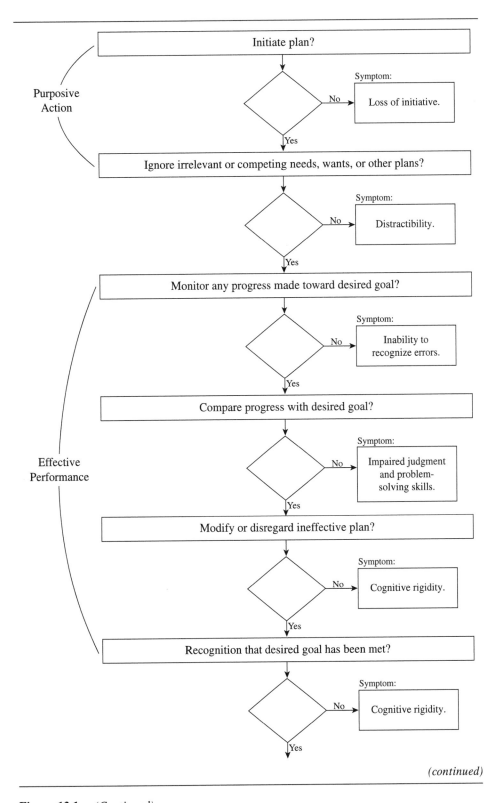

Figure 13.1.   *(Continued)*

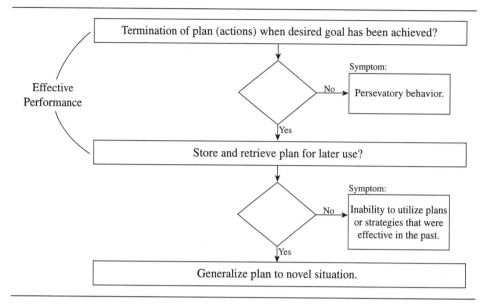

Figure 13.1. *(Continued)*

8. High need for external structure.
9. Loss of ability to enjoy life or sex.
10. Loss of goals or plans for the future.
11. Loss of motivation.

Assessment of Volitional Deficits

Patients with volitional deficits can be assessed by a direct clinical examination or through selective neuropsychological tests. In the former, the clinician should interview the patient to determine the activities that they enjoy and those that make them upset, how they spend their leisure activities, and the last time they left the confines of their home on their own. The clinician should also ask the patient to describe how he or she is doing, specifically in terms of the kinds of problems and difficulties they are having, because patients with significant volitional deficits will typically not recognize that anything is wrong with them, even though their cognitive and behavioral deficits are readily apparent to others.

As previously discussed, neuropsychological testing may not detect patients with relatively mild volitional deficits because many examiners compensate for the patient's volitional deficits by instructing them to perform a specific task (e.g., "I want you to connect these circles containing numbers ranging from 1 to 25 in numerical order") and telling them precisely when to begin the task. If the patient falters while performing this task, the examiner will frequently repeat the test instructions to the patient and/or will provide prompts and cues throughout the task so that the patient is able to perform and complete the task.

Because the curiosity and social awareness of patients with volitional deficits are generally poor, the examiner should interview family members and significant others to determine if the patient exhibits the symptoms noted. Unfortunately, many family members will attribute such symptoms to depression, even though the patient does not appear depressed, does not complain of sleep difficulties, or exhibit changes in appetite or dysphoric mood states.

Case Example

A patient (a 42-year-old, right-handed male) had recently undergone a resection of the frontal lobes at the UCLA Neuropsychiatric Institute to remove a large tumor that had invaded both lobes. He had been brought into an unfamiliar room and was instructed to sit in a chair and wait for the doctor to arrive. Observations of this patient's behavior through a one-way mirror revealed that the patient never visually or physically explored the room or showed any indication of curiosity, impatience, or frustration, even though he waited in this room for nearly two hours.

Manifestations of Deficits in Planning

Patients who have planning deficits are unable to formulate a set of plans to achieve a desired goal, to evaluate the effectiveness of such plans, or to select a particular plan to be executed. These patients typically exhibit concrete thinking and are unable to conceive of alternatives, to weigh or make choices, or to entertain sequential or hierarchial ideas that are necessary to develop the conceptual framework or structure that will provide them with the direction necessary to carry out the plan. Patients with significant planning deficits are likely to exhibit the following symptoms:

1. Loss of abstract and conceptual thinking.
2. Disorganized behavior and thinking.
3. Inflexible thinking.
4. Poor planning and organizational skills.
5. Loss of goals or plans for the future.
6. Socially inappropriate behavior.

Assessing Planning Deficits

The vast majority of neuropsychological tests are inadequate to assess the patient's planning skills because they typically focus on the patient's quantitative performance, which is frequently represented by a single numerical score (e.g., the number of errors or the time required to complete task). Although such scores are usually compared to norms that are appropriate for the patient's sex, age, and educational background, such comparisons only permit the neuropsychologist to determine how well or how poorly the patient performed on the test without being able to establish whether the patient was able to formulate a set of plans to achieve a specific goal, to evaluate the effectiveness of these plans, or to arrive at a plan to achieve a specific goal. As a consequence, the clinician must rely on a qualitative analysis of the patient's performance during neuropsychological testing to understand the patient's planning strategies and skills. However, when clinicians do this while using standardized tests, their modifications of the test protocol may prevent them from legitimately utilizing the test norms, which often creates a perplexing dilemma. In such circumstances, the examiner should rely heavily on the qualitative observations of the patient's behavior, particularly if the quantitative test data do not appear ecologically valid and/or appear discrepant from the observations of the patient's significant others.

Many examiners modify the testing protocol and/or utilize compensatory interventions during testing in order to compensate for the patient's planning deficits. For example, the examiner may: modify or simplify the test instructions, provide repetition and clarification, permit the patient to engage in considerable practice and rehearsal, provide frequent cues and prompts during testing, and redirect the patient back to the task if his or her thinking becomes tangential. Sometimes out of frustration, some examiners will even provide the patient with cognitive strategies or plans during testing so that the patient is able to complete the task. It is essential that the clinician recognize the various compensatory interventions that are provided to the patient during testing that may mask the patient's cognitive and behavioral deficits.

Modifications of the test protocol and the use of compensatory interventions during testing that are likely to significantly improve the patient's test performance have been termed "conditionality" (Sbordone, 1996, 1997) and may result in the patient's appearing relatively normal, even though the patient sustained an insult to the frontal-subcortical circuits. A similar tact was initially described by the philosopher Plato (1952) in his dialogues Cisca 380 B.C. when he discussed how Socrates was able to convince Meno that all knowledge was innate by demonstrating that an illiterate slave knew the principles of geometry: Socrates asked a slave boy, "Tell me, boy, do you know that a figure like this is a square?" to which the slave boy replied, "I do." Socrates then asked, "And you know that a square figure has these four lines equal?" to which the slave boy replied, "Certainly." Socrates then asked, "And these lines, which I have drawn through the middle of the square, are also equal?" to which the slave boy stated, "Yes." Through his leading questions, Socrates was able to convince Meno that this slave boy innately knew the principles of geometry, even though the slave boy lacked any knowledge of the subject.

Neuropsychological tests such as the Porteus Maze (Porteus, 1959, 1965), the WISC-III Mazes (1991), Tower Test (London, Hanoi, & Toronto), and the Visual Search Tests have been reported by Lezak (1995) to be helpful in assessing the patient's impaired planning skills, particularly if the examiner asks the patient to describe the strategies he or she utilized during the test and his or her motives for utilizing such strategies.

Manifestations of Deficits of Purposive Action

Purposive action involves the patient's ability to initiate a particular plan while simultaneously ignoring irrelevant or competing needs, wants, or other plans. Deficits in the patient's ability to engage in purposive action are frequently manifested by the following symptoms:

1. Distractibility.
2. Loss of initiative.
3. Difficulty processing one or more external activities simultaneously.
4. Loss of ability to maintain an ongoing cognitive or motor response set.

5. Disorganized behavior and thinking.

6. Emotional lability.

7. Impatience.

8. Disassociation between the patient's expressed verbal intentions and actions.

9. Difficulty maintaining train of thought.

10. Circumstantial or tangential thinking.

11. Difficulty performing novel tasks.

12. Difficulty functioning in novel or unfamiliar situations.

13. Poor work habits or frequent terminations.

Assessment of Deficits of Purposive Action

Although a patient with significant deficits of purposive action can often be assessed through standard neuropsychological tests, the major obstacle in assessing such deficits is the testing process itself because the physical conditions and circumstances present during testing may minimize or mask the patient's deficits in purposive action. For example, clinicians usually test a patient with brain impairments on a one-on-one basis in an environment that is typically free of extraneous stimulation. Furthermore, the examiner may utilize frequent cues and prompts to facilitate the patient's initiation; cognitive and/or compensatory strategies to minimize the influence of irrelevant or competing needs, wants, or plans; or external incentives or rewards (e.g., giving the patient a rest break or an opportunity to smoke a cigarette if he or she cooperates or performs well on the test). The examiner may provide praise or encouragement during testing or may reinforce the patient's use of a particular plan or strategy during testing by providing such feedback as "That's really good, that really works" or "You're doing it right—keep it up." When patients with impaired executive functions, particularly involving the orbitofrontal-subcortical circuit, are tested in such a manner, they may fail to display symptoms such as impatience, emotional lability, diminished frustration tolerance, irritability, aggressive outbursts, and difficulty regulating their emotions, particularly if the examiner is patient, kind, and gentle.

Lezak (1995) has recommended the following neuropsychological tests to assess the patient's deficits of purposive action, particularly the ability to initiate, maintain, switch, and stop sequences of complex behavior in an orderly and integrated manner: The Tinker Toy Test (Lezak, 1995), the Cookie Theft Picture (Mendez & Ashla-Mendez, 1991), the use of Objects or Alternative Uses Test (Guilford, Christensen, Merrifield, & Wilson, 1978), the Ruff Figural Fluency Test (Evans, Ruff, & Gualtieri, 1985; Ruff, Light, & Evans, 1987), and Luria's techniques (Luria, 1966), many of which have been incorporated into the Luria-Nebraska Neuropsychological Battery (Golden, Purisch, & Hammeke, 1985).

Manifestations of Deficits of Effective Performance

Effective performance involves monitoring any progress made toward a desired goal and comparing such progress with the desired goal. This requires that the patient is able to monitor, self-correct, and regulate goal-directed behavior. Should the patient's progress toward the desired goal be inadequate, the patient must modify or disregard the plan and replace it with a more effective one. The patient must also recognize when the desired goal has been achieved and terminate his or her actions when this occurs. Finally, the effective plan should be stored in the patient's long-term memory and retrieved whenever the patient encounters a similar or identical situation. Patients with significant deficits in effective performance will frequently exhibit the following symptoms:

1. Perseverations.
2. Cognitive rigidity.
3. Inability to successfully complete or follow through on tasks.
4. Inability to recognize or rectify errors.
5. Poor work habits or employment history.
6. Significant problem-solving difficulties.
7. Inability to utilize plans or strategies that were effective in the past.

Assessment of Deficits in Effective Performance

Deficits in effective performance can be assessed through naturalistic observation of the patient's behavior in real-world settings that are likely to have more ecological validity than the patient's performance in a highly structured test environment (Sbordone, 1997). The following case example illustrates this.

Case Example

The author was asked to evaluate the functional and everyday skills of a patient who had sustained a severe traumatic brain injury several years earlier. The patient was given a $20 bill and was instructed to go to a large supermarket, which was located approximately two blocks away, and to purchase four items: (1) a bag of chocolate chip cookies, (2) a can of frozen concentrated orange juice, (3) a bag of potato chips, and (4) a pint of vanilla ice cream. The patient (a 27-year-old man) wrote the four items on a sheet of paper, placed the money and the sheet of paper in his pocket, and walked the two blocks to the supermarket. When he arrived at the supermarket, he pulled out the sheet of paper and walked up and down the aisles until he found the first item on the list. He reached out and grabbed the item and then proceeded to walk up and down the aisles until he found the second item on the list. At that time, he put down the first item, picked up the second item, and then began walking up and down the aisles with the second item until he located the third item. When he reached for the third item, he put down the second item. After spending nearly an hour in the store, he finally arrived at the check-out counter with numerous items: a gallon of chocolate ice cream, a quart of freshly squeezed orange juice, candy, a bag of pretzels, three frozen dinners, a quart of milk, and a can of shaving cream. The total cost of the items exceeded the $20 he had been given. When he was told by the cashier that the price of the items was more than the amount of money he had, the patient did not know what to do because he did not have any additional money. As a consequence, the store manager was summoned, who informed the patient that he did not have enough money to purchase all of the items. As a result of this dilemma, the checkout line had increased to 15 customers. After the patient was unable to decide which items he did not need, the store manager was forced to make the decision for him, so that the situation could be resolved. Even though the patient had placed the original shopping list in his pocket, he apparently "forgot" to refer to this list when he was asked which items he did not need.

This case example illustrates the patient's failure to monitor any progress he had made toward the specific goal (i.e., purchasing four items). Even though the patient initially checked each item against his shopping list, he eventually completely disregarded the shopping list and began to select items based on his own needs or wants. When the cashier and the store manager told him that he did not have enough money to purchase these items, he was unable to decide which items he should disregard. He also failed to utilize the original plan that had been formulated by the examiner (i.e., purchasing the four items), which he had written down and placed in his pocket. Thus, even though he had the sheet of paper in his pocket that listed the four items to be purchased, he never referred to this list when the cashier and the store manager asked him which items he wished to either purchase or disregard. As a result, he was unable to carry out the original plan of action formulated by the examiner.

Unfortunately, very few neuropsychological techniques have been developed for the express purpose of studying self-monitoring or self-correcting behavior because the vast majority of neuropsychological tests provide quantitative scores about how a patient performed, rather than providing qualitative information about how the patient went about taking the test. Thus, to assess the qualitative aspects of effective performance, it is necessary for the examiner to carefully observe the patient's behavior during neuropsychological testing in response to such factors as: structure, organization, cues, prompts, warm-up time, practice, feedback, and external motivation. The examiner should also carefully assess the patient's ability to evaluate his or her own performance, that is, his or her ability to disregard ineffective plans and/or strategies, to evaluate the conditions of a particular problem, to formulate plans, to maintain the necessary motivation or persistence until the desired goal is achieved, to ignore distracting stimuli or competing goals, and to disregard ineffective plans. An excellent textbook written by Luria and Tsvetkova (1990), entitled *Neuropsychological Analysis of Problem Solving,* is highly recommended because it demonstrates Luria's remarkable analysis and understanding of the executive functions of the brain.

THE ECOLOGICAL VALIDITY OF NEUROPSYCHOLOGICAL TESTING FOR EXECUTIVE FUNCTIONS

Within the past several years, psychologists have become increasingly aware of the ecological validity of the various tests and measures utilized to evaluate the patient's cognitive functioning, particularly with respect to the generalizability of such tests in real-world or everyday situations. For example, the patient's score on a particular test or measure may lack ecological validity because the scores may or may not have any bearing on the patient's ability to function in his or her environment. Thus, *ecological validity* can be defined as the "functional and predictive relationship between the patient's performance on a set of neuropsychological tests and the patient's behavior in a variety of real-world settings, e.g., home, work, school, community, etc." (Sbordone, 1996).

Assessment of Executive Functions Involved in Everyday Functioning

The patient's executive functions can have a dramatic effect on his or her adaptive functioning. For example, the patient's ability to organize, plan, and coordinate a plan of action, to follow through on tasks and activities, and to modify an approach based on changing conditions in environment can have far-reaching implications for everyday functioning, particularly for complex activities such as home management and the handling of finances. Furthermore, problems of impulsivity and disinhibition can also adversely affect everyday skills. While a wide variety of neuropsychological tests that have been utilized to assess the patient's executive functions, there has been little systematic research on the ecological validity of these measures. Even though it is well known that the demands placed on the patient with brain injury within the highly structured test environment are too restrictive to capture many of the difficulties the patient may have in his or her daily life (Sbordone & Guilmette, 1999).

Acker (1990) described several factors that interfered with the clinician's assessment of the patient's executive functions. These factors included the complexity of the frontal lobe structures and functions, the heterogeneity of frontal lobe problems, the push and assistance from the examiner during testing for maximum performance, and psychology's focus on outcome scores rather than process. As a consequence, Acker stressed the importance of supplementing formal test procedures with observations and descriptions of the patient's behavior during testing and from family members and significant others, as well as with observations of the patient's behavior under more varied circumstances.

Some formal executive function procedures appear to have some promise in predicting everyday skills. For example, the Behavioral Dyscontrol Scale (BDS; Grigsby, Kaye, & Robbins, 1990, 1992) was a test instrument specifically created for the purpose of assessing the patient's ability to engage in activities of daily living. The BDS is a 10-minute measure, based primarily on simple cognitive and motor tasks used by Luria in his studies of frontal lobe functioning. The BDS has been shown to predict the executive functioning of geriatric patients (Kaye, Grigsby, Robbins, & Korzum, 1990) and has been shown to be superior to the Folstein Mini-Mental State Examination in predicting success in an independent versus an assisted-living situation and functional independence three months following discharge from a rehabilitation program (Suchy, Blint, & Osmon, 1997).

The Dementia Rating Scale developed by Mattis (1988) has been shown to significantly predict an older patient's performance of everyday functions in a hospital setting (Nadler, Richardson, Malloy, Marran, & Hostetler Brinson, 1993). In particular, the Initiation/Perseveration subscale has been shown to be sensitive to the patient's executive functions (Nadler et al., 1993).

The Behavioral Assessment of the Dysexecutive Syndrome (BADS) test is composed of six tests that are similar to real-life activities that would be expected to cause difficulties for patients with a dysexecutive syndrome. The BADS utilizes practical problem-solving tasks, paper-and-pencil problem-solving activities, route following, and tasks that require the patient to follow rules and directions. It also includes a 20-item questionnaire that samples changes in the patient's emotions or personality, behavior, and cognitive functioning. This questionnaire is completed by the patient and a significant other. BADS has been found to be a better predictor of the patient's executive functions in real-world situations than the Wisconsin Card Sorting Test (Wilson, 1993). Wilson, Alderman, Burgess, Emslier, and Evans (1996) have reported that the overall BADS profile score differentiated patients with neurological disorders, comprised largely of closed head injuries, from normal or healthy controls on all six tests. They also found a moderate negative correlation between the ratings of significant others and the patient's performance on the six individual tests (e.g., low scores were indicative of everyday executive problems). They concluded that the performance on the BADS test was significantly correlated with the ratings of executive functions of patients with brain injuries that were made by their significant others. Spreen and Strauss (1998) have suggested that the BADS may be a useful test to identify subtle impairments in planning and organization, particularly in patients who appear to be cognitively intact and functioning well in structured settings.

The Relationship Between Executive Functions and Vocational Functioning

Lezak (1987), based on a 5-year follow-up study of 42 adults who had sustained severe traumatic brain injuries, concluded that the most significant residual impairments found in these patients were due to their impaired executive functions. Similarly, Crepeau and Scherzer (1993) found that impaired executive function was one of four of the most reliable correlates of unemployment. They emphasized that deficits in planning, organization, cognitive flexibility, unawareness of deficits, and loss of initiation needed to be taken into account when assessing ability to return to work of the patient with brain injuries.

Lezak (1995) has utilized the Tinker Toy Test to assess executive functions in terms of the patient's ability to spontaneously formulate goals, engage in planning, and carry out such plans. Bayless, Varney, and Roberts (1989) administered this test to 50 patients who had sustained traumatic brain damage and 50 normal controls. They found that although a score of 6 or greater was not necessarily predictive of employment, a score of less than 6 was strongly associated with unemployment.

The Behavioral Assessment of Vocational Skills (BAVS) test, which was developed by Butler, Anderson, Furst, and Namerow (1989) to assess the patient's executive functions in a more functional manner, shows some promise in predicting employment. For example, Butler, Rorsman, Hill, and Tuma (1993) administered a variety of neuropsychological tests to a group of 20 patients who had sustained significant brain injuries and who were then being treated in an outpatient rehabilitation clinic. These patients were also given the task of assembling a wooden wheelbarrow from printed instructions. However, these patients were also intentionally interrupted while working on the latter task: they were asked to work for several minutes on another task and were given negative criticism about their performance. Trained observers rated their skills in such areas as following directions, organization, attention, frustration tolerance, problem solving, and judgment. Although standardized neuropsychological test data from the Wechsler Adult Intelligence Scale-Revised (WAIS-R), Trails A and B, Logical Memories and Visual Reproduction tests from the Wechsler Memory Scale-Revised, and the WISC were found to be related to some measures of vocational functioning during a 3-month trial of volunteer work, a multiple regression analysis demonstrated that a patient's score on the BAVS measure was the only significant predictor of vocational performance.

SUMMARY

The executive function of the brain refers to the complex process by which an individual goes about performing a novel problem-solving task from its inception to its completion. The executive functions are mediated by complex neural circuits or feedback loops that connect discrete regions in the frontal lobes with other cortical regions in the brain and subcortical structures. A variety of subcortical and psychiatric disorders can impair the executive functions as a result of either producing lesions in the feedback loops or alterations in the metabolic activity of the structures that comprise the circuits. When these circuits or loops are broken or compromised, patients may exhibit what has been commonly termed a "frontal lobe syndrome," even though their frontal lobes may be neurologically intact. Three major circuits (dorsolateral prefrontal, orbitofrontal, and medial frontal) interact with subcortical structures and provide a person with the ability to guide his or her behavior through mental representation of the perceived world (e.g., working memory) and to free him or her from dependency on the environment. The dorsolateral prefrontal cortex receives information about the internal environment, internal milieu, and the emotional state of the person and serves as the principal organ for integrating information from the three circuits.

The executive functions cannot be adequately assessed by standardized neuropsychological tests because they are exceedingly complex and variable and cannot be easily categorized or quantified. Lezak's (1995) conceptualization of the executive functions into four components (volition, planning, purposive action, and effective performance) can help psychologists evaluate patients with impaired executive functions. However, the complex problems inherent in the assessment process necessitate the use of observational techniques utilizing qualitative rather than quantitative methods and a careful examination of the examiner's behavior and interactions with patients. Unfortunately, compensatory interventions (examiner cues, prompts, etc.) may unwittingly cause patients to appear relatively normal even though they sustained damage to the frontal-subcortical circuits. In addition, the highly structured and artificial test environment may compensate for lesions in the orbitofrontal-subcortical circuit and result in the patient's failure to exhibit behavior such as impatience, irritability, and emotional lability in this setting.

A patient's score on a particular neuropsychological test or measure may lack ecological validity because it may not have any bearing on the patient's ability to function in a variety of real-world settings (e.g., home, work, school, community). Some formal executive function procedures, however, appear to have promise in predicting a patient's executive functions in a variety of everyday settings. For example, tests such as the Behavioral Dyscontrol Scale (BDS), Behavioral Assessment of the Dysexecutive

Syndrome (BADS), Tinker Toy, and the Behavioral Assessment of Vocational Skills (BAVS) tests have been found to be helpful in identifying subtle executive function problems that patients have in everyday settings.

RECOMMENDED READING

Grafman, J., Holyoak, K.J., & Boller, F. (1995). Structure and functions of the human pre-frontal cortex. *Annals of the New York Academy of Sciences, Vol. 769.*

Luria, A.R. (1980). *Higher Cortical Functions in Man, Second Edition.* New York: Basic Books.

Luria, A.R., & Tsvetkova, L.S. (1990). *Neuropsychological Analysis of Problem Solving.* Delray Beach, FL: GR/St. Lucie Press.

Rabbitt, P. (1997). *Methodology of Frontal and Executive Function.* East Sussex: Psychology Press.

Stuss, D.T., & Benson, D.F. (1986). *The Frontal Lobes.* New York: Raven Press.

REFERENCES

Acker, M.B. (1990). A review of the ecological validity of neuropsychological tests. In D.E. Tupper & K.D. Cicerone (Eds.), *The neuropsychology of everyday life: Assessment and basic competencies.* Boston: Kluwar Academic.

Albert, M.L., Feldman, R.G., & Willis, A.L. (1974). The "subcortical dementia" of progressive supranuclear palsy. *Journal of Neurology, Neurosurgery and Psychiatry, 37,* 121–130.

Alexander, G.E., & Crutcher, M.D. (1990). Functional architecture of basal ganglia circuits: Neural substrates of parallel processing. *Trends in Neuroscience, 13,* 266–271.

Alexander, M.P., Benson, D.F., & Stuss, D.T. (1989). Frontal lobes and language. *Brain and Language, 37,* 656–691.

Arlien-Soberg, P., Bruhn, P., Gyldensted, C., & Melgaard, B. (1979). Chronic painter's syndrome. *Acta Neurologica Scandinavica, 60,* 149–156.

Barkley, R., Grodzinsky, G., & DuPaul, G.J. (1992). Frontal lobe functions and attention-deficit disorder with and without hyperactivity: A review and research report. *Journal of Abnormal Clinical Psychology, 20,* 163–188.

Baxter, L.R., Phelps, M.E., Mazziotta, J.C., Guze, B.H., Schwartz, J.M., & Selin, C.E. (1987). Local cerebral glucose metabolic rates in obsessive-compulsive disorder. *Archives of General Psychiatry, 31,* 263–270.

Bayless, J.D., Varney, N.R., & Roberts, R.J. (1989). Tinker toy test performance and vocational outcome in patients with closed head injuries. *Journal of Clinical and Experimental Neuropsychology, 11,* 913–917.

Bigler, E.D. (1988). Frontal lobe damage and neuropsychological assessment. *Archives of Clinical Neuropsychology, 3,* 279–297.

Blumer, D., & Benson, D.F. (1975). Personality changes with frontal and temporal lobe lesions. In D.F. Benson & D. Blumer (Eds.), *Psychiatric aspects of neurologic disease* (pp. 151–170). New York: Grune & Stratton.

Bromfield, E.B., Altshuler, D.B., Leiderman, D.B., Balish, M., Ketter, T.A., Devinsky, O., Post, R.M., & Theodore, W.H. (1992). Cerebral metabolism and depression in patients with complex partial seizures. *Archives of Neurology, 49,* 617–623.

Butler, R.W., Anderson, L., Furst, C.J., & Namerow, N.S. (1989). Behavioral assessment in neuropsychological rehabilitation: A method for measuring vocational related skills. *Clinical Neuropsychologist, 3,* 235–243.

Butler, R.W., Rorsman, I., Hill, J.M., & Tuma, R. (1993). The effects of frontal brain impairment on fluency: Simple and complex paradigms. *Neuropsychology, 7,* 519–529.

Butters, N., Sax, D.S., Montgomery, K., & Tarlow, S. (1978). Comparison of the neuropsychological deficits associated with early and advanced Huntington's disease. *Archives of Neurology, 35,* 585–589.

Chen, S.T., Sultzer, D.L., Hinkin, C.H., Mahler, M.E., & Cummings, J.L. (1998). Executive dysfunction in Alzheimer's disease: Association with neuropsychiatric symptoms and functional impairment. *Journal of Neuropsychiatry and Clinical Neurosciences, 10,* 426–432.

Cools, A.R., Van den Bercken, J.H.L., Horstink, M.W.I., Van Spaendonck, K.P.M., & Berger, H.J.C. (1984). Cognitive and motor shifting aptitude disorder in Parkinson's disease. *Journal of Neurology, Neurosurgery and Psychiatry, 47,* 443–453.

Crepeau, F., & Scherzer, P. (1993). Predictors and indicators of work status after traumatic brain injury: A meta-analysis. *Neuropsychological Rehabilitation, 3,* 5–35.

Cripe, L.I. (1996). The ecological validity of executive function testing. In R.J. Sbordone & C.J. Long (Eds.), *Ecological validity of neuropsychological testing* (pp. 171–202). Delray Beach, FL: GR/St. Lucie Press.

Cummings, J.L. (1985). *Clinical neuropsychiatry.* New York: Grune & Stratton.

Cummings, J.L. (1992). Depression and Parkinson's disease: A review. *American Journal of Psychiatry, 149,* 443–454.

Cummings, J.L. (1995). Anatomic and behavioral aspects of frontal-subcortical circuits. In J. Grafman, K.J. Holyoak, & F. Boller (Eds.), Structure and function of the human prefrontal cortex. *Annals of the New York Academy of Sciences, 769,* 1–13.

Cummings, J.L., Gosenfeld, L.F., Houlihan, J.P., & McCaffrey, T. (1983). Neuropsychiatric disturbances associated with idiopathic calcification of the basal ganglia. *Biological Psychiatry, 18,* 591–601.

Cummings, J.L., & Mendez, M.F. (1984). Secondary mania with focal cerebrovascular lesions. *American Journal of Psychiatry, 141,* 1084–1087.

Damasio, A.R. (1985). The frontal lobes. In K.M. Heilman & E. Valenstein (Eds.), *Clinical neuropsychology* (2nd ed., pp. 339–375). New York: Oxford University Press.

Dillon, B., Dubois, B., Lhermitte, F., & Agid, Y. (1986). Heterogenicity of cognitive impairment in progressive supranuclear palsy, Parkinson's disease, and Alzheimer's disease. *Neurology, 36,* 1179–1185.

Evans, R.W., Ruff, R.M., & Gualtieri, C.T. (1985). Verbal fluency and figural fluency in bright children. *Perceptual and Motor Skills, 61,* 699–709.

Fedio, P., Cox, C.S., Neophytides, A., Canal-Frederick, G., & Chase, T.N. (1979). Huntington's disease. In T.N. Chase, N.S. Wexler, & A. Barbeau (Eds.), *Advances in neurology* (Vol. 23, pp. 239–255). New York: Raven Press.

Flowers, K.A., & Robertson, C. (1985). The effect of Parkinson's disease on the ability to maintain a mental set. *Journal of Neurology, Neurosurgery and Psychiatry, 48,* 517–529.

Golden, C.J., Purisch, A.D., & Hammeke, T.A. (1985). *Luria-Nebraska neuropsychological battery: Forms I and II.* Los Angeles: Western Psychological Services.

Grafman, J., Litvan, I., Gomez, C., & Chase, T.N. (1990). Frontal lobe function in progressive supranuclear palsy. *Archives of Neurology, 47,* 553–558.

Grant, D.A., & Berg, E.A. (1948). A behavioral analysis of the degree of reinforcement and ease of shifting to new responses in a Weigl-type card sorting problem. *Journal of Experimental Psychology, 38,* 404–411.

Grigsby, J., Kaye, K., & Robbins, L.J. (1990). Frontal lobe disorder, behavioral disturbance and independent functioning among the demented elderly. *Clinical Research, 38,* 81A.

Grigsby, J., Kaye, K., & Robbins, L.J. (1992). Reliabilities and factor structure of the behavioral dyscontrol scale. *Perceptual and Motor Skills, 74,* 883–892.

Guilford, J.P., Christensen, P.R., Merrifield, P.R., & Wilson, R.C. (1978). *Alternate uses: Manual of instructions and interpretation.* Orange, CA: Sheridan Psychological Services.

Gustafson, L., Risberg, J., Johanson, M., & Brun, A. (1984). An evaluation of organic dementia by regional cerebral blood flow measurements and clinical and psychometric methods. In M.M. Cohen (Ed.), *Monographs in neurosciences* (Vol. 11, pp. 111–117). Basel: Karger.

Hawkins, K.A. (1990). Occupational neurotoxicology: Some neuropsychological issues and challenges. *Journal of Clinical and Experimental Neuropsychology, 12,* 664–680.

Josiassen, R.C., Curry, L.M., & Mancall, E.L. (1983). Development of neuropsychological deficits in Huntington's disease. *Archives of Neurology, 40,* 791–796.

Kaye, K., Grigsby, J., Robbins, L.J., & Korzum, B. (1990). Prediction of independent functioning and behavior problems in geriatric patients. *Journal of the American Geriatrics Society, 38,* 1304–1310.

Lees, A.J., & Smith, E. (1983). Cognitive deficits in the early stages of Parkinson's disease. *Brain, 106,* 257–270.

Lezak, M.D. (1987). Relationships between personality disorders, social disturbances, and physical disability following traumatic brain injury. *Journal of Head Trauma Rehabilitation, 2,* 57–69.

Lezak, M.D. (1995). *Neuropsychological assessment* (3rd ed.). New York: Oxford University Press.

Luria, A.R. (1966). *Higher cortical functions in man.* New York: Basic Books.

Luria, A.R., & Tsvetkova, L.S. (1990). *Neuropsychological analysis of problem solving.* Delray Beach, FL: GR/St. Lucie Press.

Maher, E.R., Smith, E.M., & Lees, A.J. (1985). Cognitive deficits in the Steele-Richardson-Olzwewski syndrome (progressive supranuclear palsy). *Journal of Neurology, Neurosurgery and Psychiatry, 48,* 1234–1239.

Maruff, P., Currie, J., Malone, V., McArthur-Jackson, C., Mulhall, B., & Benson, E. (1994). Neuropsychological characterization of the AIDS dementia complex and rationalization of a test battery. *Archives of Neurology, 51,* 689–693.

Mattis, S. (1988). *Dementia rating scale.* Odessa, FL: Psychological Assessment Resources.

Mattson, A.J., & Levin, H.S. (1990). Frontal lobe dysfunction following closed head injury. *Journal of Nervous and Mental Diseases, 178,* 282–291.

Mendez, M.F., & Ashla-Mendez, M. (1991). Differences between multi-infarct dementia and Alzheimer's disease on unstructured neuropsychological tasks. *Journal of Clinical and Experimental Neuropsychology, 13,* 923–932.

Mesulam, M.M. (1986). Frontal cortex and behavior: Editorial. *Annals of Neurology, 19,* 320–325.

Morris, R.G., Rushe, T., Woodruff, P.W.R., & Murray, R.M. (1995). Problem solving in schizophrenia: A specific deficit in planning ability. *Schizophrenia Research, 14,* 235–246.

Moscovich, M. (1982). Multiple disassociations of function in amnesia. In L. Cermack (Ed.), *Human memory and amnesia* (pp. 337–370). Hillside, NJ: Erlbaum.

Nadler, J.D., Richardson, E.D., Malloy, P.E., Marran, M.E., & Hostetler Brinson, M.E. (1993). The ability of the dementia rating scale to predict everyday functioning. *Archives of Clinical Neuropsychology, 8,* 449–460.

Nieuwenhuys, R., Voogd, R.J., & van Huijzen (1988). *The human central nervous system* (3rd ed.). New York: Springer-Verlag.

Plato. (1952). The dialogues of Plato (B. Jowett, Trans.). In R.M. Hutchins (Ed.), *Great books of the western world* (Vol. 7). Chicago: Encyclopedia Brittanica.

Porteus, S.D. (1959). *The maze test and clinical psychology.* Palo Alto, CA: Pacific Books.

Porteus, S.D. (1965). *Porteus maze test. Fifty years application.* New York: Psychological Corporation.

Potegal, M. (1971). A note on spatial-motor deficits in patients with Huntington's disease: A test of a hypothesis. *Neuropsychologica, 9,* 233–235.

Reitan, R.M. (1958). Validity of the trail making test as an indicator of organic brain damage. *Perceptual and Motor Skills, 8,* 271–276.

Ruff, R.M., Light, R.H., & Evans, R.W. (1987). The ruff figural fluency test: A normative study with adults. *Developmental Neuropsychology, 3,* 37–52.

Sbordone, R.J. (1996). Ecological validity: Some critical issues for the neuropsychologist. In R.J. Sbordone & C.J. Long (Eds.), *Ecological validity of neuropsychological testing* (pp. 15–41). Orlando, FL: GR/St. Lucie Press.

Sbordone, R.J. (1997). The ecological validity of neuropsychological testing. In A.M. Horton, Jr., D. Wedding, & J. Webster (Eds.), *The neuropsychology handbook* (2nd ed.) (Vol. 1, pp. 365–392). New York: Springer.

Sbordone, R.J., & Guilmette, T.J. (1999). Ecological validity: Prediction of everyday and vocational functioning from neuropsychological test data. In J. Sweet (Ed.), *Forensic neuropsychology: Fundamentals and practice* (pp. 223–250). New York: Swets.

Sbordone, R.J., Seyranian, G.D., & Ruff, R.M. (1998). Are the subjective complaints of traumatically brain-injured patients reliable? *Brain Injury, 12*(6), 505–515.

Spreen, O., & Strauss, E. (1998). *A compendium of neuropsychological tests* (3rd ed.). New York: Oxford University Press.

Stuss, D.T. (1987). Contribution of frontal lobe injury to cognitive impairment after closed head injury: Methods of assessment and recent findings. In H.S. Levin, J. Grafman, & H.M. Eisenberg (Eds.), *Neurobehavioral recovery from head injury.* New York: Oxford University Press.

Stuss, D.T., & Benson, D.F. (1986). *The frontal lobes.* New York: Raven Press.

Suchy, Y., Blint, A., & Osmon, D.C. (1997). Behavioral dyscontrol scale: Criterion and predictive validity in an inpatient rehabilitation unit population. *Clinical Neuropsychologist, 11,* 258–265.

Taylor, A.E., Saint-Cye, J.A., Lang, A.E., & Kenny, F.T. (1986). Frontal lobe dysfunction in Parkinson's disease. The cortical focus of neostriatal outflow. *Brain, 109,* 845–883.

Tsushima, W.T., & Towne, W.S. (1977). Effects of paint sniffing on neuropsychological test performance. *Journal of Abnormal Psychology, 86,* 402–407.

Wechsler, D. (1991). *Wechsler intelligence scale for children* (3rd ed.). San Antonio, TX: The Psychological Corporation.

Wilson, B.A. (1993). Ecological validity of neuropsychological assessment: Do neuropsychological indexes predict performance in everyday activities? *Applied and Preventive Psychology, 2,* 209–215.

Wilson, B.A., Alderman, N., Burgess, P.W., Emslie, H., & Evans, J.J. (1996). *Behavioral assessment of the dysexecutive syndrome.* Bury St. Edmunds, England: Thames Valley Test Company.

Yeterian, E.H., & Pandya, D.N. (1993). Striatal connections of the parietal association cortices in Rhesus monkeys. *Journal of Comparative Neurology, 332,* 175–197.

Chapter 14

ASSESSMENT OF EMOTIONAL FUNCTIONING WITH THE MMPI-2

CARLTON S. GASS

The assessment of personality is an often-neglected component of the neuropsychological evaluation, despite the frequency with which psychological problems play a central role in both the diagnosis and the treatment of individuals who are referred to the neuropsychologist. Brain dysfunction is commonly associated with changes in personality and emotional functioning. This fact is widely recognized in relation to virtually all major forms of neuropathology. Broadly conceptualized, the general causes of these changes can be roughly classified into (1) psychological reactions to the loss of functional capacity and the associated reduction of rewarding transactions with the environment, (2) endogenous alterations in the neural substrate that influence mood and behavior, and (3) long-term adjustment to the postinjury environment that is substantially shaped by the behavior of the individual with neurological impairment. Although the precise causes of these psychological changes in an individual case are sometimes difficult to ascertain, an effective plan of intervention can be established only if the disturbances are first identified diagnostically by the clinician.

The imperative of evaluating emotional functioning in the neuropsychological context is suggested not only by the frequency of personality disturbances following brain injury, but also by the common presentation of individuals who have psychological symptoms that mimic neurologic disorder. Memory complaints are a prime example of this because they probably constitute the most common reason for a neuropsychological referral. Forgetfulness and distractibility, whether real or imagined, are often interpreted as signs of brain dysfunction (e.g., a progressive dementia, residual effects of traumatic brain injury), though these symptoms are quite common in people who are neurologically intact yet psychologically disturbed (Burt, Zembar, & Niederehe, 1995; Gass, 1996b). Such complaints are also notoriously common among individuals who consciously feign traumatic brain injury. Psychological factors are often implicated in seizures that are nonepileptic (i.e., they occur in the presence of normal brain-wave activity), as well as in headache, nausea, fatigue, confusion, paresthesia, gait disturbance, difficulty swallowing (globus hystericus), diplopia, and numerous other sensory and motor symptoms that are associated with impairment of the central nervous system (CNS; Devinsky, 1992). The assessment of psychological functioning is a critical component of the neuropsychological evaluation precisely because numerous psychiatric conditions, often undiagnosed, can present with symptoms that appear to reflect abnormal brain function.

Whether they have brain injuries or not, individuals who are referred for a neuropsychological evaluation commonly experience cognitive inefficiency that is secondary to emotional difficulties such as depression, anxiety, and health-related preoccupations. This inefficiency might not be reflected in the neuropsychological test results that are obtained under highly controlled conditions, in a testing environment that is relatively free of distraction. Normal test results can be achieved by neurologically intact individuals who genuinely experience cognitive difficulties in daily living (Gass & Apple, 1997). In isolation, the cognitive component of a neuropsychological examination can assist in determining whether a person's cognitive complaints reflect actual areas of limited capacity or deficit. However, it cannot address the broader and important question of whether cognitive inefficiency occurs on a daily basis in the individual who is affected by emotional difficulties.

Moreover, neuropsychological test performance can be impeded by adverse emotional influences. As a general rule, performance on the Halstead-Reitan Neuropsychological Battery (HRNB; Reitan & Wolfson, 1993) is relatively resilient to the effects of psychological disturbance (Calsyn, Louks, & Johnson, 1982; Gass, 1991a; Heaton, Baade, & Johnson, 1978; Heaton & Crowley, 1981; Reitan & Wolfson, 1997; Weins & Matarazzo, 1977). However, more recent data indicate that emotional variables are associated with performance on other widely used cognitive measures. This conclusion applies to neurologically intact people as well as to patients who have brain dysfunction (Burt et al., 1995; Gass, 1996b; Gass, Ansley, & Boyette, 1994; Kinderman & Brown, 1997; Richards & Ruff, 1989). Therefore, the evaluation of emotional functioning is necessary for understanding the sources of everyday cognitive inefficiency about which many emotionally disturbed individuals complain, as well as for interpreting their deficient performance on certain neuropsychological measures.

Intervention in the form of rehabilitation has not been a strong point within the field of neuropsychology, partly because of the discipline's major focus on cognition and partly because of the difficulties associated with translating this extensive base of descriptive knowledge into clinical application (Nelson & Adams, 1997). On the other hand, once identified, many neuropsychology patients who have emotional difficulties can be helped through relatively clear, straightforward methods of intervention such as psychotherapy and psychotropic medication (Prigatano, 1987). Early intervention might be particularly helpful. In relation to stroke, and possibly to other neurologic disorders, depression appears to impede rehabilitative efforts (Parikh, Robinson, & Price, 1988) and to hinder progress in the recovery of function (Sinyor et al., 1986). In cases of traumatic brain injury, psychosocial adjustment and eventual rehabilitative outcome are determined more by personality factors than by cognitive status (Fordyce, Rouche, & Prigatano, 1983; Oddy, Humphrey, & Uttley, 1978). When combined with the provision of feedback, the evaluation of personality and emotional status can ultimately assist patients and their families in addressing present and potential problem areas that fall beyond the scope of a thorough cognitive assessment (Gass & Brown, 1992). In addition, the evaluation can provide information concerning areas of competency that fall outside the scope of cognitive testing, such as stress-coping skill, self-acceptance, personal responsibility, social interest and sensitivity, and the ability to initiate and sustain satisfactory interpersonal relationships.

COMMONLY USED ASSESSMENT INSTRUMENTS

A common misconception equates neuropsychological assessment with the analysis of test scores on a battery of neuropsychological tests. Assessment, when properly conducted, is based on the expertise of a highly trained clinician who can integrate information derived from a variety of sources. A comprehensive evaluation of personality and emotional status requires more than inferences based on test scores alone. Such an evaluation depends on additional data obtained from the clinical interview, from direct observation, from the examinee's history, and from information obtained from family members or close acquaintances (Cripe, 1989). Gass and Ansley (1995) discussed the use of interview-based information, direct observation, behavior rating scales, self-report measures, and various projective tests for evaluating the psychological functioning of individuals with brain injuries. Self-report is undoubtedly the most popular medium through which clinicians gather objective data about an individual's personality and emotional status.

Self-report instruments vary widely with respect to their comprehensiveness in describing the many facets of psychological functioning. The Beck Depression Inventory (BDI; Beck, Ward, Mendelsohn, Mock, & Erbaugh, 1961), for example, is widely used to measure symptoms of depression. Although depression is relatively common in neurologic patients, the focus of this 21-item instrument is quite narrow when considered in the broader context of the many other behavioral disturbances associated with known or suspected brain dysfunction. The same general limitation applies to a myriad of other brief self-report measures (Speilberger, Gorsuch, & Luschene, 1971; Yesavage et al., 1983; Zung, 1965, 1971).

The Symptom Checklist 90-Revised (SCL-90-R, Derogatis, 1977) is a 90-item inventory that provides information related to nine primary symptom dimensions: Somatization, Obsessive-Compulsive, Interpersonal Sensitivity, Depression, Anxiety, Hostility, Phobic Anxiety, Paranoid Ideation, and Psychoticism. Although some neuropsychological investigations have included the SCL-90-R as a measure of emotional status, more detailed research focusing on the instrument itself in neuropsychological settings has been limited. Several studies suggest that potentially misleading scale elevations on the SCL-90-R occur in patients with brain injuries as the result of self-reported cognitive and physical symptoms of CNS damage (Woessner & Caplan, 1995, 1996). For example, 8 items were identified by O'Donnell, DeSoto, DeSoto, and Reynolds (1995) to be sensitive to cognitive impairment in a heterogeneous sample of individuals who had brain damage, and 5 of these are included in the 10-item Obsessive-Compulsive scale.

The Millon Clinical Multiaxial Inventory-III (MCMI-III; Millon, 1994) and its predecessors are sometimes used in the context of neuropsychological evaluations to help clarify the role of long-standing personality patterns as distinct from more transient emotional disturbances that are associated with brain injury. S. Russell and Russell (1997) describe the potential assets of this instrument as a tool to assist the neuropsychologist in differential diagnosis. Although a substantial amount of attention in the research literature has been directed at the MCMI, relatively few empirical studies have addressed the application of the MCMI in neuropsychological settings, particularly to individuals who have brain dysfunction.

THE MINNESOTA MULTIPHASIC PERSONALITY INVENTORY-2

This chapter specifically addresses the use of the Minnesota Multiphasic Personality Inventory-2 (MMPI-2; Butcher, Dahlstrom, Graham, Tellegen, & Kaemmer, 1989), which is by far the most widely used and extensively researched instrument for evaluating the personality characteristics and emotional status of individuals who have known or suspected neurological dysfunction. In forensic neuropsychological cases, for example, Lees-Haley, Smith, Williams, and Dunn (1996) reported that the MMPI-2 is used with an estimated frequency of 66%, which is far more than the Rorschach (14%), Millon Clinical Multiaxial Inventory-II (MCMI-II; Millon, 1987) (9%), or the SCL-90-R (5%; Derogatis, 1977). A recent survey of test usage by instructors of clinical neuropsychology (McCaffrey & Lynch, 1996) indicated that the MMPI/MMPI-2 was the third most widely used instrument (64%), following the Wechsler Adult Intelligence Scale-Revised (Wechsler, 1981) and the HRB. The frequency of MMPI-2 usage is matched by the voluminous amount of neuropsychological research involving the MMPI-2. The MMPI-2 and its forerunner (MMPI) have been investigated in hundreds of neuropsychological studies over the past 50 years, far more than any other personality measure.

The MMPI was originally constructed by Starke Hathaway, a clinical psychologist, and J. Charnley McKinley, a neuropsychiatrist, in the late 1930s and early 1940s for the purpose of assisting in the diagnosis of psychiatric disorders in patients who were treated at the University of Minnesota hospitals. Hathaway and McKinley initially assembled a pool of over 1,000 personality-related statements that were drawn from a wide variety of sources, including other psychological scales, clinical case reports, psychiatric interview guides, and their own clinical experience. As these statements were then evaluated, edited, simplified, and cast into a declarative format, the authors reduced the item pool to 504 statements. (Fifty-one items were subsequently added that comprised the Lie scale and additions to the Masculinity-Femininity scale.) The 504 items were presented individually on cards that were sorted by the examinee into two boxes (True and False). Item-response frequencies were contrasted between "Minnesota normals," composed primarily of relatives and visitors of patients in the University of Minnesota Hospitals, and clinical patients classified into one of several psychodiagnostic groups. Items that statistically discriminated between the normals and a specified psychodiagnostic group were cross-validated and placed on a scale representing that diagnosis.

The purported advantage of the empirical keying approach to constructing the MMPI was that, as long as the examinee was able to read the items and understand the instructions, the interpreter did not have to presume truthfulness or accuracy on the part of the subject in answering the items. This was a main concern with the earlier face-valid or content approach to personality test construction. In fact, originally and for many years, it was believed that the MMPI interpreter would be invariably misled by examining the client's responses to item content. Face validity was sometimes deemed "farce validity"; it was well known that clients commonly selected answers in order to appear healthy or to feign illness. In addition, there is a projective dimension involved in a reader's interpretation of questionnaire items (Meehl, 1945). For example, the decision to respond true or false to an item often hinges on how an individual chooses to interpret ambiguous words such as *often, usually, seldom, sometimes, like and dislike, most,* and *very.* These words mean different things to different people under different circumstances, and the interpretation of them can vary as a function of an individual's emotional status at any given moment. Rather than be misled by item content, early MMPI interpreters focused exclusively on the extent to which the examinee's item responses matched those made by patients who had a specific psychiatric diagnosis. This correlation-based approach seemed foolproof. However, one disadvantage of the empirical keying approach to test construction is that item content can easily show a systematic bias toward nonpsychiatric groups of individuals who might endorse these items in the scored direction for reasons other than having a psychiatric disturbance (Helmes & Reddon, 1993). The validity of the test has to be questioned whenever it is used with populations other than the type used in constructing the scales (Wiggins, 1973).

The MMPI was restandardized in 1989 (MMPI-2; Butcher et al., 1989). Although continuity with the original MMPI was preserved in many respects, significant improvements were made. First, the normative sample of the MMPI-2 is far better with respect to its size and its geographic, educational, and racial representation. The norms are more accurate. The fact that for many years, normal individuals have produced T-scores averaging approximately $55T$ on the MMPI is probably due to the fact that they answer virtually all of the test items, whereas the individuals who were in the original standardization sample declined to answer an average of 30 items. The literary quality of the MMPI was upgraded by eliminating and revising items that were archaic, grammatically impoverished, or perceived by some people to be offensive. Uniform T-scores were derived for the MMPI-2, which means that the percentile equivalent for any given T-score is identical across all of the scales. Finally, 15 new content scales and 12 supplementary scales were added to reflect content domains of interest to contemporary mental health professionals. Several of these scales can be particularly helpful in assessment work with patients with brain injuries. Reliability and validity issues are discussed in greater detail by Groth-Marnat (1999).

Administration of the MMPI-2

Many individuals who have sustained a brain injury or who have been diagnosed with a neurologic condition do not initially understand why they have been asked to undergo an evaluation of personality and psychological status. During this portion of the examination, patients sometimes question, "So, Doc, you want to see if I'm nuts?" This is a reasonable question because individuals who have CNS disease or other medical conditions do not readily expect to be treated as though they might have a mental illness. Yet, the MMPI-2 clearly asks very personal questions about psychological and social functioning. Medical patients expect to be asked about their symptoms, previous medical problems, diet, and family history. The patient might consider it strange to be asked by the doctor about such things as playing house as a child, stepping on sidewalk cracks, making donations to beggars, feeling afraid of mice and spiders, being fascinated with fire, enjoying gambling, auto racing, growing house plants, and flirting. Such inquiries have questionable relevance from the perspective of most medical patients. Some of these individuals respond to the test items defensively, feeling compelled to assert normalcy and to deny any problems so as not to be mistaken as "crazy." Others may be offended and refuse to cooperate with the remainder of the assessment process.

The clinician can prevent these unfortunate outcomes from occurring by preparing the patient prior to administering the MMPI-2. Patients should never be administered the MMPI-2 or other instruments without an adequate explanation of its function and the rationale for giving it. A general approach that seems to suffice is one in which the clinician introduces the MMPI-2 as a routine part of the examination process designed to measure feelings and attitudes. The clinician explains that he or she views understanding these feelings and attitudes as an important component in gaining a complete picture of the patient's general health. Although the clinician presents MMPI-2 administration to the patient as a routine procedure, he or she should be sensitive toward the patient and should leave room for questions or concerns to be expressed.

The MMPI-2 may be used with most individuals who are at least 18 years old and who have a minimum eighth-grade level of reading comprehension. The popularity of the MMPI-2 among neuropsychologists suggests that, in most clinical settings, administration is not a significant problem. However, patients who are substantially handicapped by cognitive impairment or behavioral disturbances are often unable to manage the requirements of the test and are, therefore, unable to provide valid information. A wide variety of conditions can preclude a valid administration of the MMPI-2. These include impatience and low frustration tolerance, visual disturbances, confusion, dyslexia, impaired reading comprehension, inattention and distractibility, and florid psychotic symptoms. Burke, Smith, and Imhoff (1989), using a sample of 66 patients with post-acute traumatic brain injury (TBI), reported a 20% incidence of inconsistent responding to the MMPI. On the other hand, there is evidence suggesting that patients who have mild or even moderate neuropsychological impairment secondary to brain injury are typically able to produce profiles that are valid in regard to content-response consistency (Mittenberg, Tremont, & Rayls, 1996; Paniak & Miller, 1993).

Completion of the MMPI-2 sometimes requires breaking the session into several shorter periods. For patients who are severely impaired and who are unable to manage the test's cognitive or sensorimotor demands, clinicians sometimes attempt to read the test items aloud to the patient and assume the task of filling out the answer sheet for the patient. The impact of the examiner's involvement in this situation is unknown. If this nonstandardized procedure is used (presumably as a last resort), the examiner must exercise caution in interpreting the results. In many instances, a better and effective alternative to this administrative procedure is to use an audio cassette version of the MMPI-2 that is produced and sold by National Computer Systems (NCS). Because the tape is fragile, currently costs $75.00, and has only a 6-month warranty, clinicians should exercise care in handling it. A compact disk version should be available within the next several years. The audio format for administering the MMPI provides results that are comparable to the booklet version and appears to be valid (Weiner, 1947). The tape first presents the general test instructions, followed by two readings of each item to ensure that examinees understand and have time to mark their response. On the standard MMPI-2 answer sheet, the typeset and bubbles are too small for many patients who have impaired visual and visuomotor function. This problem can be resolved often by printing a custom answer sheet with larger font and including the words "True" and "False" after each item number. The patient can then be instructed to circle the appropriate answer.

Based on clinical experience with the MMPI-2, the routine use of the audio version is strongly recommended. Many patients who have brain injuries and who are unable to manage the standard written format can effectively complete the MMPI-2 using this approach. The audio version requires no reading, very little visual concentration, and apparently less mental effort on the part of the examinee. Furthermore, the rate of compliance is better, and the time to completion is typically much less. The cassette tape version produced by NCS requires approximately 2 hours. Other administrative alternatives to the widely used booklet format include the card form and computer administered methods, both of which should be considered with individuals who have brain dysfunction or reduced visual acuity (Herrman, Dorfman, Roth, & Burns, 1997).

As the MMPI-2 administration begins, it is important to unobtrusively observe the examinee taking the first several items to ensure that the instructions are properly followed. This is particularly critical in the case of those individuals who have a more serious degree of cognitive impairment and are more likely to lose the instructional set, wander off task, or become distracted. If there are any doubts about the examinee's reading ability, the audio version should be used. Most examinees who successfully complete the first several items are able to finish the remainder of the MMPI-2, though an additional session or two may be required due to fatigue or other discomfort. In some instances, the examinee will have increasing difficulties as the testing continues. This may become apparent in several ways. First, the patient may inform the examiner directly by saying so. Unfortunately, it is common for neurologically impaired examinees to "complete" the test, answering items, but nevertheless being confused. The clinician can sometimes observe the quietly confused patient making unusual marks with the pen, writing in the wrong location on the answer sheet, skipping items, or not answering items at all. In any case, it is important for the clinician to monitor the patient throughout the course of the administration so that an appropriate intervention can be made if a problem arises. In some cases, the clinician will need to terminate the MMPI-2 administration completely because of the examinee's inability to manage the basic task requirements. If the examinee successfully completes the first 370 MMPI-2 items, this abbreviated form is perfectly adequate for scoring the basic clinical scales as well as the Harris-Lingoes subscales. In most cases, those patients who have the capacity to answer the first 370 items are quite able to complete the entire 567-item version. The complete MMPI-2 provides substantially more information than the abbreviated 370-item version and, in most cases, is well worth the extra time required to administer it.

The examinee should complete the MMPI-2 in a supervised setting where privacy can be assured and assistance is available if needed. There are two mistakes that some clinicians make in MMPI-2 administration. The first is allowing the examinee to complete the MMPI-2 unsupervised or in the presence of friends or relatives. Early in my career, I discovered that many examinees are naturally inclined to solicit help in answering the test items. They will ask their significant others for advice on how to answer specific items, or, in other cases, they will be told what answers to give on an item-by-item basis. Even the presence of other patients is a potential problem because some examinees are predisposed to make the MMPI-2 a group experience, opting for a democratic process in answering test items. On one occasion, I entered a testing room where group administration of the MMPI was being conducted and discovered that four or five examinees were voting on which answer to give for each MMPI item. In these cases, the resulting profile (should the clinician bother to score it) could not be accepted as valid. The second mistake that clinicians sometimes make is allowing patients to take the MMPI-2 home to complete. The problem in this case is that in the absence of a supervised setting, one can never know who really completed the inventory or what influences may have intervened (Pope, Butcher, & Seelen, 1993).

Scoring the MMPI-2

The MMPI-2 can be scored by hand using the templates provided by NCS, or it can be computer scored. Scores on the basic clinical scales are based on items that were assigned to these scales because of their sensitivity to the personality and the emotional characteristics of the original psychiatric samples that had well-defined diagnoses. Because Hathaway and McKinley did not originally intend to use the MMPI-2 outside of the psychiatric setting, there was no attempt to determine whether the item pool would be systematically endorsed in some way by nonpsychiatric populations who might share a particular set of characteristics. Within the limited range of Hathaway and McKinley's clinical application, content bias was not a concern. An important implication of this is that the clinician should exercise some degree of caution whenever administering the MMPI-2 in nonpsychiatric settings. Ideally, the MMPI-2 should be empirically validated before it is used in nonpsychiatric settings, particularly when the item pool shows a systematic pattern of endorsement that does not clearly reflect symptoms of psychopathology but that suggests problems that are known to be associated with that population's condition.

There are rational and empirical reasons for doubting whether reliance on the standard MMPI-2 scoring procedure is appropriate when applied to individuals who have CNS disease. First, from a rational point of view, it is reasonable to suspect that patients who have CNS disease will, if asked by their doctor, report related physical symptoms and health-related concerns. Does the MMPI-2 have such questions in it? Unfortunately, yes. In fact, Hathaway and McKinley (1940) themselves initially identified the neurologic-symptom item content on the inventory. McKinley, who had a strong interest in measuring neurologic as well as psychiatric symptoms, made certain that the MMPI-2 item pool included neurologic symptom items. These items had content referring to paresthesia (53), headache (101), dysarthric speech (106), seizure (142, 182), syncope (159), dizziness (164), tremor (172), weakness (175), poor motor coordination (177), ataxia (181), hypesthesia (247), and tinnitus (255). Hathaway and McKinley originally identified several clusters of MMPI items reflecting "general neurologic" (19 items), "cranial nerve" (11 items), and "motility and coordination" (6 items). In addition, many of the MMPI-2 items refer specifically to health concerns that a person would naturally have when faced with any serious medical condition, including brain disease.

A second rational reason for not using the MMPI-2 in the conventional way with neurologic patients is that no norms exist for use with this population, nor have any studies validated the MMPI-2 scales as applied to individuals with brain injuries. The standard use of the MMPI-2 with patients with brain injuries is therefore psychometrically indefensible. These criticisms apply similarly to other less frequently used instruments, including the Millon Clinical Multiaxial Inventory-III, the Symptom Checklist 90-R, and the Beck Depression Inventory (Christensen, Ross, Kotasek, Rosenthal, & Henry, 1995; Rattok, Ross, & Ohry, 1995; Woessner & Caplan, 1996).

From an empirical perspective, several MMPI-2 scales are problematic because neurologically relevant complaints constitute a distinctive source of variance in MMPI-2 responding by patients with neurological impairments (Gass, 1991b, 1992). Factor analytic studies, which led to the derivation of correction factors, determined that neurologic item endorsement was factorially distinct and statistically independent of psychological-symptom reporting. Prior to these studies, a review of the MMPI literature revealed that patients with brain impairments consistently produce elevated scores on Scales 1, 2, 3, 7, and 8 (Wooten, 1983). Coincidentally, these are the particular scales on which neurologically relevant items load (Lezak, 1995).

A few neuropsychologists have claimed that patients with brain injuries endorse the neurologically related physical and cognitive items because of emotional distress, rather than because the items represent bona fide neurological symptoms. If this proposition is true, then MMPI-2 interpretation with these patients is more problematic for two reasons. First, this claim discounts the veracity of patients with brain injuries in acknowledging their neurological symptoms. It suggests that examinees conceal their physical and cognitive problems, unless they happen to be in distress. This corollary is both ludicrous and contrary to the results of numerous studies of scoring patterns on the Harris-Lingoes subscales (Bornstein & Kozora, 1990; Gass, 1997; Gass & Lawhorn, 1991; Gass & Russell, 1991). Valid responding to the MMPI-2 items is predicated on the acknowledgement of existing symptoms, regardless of whether they are psychological or neurological in nature (Reitan & Wolfson, 1997).

If it is true that neurological-symptom reporting in patients with brain injuries reflects "nothing but distress," it logically follows that the MMPI-2 is invalid when applied to neurological patients. The clinical scale elevations that are caused by endorsement of these items purportedly measure a multitude of highly specified symptoms and behavioral characteristics that are not adequately represented under the amorphous label "distress." For example, prominent elevations on Scale 3, which are common in neurological samples, are not associated with emotional distress in the code-type literature. Indeed, Scale 3 correlated only .09 with the best MMPI-2 indicator of distress, Scale 7, in the MMPI-2 normative sample of men (Butcher et al., 1989). A clinician could only interpret elevated scores on Scale 3 as "distress" by completely disregarding all that is known about Scale 3 correlates.

Recent data suggest that distress can explain less than 40% of the variance in neurologically sensitive item endorsement (Brulot, Strauss, & Spellacy, 1997). It would be more accurate, perhaps, to say that the physical and cognitive sequelae of brain injury account for less than 40% of an individual's level of distress. In either case, when patients with TBI are asked directly about their MMPI-2 responses, they report that they endorse the neurologically related items because the content of these items represents specific symptoms of their head injury. Family members who presumably know the patient quite well concur with this attribution (Edwards, Holmquist, Wanless, Wicks, & Davis, 1998). Of course, neurologic symptoms might be a source of distress for most people, and so a relationship between symptoms and distress would be expected. However, the assertion that neurologic-related item endorsement primarily reflects psychopathology is counterintuitive and contradicted by numerous research studies (Gass, 1991b, 1992; Kalmar, Cicerone, & Giacino, 1996; Meyerink, Reitan, & Selz, 1988; Rayls, Mittenberg, Burns, & Theroux, 1997).

For many years, clinicians have been able to use the MMPI and MMPI-2 successfully in their work with neurologic patients because the vast majority of the MMPI-2 items are specific to personality and emotional status. There is, however, some content bias that, once eliminated, will improve the accuracy of the MMPI-2 when applied to neurologic patients. The interpretive problem that neuropsychologists confront has been addressed in several ways. One approach is to use the standard scoring and interpretive approach, a practice that implicitly ignores the possibility that bona fide neurological symptoms of a physical, cognitive, or general health-related nature affected the clinical profile. *This approach is rationally indefensible because there is an abundance of evidence suggesting that nonpsychiatric factors systematically affect MMPI-2 item endorsement in patients who differ healthwise from the Minnesota criterion groups used to construct the clinical scales.* This fact is particularly problematic in the assessment of individuals with brain injuries because of the large number of items that have neurologically related content.

The second approach, which is by far the most widely used at the present time, is to rely on "clinical judgment." According to a recent survey by Zillmer and his colleagues, 79% of the members of the National Academy of Neuropsychologists rely on clinical judgment to interpret the MMPI/MMPI-2 profiles of individuals who have brain damage (Cripe, Gass, Greene, Perry, & Zillmer, 1997); that is, they do not use a standard approach or an empirically derived correction factor. The methodology involved in the application of clinical judgment was not specified in the survey. However, anecdotal evidence suggests that clinicians ordinarily make mental adjustments of scores on some of the clinical scale scores, lowering them in an effort to compensate for the influence of nonpsychiatric medical symptoms and health-related concerns that affect item endorsement. This methodology has the advantage of requiring little time or effort. However, its accuracy is contingent on the clinician's knowledge of the identity and the number of neurologically related items on each scale, knowledge of which of these were endorsed by the examinee, and knowledge concerning the precise T-score impact of these endorsements. In the absence of empirical data, this task would require virtual omniscience. "It is highly presumptuous to believe that even an experienced and conscientious clinician can make dependable judgments about how his client has actually interpreted the content of the item or how it bears upon various special circumstances in his background and experience" (Dahlstrom, Welsh, & Dahlstrom, 1972). Empirical data are required. Nevertheless, clinicians often feel very confident in their clinical judgment, despite the systematic errors they commit due to a variety of poor judgment habits and human cognitive limitations (Faust, 1986; Garb, 1998).

MMPI-2 and the Use of a Correction Factor

A preliminary solution to the problem of neurologic content bias on the MMPI-2 involved the construction of a correction factor. The correction approach is a systematic, empirically based method of scoring and interpreting the MMPI-2 when it is used with individuals who have a medical condition. The use of a correction is warranted whenever there is reliable evidence that patients may be reporting symptoms of their disease that are not manifestations of psychological disturbance. The rationale for using the corrective strategy is to allow the MMPI-2 to more accurately assess what it was designed to assess, namely, personality characteristics and psychopathology. Some clinicians oppose the use of a correction because they feel that it removes important information from the resulting profile that has neurologic relevance. They prefer to interpret the neurological and psychological symptoms together and to work out some sort of synthesis without observing the underlying pattern of item endorsement. Ordinary clinicians are unable to perform this feat and may rely instead on data.

R.B. Page designed the first MMPI correction in 1947 as part of his dissertation at the University of Minnesota. Using a rational or face-valid approach to item selection, he attempted to "purify" the MMPI of items that reflected physical symptoms of tuberculosis. Over the next 40 years, numerous corrections were designed using this same approach that essentially relied on the opinions of expert judges to identify salient items. Multiple sclerosis was addressed in several subsequent studies, beginning with Baldwin (1952), who, using expert opinion, selected 12 MMPI items that were judged to be associated with symptoms of demyelinating CNS disease. Judges probably differ in the stringency of the criteria they employ in item identification. In addition, the author of a correction must not select too many items or else clinical profiles will be systematically overcorrected, yielding an underestimate of psychological problems. Individuals who have multiple sclerosis commonly present with unusually high scores on Scales 1, 3, and 8, and some authors questioned whether a 12-item correction was sufficient. Marsh, Hirsch, and Leung (1982) devised a 24-item correction for this population. After this, Mueller and Girace (1988) designed a 22-item version. The need for an MMPI correction in the assessment of patients with multiple sclerosis was most clearly demonstrated in an empirical investigation by Meyerink et al. (1988), and in several more recent studies (Connor, Ogden, Waller, Cullum, & Frohman, 1998; Nelson & Do, 1998).

The MMPI-2 Correction Factor for Closed Head Injury

Closed head injury has been described as an epidemic, and, considering its common impact on behavior and psychological status, as well as its widespread association with personal injury and worker's compensation litigation, it is not surprising that it has received so much empirical attention in recent years. The potential impact of reporting symptoms of TBI on the MMPI was initially investigated by Gass and Russell (1991), who examined the contribution of 42 neurologically related MMPI items that were selected by three clinical neurologists who were experts in TBI rehabilitation. The effect of neurologic-related item endorsement on the clinical profiles was substantial, *even after prorating the scores on the clinical scales to compensate for the removal of these 42 items.* Although the need for a corrective approach to MMPI scoring was evident, it seemed that reliance on the subjective judgments of experts was not a sound basis for constructing one.

A solution to this problem appeared in an earlier article authored by Kendall, Edinger, and Eberly (1978). This study outlined a rigorous empirical approach to correction derivation for use in the MMPI assessment of individuals with spinal cord injury. As further item-level data were collected on patients with closed head injury for derivation of an empirically based correction factor (Gass, 1991b), a "neurocorrective" procedure for use with the MMPI appeared in the literature (Alfano, Finlayson, Stearns, & Neilson, 1990). This correction consisted of 44 items that were selected by experts for deletion from the profiles of a mixed sample of patients with brain impairment. Several years later, Alfano, Paniak, and Finlayson (1993) used a subset of these 44 items to construct a 13-item correction for use with the MMPI in cases of closed head injury.

The MMPI-2 correction for closed head injury (Gass, 1991b) consists of 14 out of the 370 items of the abbreviated MMPI-2 that passed four successive empirical criteria. First, responses to each of the items sharply distinguished a sample of 75 patients with head injury from the MMPI-2 normative sample ($p < .001$). Second, every item was endorsed by at least 25% of the patients with head injury. Third, the items were statistically grouped together, comprising a unitary factor as determined by the application of factor analysis (varimax rotation). The results of the orthogonal analysis revealed these items to be factorially independent of a set of psychiatric symptom items that also emerged as a factor. Fourth, the content of the items showed face validity as representing physical and cognitive symptoms and concerns related to brain injury (see Table 14.1). Cross-validation of correction-factor internal consistency was provided by Barrett, Putnam, Axelrod, and Rapport (1998). Using a separate sample of patients with head injury, they reported a Cronbach's alpha coefficient of .80.

Scoring the MMPI-2 profiles of patients with closed head injury should be done twice—once in the standard manner and again after eliminating any correction items that were endorsed in the scored direction. This procedure, which is detailed in the next paragraph, provides the clinician with a systematic means of measuring the degree and the manner in which neurological-symptom endorsement influences the resulting clinical profile. The procedure eliminates the guesswork and the inherent unreliability associated with subjective-based methods. In addition, when evaluating the MMPI-2 produced by a patient with head injury, the correction procedure helps resolve the skepticism that some clinicians appropriately express in trying to determine the extent to which scores reflect psychopathology and the extent that might be

Table 14.1. The MMPI-2 correction factor for Closed-Head Injury

31.	I find it hard to keep my mind on a task or job (T).
101.	Often I feel as though there were a tight band around my head (T).
106.	My speech is the same as always (not faster or slower, no slurring; no hoarseness) (F).
147.	I cannot understand what I read as well as I used to (T).
149.	The top of my head sometimes feels tender (T).
165.	My memory seems to be all right (F).
170.	I am afraid of losing my mind (T).
172.	I frequently notice that my hand shakes when I try to do something (T).
175.	I feel weak all over much of the time (T).
179.	I have had no difficulty in walking or keeping my balance (F).
180.	There is something wrong with my mind (T).
247.	I have numbness in one or more regions of my skin (T).
295.	I have never been paralyzed or had any unusual weakness of any of my muscles (F).
325.	I have more trouble concentrating than others seem to have (T).

due to neurological-symptom reporting. Without empirical data, the task is so formidable, according to one expert, that it is akin to "a wild goose chase" that requires the clinician to initially "dim the lights, light the candles, and burn the incense" (Cripe et al., 1997). Without empirical guidance, the MMPI-2 in neuropsychological assessment is indeed a "murky" measure (Cripe, 1996).

How to Apply the Correction Factor

The correction scoring procedure initially requires checking the answer sheet for specific answers to the 14 neurologically related items listed in Table 14.2. If the examinee's answer is in the keyed direction, as indicated later, then one point is deducted from the raw score of the clinical scales that are represented on the same line. For example, if item 31 is answered "True," then one point is subtracted from the raw score of Scales 2, 3, 4, 7, 8, and 0. Table 14.2 can be used to tally the total number of pathologically endorsed items for each MMPI-2 scale. If the items (the far left column) are answered in the keyed direction indicated, then the item number is tallied wherever it appears across the entire row. After following this procedure for each item, the clinician can work columnwise counting the number of circled items in each column. The sums are recorded at the bottom of Table 14.2 above the corresponding MMPI-2 scale. These numbers located in the bottom row are the values that should be subtracted from the respective raw scores on the basic clinical profile. Once the corrected raw scores are determined, they can be plotted on a National Computer System hand-plotting MMPI-2 profile sheet, or the revised *T*-scores can be determined using Table A-1 in the MMPI-2 manual (Butcher et al., 1989, pp. 54–55).

Issues Involved in the Use of the Correction

The use of the MMPI-2 correction has been opposed on the grounds that the procedure is "too risky" (Cripe, Maxwell, & Hill, 1995) and that it assumes that the patients with head injury are a homogeneous group (Greene, Gwin, & Staal, 1997). In reality, the

Table 14.2.   MMPI-2 correction table for Closed-Head Injury

Item	F	1	2	3	4	7	8	9	0
31 True	—	—	31T	31T	31T	31T	31T	—	31T
101 True	—	101T	—	101T	—	—	—	—	—
106 False	—	—	—	—	—	—	106F	106F	106F
147 True	—	—	147T	—	—	147T	147T	—	—
149 True	—	149T	—	—	—	—	—	—	—
165 False	—	—	165F	—	—	165F	165F	—	—
170 True	—	—	170T	—	—	170T	170T	—	—
172 True	—	—	—	172T	—	—	—	—	—
175 True	—	175T	175T	175T	—	175T	—	—	—
179 False	—	179F	—	179F	—	—	179F	—	—
180 True	180T	—	—	—	—	—	180T	—	—
247 True	—	247T	—	—	—	—	247T	—	—
295 False	—	—	—	—	—	—	295F	—	—
325 True	—	—	—	—	—	325T	325T	—	—
Sum	F	1	2	3	4	7	8	9	0

conventional scoring approach, when used alone, is exceedingly more risky because of content bias in the MMPI-2. Correction usage does not assume homogeneity in the population with head injury any more than the use of any MMPI-2 scale assumes homogeneity in the psychiatric population. The correction factor is not a diagnostic scale per se, though it reliably reflects neurological symptoms in examinees with brain injuries (Edwards et al., 1998). The correction-derivation samples were heterogeneous in several important respects (e.g., age, education, time post-injury), though none of these relevant variables affected correction-item endorsement. Cross-validation support for the sensitivity of the correction items was provided by Gass and Wald (1997) using a sample of 54 patients with closed head injury—men and women with milder and more recent head trauma than existed in the original derivation sample. Barrett et al. (1998), using a sample of 353 clients with head injury, provided similar support for the 14 items in the correction. They found that the correction items were collectively associated with the presence of head injury in individuals who have no premorbid history of psychological disturbance. Netto (1997) obtained the same finding using a sample 30 Hispanic patients with TBI who were administered the Hispanic version (NCS) of the MMPI-2.

In another study, patients with head injury who were interviewed after completing the MMPI-2 reported that they endorsed these items because of injury-related symptoms and not premorbid personality characteristics (Edwards et al., 1998). Contrary to Greene et al. (1997), the use of the correction scoring strategy is based on the belief that individual differences exist with respect to the presence of bona fide medical symptoms. In contrast, the use of the standard MMPI-2 scoring procedure indiscriminately with all medical patients operationally assumes that all item responses fall on a continuum of normal to psychiatrically disturbed. Numbness or paresthesia, for example, is treated as a behavioral and psychiatric correlate of Scales 1 and 8. In actuality, the acknowledgement of bona fide CNS symptoms constitutes a second possibility. Using the standard approach that disregards the use of a correction, all MMPI-2 items that are endorsed in the keyed direction are scored on psychopathology scales for *all individuals indiscriminately,* without any consideration of a patient's medical problems and their relation to the MMPI-2 item pool. In contrast, the use of the correction customizes the MMPI-2 for specific use with individuals with brain injury and eliminates the "noise" that is introduced by confusing bona fide physical symptoms with psychological problems.

Some authors have ignored the psychometric problems inherent in applying the MMPI-2 outside of the psychiatric context and are willing to assume that the MMPI-2 is valid when applied to any and all medical populations. This stance is particularly puzzling when one considers the sheer number of health-related items in the MMPI-2. In addition, it is difficult to ignore the overwhelming weight of empirical evidence that demonstrates neurologic content bias in the item pool of the MMPI-2. Nevertheless, it is sometimes argued that because the correction items are sensitive to psychiatric disturbances (including somatoform disorders), their endorsement frequency should not be examined or corrected in individuals who have had TBI or other types of neurologic insult. This means that, for example, if a patient who had a stroke reports hemiparesis and hemisensory loss on MMPI-2 items that, in psychiatric patients, reflect emotional problems, the clinician should interpret these responses as symptoms of psychological disturbance. One consequence of this approach would be the frequent false positive diagnosis of conversion disorders and other somatoform symptoms in the stroke population, which frequently exhibits the 13/31 code type.

Dunn and Lees-Haley (1995) recommended a standard interpretive approach to litigating patients with head trauma after they found that the endorsement frequencies on the correction items did not substantially distinguish between samples of litigating head trauma and psychiatric patients, many of whom had physical injuries and pain syndromes. They demonstrated that the correction items (Gass, 1991b) can be endorsed because of problems other than brain injury. They recommend not using the correction—a conclusion with which this author fully concurs in relation to the many compensation-seeking cases in which the presence of bona fide brain injury is doubtful. As applied to patients with *bona fide brain injury* (litigating or not), the rationale behind the recommendation of Dunn and Lees-Haley is flawed. It ignores the fact that the validity of the MMPI-2 item pool rests not just on its *sensitivity* to psychopathology, but on its *specificity* to psychiatric disturbance. The MMPI-2 is not a valid measure of psychopathology if reasons other than psychopathology systematically affect item endorsement. As previously emphasized, postadministration interview data indicate that in the vast majority of cases involving bona fide brain injury, the correction items are endorsed in the scored direction as an indication of injury-related symptoms, as opposed to preexistent emotional characteristics (Edwards et al., 1998). *As long as the clinical scales on the MMPI-2 are to be interpreted as measures of psychopathology, the burden of proof lies with those who apply the scales to populations of patients who have medical diseases that systematically influence MMPI-2 item endorsement.*

If an individual claims to have a head injury without any accompanying evidence of impaired brain function, the MMPI-2 correction procedure has only one very limited application. In this case, it can be used to describe only what the profile impact would be *hypothetically* in the presence of a bona fide brain injury. Such a description is often quite useful because individuals who feign brain damage or who have somatoform disorders typically score so high on the corrected scales that they rarely derive much benefit from the application of the profile correction. In most cases, the corrected profile retains the elevated scores, providing more definitive evidence of psychological disturbance and/or feigning of psychopathology. Neuropsychologists who work as expert witnesses for the defense in personal injury cases sometimes use the MMPI-2 correction to support a presumed psychiatric diagnosis (e.g., somatoform disorder) or malingering in individuals who appear to be feigning symptoms of brain damage.

The use of the correction has been opposed on the grounds that, in litigating claimants with head injury, the correction-item responses do not correlate with presumed measures of injury severity (Brulot et al., 1997). Unfortunately, this study used an inappropriate and diagnostically obscure sample and a questionable methodology for addressing the validity of the correction approach (Gass, 1998). The standard application of the correction should be limited to the MMPI-2 protocols of individuals who have clear evidence of bona fide brain injury and no premorbid history of psychopathology or drug addiction. As a general rule, recovery from mild head injury is nearly complete within 6 months post-injury (Binder, 1997; Binder, Rohling, & Larrabee, 1997). Therefore, it is questionable whether the correction should be applied in cases in which symptoms persist beyond 6 months.

Endorsement of the correction items was correlated with injury severity (Glascow Coma Scale and positive CT [computerized tomography] findings) in a longitudinal study of 61 patients who were consecutively admitted to a general hospital for treatment of mild head trauma (Rayls et al., 1997). Unlike the individuals in the Brulot et al. (1997) study, these patients were consecutive admissions who were evaluated in the acute stage and who were not involved in litigation or seeking compensation for their injuries. The analysis indicated that the correction was indeed sensitive to the initial presenting symptoms and that item endorsement was not related to psychological stressors. Most salient, however, was the fact that the frequency of correction-item endorsement significantly decreased in these patients when they were retested 7 months later, concurrent with their recovery from head trauma.

As a general rule, clinicians are advised to first establish that there is sufficient evidence of CNS impairment before applying the correction to an MMPI-2 protocol. By implication, the correction is not appropriate for routine application with the majority of individuals who are seeking compensation for persisting symptoms following mild head injury (Brulot et al., 1997; Dunn & Lees-Haley, 1995). In these cases, there is reason to suspect that the symptomatic complaints are largely related to psychological factors, motivational pressures, incentives to acquire compensation, and other important aspects of their medico-legal context (Binder, 1997; Gasquonine, 1997; Reitan & Wolfson, 1997; Youngjohn, Burrows, & Erdal, 1995). Correction application would potentially distort rather than enhance the accuracy of profile interpretation.

MMPI-2 Correction Factor for Stroke

Cerebrovascular disease (CVD), or stroke, is another disorder that is frequently evaluated in neuropsychological settings. Strokes occur in the United States with an estimated annual incidence of 500,000 to 700,000 cases. It is the most common neurological disorder of adult life, accounting for over 85,000 fatalities and one million new disabilities annually (Adams & Victor, 1989). Gass (1992) addressed the problem of stroke-related item content on the MMPI-2 and designed a correction factor specifically for use with individuals who have had a stroke. The 21-item correction for stroke was designed using 110 patients with CVD and virtually the same statistical procedures as were used previously with patients with closed head injury (Gass, 1991b). Empirical support for the sensitivity of these 21 items was obtained in a recent cross-validation study of 50 patients with CVD (Gass, 1996a). The correction items are presented in Table 14.3. The items can be tabulated using Table 14.4 to derive corrected scores on the clinical scales. Although the corrections for use with individuals with closed head injury and stroke share some common items, there are enough differences to indicate that any corrective method should be tailored specifically for particular neurodiagnostic populations rather than for patients with brain impairment in general.

Interpretive Sequence for the MMPI-2

MMPI-2 interpretation consists of generating a series of hypotheses about an individual based on empirically derived behavioral correlates of scores and score patterns. These descriptive correlates are based on systematic studies of individuals who, in most cases, had a psychiatric diagnosis and who, in many instances, were receiving

Table 14.3.   The MMPI-2 correction factor for Cerebrovascular Disease

10.	I am about as able to work as I ever was (F).
31.	I find it hard to keep my mind on a task or job (T).
45.	I am in just as good physical health as most of my friends (F).
47.	I am almost never bothered by pains over the heart or in my chest (F).
53.	Parts of my body often have feelings like burning, tingling, crawling, or like "going to sleep" (T).
106.	My speech is the same as always (not faster or slower, no slurring, no hoarseness) (F).
141.	During the past few years, I have been well most of the time (F).
147.	I cannot understand what I read as well as I used to (T).
148.	I have never felt better in my life than I do now (F).
152.	I do not tire quickly (F).
164.	I seldom or never have dizzy spells (F).
168.	I have had periods in which I carried on activities without knowing later what I had been doing (T).
172.	I frequently notice that my hand shakes when I try to do something (T).
173.	I can read a long time without tiring my eyes (F).
175.	I feel weak all over much of the time (T).
177.	My hands have not become clumsy or awkward (F).
182.	I have had attacks in which I could not control my movements or speech but in which I knew what was going on around me (T).
224.	I have few or no pains (F).
229.	I have had blank spells in which I did not know what was going on around me (T).
247.	I have numbness in one or more regions of my skin (T).
249.	My eyesight is as good as it has been for years (F).

some form of psychological and/or psychopharmacologic treatment. Seven interpretive steps are recommended.

1. *Analysis of Test-Taking Attitude.* The interpretation of the MMPI-2 typically begins with an analysis of the examinee's test-taking attitude as reflected in the validity scales. In some cases, scores on these scales are extreme enough to indicate that the clinical profile, content scales, and other measures are completely invalid. In these cases, clinical profile interpretation is very limited, even though some important information might be gained by examining the scores on the validity scales. In interpreting highly defensive protocols, it is useful to note that any elevated scores on clinical or content scales may still provide some valid and potentially useful information about the examinee. In most cases, it is safe to conclude that, among other possible problems, the client has, at minimum, the problems identified by the elevated scale(s). Of course, additional difficulties that might have been undetected could exist. Thus, the results must be qualified, due to the likelihood that scores on some of the other clinical scales were suppressed by the examinee's defensiveness.

2. *Estimation of General Level of Psychological Adjustment.* The level of psychological adjustment can be evaluated using a combination of methods. In general, serious maladjustment is suggested whenever the basic clinical profile has scores on three or more scales (excluding Scales 5 and 0) exceeding 65*T* or a score exceeding 80*T* on

Table 14.4.   MMPI-2 correction table for Cerebrovascular Disease

Item		F	1	2	3	4	7	8	9	0
10	False	—	10F	10F	10F	—	—	—	—	—
31	True	—	—	31T	31T	31T	31T	31T	—	31T
45	False	—	45F	45F	45F	—	—	—	—	—
47	False	—	47F	—	47F	—	—	—	—	—
53	True	—	53T	—	—	—	—	—	—	—
106	False	—	—	—	—	—	—	106F	106F	106F
141	False	—	141F	141F	141F	—	—	—	—	—
147	True	—	—	147T	—	—	147T	147T	—	—
148	False	—	—	148F	148F	—	—	—	—	—
152	False	—	152F	—	152F	—	—	—	—	—
164	False	—	164F	—	164F	—	—	—	—	—
168	True	168T	—	—	—	—	—	168T	168T	—
172	True	—	—	—	172T	—	—	—	—	—
173	False	—	173F	—	173F	—	—	—	—	—
175	True	—	175T	175T	175T	—	175T	—	—	—
177	False	—	—	—	—	—	—	177F	—	—
182	True	—	—	—	—	—	—	182T	182T	—
224	False	—	224F	—	224F	—	—	—	—	—
229	True	—	—	—	—	—	—	229T	229T	—
247	True	—	247T	—	—	—	—	247T	—	—
249	False	—	249F	—	249F	—	—	—	—	—
Sum		F	1	2	3	4	7	8	9	0

any of these scales. In all cases (except malingering), more serious psychopathology is suggested by a positive or upward slope on the right side of the profile graph, with relatively high scores on Scales 6, 8, and 9, in contrast with Scales 1, 2, and 3.

3. *Clinical Code Type Interpretation.* The descriptive information obtained from the two-point code types is based on an extensive amount of research and, as such, is the most reliable source of MMPI-2-based clinical material about the examinee. In some cases, three-point codes can be used. In general, inferences based on code-type data have priority over other sources of test information (e.g., individual scales, subscales, and critical items), particularly when apparently contradictory or irreconcilable inferences emerge. In evaluating the clinical profiles of individuals who have bona fide CNS damage, the code type should be based on appropriate norms that are relatively unaffected by neurologic-related content bias in the underlying item pool. Until these norms are available for use with individuals with neurological impairment, clinicians who work with patients with head injury and stroke should consider code types that result when corrected scores are used (Gass, 1991b; Gass, 1992). When patients who have other types of neurological disorders are evaluated, other precautions should be applied (see "Considerations for Patients Other Than TBI and Stroke" on pages 516–517 in this chapter).

4. *Secondary Scale Elevations.* After the code-type descriptors have been organized, the clinician considers the psychological correlates of the remaining clinical

scales, beginning with the scale that has the highest elevation. Scales that have elevated scores should be evaluated with respect to content by examining scores on the Harris-Lingoes subscales. This is especially important in regard to clinical scales that have marginally elevated scores (60T to 70T). Hand-scoring keys for these subscales are available through NCS.

5. *Interpreting Components of the Profile Configuration.* The relationship between the scores on various clinical scales can provide very useful and rich descriptive hypotheses about the examinee. Scales 1, 2, 3, 5, 7, and 0 typically operate as control variables over the expression of serious psychopathology, possibly due, in most cases, to their association with the internalization of conflict. To the extent that the highest scores in a protocol exist on these scales, acting out is less likely to occur. In contrast, the externalization of psychological conflict is much more likely to occur when the profile configuration has generally higher scores on Scales 4, 6, 8, and 9. Elevated scores on these scales are associated with a greater likelihood of acting out. The significance of various score combinations across pairs of clinical scales will be discussed in greater detail.

6. *Interpreting the Content and Supplementary Scales.* The content and supplementary scales provide information that can help clarify the meaning of other scores, and they add to the information base derived from the basic clinical profile. For example, high scores on Scale 7 can be clarified by examining scores on Anxiety (ANX), Fears (FRS), and Obsessiveness (OBS), all of which assess certain symptomatic components of *psychasthenia*. Scores on Bizarre Mentation (BIZ) and Social Discomfort (SOD) can assist in the interpretation of high scores on Scale 8. Anger (ANG) and Antisocial Practices (ASP) scores further understanding of the significance of elevated scores on Scale 4. In addition to providing further clarification, the content scales measure reported problems in daily living that might be surmised but that are not clearly addressed by the basic clinical scales. Examples of these problems include Family Problems (FAM) and Work Interference (WRK). Additional issues, such as substance abuse, addiction potential, marital conflict, and post-traumatic stress, are examined with the use of specific MMPI-2 supplementary scales.

7. *Examining Critical Items.* Answers to certain MMPI-2 items could potentially indicate problems of critical importance to the clinician (Butcher, 1995). For example, the clinician should follow up when a client responds "true" to the item, "Nobody knows it, but I have tried to kill myself." Sets of critical items have been published by Koss and Butcher (1973) and Lachar and Wrobel (1979).

The Validity Scales

A major advantage of the MMPI-2 over other assessment instruments is its measurement of test-taking attitude and profile validity. The original intent of Hathaway and McKinley (1940) to circumvent the potential problem of faking test findings through an empirical keying strategy of test construction was not completely successful. The addition of validity scales was essential. Regardless of how self-report measures are constructed, individuals can produce test scores that may lead to an overestimate or an underestimate of psychological disturbance. An examinee's test-taking attitude and openness in reporting problems determines the test results on self-report measures of emotional functioning.

Therefore, proper interpretation of the MMPI-2 validity scales lays a necessary foundation for accurately understanding the meaning of scores on the clinical and the content scales. In addition, scores on these scales have certain personality correlates that can be very important in their own right for understanding the examinee.

Cannot Say (?)

The Cannot Say score is the number of unanswered or double-tallied (True and False) items. Most examinees answer every item, and, *as a general rule, the examinee who fails to answer items should be queried and, to whatever extent possible, encouraged to reconsider and to respond to any items that were not initially answered.* The typical impact of unanswered items is a reduction of scores on the clinical profile. If these omissions occur on items that appear after the first 370 items, the basic clinical scales and their subscales are unaffected and their scores can be interpreted. According to the MMPI-2 manual, if 30 or more items are unanswered, the profile is invalid, and it should not be interpreted. However, the clinical profile will be affected proportionately by the number of omitted items, even if there are fewer than 30. Some degree of caution should be applied if more than 10 items are omitted (Graham, 1993), and more so as the number of omitted items increases.

Omitted or double-scored items can occur for many reasons. Confusion or uncertainty over the precise meaning of a test item is often the cause. In some cases, both True and False are considered by the examinee to be valid ways of responding. In addition, brain damage can interfere with reading comprehension in a variety of ways, thereby producing uncertainty as to how to respond. Insufficient reading ability based on limited educational background can also lead to poor comprehension and item omission. In other instances, items might not be applicable; they may be perceived to be personally intrusive or offensive; or the examinee might be oppositional or defensive in disclosing problem areas.

L Scale

The L (Lie) scale consists of 15 items that measure a tendency to answer the MMPI-2 in a way that expresses a naive defensiveness as well as an unrealistically high degree of moral virtue and self-control over thoughts, emotional impulses, and behavior. High scores ($T > 60$) on the L scale suggest limited self-awareness and poor emotional insight. Higher scorers who have impaired brain functioning typically overestimate their cognitive abilities and, as a result, make poor decisions, taking on tasks that are beyond their capability to effectively handle. Increasingly higher scores on L are associated with poorer recognition of cognitive limitations, acquired deficits, and, simultaneously, worse neuropsychological test performance. In a mixed neurological sample, scores on the L scale were mildly predictive of the degree of global neuropsychological impairment on the Average Impairment Rating Scale, r (144) = −.27, $p <$ .005 (Gass, 1997). Scores on L have been linked with the extent of cognitive impairment in several studies of patients with brain injuries (Dikmen & Reitan, 1974a, 1977; Gass & Ansley, 1994).

In individuals who are neurologically intact, scores above $60T$ on Scale L are associated with a psychologically based denial and rigid, stereotypic, and ineffective style of coping with stress. High scorers on L tend to be moralistic, rigid, concrete, and unaware of the impact that their behavior has on other people. They commonly overestimate their abilities, pursue unrealistic goals, and view themselves as "above" any need for psychological intervention. Elevated scores on L are typically associated with lower scores on the clinical profile, particularly on the higher numbered scales (6, 7, 8, and 9).

Scale L is often elevated in individuals who earnestly want to present a highly moral appearance. In some cases, high scores on Scale L are accompanied by elevations on Scales 1 and 3, suggesting vague somatic symptoms and somatoform features in an individual who wants to present as responsible, moral, and concerned with integrity. Individuals who are suspected of malingering neuropsychological test findings in order to gain financial compensation commonly score high on L because they want to appear morally impeccable. When accompanied by a high score on Scale F, the individual is conveying an image of being extremely virtuous but afflicted with emotional difficulties.

Average scorers on the L scale acknowledge having normal human weaknesses and frailties. They are less likely to resort to denial as a coping strategy, and more likely to have a realistic assessment of their strengths and weaknesses. Low scores ($T < 40$) suggest the possibility of a self-critical stance, a hypothesis that can be examined more directly using other MMPI-2 scales (e.g., LSE).

F Scale

The F (Infrequency) scale consists of 60 items that were originally designed to measure random responding and unusual or deviant ways of responding to the inventory. Each of these items was endorsed in the scored direction by less than 10% of the original Minnesota normative sample in the 1930s, though they are endorsed much more frequently by contemporary normal individuals (Arbisi & Ben-Porath, 1995). In most cases, the F scale measures the degree of openness to disclosing psychological problems, including attempts to exaggerate or feign psychological disturbance. Scores on the F scale are often indicative of the severity or acuteness of psychological problems and an accompanying interest in obtaining psychological help. In some cases, high F scores ($T > 80$) are due to content-independent responding, possibly secondary to poor reading comprehension, confusion, difficulty understanding the meaning of items, or noncompliance. Examinees who are confused, disoriented, or substantially impaired in their thinking or in their perceptual processes sometimes respond randomly to items and, as a result, score quite high on the F scale. A random pattern of responding to test items can be more clearly identified using two other validity scales that are designed to measure response consistency: Variable Response Inconsistency (VRIN) and True Response Inconsistency (TRIN). These scales are described later.

The interpretation of scores on the F scale partially depends on the base rates associated with one's particular clinical setting. For example, a T-score of 70 would be unusually high and alarming in a personnel-screening setting where presumably "normal" individuals are being evaluated, whereas the same score could, in some cases, suggest a relatively benign psychological disturbance in an inpatient psychiatric context. Neuropsychological referrals in a medical center setting frequently score above a T-score of 75, particularly if they have a psychiatric history or are referred by a psychiatry service within the hospital. If a high F scale score cannot be explained on the basis of content-independent responding (i.e., VRIN and TRIN are less than $80T$), the clinician has to address the difficult challenge of differentiating between the profile impact of legitimate psychopathology versus exaggeration or malingering.

An F scale score that exceeds 80T or even 100T is often produced by patients who have serious psychopathology in the absence of marked exaggeration of symptomatology. This fact is exemplified by the finding that approximately 30% of psychiatric inpatients score higher than 90T on F (Arbisi & Ben-Porath, 1995). In these cases, the clinician should make a very careful attempt to determine whether the associated clinical profile, which, in most cases, has at least several elevated scores, is corroborated by observation and interview data. For example, individuals who have been properly assigned a diagnosis of schizophrenia, chronic paranoid type, often produce valid MMPI-2 profiles with an F scale score exceeding 100T and accompanying elevations on Scales 6 and 8. Extratest knowledge regarding the patient supports the validity of the profile, suggesting that the extremely high score on the F scale is largely due to bona fide psychopathology and not to "faking bad." On the other hand, neurotic individuals can also produce an F score of 90T or 100T as the result of exaggerating their psychological difficulties. Normal people who malinger can do the same. Extratest knowledge about these individuals will often help the clinician to determine whether exaggeration played a role in their responses on the MMPI-2.

The interpretation of high scores on the F scale can also be enhanced in some instances by meeting with the examinee for a feedback session after the test results have been initially evaluated. The MMPI-2 results can be reviewed and discussed with the patient in an effort to gain clarification of the meaning of high scores and individual item responses. When an MMPI-2 profile conflicts sharply with the observed behavior of the examinee, this exchange of information is sometimes very enlightening. However, in my experience, individuals who have a frankly psychotic disorder sometimes explain away their endorsement of specific items that have florid psychotic content, despite the fact that they exhibit these symptoms. Thus, although posttesting interview sessions can contribute to the assessment process, the clinician should not assume that all examinees will openly and candidly discuss in a face-to-face meeting the real reasons behind their item responses.

The deliberate faking or exaggeration of symptoms following mild head trauma is a very common problem confronted by neuropsychologists who are involved in personal injury and other compensation-related forensic cases. Individuals with no known impairments (e.g., college students) who are instructed to answer the MMPI-2 in a manner that will simulate brain damage and increase their chances of obtaining a financial award typically produce very high scores on the F scale (Berry et al., 1995). However, in clinical settings, claimants who consciously feign symptoms of traumatic brain injury in order to gain financial compensation are often more inclined to emphasize cognitive deficits, physical problems, and general health concerns, while minimizing any claims of severe psychopathology or highly unusual psychological symptoms. They do not want to appear "crazy," just brain-damaged. Although a subset of malingerers attempt to appear cognitively, physically, and psychologically disabled (and consequently produce high F scale scores), a substantial percentage of malingerers portray themselves as being psychologically intact but physically and cognitively disabled. The latter group typically produces marginally elevated scores on the F scale (Berry et al., 1995; Greiffenstein, Gola, & Baker, 1995) and high scores on Scales 1 and 3 (Larrabee, 1997; Suhr, Tranel, Wefel, & Barrash, 1997).

Moderate elevations on the F scale (65*T* to 79*T*) are within an acceptable validity range in most clinical settings. These scores typically reflect open disclosure of multiple problems. In many cases, they are produced by people who have psychotic or severely neurotic symptoms. Individuals who adhere to ideological beliefs and social values that are sharply divergent from the mainstream of the surrounding culture sometimes produce scores on the F scale in this range. Individuals who have traumatic brain injury and who score higher than 65*T* on the F scale show marked variability in the number of cognitive complaints they express. In nonlitigating patients with head injury, high scores on F do not predict a large number of cognitive complaints. On the other hand, those who complain of substantial cognitive difficulties almost invariably produce F scale scores that exceed 65*T* (Gass & Freshwater, 1998).

Marginal elevations (60*T* to 64*T*) on the F scale suggest openness in reporting problems that are relatively circumscribed in nature. A very large percentage of patients with brain injuries produce F scores within this range. From a treatment perspective, individuals who score in this range appear to be good candidates for intervention because they are open in disclosing their difficulties, yet they are not overwhelmed by so many problems and symptoms that they easily lose their focus in psychotherapy. Victims of bona fide traumatic brain injury who score below 65*T* very rarely report a substantial number of cognitive complaints (Gass & Freshwater, 1998). In clinical settings involving general medical and psychiatric patients, a score below 50*T* is rather unusual and is likely to be accompanied by additional and more reliable evidence of defensiveness (L and K scales). Even medical patients who do not have a history of psychiatric disturbance typically produce mildly elevated scores on the F scale.

K Scale

Early work with the MMPI led to a realization that profile validity was often compromised by a form of defensiveness that was too subtle and sophisticated to be detected using the L scale. Individuals with psychological disturbances might be willing to admit to having certain common human frailties and limitations (L scale), yet, at the same time, attempt to respond to MMPI items in a manner that conveys an image of psychological health and adjustment. The K (Correction) scale consists of 30 items that were designed to measure this type of defensiveness (Meehl & Hathaway, 1946). High scorers on the K scale ($T > 60$) are defensive and usually unwilling to disclose their emotional difficulties and other problems in living. They have a need to appear psychologically healthy and emotionally well-adjusted. They often use denial as a defense mechanism and, in many cases, have very limited self-insight and awareness about their own behavior and emotions. They do not see themselves as being in need of any psychological intervention and generally meet such attempts with resistance. Therapy clients who have a high K scale score are generally unwilling to disclose or discuss their feelings.

High scores on K are associated with low scores on the clinical profile. Meehl and Hathaway (1946) had originally hoped that the suppressant profile effect of K-related defensiveness could be statistically offset by adding a fraction of the K raw score to five MMPI scales: 1, 4, 7, 8, and 9. Unfortunately, the K correction does not adequately compensate for a defensive test-taking response style, and even K-corrected scores are often lower than would be the case in the presence of open problem disclosure (Graham, Watts, & Timbrook, 1991). When the score on K is high ($T > 60$), the MMPI-2 results have questionable validity. In most cases, the resulting clinical profile consists of low-to average-range scores across the clinical and content scales. An important exception to this generality involves individuals who have somatoform disorders, including conversion, psychogenic pain, somatization, and hypochondriasis. These individuals sometimes produce high scores on K in conjunction with elevated scores on Scales L, 1, and 3, indicating a willingness to admit to problems of a physical nature while denying any difficulties of an emotional or psychological nature. The clinician should interpret high scores on the clinical scales in a defensive protocol. However, the clinical profile is still likely to underestimate certain psychological problems. Cautious interpretation is warranted because one does not know what additional scale elevations might have occurred with open disclosure or what the overall profile configuration would have been in the absence of a defensive test-taking approach.

Marginal elevations on K (55T to 60T) suggest mild defensiveness, positive psychological adjustment, or a combination of the two. Unfortunately, the K scale is not a pure measure of defensiveness. It correlates to some extent with psychological health, ego strength, adaptive skill, and perhaps even breadth of intellectual interests. However, in clinical settings, even a marginally elevated score on K might reflect some defensiveness or nondisclosure of symptoms, particularly in the presence of a low score on the F scale. Low scores on K (below 40T) sometimes reflect an attempt to present oneself as extremely disturbed psychologically, particularly when the score on F is high. Although exaggeration of psychopathology often leads to a low score on K, low K scores commonly suggest that an individual feels extremely overwhelmed by problems and is defenseless and vulnerable.

F − K Index

The combination of an elevated score on the F scale and a very low score on the K scale was reported by Gough (1950) to be especially sensitive to symptom exaggeration or claims of nonexistent problems (dissimulation). When F minus K (F − K) is large (e.g., more than 11 raw score points), it has been suggested that the examinee is likely to be exaggerating psychopathology. Some clinicians attempt to identify defensiveness, or "faking good," using an F − K raw score cutoff that is negative and greater than 12, though it is generally agreed that this approach is much more problematic and results in a dismissal of interpretable protocols (Butcher & Williams, 1992). As a general rule, the use of formal cutoff scores to draw such inferences should be cautiously considered. Clinical settings vary considerably in the base rates with which examinees "fake good" or "fake bad," as well as in the particular risks involved in protocol misclassification. For these reasons, no single cutoff score can be optimal across all clinical settings, and recommended cutoffs should be viewed as tentative and suggestive. Recent research has suggested that the F scale in isolation might be equally as effective as F − K in detecting feigning and that the incremental value derived by including K in an index is minimal (Graham et al., 1991).

Fb Scale

The Fb, or F Back, scale was developed for the MMPI-2 to detect deviant or random responding to the items that are presented later in the test. The rationale behind the construction of this 40-item scale was based on the fact that the F scale does not adequately assess the validity of answers that occur beyond the initial 370 items of the inventory. During the course of test administration, individuals could conceivably become fatigued, frustrated, or careless in answering items in the latter portion of the test or could modify their degree of openness or truthfulness in disclosing problem areas. In these situations, the validity of the scores produced on the supplementary and content scales could be compromised and yet be undetected by the clinician who relies solely on a consideration of scales L, F, and K. The scale was developed in the same manner that was originally used to construct the F scale. Items in the latter part of the inventory were included in Fb if they were endorsed in the scored direction by less than 10% of the MMPI-2 normative sample.

The interpretive guidelines for the Fb scale resemble those used in the analysis of the F scale. In clinical settings, Fb scores usually reflect the degree of openness in reporting psychological symptoms and problem areas, including attempts to exaggerate or feign psychopathology. Very high scores ($T > 100$) are common in psychiatric patients who have psychotic symptoms and who may be in substantial distress. Scores in this range do not necessarily indicate invalidity of the test protocol. In many cases, these scores reflect a mild to moderate degree of symptom exaggeration in patients who have severe psychopathology. The interpretation of very high scores should be considered in the context of clinical observations and of detailed interview-based information. Contextual considerations are also critical in many settings because elevated scores may reflect a plea for special assistance in the form of psychological intervention, disability status, or financial compensation. In some cases, the extratest data and situational context suggest that the high Fb score indicates profile invalidity, whereas in other cases, the profile is judged to be accurate.

Although health problems often pose challenges to psychosocial adjustment, medical patients who have a relatively normal premorbid psychiatric history rarely produce extremely high F or Fb scores. Individuals who have brain injury can report a wide variety of cognitive and sensorimotor symptoms and health-related concerns without substantially elevating the F or Fb scale score. When very high scores on these scales are observed, they almost invariably reflect severe psychiatric disorder, symptom exaggeration, malingering, confusion, or random responding or a combination of these factors. These potential influences can be distinguished to a large extent by considering other validity scales. If a score on either VRIN or TRIN is greater than 80T, then the elevated score on F or Fb is at least partly due to content-independent responding, and the profile may be uninterpretable. If scores on the VRIN and TRIN scales are less than 80T and if Fb is greater than 100T, then the examinee might be exaggerating symptoms or, alternatively, could have severe psychopathology. In either case, the fact that TRIN and VRIN are less than 80T indicates that the examinee paid attention to the test items and was rationally consistent in responding to MMPI-2 item content.

F(p) Scale

The interpretive problem of disentangling bona fide psychopathology from symptom exaggeration when confronted with very high scores on the F and Fb scales was the basis for developing the F(p) scale (Arbisi & Ben-Porath, 1995). F(p) consists of 27 items that are rarely endorsed in the keyed direction by psychiatric inpatients or by individuals with no known impairments. F(p) primarily measures an attempt to exaggerate or fabricate the presence of psychological symptoms. The authors found evidence that, when compared to F and Fb, F(p) is more sensitive and specific to feigned psychopathology (faking bad) and is less sensitive to bona fide psychopathology. As a general rule, a high score on F is more likely to suggest serious psychological disturbance (as opposed to exaggeration) in a psychiatric patient who scores low on F(p). To the extent that the score on F(p) exceeds 80T in a consistent protocol (VRIN and TRIN < 80T), the clinician should suspect symptom exaggeration, perhaps as a plea for help, or malingering.

Variable Response Inconsistency Scale (VRIN)

Response inconsistency across the MMPI-2 item pool is measured by VRIN (Tellegen, 1988). Protocol validity is predicated on the assumption that the examinee read, understood, and responded in a meaningful way to the content of the individual items. However, some individuals are unable to manage this requirement due to poor verbal comprehension; impaired reading ability; or tiredness, confusion, or inability to adequately sustain an attentional focus. Depending on its severity, brain dysfunction sometimes interferes with an individual's ability to complete the MMPI-2, though this problem is probably less common if an audio version (cassette or compact disk) or cardsort format is used. VRIN is a very important scale because, in some instances, examinees are incapable of or choose not to fully comply with the test instructions, resulting in a haphazard approach to answering the test items. Difficulties with verbal comprehension in patients with brain injuries make VRIN a very important scale.

VRIN consists of 67 pairs of items that have either similar or opposite meanings. Each pair is scored one point if the two answers to the item pair are inconsistent or contradictory. A score of 13 or greater (80T or more) suggests invalidity due to content-independent responding. In these cases, the protocol is uninterpretable. This is invariably the case with the content scales, which are based on many items located in the second half of the inventory. However, it is theoretically possible for VRIN to be elevated and for the basic scales to be valid if the random responding occurred exclusively toward the end of the inventory. This scenario is more likely to the extent that the F scale score is low rather than high. VRIN should always be checked for evidence of inconsistent responding when the protocol has a high score ($T > 80$) on the F or Fb scales. If VRIN and TRIN are below 80, then it can be concluded that the high score on F or Fb is not merely due to careless responding.

True Response Inconsistency Scale (TRIN)

Examinees sometimes lapse into a mode of repeatedly answering test items with the same answer (True or False), without attending to or giving due consideration to the content of test statements. Individuals who have frontal lobe dysfunction occasionally do this in the context of other perseverative behaviors. TRIN was designed by Tellegen (1988) to detect the tendency of an examinee to consistently answer either True or False to MMPI-2 statements, disregarding item content. TRIN consists of 23 pairs of items that have opposite content. An all-True response style shows contradictions on 14 of these pairs (adding one point for each), whereas an all-False endorsement pattern is contradictory on 9 pairs (subtracting one point for each). This scale is bipolar. High raw scores indicate acquiescence, and the scaled score is designated with a "T." Low raw scores indicate responding False to items, and the scaled score is designated with an "F." Scores that exceed 80T or 80F suggest protocol invalidity.

Basic Clinical Scales

Scale 1. Hypochondriasis (Hs)

This 32-item scale was originally referred to as the Hypochondriasis scale because item selection was based on the responses of a group of patients with neuroses who had multiple physical complaints and health-related preoccupations in the absence of any discernible medical condition or abnormal physical findings. When scores on Scale 1 are high (T > 70) and prominently elevated in the profile configuration, they often suggest a diagnosis of a somatoform disorder. Studies of psychiatric patients indicate that high scorers on Scale 1 report numerous somatic complaints, many of which are vague or poorly described. High scorers are overly focused on their physical health status, their own bodily functions, and physical sensations. They often interpret unusual physical sensations as a sign of underlying disease. As a result, they require substantial medical attention and have frequent doctor visits.

High scorers on Scale 1 (T > 65) report numerous vague physical symptoms. These symptoms often show fluctuation and appear to be related to periods of psychological stress and poorly managed emotional conflict. Secondary gain is commonly associated with the physical complaints expressed by these individuals, and an underlying intense emotional dependency is usually evident. The physical preoccupations sometimes function to divert one's attentional focus away from painful circumstances surrounding a significant relationship. The physical symptoms may also serve the purpose of expressing anger or insecurity and control over significant others. High scorers on Scale 1 are often pessimistic and convey very negative attitudes. They whine, complain, and demand a great deal of attention and sympathy from others. When these intense needs are not satisfied, they retaliate by causing aggravation and behaving in a passive-aggressive manner.

In the neuropsychological context, elevations on Scale 1 are quite common. Individuals with brain injuries commonly score moderately high on Scale 1 (65T to 75T) because of their frank endorsement of neurologically related items. These include references to diminished general health status (45), paresthesias (53), tiredness and fatigue (152), weakness (175), pain (224), periodic dizzy spells (164), difficulty walking (179), and numbness (247). Although there are exceptions, empirical data suggest that scored responses to neurologically related items such as these account for an average increase of 10 to 15 T-score points on Scale 1, with a range of 0 to 30 points (Gass, 1991b, 1992).

Gass (1997) examined the MMPI-2 scoring characteristics of samples of 54 patients with closed head injury and 40 patients with CVD (all men) who were referred for neuropsychological evaluation at the Miami Veterans Affairs Medical Center (VAMC). This data, which will be alluded to throughout this section, was based exclusively on valid protocols that were not corrected for neurologically related item endorsement. None of these individuals had a premorbid history of psychiatric treatment or addictive disorder.

All had documented brain injuries, and none were seeking compensation benefits; their average ages were 45 and 61, respectively, with an average education of 12 years. Fifty percent of the patients with closed head injury and 45% of the patients with CVD scored above 65T on Scale 1, though clinical experience with these patients suggests that the incidence of somatoform symptoms is substantially less than this. In contrast, these percentages grossly underestimate the frequency of elevated Scale 1 scores in litigating head-trauma cases (Youngjohn, Davis, & Wolf, 1997) and personal injury plaintiffs (Lees-Haley, 1997), many of whom lack any objective evidence of structural brain damage. The physical and cognitive disabilities that are claimed by individuals who pursue legal means of obtaining compensation are generally associated with high scores on the same scales that have neurologic-related content, though the specific items that they endorse are often different (Dunn & Lees-Haley, 1995). Secondary gain is clearly a critical factor in a large number of compensation-related cases, and elevated scores on Scales 1, 2, and 3 sometimes reflect feigning of physical symptoms and health-related preoccupations. Elevated scores on these scales have been associated with incomplete effort on neuropsychological testing and an atypical *decline* in cognitive test performance on repeated testing following head trauma (Putnam, Kurtz, Fichtenberg, O'Leary, & Adams, 1995). Elevated scores are also associated with the presence of physical and cognitive complaints well beyond the period within which individuals normally recover from mild head trauma (Putnam, Kurtz, Adams, et al., 1995).

Scores on Scale 1 (and probably on other scales) are unlikely to be helpful to the clinician who is confronted with the task of differentiating between frank malingering and a somatoform disorder. Individuals who malinger or who have somatoform symptoms commonly score between 70T and 90T on Scale 1, though people who malinger might tend to score slightly higher (Suhr et al., 1997). The client's history and other pertinent data, including life-contextual considerations, are likely to contribute far more useful information to the clinician who has to make this differential diagnosis. Also problematic is the fact that conscious and unconscious feigning of somatic symptoms can occur simultaneously and in conjunction with brain damage. For example, certain individuals undoubtedly develop very intense physical concerns and heightened somatic sensitivities as part of a psychological reaction to brain injury or CNS disease. In these cases, symptoms of hypochondriasis or somatization disorder can contribute substantially to scores on Scale 1, well beyond the direct influence of reporting bona fide symptoms of neurological impairment.

Individuals who have the psychological characteristics represented in Scale 1 usually obtain some form of secondary gain from their symptoms and are not usually interested in psychologically or behaviorally based solutions. However, they often seek medical solutions (e.g., medicine or surgery) that offer potentially rapid relief, and they are subject to potential medication or substance abuse. These individuals are sometimes open to accepting the rationale that stress plays a contributory role in their problems, and symptom-focused interventions that are directed toward reducing stress, pain, and other discomfort may be helpful in some cases. Accompanying symptoms of depression may warrant the use of other directive intervention strategies aimed at increasing the individual's involvement in rewarding activities, promoting physical exercise, and improving the quality of their interpersonal relationships.

Scale 2. Depression (D)

The 57-item Depression scale assesses common symptoms of depression, including subjective dysphoria, sadness, low self-esteem, psychomotor retardation, a sense of hopelessness about the future, and vegetative features such as poor appetite, fatigue, and insomnia. High scorers ($T > 70$) are also socially withdrawn and often isolate themselves. They feel very inadequate, lack self-confidence, and are prone to feeling guilty. They experience cognitive inefficiency in daily living, such as poor concentration and forgetfulness, though their actual capability in these neurobehavioral domains may be intact (Gass & Russell, 1986a; Gass, Russell, & Hamilton, 1990). They are often indecisive and plagued by doubts about themselves, their circumstances, and their future.

Clinicians can often obtain a better understanding of the meaning of elevated scores on Scale 2 (as well as on Scales 3, 4, 6, 8, 9, and 0) by examining scores on the subscales that reflect specific underlying content domains. Harris and Lingoes (1955, 1968) divided the item content of Scale 2 into five rationally constructed component subscales:

1. *Subjective Depression (D1,* 32 items) has content that refers to subjective feelings of unhappiness, diminished interest, low energy for coping, feelings of inadequacy, and social uneasiness.

2. *Psychomotor Retardation (D2,* 14 items) suggests lack of energy, emotional immobilization, and social avoidance.

3. *Physical Malfunctioning (D3,* 11 items) contains content related to somatic preoccupations, specific physical symptoms, and generally poor health.

4. *Mental Dullness (D4,* 15 items) refers to diminished attention, concentration, and memory; lack of energy; and self-doubt.

5. *Brooding (D5,* 10 items) suggests crying, ruminating, and, in some cases, feelings of hopelessness.

In inspecting the scores on these subscales, the clinician will frequently note that individuals who have neurological impairment score relatively high on *Mental Dullness (D4)* and *Physical Malfunctioning (D3)* as an expression of their cognitive and somatic difficulties (Gass & Lawhorn, 1991; Gass & Russell, 1991; Gass et al., 1990). They also commonly score high on *Subjective Depression (D1),* which is consistent with the fact that symptomatic depression is probably the most common psychological sequelae of brain disease or injury.

Individuals with brain injuries frequently produce marginally elevated scores ($60T$ to $70T$) on Scale 2. Scores in this range are difficult to interpret because of the heterogeneous item content comprising the 2 scale and because of the related fact that not all of the traditionally described D scale correlates will apply. For this reason, an analysis of the scoring pattern on the Harris-Lingoes subscales is especially helpful in clarifying the meaning of marginally elevated scores on Scale 2. Individuals who have CNS impairment and report their neurological symptoms on the MMPI-2 will typically increase their scores on the 2 scale regardless of whether they are depressed. This occurs because the 2 scale contains a subset of items that are related to bona fide physical and cognitive manifestations of brain damage.

Scale 2 includes items that refer specifically to problems with distractibility (31), convulsions (142), diminished reading comprehension (147), memory difficulty (165), generalized weakness (175), and walking or balance (179). Acknowledgment of these symptoms increases the T-score on the 2 scale by an average of 5 to 10 points, with a range of 0 to 12 points (Gass, 1991b, 1992). When protocols were not corrected for neurological item endorsement, half of the patients with closed head injury and 43% of the those with CVD comprising the Miami VAMC referral sample scored above $65T$ on Scale 2. Scores on Scale 2 that exceed $75T$ in individuals with brain injuries almost invariably reflect depressive symptoms in addition to any neurologic item-related artifact that might exist. Clinicians examining the protocols of patients with brain injuries can obtain more reliable information pertaining to depression by using the content scale Depression (DEP).

Although depression is widely believed to adversely affect cognitive-test performance, scores on Scale 2 are not usually predictive of neuropsychological test performance. Studies have suggested that Scale 2 scores in neuropsychological referrals are independent of level of performance on measures of attention and memory (Gass, 1996b; Gass & Russell, 1986a; Gass et al., 1990), fluency or mazes (Gass et al., 1994) or of alternating attention on the Trail-Making Test, Part B (Gass & Daniel, 1990).

High scores on Scale 2 typically have an interest in obtaining psychological help as a means of resolving emotional distress. They usually become engaged in therapy and show steady progress. Viable treatment options vary, but the specific type of recommended intervention may depend, in part, on the individual's psychological-mindedness, insight, and level of verbal skills. Antidepressant medication may be an effective adjunct to psychotherapy.

Scale 3. Hysteria (Hy)

The Hysteria scale is comprised of 60 items that were originally selected on the basis of their association with psychologically based sensory or motor abnormalities (conversion disorder). Accordingly, when individuals' scores on Scale 3 are high ($T > 70$) and have a prominently elevated position in the profile, these individuals show a tendency to report a variety of somatic complaints and develop physical symptoms in response to psychological conflict or stressful circumstances. Behind these symptoms, in many cases, is secondary gain in the form of obtaining affectionate attention from others or a reduction in stressful responsibilities (e.g., work). The complaints are often rather vague, transient, and intermittent, and they may include pain, headache, sleep disturbance, tiredness, fatigue, malaise, and gastrointestinal discomfort. High scorers are overly dependent and demanding, dramatic, and self-centered and are lacking in maturity. They are often socially active, friendly, and engaging, though other people might find them to be superficial.

High scores on Scale 3 suggest very poor psychological insight or self-awareness, including denial of anger or other unacceptable emotions or internal impulses. High scorers engage in substantial denial and expend a great deal of energy in order to sustain a naively positive and unrealistically optimistic outlook on circumstances and on themselves. They resist psychological interpretations of their symptoms and seek medical explanations. Harris and Lingoes (1955, 1968) identified five content domains on Scale 3 that are routinely scored as subscales:

1. *Denial of Social Anxiety (Hy1,* 6 items) suggests ease in social interaction and a resilience to the influence of social mores.
2. *Need for Affection (Hy2,* 12 items) assesses an emotional dependency on others, denial of unacceptable emotion, and a tendency to suppress negative feelings that would jeopardize such relationships.
3. *Lassitude-Malaise (Hy3,* 15 items) has content that refers to generalized weakness, discomfort, and fatigue, as well as to unhappiness, sleep disturbance, and poor concentration.
4. *Somatic Complaints (Hy4,* 17 items) consists of multiple symptomatic complaints of a physical nature.
5. *Inhibition of Aggression (Hy5,* 7 items) suggests a denial of hostile impulses and a sensitivity to other people's reactions.

Patients who are referred for neuropsychological evaluation produce high scores on the *Lassitude-Malaise* and *Somatic Complaints* subscales far more commonly than on the other Scale 3 subscales, indicating a prominence of physical discomfort, fatigue, and various other physical complaints in this population. These two subscales include several items that are descriptive of neurological symptoms. Not surprisingly, these subscales are usually elevated to some degree in patients with brain injuries, even in the absence of hysterical or histrionic personality characteristics (Gass & Lawhorn, 1991).

Because of the relatively high frequency of somatoform disorders in neuropsychological settings, Scale 3, like Scale 1, plays an important role in neuropsychological diagnosis. In numerous settings, individuals are referred for a neuropsychological evaluation because of symptoms that mimic a neurological condition. In some cases, these individuals have been misdiagnosed and have been prescribed inappropriate treatments over a period of many years. Although individuals with brain impairments often produce moderately high Scale 3 scores ($60T$ to $70T$) without having symptoms of a somatoform disorder, very high scores on Scale 3 ($T > 75$) usually indicate the presence of somatoform symptomatology or malingering or a combination of the two. The same generalization applies to Scale 1. For example, scores on both 1 and 3 are typically higher in patients with nonepileptic seizure (NES) disorder than in patients with epilepsy, who commonly exhibit primary elevations on Scales 2 and 8 (Ansley, Gass, Brown, & Levin, 1995).

Scale 3 scores are clearly increased when examinees report CNS symptoms on the MMPI-2 and show no evidence of conversion hysteria or other somatoform characteristics. As is the case with Scales 1, 2, 7, and 8, the amount of the score increase varies widely across individuals and possibly across neurological diagnoses. Neurologically relevant item content includes references to work capacity (10), distractibility (31), general health (45, 148), pain (47, 224), tiredness and fatigue (152, 173), periodic dizzy spells (164), tremor (172), weakness (175), and vision (249). The *T*-score on Scale 3 is increased by an average of 5 to 10 points as a result of reporting neurologically relevant items, though the potential increase ranges from 0 to 23 points (Gass, 1991b, 1992). In the Miami VAMC study of noncorrected MMPI-2 profiles, 32% of the patients with closed head injury and 25% of the patients with CVD had scores on Scale 3 exceeding $65T$. However, a Massachusetts private practice sample of 54 patients (both men and women), who had experienced more recent (less than 6 months) and milder head injuries than those in the Miami study, produced high scores on Scale 3 ($T > 65$) with a frequency of 66%. It is significant that many of these Massachusetts patients had retained the services of an attorney in order to ensure the maintenance of insurance benefits. Persisting symptoms following mild head injury and legal involvement are both associated with higher scores on Scale 3 (Youngjohn et al., 1995, 1997).

Individuals who have prominent elevations on Scale 3 are usually resistant to psychological treatment because they adhere to the belief that there is an organic etiology for their symptoms and, in any case, derive some benefits (secondary gain) from their symptoms. Insight-oriented psychotherapy in such cases is rarely successful. However, these individuals are sometimes responsive to the suggestion that their symptoms are at least partly related to stress and that, therefore, they may benefit from training in the use of stress management techniques. In addition, proposed interventions that are framed in medical terminology, such as "neurocognitive retraining," are more likely to be acceptable to these patients. The combination of supportive contact with an empathic therapist and coaching in the application of methods such as relaxation training, biofeedback, guided imagery, or hypnosis is sometimes effective. The underlying emotional conflict and secondary gain that create or exacerbate the presenting symptoms are sometimes rooted in a problematic relationship with a significant other, in which case marriage or couples therapy may be essential.

Scale 4. Psychopathic Deviate (Pd)

Psychopathic or antisocial personality disorder characterized the individuals in the clinical sample used by Hathaway and McKinley to construct the 50-item Psychopathic Deviate scale. A variety of asocial or antisocial behaviors and attitudes are associated with high scores ($T > 65$) on Scale 4. High scorers on Scale 4 show limited identification with conventional ethical values and societal standards of behavior. They are typically viewed as rebellious and defiant, harboring unresolved anger, and predisposed to acting impulsively without regard for the long-range consequences of their actions. They display an inability or an unwillingness to postpone gratification of their impulses and desires, even when doing so would be ultimately in their own best interest. High scorers on Scale 4 are often substance abusers. They have a proclivity for behaving in ways that violate societal standards, such as lying, stealing, and exploiting other people in order to satisfy their own needs. Although adventurous and sometimes socially engaging and charming, these individuals are usually self-centered, manipulative, and lacking in empathy for other people.

The item content of Scale 4 was divided into five subscales by Harris and Lingoes (1955, 1968):

1. *Familial Discord (Pd1,* 11 items) refers to an unpleasant family life characterized by little love, emotional support, or understanding.
2. *Authority Problems (Pd2,* 10 items) measures attitudes and behaviors that indicate a rejection of authority and run-ins with societal limits.
3. *Social Imperturbability (Pd3,* 12 items) assesses self-confidence and comfort in social situations.

4. *Social Alienation (Pd4,* 18 items) refers to feelings of estrangement and rejection by others, most likely resulting from behavior that is self-centered, insensitive, and inconsiderate of other people.

5. *Self-Alienation (Pd5,* 15 items) measures frustration both with oneself and with the inability to find life interesting or rewarding.

The interpretation of scores on Scale 4 in people who have CNS impairment is straightforward. The items comprising this scale appear to have little or no neurological content bias. It is conceivable that Scale 4 is sensitive to some of the personality and behavioral changes that occur in a subset of individuals with brain injuries who display a loss of self-control, outbursts of anger, and a diminished concern with other people's needs and interests. In most cases, however, elevated scores on Scale 4 reflect premorbid personality characteristics and not secondary effects of brain damage. Among the various neurodiagnostic groups, high scores on Scale 4 are most frequently produced by chronic substance abusers and people with traumatic brain injury (Gass & Russell, 1991). In the Miami VAMC study, high scores ($T > 65$) on Scale 4 were produced by 34% of the patients with closed head injury and by 18% of those with CVD, though both groups had been screened for addictive disorders.

Psychological intervention with high scorers on Scale 4 is difficult because of their poor impulse control, apparent inability to profit from experience, their tendency to reject responsibility and to blame others, and their self-centered orientation. When external pressures to obtain treatment are removed, high scorers often terminate treatment prematurely.

Scale 5. Masculinity-Femininity (Mf)

The Masculinity-Femininity scale was originally designed to identify problems in sex-role adjustment and particularly ego-dystonic impulses of a homoerotic nature. In clinical settings, general problems with sexual adjustment and gender identification are often associated with high scores on Scale 5 ($T > 75$). However, a substantial number of the items on this scale pertain to interests, attitudes, and preferences that were more gender-specific in the 1930s and 1940s than they are today. For this reason, mild to moderate elevations on Scale 5 ($60T$ to $75T$) are conservatively interpreted as representing traditional and stereotypic opposite-sex gender-related interest patterns. Women who score in this range are likely to have interests and preferences that are stereotypically masculine, for example sports, science, and outdoor activities such as camping or hunting. Men who score in this range lack many of the stereotypically masculine interests and values and tend to be more "culturally refined," interested perhaps in art, music, and aesthetics.

Low scorers ($T < 40$) on Scale 5 identify to some extent with their own traditional sex-role stereotype in terms of interest patterns. This generalization probably applies more to men than to women. In fact, many women who possess academic and professional ambition produce low scores on Scale 5. Low-scoring men, on the other hand, generally have traditionally masculine interests and, in the extreme, might be described as "macho." In men, educational background shows a slight relationship with the 5 scale, with poorly educated individuals tending to score at a slightly lower level on Scale 5. In neuropsychological settings, Scale 5 scores do not appear to be affected by self-reported physical and cognitive symptoms of neurological dysfunction. In most clinical settings, the Scale 5 score typically falls well within the average range. The prevalence of elevated Scale 5 scores ($T > 65$) in the Miami VAMC male veteran sample was less than 4%, which is lower than would be expected in nonmilitary settings.

Scale 6. Paranoia (Pa)

The criterion sample used by Hathaway to select the 40 items on the Paranoia scale consisted of individuals who had frank paranoid features or a diagnosed paranoid disorder. High scorers ($T > 75$) are occasionally psychotic and may harbor paranoid ideation and delusions, especially when Scale 6 is elevated above Scale 7 and has a prominent position with the profile configuration. In the moderately elevated range ($65T$ to $75T$), scorers are usually rigid, hypersensitive, and predisposed to misinterpret and overpersonalize the words and actions of other people. They readily view themselves as being mistreated, and they respond with anger and resentment. Projection and rationalization are their most prominent defense mechanisms. Individuals who have high scores on Scale 6 tend to overemphasize "rationality" and moralism at the expense of sensitivity to broader considerations, particularly of an emotional nature. Although high scorers on Scale 6 generally have paranoid characteristics, some paranoid individuals answer the MMPI-2 defensively in order to conceal their symptoms. In fact, in clinical settings, very low scores ($T < 35$) on Scale 6 in the context of a defensive protocol (L and K greater than $60T$ and higher than F), and in which Scale 6 has the lowest score, sometimes occur in persons who are frankly psychotic.

Harris and Lingoes (1955, 1968) constructed subscales that assess 3 content domains on Scale 6:

1. *Persecutory Ideas* (*Pa1*, 17 items) measures feelings and perceptions of being mistreated and victimized.
2. *Poignancy* (*Pa2*, 9 items) refers to feeling high-strung, sensitive, lonely, misunderstood, and distant from others.
3. *Naiveté* (*Pa3*, 9 items) refers to optimism about people, naive trust in others, and associated feelings of vulnerability to hurt.

Scale 6 contains few, if any, items that refer directly to physical, cognitive, or health-related symptoms of brain dysfunction. There is no correction applied to this scale. Studies suggest that most individuals with neurological impairments score within the average range on the 6 scale. However, individuals with traumatic brain injury endorse Scale 6 items with some frequency, particularly if they are examined very soon after injury. Their scores are sometimes sufficiently elevated ($T > 65$) to suggest suspiciousness, distrust, and a sense of having received a "raw deal" from life. Post-traumatic paranoia is not uncommon, particularly in people with acute head injury, though the paranoia rarely persists over a period of months (Grant & Alves, 1987). In the Miami VAMC sample, 35% of the patients with closed head injury scored above $65T$, whereas only 15% of the patients with CVD scored that high (Gass, 1997). Individuals who are involved in litigation proceedings are more likely to experience (or at least report) symptoms that increase scores on Scale 6. In the forensic neuropsychological context, compensation-seeking patients with mild head trauma who have persisting symptoms commonly produce Scale 6 scores between 65T and 75T, with a mean T-score that is about 10 points higher than that found in the Miami VAMC sample (Youngjohn et al., 1997).

High scorers on Scale 6 may be amenable to psychological intervention because of emotional distress that they experience in addition to their problems with anger, resentment, and a sense of being victimized. Intervention with high scorers on Scale 6 must invariably overcome the barriers posed by their distrust, suspiciousness, and tendency to deny personal responsibility for problems. An empathic and unconditionally accepting therapeutic focus may be a critical initial step to forming any kind of meaningful working alliance. If these individuals can feel understood and supported by the therapist, they may go on to derive some benefit from interventions aimed at reducing anger and associated tendencies to be hypervigilant and overreactive to the social environment. Antipsychotic medication may be a necessary adjunct to psychological intervention.

Scale 7. Psychasthenia (Pt)

The 48 items that comprise this scale were intended to measure psychasthenia, which is roughly synonymous with obsessive-compulsive disorder. High scorers ($T > 65$) on Scale 7 are very distressed, anxious, and worried, often over an abundance of seemingly minor issues. They suffer intense feelings of insecurity and inadequacy and tend to ruminate excessively. Obsessional behavior and ritualistic compulsions are sometimes observed. Interpersonally, high scorers are emotionally dependent, socially anxious, unassertive, and difficult to get to know. They are commonly achievement oriented, perfectionistic, demanding, conscientious, meticulous, and prone to feeling guilt. From a cognitive standpoint, high scorers are fearful of making decisions (hence, indecisive), and complain of problems with concentration.

A substantial number of individuals with neurological impairments score above 65T on Scale 7. In the Miami VAMC study, 50% of the patients with closed head injury and 33% of the patients with CVD produced elevated (noncorrected) scores on this scale. Although many individuals with brain injuries become highly distressed and worried about their health condition, the frequency of high scores in this population is partially due to the endorsement of items that fall within the larger cluster of empirically identified, neurologically related items. These items include references to distractibility (31), reading problems (147), memory difficulty (165), generalized weakness (175), forgetfulness (308), and concentration difficulty (325). Acknowledgment of these symptoms increases the T-score on Scale 7 by an average of 5 points, though the effect can be as large as 12 points in an individual case (Gass, 1991b). Thus, slightly elevated scores on Scale 7 do not necessarily reflect anxiety and distress in individuals who have bona fide brain injury. Scores that exceed 70T, however, almost always indicate the presence of these symptoms.

No subscales exist for Scale 7, though the results of a factor analytic study suggest that the scale includes components of maladjustment, neuroticism, anxiety, psychotic tendencies, withdrawal, denial of antisocial behavior, poor concentration, agitation, and poor physical health (Comrey, 1958). To assist in making inferences about anxiety, fearfulness, or obsessional thinking, scores on Scale 7 can be compared with scores on several content scales that measure anxiety-related symptoms: generalized anxiety (ANX), obsessional thinking (OBS), specific phobias, apprehensions, and a general tendency to be fearful (FRS).

Individuals who score moderately high on Scale 7 ($60T$ to $80T$) want relief from their distress and may benefit from cognitive-behavioral interventions that help to reduce their anxiety, worry, guilt, and self-deprecating tendencies. Training in the use of relaxation methods may effectively target the somatic manifestations of generalized anxiety and stress. The ruminative and intellectualized approach of these individuals generally contraindicates traditional insight-oriented methods. Instead, they seem to benefit at least initially from more directive and structured approaches to intervention. Patients who score extremely high on Scale 7 ($T > 90$) are often so overwhelmed with worrisome thoughts and preoccupations, as well as perfectionistic tendencies, that they are effectively immobilized when presented with cognitive strategies, and they may even fail to benefit from more somatically focused relaxation training techniques. In such cases, psychotropic medication may be a necessary adjunct to psychological intervention.

Scale 8. Schizophrenia (Sc)

The Schizophrenia scale consists of 78 items that were pooled by Hathaway and McKinley (1940) from several groups of items that were originally intended (but failed) to be specific to four subtypes of schizophrenia (paranoid, simple, hebephrenia, and catatonic). The resulting scale was both lengthy and heterogeneous in content. The heterogeneity of Scale 8 partially accounts for the fact that scores on it can be increased by factors that are largely unrelated to schizophrenia. For example, Graham (1993) reported that slightly higher scores frequently occur in adolescents, college students, African-American men, amphetamine users, and people who have certain medical conditions, such as epilepsy. Butcher and Williams (1992) further observed that scores on Scale 8 are sometimes increased in individuals who adhere to nontraditional or countercultural values, as well as in individuals who have severe sensory impairment or organic brain dysfunction.

In the absence of confounding influences on Scale 8 scores, extreme elevations ($T > 80$) that have a prominent place in a valid protocol (i.e., minimal or no exaggeration) suggest florid psychotic symptoms, confusion, and poor judgment. This is more likely to be true when the score on Scale 8 is higher than scores on Scales 7 or 2. However, such scores are common in nonpsychotic psychiatric patients who are acutely disturbed—they exaggerate their symptoms to some extent in order to communicate a special need for help. Additional sources of information, such as interview and observational data, relevant history, contextual considerations, and scores on scales F and F(p), can be especially useful in interpreting high scores on Scale 8.

High scores on Scale 8 ($T > 70$) suggest social detachment, withdrawal, and isolation in an individual who displays eccentric attitudes and behaviors and is alienated from the mainstream. These individuals tend to be generally anxious and often angry, though they typically deal with emotional stress by retreating into daydreaming or fantasy and detaching themselves from the pressures of daily existence. Sexual preoccupations and physical complaints are common. Moderately elevated scores ($65T$ to $69T$) should be carefully evaluated using the Harris-Lingoes subscales because a variety of factors (including neurological symptoms) can produce Scale 8 scores in this range. In many cases, individuals who have a psychiatric disturbance and who produce scores within this range exhibit milder degrees of alienation and isolation, in addition to unconventional behavior and mild detachment from other people.

Six subscales reflect areas of rationally discerned content domains on Scale 8 (Harris & Lingoes, 1955, 1968):

1. *Social Alienation (Sc1,* 21 items) refers to feelings of having been mistreated, misunderstood, and unloved.
2. *Emotional Alienation (Sc2,* 11 items) assesses feelings of depression, apathy, fear, and despair.
3. *Lack of Ego Mastery, Cognitive (Sc3,* 10 items) refers to strange thoughts, feelings of unreality, and difficulties with concentration and memory.
4. *Lack of Ego Mastery, Conative (Sc4,* 14 items) refers to life as a strain, excessive worry, and coping with stress by withdrawing into fantasy and daydreaming.
5. *Lack of Ego Mastery, Defective Inhibition (Sc5,* 11 items) refers to feeling out of control, restless, and hyperactive.
6. *Bizarre Sensory Experiences (Sc6,* 20 items) assesses unusual sensory experiences and physical changes, in addition to hallucinations and bizarre thought content.

Despite the general association of schizophrenia with disordered thinking, it should be emphasized that Sc2 and Sc4 measure primarily *affective* components (depression and despair) that commonly exist as part of the symptom picture within the spectrum of schizophrenic disorders. In psychiatric settings, high scores on Sc3 and Sc6 suggest a more severe psychotic-symptom picture than do scores on the other subscales. However, the characteristics that are measured by these two subscales are certainly not specific to psychosis or even to psychopathology; they often reflect cognitive and sensorimotor complaints that are common in individuals with neurological impairments (Bornstein & Kozora, 1990; Gass, 1991b; Gass & Russell, 1991).

Individuals who have CNS impairment and who report their neurological symptoms and related concerns on the MMPI-2 will typically increase their scores on Scale 8, independent of psychotic tendencies. Items that are commonly endorsed include references to blank spells (229), distractibility (31, 299), speech changes (106), poor concentration (325), reading difficulty (147), memory problems (165), problems walking (179), anosmia (299), tinnitus (255), numbness (247), and paralysis or weakness (177, 295). The endorsement of neurologically related symptoms on the MMPI-2 increases the T-score on Scale 8 by an average of 5 to 10 points, with a potential increase of as many as 20 points (Gass, 1991b, 1992). There is some evidence that symptom reporting that is restricted to medically refractory seizure disorder has a minimal mean impact on Scale 8 and on other MMPI-2 scores (Derry, Harnadek, McLachlan, & Sontrop, 1997), though the results of other studies suggest otherwise (Bornstein & Kozora, 1990). In the Miami VAMC referral samples, uncorrected scores exceeding $65T$ on Scale 8 were produced by 48% of the patients with closed head injury and CVD. This figure approximates the 44% reported by Alfano et al. (1990) in an MMPI study of 115 heterogeneous patients with brain impairments and the 55% reported by Bornstein and Kozora in a sample of 152 patients with epilepsy ($T > 70$). Although scores in this range are not invariably associated with the presence of psychotic symptoms, these percentages still contrast sharply with the estimated 10% frequency of psychosis following brain injury secondary to trauma (Grant & Alves, 1987).

Individuals who feign traumatic brain injury commonly produce mildly to moderately high scores on Scale 8, often because of their endorsement of MMPI-2 items that have content related to cognitive difficulties (Sc3) and physical abnormalities (Sc6). The interpretation of high scores on Scale 8 should be made in the context of (1) knowledge of the examinee's history, (2) clinical observation, (3) the examinee's test-taking attitude as measured by the validity scales, and (4) understanding the medico-legal particulars surrounding the evaluation.

Prominent scorers on Scale 8 vary widely in regard to their cognitive abilities and psychological status, though, in general, they pose several treatment difficulties. Establishing rapport in the therapeutic dyad is difficult because of their tendency toward interpersonal isolation, withdrawal, and emotional detachment. Therapists find it problematic to connect with these individuals or to form a productive working alliance. High scorers on Scale 8 typically lack the practical skills, ego resources, or personal incentives to work toward problem resolution. They have a low tolerance for stress, and they cope by mentally withdrawing from the concrete demands of everyday living, often into an ideational world consisting of abstract themes and bizarre preoccupations. In some cases, they respond favorably to a supportive approach involving an interpersonal focus and may benefit from group psychotherapy. Concurrent symptoms of depression and anxiety are often present and may be severe enough in their own right to warrant medication. The presence of a thought disorder and impaired reality testing is more likely when Scale 8 is significantly higher than Scale 7 and when scores on the Bizarre Mentation content scale are high ($T > 70$).

Scale 9. Hypomania (Ma)

The 46 items on this scale measure characteristics of hypomania, including overactivity, heightened energy level, emotional excitement, and flight of ideas. Marginally elevated scores ($60T$ to $69T$) suggest a high level of energy and activity in an outgoing, gregarious individual. As scores reach a higher level ($70T$ to $79T$), the individual's activity typically becomes less efficient and less productive, though he or she may express many ambitious plans. Scorers in this range overestimate their abilities, develop superficial involvements, and derive little insight from their failures. They are often hyperverbal and domineering. Very high scorers ($T > 80$) exhibit poor control over their impulses. They seem to thrive on stimulation, are easily bored and restless, and show a low tolerance for frustration. They are often expansive and grandiose. High scores on the 9 scale are associated with a potentiation of behavioral correlates of high scores on the other clinical scales. For example, a moderately high score on Scale 6, when accompanied by a high score on Scale 9, is more likely to be associated with overt paranoid features. Low scores on Scale 9 ($T < 40$) have traditionally been associated with low energy, psychomotor retardation and other symptoms of depression. However, recent empirical data suggest that low scores on Scale 9 indicate a probable absence of hypomanic features and nothing more specific (Graham, Ben-Porath, & McNulty, 1997).

Harris and Lingoes divided Scale 9 into four major content domains and representative subscales:

1. *Amorality (Ma1,* 6 items) measures characteristics of selfishness, dishonesty, and vicarious satisfaction over others' manipulative exploits.
2. *Psychomotor Acceleration (Ma2,* 11 items) assesses an increased rate of speech, thought, and motor activity and an unusual need for stimulation and excitement.
3. *Imperturbability (Ma3,* 8 items) represents a denial of social anxiety and a lack of concern with the feelings, attitudes, and opinions of other people.
4. *Ego Inflation (Ma4,* 9 items) measures an unrealistically optimistic self-evaluation.

Most patients with brain injuries score well within the average range on the 9 scale. In the Miami VAMC study of uncorrected MMPI-2 protocols, only 20% of the patients with closed head injury and 23% of the patients with CVD scored higher than 65*T*. The incidence of elevated Scale 9 scores in a sample of patients with milder and more recent head injury who where undergoing rehabilitation was 4% (Gass & Wald, 1997). However, Gass, Luis, Rayls, and Mittenberg (1998) reported a 25% incidence of high ($T > 65$) Scale 9 scores in a sample of 67 nonlitigating patients with acute head injury who averaged 7 days post-injury. High scorers on this scale are often referred for a neuropsychological assessment because of problems with distractibility and forgetfulness, symptoms that are not uncommon in bipolar disorder, schizoaffective disorder, and schizophrenia.

Psychological intervention with individuals who have a prominent profile elevation on Scale 9 ($T > 70$) is challenging for several reasons. Such persons are generally lacking in insight and tend to deny having any need for assistance. They overestimate their abilities, have an inflated sense of self-importance, and rarely admit to weaknesses. When they do become involved in therapy, it is generally short-lived because these individuals avoid introspection, are very unsettled and restless, and readily abandon many of the plans they make. High scorers are at risk for substance abuse. The most likely scenario in which psychological intervention might be beneficial to these people probably involves a highly structured approach with very specific, short-term behavioral goals, substantial use of reinforcement, and an avoidance of any methods or procedures that would evoke negative introspection. More commonly, there is a positive therapeutic response to lithium carbonate or other medical treatment that targets manic symptoms.

Scale 0. Social Introversion (Si)

The Social Introversion scale was designed by L.E. Drake (1946) using a sample of female college students. It consists of 69 items that assess shyness, discomfort and avoidance of social situations, and self-doubt. High scorers ($T > 65$) are socially anxious, timid and retiring, lacking in self-confidence, and bothered by their shyness. They seek comfort in solitary pursuits and interests and are difficult to get to know. High scorers on Scale 0 are described as being very reserved, emotionally constricted, and overcontrolled. In social settings, their behavior shows aloofness, limited interests or pursuits, a slow tempo, lack of energy, moodiness, indecisiveness, conventionality, and rigidity in attitudes. However, high scorers also tend to be reliable and dependable, and they derive pleasure from work-related achievements.

Low scorers on Scale 0 ($T < 40$) are gregarious, friendly, energetic, and outgoing. They prefer social interaction and group activities, and they seek out competitive situations. Although they mix well in social settings, their relationships are often shallow, and eventually they evoke resentment or hostility. In addition to fitting in socially, low scorers are often self-indulgent, manipulative, and opportunistic in their relationships. Poor impulse control and short-range decision making are characteristic.

Scale 0 measures personality characteristics that appear to be relatively stable across the life span and are more traitlike than those assessed using the other clinical scales. Three subscales were designed by Ben-Porath, Hostetler, Butcher, and Graham (1989) using rational and empirical techniques:

1. *Shyness* (*Si1*, 14 items) refers to interpersonal discomfort and a lack of sociability.
2. *Social Avoidance* (*Si2*, 8 items) measures a tendency to socially withdraw and to avoid group situations.
3. *Self/Other Alienation* (*Si3*, 17 items) refers to a negative self-perception and to feelings of alienation and estrangement from other people. High scorers report experiencing distrust, disappointment, and social apprehension.

In neuropsychological settings, the interpretation of Scale 0 scores is straightforward. This scale contains very few neurologically related items and, as such, does not require a consideration of content bias or correction. High scores are more likely to be found in patients referred for psychiatric assessment than in general medical patients. In the Miami VAMC study of neurologic patients, none of whom had a premorbid psychiatric history, only 23% of the patients with closed head injury and 20% of the patients with CVD had high scores on Scale 0 ($T > 65$).

Scale 0 scores have several implications related to treatment planning. Low scorers may be pressured by external forces to attend therapy. They rarely perceive any need for psychological assistance. Although they are quite verbal in therapy, they are rarely self-critical or genuinely introspective. Conflicts with other people may result from their impulsive or irresponsible behavior. However, they are not inclined to scrutinize their actions (Butcher, 1990). High scorers on Scale 0 ($T > 70$) are anxious and uncomfortable with self-disclosure of feelings and may have limited social skills to utilize in therapy. The effective therapist must overcome the client's initial distrust and fear of being judged or misunderstood and must tolerate sessions that are slow-paced and filled with periods of silence. The therapist's consistent display of empathy and communication of positive regard may lay the groundwork for interventions aimed at improving social skills, developing self-confidence, and fostering self-esteem.

Clinical Scale Configurations

Before the original development of the MMPI clinical scales was complete, Hathaway and McKinley were convinced that configural analysis of the MMPI profile would yield richer and more detailed diagnostic information than would individual scale interpretation. Although configural analysis and clinical profile interpretation were once thought to require a consideration of numerous formulas often involving multiple scale elevations, the modern approach generally involves analyzing simple combinations of high-point clinical-scale elevations. Over the past five decades, a substantial amount of empirical research has addressed the behavioral correlates of high-point codes (code types) in psychiatric patients and normal individuals. Unfortunately, code-type behavioral correlates of individuals with brain injuries have not been established. In any case, the reliability of such code types would probably be compromised by the presence of item-content bias in many of the basic clinical scales. In general applications of the MMPI-2, code types are the most reliable source of descriptive information derived from the MMPI-2 because a substantial portion of research has been devoted to code-type behavioral correlates.

A set of useful guidelines for code type interpretation was outlined by Graham (1997). Code types identify and label a protocol on the basis of the highest scores on the basic clinical scales, excluding Scales 5 and 0, which are primarily personality measures and which have received limited attention in the psychopathology-oriented code-type research. The characteristics of many potential code types are not described in any studies because they are so rarely found. The 27 code type signifies that scales 2 (D) and 7 (Pt) have the highest T-scores. In most cases, the order of the scales in the two- and three-point code types is not important. For example, the 27 code and the 72 code are given basically the same interpretation. Only protocols containing scores that provide clearly defined code types should be identified and interpreted as such. Adequate code-type definition is defined operationally on the basis of at least 5 T-score points between the lowest scale in the code type and the next highest clinical scale in the profile (excluding Scales 5 and 0). Some confusion in the past undoubtedly resulted from ignoring measurement error and from granting code-type status to protocols that were configurally unstable (i.e., too many scores were too close together). Many protocols do not have well-defined code types, and the interpretation of these profiles should focus on the individual scales, beginning with the scale that has the highest score. Interpretations of code types that are not elevated ($T < 65$) should be limited to inferences about personality functioning, without reference to psychopathology. Code types that exceed $65T$ are interpreted with reference to both personality functioning and symptoms of psychopathology.

Clinical inferences derived from profile code types are based on the results of studies of normal individuals and psychiatric patients. When applied to individuals who have CNS dysfunction, neurological symptom reporting can significantly influence clinical scale elevations and result in code types that are misleading when interpreted from the traditionally applied framework of psychopathology. For example, the 13/31 code type is common in patients with CVD and multiple sclerosis, though a minority of these patients have conversion or other somatoform disorders. Similarly, peak elevations on Scale 8 are common in patients with traumatic brain injury, whereas psychotic symptoms are atypical. *To prevent the configural distortion that often results from neurological symptom reporting, the clinician is advised to remove the influence of neurologically related test items by using an appropriate correction factor or, when available, a restandardized MMPI-2 that has norms that will more accurately assess psychopathology in individuals who have brain dysfunction.* New norms should be available within the next several years. There is probably no need to correct the MMPI-2 content scales because, with the exception of HEA (Health Concerns), these scales contain few or no neurologically related items. The supplementary scales have not been investigated in this regard, so some caution is warranted in their interpretation.

The following code-type descriptions consist of inferences that, in many cases, will not apply to the uncorrected standard protocols of patients with brain injuries. However, these descriptions are likely to be accurate when applied to neuropsychologically intact individuals who are referred for neuropsychological evaluation. Numerous books on psychological and MMPI-2 assessment contain these descriptions, including those by Butcher and Williams (1992), Golden (1979), Graham (1993), and Groth-Marnat (1999). In general, the descriptive correlates are more likely to have broad application and to include the more severe symptoms (e.g., floridly psychotic) when the profile configuration is quite elevated ($T > 75$). Code-type scores that are only slightly elevated ($60T$ to $65T$) are still interpretable in terms of personality correlates, but as a rule they should not be interpreted in terms of psychopathology (Graham, 1997).

12/21

This code type indicates a combination of physical preoccupations and depressive symptomatology. Individuals with this code type often wallow in misery, expressing pervasive unhappiness and poor physical functioning. They appear to be immobilized by psychological inertia, showing a reluctance to make behavioral changes that would improve their circumstances. The physical complaints are usually associated with stress and unresolved emotional conflict. In some cases, these symptoms are purportedly disabling.

Interpersonally, these individuals are typically withdrawn, passive-dependent, hypersensitive, suspicious, and very resentful toward others who are perceived as insufficiently affectionate, attentive, or nurturing. They require a great deal of reassurance to compensate for their inner insecurity and self-doubt. Heavy alcohol consumption is sometimes an attempted means of reducing stress.

Individuals who have the 12/21 code type are very passive and tolerate a substantial degree of misery before attempting to change their circumstances. Insight-oriented psychotherapy is usually ineffective, whereas symptom-focused treatments are sometimes beneficial. Marriage or relational therapy involving significant others is often indicated.

13/31

The 13/31 pattern is associated with exaggerated complaints of physical problems and, in many cases, pain. These symptoms are not always incapacitating, though they may interfere with efficiency in daily living. In many cases, the physical symptoms or complaints relieve the sufferer of normal or routine responsibilities, such as work. Individuals who produce this code type often develop these (conversion) symptoms as a reaction to stressful circumstances, while showing few, if any, signs of anxiety or depression. The symptoms often remit when the source of stress abates. To the extent that Scale 1 is higher than Scale 3, a negativistic, whining, and complaining style of behavior is likely. If Scale 3 is significantly elevated above Scale 1, the individual is more apt to convey a general attitude that is overly optimistic and Pollyanna-ish. If Scale 2 is much lower than Scale 1 and Scale 3 resulting in the classic conversion V configuration, *la belle* indifference characterized by an absence of manifest depression and anxiety is likely.

Interpersonally, persons with this code type are usually very dependent emotionally, in dire need of affectionate attention, egocentric, and lacking in maturity. They are often charming, outgoing, and engaging, though their relationships are typically superficial. Outward appearances are important to these individuals, and they are mostly or totally unaware of underlying anger and inner conflict. They secretly resent their own dependency strivings. They are emotionally overcontrolled and, in addition to channeling emotional conflict into physical symptoms, they often express their anger through passive-aggressive behavior that frustrates other people. However, when the anger is sufficiently intense, they exhibit dramatic outbursts of anger.

Individuals with this profile prefer medical explanations for their problems and resist formulations based on psychological factors. They typically seek instant cures. Although they thrive on attention, they respond poorly to insight-oriented psychotherapy (when they agree to it). The psychological interventions that are most likely to succeed are usually aimed initially at alleviating the physical symptoms. These include relaxation training, hypnosis, biofeedback, and other methods of a behavioral nature.

The 13/31 code type occurs in a subset of patients who have neurological dysfunction, particularly following stroke or the progression of multiple sclerosis. The clinician should exercise caution in using the standard approach to scoring and in interpreting the MMPI-2 profiles of these patients because many of them produce elevations on Scales 1 and 3 by acknowledging CNS symptoms in their responses to items on the inventory. On the other hand, somatoform symptoms can occur following brain injury, and the feigning of neurological symptoms (whether conscious or unconscious) will often result in the 13/31 profile configuration.

14/41

These individuals are typically very hypochondriacal and overly focused on bodily functions. Physical symptoms are generally used as a means to manipulate others and to avoid responsibilities. Although they often abuse alcohol and display anti-authoritarian attitudes, they rarely exhibit a pattern of antisocial behavior. More commonly, they exhibit problems in academic, occupational, or marital functioning. These individuals have poorly defined goals, are indecisive, lacking in drive, and express a great deal of dissatisfaction and pessimism. They may be narcissistic and blame their lack of success on their poor physical condition. Interpersonally, this profile suggests a sociable, outgoing individual who is often demanding, grouchy, complaining, and rebellious toward home and parents.

18/81

This code type suggests substantial difficulties in managing underlying hostility. These individuals express anger through either passive-aggressive or belligerent and abrasive behavior. A diagnosis of schizophrenia is common. These individuals sometimes have delusions about bodily functions. They are unhappy, distrusting of other people, and often isolated. They sometimes adopt a nomadic lifestyle and an associated poor work history.

19/91

This pattern suggests acute distress in a restless, anxious individual who is frustrated by an inability to achieve high goals. In many cases, their goals are vaguely defined, despite their expression of great ambition. Such individuals are conflicted over their underlying passivity and strong dependency needs, and they strive to deny this through an outward display of achievement, aggressiveness, belligerence, and extroversion. They are usually tense and report somatic complaints and preoccupations.

23/32

This code is associated with chronic tension, worry, sadness, apathy, fatigue, and other physical symptoms in an emotionally overcontrolled individual who is overwhelmed by life pressures. These people are usually depressed and function at a reduced level of efficiency, with decreased physical activity, interest, and involvement in normal life situations. They actively pursue achievement, power, and recognition, yet they are unable to handle the pressures that accompany the increased responsibility. In reality, they are passive-dependent individuals who crave special attention, are hypersensitive to criticism, and often feel that they do not receive the recognition they deserve.

Individuals with this code type feel insecure, inadequate, and helpless and behave in ways that solicit nurturance from others. However, they commonly feel uncomfortable around members of the opposite sex. Sexual impotence and frigidity are common. These individuals often internalize or deny underlying emotional conflict and have little psychological insight or self-awareness. They tend to hold onto a great deal of unhappiness and misery before deciding to make any constructive changes. As a result, insight-oriented psychotherapy is generally contraindicated.

24/42

This configuration is commonly produced by socially deviant individuals who have been caught and are facing the consequences of their impulsive acting out. They may appear to be depressed and remorseful over their misbehavior, though when external pressures subside and circumstances permit, they typically return to their pattern of acting out, thus continuing the cycle. Their behavior often shows a self-defeating pattern. These individuals lack many societal values and standards of conduct. The profile suggests poor impulse control and an unwillingness to delay gratification of desires. Run-ins with societal limits and problems with alcohol and substance abuse are common.

Individuals with this code type are usually energetic, outgoing, sociable, and good at making initially favorable impressions on other people. They present a facade of self-confidence, though they are actually passive-dependent and dissatisfied with their limited achievement. Ultimately, other people discover that these individuals are self-centered, manipulative, and insensitive. Suicide gestures are sometimes expressed and often have a manipulative quality. These individuals rarely participate in psychotherapy voluntarily. Usually they participate because of a required part of a legal agreement, or they have been coerced and enter therapy as a means of alleviating external pressures. Quick "cures" are commonly claimed by these individuals in order to avoid the discomfort, inconvenience, and expense of psychotherapy.

26/62

These individuals harbor a vast amount of unresolved anger that is both internalized and projected. They are typically depressed, hypersensitive, hostile, and aggressive. Their suspiciousness and resentfulness induce rejection by other people and lead to generally poor social adjustment.

27/72

This code type occurs in individuals who have a wide variety of neurotic symptoms and characteristics. These persons are very tense, nervous, anxious, and depressed. They worry and ruminate over real and imagined issues. Fatigue, weakness, lack of initiative, and pessimism are characteristic. In addition, physical complaints and somatic preoccupations are common. They often report disturbed sleep and loss of appetite, with associated tiredness and weight loss, respectively, and problems with concentration and memory.

These individuals have high standards of achievement and tend to be perfectionistic and demanding of themselves and other people. They view themselves as inadequate and inferior, having failed to meet these high standards. They are guilt-prone and intropunitive, often preoccupied with their personal deficiencies. Self-concept is very poor. Individuals with this code type are generally conscientious, meticulous, and focused on details. Their thinking is rigid.

Interpersonal functioning shows a passive-dependent orientation in relationships. These individuals are very insecure, fearful of rejection, and self-castigating, and they manage anger through internalization. Consequently, they find it very difficult to be assertive in social situations. Their high level of distress and, in many cases, sense of hopelessness are often associated with suicidal ideation. Suicide potential should be closely investigated. Diagnostically, these individuals are usually classified primarily on the basis of their depression, anxiety, or obsessional features. As a general rule, they are highly motivated for psychological assistance.

28/82

Individuals with this configuration are typically anxious, tense, agitated, and depressed. Unusual physical complaints and pervasive apathy may be present. They complain of difficulties with distractibility, forgetfulness, periodic confusion, and inefficiency in managing daily responsibilities. Hysterical features, particularly involving dissociation, are likely. "Blank spells" may be reported. In some cases, episodes of acting out occur purportedly without the individual's awareness or recollection.

Individuals with this profile commonly have a long history of experiencing emotional hurt in interpersonal relationships, and they avoid closeness or emotional involvement in order to protect themselves from further harm. They are distrusting of other people, doubting their motives and showing heightened sensitivity to their reactions. They are seen as unsociable. Their alienation and isolation increases their sense of despair and worthlessness. Individuals with this code type often have a history of suicide attempts and commonly report suicidal ideation. Suicide potential should be carefully evaluated. Diagnostically, this code type is very nonspecific. It is often associated with major depression and post-traumatic stress disorder and, in some cases, schizoaffective disorder, schizophrenia, and bipolar disorder.

29/92

Individuals with this profile have serious conflicts centered on self-worth. They are self-absorbed and preoccupied with high achievement, though their performance is ineffective, if not self-defeating. Symptomatically, these individuals are anxious, restless, energetic, and overly active. In some cases (bipolar or cyclothymic disorder), periods of restlessness and accelerated activity are cycled with episodes involving depression and withdrawal. These individuals commonly present physical complaints, often involving the gastrointestinal area. Although traditional lore and earlier research suggested brain dysfunction as a common diagnosis for this code type, it is rarely represented in samples of individuals who have brain damage (Golden, 1979; Wooten, 1983).

20/02

This profile suggests depression and social withdrawal. Individuals with this profile feel very insecure and inadequate in social situations. Their shyness and social avoidance is often accompanied by poor interpersonal skills and ineptitude in social interaction.

34/43

Individuals with this profile configuration have conflict centering on control over hostile impulses and social conformity. Repressive overcontrol related to intense underlying anger is generally characteristic. Occasional brief episodes of explosive aggression may occur in the absence of a justifiable provocation. This is particularly true to the extent that Scale 4 is higher than Scale 3 (by at least 5 T-score points). In this case, self-control is tenuous. Other forms of acting out may also be expressed episodically, including substance abuse, promiscuity, and other asocial behaviors. These individuals have poor insight into the causes and effects of their unusual behavior and sometimes show a complete disregard for its significance. When Scale 3 is significantly higher than 4, hostility may be more commonly expressed through indirect and passive ways, and episodic acting out may be less likely.

   Somatic complaints may be expressed. People who have this code type are basically rebellious individuals who struggle with outward conformity. Periods of acting out are sometimes followed by suicidal thoughts or behavior. The high Scale 3 indicates a strong need for others' attention and approval, which is counter to the defiance and rebelliousness of Scale 4. These individuals become quite angry when criticized. They have very poor psychological insight and are likely to resist psychological interpretations of their difficulties.

36/63

Individuals with this code type typically report somatic symptoms and exhibit a moderate degree of anxiety. These persons are sometimes described as narcissistic and self-centered. They are viewed as defiant, uncooperative, and difficult to get along with. Individuals with this profile lack insight about their underlying feelings (especially anger) and do not usually express them directly. Although they are mildly suspicious, hypersensitive, and resentful toward other people, they overtly promote themselves as naïve and optimistic about the world. They inwardly harbor a substantial amount of unresolved hostility toward family members, and, as a result, they often have marital and family problems.

38/83

These individuals are in substantial psychological turmoil. They report feeling anxious, tense, fearful, and worried, as well as depressed, apathetic, pessimistic, and hopeless. A wide range of vague or unusual physical complaints may be expressed. In addition, these individuals sometimes report disturbed thinking manifested in confusion, poor concentration, memory lapses, unusual ideas, loose ideational associations, and blank spells that occasionally reflect dissociative reactions. To the extent that Scale 8 is higher than Scale 3, delusions and hallucinations become more likely, as does a diagnosis of schizophrenia.

This code type is found in individuals who are described as somewhat unusual and peculiar. Although socially withdrawn in many cases, they are viewed as being emotionally dependent, immature, and hostile and as having a strong need for attention and affection. They exhibit a stereotyped style of responding to problems. Schizoid adaptation is common, though a thought disorder should be ruled out. Supportive psychological intervention is sometimes helpful.

46/64

These individuals typically have interpersonal difficulties that are associated with chronic, unresolved anger and a propensity to see themselves as a victim. They are self-absorbed and grandiose, viewing themselves in an unrealistically favorable light. Authority figures are typically resented. They distrust other people in general, are hypersensitive, and easily hurt, deny responsibility for their actions, and characteristically rationalize situations in a way so as to blame others for alleged wrongdoing. These individuals are often described as being irritable, bitter, sullen, rigidly argumentative, and obnoxious. Their conflict, in part, involves the fact that their sense of self-worth and security is highly dependent on the attention and sympathy that they receive from other people. Relationships with the opposite sex are especially difficult. They often use passive-aggressive strategies for handling interpersonal conflict. These individuals typically reject the notion that they would benefit from psychotherapy, rarely benefit from it, and typically generate a substantial amount of countertransference. Diagnostically, these individuals are often classified as passive-aggressive personality or, when Scale 8 is also elevated, schizophrenia, chronic paranoid type.

47/74

This profile denotes an individual who is insensitive, self-centered, and manipulative on the one hand, yet, on the other hand, is excessively concerned with pleasing other people and winning approval and acceptance. Classically, these persons display a cyclical pattern of acting out selfishly, perhaps in asocial ways, followed by a period of expressed guilt, worry, and contrition that eventually fade. These individuals are impulsive yet emotionally insecure, highly dependent, tense, fatigued, and preoccupied with their self-worth. They often report vague physical complaints. In psychotherapy, their symptoms generally respond to supportive intervention and reassurance, though the prognosis for behavior change is less optimistic.

48/84

Individuals with this code type combine a defiance of conventional standards of behavior with alienation, introversion, and peculiar thinking. They are notably unpredictable, but often angry, irritable, and resentful. Behavioral controls are weak because these individuals exhibit poor impulse control and commonly indulge in asocial or antisocial forms of acting out. Substance abuse, sex-related crime, promiscuity, physical assault, delinquency, and various criminal behaviors are often part of their histories. These people show a pattern of underachievement and marginal adjustment.

People with this profile pattern view the world as threatening and rejecting. At times, their behavior suggests a pattern of striking out aggressively to avoid being hurt. They blame other people for their problems and are reluctant to accept personal responsibility for the consequences of their actions. They lack the normal capacity for empathizing with other people's feelings. In many cases, they show poorly developed social skills and are withdrawn and isolated. Other people tend to view these individuals as being rather odd or peculiar. In some cases, these people espouse unusual belief systems or ideological commitments. They avoid emotional involvement with other people.

Concerns about their own masculinity or femininity are often present, alongside of fears regarding the adequacy of their sexual performance. Antisocial sexual behavior sometimes occurs as a means of demonstrating adequacy in this area. These individuals exhibit poor judgment in addition to their lack of impulse control. They sometimes have a history of committing crimes that are poorly planned and executed and that may involve bizarre or violent behaviors. Diagnostically, these individuals usually fall somewhere between antisocial personality and schizophrenia, chronic paranoid type, combining elements of both.

49/94

Individuals who produce this code type are very energetic, impulsive, and inclined to act out in asocial or antisocial ways. They disregard societal standards and customs, and they reject any responsibility for the consequences of their behavior. These individuals are self-focused, self-indulgent, and often narcissistic. They do not tolerate frustration effectively and seek immediate gratification of their desires, even when postponement would be in their best interest. Sometimes described as overactive, they appear to have a strong need for stimulation and excitement. Substance abuse and alcohol addiction are common. Antisocial or criminal behavior is frequently a problem. Failure to follow through in pursuit of goals is also common because these individuals are easily distracted or sidetracked. In regard to their deviant behavior, these people do not learn from their mistakes or profit from experience. They rationalize their actions and blame other people for any difficulties.

Interpersonally, this code type suggests a pattern of exploiting and manipulating other people for self-gratification. Individuals with this code type are usually very outgoing, sociable, and active. They convey a sense of security and self-confidence, create a positive first impression, and are sometimes quite charming. Their interpersonal relationships are generally shallow. Emotional attachments are feared, despite their strong underlying dependency needs. These individuals are often unreliable, irresponsible, and untrustworthy. They are commonly described as impatient, irritable, moody, caustic, and prone to occasional temper outbursts. Diagnostically, these people often have drug dependency and sometimes fit under the category of antisocial personality disorder.

68/86

This code type occurs in individuals who exhibit intense feelings of insecurity and inferiority associated with perceived failures. Pervasive emotional apathy sometimes conceals underlying depression and despair. These individuals feel mistreated and victimized. They are described as being irritable, unfriendly, moody, and negativistic. Poor social skills and unpredictable behavior are characteristic. Individuals who produce this code type are psychologically detached and alienated, and they withdraw from other people. They are suspicious and distrusting of people's motives and typically prefer isolation to social interaction.

Cognitive functioning shows a variety of potential disturbances, including attentional difficulties and poor concentration. Stream of thought may be slow. A retreat into daydreaming and fantasy is their characteristic manner of responding to stress. Individuals with this code type often become preoccupied with abstract matters to the exclusion of involvement in the real world. Their thought content typically includes unusual ideas or preoccupations that are often related to themes of a political, religious, or sexual nature. Persecutory ideation is very common, and paranoid delusions are sometimes evident. Thinking may be fragmented, circumstantial, or tangential. Florid psychotic symptoms may be evident. Diagnostically, this code type is commonly associated with paranoid schizophrenia.

69/96

These individuals are tense, anxious, insecure, and emotionally dependent, and they have an intense need for attention and affection. They overreact to minor stress and respond to major stress by withdrawing into fantasy. They are sometimes described as hostile and grandiose. In handling emotions, they lack adaptive modulation and alternate between emotional overcontrol and explosive outbursts.

Interpersonal functioning is poor due to poorly controlled anger, suspiciousness, and pervasive distrust. They are sometimes overly energetic, overactive, and show poor self-control. They tend to ruminate a great deal and show problems with concentration and organized, goal-directed thinking.

78/87

This code type suggests substantial inner turmoil marked by anxiety, tension, depression, worry, and agitation. These individuals are overideational and ruminate obsessively about real or imagined dangers. They feel defenseless. At times, they present with symptoms of episodic confusion and panic attacks. Indecision and other cognitive complaints are common. They also lack common sense and show poor judgment and a tendency to repeat mistakes over and over again.

Interpersonally, these persons are shy, introverted, and lacking in both self-confidence and social poise. As a result of their social discomfort, they are typically withdrawn and isolated. They have difficulty establishing close relationships. They assume a passive-submissive role in relationships with other people. To the extent that Scale 7 is higher than 8, problems may be more acute, reality contact firmly established, and the individual struggling to maintain control. If Scale 8 is significantly higher than 7, they may be adapting to and accepting the presence of their psychopathology. In this case, a distortion of reality (e.g., delusions, loose thinking) is more likely.

79/97

Anxiety, restlessness, tenseness, and agitation are characteristic of individuals who produce this code type. Stress-related symptoms and excessive worry are characteristic. People with this profile configuration are commonly achievement oriented and may exhibit a heightened energy level and periods of overactivity and inefficiency. These episodes may lead to feelings of guilt and self-deprecation.

89/98

Individuals with this code type exhibit restlessness, labile emotionality, and hyperactivity with varying degrees of confusion and disorientation. From an emotional standpoint, they are depressed, anxious, angry, and irritable. They have low self-esteem and a negative self-concept. Their behavior suggests an intense pressure to achieve, combined with only mediocre performance. Their judgment is poor, and their behavior is often erratic and unpredictable. A great deal of time may be spent in fantasy and daydreaming.

Interpersonal functioning is very poor. These individuals are infantile in their expectations of others and demand an inordinate amount of attention. When others fail to meet their expectations, they become hostile and belligerent. In general, they are afraid of emotional involvement and avoid forming close relationships. Many of these individuals show evidence of paranoid mentation and a thought disorder. In some cases, their social transactions and relationships are adversely affected by the difficulties they have remaining focused and following through on a topic of discussion. Furthermore, they display poor social judgment.

Clinical Scale Combinations

Regardless of the profile code type, the following classic clinical scale combinations can provide additional information regarding an individual's style of coping. In some cases, these score combinations are specific applications of the following general principle: Scales 1, 2, 3, 5, 7, and 0 represent tendencies related to self-control or regulation of impulses, whereas elevated scores on Scales 4, 6, 8, and 9 are more closely associated with diminished control and acting out behaviors.

"Conversion V"

If Scales 1 and 3 are prominently elevated and at least 10 T-score points higher than Scale 2, this conversion V pattern suggests the presence of physical manifestations of psychological conflict combined with an attitude of relative indifference toward the symptoms. This pattern is also common in individuals who sustain mild head trauma and who, for many months or even years thereafter, continue to report a variety of problems (e.g., distractibility, forgetfulness, headache, diffuse pain, dizzy spells, fatigue) that are difficult to explain on the basis of current medical knowledge. These individuals are typically pursuing financial compensation for their alleged injury. Many are presumed to have a somatoform disorder or to be consciously malingering, or a combination of the two. In the absence of sufficient evidence of actual brain injury, the MMPI-2 correction for closed head injury (Gass, 1991b) should not be used. The conversion V pattern on the MMPI-2 is also common in individuals following stroke. In these cases, evidence of brain damage is usually unequivocal, and the correction factor for stroke (Gass, 1992) should be applied to help control for the effects of neurological symptom reporting. The exception to this guideline occurs if the stroke patient has a premorbid history of psychopathology.

Control of Anger

Control over and modulation of anger is a central issue when Scales 3 and 4 are both prominently elevated in the profile. If Scale 3 is higher than Scale 4 by at least 5 *T*-score points, then emotional overcontrol and repressive defenses are predominant, and the likelihood of acting out anger is considerably reduced. If, however, Scale 4 is higher than the Scale 3 by at least 5 *T*-score points, then the general pattern of emotional overcontrol is usually accompanied by intermittent periods of angry outbursts and hostility. Other forms of acting out are also more likely to occur.

Control of Cognitive Functioning

If Scales 7 and 8 are both prominently elevated, their relative scores provide information regarding the degree of control an individual has over cognitive processes, perceptual accuracy, and reality testing. If Scale 7 is higher than Scale 8 by at least 5 *T*-score points, then anxiety, acute distress, and obsessional characteristics are more likely to be present than psychosis. If Scale 8 is greater than 80*T* and higher than Scale 7 by at least 5 *T*-score points, then the psychological disturbance is more likely to involve cognitive slippage, impaired reality testing, and problems of a more chronic nature. In this case, control over thought processes is much more fragile, and the likelihood of psychotic thought content is higher.

Impulse Control

Acting-out potential and poor impulse control increase as Scale 0 falls below 40*T* while either Scale 4 exceeds 65*T* or Scale 9 exceeds 70*T*. Aggressive acting out is more likely as ANG exceeds 65*T*. Suicidal behavior is more likely to occur following a period in which an individual feels hopeless and in despair (Scale 8); depressed and worthless (Scale 2); guilty, or in high distress and desperate for a solution (Scale 7); aggressive, impulsive, impatient, and intolerant of negative emotions (Scale 4); and sufficiently energetic and prepared to act with minimal forethought or consideration of long-range consequences (Scale 9).

Social Withdrawal

When Scales 8 and 0 are both elevated (*T* > 70) and more than 10 *T*-score points higher than Scale 9, this "avoidant V" pattern suggests the presence of social anxiety and an intense fear of rejection, resulting in social withdrawal, loneliness, and isolation. The elevated score on Scale 0 suggests that the individual is uncomfortable with this degree of interpersonal distance. In slight contrast with this avoidant pattern, a schizoid detachment from others might be more likely when Scale 0 is lower than 70T and Scale 8 is elevated ($T > 70$).

Content Scales

The 15 MMPI-2 content scales were developed using a multistep approach that combined rational and empirical analytic procedures (Butcher, Graham, Williams, & Ben-Porath, 1990). These scales provide important information that augments and supplements the data derived from the basic clinical scale profile. Empirical studies (Butcher et al., 1990) indicate that these scales are psychometrically sound with respect to both reliability and validity. Unlike the basic clinical scales, the content scales are composed entirely of test items that have clear (face valid) and obvious meaning to the reader. As a result, scores on these scales provide a much clearer and more direct reflection of how the examinee wants his or her problems to be portrayed to the clinician. Individuals who minimize or deny problem areas typically score low on these scales ($T < 40$). Those who exaggerate or malinger commonly score high across many of the scales ($T > 80$). Interpretation of the content scales is always preceded by a preliminary analysis of the MMPI-2 validity scales, including Fb, VRIN, and TRIN.

Component subscales for many of the content scales were designed by Ben-Porath and Sherwood (1993) using rational and empirical procedures. Scoring can be done through NCS either by computer or by using hand-scoring templates. Butcher et al. (1990) described four general clinical areas that are addressed by the content scales: (1) internal symptomatic behaviors; (2) external aggressive tendencies; (3) negative self-views; and (4) general problem areas—social, family, work, and treatment. The content scales can be classified under one of these four general clinical domains.

Internal Symptomatic Behaviors

The first group of content scales measures a variety of classically neurotic symptoms that generally reflect internalized psychological conflict. The following descriptions of the content scales were provided primarily by Butcher et al. (1990) and Ben-Porath and Sherwood (1993).

Anxiety (ANX, 23 items).   High scorers on ANX report general symptoms of anxiety, including tension, somatic problems (e.g., heart pounding and shortness of breath), sleep difficulties, worries, and poor concentration. They fear losing their minds, find life a strain, and have difficulty making decisions. They appear to be aware of having these symptoms and problems and admit to having them. ANX is closely related to Scale 7, with a correlation of .82 in the MMPI-2 restandardization sample. In the Miami VAMC study (Gass, 1997), 34% of the patients with closed head injury and 28% of the patients with CVD had scores exceeding 65T on ANX. No correction for neurologically related content is needed on ANX.

Fears (FRS, 23 items).   A high score on FRS indicates the presence of many specific fears, including the sight of blood; high places; money; animals such as snakes, mice, or spiders; leaving home; fire; storms and natural disasters; water; the dark; being indoors;

and dirt. Factor analytic work suggested that this scale has two major components, which were subsequently developed into subscales (Ben-Porath & Sherwood, 1993):

1. *Generalized Fearfulness (FRS1,* 12 items) reflects a general pattern of fearfulness in daily living and a proneness to be nervous and to overidentify danger in one's environment.
2. *Multiple Fears (FRS2,* 10 items) consists of items that reflect phobic reactions to a large number of specific stimuli.

The FRS scale does not correlate substantially with any of the other MMPI-2 scales ($r < .40$). In the Miami VAMC study, high FRS scores ($T > 65$) were produced by 38% of the patients with CVD and 15% of the patients with closed head injuries. FRS seems to be unique and relatively powerful as a predictive variable in certain specific areas of neuropsychological test performance. Scores on FRS appear to be inversely related to the quality of performance on a variety of widely used cognitive measures, particularly those of a nonverbal nature. In a neuropsychological referral sample of 70 male veterans (Gass et al., 1994), none of whom had evidence of impaired brain function, higher scores on FRS predicted poorer performance on the Design Fluency Test ($r = -.48$), Mazes ($r = -.40$), and the Controlled Oral Word Association Test ($r = -.36$). In another study, Gass (1996b) used a similar sample of 80 psychiatric patients and found that FRS was inversely related to visual memory performance (Visual Reproduction) on the Wechsler Memory Scale-Revised (WMS-R; $r = -.40$). These general findings were replicated in a study of 326 men and women who sustained traumatic brain injury (Ross, Putnam, Gass, & Adams, 1997). Finally, scores on FRS showed a correlation of $-.34$ ($p < .005$) with the global level of neuropsychological test performance (Average Impairment Rating Scale; E. Russell, Neuringer, & Goldstein, 1970) in a sample of 95 male psychiatric patients who had normal neurodiagnostic findings and no medico-historical record of brain damage (Gass, 1997). FRS does not contain neurological symptom content.

Obsessiveness (OBS, **16 items).**   High scorers on OBS have tremendous difficulty making decisions and are likely to ruminate excessively about issues and problems, causing others to become impatient. Having to make changes distresses them, and they may report some compulsive behaviors like counting or saving unimportant things. They are excessive worriers who frequently become overwhelmed by their own thoughts. This scale has homogeneous item content. OBS is most closely associated with Scale 7, showing a correlation of .78 in the MMPI-2 restandardization sample.

Gass (1996b) reported that in a sample of 80 neurologically normal male psychiatric inpatients who were referred for neuropsychological evaluation, scores on OBS were inversely related to verbal memory (Logical Memory) performance on the WMS-R ($r = -.36$, $p < .01$). This relationship was not found in a sample of 48 patients with closed head injury. In the Miami VAMC study, OBS scores exceeded 65T in 22% of the patients with closed head injury and 35% of the patients with CVD. OBS has very few items that commonly represent physical or cognitive symptoms of CNS impairment.

Depression (DEP, **33 items).**   High scores on DEP characterize individuals with significant depressive thoughts. They report feeling blue, uncertain about their future, uninterested in their lives. They are likely to brood, to be unhappy, to cry easily, and to feel hopeless and empty. They may report thoughts of suicide or wishes that they were dead. They may believe that they are condemned or have committed unpardonable sins. Other people may be viewed as nonsupportive. Unlike Scale 2, the item composition of DEP is relatively free of neurologically related content and, as a result, is often a better measure of depression in individuals with neurological conditions.

DEP has item content that falls into four categories (Ben-Porath & Sherwood, 1993):

1. *Lack of Drive (D1,* 12 items) suggests that the individual reports feeling unable to get going and get things done. The person is likely to be experiencing a general lack of drive and motivation, perhaps also lacking an interest in important aspects of her or his life.

2. *Dysphoria (DEP2,* 6 items) indicates symptoms of depressed mood and recurrent spells of the blues that are rather persisting.

3. *Self-Depreciation (DEP3,* 7 items) represents a negative self-concept, feelings of uselessness, underestimation of one's abilities, lack of self-confidence, helplessness, and, in some cases, worthlessness.

4. *Suicidal Ideation (DEP4,* 5 items) suggests current contemplation of suicide and, in some cases, a history of one or more attempts. An elevated score on this scale is a red flag indicating a need for further assessment of self-destructive potential.

DEP is a good indicator of general distress, worry, and unhappiness in neuropsychological referrals. Unlike the more heterogeneous Scale 2, DEP has very little item content that potentially reflects physical or cognitive symptoms of brain damage. For this reason, DEP is better than Scale 2 as a measure of emotional distress and dissatisfaction in neurologic patients. DEP is more closely related to Scale 7 ($r = .82$) than to Scale 2 ($r = .58$). High DEP scores ($T > 65$) were produced by 49% of the patients with closed head injury and 30% of the patients with CVD in the Miami VAMC study (Gass, 1997).

Health Concerns (HEA, 36 items). High scores suggest the acknowledgement of physical symptoms across several body systems and worry over general health status. This scale has three components:

1. *Gastrointestinal Symptoms (HEA1,* 5 items) consists of items that reflect chest and stomach pain and general malfunctioning of the digestive system.

2. *Neurological Symptoms (HEA2,* 12 items) consists of items that refer to various symptoms of CNS disease, such as tinnitus, paresthesia, numbness, syncope, dizziness, and ataxia.

3. *General Health Concerns (HEA3,* 6 items) suggests the perception of poor general health. High scorers worry about catching diseases and report vague symptoms of pain and weakness.

Individuals who report symptoms of brain dysfunction typically produce marginal elevations on the HEA scale ($65T$ to $75T$), even in the absence of any neurotic preoccupations or somatoform symptoms. In the Miami VAMC study of MMPI-2 protocols that were not corrected for neurologically related item endorsement, 51% of the patients with closed head injury and 48% of the patients with CVD produced HEA scores exceeding 65T. Analysis of the component scales in these cases usually reveals a prominent elevation on HEA2, indicating the major contribution of neurologically related item endorsement to the HEA score. HEA is psychometrically very similar to Scale 1. In the normative sample, an analysis of HEA and Scale 1 showed a correlation of .90 between the two scales (Butcher et al., 1990). Not surprisingly, high scorers on HEA exhibit hypochondriacal tendencies and are overly focused on somatic functioning.

Bizarre Mentation (BIZ, 24 items).   Psychotic thought processes and unusual experiences characterize high scorers on BIZ ($T > 65$). This scale has two major components.

1. *Psychotic Symptomatology (BIZ1,* 11 items) refers to frankly psychotic symptoms, including delusions, and hallucinations and, more generally, to what has been referred to as "positive" symptoms of schizophrenia.
2. *Schizotypal Characteristics (BIZ2,* 9 items) suggests a variety of peculiar and unusual experiences, including illusions and ideas of reference.

In the MMPI-2 standardization sample, the correlation between BIZ and Scale 8 was .64. BIZ is generally more effective than Scale 8 in identifying psychotic symptoms, probably because of its homogeneous item content. Unlike Scale 8, BIZ is unaffected by the endorsement of common neurological symptoms. For these reasons, the clinician should rely more heavily on BIZ in making inferences regarding the presence of psychotic features, especially in examinees who have impaired brain functioning. From the standpoint of cognitive testing, BIZ, like FRS, has a potentially important role as a variable in the quality of certain types of neuropsychological test performance. Gass (1996b) observed that higher BIZ scores were associated with worse performance on attention tasks ($r = -.40, p < .01$) in a sample of patients with closed head injury ($n = 48$) and visual retentive memory ($r -.38, p < .001$) in a sample of 80 neurologically intact patients who were referred for a neuropsychological evaluation. These findings were replicated in an investigation of patients with head injury by Ross et al. (1997).

External Aggressive Tendencies

The second group of content scales measures characteristics that reflect outward manifestations of conflict, primarily centering on impulses of anger and hostility. These scales assess several different ways in which anger is channeled and expressed.

Anger (ANG, 16 items).   Problems with anger control are characteristic of high scorers on ANG. The scale has two components:

1. *Explosive Behavior (ANG1,* 7 items) refers to a person's violent, explosive tendencies when angry, such as hitting or smashing objects, throwing a tantrum, engaging in loud argumentation, and fights.
2. *Irritability (ANG,* 7 items) suggests somewhat better control and modulation over anger, but anger is still problematic.

High scores on this scale are associated with frequent displays of irritability, grouchiness, and impatience toward people. High scorers are easily annoyed and are often viewed as argumentative and petty. Scores on ANG are useful for clarifying the manner in which anger is handled and expressed in the presence of elevated scores on Scales 4, 6, 8, and/or 9. High scores on ANG were produced by 24% of the patients with closed head injury and 20% of the patients with CVD in the Miami VAMC study. ANG does not contain neurologic symptom items.

Cynicism (CYN, **23 items).**   This scale assesses a misanthropic outlook about people generally, as well as a more specific tendency to mistrust other people in interpersonal transactions. It has two components:

1. *Misanthropic Beliefs (CYN1,* 15 items) refers to negative perceptions about people in general. People are judged to be purely self-serving, out for themselves, and unwilling to help other people. They are also perceived to be opportunistic, manipulative, and untrustworthy.
2. *Interpersonal Suspiciousness (CYN2,* 8 items) reflects a pervasive distrust toward people involved in the individual's world.

High scorers distrust positive outward appearances in social situations and are suspicious of other peoples' motives. They have doubts about others' true intentions. They feel that they are often misunderstood, treated unfairly, and exploited.

Antisocial Practices (ASP, **22 items).**   This scale has two main components:

1. *Antisocial Attitudes (ASP1,* 16 items) consists of items that refer to (1) self-serving attitudes that defy societal standards of conduct, (2) an endorsement of others' asocial behavior, and (3) cynical beliefs about human nature, in general. High scorers place a priority on expedience in self-gain over moral decision making.
2. *Antisocial Behavior (ASP2,* 5 items) refers to misconduct during the school years (e.g., suspension) and problems such as being in trouble with the law or stealing.

Type A Behavior (TPA, **19 items).**   This scale assesses a tendency to be hard-driving, demanding, irritable, fast-paced, impatient, and work oriented. There are two major components to this scale:

1. *Impatience (TPA1,* 6 items), assesses irritability, demandingness, and an unwillingness to tolerate delays.
2. *Competitive Drive (TPA2,* 9 items) assesses an aggressive, hard-driving, achievement orientation and a need to demonstrate dominance and superiority. High scorers may be viewed as ruthlessly competitive, insensitive, and hostile in their pursuit of success.

Low Self-Esteem (LSE, **24 items)***.*   Two primary components comprise this scale:

1. *Self-Doubt (LSE1,* 11 items) refers to a sense of being inadequate, incapable, unsuccessful, unattractive, disliked, and lacking in importance.
2. *Submissiveness (LSE2,* 6 items) refers to a self-effacing tendency to defer to other people across a variety of interpersonal situations. High scorers doubt themselves to such an extent that they allow other people to take charge, to make decisions, to win arguments, and generally to assume a dominant role.

General Problem Areas: Social, Family, Work, and Treatment

Four content scales address the examinee's level of adjustment and attitudes in several specific environmental contexts: (1) social, (2) family, (3) work, and (4) psychological treatment. These measures provide broader contextual information that is very relevant to rehabilitation and psychosocial intervention following brain injury.

Social Discomfort (SOD, 24 items)*.*   This scale assesses an individual's level of social anxiety and discomfort, as well as a tendency to actively avoid being in situations that might require social interactions or group involvement.

1. *Introversion (SOD1,* 16 items) suggests an avoidance of interpersonal contact and a general preference to keep other people at a distance. High scorers attempt to avoid parties, social gatherings, and other group situations.
2. *Shyness (SOD2,* 7 items) refers to the subjective anxiety that the individual experiences in social situations. High scores suggest substantial discomfort in meeting new people, speaking in front of people, or being made the center of attention in group situations.

Family Problems (FAM, 25 items)*.*   Family relationship problems are measured by this scale.

1. *Family Discord (FAM1,* 12 items) reflects considerable family strife and discord, with animosity, quarrels, and ill feelings.
2. *Family Alienation (FAM2,* 5 items) addresses the individual's degree of attachment to the family. High scorers deny feeling family-based emotional support and do not have strong ties to their families.

Work Interference (WRK, 33 items)*.*   This scale addresses negative attitudes related to work or achievement. High scorers typically possess negative work attitudes and personal problems that interfere with work performance. They report low self-confidence, concentration difficulties, obsessional thinking, tension, and indecision.

Negative Treatment Indicators (TRT, 26 items)*.*   This scale measures attitudes and beliefs regarding receiving help and making behavioral changes.

1. *Low Motivation (TRT1,* 11 items) suggests that the individual lacks the incentive for self-help and perhaps feels helpless about making changes. High scorers are described as apathetic, skeptical, and lacking in self-confidence.

2. *Inability to Disclose (TRT2,* 5 items) measures subjective discomfort and reluctance to disclose personal information. High scorers are skeptical about the likelihood of being understood.

Supplementary Scales

In addition to the basic validity and clinical scales, numerous supplementary scales were created for the original MMPI, some of which continue to be particularly useful in MMPI-2 work. Several new scales have also been constructed for the MMPI-2. This section provides a brief overview of some of the more widely used scales.

Anxiety (A, 39 items).   This scale, which is comprised of basic-scale items that emerged as the first dimension in a factor analysis of items on the standard validity and clinical scales (Welsh, 1956), measures "general maladjustment." High scorers on A $(T > 65)$ are anxious, distressed, indecisive, inhibited, conforming, overcontrolled, and easily upset in social situations. Low scorers are typically outgoing, energetic, competitive, and lacking in distress.

Repression (R, 37 items).   This scale consists of the second factor that emerged in Welsh's (1956) analysis of items on the standard validity and clinical scales. High scorers on R tend to be conventional, submissive individuals who strive excessively to avoid interpersonal conflict or psychological discomfort. Low scorers are typically energetic, outgoing, expressive, and enthusiastic. They are also described as dominant, shrewd, and aggressive.

Ego Strength (Es, 52 items).   Originally designed to measure the probability of benefiting from psychological treatment (Barron, 1953), the Es scale more accurately assesses an individual's personal resources for adapting and coping with stressful situations. Low scorers $(T < 40)$ show pervasive psychological maladjustment, are ineffective at managing stressful circumstances, and, as a result, are less likely to benefit from psychotherapy.

MacAndrew Alcoholism Scale-Revised (MAC-R, 49 items).   Originally designed to identify alcoholism in psychiatric patients (MacAndrew, 1965), this scale appears to measure personality characteristics that are commonly associated with addiction proneness. The MAC-R consists of items that statistically differentiated alcohol abusers from individuals experiencing psychiatric problems. The items include references to cognitive difficulties, school-related behavioral problems, risk-taking behavior, interpersonal competence, extroversion and exhibitionism, and moral indignation (Graham, 1993). High scorers $(T > 65)$ often have a history of drinking alcohol excessively, of overusing nonprescription drugs, and of overstepping the boundaries of socially acceptable and legally sanctioned behavior. These individuals exhibit deficient impulse control, poor judgment, and high risk-taking behavior. Although outgoing and sociable, they are often insensitive, dishonest, and quick to lose their tempers. Although high scorers on MAC-R do not invariably have a history of substance abuse, they appear to be predisposed to become chemically dependent. Substance abusers who produce low scores on MAC-R usually have other psychological problems. If those problems are effectively treated, the individuals are more likely to stop their abuse of drugs.

Responsibility Scale (Re, 32 items).   This scale measures behavior associated with social responsibility. The scale consists of items that discriminated students who were judged by peers or teachers to be "most" responsible from those considered to be "least" responsible (Gough, McClosky, & Meehl, 1952). High scorers on Re ($T > 65$) value fairness and justice, have social concern, and live in accordance with conventionally sanctioned moral standards. They tend to be reliable, trustworthy, optimistic, and self-confident. In contrast, low scorers ($T < 40$) are described as unconventional, unreliable, and lacking in personal integrity.

Addiction Potential Scale (APS, 39 items).   Using the complete MMPI-2 item pool, Weed, Butcher, Ben-Porath, and McKenna (1992) derived the APS using the same empirical keying strategy that was used in constructing the MAC-R. In some clinical settings, the APS may be more effective than the MAC-R in identifying substance abusers from among psychiatric patients and individuals with no known impairments (Greene, Weed, Butcher, Arrendondo, & Davis, 1992; Weed et al., 1992).

Addiction Acknowledgment Scale (AAS, 13 items).   Developed by Weed et al. (1992) using a combined rational and empirical strategy of scale construction, the AAS measures the open admission of problems associated with alcohol or substance abuse. High scorers on AAS should be suspected of substance abuse because of their open admission to it, regardless of their scores on MAC-R and APS.

Marital Distress Scale (MDS, 14 items).   This scale, designed by Hjemboe, Almagor, and Butcher (1992), consists of items that were empirically associated with scores on a measure of marital distress, the Spanier Dyadic Adjustment Scale (Spanier & Filsinger, 1983). High scores ($T > 65$) suggest the presence of marital problems that could potentially play an important role in an individual's presenting symptoms.

Over-Controlled Hostility Scale (O-H, 28 items).   This scale measures a tendency to periodically exhibit assaultive or hostile behavior within the backdrop of emotional overcontrol and repressed anger. Such behavior characterized the prison sample of convicted felons used in the empirical derivation of O-H (Megargee, Cook, & Mendelsohn, 1967). High scores on O-H should be cautiously interpreted for two reasons. First, outside of the prison setting, assaultive behavior has a lower base rate; and for this reason O-H has relatively poor predictive power. Second, individuals who produce defensive MMPI-2 protocols as evidenced by elevated scores on L and K often produce higher scores on O-H, even though they may not exhibit assaultive behavior or tenuous control over hostile impulses. This phenomenon occurs with airline pilot applicants and other "normal" individuals who attempt to present themselves in a favorable light. In most cases, high scores on O-H simply reflect a tendency to deny aggressive behavior

(Butcher & Williams, 1992). Nevertheless, high scorers ($T > 65$) who also have a history of committing assault are likely to be overcontrolled, rigidly repressive, and constricted in handling everyday frustration and anger. Thus, in these individuals, O-H may be useful in providing a *post-hoc* understanding of the dynamics of their assaultive behavior.

Post-Traumatic Stress Disorder Scale (PK, 49 items).   This scale is comprised of MMPI-2 items that differentiated 100 military veterans who had a diagnosis of PTSD from 100 veterans who had other psychiatric conditions (Keane, Malloy, & Fairbank, 1984). It measures symptoms that commonly occur in PTSD, including distress, anxiety, depression, insomnia, intrusive thoughts, suspiciousness, distrust, and feelings of alienation. High scores ($65T$ to $85T$) are not specific to PTSD; they are commonly produced by acutely distressed individuals and by patients who have chronic and severe psychopathology. In the absence of malingering, very high scores ($T > 90$) indicate a higher probability of a formal diagnosis of PTSD, particularly in settings where PTSD has a relatively high base rate. However, the many symptoms of PTSD occur in other disorders. Therefore, even in the presence of high scores on PK, the accuracy of this scale in predicting PTSD is largely a function of the frequency with which PTSD occurs in a given clinical setting.

Additional Interpretive Considerations for Neurologic Patients

Considerations for Patients Other Than TBI and Stroke

Any type of CNS impairment is likely to lead individuals to produce inflated scores on Scales 1, 2, 3, 7, and 8. If an individual has brain damage, the clinician must take special precautions to reduce interpretive error when there is an absence of appropriate norms or a diagnostic-specific correction factor for the MMPI-2. In these cases, the clinician should exhibit a greater degree of reliance on information derived from the Harris-Lingoes subscales and the Content scales. These measures enable one to estimate the extent to which neurological symptom reporting affects scores on several of the affected clinical scales.

In interpreting scores on Scale 2, the standard psychological correlates are less likely to apply to individuals with brain injury who have normal-range scores on D1 (Subjective Depression), D2 (Psychomotor Retardation), and D5 (Brooding). If Scale 2 is less than $75T$ and if high subscale scores are restricted to D3 (Physical Malfunctioning) and D4 (Mental Dullness), one must consider the possibility that self-reported physical and cognitive symptoms of brain damage (not necessarily depression) explain the elevated score. Very high scores on Scale 2 ($T > 75$) are usually indicative of depressive symptoms, regardless of the subscale results. The score on DEP (Depression) is also very helpful in understanding the significance of high scores on Scale 2 because DEP is a more specific measure of depression and contains very few, if any, items that reflect the physical and cognitive effects of brain dysfunction. Depressive symptoms are less likely to exist if DEP is less than $60T$.

In regard to Scale 3, the traditional behavioral correlates are more likely to apply to an individual with brain injury if an elevated score is accompanied by a high score on Hy1 (Denial of Social Anxiety), Hy2 (Need for Affection), or Hy5 (Inhibition of Aggression). If Scale 3 is less than 75T and only Hy3 (Lassitude-Malaise) and Hy4 (Somatic Complaints) are elevated, many of the Scale 3 descriptors are probably inaccurate. Very high scores on Scale 3 ($T > 75$) are likely to be associated with the presence of somatoform symptoms, regardless of the subscale results. Research has yet to address the potential discriminative value of the Neurological Symptoms component subscale of HEA.

Marginally elevated scores (60T to 65T) on Scale 7 produced by individuals with brain impairment are less likely to represent the traditionally ascribed behavioral correlates of this scale when scores on ANX, FRS, and OBS are low ($T < 60$).

Scale 8 elevations in neurologic patients are more likely to reflect the standard behavioral correlates when they are accompanied by high scores on Sc1 (Social Alienation), Sc2 (Emotional Alienation), Sc4 (Lack of Ego Mastery, Conative), or Sc5 (Lack of Ego Mastery, Defective Inhibition). Many Scale 8 behavioral correlates do not apply to patients with brain injury who produce high scores that are limited to Sc3 (Lack of Ego Mastery, Cognitive) and Sc6 (Bizarre Sensory Experiences). In addition, psychotic symptoms are less likely to exist if BIZ is less than 65T.

Factors Affecting MMPI-2 Scores in Individuals with Brain Injury

Location of Brain Lesion

The MMPI-2 is somewhat sensitive to the presence of CNS symptoms. However, numerous attempts to find ways of using the MMPI as a tool for identifying brain dysfunction have been unsuccessful. During the 1960s, attempts to identify "organic code types" failed because very few individuals with brain damage produce these code types (e.g., 29/92 and 139). Attempts to derive special "organic scales" were successful in research settings in discriminating between "organics" and patients with schizophrenia or other psychiatric disorders. However, the efficacy of these scales was based on the sensitivity of the MMPI to symptoms of psychopathology. Individuals who had brain dysfunction were identifiable, but it was primarily on the basis of their relatively infrequent endorsement of psychological symptoms (see Farr & Martin, 1988, for a review). More complex discriminant functions involving numerous MMPI scales have been designed to assist in identifying brain damage. A major weakness of these studies involves the fact that their research subjects, who fall into clearly identifiable diagnostic categories, are rarely representative of the more challenging diagnostic cases commonly encountered in clinical practice. Cross-validation data in clinical settings has been either nonsupportive or absent.

The MMPI-2 is apparently insensitive to the general location of a brain lesion, whether the lesion is classified by right versus left (Gass & Russell, 1986b) or by left-right, anterior-posterior quadrants (Dikmen & Reitan, 1974b). Several studies have found a greater incidence of psychopathology in patients with right hemisphere damage (RHD; Cullum & Bigler, 1988; Folstein, Maiberger, & McHugh, 1977; Gass & Lawhorn, 1991), and some have reported greater problems when the lesion is located in the left hemisphere (Black, 1975; Gasparrini, Satz, Heilman, & Coolidge, 1978). It is conceivable that greater precision in lesion location would yield significant findings, but this proposition remains speculative.

Type of Neurobehavioral Deficit

Earlier studies using the MMPI suggest that, in general, acquired verbal deficits might have a mild impact on MMPI-2 scores (Burke, Imhoff, & Kerrigan, 1990; Dikmen & Reitan, 1974a, 1974b, 1977; Gass & Ansley, 1994; Reitan, 1976). Higher scores on the L and F scales have been consistently reported in association with the severity of verbal deficit. Similar findings were reported by Dikmen and Reitan (1977) for Scales 6 and 8 using a sample of 129 individuals with neurological impairments associated with a variety of brain disorders. These results might be mediated, in part, by a patient's educational background because more highly educated individuals appear to cope more effectively with their verbal deficits (Burke et al., 1990; Gass & Russell, 1985). Lower scores on Scale 3, which probably reflect a decline in verbal facility, have been reported in conjunction with verbal-intellectual decline in patients with CVD (Gass & Ansley, 1994) and with TBI (Burke et al., 1990).

Deficits in the areas of visuospatial and nonverbal intellectual functioning seem to have a minimal effect on the MMPI. Lower Performance IQs were associated with slightly higher scores on Scales L and F in a sample of individuals who varied with respect to lesion location (Dikmen & Reitan, 1977). These results were not replicated in a subsequent study of 50 patients who had unilateral lesions restricted to the right cerebral hemisphere (Gass & Russell, 1987). An association between acquired deficits and psychological status appears to be less likely in the presence of RHD, probably because the right hemisphere plays a somewhat greater role than the left in mediating individuals' appreciation of their deficits (Prigatano & Altman, 1990). Lower Performance IQs were associated with slightly lower scores on Scales 1 and 3 in a sample of post-acute patients with TBI (Burke et al., 1990). Visuospatial deficits were not significantly related to MMPI scores in a study of 130 patients with CVD (Gass & Ansley, 1994).

Sensory-perceptual and motor deficits generally showed little or no evidence of an effect on MMPI scores in a mixed neurodiagnostic sample (Dikmen & Reitan, 1977). However, sensorimotor impairment as measured by the HRNB was related to higher scores on Scale 7 in a sample of 55 stroke patients with left hemisphere, but not in patients who had right hemisphere stroke (Gass & Ansley, 1994).

Reitan and Wolfson (1997) presented a series of excellent guidelines for evaluating the MMPI-2 profiles of individuals with head trauma. In these cases, elevated MMPI-2 scores are more likely to be secondary to the brain injury if the individual has bona fide neurobehavioral deficits demonstrated on neuropsychological testing. Patients with head injuries who produce normal neuropsychological examination results, especially several months after the injury, but who have deviant MMPI-2 profiles, may have psychological difficulties that are not attributable to the head injury. These psychological problems may predate the injury.

Group studies are often useful in clarifying common (and therefore expected) patterns of psychological adjustment following brain injury. From a clinical standpoint, individuals show considerable variability in post-injury adjustment to acquired deficits. A comprehensive evaluation is required in each individual case (Reitan & Wolfson, 1997). A particular deficit can have very different implications depending on an individual's specific needs and life situation. For example, a visuospatial impairment might have little or no psychological impact on a language teacher but substantial consequences for an engineer or an architect. A hemiparesis caused by a subcortical lesion might be critical to a professional athlete but less so to an accountant. MMPI-2 scores partially reflect the degree to which acquired neurobehavioral deficits interfere with an individual's lifestyle and accessibility to rewarding experiences.

Severity of Head Trauma and Duration of Recovery Period

The research literature concerning the relationship between severity of head injury and MMPI-2 scores provides mixed findings. A review of these studies shows that different sampling methods often yield markedly varied results. The natural course of mild TBI involves substantial recovery within 3 months (Levin et al., 1987), with 85% to 90% of patients effectively recovered though not necessarily symptom-free after one year (Alexander, 1995). Consistent with this are the findings of studies that recruit individuals who are consecutively admitted to hospital programs following acute injury—they almost invariably show an improvement (normalizing) of MMPI scores over time in conjunction with a recovery of cognitive functions. This improvement is particularly evident in lower scores on Scales 1, 2, 3, 7, and 8 (Dikmen & Reitan, 1977; Dikmen, Reitan, Temkin, & Machemer, 1992; Rayls et al., 1997). Longitudinal studies suggest that, at least to a point, greater neurological compromise is associated with higher MMPI-2 scores. It should be emphasized, however, that many individuals with severe injuries have impaired awareness of their deficits (Prigatano & Altman, 1990). These patients often exhibit naïve defensiveness in taking the MMPI-2 and produce lower scores on the clinical scales. As recovery occurs in these cases, improved awareness is sometimes associated with the emergence of significant emotional difficulties (Thomsen, 1989).

Selection bias characterizes samples that are studied cross-sectionally with respect to time post-injury because the patients who have a longer time post-injury are much more likely to be referred for evaluation due to the emergence or persistence of psychological problems. Individuals who have chronic brain injury but who are psychologically healthy are less likely to be referred for evaluation. In contrast, in many settings, the evaluation of individuals who have acute and subacute brain injuries is a routine clinical procedure or part of a research protocol. Many individuals who are examined in these settings display a relatively normal degree of psychological adjustment. Selection bias in cross-sectional studies partially explains the paradox of higher MMPI scores in some patients who have had a longer period of recovery.

Patients with mild head trauma who complain of multiple symptoms many months or even years after their injury often have higher MMPI-2 scores than do individuals who have sustained moderate or severe brain injuries (Leininger, Kreutzer, & Hill, 1991; Youngjohn et al., 1997). It is evident that although the biological effects of mild brain trauma typically resolve within months, various psychological factors lead individuals with mild brain trauma into a downward spiral in functional status. This decline is undoubtedly exacerbated in many cases by potential rewards in the form of financial gain and relief from the stressful responsibilities of daily living (Berry et al., 1995;

Youngjohn et al., 1995). The MMPI-2 commonly shows evidence of exaggerated or feigned symptoms of emotional disturbance, with elevated scores on F, Fb, and F(p). In some cases, somatic symptoms are exaggerated on Scales 1, 2, and 3, while problems of a specifically emotional nature are minimized, resulting in an average or marginally elevated score on F.

The MMPI-2 correction for closed head injury should not be applied to the protocols of head trauma unless there is clear evidence of underlying brain dysfunction secondary to TBI. Such evidence is unlikely to exist in patients with mild head trauma who are well beyond the normally required recovery period. In these cases, persisting complaints are more likely to be secondary to psychological factors, motivational pressures, incentives to acquire compensation, and other important aspects of their medico-legal situation (Binder, 1997). In addition, the MMPI-2 correction should probably not be applied to the protocols of individuals with brain injury who have a premorbid history of psychological disturbance or chronic substance abuse. In these cases, the correction items are not as likely to be reflective of CNS symptomatology and may, instead, reflect psychological symptoms.

Case Example

Bob is a 20-year-old, right-handed, single man who, 5 months previously, was struck by a car (hit-and-run) as he was walking along the side of a road. He sustained a closed head injury, a broken rib and nose, and a severed optic nerve in his right eye. He was in a coma for 10 days. His presenting complaints consist of residual symptoms of depression, forgetfulness, and headaches. Bob describes himself as feeling "down," unhappy, somewhat listless, and socially withdrawn.

Bob denied any premorbid history of psychological problems or substance abuse. He has a 10th grade education and has been unemployed for several months after being laid off by his employer at a furniture manufacturing company. He had been employed with this company for 2 years. Bob lives with his mother and younger sister. Since being laid off work, Bob has spent much of his time at home "just sitting around and watching television." However, he spends several hours a week earning small wages doing general repair work for people in his neighborhood. Prior to feeling depressed, he had a moderately active social life. Bob did not become involved in any legal action, nor did he consider pursuit of any type of compensation for his injury.

In the clinical interview, Bob was alert and oriented to person, place, and time. His insight was good. Affect was slightly constricted, and mood was mildly dysphoric. He spoke softly and slowly, with slight dysarthria. His speech was otherwise normal with respect to fluency and appropriate with respect to grammar, content, and substance. Bob denied ever having had any hallucinations, strange experiences, or ideas of a potentially delusional nature. He denied any suicidal ideation.

The neuropsychological examination results suggested mild residual impairment of Bob's auditory attention and ability to retain verbal material in long-term memory. In addition, his verbal skills generally showed evidence of marginal to mild impairment. His nonverbal abilities were within normal limits. Bob performed within the Average range on the WAIS-R (Full Scale IQ = 97). Collectively, the results suggested substantial but not complete recovery from his (severe) head injury.

Bob obtained the following MMPI-2 results on the basic clinical profile shown in Figure 14.1. The solid line depicts his standard profile results. Elevated scores ($T > 65$) were produced on Scales 1, 2, 7, and 8. The following list shows Harris-Lingoes subscale scores on Scales 2 and 8:

D1	69	Sc1	64
D2	59	Sc2	50
D3	83	Sc3	78
D4	82	Sc4	60
D5	51	Sc5	54
		Sc6	80

On the content scales, Bob obtained the results shown in Figure 14.2.

TEST-TAKING ATTITUDE

Bob completed the audio cassette administration of the MMPI-2 in one session. He answered every item. His score of 43 on the L scale is below average, indicating that he is open in admitting common human frailties and is not naively defensive in his approach to the inventory. Bob's T-score of 67 on F suggests that he is

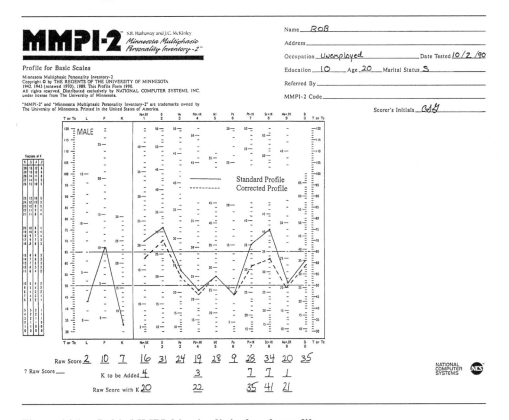

Figure 14.1.   Bob's MMPI-2 basic clinical scale profile

Basic Scales: Minnesota Multiphasic Personality Inventory-2 (MMPI) Profile for Basic Scales. Copyright © 1989 the Regents of the University of Minnesota. All rights reserved. "MMPI-2" and "Minnesota Multiphasic Personality Inventory-2" are trademarks owned by the University of Minnesota.

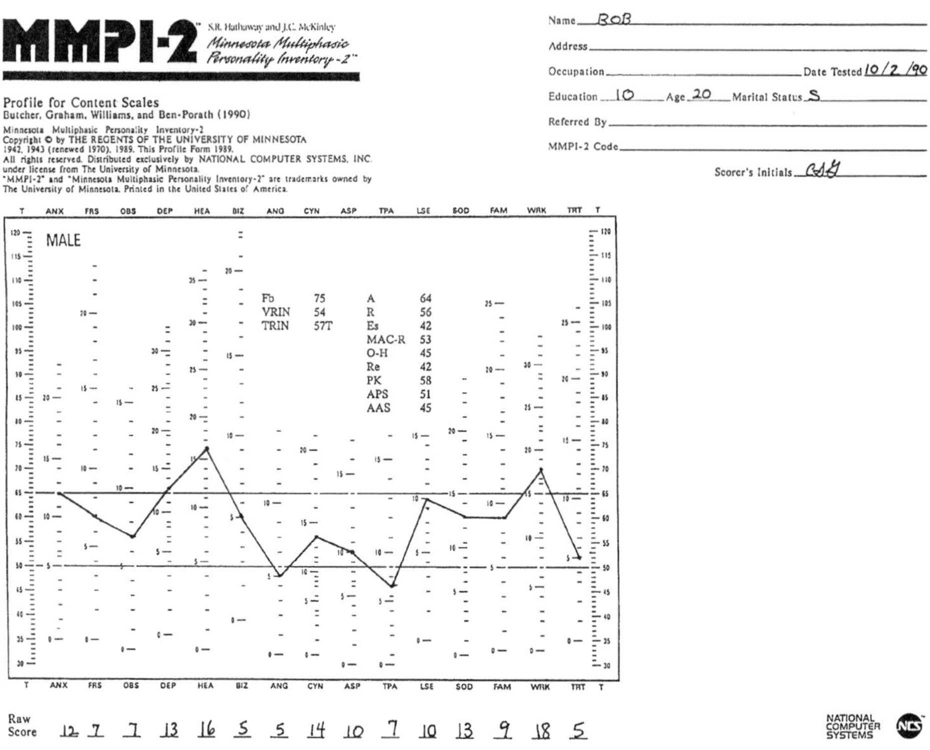

Figure 14.2. Bob's MMPI-2 content scale profile
Content Scales: Minnesota Multiphasic Personality Inventory-2 (MMPI-2) Profile for Content Scales.
Copyright © 1989 the Regents of the University of Minnesota. All rights reserved. "MMPI-2" and
"Minnesota Multiphasic Personality Inventory-2" are trademarks owned by the University of Minnesota.

openly reporting some significant problems that are probably fairly circumscribed in nature. This score is certainly not high enough to consider either exaggerated or content-independent responding to the test items. VRIN and TRIN scores are well within the acceptable range, indicating that he responded meaningfully to item content. Bob's Fb score of 75 is sufficiently similar to his F-scale score (within 15 T-score points) to suggest that he maintained the same general test-taking attitude in answering items that appear later in the test. Bob's T-score of 33 on the K scale is quite low. It suggests a very self-critical attitude in an individual who feels overwhelmed by the pressures of daily living.

APPLICATION OF THE MMPI-2 CORRECTION FOR CLOSED HEAD INJURY

Bob sustained a severe head injury resulting in a 10-day coma, with brain damage evident on the basis of clinical history, CT scan results, and current neuropsychological test findings. He did not have a premorbid history of psychopathology or substance abuse that might conceivably explain his positive endorsement of the correction items. Therefore, his responses to the 14 correction items were examined using the correction scoring table (Gass, 1991b). Bob endorsed nine of these items in the scored direction:

101. Often I feel as though there were a tight band around my head (T).

106. My speech is the same as always (not faster or slower, no slurring or hoarseness) (F).

147. I cannot understand what I read as well as I used to (T).

149. The top of my head sometimes feels tender (T).

165. My memory seems to be alright (F).

170. I am afraid of losing my mind (T).

247. I have numbness in one or more places on my skin (T).

295. I have never been paralyzed or had any unusual weakness of any of my muscles (F).

325. I have more trouble concentrating than others seem to have (T).

Collectively, these responses accounted for raw-score increments of 8 points on Scale 8 ($T = 13$), 4 points on Scale 7 ($T = 8$), 3 points on Scales 1 and 2 ($T = 6$), and 1 point on Scales 3, 9, and 0 ($T < 4$). The basic clinical profile after the application of the correction is presented as the dotted line in Figure 14.1.

This revised profile suggests that Bob's original scores on several clinical scales may have been increased because of his disclosure of physical and cognitive symptoms of brain injury. The original profile had clinically significant elevations on Scales 1, 2, 7, and 8. After correction, only Scale 2 had a score that exceeded 65T. In regard to code-type interpretation, the emphasis in this case should be on the corrected profile with a spike on Scale 2, rather than on the combination of 1, 2, 7, and 8. This is because a standard interpretation of his original scores on Scales 1, 7, and 8 would most likely lead to inaccurate inferences about Bob's current psychological status and personality characteristics.

GENERAL LEVEL OF PSYCHOLOGICAL ADJUSTMENT

The clinical profile, after correction, suggests a mild degree of psychological disturbance and maladjustment. The basic profile has only one elevated scale, a marginally elevated score on the F scale, and a negative (neurotic) slope.

CLINICAL CODE TYPE AND SECONDARY SCALE INTERPRETATION

The spike 2 code type suggests that Bob feels mildly depressed, unhappy, and somewhat pessimistic. He is likely to feel useless, lacking in self-confidence, and largely unable to function. Because he is somewhat withdrawn, he is less actively involved in former interests. Problems with guilt, self-doubt, and indecision may be present. The noncorrected scores on the Harris-Lingoes subscales suggest that Bob has a number of complaints related to physical malfunctioning (D3 = 83) and mental dullness (D4 = 82), in addition to the depressive symptoms described earlier (D1 = 69). Marginal elevations on Scale 1 ($T = 62$) suggest that Bob indeed has greater than average concerns about his physical health, but the corrected score is not high enough to suggest neurotic preoccupations or unrealistic worries about his health. The marginal elevation on Scale 8 ($T = 62$) is consistent with the fact that, in addition to difficulties related to sensory and somatosensory functioning (Sc6 = 80) and to cognitive efficiency (Sc3 = 78), he might also feel somewhat withdrawn, lonely, and misunderstood (Sc1 = 64).

CONTENT AND SUPPLEMENTARY SCALE INTERPRETATION

Bob understandably has concerns regarding his health status (HEA = 74T). His acknowledgement of bona fide physical symptoms undoubtedly affected his score on HEA. This scale has 12 items that have been classified as representing neurological complaints (Ben-Porath & Sherwood, 1993). The DEP score (71T) underscores Bob's mild depressive status, including his feelings of distress, unhappiness, worry, and pessimism. Bob is somewhat anxious and tense (ANX = 65T). He perceives that his ability to manage a job or to function in a work setting is compromised (WRK = 70T). Specifically, he believes that his work performance is adversely affected by concentration difficulties, worry, indecisiveness, and self-doubt. Bob's self-image currently includes a sense of inadequacy, ineffectiveness, and failure (LSE = 64T).

Scores on the supplementary scales were technically within normal limits. However, his marginally low score on Es (T = 42) suggests somewhat limited resources for adapting to life changes and coping with stress. Similarly, his T-score of 64 on A indicates a mild degree of general maladjustment.

CRITICAL ITEM INSPECTION

Bob responded "True" to item 71 ("These days I find it hard not to give up hope of amounting to something") and to item 146 ("I cry easily"). Further inquiry verified that Bob has been experiencing these problems since the loss of his job.

CASE DISPOSITION

The results of the neuropsychological evaluation, including the MMPI-2 findings, were discussed with Bob in a feedback session (Gass & Brown, 1992). The results of the examination were quite consistent with the difficulties that Bob had been experiencing, and he eagerly accepted the recommendation of psychological intervention on a weekly basis. The therapeutic goals consisted of helping Bob improve his morale, increase his sense of self-worth, and improve his social and work-related functioning. Bob responded quite well to his therapist and became readily engaged in the therapy process. Early in therapy, Bob indicated that he valued the process of being listened to, understood, and gently encouraged to pursue rewarding activities. Over the course of 3 months, his emotional status improved considerably as he began developing his repair work into a small business and, in addition, increasing his social and recreational activity. Through this process, his morale improved and he began to rediscover a more favorable image of himself.

RECOMMENDED READING

Butcher, J.N., & Williams, C.L. (1992). *Essentials of MMPI-2 and MMPI-A interpretation.* Minneapolis, MN: University of Minnesota Press.

Gass, C.S., & Ansley, J. (1995). Personality assessment of neurologically impaired patients. In J.N. Butcher (Ed.), *Clinical Personality Assessment: Practical Approaches* (pp. 192–210). New York: Oxford University Press.

Graham, J.R. (1993). *MMPI-2: Assessing personality and psychopathology* (Second edition). New York: Oxford University Press.

Reitan, R.M., & Wolfson, D. (1993). *The Halstead-Reitan Neuropsychological Test Battery: Theory and clinical interpretation.* Tucson, AZ: Neuropsychology Press.

Reitan, R.M., & Wolfson, D. (1997). Emotional disturbances and their interaction with neuropsychological deficits. *Neuropsychology Review, 7,* 3–19.

REFERENCES

Adams, R.D., & Victor, M. (1989). *Principles of neurology* (4th ed.). New York: McGraw-Hill.

Alexander, M.P. (1995). Mild traumatic brain injury: Pathophysiology, natural history, and clinical management. *Neurology, 45,* 1253–1260.

Alfano, D.P., Finlayson, M.A., Stearns, G.M., & Neilson, P.M. (1990). The MMPI and neurological dysfunction: Profile configuration and analysis. *Clinical Neuropsychologist, 4,* 69–79.

Alfano, D.P., Paniak, C.E., & Finlayson, A.J. (1993). The MMPI and closed head injury: A neurocorrective approach. *Neuropsychiatry, Neuropsychology, & Behavioral Neurology, 6,* 111–116.

Ansley, J., Gass, C.S., Brown, M.C., & Levin, B.E. (1995). Epileptic and non-epileptic seizure disorder: A comparison of MMPI-2 profile characteristics [Abstract]. *Journal of the International Neuropsychological Society, 1,* 135–136.

Arbisi, P.A., & Ben-Porath, Y.S. (1995). An MMPI-2 infrequent response scale for use with psychopathological populations: The infrequency-psychopathology scale, F(p). *Psychological Assessment, 7,* 424–431.

Baldwin, M.V. (1952). A clinic-experimental investigation into the psychologic aspects of multiple sclerosis. *Journal of Nervous and Mental Disease, 115,* 299–343.

Barrett, P., Putnam, S.H., Axelrod, B.N., & Rapport, L.J. (1998). Some statistical properties of 2 MMPI neurocorrection factors for individuals with closed head injury [Abstract]. *Archives of Clinical Neuropsychology, 13,* 16.

Barron, F. (1953). An ego strength scale which predicts response to psychotherapy. *Journal of Consulting Psychology, 17,* 327–333.

Beck, A.T., Ward, C., Mendelsohn, M., Mock, J., & Erbaugh, J. (1961). An inventory for measuring depression. *Archives of General Psychiatry, 4,* 561–571.

Bennett-Levy, J. (1984). Long-term effects of closed-head injury on memory: Evidence from a consecutive series of young adults. *Acta Neurologica Scandinavica, 70,* 285–298.

Ben-Porath, Y.S., Hostetler, K., Butcher, J.N., & Graham, J.R. (1989). New subscales for the MMPI-2 social introversion (Si) scale. *Psychological Assessment, 1,* 169–174.

Ben-Porath, Y.S., & Sherwood, N.E. (1993). *The MMPI-2 content component scales: Development, psychometric characteristics, and clinical application.* Minneapolis: University of Minnesota Press.

Berry, D.T.R., Wetter, M.W., Baer, R.A., Youngjohn, J.R., Gass, C.S., Lamb, D.G., Franzen, M.D., MacInnes, W.D., & Buchholz, D. (1995). Overreporting of closed-head injury symptoms on the MMPI-2. *Psychological Assessment, 7,* 517–523.

Binder, L.M. (1997). A review of mild head trauma. Part II: Clinical implications. *Journal of Clinical and Experimental Neuropsychology, 19,* 432–457.

Binder, L.M., Rohling, M.L., & Larrabee, G.L. (1997). A review of mild head trauma. Part I: Meta-analytic review of neuropsychological studies. *Journal of Clinical and Experimental Neuropsychology, 19,* 421–431.

Black, F.W. (1975). Unilateral brain lesions and MMPI performance: A preliminary study. *Perceptual and Motor Skills, 40,* 87–93.

Bornstein, R.A., & Kozora, E. (1990). Content bias of the MMPI Sc scale in neurologic patients. *Neuropsychiatry, Neuropsychology, & Behavioral Neurology, 3,* 200–205.

Bornstein, R.A., Miller, H.B., & van Schoor, T. (1989). Neuropsychological deficit and emotional disturbance in head-injured patients. *Journal of Neurosurgery, 70,* 500–513.

Brulot, M.M., Strauss, E., & Spellacy, F. (1997). Validity of the Minnesota multiphasic personality inventory-2 correction factors for use with patients with suspected head injury. *Clinical Neuropsychologist, 11,* 391–401.

Burke, J.M., Imhoff, C.L., & Kerrigan, M. (1990). MMPI correlates among post-acute TBI patients. *Brain Injury, 4,* 223–231.

Burke, J.M., Smith, S.A., & Imhoff, C.L. (1989). The response styles of post-acute traumatic brain-injured patients on the MMPI. *Brain Injury, 3,* 35–40.

Burt, D.B., Zembar, M.J., & Niederehe, G. (1995). Depression and memory impairment: A meta-analysis of the association, its pattern, and specificity. *Psychological Bulletin, 117,* 285–305.

Butcher, J.N. (1990). *The MMPI-2 in psychological treatment.* New York: Oxford University Press.

Butcher, J.N. (1995). Item content in the interpretation of the MMPI-2. In J.N. Butcher (Ed.), *Clinical personality assessment: Practical approaches* (pp. 302–316). New York: Oxford University Press.

Butcher, J.N., Dahlstrom, W.G., Graham, J.R., Tellegen, A., & Kaemmer, B. (1989). *MMPI-2 (Minnesota multiphasic personality inventory-2): Manual for administration and scoring.* Minneapolis: University of Minnesota Press.

Butcher, J.N., Graham, J.R., Williams, C.L., & Ben-Porath, Y.S. (1990). *Development and use of the MMPI-2 content scales.* Minneapolis: University of Minnesota Press.

Butcher, J.N., & Williams, C.L. (1992). *Essentials of MMPI-2 and MMPI-A interpretation.* Minneapolis: University of Minnesota Press.

Calsyn, D.A., Louks, J.L., & Johnson, J.S. (1982). MMPI correlates of the degree of generalized impairment based on the Halstead-Reitan battery. *Perceptual and Motor Skills, 55,* 1099–1102.

Christensen, B.K., Ross, T.P., Kotasek, M., Rosenthal, M., & Henry, R.R. (1995). *Factor structure of the Beck depression inventory in a sample of persons with traumatic brain injury.* Poster session presented at the 23rd annual meeting of the International Neuropsychological Society, Seattle, WA.

Comrey, A.L. (1958). A factor analysis of items on the MMPI psychasthenia scale. *Educational and Psychological Measurement, 18,* 99–107.

Connor, B., Ogden, M.L., Waller, K., Cullum, C.M., & Frohman, E.M. (1998). MMPI-2 interpretation and multiple sclerosis [Abstract]. *Archives of Clinical Neuropsychology, 13,* 109.

Cripe, L.I. (1989). Neuropsychological and psychosocial assessment of the brain-injured person: Clinical concepts and guidelines. *Rehabilitation Psychology, 34,* 93–100.

Cripe, L.I. (1996). The MMPI in neuropsychological assessment: A murky measure. *Applied Neuropsychology, 3,* 97–103.

Cripe, L.I., Gass, C.S., Greene, R., Perry, W., & Zillmer, E. (1997). *Using the MMPI-2 in neuropsychology.* Symposium conducted at the 17th annual National Academy of Neuropsychology Conference, Las Vegas, NV.

Cripe, L.I., Maxwell, J.K., & Hill, E. (1995). Multivariate discriminant function analysis of neurologic, pain, and psychiatric patients with the MMPI. *Journal of Clinical Psychology, 51,* 258–268.

Cullum, C.M., & Bigler, E.D. (1988). Short-form MMPI findings in patients with predominantly lateralized cerebral lesions. *Journal of Nervous and Mental Disease, 176,* 332–342.

Dahlstrom, W.G., Welsh, G.S., & Dahlstrom, L.E. (1972). *An MMPI handbook: Clinical interpretation* (Vol. 1, 2nd ed.). Minneapolis: University of Minnesota Press.

Derogatis, L.R. (1977). *SCL-R administration, scoring, and procedures manual.* Baltimore: Clinical Psychometrics Research Unit, Johns Hopkins School of Medicine.

Derry, P.A., Harnadek, M.C., McLachlan, R.S., & Sontrop, J. (1997). Influence of seizure content on interpreting psychopathology on the MMPI-2 in patients with epilepsy. *Journal of Clinical and Experimental Neuropsychology, 19,* 396–404.

Devinsky, O. (1992). *Behavioral neurology.* St. Louis, MO: Mosby Year Book.

Dikmen, S., & Reitan, R.M. (1974a). Minnesota multiphasic personality inventory correlates of dysphasic language disturbances. *Journal of Abnormal Psychology, 83,* 675–679.

Dikmen, S., & Reitan, R.M. (1974b). MMPI correlates of localized cerebral lesions. *Perceptual and Motor Skills, 39,* 831–840.

Dikmen, S., & Reitan, R.M. (1977). MMPI correlates of adaptive ability deficits in patients with brain lesions. *Journal of Nervous and Mental Disease, 165,* 247–254.

Dikmen, S., Reitan, R.M., Temkin, N.R., & Machemer, J.E. (1992). Minor and severe head injury emotional sequelae. *Brain Injury, 6,* 477–478.

Drake, L.E. (1946). A social I.E. scale for the MMPI. *Journal of Applied Psychology, 30,* 51–54.

Dunn, J.T., & Lees-Haley, P.R. (1995). The MMPI-2 correction factor for closed-head injury: A caveat for forensic cases. *Assessment, 2,* 47–51.

Edwards, D.W., Holmquist, L., Wanless, R., Wicks, J., & Davis, C. (1998). Comparing three methods of "neuro-correction" for the MMPI-2 [Abstract]. *Journal of the International Neuropsychological Society, 4,* 27–28.

Edwards, D.W., Weissman, H.N., & Morrison, T.L. (1993). "Neuro-corrected items" on the MMPI-2: Endorsement rates in a psychiatric sample [Abstract]. *Archives of Clinical Neuropsychology, 9,* 125–126.

Farr, S.P., & Martin, P.W. (1988). Neuropsychological dysfunction. In R.L. Greene (Ed.), *The MMPI: Use with specific populations* (pp. 214–245). Philadelphia: Grune & Stratton.

Faust, D. (1986). Research on human judgment and its application to clinical practice. *Professional Psychology: Research and Practice, 17,* 420–430.

Folstein, M.F., Maiberger, R., & McHugh, P.R. (1977). Mood disorder as a specific complication of stroke. *Journal of Neurology, Neurosurgery, and Psychiatry, 40,* 1018–1020.

Fordyce, D.J., Rouche, J.R., & Prigatano, G.P. (1983). Enhanced emotional reactions in chronic head trauma patients. *Journal of Neurology, Neurosurgery, and Psychiatry, 46,* 620–624.

Garb, H.N. (1998). *Studying the clinician: Judgment research and psychological assessment.* Washington, DC: American Psychological Association.

Gasparrini, W.G., Satz, P., Heilman, K.M., & Coolidge, F.L. (1978). Hemispheric asymmetries of affecting processing as determined by the MMPI. *Journal of Neurology, Neurosurgery, and Psychiatry, 41,* 470–473.

Gasquonine, P.G. (1997). Postconcussion symptoms. *Neuropsychology Review, 7,* 77–86.

Gass, C.S. (1991a). Emotional variables in neuropsychological test performance. *Journal of Clinical Psychology, 47,* 100–104.

Gass, C.S. (1991b). MMPI-2 interpretation and closed-head injury: A correction factor. *Psychological Assessment, 3,* 27–31.

Gass, C.S. (1992). MMPI-2 interpretation of patients with cerebrovascular disease: A correction factor. *Archives of Clinical Neuropsychology, 7,* 17–27.

Gass, C.S. (1996a). MMPI-2 interpretation and stroke: Cross-validation of a correction factor. *Journal of Clinical Psychology, 52,* 569–572.

Gass, C.S. (1996b). MMPI-2 variables in attention and memory test performance. *Psychological Assessment, 8,* 135–138.

Gass, C.S. (1997, June 5). *Assessing patients with neurological impairments.* Presented at the University of Minnesota MMPI-2 Clinical Workshops & Symposia, Minneapolis.

Gass, C.S. (1998). *MMPI-2 correction factor validity and closed-head injury: A response to Brulot, Strauss, and Spellacy.* Manuscript submitted for publication.

Gass, C.S., & Ansley, J. (1994). MMPI correlates of poststroke neurobehavioral deficits. *Archives of Clinical Neuropsychology, 9,* 461–469.

Gass, C.S., & Ansley, J. (1995). Personality assessment of neurologically impaired patients. In J.N. Butcher (Ed.), *Clinical personality assessment: Practical approaches* (pp. 192–210). New York: Oxford University Press.

Gass, C.S., Ansley, J., & Boyette, S. (1994). Emotional correlates of fluency test and maze performance. *Journal of Clinical Psychology, 50,* 586–590.

Gass, C.S., & Apple, C. (1997). Cognitive complaints in closed-head injury: Relationship to memory test performance and emotional disturbance. *Journal of Clinical and Experimental Neuropsychology, 19,* 290–299.

Gass, C.S., & Brown, M.C. (1992). Neuropsychological test feedback to patients with brain dysfunction. *Psychological Assessment, 4,* 272–277.

Gass, C.S., & Daniel, S.K. (1990). Emotional impact on trail making test performance. *Psychological Reports, 67,* 435–438.

Gass, C.S., & Freshwater, S. (1999). MMPI-2 symptom disclosure and cognitive complaints in a closed-head injury sample [Abstract]. *Archives of Clinical Neuropsychology, 14,* 29–30.

Gass, C.S., & Lawhorn, L. (1991). Psychological adjustment following stroke: An MMPI study. *Psychological Assessment, 3,* 628–633.

Gass, C.S., Luis, C.A., Rayls, K., & Mittenberg, W.B. (1999). Psychological status and its influences in acute traumatic brain injury: An MMPI-2 study. *Archives of Clinical Neuropsychology, 14,* 30.

Gass, C.S., & Russell, E.W. (1985). MMPI correlates of verbal-intellectual deficits in patients with left hemisphere lesions. *Journal of Clinical Psychology, 41,* 664–670.

Gass, C.S., & Russell, E.W. (1986a). Differential impact of brain damage and depression on memory test performance. *Journal of Consulting & Clinical Psychology, 54,* 261–263.

Gass, C.S., & Russell, E.W. (1986b). MMPI correlates of lateralized cerebral lesions and aphasic deficits. *Journal of Consulting & Clinical Psychology, 54,* 359–363.

Gass, C.S., & Russell, E.W. (1987). MMPI correlates of performance intellectual deficits in patients with right hemisphere lesions. *Journal of Clinical Psychology, 43,* 484–489.

Gass, C.S., & Russell, E.W. (1991). MMPI profiles of closed-head trauma patients: Impact of neurologic complaints. *Journal of Clinical Psychology, 47,* 253–260.

Gass, C.S., Russell, E.W., & Hamilton, R.A. (1990). Accuracy of MMPI-based inferences regarding memory and concentration in closed-head trauma. *Psychological Assessment, 2,* 175–178.

Gass, C.S., & Wald, H. (1997). MMPI-2 interpretation and closed-head trauma: Cross-validation of a correction factor. *Archives of Clinical Neuropsychology, 12,* 199–205.

Golden, C.J. (1979). *Clinical interpretation of objective psychological tests.* New York: Grune & Stratton.

Gough, H.G. (1950). The F minus K dissimulation index for the MMPI. *Journal of Consulting Psychology, 14,* 408–413.

Gough, H.G., McClosky, H., & Meehl, P.E. (1952). A personality scale for social responsibility. *Journal of Abnormal and Social Psychology, 47,* 73–80.

Graham, J.R. (1993). *MMPI-2: Assessing personality and psychopathology* (2nd ed.). New York: Oxford University Press.

Graham, J.R. (1997, June 4). *Interpretation of MMPI-2 code types.* Presented at the University of Minnesota MMPI-2 Clinical Workshops & Symposia, Minneapolis.

Graham, J.R., Ben-Porath, Y.S., & McNulty, J.L. (1997). Empirical correlates of low scores on MMPI-2 scales in an outpatient mental health setting. *Psychological Assessment, 9,* 386–391.

Graham, J.R., Watts, D., & Timbrook, R.E. (1991). Detecting fake-good and fake-bad MMPI-2 profiles. *Journal of Personality Assessment, 57,* 264–277.

Grant, I., & Alves, W. (1987). Psychiatric and psychosocial disturbances in head injury. In H.S. Levin, J. Grafman, & H.M. Eisenberg (Eds.), *Neurobehavioral recovery from head injury* (pp. 232–261). New York: Oxford University Press.

Groth-Marnat, G. (1999). *Handbook of psychological assessment* (3rd ed. rev.). New York: Wiley.

Greene, R.L., Gwin, R., & Staal, M. (1997). Current status of MMPI-2 research: A methodologic overview. *Journal of Personality Assessment, 68,* 20–36.

Greene, R.L., Weed, N.C., Butcher, J.N., Arrendondo, R., & Davis, H.G. (1992). A cross-validation of MMPI-2 substance abuse scales. *Journal of Personality Assessment, 58,* 405–410.

Greiffenstein, M.F., Gola, T., & Baker, W.J. (1995). MMPI-2 validity scales versus domain specific measures in detection of factitious traumatic brain injury. *Clinical Neuropsychologist, 9,* 230–240.

Harris, R., & Lingoes, J. (1955, 1968). *Subscales for the Minnesota multiphasic personality inventory.* Mimeographed materials. Los Angeles, CA: The Langley Porter Clinic.

Hathaway, S.R., & McKinley, J.C. (1940). A multiphasic personality schedule (Minnesota): I. Construction of the schedule. *Journal of Psychology, 10,* 249–254.

Heaton, R.K., Baade, L.E., & Johnson, K.L. (1978). Neuropsychological test results associated with psychiatric disorders in adults. *Psychological Bulletin, 85,* 141–162.

Heaton, R.K., & Crowley, T.J. (1981). Effects of psychiatric disorders and their somatic treatments on neuropsychological test results. In S.B. Filskov & T.J. Boll (Eds.), *Handbook of clinical neuropsychology* (Vol. 1, pp. 481–525). New York: Wiley Interscience.

Helmes, E., & Reddon, J.R. (1993). A perspective on developments in assessing psychopathology: A critical review of the MMPI and MMPI-2. *Psychological Bulletin, 113,* 453–471.

Herrman, E.J., Dorfman, W.I., Roth, L., & Burns, W.J. (1997). *Utility of the MMPI-2 with a geropsychiatric population: Comparison of four formats.* Unpublished manuscript.

Hjemboe, S., Almagor, M., & Butcher, J.N. (1992). Empirical assessment of marital distress: The marital distress scale (MDS) for the MMPI-2. In C.D. Spielberger & J.N. Butcher (Eds.), *Advances in personality assessment* (Vol. 9, pp. 141–152). Hillsdale, NJ: Erlbaum.

Kalmar, K., Cicerone, K., & Giacino, J. (1996). Persistent post-concussion syndrome: A distinct disorder, or part of a general distress syndrome identified with the MMPI [Abstract]? *Archives of Clinical Neuropsychology, 11,* 405.

Keane, T.M., Malloy, P.F., & Fairbank, J.A. (1984). Empirical development of an MMPI subscale for the assessment of combat-related posttraumatic stress disorder. *Journal of Consulting & Clinical Psychology, 52,* 888–891.

Kendall, P.C., Edinger, J., & Eberly, C. (1978). Taylor's MMPI correction for spinal cord injury: Empirical endorsement. *Journal of Consulting and Clinical Psychology, 46,* 370–371.

Kinderman, S.S., & Brown, G.G. (1997). Depression and memory in the elderly: A meta-analysis. *Journal of Clinical and Experimental Neuropsychology, 19,* 625–642.

Koss, M.P., & Butcher, J.N. (1973). A comparison of psychiatric patients' self-report with other sources of clinical information. *Journal of Research in Personality, 7,* 225–236.

Lachar, D., & Wrobel, T.A. (1979). Validating clinicians' hunches: Construction of a new MMPI critical item set. *Journal of Consulting and Clinical Psychology, 46,* 277–284.

Larrabee, G.J. (1997). Somatic malingering on the MMPI/MMPI-2 in litigating subjects [Abstract]. *Archives of Clinical Neuropsychology, 12,* 353–354.

Lees-Haley, P.R. (1997). MMPI-2 base rates for 492 personal injury plaintiffs: Implications and challenges for forensic assessment. *Journal of Clinical Psychology, 53,* 745–755.

Lees-Haley, P.R., Smith, H.H., Williams, C.W., & Dunn, J.T. (1996). Forensic neuropsychological test usage: An empirical survey. *Archives of Clinical Neuropsychology, 11,* 45–52.

Leininger, B.E., Kreutzer, J.S., & Hill, M.R. (1991). Comparison of minor and severe head injury emotional sequelae using the MMPI. *Brain Injury, 5,* 199–205.

Levin, H.S., Mattis, S., Ruff, R.M., Eisenberg, H.M., Marshall, L.F., Tabbador, K., High, W.M. Jr., & Frankowski, R.F. (1987). Neurobehavioral outcome of minor head injury: A three center study. *Journal of Neuroscience, 66,* 234–243.

Lezak, M.D. (1995). *Neuropsychological assessment* (3rd ed.). New York: Oxford University Press.

MacAndrew, C. (1965). The differentiation of male alcoholic out-patients from nonalcoholic psychiatric patients by means of the MMPI. *Quarterly Journal of Studies on Alcohol, 26,* 238–246.

Marsh, G., Hirsch, S., & Leung, G. (1982). Use and misuse of the MMPI in multiple sclerosis. *Psychological Reports, 51,* 1127–1134.

Mateer, C.A., Sohlberg, M.M., & Crinean, J. (1987). Perceptions of memory function in individuals with closed-head injury. *Journal of Head Trauma Rehabilitation, 2,* 74–84.

McCaffrey, R.J., & Lynch, J.K. (1996). Survey of the educational backgrounds and specialty training of instructors of clinical neuropsychology in APA-approved graduate training programs: A 10-year follow-up. *Archives of Clinical Neuropsychology, 11,* 11–19.

Meehl, P.E. (1945). The dynamics of "structured" personality tests. *Journal of Clinical Psychology, 1,* 296–303.

Meehl, P.E., & Hathaway, S.R. (1946). The K factor as a suppresser variable in the MMPI. *Journal of Applied Psychology, 30,* 525–564.

Megargee, E.I., Cook, P.E., & Mendelsohn, G.A. (1967). Development and validation of an MMPI scale of assaultiveness in overcontrolled individuals. *Journal of Abnormal Psychology, 72,* 519–528.

Meyerink, L.H., Reitan, R.M., & Selz, M. (1988). The validity of the MMPI with multiple sclerosis patients. *Journal of Clinical Psychology, 44,* 764–769.

Millon, T. (1987). *Manual for the MCMI-II* (2nd ed.). Minneapolis: National Computer Systems.

Millon, T. (1994). *Millon clinical multiaxial inventory-III manual.* Minneapolis: National Computer Systems.

Mittenberg, W., Tremont, G., & Rayls, K.R. (1996). Impact of cognitive function on MMPI-2 validity in neurologically impaired patients. *Assessment, 3,* 157–163.

Mueller, S.R., & Girace, M. (1988). Use and misuse of the MMPI, a reconsideration. *Psychological Reports, 63,* 483–491.

Nadolne, M.J., Hoffman, R.G., Tremont, G., Scott, J.G., & Adams, R.L. (1997). Effects of head injury severity and litigation on self-reported post-concussion symptoms [Abstract]. *Archives of Clinical Neuropsychology, 12,* 374–375.

Nelson, L.D., & Adams, K.M. (1997). Challenges for neuropsychology in the treatment and rehabilitation of brain-injured patients. *Psychological Assessment, 9,* 368–373.

Nelson, L.D., & Do, T. (1998). Using the MMPI-2 in patients with multiple sclerosis [Abstract]. *Archives of Clinical Neuropsychology, 13,* 92.

Netto, D. (1997). *Brain injury and the MMPI-2: Neuro-correction for Hispanics.* Unpublished doctoral dissertation, Nova Southeastern University, Fort Lauderdale, FL.

Oddy, M., Humphrey, M., & Uttley, D. (1978). Stresses upon the relatives of head-injured patients. *British Journal of Psychiatry, 133,* 507–513.

O'Donnell, W.E., DeSoto, C.B., DeSoto, J.L., & Reynolds, D. McQ. (1995). *Neuropsychological impairment scale (NIS): Manual.* Los Angeles: Western Psychological Services.

Paniak, C.E., & Miller, H.B. (1993). Utility of the MMPI-2 validity scales with brain injury survivors [Abstract]. *Archives of Clinical Neuropsychology, 9,* 172.

Parikh, R.M., Robinson, R.G., & Price, T.R. (1988). Disability and rehabilitation after stroke. *Stroke, 19,* 1055.

Pope, K.S., Butcher, J.N., & Seelen, J. (1993). *The MMPI, MMPI-2, and MMPI-A in court.* Washington, DC: American Psychological Association.

Prigatano, G.P. (1987). Personality and psychosocial consequences after head injury. In M. Meier, A. Benton, & L. Diller (Eds.), *Neuropsychological rehabilitation* (pp. 355–378). New York: Plenum Press.

Prigatano, G.P., & Altman, I.M. (1990). Impaired awareness of behavioral limitations after traumatic brain injury. *Archives of Physical Medicine Rehabilitation, 71,* 1058–1064.

Putnam, S.H., Kurtz, J.E., Adams, K.M., Millis, S.R., Fichtenberg, N.L., & O'Leary, J.F. (1995). MMPI-2 neurotic triad configurations among a TBI sample [Abstract]. *Clinical Neuropsychologist, 9,* 295.

Putnam, S.H., Kurtz, J.E., Fichtenberg, N.L., O'Leary, J.F., & Adams, K.M. (1995). MMPI-2 correlates of unexpected cognitive deterioration in traumatic brain injury [Abstract]. *Clinical Neuropsychologist, 9,* 296.

Rattok, J., Ross, B., & Ohry, A. (1995). The use of the SCL-90-R with the traumatically head injured [Abstract]. *Journal of the International Neuropsychological Society, 1,* 213.

Rayls, K., Mittenberg, W.B., Burns, W.J., & Theroux, S. (1997). Longitudinal analysis of the MMPI-2 neurocorrection factor in mild head trauma [Abstract]. *Archives of Clinical Neuropsychology, 12,* 390–391.

Reitan, R.M. (1976). Neurological and physiological bases of psychopathology. *Annual Review of Psychology, 27,* 275–284.

Reitan, R.M., & Wolfson, D. (1993). *The Halstead-Reitan neuropsychological test battery: Theory and clinical interpretation* (2nd ed.). Tucson, AZ: Neuropsychology Press.

Reitan, R.M., & Wolfson, D. (1997). Emotional disturbances and their interaction with neuropsychological deficits. *Neuropsychology Review, 7,* 3–19.

Richards, P.M., & Ruff, R.M. (1989). Motivational effects on neuropsychological functioning: Comparison of depressed versus nondepressed individuals. *Journal of Consulting and Clinical Psychology, 57,* 396–402.

Ross, S.R., Putnam, S.H., Gass, C.S., & Adams, K.M. (1997, June 8). *MMPI-2 predictors of cognitive test performance in traumatic brain injury.* Presented at the University of Minnesota MMPI-2 Clinical Workshops & Symposia, Minneapolis.

Russell, E.W., Neuringer, C., & Goldstein, G. (1970). *Assessment of brain damage: A neuropsychological key approach.* New York: Wiley Interscience.

Russell, S.K., & Russell, E.W. (1997). Using the MCMI in neuropsychological evaluations. In T. Millon (Ed.), *The Millon inventories: Clinical and personality assessment* (pp. 154–172). New York: Guilford Press.

Sinyor, P., Jacques, P., Kaloupek, D., Becker, R., Goldenberg, M., & Coopersmith, H. (1986). Post-stroke depression and lesion location: An attempted replication. *Brain, 109,* 537–546.

Spanier, G.B., & Filsinger, E.E. (1983). The dyadic adjustment scale. In E.E. Filsinger (Ed.), *Marriage and family assessment* (pp. 155–168). Beverly Hills, CA: Sage.

Speilberger, C.D., Gorsuch, R.L., & Luschene, R.E. (1971). *Manual for the state-trait anxiety inventory.* Palo Alto, CA: Consulting Psychologists Press.

Suhr, J., Tranel, D., Wefel, J., & Barrash, J. (1997). Memory performance after head injury: Contributions of malingering, litigation status, psychological factors, and medication use. *Journal of Clinical and Experimental Neuropsychology, 19,* 500–514.

Tellegen, A. (1988). The analysis of consistency in personality assessment. *Journal of Personality, 56,* 621–663.

Thomsen, I.V. (1989). Do young patients have worse outcomes after severe blunt head trauma? *Brain Injury, 3,* 157–162.

Wasserman, J.D., & Black, F.W. (1993). *MMPI outcome and severity of closed-head injury.* Paper presented at the 13th annual National Academy of Neuropsychology Conference, Phoenix, AZ.

Wechsler, D. (1981). *Manual for the Wechsler adult intelligence scale-revised (WAIS-R).* San Antonio, TX: The Psychological Corporation.

Weed, N.C., Butcher, J.N., Ben-Porath, Y.S., & McKenna, T. (1992). New measures for assessing alcohol and drug abuse with the MMPI-2: The APS and AAS. *Journal of Personality Assessment, 58,* 389–404.

Weiner, D.N. (1947). Differences between the individual and group forms of the MMPI. *Journal of Consulting Psychology, 11,* 104–106.

Weins, A.N., & Matarazzo, J.D. (1977). WAIS and MMPI correlates of the Halstead-Reitan neuropsychological battery in normal male subjects. *Journal of Nervous and Mental Disease, 164,* 112–121.

Welsh, G.S. (1956). Factor dimensions A and R. In G.S. Welsh & W.G. Dahlstrom (Eds.), *Basic readings on the MMPI in psychology and medicine.* Minneapolis: University of Minnesota Press.

Wiggins, J.S. (1973). *Personality and prediction: Principles of personality assessment.* Reading, MA: Addison-Wesley.

Woessner, R., & Caplan, B. (1995). Affective disorders following mild to moderate brain injury: Interpretive hazards of the SCL-90-R. *Journal of Head Trauma Rehabilitation, 10,* 78–89.

Woessner, R., & Caplan, B. (1996). Emotional distress following stroke: Interpretive limitations of the SCL-90-R. *Assessment, 3,* 291–306.

Wooten, A.J. (1983). MMPI profiles among neuropsychology patients. *Journal of Clinical Psychology, 39,* 392–406.

Yesavage, J.A., Brink, T.I., Rose, T.L., Lum, O., Huang, V., Adey, M., & Leirer, V.O. (1983). Development and validation of a geriatric depression screening scale: A preliminary report. *Journal of Psychiatric Research, 17,* 37–49.

Youngjohn, J.R., Burrows, L., & Erdal, K. (1995). Brain damage or compensation neurosis? The controversial post-concussive syndrome. *Clinical Neuropsychologist, 9,* 595–598.

Youngjohn, J.R., Davis, D., & Wolf, I. (1997). Head injury and the MMPI-2: Paradoxical severity effects and the influence of litigation. *Psychological Assessment, 9,* 177–184.

Zung, W.W. (1965). A self-rating depression scale. *Archives of General Psychiatry, 12,* 63–70.

Zung, W.W. (1971). A rating instrument for anxiety disorders. *Psychosomatics, 12,* 371–379.

PART FOUR

INTEGRATION OF TEST RESULTS

Chapter 15

NEUROPSYCHOLOGICAL ASSESSMENT AND TREATMENT PLANNING

Carolyn M. Lemsky

Clinical neuropsychology has evolved from lesion localization, through differential diagnosis, and toward the application of neuropsychological methods in treatment planning and therapeutic interventions. Despite this evolution and despite the fact that neuropsychologists have become well-accepted members of rehabilitation treatment teams, their role still remains poorly defined (Diller, 1994; Johnstone & Callahan, 1996; Nelson & Adams, 1997). Neuropsychologists bring knowledge of brain-behavior relationship and well-developed measurement strategies, as well as an understanding of coping styles and psychopathology to rehabilitation settings. Given the growth of neuropsychology positions in rehabilitation settings (Willer & Corrigan, 1994) the services neuropsychologists provide are seen as beneficial to the development, implementation, and evaluation of treatment plans.

There is little consensus about the role of neuropsychologists in rehabilitation (see reviews in Diller, 1994 and Nelson & Adams, 1997), but there are some points of general agreement. The most popular assertion is that neuropsychologists lend their expertise in brain-behavior relationships to help treatment teams better understand the condition of their patients. Neuropsychologists have also generated theoretical models and treatment paradigms that have proven useful in the development of rehabilitation in acquired brain injury. The behavioral, psychometric, and research expertise of psychologists has been essential to outcomes research. Additionally, the use of single case and behavioral methodologies in the rehabilitation literature provides evidence of the presence of psychologists both as practitioners and as consultants to other fields. While other rehabilitation team members may participate in counseling, psychologists are also primary providers of psychological assessment, psychotherapy, and family therapy.

Knowledge of brain-behavior relationships is useful, but what is invaluable to the treatment team is the ability to predict functional impairment and guide treatment efforts. When discussing the application of psychometric assessment in rehabilitation settings, many authors have noted the existing gap between information gleaned through neuropsychological assessment and the information needed to predict everyday functioning and plan treatment efforts (e.g., K.D. Cicerone & Tupper, 1991; Fordyce, 1994; Johnstone & Callahan, 1996; Sbordone, 1991; Stuss, Mateer, & Sohlberg, 1994). This is a survival issue for clinical neuropsychologists because, in many clinical settings, neuropsychological assessments are useful only if they provide guidance for treatment planning in addition to diagnosis (Long, 1996). This is consistent with surveys indicating that neuropsychological assessment reports are often overly technical and, even after pages of descriptive information, may offer little in the way of practical advice (Tallent, 1993). Writing readable and useful reports is critical to rehabilitation neuropsychology since cognitive rehabilitation is best accomplished by interdisciplinary teams who are expert in involving the families, employers, and others who share the lives of rehabilitation participants. To be effective, neuropsychologists must not only be able to assess cognitive impairments, but to transmit this information to the persons to whom it will be most useful.

Faced with the relatively new goal of treatment planning, neuropsychologists are now more frequently seeking information about the ecological validity of assessment procedures that may originally have been developed for lesion localization or discrimination between clinical groups (Johnstone & Callahan, 1996; Sbordone, 1991). Many common neuropsychological measures demonstrate poor ecological validity. For example, it is widely agreed that formal measures of executive functioning and attention may not reflect impairments in day-to-day living because they are administered in a structured assessment session that may compensate for a client's deficits in initiating, monitoring, and redirecting their behavior (see Chapter 13). Similarly, measures of attention conducted as a part of traditional neuropsychological batteries have frequently been criticized for their poor ecological validity (Johnstone & Callahan, 1996; Sloan & Ponsford, 1996). In addition, some of the most popular working memory and attention tasks may be confounded by verbal, mathematical, or motoric requirements in addition to attention (Sohlberg & Mateer, 1989). It has been hypothesized that the high level of structure, relatively brief duration, and simplified environment provided in most neuropsychological examinations can mask attentional deficits that prove to be of great functional significance in real life settings (Ponsford & Kinsella, 1992). As a result, many neuropsychologists have suggested that the richest source of information about attentional processes may come from the qualitative aspects of test performance and behavioral observations during testing rather than from actual test scores (Stuss, 1991).

In contrast, there is ample data in many cognitive domains to support the use of neuropsychological measures to predict functional independence (Sbordone & Long, 1996). However, even when studies show strong correlations between functional activities, neuropsychologists must rely on clinical judgment when evaluating individual cases. For this reason, many authors have called for the use of functional assessments in rehabilitation settings (Parenté & Herrmann, 1996; Prigatano, 1996; Sloan & Ponsford, 1996; Sohlberg & Mateer, 1989; Wilson, 1997).

Despite the relevance of functional assessments, data collection in the natural environment can be quite costly. Ecological validity is therefore as difficult to evaluate with psychometric rigor as it is to reconcile with the economic and human demands of most clinical settings (Sbordone & Long, 1996). When in vivo assessment is not practical, assessment of functional status through interviews and self-report measures completed with clients and care providers has been shown to have good clinical utility (Crew & Dijkers, 1995). It has become customary in many rehabilitation, medical, and geriatric settings to include these kinds of measures in a comprehensive neuropsychological evaluation.

Over the past decade, neuropsychologists have begun to develop measurement strategies to address the need for information about cognitive functioning in day-to-day situations along with the behavioral sequela of brain injury. Unfortunately, some of these measures (e.g., The Rivermead Behavioral Memory Test; Wilson, Cockburn, & Baddeley, 1985, and the Behavioral Assessment of the Dysexecutive Syndrome; Wilson, Alderman, Burgess, Emslie, & Evans, 1996) have sacrificed desirable psychometric scaling properties to resemble functional tasks. While they should generally not be used to determine the presence of neurocognitive impairment, measures of this type are certainly useful in describing deficits in reference to an individual's functional status (Spreen & Strauss, 1998).

Recent discussions of neuropsychological rehabilitation generally include reference to the need to obtain information about functional status prior to planning interventions (e.g., Kreutzer & Wehman, 1991; Parenté & Herrmann, 1996; Ponsford & Sloan, 1995; Sohlberg & Mateer, 1989; Wilson, 1997). The precise nature of the functional assessment differs across authors, disability groups, deficits, and treatment orientations, but there are several common themes. First, cognitive impairments exist in a matrix of personal, social, physical, and environmental factors that interact in unpredictable ways. For this reason, it is necessary to evaluate how an individual understands their cognitive functioning and how their cognitive functioning affects their ability to meet particular environmental demands. For example, the finding of constructional dyspraxia is likely to have very different consequences for an architect as opposed to a psychologist. Second, the personal relevance of a treatment goal to a client may cause it to take priority in treatment planning. Sometimes this means working with a client to attempt remediation of a cognitive impairment—even when success is considered unlikely—until the client is willing to accept compensatory strategies as a part of the treatment plan. Third, although self-report is important, the perspective of others in the individual's environment should also be considered. Finally, functional assessment should be informed by neuropsychological test performances. For example, findings of an impairment of attention on a particular measure may lead to an exploration of how this test performance relates to functioning in a particular environment or on a particular task.

It is difficult to clearly delineate how neuropsychological data can be used to inform treatment decisions. Some authors have suggested that, in fact, this process is ideographic, resting on the laurels of clinical experience and expert judgment (Johnstone & Callahan, 1996). What is implied by several authors, but not directly stated, is that areas of deficit as defined in neuropsychological examinations should be used to direct efforts toward functional assessment by identifying the nature and extent of damage to specific cognitive systems. This approach makes sense, since, expensive as they are, neuropsychological evaluations are often less expensive than the person-hours required to complete exhaustive evaluations of day-to-day functioning.

To complicate the process of making treatment recommendations based upon neuropsychological data, treatments for persons with neurocognitive impairment are relatively new in that they have experienced their greatest growth over the past 15 years. Although the clinical application of cognitive neuroscience is moving rapidly forward, there is still relatively little evidence to substantiate the success of many specific cognitive remediation strategies (Cope, 1995; Wilson, 1997). Holistic treatment approaches for persons with acquired brain injury show promise, but the long-term outcome data are only newly collected and research to determine the active ingredients of comprehensive programs is limited (Ashley, Persel, Clark, & Krych, 1997; Carney, et al., 1999; Ponsford, Oliver, & Curran, 1995; Prigatano, 1997).

During the past several years, the need for guidelines for the delivery of cognitive rehabilitation have received the attention of national organizations. The Head Injury Interdisciplinary Special Interest Group of the American Congress of Rehabilitation (ACRM) has published ethical and clinical guidelines (Head Injury Special Interest Group of the American Congress of Rehabilitation Medicine, 1992). In October 1998, the National Institutes of Health (NIH) held a consensus conference on the Rehabilitation of Persons with Traumatic Brain Injury. In 1999, ACRM will formulate clinical guidelines for cognitive rehabilitation based upon available empirical research. Clinicians practicing in this area should be well aware of the information contained in these documents as they are published.

Study of individual and group psychotherapy and behavioral interventions in persons with cognitive impairments is also a relatively new pursuit. Systematic approaches were first described as a part of the milieu therapies offered by Yehuda Ben-Yishay and Leonard Diller for patients with head injury near Tel Aviv in the mid-1970s (Ben-Yishay & Prigatano, 1990). Group interventions are fairly well established as a treatment of choice for persons with acquired brain injuries, particularly those with impaired awareness. There is also a growing body of knowledge delineating the relationship between insight, psychiatric symptoms, and behavioral difficulties, but the understanding of how lesion location affects psychotherapy is still in the earliest stages of exploration (Prigatano, 1994).

Even though much of the knowledge related to assessment and treatment planning is newly emerging, neuropsychologists have much to offer to the process of treatment planning. This chapter introduces the bodies of knowledge relevant to the process of treatment planning for adults with acquired neurocognitive impairment. The intention is to illustrate the scope of basic information that can be used to formulate treatment recommendations. A brief review of models of cognitive rehabilitation and treatments developed for specific areas of cognitive functioning as well as some recent research findings are presented. The use of cognitive data to make recommendations about driving and vocational placement are also discussed. The majority of research in the area of cognitive rehabilitation was conducted with persons with stroke and traumatic brain injury. Where available, information about treatment of persons with cognitive disorders of other etiologies is presented. Information about facilitating adjustment in persons with cognitive impairment also is addressed.

A table of suggestions for treatment planning will be provided at the end of many of the sections describing clinical interventions. These suggestions may be used in report writing. However, it is strongly recommended that the neuropsychologist using them spend time in treatment settings to ensure that their recommendations are both practical and appropriate. Although the process of treatment planing often begins with recommendations from an evaluating professional, the process continues with the patient, family, and treatment team working together. This enables the development of goals that are realistic when the individual's desires, needs, resources, and environment are considered. As the practitioner becomes more familiar with individuals providing the treatment as well as the treatments being provided, treatment reports and recommendations may become more relevant. It is highly recommended to get feedback on the utility of treatment recommendations from the consumers of written reports. Table 15.1 summarizes these considerations in a model for the integration of patient-related data, clinical knowledge areas, and categories of treatment planning.

Table 15.1. Model for neuropsychological assessment and treatment planning

Sources of Patient Data	Clinical Knowledge Areas	Treatment Recommendations
Standardized neuropsy-chological tests	Models of cognitive rehabilitation	Cognitive remediation
Behavioral observations	Research on treatment outcomes:	Compensation for cognitive impairment
Self, caregivers, profession-als, others	Memory and learning	
	Verbal functions	Behavioral interventions
Interviews (patient and others)	Mental activities (processing speed)	Vocational re-entry
Records (medical, educa-tional, etc.)	Visual/spatial perceptual	Driving
	Executive functioning	
	Awareness	Facilitating adjustment
Behavioral analysis	Milieu/comprehensive programs	Family intervention
History	Behavioral modification	Community resources
	Psychotherapy/family therapy	
	Adjustment to disability	
	Ecological validity of neuropsy-chological tests	

MODELS OF COGNITIVE REHABILITATION

Wilson (1995) defines cognitive rehabilitation as "... a process whereby brain injured people work together with health professionals to remediate or alleviate cognitive deficits arising from a neurological insult" (p. 637). Similar to neuropsychological assessment, cognitive rehabilitation began with a focus on the direct relationship between damage to brain tissue and its cognitive and behavioral consequences. (Malec, 1996; Prigatano, 1996; Wilson, 1997). Early interventions were predicated on the belief that successful treatment of cognitive disorders would also ameliorate the emotional, behavioral, and social consequences of a brain injury (Malec, 1996). Over the past 15 to 20 years, clinicians and researchers have come to acknowledge and explore the complex relationships between the individuals' premorbid self and circumstances, and their injury-related sequelae. The effects of social and environmental circumstances, including legal, ethical, societal, and familial aspects of acquired disability are now seen as important determinants of an individual's ability to achieve a satisfying, productive lifestyle in the context of cognitive impairments.

Models of cognitive rehabilitation vary according to whether the primary target of treatment is related to an individual's cognitive impairment or its implications for adaptive functioning. It has become customary to use the World Health Organization's 1980 model of the effects of illness, disease, and injury as a framework to describe cognitive rehabilitation (Sloan & Ponsford, 1996; Trexler, Webb, & Zappala, 1994; Wilson, 1997). In this model, *impairment* refers to the actual damage done to physical or mental structures. *Disability* is used to indicate the functional difficulties that are caused by the impairment, and *handicaps* are the ways in which disabilities (i.e., reduced functional abilities) impair an individual's ability to meet the expectations of a desired social role.

In the 1998 revision of this document, impairments are divided into "impairments of function and impairments of structure," disabilities are renamed *activities* (or restriction in activities) and handicaps are renamed *participation* (or restriction in participation), but the basic model is essentially unchanged (World Health Organization, 1998). The major models of cognitive rehabilitation focus either on impairments of function, or restrictions in activities or participation (Sloan & Ponsford, 1995; Trexler et al., 1994).

Sloan and Ponsford (1995) divide cognitive rehabilitation strategies into four categories:

1. Restorative
2. Compensatory
3. Environmental
4. Behavioral

Restorative approaches focus on remediating impairments that are felt to underlie functional difficulties. *Compensatory* and *environmental* approaches address disability either by assisting the individual to identify alternative methods for completing everyday tasks or by implementing environmental supports to prevent or reduce handicaps. *Behavioral* approaches employ the technology of behavioral analysis to maximize treatment gains.

Holistic approaches include cognitive remediation strategies, but also integrate treatments focused on adaptation to disability and behavioral disturbances. Treatment occurs within the context of a therapeutic milieu and emphasis is placed upon the development of insight and the formulation of personal goals, as well as the remediation of functional deficits (Ben-Yishay & Prigatano, 1990; Prigatano, 1997). Goals of treatment may include improved psychological adaptation, and identification of appropriate community supports. Individual and family therapy are also often included in the treatment program.

TREATMENT OUTCOMES IN COGNITIVE REHABILITATION

To make recommendations for cognitive rehabilitation, it is helpful to have an understanding of recent outcomes research in this area. When level of impairment, disease state, and premorbid characteristics are well controlled, research findings have generally been less supportive of cognitive retraining or restorative approaches than training in compensatory strategies and holistic approaches, although this varies according to the cognitive function being addressed (Diller & Gordon, 1981; Malec, 1996; Wilson, 1997). A basic overview of the findings from research evaluating the efficacy of cognitive rehabilitation will be presented for memory and learning, verbal functions, mental activities, visual-spatial/perceptual skills, executive functioning, and awareness.

Memory and Learning

In general, research on the efficacy of treatments to restore *declarative memory* using computerized or other structured exercises have been discouraging (see reviews in

Glisky, 1995; Malec, 1996; Wilson, 1997). Although persons with memory impairment may be able to demonstrate improved performance on memory tasks using specific learning strategies during treatment sessions, they often fail to generalize the use of these strategies in their natural environment (Franzen & Haut, 1991; Richardson, 1992; Rimmele & Hester, 1987; Tate, 1997). This is not surprising considering that memory deficits often occur in the context of executive impairment. As a result, individuals who are able to learn the use of a technique when structure is provided may fail to initiate the strategy when there is less structure. Initiation failures may be the result of poor insight, or an impaired ability to see how the strategy that was learned might apply to situations outside of the therapy context. For this reason, multimodal memory programs that combine the use of learning strategies with organizational techniques while addressing executive dysfunction seem to be more effective than teaching memory strategies alone (Malec, 1996).

There is a growing literature on the use of memory books and external aids to help persons with memory impairments remind themselves of past events *(episodic memory)* and keep track of appointments and tasks to be done *(prospective memory)*. Memory books have become standard tools in most comprehensive brain injury programs and multimodal cognitive rehabilitation programs (Malec, 1996; Tate, 1997). Although the technique itself is relatively simple, memory book training may be complicated by several factors. First, clinical researchers often report that there is a strong tendency for clients to reject the use of memory aids, particularly in the acute and early post-acute phases of rehabilitation (Burke, Danick, Bemis, & Durgin, 1994; Squires, Hunkin, & Parkin, 1996; Tate, 1997). Further, learning to use a memory book is in itself a task that requires learning and memory as well as insight (Wilson & Hughes, 1997). For these reasons, introducing the use of a memory book usually requires weeks to months of focused treatment. Memory book training generally includes tailoring the memory book or day planner to the needs and interests of the individual, supportive counseling, and modeling by professionals and peers to facilitate acceptance of the strategy. Behavioral strategies to reinforce the appropriate use of compensatory strategies may also be helpful. Consideration must also be given to teaching the client to make appropriate entries at the appropriate times and in the correct places, to check the diary at appropriate times—ideally using alarms along with personal cues, and to use the diary to plan ahead or remember past events. Systematic training strategies, such as those described by Burke et al. (1994) may be used when creating a treatment plan that includes the use of memory books.

In a follow-up survey of persons with acquired brain injury, Wilson (1991) found that some traumatically injured persons actually improved in their use of memory strategies years after their original injury. She interpreted this finding to suggest that some people begin to recognize the utility of a memory book after years of living with their disability. When motivation and insight are good, individuals may develop highly adaptive strategies that serve to remediate most of the disability associated with their memory impairment. For example, Wilson et al. (1997) document the evolution of a memory compensatory system over the course of years in an individual (JC) with severe declarative memory impairment as the result of an intracranial hemorrhage, demonstrating how an individual learned to develop and teach himself to use new organizational and memory strategies.

Clients often enter treatment with a desire to remember more of what they read. Wilson (1987) found that teaching an organizational strategy aided comprehension and recall of written material. The technique is referred to as PQRST, which is an acronym to cue learners to first *preview* material to be read, then create *questions* to be answered by the text, *read* the text, *state* the contents of the reading and *test* themselves on what was learned. Similarly, Kreutzer and Wehman (1991, p. 153) found that simply restating what was read in one's own words was generally sufficient to improve recall of texts.

Even in persons with severe acquired injury or progressive neurological disease, procedural memory is often less affected than declarative memory (see Chapter 9). Consistent with this finding, techniques such as the method of vanishing cues, which rely on *procedural memory,* have been used successfully to teach domain-specific information (e.g., Glisky, Schacter, & Tulving, 1986; Kime, Lamb, & Wilson, 1996). This can be useful, for example, in teaching medication regimens. However, difficulty with generalization of learning is often observed, particularly in persons with greater impairment (Glisky et al., 1986).

Severely amnesic individuals cannot recall the context of an action (i.e., whether they were right or wrong), any action performed or response given is strengthened or "learned." The learner, unable to distinguish correct from incorrect responses, may continue to give an erroneous response because rehearsal has strengthened it. Wilson and Evans (1996) found that prevention of errors when teaching persons with severe impairments of declarative memory speeds up the learning process. A number of researchers have found that by using slowly vanishing cues and providing information without allowing guessing, information is learned more quickly and accurately (e.g., Squires et al., 1996; Wilson & Evans, 1996).

Memory loss is a common complaint that often brings older adults and persons with mood disorders in for neuropsychological assessment. Those in the early stages of dementing disease, as well as those whose memory impairments are considered "normal" or "benign" may benefit from multimodal memory groups (Verhaeghen, Marcoen, & Goossens, 1992). However, it is generally agreed that the use of imagery and organizational strategies are quite effortful. Unless the learner is highly motivated and has good executive abilities, these tools tend to be abandoned after therapy ends (see review in West, 1995). Interventions for specific populations, including stroke, Alzheimer's disease (West, 1995), and learning disabled children (Rourke & Tsatsanis, 1995) have also been found to be effective if appropriate measures are taken to help clients generalize their learning to real-life settings. The available literature on memory intervention as a whole strongly suggests that groups include direct instruction in several techniques, allow sufficient time for practice (generally more than five hours over the course of several weeks) and include assistance in adapting the strategies reviewed to problems of particular concern to the learner. Table 15.2 lists sample recommendations to address memory impairment.

Verbal Functioning

The *aphasias, dysarathrias,* and *apraxias* that are traditionally the treatment targets of speech and language pathologists have a long history of treatment and a large existing literature. Interventions are primarily the domain of speech and language specialists

Table 15.2.   Recommendations for memory and learning

Strategy	Treatment Considerations
Training in mneumonic devices	Client motivation must be high and impairment mild. Training for generalization is necessary. Instruction should be combined with practice. Multi-modal memory groups have been shown to be most effective.
PQRST/reading summaries	Useful for persons wanting to recall more of what they read. Generally requires high level of motivation, direct instruction and practice.
Memory books/diaries	Book design should be consistent with level of memory deficit and impairment in other areas. Tailor the design of the book to the needs/goals of the client. Counseling and/or reinforcement strategies to facilitate use/acceptance may be necessary. Modeling, direct instruction, and generalization training are usually required.
Environmental structuring	Useful with all levels of impairment. When impairment is more severe, cooperation of a caregiver is required. Use old, overlearned information and behavior patterns when possible. Cues may require alternation of changes to remain salient.
Learning strategies (Method of vanishing cues, errorless learning, massed practice)	

(e.g., see review in Ylvisaker & Urbanczyk, 1994; also see Chapter 10). However, cognitive communication disorders, which have been regarded as presenting a significant barrier to reintegration in the community, are more often overlooked in clinical practice and require special attention in the context of neuropsychological rehabilitation (DePompei & Blosser, 1991; Sohlberg & Mateer, 1989; Ylvisaker et al., 1990).

Cognitive communication disorders may be defined as the impairments in communication that result from deficits in both linguistic and nonlinguistic cognitive functioning (DePompei & Blosser, 1991). Even in the absence of dysarthria, aphasia, or apraxia, an individual's ability to communicate can be quite disturbed because of the impaired use of language pragmatics. Language pragmatics are those aspects of communication that allow good communication in the natural environment. Pragmatics include overt behaviors (gestures, eye contact, tonal variation while speaking) as well as the qualitative aspects of the content of a communication (e.g., topic maintenance, and use of information). Difficulty appreciating the nonverbal aspects of behavior *(aprosodias),* and impaired attention and executive abilities often result in verbosity, tangentiality, and poorly organized communication. Pragmatic errors in communication may reflect an individual's difficulty in taking the perspective of the listener, keeping track of the goal of the conversation, and soliciting and receiving enough information to keep a communication moving forward.

The study of language pragmatics is a relatively new pursuit, but since the early 1980s significant progress has been made in identifying the components of language pragmatics that may become the targets of intervention. For example, the Pragmatic Profile (Prutting & Kirchner, 1983) is designed to assess an individual's strengths and weaknesses using clinician ratings of the appropriate or inappropriate use of 32 pragmatic behaviors. The Clinical Discourse Analyses (Damico, 1985) arrives at a frequency count of observable behaviors (i.e., total utterances, discourse errors, total utterances with errors, and percentage of utterances with errors). Quantifying discourse allows the clinician to focus treatment and assess changes in communication after treatment.

Interventions to address cognitive-linguistic impairments overlap considerably with interventions designed for executive impairments and social skills training. In the acute phases of recovery, environmental interventions may be used to facilitate communication. These might include providing instruction to caregivers to remove distractions (e.g., turnoff the television or radio and close doors) simplify their communications, allow additional time for processing, and ask for clarification to ensure that good communication has occurred. If there are impairments of speech and language, involvement of a speech and language therapist can ensure selection of appropriate treatment strategies and augmentative communicative devices, as needed.

As recovery progresses, goals for therapy change. The first phase of therapy should include an educational component to assist the patient, family, and caregivers to understand the observed deficit and the need for intervention. In the case of communication impairments, compensatory strategies, an initial phase of therapy, may also include teaching the individual to monitor the nature of their communication for specific errors. Patients may then be taught rules to use when attempting to alter their behavior. For example, individuals with a tendency to be tangential could be provided with instruction and practice in identifying the topic of conversations. Once they are able to identify the topic of conversation they may be cued to write notes before speaking in order to organize their thoughts and consider how well what they want to say fits into the conversation. Environmental cues, such as a note stating the topic of conversation may be used as a reminder in the beginning of treatment, and then faded as communication skills are developed. Research provides evidence that groups designed to improve communication and social skills following acquired brain injury have achieved positive results (e.g., Ben-Yishay & Prigatano, 1990). Table 15.3 provides several examples of recommendations to address language disorders.

Mental Activities (Attention and Processing Speed)

Studies using a remediation approach to attention training have yielded mixed results. In making sense of the varied findings, Malec (1996) reviewed research indicating that, early in the process of recovery from traumatic injury, it is common for individuals to demonstrate impairments in both the perceptual and response formulation aspects of attentional processing. Later in the recovery process, deficits are typically limited to the response formulation phase that is usually demonstrated by increased response latencies. Malec observed that studies using subjects less than one year

Table 15.3. Recommendations for language functioning

Strategy	Treatment Considerations
Consultation with a speech and language therapist	For known or suspected language impairments
Education • Explanation of disorder • Demonstration of communication • And compensatory strategies	All cognitive/language disorders
Ensure comprehension and attention • Remove environmental distractions • Simplify communications • Request repetition of information • Allow extra processing time	When attention, concentration of specific language impairments are observed
Self-management strategies • Development of rules to direct behavior • Write notes before speaking • Use of environmental cues	For pragmatic language impairments
Group interventions	Useful to increase social interaction and to address social skills

following their injury or that focused on sustained attention to stimulus features were less likely to show treatment effects, while those studies with a focus on reducing response time and increasing response accuracy yielded more positive results.

While the treatment findings seem positive, there is evidence to suggest that treatment gains made on training tasks do not generalize to functional improvements in the natural environment (e.g., Ponsford & Kinsella, 1988; Sturm & Willmes, 1991). Additionally, the type of functional deficits that are related to impairments of attentional processes may not always be captured by neuropsychological tests used as outcome measures (see Chapter 11). Potential recommendations to address attentional deficits are provided in Table 15.4.

Visual-Spatial/Perceptual Functioning

There is accumulating evidence to suggest that, in some cases, acquired visuoperceptual disorders respond favorably to treatment which can generalize day-to-day behavior (Gouvier & Cubic, 1991). Gianutsos and Matheson (1987) make a convincing argument that prior to beginning treatment all persons with acquired brain injury or known perceptual impairment should have visual acuity and binocular functioning (i.e., *diplopia, accommodation,* and *suppression*) carefully assessed prior to the outset of treatment. They site their own finding that of 39 head injured clients, 19 warranted the services of a rehabilitative optometrist who specialized in low vision. Services rendered included prescription for new refraction, occlusion of one lens, prism lenses, and fusion training. They concluded that 18 of their subjects benefited from the treatment provided.

Table 15.4.   Recommendations for attention, processing speed, and executive functions

Strategy	Treatment Considerations
Environmental manipulation • Remove hazards (e.g., remove stove fuse) • Remove clutter • Make important features more salient (e.g., keep bathroom door open, label drawers)	Appropriate for all levels of functioning, but most useful for lower functional levels
Use alarms	Helpful when initiation is mildly impaired
Use written notes to structure activities	Useful to address impaired organization
Self-management strategies • Develop a script for self-cueing • Structured goal-setting procedure • Written notes to increase awareness of goals set	Strategies need to be taught and rehearsed Most useful when insight is good
Videotaped feedback	To increase social awareness Feedback must be offered in a supportive atmosphere
Group interventions	Useful if peer feedback and support are facilitated Peer models often increase compliance and insight

Researchers and reviewers typically divide observed visuospatial impairments into three categories: (1) primary visual field defects, (2) visual hemi-inattention, and (3) complex visuoperceptual and visuomotor impairments. Because primary visual field deficits and hemi-inattention are common sequelae of stroke, most studies were conducted with this patient population. Some studies, however, have included persons with other acquired injuries. While there were positive findings from a single German study, Gianutsos (1991) summarized findings related to remediation of visual field deficits to indicate that the tedious training, which requires visual stimulation to the boundaries of affected fields, is impractical for clinical settings.

Training to reduce neglect and to compensate for a visual field deficit has proven more successful. A series of studies conducted at the Rusk Institute at NYU Medical Center provides evidence that training in visual scanning, size estimation, tactile location training, and the use of cancellation tasks are successful in treating visual neglect (e.g., Weinberg et al., 1977, 1979; Weinberg, Piasetsky, Diller, & Gordon, 1982). These studies compared persons receiving the intervention with patients who received standard treatment, making their findings all the more impressive.

In their reviews of the available literature, Malec (1996), Gianutsos (1991) and Warren (1993a) each note that there are variable findings as to whether or not training in the basic skill (e.g., scanning) translates to actual functional gains. The most practical approaches to visual-spatial training are outlined in detail by Warren (1993a, 1993b) and Sohlberg and Mateer (1989). They suggest that training in scanning may begin with simplified therapy materials that have cues or "visual anchors" on the neglected side to encourage increased attention. As therapy progresses, anchors are removed and materials resembling functional skills are added. The final portion of therapy involves practice of the functional skills in the environment(s) in which difficulties are most likely to occur. Taken together, available data suggest that treatment of visual-spatial disorders is most likely to be successful in persons who have more localized lesions. In addition, gains in functionally relevant skills are most likely to be observed when training includes a variety of tasks that are practiced across environmentally relevant settings (Gouvier & Cubic, 1991). Table 15.5 provides an overview of several recommendations for visual/spatial impairments.

Executive Functioning

Impairments of executive functioning are among the most common and vexing of assessment and rehabilitation issues. As discussed in Chapter 13, structured measures of "frontal lobe functioning" are usually not sufficient to tap the behavioral effects of lesions to these or interconnected brain structures. Definitions of executive functioning vary from author to author, but generally include processes involved in modulating attention (i.e., sustained and selective attention and cognitive flexibility) as well as planning, organization, initiation, self-monitoring, and anticipation (see Chapter 13). At its lowest level, executive functioning involves paying attention to the right stimulus (or stimuli) at the right time. At higher levels of performance, it means making a well-sequenced and timed plan of action and the ability to understand and anticipate feedback from the environment (i.e., insight). It is easy to understand how executive abilities affect the ability to use other cognitive functions. If emotion and interpersonal interactions can be seen as cognitive constructs, the effect of executive abilities on social relationships and behavior is also quite obvious. The term "metacognition" is gaining popularity among rehabilitation professionals to describe those aspects of executive functioning that require conscious awareness of one's own thought process (e.g., Baddeley, 1990; McCarthy & Warrington, 1990; Stuss et al., 1994). The concept, as applied in rehabilitation settings, has its roots in Meichenbaum's work in self-instructional techniques with children (Meichenbaum & Goodman, 1971).

Stuss et al. (1994) present a hierarchical model of remediation of disturbances of executive functioning that is based upon a three level model (see Stuss, 1991 for a

Table 15.5. Recommendations for visual/spatial impairments

Strategy	Treatment Considerations
Referral to rehabilitation optometrist	Ideally all patients with acquired brain injury during the acute phase of rehabilitation
Training to reduce neglect and compensate for visual field deficits • Visual scanning • Size estimation • Cancellation tasks	For all persons with visual field impairments or neglect who continue to demonstrate impairment on functional tasks Therapy tasks should be followed by training in day-to-day situations (e.g., reading menus/newspapers, using a wheelchair)
Use of visual anchors placed on the neglected side, and verbal cues to attend to neglected side	Cues (visual and verbal) should be faded as mastery is demonstrated

complete description of the model). Briefly, this model posits that the most basic aspect of frontal lobe functioning is comprised of basic knowledge. Processing at this level is fast, automatic, and routine, and consists of behaviors that can be completed without much (if any) conscious processing. The next level of processing includes executive control, which requires decision making about initiating and altering the automatic behaviors of the first level. The highest level of frontal lobe functioning involves the ability to reflect on the process of cognition (metacognition) and involves mainly abstract mental representations. Treatment based upon this model is designed to provide a prosthetic for the missing frontal lobe function. This means that if the routines of level one are not present, therapy focuses on re-training the routine. If the ability to initiate the appropriate routine is impaired (a level two dysfunction), then therapy would focus on providing environmental cues to facilitate appropriate initiation. If knowledge of the process of planning and initiation are missing (a level three dysfunction), then therapy focuses on highlighting environmental feedback and providing assistance in creating appropriate schema to plan and self-direct the activities of the lower levels of functioning. Even when treatment for impairments of executive functioning do not explicitly rely on this conceptual model, they can generally fit this conceptualization.

As an example, failure to complete bathing in an individual physically capable of bathing may be the result of a lack of the basic routines, which would be addressed by listing the necessary behaviors in a checklist. Failure to initiate or regulate the ongoing behaviors can be addressed by using a cue to indicate when to initiate the bathing (e.g., an alarm or structured morning routine) or a cue to indicate where the individual is in the process of bathing (e.g., a marker that is moved when each task is completed). Failure to bathe may also be a failure to understand the hygienic and social reasons for doing so. In this case, intervention focuses on the provision of social feedback and reinforcement to encourage the desired behavior.

Specific interventions for executive functioning, particularly for those with severe impairment, often begins with environmental alterations, (e.g., simplifying stimuli, providing labels, alarms, and action lists). While this type of treatment recommendation is commonplace, there have only been a handful of case studies to substantiate its usefulness in persons with acquired brain injury. However, the behavioral geriatrics literature does provide a number of examples of how structuring the environment can help to address the dysexecutive symptoms of persons with dementing illnesses (see review in Fisher & Carstensen, 1990). A notable example of this type of intervention comes from Panella (1986) who observed that incontinence in persons with dementia is sometimes the result of difficulty locating a bathroom or recognizing whether or not one is in a bathroom. They found that increasing the visibility of toilets significantly reduced the incidence of incontinence in a nursing home environment. This literature also provides advice about how to make simple environmental modifications, such as removing the fuses from a stove or installing childproof locks. These modifications can sometimes be the determining factor that allows patients with significant impairments to stay in less restrictive environments (see examples of environmental interventions Kreutzer & Wehman, 1991; Parenté & Herrmann, 1996; Ponsford & Sloan, 1995; Sohlberg & Mateer, 1989). Parenté and Herrmann (1996) present a taxonomy of cognitive aids. Table 15.6, adapted from their text, is presented to illustrate the variety of cognitive aids that may be used. Stuss, Mateer, and Sohlberg (1994) point out that to be effective,

Table 15.6.   Types of external aids

Type	Description	Example
Behavioral prosthetics	Behaviors that remind	Ask someone to remind you Put something in a special place Wear a colored rubber band
Cognitive prosthetics	Obviate memory and cognitive problems	Use a tape recorder
Cognitive robots	Carry out a routine cognitive task for an individual	Use a calculator
Cognitive correctors	Find and correct errors	Use a spell-checker
Cognitive assessors	Evaluate a client's cognitive ability	Use hand-held electronic game to test one's abilities
Cognitive trainers	Provide stimulation therapy, instruction and performance feedback	Computer-assisted rehabilitation
Cognitive sources	Maintain or supplement knowledge	Reference materials
Cognitive art	Visual memory and problem-solving summaries	Chart that summarizes important information/floor plan or map
Nonelectronic cognitive aids	Employ low-tech solutions	Checklists Medication organizers Cue cards Post-It Notes
Superstitious possessions	E.g., a lucky pencil	Rabbit's foot that gives an individual confidence

Source: Adapted from Parenté and Herrmann (1996).

recommendations for environmental modifications must be based upon a behavioral analysis of the difficulty being addressed. These interventions should also utilize existing cognitive strengths, and include education of the client and significant others in the environment. Treatment would include a phase of evaluation and modification to ensure the environmental change was effective. As with any intervention, care must be taken to identify which strategies an individual is willing to use. As Parenté and Herrmann (1996) point out, "The extent to which the environment aids cognition depends largely on the client's perception that the device will solve more problems than it creates."

Direct training has been shown to help individuals compensate for impaired executive functioning. These interventions include the use of learning and behavior therapy methods to teach domain-specific behavior. Again, there are many case examples in the literature that demonstrate the efficacy of behavioral methods in individuals with acquired brain injuries (e.g., Wilson, 1991) or dementia (see review in Fisher & Carstensen, 1990). Given the individualized nature of the treatments, it is not surprising that group studies are very few in number. Even so, behavioral methods clearly have a place in neuropsychological rehabilitation (Malec & Lemsky, 1996; Wilson, 1997).

When lower levels of frontal lobe functioning are intact, but there is evidence of impaired planning and self-regulation and organization, training in metacognitive strategies can be undertaken. This category of interventions includes the use of self-instruction techniques in which the individual is trained to state their goals and narrate their actions, first aloud and then covertly (K.A. Cicerone & Wood, 1987; Meichenbaum & Goodman, 1971). Case studies have demonstrated the efficacy of this approach to increase accuracy on training tasks (K.A. Cicerone & Wood, 1987) and motor impersistence (Stuss, Delgado, & Guzman, 1987). With specific training, use of this strategy may generalize to functional tasks (K.A. Cicerone & Wood, 1987). Other methods have been developed to retrain organizational skills, problem solving, and conceptual skills (Parenté & Herrmann, 1996). These methods involve creating rules to address the cognitive process that is lacking. Although there are no studies employing these strategies in groups of persons with executive impairments, they are usually included in the cognitive retraining aspect of multi-modal integrated treatment programs that have been found to be effective in treating the behavioral impairments associated with acquired brain injury (Ben-Yishay & Prigatano, 1990; Malec, Schafer, & Jacket, 1992; Malec, Smigielski, DePompolo, & Thompson, 1993).

Impairments of Awareness

In recent years, the terms *awareness deficit* and *lack of awareness* have been used by many authors to refer to the inability to recognize deficits as a direct result of neurological impairment. This phenomenon is generally agreed to differ from *denial,* which is described as a refusal to acknowledge a deficit for psychological reasons. In practice, it is difficult to differentiate organic from psychological etiologies in persons with denial or lack of awareness, except that psychological denial is generally thought to be more amenable to psychotherapy once the intrapsychic need filled by the denial can be identified and addressed.

The precise cause of lack of awareness is unclear. Some studies have found that deficits seem to be related to neurological indices of injury severity (e.g., Prigatano & Altman, 1990) but other have found that these deficits are unrelated to injury severity (Alan & Ruff, 1990; Anderson & Tranel, 1989; Gasquonine, 1992). While there is speculation that awareness deficits occur more frequently in persons with frontal lobe (Damasio & Anderson, 1993; Stuss, 1991), and right hemispheric lesions (Heilman, Watson, & Valenstein, 1993), findings from other studies have not found a strong relationship between lack of awareness and lesion site (Sherer, Bergloff, et al., 1998). Research also indicates that persons with traumatic brain injury are more aware of their physical deficits than their nonphysical (cognitive and behavioral) impairments, and are more likely to identify their deficits correctly if asked about specific skills as opposed to general abilities (Sherer, Boake, et al., 1998).

A model of impaired awareness proposed by Crosson et al. (1989) provides a framework for understanding the range of impairments of awareness that occur. In this model, the most basic type of awareness is "intellectual" awareness. Persons with intellectual awareness are able to name their deficits, but lack an understanding of the implication of the deficits. They may state their impairments more in terms of what they have been told about themselves. Persons with "emergent" awareness are able to name their deficits, and indicate knowledge of the deficit when it occurs. In the most advanced stage of awareness "anticipatory awareness" individuals are able to name the deficit, recognize when it is occurring and anticipate situations in which the deficit might create a problem.

Fordyce and associates have shown that a behaviorally-oriented program including education regarding the impact of the injury, patient self-monitoring of observed deficits, and videotaped feedback of target behaviors resulted in reduced discrepancies between self-report and observer-rated behavior (Fordyce & Rouche, 1986; Prigatano & Fordyce, 1986). Several authors have noted that even when attempts to restore specific areas of cognitive functioning are not expected to be successful, the process of cognitive rehabilitation may help to build awareness if treatment includes direct and immediate feedback about performance (Ben-Yishay & Prigatano, 1990; Klonoff, O'Brien, Prigatano, Chiapello, & Cunningham, 1989; Tate, 1997).

Crosson et al. (1989) present a model of clinical decision making based upon the stage of awareness demonstrated in an individual. In the absence of intellectual awareness, external compensation is recommended. When intellectual (but not emergent) awareness is achieved, compensation that is specific to particular situations may be trained. In this case the strategies to be used are trained as habitual in all situations where they might be appropriate so that there is no need to recognize the problem as it is occurring. When emergent awareness is present, then compensation strategies to be employed "as needed" can be trained. With anticipatory awareness the individual may use training compensation strategies and be offered guidance about generalizing the strategy across situations.

Impaired awareness has been shown to be an impediment to rehabilitation, resulting in diminished participation and motivation (Prigatano & Fordyce, 1986). Although deficits of awareness may resolve in the first years following injury, patients who have shown the most successful long-term outcomes receive early intervention (Cope, Cole, Hall, & Barkan, 1991; Cope & Hall, 1982; Malec et al., 1993). Some persons may require intensive, multimodal treatment of the type offered in comprehensive outpatient or milieu therapies, to successfully improve their awareness (Ben-Yishay & Prigatano, 1990; Malec et al., 1992, 1993). Table 15.7 provides a list of potential recommendations to address deficits of awareness.

Table 15.7.   Recommendations for lack of awareness

Strategy	Treatment Considerations
Education and feedback from testing	Useful for all levels of impairment if information is tailored to level of comprehension
Self-monitoring of areas of impairment	Useful at lower levels of impairment Helpful to encourage development of anticipatory insight
Feedback using videotapes	Useful at all levels of impairment Effective review of tapes requires good rapport with clinician Most useful in the context of a structured program
Training to compensate for the deficit in particular situations	Useful when the individual cannot anticipate situations in which a deficit will occur

COMPREHENSIVE OUTPATIENT
PROGRAMS/MILIEU THERAPY

Each of the treatment approaches reviewed above have demonstrated some utility in managing the cognitive deficits associated with acquired brain injury and neurological disease. However, the greatest barriers to reintegration into the community and gainful employment are the emotional and behavioral rather than physical or strictly cognitive in nature (Lezak, 1988). Because of the need to address impairments of awareness and the emotional and behavioral outcomes of traumatic injuries, comprehensive models of rehabilitation were developed (Ben-Yishay & Prigatano, 1990; Malec et al., 1992). These interventions, referred to as "milieu," "holistic," or "comprehensive-integrated" programs, are designed to address the multiple and interacting cognitive, emotional, and social factors in an integrated fashion (Ben-Yishay & Gold, 1990).

Ben-Yishay and Gold (1990) review three basic tenants that led to the formulation of integrated treatment models. First, because the emotional and cognitive aspects of injury have been found to be correlated, it is only sensible that these factors should not be treated in isolation from one another. Second, programs designed to integrate treatment of emotional and cognitive sequelae of brain injury should be organized in a systematic manner that allows an individual to integrate gains in one area of functioning with gains and goals in other areas of functioning. Third, the psychotherapy process must be modified to accommodate the organically based difficulties some persons with brain injury have in developing insight and creating a balanced, well-integrated, and realistic self-image.

Over the past 10 years, comprehensive programs have addressed the needs of persons with traumatic brain injuries as well as impairments of a stable nature resulting from tumors, stroke, exposure to neurotoxins, hypoxic ischemic encephalopathy and other medical conditions. For the most part, these programs are open to persons with mild to moderately severe injuries who are in the post-acute phase of their rehabilitation. Although there is variance across programs, the post-acute phase of rehabilitation is generally defined as being at least 6 to 12 months post injury, though some programs admit clients as little as one month following injury (e.g., Malec et al., 1993). To be admitted, patients must be able to participate in an intensive program in an outpatient setting. Again, this varies from program to program, but clients are generally required to have at least minimal residual ability to learn new information, are capable of handling basic activities of living on an independent basis, and are able to communicate sufficiently to participate in group discussion. Because the most common form of this program occurs in an outpatient setting, clients are generally required to be medically stable and be free of aggressive behaviors likely to endanger themselves or others. Often, clients are admitted many years after their injuries when repeated treatment and vocational failures have caused them to seek additional rehabilitation.

The defining characteristics of holistic programs are that the majority of treatment is delivered in the context of a group and that interventions to address insight, emotional and personal adjustment, and functional abilities are all intertwined (Ben-Yishay & Gold, 1990). The programs are highly structured, generally occurring five days per week, four to six hours per day. Clients are well aware of the goals of each phase of treatment. Treatment occurs in six phases that are hierarchical, but overlap to some degree. The first phase of treatment is designed to optimize awareness. This occurs in the context of feedback on cognitive tasks during cognitive rehabilitation sessions and the feedback of staff members and other clients in the course of all daily activities. The second phase of treatment focuses on increasing the individual's willingness to make changes that will address the newly discovered or understood difficulties. The third phase of treatment focuses on acceptance of the "existential predicament" presented by having a brain injury. Success in this phase of therapy is demonstrated by a resignation to reality with a hopeful attitude about making the most of one's strengths. In the fourth phase of treatment, the emphasis is on honing compensatory skills to manage desired activities and social roles. The fifth phase of therapy is designed to determine the degree of autonomy the individual is able to achieve when treatment is ended. The final, sixth, phase of treatment involves marshaling environmental supports that can be made available to ensure optimal functioning on a long-term basis.

The logistics of these programs may vary to some degree. Some programs admit participants as a cohort, and use a standard length of program (usually around 12 to 20 weeks), after which clients may advance to a vocationally or educationally centered program or repeat the initial treatment cycle (e.g., Ben-Yishay & Prigatano, 1990). Other programs (e.g., Malec, Smigielski, DePompolo, & Thompson, 1993) using a rolling admission scheme in which clients graduate when they have met their individual goals. An advantage of this approach is that more experienced participants are available as role models to persons newer to the program and more advanced participants are able to consolidate their treatment gains through mentoring less advanced participants. All programs emphasize the need to involve families in treatment.

A typical day in comprehensive programs includes a daily orientation session that is used to renew attention to treatment goals; interpersonal skills training that typically involves participation in structured group exercises that may be videotaped for the purpose of providing specific feedback on behavior; individualized cognitive rehabilitation that may have the aim of increasing awareness as well as improving cognitive function; community meetings designed to manage interpersonal and logistic issues occurring in the program; personal counseling sessions and family therapy. In the later phases of therapy, transition into educational, vocational, or homemaking duties is completed, first in therapy simulations and later in the community.

Research related to the outcomes of holistic programs is generally quite positive, although most studies rely on quasi-experimental designs (Cope, 1995). Findings from recent studies suggest that participation in holistic programs results in benefits at the level of reduced handicap, including decreased dependence in activities of daily living (Malec et al., 1992), improvements in employment status (e.g., Ben-Yishay, Silver, Piasetsky, & Rattock, 1987; Malec et al., 1992; Prigatano et al., 1984) and decreased emotional distress (e.g., Prigatano et al., 1984). Future directions in research are likely to include defining the characteristics of clients most likely to benefit from holistic programs.

BEHAVIOR MODIFICATION

Behavioral disturbances associated with neurological insults such as aggressiveness, impulsiveness, disinhibition, and apathy can disrupt the rehabilitation process, and, as a result, their treatment may become a primary goal of rehabilitation. Families often find the personality and behavioral changes caused by injury or disease more distressing than cognitive or functional losses, which provides another reason why behavioral difficulties may become a prime treatment priority. Behavioral disorders occurring after brain injury include behavioral excesses (i.e., aggression and self-stimulation), deficits (lack of a specific social skill), or inappropriate stimulus control (when a behavior occurs at the wrong time and/or place), and syndromal disorders (i.e., depression and paranoid conditions; Eames, 1988). The use of behavioral procedures to manage sequelae of neurological insults is predicated on the notion that provision of a new learning experience will alter behavior. This definition implies that behavioral procedures will be effective despite the neurological contribution to the behavioral problem. Behavioral procedures including discrimination training, chaining, stimulus control, operant conditioning, and response cost have been applied to improve patients' abilities to complete basic activities of living as well as decrease the intensity and frequency of unwanted behaviors (see reviews in Davis & Goldstein, 1994; Malec & Lemsky, 1995; Wood, 1990). Although, the efficacy of behavioral approaches has mainly been demonstrated with case studies and quasi-experimental designs, knowledge of behavioral principles is generally regarded as essential for implementation of rehabilitation programs. The reader is directed to manuals written by Matthies, Kreutzer, and West (1997) and Jacobs (1993) and the chapter by Malec and Lemsky (1995) for specific information about behavioral analytic techniques and their use in persons with neurological disorders.

When behavior or cognitive impairments interfere with completion of activities of daily living and/or participation in rehabilitation, consultation with a behaviorally trained psychologist may be useful. Typically, a formal behavioral modification program is reserved for problems that have not responded to less formal changes in contingencies that may be implemented through consultation with caregivers (Matthies, Kreutzer, & West, 1997).

Matthies and coworkers (1997) review ways that staff may be taught to provide feedback about socially inappropriate behavior and to avoid unintentional reinforcement of disruptive behavior. For example, when a client becomes aware that certain types of behavior will allow escape from an unwanted activity, the behavior is negatively reinforced. By teaching staff to attend to appropriate behavior, contract for a desired outcome, and modify the structure of the day to provide pleasant activities following less-desired activity, the need for a formal program requiring behavioral analysis can be avoided. However, when these interventions fail to remediate the behavioral difficulty, a formal program of behavioral therapy may be advised.

Whether the intervention is formal or informal, selecting the optimal targets of treatment requires careful attention to ethical principles as well as an overall assessment of an individual's treatment needs. It is necessary to be sensitive to cultural factors when determining definitions of desirable and appropriate behavior, particularly when the individual with acquired brain injury, family members, and the treatment team do not share the same goals for treatment. For example, it may be justified to override an individual's right to refuse treatment if the likely result is self-harm or loss of needed care giver support. The most difficult and critical phase of the treatment planning processes may be building consensus about both the nature of the desired change and the means to achieve it. While some authors have found it successful to use family members to assist in the process of behavior modification, not all family members are willing and able to take on this role (Malec & Lemsky, 1995).

Cognitive changes that occur with neurological insults change the process of learning new behaviors. In operant programs, it is necessary for the individual in training to learn the stimulus conditions and behaviors that result in reinforcement. If their cognitive impairments result in difficulty discriminating stimuli or recalling the conditions of reinforcement, learning may be protracted or impossible (Wilson, 1991; Wood, 1990). Alderman and Ward (1991) observed that persons with severe memory or executive deficits sometimes do not respond well to reinforcement or time-out programs. These authors found that a response-cost paradigm (relinquishing a token/reinforcer immediately following an unwanted behavior) was more effective in persons with these severe deficits, apparently because it made the relationship between the response and the consequence more obvious and immediate. Additionally, several authors have observed that behavioral problems that were present prior to the injury or illness may be particularly difficult to change, though there is no data to support this claim (Matthies et al., 1997; Ponsford, 1995a).

Matthies and colleagues (1997) present a framework for selecting treatment based upon level of impairment. They suggest that in cases where there is a high level of impairment, restraints, environmental manipulation allowing extinction, and pharmacological intervention may achieve the best results. At moderate levels of cognitive impairment, positive feedback, gestural cues, verbal reprimands, repetition, and redirection, or substitution are recommended. When cognitive impairment is mild, negotiating, oral agreements and contracts as well as negative feedback and self-management may be in order.

It is unclear from the literature what the minimum cognitive requirements are for conditioning to occur in the context of a formal behavioral program. Evidence from implicit learning studies demonstrate that under the right conditions, complex learning may occur without conscious awareness (Baddeley, 1992; Glisky et al., 1986). It seems obvious that procedural learning may be the basis of success in a behavioral program. It is also reasonable to hypothesize that conditioning may occur differently in persons with damage to the central nervous system, particularly when damage is diffuse and involves multiple cognitive systems.

Based on clinical observation, some of the behavioral disorders of persons with dense amnesia may be related to their greater susceptibility to "accidents" of conditioning. In these cases, an unconditioned stimuli becomes spuriously associated with a misperceived stimuli. In persons with normal neurological functioning, extreme affect may become associated with fragmented stimuli as in the case of post-traumatic stress disorder. However, in the person with cognitive impairment, this type of mistaken association may occur more easily, either because of labile affect owing to limbic interconnections with mesial temporal structures, or because significant aspects of the learning experience are not perceived or are forgotten. For example it is not unusual for persons with dense amnesia to develop an aversion to therapy, even without explicit memories of what occurred there. It therefore becomes necessary to carefully monitor the emotional responses of persons with dense amnesia and work to help them enjoy the experience of therapy in order to avoid future noncompliance.

Table 15.8.   Recommendations for behavioral interventions

Strategy	Treatment Considerations
Informal behavioral interventions	Most appropriate for relatively mild behavioral disturbances
• Teach staff to attend to appropriate behavior	Consistency across settings facilitates success
• Contract for desired outcome	Should be supervised by behaviorally trained clinician
• Modify the structure of the day	
• Positive feedback	
• Reprimands	
• Gestural cues	
• Redirection	
• Substitution	
Formal behavioral analysis	Should be completed by a behaviorally trained clinician
• Operant conditioning	Build consensus regarding the nature of the desired change and how to achieve it
• Chaining	
• Stimulus control	To be effective, the individual must be able to learn the stimulus conditions and behaviors that result in reinforcement
• Discrimination training	
• Response cost	Individuals with greater cognitive impairment may take longer to achieve positive results
	Interventions should be conducted in consideration of community standards of behavior
	Review of the ethical implications of all procedures should be undertaken before implementation

When there is an internal, physiological etiology of the behavior, it stands to reason that behavioral methods may not be effective. Wood (1990) reported on a series of studies demonstrating that persons with episodic dyscontrol (as confirmed by EEG abnormalities) were unlikely to benefit from a response-consequence contingency program unless behavioral treatment was accompanied by anticonvulsant therapy. They also found that patients with a form of "frontal dyscontrol" had a more variable and longer (six to eight months) course of treatment using a "time out" paradigm than persons whose aggressive behaviors were clearly acquired well after the brain injury and were not accompanied by EEG changes (six to eight weeks). They concluded that if treatment is consistent enough and sustained enough, operant programs can be effective, even in persons with severe amnesia. Table 15.8 reviews possible recommendations for behavioral interventions.

VOCATIONAL RE-ENTRY

Vocational re-entry is considered one of the most important indicators of rehabilitation success. Neuropsychological examination is commonly regarded as a prerequisite to vocational rehabilitation efforts. Guilmette and Kastner (1996) found that predicting behavior on the job was the second most frequent reason (out of eight listed) for referral to a neuropsychologist. Questions about vocational functioning have significance for the determination of compensation after traumatic brain injury as well as planning rehabilitation efforts. Unfortunately, many vocational rehabilitation counselors may regard neuropsychologists as "too preoccupied with identifying deficits rather than areas of cognitive and psychological strengths and too soft or general regarding treatment recommendations" (McMahon & Shaw, 1996). Shaw and McMahon also comment that the most effective cognitive rehabilitation occurs on the job site, where skills can be assessed and deficits remediated in the setting where they will be used. From this perspective, neuropsychological data are only important when the goal of testing is to gain information about why cognitive functioning is having a negative impact on job performance.

Unfortunately, the existing literature provides very little explicit guidance as to how vocational recommendations can be extracted from neuropsychological test performances. Typically, for authors addressing this issue state that neuropsychological assessment can be used to characterize an individual's strengths and weaknesses, quantify the degree of impairment relative to a normative sample, and track neurological recovery (e.g., Fordyce, 1994; Prigatano, 1996). Since few studies have attempted to assess the relationship between test performance and functioning in specific professions, this process involves inferring how underlying cognitive impairment relate to functional vocational outcome (Guilmette & Kastner, 1996).

Several studies have found a relationship between severity of traumatic brain injury and subsequent return to work (e.g., Paniak, Shore, Rourke, Finlayson, & Moustacalis, 1992; Ponsford et al., 1995). Studies have also suggested that age (over 40) and pre-injury unemployment are related to long-term unemployment (see reviews in Ponsford, 1995b and Guilmette & Kastner, 1996). Regression studies have identified that verbal memory, level of depression, reading comprehension, verbal communication ability (see review in Crisp, 1992) substance abuse (Sander, Kreutzer, & Fernandez, 1997), and lack of awareness (Sherer, Bergloff, et al., 1998) are related to vocational outcomes. However, findings from studies such as these do not provide explicit guidance regarding how to write rehabilitation recommendations.

Guilmette and Kastner (1996) abstract thirteen principles that may be used to write vocational recommendations based upon neuropsychological data. In general, they suggest that questions about employability may be best addressed if particular jobs are considered, rather than employability in general. This allows appropriate tailoring of the test battery and the use of vocational tests developed to predict job performance (e.g., clerical proficiency tests). They also discuss the fact that intellectual measures may be better at predicting performance in job settings that place a greater demand on cognitive functioning, and that neuropsychological tests are better at predicting failure (at lower levels of performance) than assessing minimal acceptable levels of performance. Additionally, they suggest that when there are questions about vocational outcomes, measures which have been shown to be more predictive of occupational success should be included in test batteries, while inclusion of extraneous measures may decrease the accuracy of clinical judgment. Finally, they note the importance of carefully evaluating an individual's history and current psychological and social functioning since socially inappropriate behavior and psychiatric symptoms are predictive of poorer vocational outcomes.

A number of rehabilitation models have been developed to address return to work. Most include a pre-employment phase in which abilities are assessed and basic behavioral and cognitive needs addressed. Work simulation or situational assessments may be conducted in order to explore the relationship between cognitive and behavioral difficulties and work-related behavior. After difficulties identified in this stage of rehabilitation have been addressed, job placement may be made.

Although the best placement for some individuals is a sheltered workshop or other segregated work setting, the trend is toward vocational placement in community settings. Wehman (1996) contends that rehabilitation that occurs on the job site may be preferable to rehabilitation in medical settings because clients find the skills learned more "face-valid" and there are fewer concerns about generalizability of the skills learned. Use of a *supported employment* model has been gaining popularity. Supported employment is defined as paid employment at or above the minimum wage for the person with disabilities who would otherwise not be able to get or retain employment (Wehman, 1996). Supportive services to the disabled employee include supervision, training, and transportation. Work sites are in the mainstream of society and emphasis is placed upon creating real work, social integration, and offering a range of opportunities so that individual strengths and preferences can be accommodated. Buffington and Malec (1997) emphasize the need for coordinated intervention as soon as possible following the onset of cognitive impairment to enable a smoother transition from medical to community and vocational settings.

It is common to have a referral question related to an individual's ability to return to a job he or she has held for sometime prior to becoming injured or ill. In general, decline from presumed premorbid abilities is always important when assessing whether an individual may return to a previous job. However, decline in cognitive functioning does not preclude good readjustment to the work environment. Care should be taken to review the nature of the observed deficit and make hypotheses about how they may relate to particular job duties. For example, while an individual may be found to be slow in solving novel visual-spatial problems, they may have little difficulty returning to a job as a telephone operator. On the other hand, an individual with a similar configuration of scores may have some difficulty in returning to work as an architect. This may appear obvious, but clinicians may be tempted to predict poor work-place re-integration even when the observed impairment is essentially unrelated to the job to which the individual will return. Consideration of work history and work skills as well as the likely level of support at the workplace is necessary before planning a return to work. When in doubt, it is always desirable to arrange a work trial in a setting that will allow the individual to create compensatory strategies if needed. This is best accomplished by enlisting the aid of a vocational rehabilitation counselor.

Whether planning return to previous employment or seeking new employment, it is important to consider the responsibilities of the employer under the law. The United States is fortunate to have one of the most advanced laws related to community integration of persons with disabilities (Americans with Disabilities Act of 1990). In other countries, specific legislation may apply. An important part of vocational rehabilitation is education about the rights and responsibilities of persons with disabilities entering the workplace. It is also important to teach individuals how to represent their disability in job interviews. Additionally, the social psychology of disability must

Table 15.9. Recommendations for vocational re-entry

Strategy	Treatment Considerations
Pre-employment assessment of basic behavioral and cognitive needs	Should be conducted before job placement or return to previous work setting
	Assessment should resemble job tasks and situations as closely as possible
Referral to a vocational rehabilitation counselor	Counselors may provide an analysis of job tasks, job coaching, and referral to appropriate positions/programs
	Useful to evaluate all job-related behaviors
Work trial	May include completion of job-tasks from the job to which an individual will return
	May include light duty or gradual re-entry to a previous job
	May include feedback sessions with a trusted co-worker or a supervisor
Supported employment	Useful for individuals who may require assistance to learn or stay on a job or require a specialized work setting
	Should be supervised by a person knowledgeable of the injury as well as the individual's cognitive impairment
Education about rights under the law	Useful for all workers with a disability

be considered when preparing individuals to re-enter any community situation. The tendency of able-bodied persons to overestimate or overgeneralize disability based on limited information is an important part of the life of all persons with disabilities. Education and the development of strategies to manage awkward situations can be helpful in ensuring a smooth transition to the community.

It is important to warn clients against taking the risk of returning to a job too soon after an illness or injury before they have adequately adapted to their disability or before recovery is optimal. Errors made during a premature return to work may erode confidence in the worker and sabotage their future at work. When behavioral difficulties are considered a barrier to return to a particular job, it may be best to defer placement until the difficulty has been addressed or care taken to place the individual in an environment in which the problematic behavior is less likely to occur. For example, an individual known to have difficulty relating appropriately to women in a work setting may be placed in a work setting that is largely male until this issue has been addressed through rehabilitation. Examples of recommendations for vocational re-entry are reviewed in Table 15.9.

DRIVING

It is not uncommon for families, rehabilitation team members, and persons with cognitive changes to solicit neuropsychologists' opinions regarding returning to driving.

However, neuropsychological tests (by themselves) are generally not good predictors of fitness to drive for elders and persons with acquired brain injury (Brouwer & Withaar, 1997; Gouvier et al., 1989). Evidence also suggests that many, if not the majority of persons who drive following a traumatic brain injury do so without direct guidance from a professional. A recent survey by Fisk and colleagues (Fisk, Schneider, & Novack, 1998) found that 60.2% of a sample of 83 persons who had sustained a moderate to severe TBI an average of 3.3 years prior to responding were currently driving. Of the active drivers, 64% had returned to driving seven days per week, although only 10.8% of the total sample had received approval for unlimited driving. Of those who returned to driving, only 24% had completed on-road-testing (Fisk et al., 1998). Despite the lack of formal approval to return to driving, persons with acquired brain injury and stroke did not demonstrate an increased incidence of accidents or driving violations (Haselkorn, Mueller, & Rivara, 1998; Katz et al., 1990). In contrast, evidence suggests that the incidence of accidents in persons with suspected dementia is high (Drachman, 1988; Lambert & Engum, 1992).

Brouwer and Withaar (1997) present a useful literature review related to return to driving in persons with traumatic brain injury. They also present a conceptual model for considering the necessary conditions for a safe return to driving after TBI which may be applied to other populations. They define fitness to drive as: (a) low probability of sudden lapses of attention; (b) perceptual, cognitive, and motor skills sufficient to manage the task of driving; and (c) social judgment sufficient to refrain from driving in unsafe circumstances (e.g., after drinking, high traffic, or with other distractions).

Brouwer and Withaar (1997) reviewed a series of Dutch studies and summarized the findings to indicate that reduced speed and impaired precision in operating a vehicle was often observed in persons after traumatic brain injury. Subjects tended to perform best in their own cars. Assessments measuring information processing and visual-motor coordination were the cognitive tests most related to driver's behind-the-wheel performance, but the correlation between neuropsychological tests and expert's evaluation of driving quality was low. Finally, these studies found that experienced drivers were better in judging traffic conditions.

Composite measures of cognitive speed have shown the most promise of acting as predictors of fitness to return to driving. A series of studies evaluated a composite variable made up of 27 simple information processing tasks (E.S. Engum, Cron, Hulse, Pendergrass, & Lambert, 1988; E.S. Engum, Lambert, & Scott, 1990; E.S. Engum, Lambert, Scott, Pendergrass, & Womac, 1989) which correlate well (approximately 0.75) with Trials A and the WAIS Digit Symbol substitution tests. Although these authors found that their model was good at identifying drivers at the extremes of the risk continuum, persons with "borderline" performances were most likely to be misclassified. Lambert and Engum (1992) suggested that the judgment of a neuropsychologist was more accurate than the index in predicting driving in elders (whom the index underestimated). However, there was a subgroup of persons with TBI under the age of 26 who achieved passing index scores and were judged by neuropsychologists as "possibly safe drivers" but who failed the behind-the-wheel test. These findings suggest that cognitive and psychomotor speed are not predictive of safe driving in either elders or young drivers.

Brouwer and Withaar (1997) concluded that persons whose performances fall outside of the normal range on tests of psychomotor, cognitive processing speed, and perceptual

motor abilities should be advised against driving. Likewise, persons with poor judgment, a tendency toward hostility, or excessive risk-taking should also be advised not
to drive. They suggest that persons scoring in or near the borderline range should be assessed on the road and provided with rehabilitation in order to assess whether or not
they can become fit drivers. Among elderly drivers, some experience-based driving
skills, such as the ability to judge traffic conditions and foresee potential hazards, may
serve as a buffer against changes in motor skills, cognitive flexibility, and processing
speed. However, given that there are data to suggest that persons with dementing illnesses have a high rate of traffic accidents and violations, care should be taken to refer
clients for driver evaluations when there is cause to be concerned about their sensory
or motor ability to drive. This is also necessary when cognitive test findings are suggestive of impaired performance when age-appropriate norms are used. Brouwer and
Withaar also advocate offering assessment and training to persons in the borderline
range of abilities. They state that this may mitigate the conservative bias of rehabilitation professionals who may tend to recommend against driving, even in persons who
might be able to manage to operate a motor vehicle safely after some rehabilitation.

FACILITATING ADJUSTMENT: INDIVIDUAL AND
FAMILY PSYCHOTHERAPY

The development of cognitive impairment, either through injury or disease, may occasion the development of emotional difficulties, or exacerbate existing psychological or
psychiatric disorders (see Chapter 14). Contextual factors, ranging from family constel-
lation and psychosocial history to local and societal resources can all impact upon an
individuals' outcome. When there is a known history of premorbid psychosocial, psychological, substance abuse, or psychiatric difficulties, it is important to assess their
current impact on adjustment and functioning. Old issues may be temporarily ignored
during the acute phase of an illness or injury in order to allow the individuals involved
to manage the crisis caused by the onset of a disability. Even when a full assessment is
not immediately possible or appropriate, it is important that the clinician not lose track
of the existence of premorbid difficulties. They can be more fully assessed when the resources and willingness to seek treatment are present.

In the acute phase of an illness, the individual and their family may be more focused
on addressing the observed impairment. In the case of stroke and TBI, the initial phase
of recovery is generally focused on restoring lost abilities. Hope for a full recovery
may be enough to facilitate coping with difficult behavior and arduous therapies. When
an illness is clearly degenerative, or in the post-acute phase of illness and injury, the
process of learning to live with a deficit occurs. In the case of mild cognitive impairment—such as occurs in mild traumatic brain injury and clinical depression—cognitive and emotional factors may interact in a manner that masks or limits recovery.

In order to prevent excess disability, anxiety, and adjustment difficulties, rehabilitation programs generally advocate that treatment begin with education about the individual's illness or disability and its known natural history. Information should be timed
according to the individual's emotional needs and abilities. Families should be informed about the nature of cognitive impairment and what they might do to optimize

the environment of the person for whom they are providing support. The process of educating clients about illness and disability may begin with the diagnosing clinician and continue when feedback from neuropsychological testing is provided.

Although many clients and family members do not foresee issues related to sexuality developing, it is important to provide information about where help may be obtained to address these issues. Some illnesses and injuries may cause a change in sex-drive or lead to sexual disinhibition. Partners may lose interest in each other because of a change in relationship roles necessitated by the injury. Disability may lead to the need for education about sexual functioning, body image, and/or suggestions for changes in technique to accommodate the disability. It is up to the clinician to validate the need to address these issues and to provide or point clients toward needed services.

Psychotherapy

Psychotherapy with persons who have sustained an injury to the brain is a recent enterprise. Nearly all of the work in this area has been published over the past 10 to 15 years. Although a number of authors have proposed theoretical models (e.g., Ellis, 1991; León-Carrión, 1997a; Lewis, 1991; Prigatano, 1991) for psychotherapy for persons with acquired cognitive impairments, empirical studies of their efficacy is entirely lacking. Lewis suggests that one reason that psychotherapy lags behind other treatments for persons with brain injury is that persons with acquired brain injury (ABI) were traditionally rejected by psychotherapists. She posits that rejections for therapy occurred because persons with ABI present the therapist with particularly difficult countertransference issues. That is, therapists may become overwhelmed by the chronicity of problems associated with ABI, or therapists may find resentment toward them, on the part of clients for not being disabled, is difficult to manage. Lewis also suggests that therapists tended to overestimate the difference between neurologically normal and neurologically impaired persons and the goals they wish to achieve through therapy. There is no doubt that persons with cognitive impairments are difficult to treat and require special consideration in treatment planning.

It is generally agreed that psychotherapy treatment plans should consider the nature of the neurological insult, the psychological meaning of the insult, the individual's personality (irrespective of the neurological insult) and the social context in which the individual functions. The most concise description of psychotherapy for persons with ABI comes from Prigatano (1991) who defined psychotherapy with persons with acquired brain injury as the process of "teaching the patient . . . to learn to behave in his or her own best self-interest" (p. 2). To complete this task, it is necessary to help the individual understand what has changed as a result of the injury, and to learn ways of coping that are consistent with the existence of the injury.

Prigatano (1991) has written about the essential questions that persons ask following traumatic changes in their cognitive status. The first of these questions is "Will I be normal?" In general, this refers to whether or not deficits will abate, but may also include the individual's concerns about return to specific roles or activities. In many cases, individuals wonder whether they will ever have the feeling of being a "whole human being" again. In therapy, individuals may also question the reason why they were fated to have an injury and whether or not they will find their life worth living after the injury. Together, these questions may be referred to as the existential crisis of traumatic injury.

Prigatano (1991) also wrote that the first goal of therapy is to help the individual become as fully engaged as possible in the process of rehabilitation. This may mean facilitating insight and providing direct education about the social, behavioral, and emotional implications of an injury. The second goal is to help the individual arrive at a meaningful interpretation of their situation and to develop a means to seek meaning in living out their life. Achievement of self-acceptance and the development of realistic plans for a return to desired social roles is, perhaps, the most difficult goal of psychotherapy with this client group. Most authors incorporate the goals outlined for psychotherapy by Prigatano (1991) in their models of treatment (e.g., León-Carrión, 1997a; Miller, 1992; Ponsford, 1995b; Schefft, Malec, Lehr, & Kanfer, 1994).

As stated by Prigatano, and reiterated by many others, the therapist's goal throughout the psychotherapy process is to understand the patient's experience of his or her situation and to engender a realistic sense of hope. Most authors also agree that psychotherapeutic efforts are ideally a part of a comprehensive program of care that includes interventions to teach necessary social skills and compensatory strategies for cognitive impairments. This is because cognitive rehabilitation provides information about cognitive abilities (and disabilities) through treatment successes and failures, while contacts with a therapist and/or peers can facilitate the development of insight and appropriate coping strategies. In the absence of structured feedback, psychotherapy is often not successful in engendering insight. Cognitive rehabilitation in the absence of supportive psychotherapy may prove intolerable to the participant and result in more entrenched forms of denial.

The nature of the psychotherapeutic process varies across functional levels. With appropriate modifications, persons with moderate to severe brain injury may be able to benefit from psychotherapeutic approaches, even when they have difficulty expressing themselves in the context of a one-on-one conversation or in a group setting. An individual's cognitive impairment may reduce their ability to formulate a reasonable interpretation of their emotional state. This can occur because memory deficits cause a discontinuity of experiences that results in a dissociation of emotional states from environmental events or thoughts. This can also occur because of difficulty in maintaining continuity of thought, preventing progression through a problem-solving process.

It is up to the therapist to understand which aspects of an individual's cognitive impairments may interfere with the process of therapy and design a means to compensate. Modifications may include the use of pictures and visual symbols to increase comprehension, tape recordings to allow review of the session (Lemsky, 1996), as well as the use of art and music (Prigatano, 1991). For example, when an individual is capable of completing problem solving, but forgets the resolution that they have reached, notes or tape recordings may be used to compensate. Homework may include rehearsal or review of the session tape to reinforce gains made during the treatment session. When an individual's thought process is tangential, the therapist may diagram the conversation, using key words and arrows to remind the client of the conversation that occurred and the conclusions drawn. The diagram can be used by both the therapist and the client to reconstruct the problem-solving process and to reinforce the progress made.

When impairment is severe, but the individual has a supportive relationship with a caregiver, inclusion of the caregiver in psychotherapy sessions can be invaluable. In this case, sessions can be used to model effective ways of coping with affectively laden conversations and to demonstrate management of emotional lability or inappropriate social behaviors. The caregiver may also promote communication by providing information the individual is unable to recall or communicate. It is essential for the therapist to be aware of how well information is being understood and retained in order to adequately assess whether a given treatment approach is effective. It is also important to allow clients to have treatment time without the caregiver present to ensure that the presence of the caregiver does not interfere with the individual's willingness to discuss some issues. As in therapy with the general population, it is often useful to provide regular review of the goals of treatment and to create written summaries of sessions with clients. This enables the client's participation in the treatment planning process, provides a vehicle for reinforcing insights achieved in the session, and serves as a mean of reviewing information between sessions.

Interventions with Families

Many authors have written about the central role that families play in the adaptation to cognitive disorders (Kay & Cavallo, 1994; Lezak, 1978, 1988; Novak, Bergquist, & Bennett, 1992; Proulx, in press). As Proulx (in press) points out, the shift of health care funding away from hospitals and toward home care has caused an even greater emphasis on the role of family members as caregivers. Additionally, family members have information essential to understanding the functional impact of cognitive impairments and they play a key role in the maintenance and generalization of treatment gains. Caregiver training has been shown to be successful in reducing the rate of admission to institutions in dementia patients (Broadaty, McGilchrist, Harris, & Peters, 1993).

There are several categories of information that families commonly request:

1. The prognosis and natural history of an injury or illness
2. The nature of cognitive impairments and strengths and how they relate to brain functioning
3. The relationship between impairments and functional capacity
4. What they might do to address cognitive and behavioral problems.

Families are also often curious to know how other families are coping, and what community resources are available for support and treatment (Proulx, in press). It is important to note that clinical experience has suggested that information often needs to be offered several times over the course of an individual's rehabilitation in order to accommodate the evolution (and exhaustion) of a family's coping resources. Reviewing the nature and facts of a deficit, even many years after the onset of an illness or injury, may result in incorporation of information that may not have been well integrated in the past.

Involvement of family members should take place as early as possible in the treatment process. As noted above, the first step in involving family members is often providing information about the injury or illness that caused the cognitive impairment. It is natural, not pathological, that family members attempt to return to familiar, premorbid patterns of interaction. When cognitive impairment or the need for care require a change in family members' behavior, many problems can be avoided by simply providing appropriate information (Kay & Cavallo, 1994; Lezak, 1988). It is human nature to assume that individuals are capable of controlling their own behavior; however, in the case of brain dysfunction, self-control is often impaired. It is also commonly assumed that people are more or less consistent in their abilities. In contrast, persons with impaired cognition often fluctuate in their abilities because of fatigue, level of stimulation, and other factors. Finally, because most people believe in their own free will, it is sometimes difficult to accept that personality changes can be the result of a biological or structural changes in the brain.

For example, emotional lability (or *pseudobulbar affect*), blunted affect, rage, and other organically induced emotional states are difficult for clients and their care providers to understand. Explanation of these phenomenon, along with the development of coping strategies is often quite useful, particularly in the acute phases of acquired injury. In mild cases, uncontrolled crying may be managed behaviorally using distraction and redirection Clients and families can be encouraged not to view the affect as a sign of extreme distress, but rather as a lowered threshold for exhibiting a behavior that is usually associated with distress. They can learn to cue the client to use the appropriate coping strategy.

Helping family members to understand and accept changes in their loved one can be a very complex issue that may occur in the context of a long history of family interaction. The individual who was once a prime decision maker in a family, after an injury may become the subject of care and supervision. Making the transition from partner to caregiver, or taking a family member's freedom away can be an emotionally difficult situation that may be assisted by timely and sensitive intervention. Novak et al. (1992) discuss the importance of helping family members adapt to role changes that may have occurred as the result of cognitive changes. They also point out that it is the responsibility of the treatment team to help family members understand their role in the recovery of their loved one and to address the barriers to a fruitful partnership between family members and clinicians.

In general, referral for family intervention is recommended in the following situations:

1. When there is a history of family conflict that may continue to be present
2. When there appears to be a misapprehension of an individuals abilities or deficits
3. When emotional stress is evident
4. The individual is presenting with behavioral difficulties likely to impact upon functioning in the home.

Evaluation of family functioning may also be helpful when the causes for treatment failures are difficult to understand. Additionally, family support and education are often welcomed by families who are coping well, but interested in making the most of

Table 15.10.   Recommendations for facilitating adjustment

Strategy	Treatment Considerations
Education for the client and family related to the client's disability, prognosis, and course	Useful at all stages of treatment and at all levels of disability
	Should be tailored to the needs and abilities of the client and family
	Should include information about sexuality or resources for information about sexuality
Individual and group psychotherapy to address • Grief associated with disability-related losses • Develop a meaningful interpretation of the situation • Develop a realistic sense of hope and plans for the future	Methods used should accommodate the individual's cognitive status (e.g., simplified explanations, tape recordings, written notes, symbols) Referral to local/national organizations
Caregiver support • To manage caregiver grief, burnout, and role changes • Training and information to manage behavioral/cognitive issues	Support may be offered individually or in groups Reading material is often helpful Referral to local/national organizations Identification of community resources

available resources. Reading, family support groups, or family therapy may be offered depending upon the level of need presented and the willingness of the family to participate in intervention. Here again, invitations to participate in therapy ideally occur through the course of rehabilitation so that families know how to access assistance when they are ready, willing, and able to do so. Suggestions for recommendations to facilitate adjustment may be found in Table 15.10.

CONCLUSION

This chapter reviewed only a portion of a relatively recent, but now large and growing literature relevant to treatment planning for persons with cognitive impairment. This literature indicates that there is growing confidence that focused intervention can help individuals compensate for cognitive impairments and thereby prevent disabilities and handicaps. When the desired outcome is a change in day-to-day functioning, treatment should include training in the client's natural environment, restructuring of this environment, and practice with real-life problems. Evaluation of an individual's cognitive impairment and emotional functioning as well as the context of his or her life is crucial in making practical, and helpful plans for treatment. Treatment should be evaluated in terms of functionally relevant changes, not simply changes on cognitive measures. Finally, treatment is most likely to be successful if it addresses emotional, behavioral, social, and cognitive factors in an integrated fashion. Where there is a lack of awareness, denial, or difficulty in coping with a disability, psychotherapy and cognitive rehabilitation offered in concert maximizes benefits.

RECOMMENDED READING

Jacobs, H.E. (1993). *Behavioral analysis guidelines and brain injury rehabilitation: People, principles, and programs.* Gathersburg, MD: Aspen.

Kreutzer, J.S., & Wehman, P.H. (1991). *Cognitive rehabilitation for persons with traumatic brain injury: A functional approach.* Baltimore: Brookes.

Matthies, B.K., Kreutzer, J.S., & West, D.D. (1997). *The behavior management handbook: A practical approach to patients with neurological disorders.* San Antonio, TX: Therapy Skill Builders.

McMahon, B.T., & Shaw, R.L. (1991) *Work worth doing.* Orlando, FL: Deutsch Press.

Ponsford, J., Sloan, S., & Snow, P. (1995). *Traumatic brain injury: Rehabilitation in everyday adaptive living.* Hillsdale, NJ: Erlbaum.

Sohlberg, M.M., & Mateer, C. (1989). *Introduction to cognitive rehabilitation: Theory and practice.* New York: Guilford Press.

Stuss, D.T. (1991). Self, awareness and the frontal lobes: A neuropsychological perspective. In G.R. Goethaals & D.T. Stuss (Eds.), *The self: An interdisciplinary approach.* New York: Springer-Verlag.

REFERENCES

Alan, C.C., & Ruff, R.M. (1990). Self-rating versus neuropsychological performance of moderate versus severe head-injured patients. *Brain Injury, 4,* 7–17.

Alderman, N., & Ward, A. (1991). Behavioural treatment of the dysexecutive syndrome: Reduction of repetitive speech using response cost and cognitive overlearning. *Neuropsychological Rehabilitation, 1,* 65–80.

Americans with Disabilities Act of 1990, Pub.L. No. 101-136, § 2, 104 Stat. 328. (1991).

Anderson, S.W., & Tranel, D. (1989). Awareness of disease states following cerebral infarction, dementia and head trauma: Standardized assessment. *Clinical Neuropsychologist, 3,* 327–339.

Ashley, M.J., Persel, C.S., Clark, M.C., & Krych, D.K. (1997). Long-term follow-up of post-acute traumatic brain injury rehabilitation: A statistical analysis to test for stability and predictability of outcome. *Brain Injury, 11,* 677–690.

Baddeley, A.D. (1990). *Human memory: Theory and practice.* New York: Allyn & Bacon.

Baddeley, A.D. (1992). Implicit memory and errorless learning: A link between cognitive theory and neuropsychological rehabilitation? In L.R. Squire & N. Butters (Eds.), *Neuropsychology of memory* (pp. 309–314). New York: Guilford Press.

Ben-Yishay, Y., & Gold, J. (1990). Therapeutic milieu approach to neuropsychological rehabilitation. In R.L. Wood (Ed.), *Neurobehavioural sequelae of traumatic brain injury* (pp. 195–215). New York: Taylor & Francis.

Ben-Yishay, Y., & Prigatano, G.P. (1990). Cognitive remediation. In M. Rosenthal, E.R. Griffith, M.R. Bond, & J.D. Miller (Eds.), *Rehabilitation of the adult and child with traumatic brain injury* (2nd ed.). Philadelphia: Davis.

Ben-Yishay, Y., Silver, S.M., Piasetsky, E., & Rattock, J. (1987). Relationship between employability and vocational outcome after intensive holistic cognitive rehabilitation. *Journal of Head Trauma Rehabilitation, 2,* 35–48.

Boake, C. (1996). History of cognitive rehabilitation following head injury. In J. Kreutzer & P. Wehman (Eds.), *Cognitive rehabilitation for persons with traumatic brain injury* (pp. 3–12). Baltimore: Brookes.

Broadaty, H., McGilchrist, C., Harris, L., & Peters, F. (1993). Time until institutionalization and death in patients with dementia. *Archives of Neurology, 50,* 643–650.

Brouwer, H.W., & Withaar, F.K. (1997). Fitness to drive after traumatic brain injury. *Neuropsychological Rehabilitation, 3,* 177–193.

Buffington, A.L., & Malec, J.F. (1997). The vocational rehabilitation continuum: Maximizing outcomes through bridging the gap from hospital to community-based services. *Journal of Head Trauma Rehabilitation, 12,* 1–13.

Burke, J.M., Danick, J.A., Bemis, B., & Durgin, C.J. (1994). A process approach to memory book training for neurological patients. *Brain Injury, 8,* 71–81.

Carney, N., Chesnut, R.M., Maynard, H., Mann, N.C., Patterson, P., & Helfand, M. (1999). Effect of cognitive rehabilitation on outcomes for persons with traumetic brain injury: A systematic review. *Journal of Head Trauma Rehabilitation, 14,* 277–307.

Christensen, A. (1989). The neuropsychological investigation as a therapeutic and rehabilitative technique. In D. Ellis & A. Christensen (Eds.), *Neuropsychological treatment after brain injury.* Boston: Kluwer Academic.

Cicerone, K.D., & Tupper, D.E. (1991). Neuropsychological rehabilitation: Treatment of errors in everyday functioning. In D.E. Tupper and K.D. Cicerone (Eds.), *The neuropsychology of everyday life: Issues in development and rehabilitation* (pp. 271–292). Boston: Kluwer Academic.

Cicerone, K.D., & Wood, J.C. (1987). Planning disorder after closed head injury: A case study. *Archives of Physical Medicine and Rehabilitation, 68,* 11–115.

Cope, D.N. (1995). The effectiveness of traumatic brain injury rehabilitation: A review. *Brain Injury, 9,* 649–670.

Cope, D.N., Cole, J.R., Hall, K.M., & Barkan, H. (1991). Brain injury: Analysis of outcome in a post-acute rehabilitation system: Part 2. Subanalyses. *Brain Injury, 5,* 127–139.

Cope, D.N., & Hall, K. (1982). Head injury rehabilitation: Benefit of early intervention. *Archives of Physical Medicine and Rehabilitation, 63,* 433–437.

Crew, N.M., & Dijkers, M. (1995). Functional assessment. In L.A. Cushman & M.J. Scherer (Eds.), *Psychological assessment in rehabilitation settings.* Washington: American Psychological Association.

Crisp, R. (1992). Return to work after traumatic brain injury. *Journal of Rehabilitation, 58,* 27–32.

Crosson, B.C., Barco, P.P., Velozo, C.A., Bolesta, M.M., Werts, D., & Brobeck, T. (1989). Awareness and compensation in post-acute head injury rehabilitation. *Journal of Head Trauma Rehabilitation, 4,* 46–54.

Damasio A., & Anderson, S.W. (1993). The frontal lobes. In K. Heilman & E. Valenstein (Eds.), *Clinical neuropsychology* (pp. 409–460). New York: Oxford University Press.

Damico, J.S. (1985). A functional approach to language assessment. In C.S. Simon (Ed.), *Communication skills and classroom success* (pp. 165–203). Eau Clare, WI: Thinking.

Davis, J.R., & Goldstein, G. (1994). Behavior therapy in brain injury rehabilitation. In M.A.J. Finlayson & S.H. Garner (Eds.), *Brain injury rehabilitation: Clinical considerations* (pp. 279–312). Baltimore: Williams & Wilkenson.

DePompei, R., & Blosser, J.L. (1991). Functional Cognitive-Communicative impairments in children and adolescents: Assessment and intervention. In J.S. Kreutzer & P.H. Wehman (Eds.), *Cognitive rehabilitation for persons with traumatic brain injury: A functional approach* (pp. 215–235). Baltimore: Brookes.

Diller, L. (1994). Finding the right treatment combinations: Changes in rehabilitation over the past five years. In A. Christensen & B. Uzzell (Eds.), *Brain injury and neuropsychological rehabilitation: International perspectives* (pp. 1–17). Hillsdale, NJ: Erlbaum.

Diller, L., & Gordon, W.A. (1981). Rehabilitation and clinical neuropsychology. In S. Filskov & T. Boll (Eds.), *Handbook of clinical neuropsychology* (Vol. 1, pp. 702–733). New York: Wiley.

Drachman, D.A. (1988). Who may drive? Who may not? Who shall decide? *Annals of Neurology, 24,* 787–788.

Eames, P. (1988). Behavior disorders after severe head injury: Their nature, causes and strategies for management. *Journal of Head Trauma Rehabilitation, 3,* 1–6.

Eames, P., & Wood, R. (1985). Rehabilitation after severe brain injury: A follow-up study of a behavior modification approach. *Journal of Neurology and Neurosurgery and Psychiatry, 48,* 613–619.

Ellis, D.W. (1991). Neuropsychotherapy. In D.W. Ellis & A.L. Christensen (Eds.), *Neuropsychological treatment after brain injury* (pp. 241–270). Norwell, MA: Kluwer Academic.

Engum, E.S., Lambert, E.W., & Scott, K. (1990). Criterion-related validity of the cognitive behavioral drivers inventory: Brain-injured patients versus normal controls. *Cognitive Rehabilitation, 8,* 20–26.

Engum, E.S., Lambert, E.W., Scott, K., Pendergrass, T.M., & Womac, J. (1989). Criterion-related validity of the cognitive behavioral drivers index. *Cognitive Rehabilitation, 7,* 22–31.

Engum, E.S., Pendergras, T.M., Cron, S., Lambert, E.W., & Hulse, C.K. (1988). Cognitive behavioral drivers inventory. *Cognitive Rehabilitation, 6,* 34–50.

Fisher, J.E., & Carstensen, L.L. (1990). Behavior management of the dementias. *Clinical Psychology Review, 10,* 611–629.

Fisk, G.D., Schneider, J.J., & Novack, T.A. (1998). Driving following traumatic brain injury: Prevalence, exposure, advice and evaluations. *Brain Injury, 12,* 683–695.

Fordyce, D.J. (1994). Neuropsychologic assessment and cognitive rehabilitation: Issues of psychologic validity. In M.A.J. Finlayson & S.H. Garner (Eds.), *Brain injury rehabilitation: Clinical considerations* (pp. 187–211). Baltimore: Williams & Wilkenson.

Fordyce, D J., & Rouche, J.R. (1986). Changes in perspective of disability among patients, staff and relatives during rehabilitation of head injury. *Rehabilitation Psychology, 31,* 217–229.

Franzen, M.D., & Haut, M.W. (1991). The psychological treatment of memory impairment: A review of empirical studies. *Neuropsychology Review, 2,* 229–263.

Gasquonine, P.G. (1992). Affective states and awareness of sensory and cognitive effects after head injury. *Neuropsychology, 6,* 187–196.

Gasquonine, P.G., & Gibbons, T.A. (1994). Lack of awareness of impairment in institutionalized, severely and chronically disabled survivors of traumatic brain injury: A preliminary investigation. *Journal of Head Trauma Rehabilitation, 9,* 16–24.

Gianutsos, R. (1991). Cognitive rehabilitation: A neuropsychological specialty comes of age. *Brain Injury, 5,* 353–368.

Gianutsos, R., & Matheson, P. (1987). The rehabilitation of visual perceptual disorders attributable to brain injury. In M.J. Meier, A.L. Benton, & L. Diller (Eds.), *Neuropsychological rehabilitation* (pp. 202–241). New York: Guilford Press.

Glisky, E. L (1995). Computers in memory rehabilitation. In A.D Baddeley, B.A. Wilson, & F.N. Watts (Eds.), *Handbook of memory disorders* (pp. 557–575). New York: Wiley.

Glisky, E.L., Schacter, D.L., & Tulving, E. (1986). Computer learning by memory-impaired patients: Acquisition and retention of complex knowledge. *Neuropsychological Rehabilitation, 24,* 313–328.

Gouvier, W.D., & Cubic, B. (1991). Behavioral assessment and treatment of acquired visuoperceptual disorders. *Neuropsychological Review, 2,* 3–28.

Gouvier, W.D., Maxfield, M.W., Schweitzer, J.R., Horton, C.R., Shipp, M., Neilson, K., & Hale, P.N. (1989). Psychometric prediction of driving performance among the disabled. *Archives of Physical Medicine and Rehabilitation, 70,* 745–750.

Guilmette, T.J., & Kastner, M.P. (1996). The prediction of vocational functioning from neuropsychological data. In R.J. Sbordone & C.J. Long (Eds.), *Ecological validity of neuropsychological testing* (pp. 387–412) Delray Beach, FL: GR/St. Lucie Press.

Haselkorn, J.K., Mueller, B.A., & Rivara, F.A. (1998). Characteristics of drivers and driving record after traumatic and non-traumatic brain injury. *Archives of Physical Medicine and Rehabilitation, 79,* 738–742.

Head Injury Special Interest Group of the American Congress of Rehabilitation Medicine: Guidelines for Cognitive Rehabilitation. (1992). *Neurorehabilitation, 2,* 62–67.

Heilman, K.M., Watson, R.T., & Valenstein, E. (1993). Neglect and related disorders. In K.M. Heilman & E. Valenstein (Eds.), *Clinical neuropsychology* (3rd ed., pp. 279–336). New York: Oxford University Press.

Jacobs, H.E. (1993). *Behavioral analysis guidelines and brain injury rehabilitation: People, principles, and programs.* Gathersburg, MD: Aspen.

Johnstone, B., & Callahan, T.S. (1996). Neuropsychological evaluation of traumatic brain injury in the United States: A critical analysis. In B.P. Uzzell & H.H. Stonnington (Eds.), *Recovery after traumatic brain injury* (pp. 115–128). Mahwah, NJ: Erlbaum.

Katz, R.T., Golden R.S., Butter, J.A., Tepper, D., Rothke, S., Holmes, J., & Sahgal, V. (1990). Driving safety after brain damage: Follow-up of twenty-two patients with matched controls. *Archives of Physical Medicine and Rehabilitation, 71,* 133–137.

Kay, T., & Cavallo, M.M. (1994). The family system: Impact, assessment and intervention. In J.M. Silver, S.C. Yudofsky, & R.E. Hales (Eds.), *Neuropsychiatry of traumatic brain injury* (pp. 533–567). Washington, DC: American Psychiatric Press.

Kime, S.K., Lamb, D.G., & Wilson, B.A. (1996). Use of a comprehensive programme of external cueing to enhance procedural memory in a patient with dense amnesia. *Brain Injury, 10,* 17–25.

Klonoff, P.S., O'Brien, K.P., Prigatano, P.G., Chiapello, D.A., & Cunningham, M. (1989). Cognitive retraining after traumatic brain injury and its role in facilitating awareness. *Journal of Head Trauma Rehabilitation, 4,* 37–45.

Kreutzer, J.S., & Wehman, P.H. (1991). *Cognitive rehabilitation for persons with traumatic brain injury: A functional approach.* Baltimore: Brookes.

Lambert, E.W., & Engum, E.S. (1992). Construct validity of the cognitive behavioral driver's inventory: Age, diagnosis, and driving ability. *Journal of Cognitive Rehabilitation, 10,* 32–45.

Lemsky, C.M. (1996). Adapting behavioral intervention for brain injured older adults. *Behavior Therapist, 19,* 126.

Leon-Carrion, J. (1997a). An approach to the treatment of affective disorders and suicide tendencies after TBI. In J. Leon-Carrion (Ed.), *Neuropsychological rehabilitation: Fundamentals, innovations and directions* (pp. 371–398). Delray Beach, FL: GR/St. Lucie Press.

León-Carrión, J. (1997b). Rehabilitation of memory. In J. Leon-Carrion (Ed.), *Neuropsychological rehabilitation: FundamEntals, Innovations, And Directions* (pp. 415–428). Delray Beach, FL: GR/St. Lucie Press.

Lewis, L. (1991). A framework for developing a psychotherapy treatment plan with brain injured individuals. *Journal of Head Trauma and Rehabilitation, 6,* 22–29.

Lezak, M.D. (1978). Living with the characterologically altered brain injured patient. *Journal of Clinical Psychiatry, 39,* 592–598.

Lezak, M.D. (1988). Brain damage is a family affair. *Journal of Clinical and Experimental Neuropsychology, 10,* 111–123.

Lezak, M.D. (1995). *Neuropsychological assessment* (3rd ed.). New York: Oxford University Press.

Long, C. (1996). Neuropsychological tests: A look at our past and the impact that ecological is-sues may have on our future. In R.J. Sbordone & C.J. Long (Eds.), *Ecological validity of neuropsychological testing* (pp. 1–15). Delray Beach, FL: GR/St. Lucie Press.

Malec, J.F. (1996). Cognitive rehabilitation. In R. Evans (Ed.), *Neurology and trauma* (pp. 231–248). Philadelphia: Sanders.

Malec, J.F., & Lemsky, C.M. (1995). Behavioral assessment: Traditional and concensual mod-els. In L. Cushing & M. Scherer (Eds.), *Assessment in rehabilitation and medical settings* (pp. 199–236). Washington, DC: American Psychological Association.

Malec, J.F., Schafer, D., & Jacket, M. (1992). Comprehensive-integrated post acute outpatient brain injury rehabilitation. *Neurorehabilitation, 2,* 1–11.

Malec, J.F., Smigielski, J.S., DePompolo, R.W., & Thompson, J.W. (1993). Outcome evaluation and prediction in a comprehensive-integrated postacute outpatient brain injury rehabilita-tion program. *Brain Injury, 7,* 12–29.

Matthies, B.K., Kreutzer, J.S., & West, D.D. (1997). *The behavior management handbook: A practical approach to patients with neurological disorders.* San Antonio, TX: Therapy Skill Builders.

McCarthy, R.A., & Warrington, E.K. (1990). *Cognitive neuropsychology: A clinical introduc-tion.* San Diego: Academic Press.

McGlynn, S.M., & Shacter, D.L. (1989). Unawareness of deficits in neuropsychological syn-dromes. *Journal of Clinical and Experimental Neuropsychology, 2,* 143–205.

McMahon, B.T., & Shaw, R.L. (1991). *Work worth doing.* Orlando Florida: Deutsch Press.

McMahon, B.T., & Shaw, R.L. (1996). Neuropsychology and rehabilitation counseling: Bridg-ing the gap. In R.J. Sbordone & C.J. Long (Eds.), *Ecological validity of neuropsychological testing* (pp. 369–388). Delray Beach, FL: GR/St. Lucie Press.

Meichenbaum, D., & Goodman, J . (1971). Training impulsive children to talk to themselves: A means of developing self-control. *Journal of Abnormal Psychology, 77,* 115–126.

Miller, L. (1992). Cognitive rehabilitation, cognitive therapy and cognitive style: Toward an integrative model of personality and psychotherapy. *Cognitive Rehabilitation, 10,* 18–28.

National Institute of Health. (1998, October 26–28). *Rehabilitation of persons with traumatic brain injury consensus statement* [online]. Available: odp.od.nih.gov./consensus/cons /109/109_statement.htm.

Nelson L.D., & Adams K.M. (1997). Challenges for neuropsychology in the treatment and re-habilitation of brain injury patients. *Psychological Assessment, 9,* 368–373.

Novak, T.A., Bergquist, T.F., & Bennett, G. (1992). Family involvement in cognitive recovery following traumatic brain injury. In C.J. Long & L.K. Ross (Eds.), *Handbook of head trauma: Acute care to recovery* (pp. 327–365). New York: Plenum Press.

Panella, J. (1986). Toileting strategies in day care programs for dementia. *Clinical Gerontolo-gist, 4,* 61–63.

Paniak, C.E., Shore, D.L., Rourke, B.P., Finlayson, M.A.J., & Moustacalis, E. (1992). Long-term vocational functioning after severe closed head injury: A controlled study. *Archives of Clinical Neuropsychology, 7,* 529–540.

Parenté, R., & Herrmann, D. (1996). *Retraining cognition: Techniques and applications,* Gaithersberg, MD: Aspen.

Persson, D. (1993). The elderly driver: Deciding when to stop. *Gerontologist, 33,* 88–91.

Ponsford, J.L. (1995a). Assessment and management of behavior problems associated with TBI. In J. Ponsford, S. Sloan, & P. Snow (Eds.), *Traumatic brain injury: Rehabilitation in everyday adaptive living* (pp. 165–194). Hillsdale, NJ: Erlbaum.

Ponsford, J.L. (1995b). Dealing with the impact of traumatic brain injury on psychological ad-justment and relationships. In J. Ponsford, S. Sloan, & P. Snow (Eds.), *Traumatic brain in-jury: Rehabilitation in everyday adaptive living* (pp. 231–264). Hillsdale, NJ: Erlbaum.

Ponsford, J.L., & Kinsella, G. (1988). Evaluation of a remedial programme for attentional deficits following closed head injury. *Journal of Clinical and Experimental Neuropsychology, 10,* 693–708.

Ponsford, J.L., & Kinsella, G. (1992). Attentional deficits following closed-head injury. *Journal of Clinical and Experimental Neuropsychology, 14,* 822–838.

Ponsford, J.L., Oliver, J.H., & Curran, C. (1995). A profile of outcome: Two years after traumatic brain injury. *Brain Injury, 9,* 1–10.

Ponsford, J.L., & Sloan, S. (1995). Assessment of cognitive difficulties following TBI. In J. Ponsford, S. Sloan, & P. Snow (Eds.), *Traumatic brain injury: Rehabilitation in everyday adaptive living* (pp. 65–101). Hillsdale, NJ: Erlbaum.

Prigatano, G.P. (1991). Disordered mind, wounded soul: The emerging role of psychotherapy in rehabilitation after brain injury. *Journal of Head Trauma Rehabilitation, 6,* 1–10.

Prigatano, G.P. (1994). Individuality, lesion location, and psychotherapy after brain injury. In A. Christensen & B. Uzzell (Eds.), *Brain injury and neuropsychological rehabilitation: International perspectives* (pp. 173–186). Hillsdale, NJ: Erlbaum.

Prigatano, G.P. (1996). Neuropsychological testing after traumatic brain injury. In R. Evans (Ed.), *Neurology and trauma* (pp. 222–230). Philadelphia: Sanders.

Prigatano, G.P. (1997). Learning from our successes and failures: Reflections and comments on "Cognitive rehabilitation: How it is and how it might be." *Journal of the International Neuropsychological Society, 3,* 497–499.

Prigatano, G.P., & Altman, I.M. (1990). Impaired awareness of behavioral limitations after traumatic brain injury. *Archives of Physical Medicine and Rehabilitation, 71,* 1058–1064.

Prigatano, G.P., & Fordyce, D.J. (1986). Cognitive dysfunction and psychosocial adjustment after brain injury. In G.P. Prigatano, D.J. Fordyce, H.K. Zeiner, J.R. Roueche, M. Pepping, & B.C. Wood (Eds.), *Neuropsychological rehabilitation after brain injury* (pp. 1–17) Baltimore: Johns Hopkins University Press.

Prigatano, G.P., Fordyce, D.J., Zeiner, H.K., Rouche, J.R. Pepping, M., & Wood, B.C. (1984). Neuropsychological rehabilitation after closed head injury in young adults. *Journal of Neurology, Neurosurgery and Psychiatry, 47,* 505–513.

Proulx, G. (in press). Family education and family partnership in cognitive rehabilitation. In D.T. Stuss, G. Winocur, & I. Robertson (Eds.), *Cognitive rehabilitation.* London, England: Cambridge University Press.

Prutting, C.R., & Kirchner, D.M. (1983). A clinical appraisal of the pragmatic aspects of language. *Journal of Speech and Hearing Disorders, 52,* 105–119.

Richardson, J.T. (1992). Imagery, mnemonics and memory remediation. *Neurology, 42,* 283–286.

Rimmele, C.T., & Hester, R.K. (1987). Cognitive rehabilitation after traumatic head injury. *Archives of Clinical Neuropsychology, 2,* 151–163.

Rourke, B.P., & Tsatsanis, K.D. (1995). Memory disturbances of children with learning disabilities: A neuropsychological analysis of two academic achievement subtypes. In A.D. Baddeley, B.A. Wilson, & F.N. Watt (Eds.), *Handbook of Memory Disorders* (pp. 501–531). New York: Wiley.

Sander, A.M., Kreutzer, J.S., & Fernandez, C. (1997). Neurobehavioral functioning, substance abuse, and employment after brain injury: Implications for vocational rehabilitation. *Journal of Head Trauma Rehabilitation, 12,* 28–41.

Sbordone, R.J. (1991). Overcoming obstacles in cognitive rehabilitation of persons with severe traumatic brain injury. In J.S. Kreutzer & P.H. Wehman (Eds.), *Cognitive rehabilitation for persons with traumatic brain injury: A functional approach* (pp. 105–126) Baltimore: Brookes.

Sbordone, R.J., & Long, C.J. (1996). *Ecological validity of neuropsychological testing.* Delray Beach, FL: GR/St Lucie Press.

Schefft, B.K., Malec, J.F., Lehr, B.K., & Kanfer, F.H. (1994). The role of self-regulation therapy with the brain injured patient. In M. Maruish & J.A. Moses, Jr. (Eds.), *Clinical neuropsychology: Theoretical foundations for practitioners* (pp. 210–245) New York: Erlbaum.

Sherer, M., Bergloff, P., Levin, E., High, W.M., Oden, K.E., & Nick, T.G. (1998). Impaired awareness and employment outcome after traumatic brain injury. *Journal of Head Trauma Rehabilitation, 13,* 52–61.

Sherer, M., Boake, C., Levin, E., Silver, B.V., Ringholz, G., & High, W. (1998). Characteristics of impaired awareness after traumatic brain injury. *Journal of the International Neuropsychological Society, 4,* 380–387.

Sloan, S., & Ponsford, J. (1995). Assessment of cognitive function. In J. Ponsford, S. Sloan, & P. Snow (Eds.), *Traumatic brain injury: Rehabilitation in everyday adaptive living.* Hillsdale, NJ: Erlbaum.

Sohlberg, M.M., & Mateer, C. (1989). *Introduction to cognitive rehabilitation: Theory and practice.* New York: Guilford Press.

Spreen, O., & Strauss, E. (1998). *A compendium of neuropsychological tests: Administration, norms and commentary* (2nd ed.). New York: Oxford University Press.

Squires, E., Hunkin, N.M., & Parkin, A. (1996). Memory notebook training in a case of severe amnesia: Generalizing from paired associate learning to real life. *Neuropsychological Rehabilitation, 6,* 55–65.

Sturm, W., & Willmes, K. (1991). Efficacy of reaction training on various attentional and cognitive functions in stroke patients. *Neuropsychological Rehabilitation, 1,* 259–280.

Stuss, D.T. (1991). Self, awareness and the frontal lobes: A neuropsychological perspective. In G.R. Goethaals & D.T. Stuss (Eds.), *The self: An interdisciplinary approach* (pp. 255–278). New York: Springer-Verlag.

Stuss, D.T., Delgado, M., & Guzman, D.A. (1987). Verbal regulation in the control of motor impersistence: A proposed rehabilitation procedure. *Journal of Neurological Rehabilitation, 1,* 19–24.

Stuss, D.T., Mateer, C.A., & Sohlberg, M.M. (1994). Innovative approaches to frontal lobe deficits. In M.A.J. Finlayson & S.H. Garner (Eds.), *Brain injury rehabilitation, clinical considerations* (pp. 212–237) Baltimore: Williams & Wilkins.

Tallent, N. (1993). *Psychological report writing* (4th ed.). Englewood Cliffs, NJ: Prentice Hall.

Tate, R.L. (1997). Beyond one-bun, two-shoe: Recent advances in the psychological rehabilitation of memory disorders after acquired brain injury. *Brain Injury, 11,* 907–918.

Trexler, L.E., Webb, P.M., & Zappala, G. (1994). Strategic aspects for neuropsychological rehabilitation. In A. Christensen & B. Uzzell (Eds.), *Brain injury and neuropsychological rehabilitation: International perspectives* (pp. 99–123). Hillsdale, NJ: Erlbaum.

Verhaeghen, P., Marcoen, A., & Goossens, L. (1992). Improving memory performance in the aged through mnemonic training: A meta-analytic study. *Psychology and Aging, 7,* 242–251.

Warren, M. (1993a). A hierarchical model for evaluation and treatment of visual perceptual dysfunction in adult acquired brain injury, Part 1. *American Journal of Occupational Therapy, 47,* 442–454.

Warren, M. (1993b). A hierarchical model for evaluation and treatment of visual perceptual dysfunction in adult acquired brain injury, Part 2. *American Journal of Occupational Therapy, 47,* 455–466.

Watts, F.N. (1995). Depression and anxiety. In A.D. Baddeley, B.A. Wilson, & F.N. Watt (Eds.), *Handbook of memory disorders* (pp. 293–317). New York: Wiley.

Wehman, P. (1996). Work outcome and supported employment. In B.P. Uzzzell & H.H. Stonnington (Eds.), *Recovery after traumatic brain injury* (pp. 257–276). Mahwah, NJ: Erlbaum.

Weinberg, J., Diller, L., Gordon, W.A., Gerstman, L.J., Lieberman, A., Lakin, P., Hodges, G., & Ezrachi, O. (1977). Visual scanning training effect on reading-related tasks in acquired right brain damage. *Archives of Physical Medicine and Rehabilitation, 60,* 491–496.

Weinberg, J., Diller, L., Gordon, W.A., Gerstman, L.J., Leiberman, A., Lakin, P., Hodges, G., & Ezrachi, O. (1979). Training sensory awareness and spatial organization in people with right brain damage. *Archives of Physical Medicine and Rehabilitation, 60,* 709–28.

Weinberg, J., Piasetsky, E., Diller, L., & Gordon, W. (1982). Treating perceptual organization deficits in non-neglecting RBD stroke patients. *Journal of Clinical Neuropsychology, 4,* 59–79.

West, R.L. (1995). Compensatory strategies for age-associated memory impairment. In A.D. Baddeley, B.A. Wilson, & F.N. Watt (Eds.), *Handbook of memory disorders* (pp. 481–500). New York: Wiley.

Willer, B., & Corrigan, J. (1994). What ever it takes: A model for community-based services. *Brain Injury, 8,* 647–659.

Wilson, B.A. (1991). Behavior therapy in the treatment of neurologically impaired adults. In P.R. Martin (Ed.), *Handbook of behavior therapy and psychological science: An integrative approach* (pp. 227–252), Elmsford, NY: Pergamon Press.

Wilson, B.A. (1995). Management and remediation of memory problems in brain-injured adults. In A.D. Baddeley, B.A. Wilson, & F.N. Watt (Eds.), *Handbook of memory disorders* (pp. 451–479). New York: Wiley.

Wilson, B.A. (1997). Cognitive rehabilitation: How it is and how it might be. *Journal of the International Neuropsychological Society, 3,* 487–496.

Wilson, B.A., Alderman, N., Burgess, P.W., Emslie, H., & Evans, J.J. (1996). *Behavioral assessment of the dysexecutive syndrome.* Bury St. Edmunds, England: Thames Valley Test.

Wilson, B.A., Cockburn, J., & Baddeley, A. (1985). *The Rivermead behavioral memory test.* Bury St. Edmunds, England: Thames Valley Test.

Wilson, B.A., & Evans, J.J. (1996). Error-free learning in the rehabilitation of people with memory impairments. *Journal of Head Trauma Rehabilitation, 11,* 45–64.

Wilson, B.A., & Hughes, E. (1997). Coping with amnesia: The natural history of a compensatory memory system. *Neuropsychological Rehabilitation, 7,* 43–46.

Wood, R.L. (1990). Conditioning procedures in brain injury rehabilitation. In R.L. Wood (Ed.), *Neurobehavioural sequelae of traumatic brain injury* (pp. 153–193). New York: Taylor & Francis.

World Health Organization. (1998). *Classification of impairments, activities and participation.* Available: http: www.who.int/sma/mnh/ems/icidh/index.htm.

Ylvisaker, M., Chorazy, A., Cohen, S., Mastrill, J., Molitor, C., Nelson, J., Szekeres, S., Valko, A., & Jaffee, K. (1990). Rehabilitation assessment following head injury in children. In M. Rosenthal, E. Griffith, M. Bond, & J.D. Miller (Eds.), *Rehabilitation of the adult and child with traumatic brain injury* (2nd ed., pp. 558–584). Philadelphia: Davis.

Ylvisaker, M., & Urbanczyk, B. (1994). Assessment and treatment of speech, swallowing and communication disorders following traumatic brain injury. In M.A.J. Finlayson & S.H. Garner (Eds.), *Brain injury rehabilitation: Clinical considerations* (pp. 157–211). Baltimore: Williams & Wilkenson.

Chapter 16

REPORT WRITING IN CLINICAL NEUROPSYCHOLOGY

MARK A. WILLIAMS and THOMAS J. BOLL

The neuropsychological report is a written document prepared by a neuropsychologist to communicate the results of a neuropsychological evaluation. While this might seem obvious, this point deserves discussion. The term *neuropsychological evaluation* is usefully distinguished from the term *neuropsychological testing* (e.g., Boll, Williams, Kashden, & Putzke, 1998; Matarazzo, 1990). Neuropsychological testing represents one of the tools employed as part of the neuropsychological evaluation. Neuropsychological test results alone provide incomplete data for completion of a neuropsychological evaluation and neuropsychological report. The skilled neuropsychologist uses his or her knowledge of brain-behavior relationships, psychopathology, behavioral science, and psychometrics to evaluate the meaning of available data that includes neuropsychological test performance (quantitative and qualitative aspects), and pertinent historical variables such as medical history, educational history, occupational history, and social/cultural history. Therefore, when reading a neuropsychological report, it is not at all unreasonable to begin with an understanding of the clinician's credentials (e.g., Hannay et al., 1998). As with all professional efforts, the neuropsychological report is only as good as the data that goes into it combined with the skill and knowledge of the clinician utilizing that data.

COGNITIVE AND BEHAVIORAL FUNCTIONING

Large advances in neuroradiology have occurred during the past 30 years allowing for sensitive structural and physiological examination of the brain. As a result, there has been a shift in focus from using neuropsychological tests to detect "brain damage" to emphasizing the use of neuropsychological tests to provide a comprehensive evaluation of functionally important cognitive and behavioral sequelae of known or suspected brain damage. Tramontana and Hooper (1988) call this the "functional profile stage." This approach emphasizes neuropsychological evaluation as a descriptive activity which is useful for informing treatment planning and making decisions about patients' capacity for performing activities in their daily lives. Tests are selected to cover a broad range of capacities that are broadly termed "cognitive" for convenience but that typically also include assessment of motor, somatosensory, perceptual, and emotional functioning. Selection of specific tests to be used is governed by a number of issues including psychometric considerations (e.g., validity and reliability of specific tests), clinician's preference, nature of the referral question, practical limitations, patient's age, and the nature and severity of the patient's neuropsychological impairments. However, under almost all circumstances, coverage of several domains of neuropsychologic functions (see Chapters 9–14) is needed to obtain a profile of areas of strength and weakness.

Descriptive activity in neuropsychological evaluation can be categorized in terms of neuropsychological syndromes or descriptive diagnoses (Stringer, 1996). Examples of syndromes include specific learning disorders, the Korsakoff amnestic syndrome, or the Gerstman syndrome. These labels reflect a cluster of neuropsychological deficits or defects that are found. Descriptive diagnostic labels are used to characterize domain-specific defects or deficits. For example, terms such as aphasia, apraxia, and agnosia refer to disorders within separate neuropsychological domains (language, skilled movement, perception). In the neuropsychological report, a major goal is to describe functioning in a summary. The use of established neuropsychological syndromes and descriptive labels facilitates this.

Clinicians should not use esoteric terminology without providing adequate descriptive explanation that will allow the intended reader to appropriately understand the patient's neuropsychological functioning. Caution is advised in the use of certain terminology, that while it may be somewhat commonly used, its use may lead to confusion. For example, the term *post-concussive syndrome* is familiar to many. However, its establishment as a syndrome with scientific or even descriptive merit is questionable. This is partly due to the fact that a strict definition of what is meant by the term has not been universally accepted. Therefore, while some persons may use the term to globally reflect any neuropsychological difficulties a person complains of following a head injury, others are more narrow in their use of the term. Also, some persons use the term to reflect their belief that neurologic-based dysfunction is present, while others use the term as a label for complaints made following head injury which are believed to be due to psychological and not necessarily neurological dysfunction. If a term has potential for misleading or confusing the intended reader, it is best to chose other more appropriate terms. Even when terms are appropriate and generally understood by the reader, adequate descriptive information given in general language should be included to accurately communicate the severity of the impairment in the patient's functioning. For example, the statement, "the patient was moderately aphasic" clearly indicates that the patient has some kind of language impairment, however, additional information of a descriptive nature is required to accurately describe the patient's language impairment.

TREATMENT PLANNING

Neuropsychological evaluation is also commonly used as a source of information for developing intervention programs (see Chapter 15). The first intervention is the provision of feedback to the patient and other interested parties as to the results and implications of the evaluation. This information often helps the patient and family understand problems and can help reduce emotional distress. Receiving feedback sets the stage for subsequent activities such as learning compensatory strategies, making vocational changes, and appropriate goal setting.

Interventions may be prescriptive or rehabilitative. *Prescriptive interventions* include providing an opinion about the patient's current ability to return to his or her previous job or other work, ability to drive safely, or competency to manage finances or engage in other specific components of activities of daily living. Test results can help guide *rehabilitative efforts* by clarifying specific areas of strength and weakness that can logically lead to development of compensatory strategies to improve overall functioning in the face of continued areas of neuropsychological deficits.

When writing reports for rehabilitation purposes, it is useful to describe in substantial detail the interaction of specific areas of deficit and strengths. This will help in the development of compensatory strategies. For example, the patient who has substantial new learning difficulties for verbally presented material, but performs within the average range on visual-spatial learning tests, may benefit from learning to emphasize visual-spatial encoding of verbal information. For other patients, efficiency of new learning may appear to be mostly related to attentional deficits. Adequate discussion in the evaluation report of how this conclusion was inferred from the testing will provide helpful data that can lead to rehabilitation efforts.

FRAMEWORK FOR THE NEUROPSYCHOLOGICAL EVALUATION

The neuropsychological report is organized around the neuropsychological evaluation. Previous chapters have described in more detail the neuropsychological evaluation so only brief mention of the more salient aspects of the neuropsychological evaluation will be made in order to provide a context for the ensuing discussion about report writing. The neuropsychological evaluation and report stands on the three "legs" of (1) presenting problems/behavioral observations, (2) history, and (3) testing (see Chapter 4, Interviewing).

Presenting Problems and Behavioral Observations

The patient's presentation of complaints may or may not be an accurate and articulate report of problems, but may well be the best presentation the patient or even the referral source can make of the individual's difficulties and subjective problems as they perceive them (see Chapter 4). For example, patients commonly use the phrase "memory problems" to encompass a broad range of difficulties that may or may not include an actual primary impairment in memory functioning. Presenting complaints, however, are useful in determining what the focus of difficulty is and the degree of concern that a patient has for one versus another characteristic that may either be pointed out initially or emerge throughout the evaluation. Patients will vary in regards to the saliency that a particular problem will have for them and this can be elicited in the interview. As an example of this, if a right-handed neuropsychologist lost his or her left little finger, that may not have much importance on a day-to-day basis, and if the neuropsychologist began to experience difficulties in one area or another of his life, it is quite unlikely that reference would be made to the little finger as a source of those difficulties, given what a neuropsychologist is called on to do. If, on the other hand, the individual who lost the left little finger was a Major League left-handed pitcher, the amputated left finger may reasonably account for that person's economic, social, psychological, and emotional difficulties, as it would be a life-altering condition. Therefore, the patient's own presentation of complaints provides much by way of salience about the impact that certain real or perceived impairments have on his life.

Behavioral observations are an extremely important source of data for the neuropsychologist. The fashion in which a patient presents himself is by itself important data that speaks to the nature and extent of both abilities and deficits. It also provides direct data by which certain aspects of the patient's self-report can be compared for hypothesis testing, inferential reasoning, and verification. For example, the patient whose self-report includes comments such as "I can't remember a thing since my accident" is making a statement that is subject to confirmation from behavioral observation data. The extent to which the patient is able to provide detailed recollection of recent activities or even to remember questions from earlier in the interview provides important data about memory functions which then is rationally considered in combination with the self-report, medical history, and formal test results in coming to a conclusion about the "true" status of the patient's memory functioning. All serious neuropsychiatric disorders include behavioral signs that should be apparent to the skilled neuropsychologist and are of great importance in providing both specific diagnoses and drawing conclusions about severity level. Self-reports are subject to intentional and unintentional distortion stemming from numerous factors. Therefore, self-report verification by considering this data against data derived from behavioral observations is an important part of the diagnostic reasoning process. For example, the severely depressed patient will show signs of affective and mood disturbance, slowed movements, and decreased motivation. Absence of these signs in a patient whose self-report is that of experiencing severe levels of depression represents a conflict that must be resolved by the clinician. In contrast, the patient with observable signs of mania or dementia who presents with a self-report indicating no functional difficulties is another example of how considering the continuity or discontinuity of self-report and observable behavior represents a major component of the diagnostic conceptualization process that will be presented in the report.

History

The second leg of the neuropsychological evaluation and report is history (see Chapters 3, 4, and 5 on context, neurology, and interviewing). This can encompass information from multiple sources including reports about a child's developmental milestones, medical history, and longstanding functioning in behavioral, social, emotional, and cognitive domains. In some settings, such as on an acute stroke unit, a great deal of information about a patient's life history may not be available on first evaluation, and the effect of the acute cerebral vascular disease on behavioral functioning may be quite easily identified without detailed gathering of one's history. On the other hand, the patient who complains of difficulty secondary to a mild head injury, which may or may not have included an injury to the brain, will be very difficult to assess regarding whether or not changes have occurred in their behavioral capabilities without obtaining substantial historical data (e.g., medical history, educational history, vocational history). Results of medical tests such as neuroradiologic procedures can be very helpful, in ruling specific entities in or out. While normal neuroradiologic and normal neurological examinations are not definitive in ruling out all neurological impairment, they certainly do represent some degree of limiting factor with regard to the type and severity of neurological disorder that may exist. It is also true that at times even when radiographic tests show "abnormal" findings, these are not necessarily the cause of any neuropsychological difficulties. Just because neuropsychological test scores are somewhat unusual or not average, it does not necessarily mean that they are "abnormal" for the particular patient being evaluated. The neuropsychological evaluation and report considers all of the data within the context of what is known about the etiology and expression of neurological disorders to formulate the case conceptualization.

Testing

The third leg is neuropsychological testing itself (see Chapters 5–14). This includes direct testing of the patient across a variety of neuropsychological domains. The neuropsychological evaluation typically covers:

1. The domains of past background knowledge, often including tests of IQ and academic achievement
2. Motor functioning
3. Sensory functioning
4. Language
5. Perception
6. Memory
7. Mental speed
8. Attentional abilities
9. Problem-solving capacity
10. Personality or psychiatric functioning.

Tests are selected to sufficiently cover each of these areas. In reality, multiple integrated neuropsychological skills are required to perform well on any given test. Therefore, just because the test being used is typically referred to as a "memory" test, for example, does not preclude a particularly poor performance due to some other problem such as attentional difficulties, language disorder, or visuospatial disorder. Use of both *broad-band* tests, which require integration of a number of neuropsychological functions, and *narrow-band* tests, which examine neuropsychological functions in greater isolation, are helpful for deriving an accurate description of patients neuropsychological deficits.

FORMAT OF THE NEUROPSYCHOLOGICAL REPORT

It is the integration of the presenting problem and behavioral observations, historical data, and neuropsychological test results that make up the neuropsychological report. There are multiple ways in which reports can be organized, and this should depend on the nature of the question, the audience to which the report is directed, and the use to which the report will be placed (Groth-Marnat, 1999; Spreen & Strauss, 1998). For instance, a report done in the context of ongoing trials for medication effect, or readiness for rehabilitation, or as a baseline and follow-up for other procedures (e.g., neurological surgery) may be one to two pages in length. Such a report might be focused specifically on changes made by the patient over multiple evaluations and have little ongoing clinical description. On the other hand, a report may require a substantial amount of detail if one is to compare various in-depth evaluative efforts that have been done over a longer period of time. For example, a report designed to make specific recommendations with regard to interventions and life planning will be quite lengthy because of the need to address a multitude of specific questions.

Some clinicians write lengthy reports (e.g., 10–20 single-spaced pages) when neuropsychological evaluation of a patient for forensic purposes has been conducted. Others, including ourselves, find that forensic neuropsychological reports usually only slightly exceed the length typically obtained in our nonforensic comprehensive neuropsychological reports (e.g., 3–5 single-spaced pages). Increased report length in forensic cases are likely due to two general factors. First, in forensic cases, verification of historical information (e.g., medical history, educational history, past test scores) is always important. This is because in most cases, the attorneys involved are debating whether or not a neurological injury has occurred and, if so, the extent of the related impairment in functioning. Discussion of relevant background information in substantial detail to provide a pre-injury (or pre-event) estimate of neuropsychological functioning is important to the referral question. While consideration and discussion of historical information is also of importance in nonforensic neuropsychological evaluations, the difference is one of emphasis and relative importance for answering the referral question. Another practice that adds length to the forensic neuropsychological reports is that of spending substantial space addressing anticipated challenges to one's conclusions. Without appropriate restraint, this can lead to a very large document that reads more like a monograph than an evaluation report. Our practice is to limit this kind of debate. General conclusions reached and inferences drawn can be stated simply and clearly. Substantially more detail including making references to published research findings pertinent to the case can be elicited by attorneys during deposition.

The neuropsychological report should be primarily conclusory in nature. How much individual test description, data presentation, and discussion provided will be determined mostly by the need of the referral source for that sort of information and the utility of that information in actually bolstering the message rather than simply filling pages. Groth-Marnat (1999) made this point by stating, "It is crucial to stress that the purpose of providing raw data and behavioral descriptions is to enrich and illustrate the topic and not to enable the reader to follow the clinician's line of reasoning or document the inferences that have been made. In drawing inferences, clinicians must draw on a wide variety of data. They cannot possibly discuss all the patterns, configurations, and relationships they used to come to their conclusions. Any attempt to do so would necessarily be overly detailed, cumbersome, and incomplete" (p. 628).

The format of a neuropsychological report will vary. Nevertheless, the internal organization of the report should be apparent and no report should contain internal inconsistencies, much less surprise endings. In addition to the difficulty in utilizing basic and clear English rather than jargon and reverting to nominalisms, one of the biggest errors is that a neuropsychological report may proceed as if the clinician is not sure how the story is going to come out. The report should be clearly organized in the mind of the neuropsychologist prior to its initiation. It should represent a coherent whole in the form of a story that is supported by evidence from the several points of data considered that leads inevitably to a diagnosis, comprehensive description, and coherent recommendations. Using a grid, such as that shown in Figure 16.1, can be helpful in organizing the data in the mind of the clinician prior to beginning the report.

While the format of neuropsychological reports can vary considerably, the following categories of basic information are typically covered in comprehensive neuropsychological reports performed for clinical purposes with the primary goal being diagnosis, description, and treatment recommendations:

1. Identifying information
2. Reason for referral
3. Presenting problems
4. Relevant history
5. Behavioral observations
6. Test results and interpretation
7. Summary and conclusions
8. Recommendations
9. Appendix: Tests given and obtained scores

While many individuals use these headings, many other report writers prefer to use a letter format. This allows for more flexibility in terms of ordering the presentation of information and a more personalized presentation.

Identifying Information

It is customary and appropriate to include some amount of basic demographic information. This can be placed at the top of the first page and/or in the first paragraph of the report. This includes the patient's name, age, race, sex, education, date of evaluation, and administrative identification such as medical record number. Brief information about the diagnosis, if already known, may be appropriate at this point. Also, any salient data that needs to be understood early on in order to understand the rest of the data should be mentioned. Examples include a patient who is significantly visually impaired, hemiplegic, or minimally cooperative.

Reason for Referral

It is helpful to briefly state the purpose for the evaluation and to clarify, if needed, the relationship of the clinician to the referring source and patient. At times, the neuropsychologist may need to help the referral source in refining the specific evaluation questions to be addressed. Referral requests such as "rule-out organicity" or "please evaluate" are too vague. More appropriately, a patient referred by a neurosurgeon subsequent to a subarachnoid hemorrhage and clipping of a cerebral aneurysm may be most interested in addressing the question of the patient's capacity to return to work or

Domains	History	Interview	Observe	WAIS-III	WRAT-III	Grooved Pegboard	Sensory Percep. Exam	Boston Naming	WMS-III	SDMT, PASAT	Category Test	MMPI-2
General intelligence												
Academic skills												
Motor skills												
Sensory-perceptual												
Language												
Mental Speed												
Atten./concentration												
Memory												
Executive												
Emotional												

Figure 16.1. Sample grid of neuropsychological domains by test or evaluation procedure.

resume driving. Having specific referral questions clearly understood and described will help the neuropsychologist to shape the report so that it clearly emphasizes the referral questions throughout the report. In the summary and recommendations sections, it is important to refer back to the specific referral questions and provide concise answers. It should be noted, however, that typically the specific referral questions given by the referral source does not prevent the clinician from addressing other questions that he or she feels are important. If the current evaluation represents a follow-up evaluation, then it is helpful to note this early in the report. A brief statement of the earlier findings and disposition of the patient can help set the stage for the current evaluation report.

Presenting Problems

Presenting complaints and patient's perceptions of his or her problems are a very important part of the evaluation and report. Complaints and concerns about the patient obtained from informed third parties are also incorporated here. The comprehensive evaluation will illicit symptom reports in physical, emotional, and cognitive domains and obtain examples of how these symptoms interfere with social and occupational functioning. It is common practice to characterize behavioral difficulties in terms of current psychiatric nomenclature (e.g., *DSM-IV;* American Psychiatric Association, 1994). The bulk of the data obtained from the clinician's diagnostic interview of the patient will be covered in this section.

Relevant History

Consideration of relevant historical data represents a major component of neuropsychological evaluation and is therefore an important part of the report. Areas of coverage include history of the injury/illness, background history (developmental, dominance, language, education, military, occupational, legal, cultural, family, religious, marital, sexual, psychiatric, substance abuse, neurologic, current stressors), and information from collateral sources (see Chapter 4). Pertinent data from previous reports may be mentioned provided this is relevant and not redundant. Sometimes aspects of the social history and other data that are available but not specifically pertinent to the patient may come under the category of gossip or irrelevant or at least unduly burdensome, and should not be included in the report.

Behavioral Observations

The comprehensive neuropsychological interview and testing will take several hours which provides the clinician with a rich sample of overt patient behavior. Aspects of observed behavior that are important to case conceptualization, diagnosis, and recommendation should be emphasized. For patients with serious psychiatric or neurobehavioral disorders, observable signs of dysfunction will be apparent and should be described. The patient's capacity to participate in the interview and understand questions and instructions itself speaks to cognitive functions and should be documented. Observations about the patient's level of cooperativeness with testing, response to encouragement or failure, and degree of effort have obvious implications for the validity of test scores and therefore should be adequately described. The amount of detail included in the behavioral observations section will depend on the extent to which the patient's behavior deviates from that which would be considered "normal" for the patient's age and the testing environment. For individuals who present with no unusual features in their appearance, communication, alertness, task persistence, motor behavior, interpersonal behavior, or emotional expression, behavioral descriptions will be brief, taking only enough space to note in summary fashion that there was no overt evidence of impairment in these areas. When evidence of overt impairment in functioning or significant uniqueness in presentation is evident, it is important to describe these in enough detail to allow the reader to accurately capture the overt appearance and behavior of the patient. These should be direct descriptions of relevant behavior rather than conclusory statements. Rather than simply concluding that the patient appeared depressed, the specific behaviors which led the clinician to this hypothesis should be described. For example, the report may read, "The patient's affect remained flat throughout the interview and most of the testing with only brief episodes of smiling after completing some of the more challenging cognitive tests. His conversational speech was slightly monotone, slightly reduced in volume, and mildly slowed. Nevertheless his conversational speech was well organized with no apparent word-finding difficulties. He sighed on a few occasions and complained that he didn't feel that he was quite up to doing his best on testing. Nevertheless, he showed no overt refusal and made an effort on each of the tests presented. His behavior suggested the presence of depression which is consistent with his complaints on interview and I suspect his performance on some of the cognitive testing (i.e., particularly those requiring substantially more effortful processing) may have been detrimentally affected by this."

Test Results and Interpretation

Differing opinions exist among neuropsychologists as to whether or not the results of each specific test given should be reported and whether or not a descriptive label such as "average," "normal," "mild impairment" and so on should be used versus standard scores such as T-scores or percentile ranks. Our general approach is to provide a description of the patient's functioning across each neuropsychological domain (see Figure 16.1). Specific tests will only be described if this is helpful in more clearly describing the nature of the patient's deficits in a fashion that the reader can appreciate. Within each domain, emphasis is placed upon interpreting the meaning of the performance for the specific individual being evaluated. For example, performance on a memory test that falls 1 to 2 standard deviations below the average of the normative group has a different interpretation for a person whose lifelong level of global cognitive functioning has been in the borderline range versus an individual whose background includes completing a master's degree in electrical engineering. Therefore, such a performance may be described as being within the expected range of normal for the first case but represent an acquired deficit for the later patient.

The order in which neuropsychological domains are discussed in the report is not inflexible. The clinician should consider the most appropriate order dependent upon the specifics of each case. It is often useful to begin with a description of past background information, such as that obtained with IQ testing and standardized academic achievement measures. This helps to lay the context and understanding of the person's lifelong ability level and their capacity currently to utilize certain skills, such as those necessary for basic academic pursuits and other parts of the remaining tests.

Other times, however, noncognitive and somewhat lower level functions, as embodied in tests of motor functioning and sensory capacity can set practical limitations on the patient's ability to perform certain tests. If, for instance, the patient is paralyzed or in some other way limited with regard to the utilization of his hands or arms or has a difficult time seeing or hearing, then clearly the data to follow, having been affected by that, will have to have been interpreted in that context. Warning the reader ahead of time that this has not only been evaluated and understood, but taken into account is important.

Language abilities are skills necessary for participation in most forms of neuropsychological evaluation and are therefore appropriately discussed relatively early in the report. Again, this is not only to describe an important aspect of human cognitive processing, but also to determine the conditions under which the examination was provided. If the patient is illiterate or dysphasic, then tests such as the Minnesota Multiphasic Personality Inventory, Verbal IQ, and other tests requiring language skills have to be considered in the context of the patient's language functions.

Tests of more complex mental processes, such as attention, memory, problem solving, cognitive speed, mental flexibility, multiple simultaneous tracking, and executive functions typically represent the heart of the neuropsychological enterprise and evaluation. It is these functions that are least likely to have been evaluated elsewhere (e.g., by the referring physician). These capacities are typically reported rather late in the evaluation because it is not unusual for a neuropsychologist to move from neuropsychological functions that are relatively less to those that are relatively more sensitive to impairment from common neurological injuries and diseases. Very commonly, it is in the area of more complex mental processing that neurological diseases have their first expression.

The placement of personality evaluation depends entirely on its pertinence to the overall report. If the patient is most notably disabled or distinguished by significant personality characteristics or psychiatric disorder, it will be important to raise this issue early. Again, this helps to set the context in which the examination has been conducted and the results conceptualized. In some cases, it will be most beneficial to note in the opening paragraph salient features of the patient's psychiatric presentation. For example, "Mr. Jones presented to the clinic in a stuporous state requiring repeated vocal and physical prompts to elicit even minimal and short-term attentional focus." This immediately orients the reader to the seriousness of the patient's condition and sets the stage for explaining the nature of the more limited examination that would be undertaken under these circumstances. In cases where the patient's personality, behavior, or psychiatric disturbance does not prevent participation in a comprehensive neuropsychological evaluation, but nevertheless may have a direct affect on explaining the results of the neuropsychological testing, a description of these factors should typically precede discussion of neuropsychological testing results. By contrast, if the patient's personality or emotional functioning is not believed to have an important influence on the neuropsychological testing, then description of results of formal personality testing (e.g., self-report measures) can be included after a discussion of the neuropsychological test results.

Summary and Conclusions

A summary and conclusions paragraph can be very helpful in terms of concisely answering the referral question and conceptualizing the case. This usually follows the test interpretation paragraphs. Some clinicians, however, will place this paragraph along with recommendations on the first page. This provides a convenient format for individuals who may be interested in the conclusions and recommendations and are not particularly interested in reviewing the remainder of the report. This situation occurs most commonly when reports are filed in charts on inpatient units where they need to be briefly reviewed by a number of persons interested in the care and progress of the patient.

Recommendations

A separate section for recommendations is typically included and usually represents the final component of the report. Recommendations related to the primary referral questions should be specifically addressed as well as those deemed important by the neuropsychologist as a result of having conducted the evaluation. These may include recommendations regarding return to work, competency to perform certain instrumental activities of daily living, and specific referral for intervention. If retesting at a later time is clinically indicated, this should be stated here with a specific time frame noted. If indicated, a detailed treatment planning program can be outlined in this section (see Chapter 15).

Appendix: Tests Given and Obtained Scores

At times, the clinician may chose to attach an Appendix to the report that includes listing the specific tests given, the raw scores, and standard scores obtained using appropriate available normative data. This information can be helpful if the report is being read and evaluated by another neuropsychologist. The specific test scores may help in deriving specific intervention plans or will be helpful for comparison purposes if the patient is to undergo repeat evaluation by the second neuropsychologist. In most cases, however, referral sources are not likely capable of using the specific test scores to improve their understanding of the case and for this reason, many clinicians will not typically include this information.

PATIENT FEEDBACK

Following the evaluation, a feedback session is desirable. Such information is often the best ally in treating a patient (Finn & Tonsager, 1992; Gass & Brown, 1992). The patient's behavior, which may have been seen by the patient and/or family as bothersome, frightening, or puzzling, may become more understandable and therefore tolerable when it is recognized as being due to a specific neurological disorder. This is particularly true when additional behavioral expressions of the neurological disorder can be described to the family so that the family understands that the clinician truly grasps the patient's difficulties. It is also helpful for family members to have a clinician help them anticipate those difficulties which the patient may later develop. Recommendations such as not returning to work can often be helpful in avoiding unnecessary difficulties which, with recovery, may be spontaneously taken care of. Avoidance of alcohol following traumatic brain injury and help with managing financial affairs can often be addressed during the feedback session. In addition, it might be stressed that behaviors such as irritability and emotional lethargy are not necessarily signs of anger or withdrawal stemming from deep psychological conflict, but may be normal manifestations of neurological disorder that might improve over time or be treatable. Addressing questions such as these in a feedback session can be both soothing and therapeutic to family members and patient alike. Such an initial feedback session can often lay the groundwork for additional types of treatment activities based on the recommendations developed from the evaluation.

Follow-up evaluations are also important. These are used to determine if changes have occurred which have relevance for issues such as return to work, diagnosis, activities of daily living, and specific intervention needs. The importance of follow-ups can often be stressed during a feedback session.

SAMPLE REPORTS

We have included three sample reports of neuropsychological evaluations. Note that the style, organization, and emphases differ substantially between the reports while the major components of the neuropsychological report as described in this chapter are maintained. Identifying information included in the reports are fictional.

Commentary on Sample Report 1 (The Neurology Clinic)

The first report was written in the context of following a patient who was initially referred from an inpatient neurology department and was being reevaluated to determine changes in neuropsychological status. At the time of the current evaluation, the patient was being treated by a psychiatrist, psychotherapist, and pediatrician. Note that the report begins with a brief summary of the medical history and findings from previous neuropsychological evaluations. This provides a reference point for the reader and helps to establish early in the report that one main purpose of the report is to describe current functioning in the context of changes that have occurred since the onset of the neurological illness. The most space is allotted to a description of the patient's behavioral problems. This was done because the patient's behavioral difficulties were the most disruptive to daily functioning and were the primary target of treatment. The patient's cognitive impairment was also very serious but less space was required to sufficiently describe the cognitive impairments. The primary purpose of this evaluation was to assist in updating the patient's treatment plan. Since pharmacological interventions were being used, the patient's problems were characterized according to standard psychiatric nomenclature. Relatively detailed behavioral descriptions (e.g., frequency, severity, antecedents, consequences) were included to be helpful in developing behavior management plans. The terminology used was judged appropriate to the intended audience (psychiatrist, psychotherapist, pediatrician). Specific tests used were not reported, because they would not benefit the intended readers. An appendix with a list of tests given and the obtained scores is maintained in the patient's file for future reference. In this case, the referral question was broad. The neuropsychologist was asked to provide an appropriately comprehensive evaluation that would be informative for assisting with ongoing treatment and placement.

Sample Report 1: The Neurology Clinic

April 27, 1998
Shelly Hardaway, M.D.
Pediatric Associates
4564 Anyplace Road
Somewhere, AZ 35000

RE: Mark Alias
MR#: 000-0000
DOE: 4/15/98
DOB: 1/10/81
AGE: 17
EDUCATION: In 10th grade

Dear Doctor Hardaway,

We conducted a repeat neuropsychological evaluation on your patient, Mark Alias, a 17-year-old, right-handed, single white male who is status post herpes simplex virus encephalitis in 12/96. We have conducted two previous neuropsychological evaluations, one in 1/97 and the other in 6/97. Results from those evaluations found Mark to have a profound anterograde amnesia, significant dysnomia, and an organic personality syndrome with lability of mood, confabulation, poor awareness of his deficits, and a number of compulsive behaviors including **polydipsia,** all of which began following the 12/96 encephalitis.

Mark was brought to the clinic today by his mother, Mrs. Wanda Alias, who served as the informant. Since the last time that I saw Mark, he has been followed at Meridian Mental Health Center by a psychiatrist, Dr. Frank Oz, and a psychotherapist, Ms. Lenne Walker. He is also enrolled in special education at Valley High School. Mrs. Alias indicates that Mark's memory is still very poor but he does show evidence of learning some new information, particularly that which is redundant and part of his daily routine. For example, when I spoke with Mark, he demonstrated that he has learned the name of his new teacher and new school. He also apparently has had some success with regard to learning some very simple manual tasks in a vocational training program he attends. Of course he requires more supervision than normal individuals and the demands of the work are not even close to the level of demands that would be required of a "normal" job. Mrs. Alias's main concern is that Mark's behavior has become more aggressive during the past couple of months. This is targeted entirely toward his three younger brothers (ages 14, 15, 15). He does not engage in aggressive behaviors in school or in other settings. Triggers for aggression include his brothers laying objects on his couch. Apparently Mark sleeps on a couch. His clothes and other belongings are kept neatly arranged near the couch. Mark frequently will count his clothes and arrange them in a particular fashion. He appears to show some awareness when they have been bothered (or at least when he believes they have been bothered) and this causes him to become angry and aggressive toward one or more of his brothers. His aggression includes chocking, "pushing on their temples," and making verbal threats that he will kill them. He has thrown small objects at them but has not threatened or actually used any seriously dangerous objects such as knifes.

The second major concern is that Mark continues to show an odd pattern of eating. He eats very little at meal times but will snack throughout the day and night. He gets out of bed several times a night, takes food to the bathroom, and then hides any remains such as empty cans, bones, and so on. He episodically complains of stomachaches and Mrs. Alias thinks that this is related to his compulsive eating pattern. The frequency of Mrs. Alias finding objects hidden in the bathroom is about 1 to 2 times per week. Mark had a history of polydipsia that began soon after his acute illness from encephalitis. This has improved substantially. In the past, he would grab other persons' drinks in public. At present, Mark may drink from a glass of liquid setting on a table at home but he no longer goes to the refrigerator to get fluids and he is not believed to be drinking from the sink in the bathroom anymore.

Mrs. Alias indicates that Mark has done well in terms of his behavior at school. He typically gets up at 6:00 A.M., and catches the disabled persons' bus to school. He has had no problems in riding the school bus. He is enrolled in a full-time special education class and is reported by the teacher to be helpful with regard to assisting some of the children who are in wheelchairs. He changes classes three to four times a day. He has an aide who walks him from class to class. He has never wandered off from school and has only wandered away from home once. At school he writes notes to himself to help him remember things and he puts the notes in his pocket. He has been involved in simple vocational activities where he worked in a hardware store counting inventory. Mark has had some mild school refusal lately. He has complained about somatic problems prior to going to school but once he is at school he stops complaining.

Mark also has stolen money from his grandmother, a family friend, and his mother. He says that he does not remember doing this and, when his mother confronts him about this, he becomes upset. He does not engage in compulsive cleaning, picking behaviors, or **pica.** His compulsive checking, arranging, and hoarding appear to be limited to his own belongings. He continues to show a frequent twitch in his eyelids and also will engage in inappropriate clapping when he gets excited. His weight fluctuates. His mother denies any known inappropriate sexual activity. Mark continues to confabulate.

Mark's mood became more depressed during November and December of 1997. He was started on Prozac which has improved his mood. Mrs. Alias does not think that the medicine has helped in controlling his compulsive behaviors. Currently he continues to be sad for brief periods of time but a persistently depressed mood is not reported. At times Mark continues to show brief outbreaks of crying and being emotionally distraught. Redirecting him to another topic has reliably worked in "derailing" him from his emotional outbursts. Mark enjoys attending church on Sundays and Wednesdays and is upset if he is unable to go. Mrs. Alias notes no observable signs of anxiety or fear. She also denies any observable signs suggesting delusions, or hallucinations.

Mark typically goes to bed between 8 and 10 at night. Mrs. Alias believes that he sleeps best between 1:00 A.M. and 5:30 A.M. He gets up several times per night and eats. He continues to show problems with restlessness. He paces around the house and yard. He plays Nintendo off and on. He seems too distracted or restless to watch an entire television show. He is able to listen to the radio for up to 30 minutes at a time.

Mark's living situation has not changed since the last time we saw him. He continues to live with his mother, stepfather, and three brothers. Mrs. Alias reports that Mark gets along well with his stepfather. Mark's 15-year-old brothers (twins) apparently have Attention Deficit Hyperactivity Disorder and this contributes to the difficulty that Mrs. Alias has had with preventing them from irritating Mark and provoking him to aggression. No new medical problems have developed. Current medications are Prozac and Indural.

Behavioral observations today found Mark to be casually but appropriately dressed and groomed. He presented with a broad smile and was pleasant throughout the interview and testing. He displayed repetitive twitching in his eyes and fumbling with a pencil. He approached all of the testing without any complaints. His performance is viewed as a generally accurate reflection of his capabilities. He was euthymic in mood and did not show hypomanic behavior as he did during the previous two evaluations.

Current intelligence testing with the WAIS-R found his performance to be within the average range with no significant difference between PIQ and VIQ. This performance is consistent with that obtained from testing done in 1/97 and 7/97. Assessment of basic academic achievement with the WRAT-3 found Word Recognition, Spelling, and Math performances all to fall within the average range. Again, these results are entirely consistent with testing performed in 1/97 and 7/97.

Observations of Mark's speech and conversation showed no obvious signs of expressive or receptive difficulties. He continues to show a child-like demeanor with some inappropriate giggling as he had in the past. His performance on quantitative measures of language functions continues to show a number of semantic paraphasic errors on a test of confrontational naming but his spontaneous verbal fluency is only slightly below average.

Sensory perceptual examination found no evidence of agraphesthesia or astereognosis.

Motor examination continues to show no signs of impairment in fine motor coordination and motor speed.

Tests of simple attention found his performance to be within the average range. Tests of information processing speed were performed somewhat variably but overall there is no indication of significant impairment.

Tests of visuospatial and visuoconstructional skills found no significant difficulties and this is consistent with past evaluations.

Mark's performance on tests of both verbal and visual spatial memory provides evidence for profound anterograde amnesia consistent with previous test results. Specifically, his immediate recall for narrative information was low average, but his 30-minute delayed recall for the same information was zero. This profound forgetting curve is consistent with his performance on previous evaluations. His performance on a visual spatial memory task was somewhat better with regard to his ability to immediately recall the information but again, after a 30-minute time delay, he was able to recall nothing. These results show a profound anterograde memory disorder for both verbal and visuospatial material with no evidence of improvement relative to the past evaluations.

In summary, Mark Alias is a 17-year-old male who is status post herpes simplex encephalitis in 12/96. The current neuropsychological evaluation continues to find evidence for a profound anterograde amnesia and moderate dysnomia, in the context of an individual whose background abilities and skills were within the average range. Although his performance on the IQ and achievement tests are still within the average range, his profound anterograde amnesia prevents him from being able to adaptively use this knowledge and skill to support independent functioning. The history obtained from Mrs. Alias also continues to show significant personality change secondary to encephalitis with the primary features being lability of mood, disinhibited behavior, and compulsive behavior. The hypomania and polydipsia, which prominently characterized his behavioral problems in the first several months following the infection, have been eliminated. However, he continues to present with inappropriate interpersonal behaviors and a multitude of other compulsive behavioral disorders.

The following recommendations are given:

1. Mark's aggressive behavior appears to be focused on his younger brothers. I had a long discussion with Mrs. Alias about the importance of working with his brothers on preventing them from engaging in activities that trigger Mark's aggression. In addition, she will need to continue to provide adequate supervision and insure that Mark does not have access to any dangerous objects.

2. With regards to Mark's compulsive and irregular eating habits, I think that it is important to obtain some direct control over his access to food. I suggested to Mrs. Alias that she place all of the nonrefrigerated items in one locked cabinet. Also, she was asked to place a sign on the cabinet and refrigerator stating "Mark, please ask your mother before taking any food." When Mark looks as if he wants a snack, I suggested that Mrs. Alias provide him with small portions of snacks that he likes. I asked her to fix some of Mark's favorite meals to encourage him to get into the habit of eating more at meal times.

3. It appears that Mark's repetitive folding and arranging of his items near his couch/bed and his tendency toward aggression when he believes those items have been disturbed are part of a compulsive disorder. Medication adjustment targeting his compulsive behaviors seems to be a reasonable plan.

4. Mark is now about 16 months status post-encephalitis. He may continue to show subtle improvement in cognitive functions and personality functioning. However, I think that it is very unlikely that Mark will be able to function independently. Due to his profound anterograde amnesia and overall poor self-management skills, Mark will require supervision the rest of his life. He will not likely benefit from any kind of intensive treatment program designed to teach self-management skills due to his profound deficits in new learning and executive functions. Some behavior changes and behavioral control, however, can likely be obtained through use of structured environments and behavior modification techniques when consistently applied. Mrs. Alias could benefit from obtaining further information about available long-term supervised placement resources that Mark may qualify for. At some point in the future, she may need to consider residential placement for Mark at least for periods of respite.

Thank you for the opportunity to follow Mark and to participate in his care. Please let me know if I can provide additional information, or be of any further help.

Sincerely,

Frank A. Psychologist, Ph.D.
Department of Neuropsychology

Sample Report 2: The Vocational/Rehabilitation Context

June 3, 1998

Ms. Gloria Robinson
Vocational Rehabilitation Services
P.O. Box 99999
Anywhere, AZ 87878

RE: John Wise
DOE: 05/21/98 & 06/01/98
DOB: 06/28/80
AGE: 17
EDUCATION: 11th grade

Dear Ms. Robinson:

We had the opportunity to conduct a neuropsychological evaluation on your client, John Wise, a 17-year-old, right-handed, white, single male who was referred for evaluation due to a history of learning difficulties and psychiatric problems. John underwent a battery of neuropsychological tests, personality testing, and clinical interview. This was started on 05/21/98. This session was cut short due to a medical emergency where John had to leave to check on his ill father. The remainder of the testing and interview was completed on 06/02/98. Information was obtained from John, as well as his mother who was interviewed by phone. John presented himself to the clinic casually dressed and appropriately groomed. He was alert and fully oriented. He was pleasant and cooperative with the interview and testing, although at times he seemed to be a little bit hesitant to go into detail about his history. Observations of his behavior during testing suggested that he put forth good effort, persistence, and was appropriately motivated, making the obtained test scores valid indicators of his capabilities.

The history shows that John has had documented difficulties in learning since beginning school. He repeated the first grade due to these difficulties and has been receiving special education services (LD) since then. He has been diagnosed in the past with dyslexia. I have reviewed some records of past Individual Educational Programs, which also show, however, that he has had significant difficulties in other academic areas, including mathematics, despite what appears to be generally average intellectual abilities. About three months ago, John stopped attending school and is being educated in a home-bound program by his mother. He describes no specific curriculum and it is not clear to me the exact nature of this program. He states that he quit attending public school because he was having conflicts with teachers and peers, and also was having what he referred to as a sleep disorder. He denies having any medical evaluation for a sleep disorder, however. When I ask him about this, he says that basically he has a hard time getting up early in the morning. He went on to describe a sleep pattern where he is accustomed to staying up until around 4 A.M. and sleeping until noon or later. He states that if he gets eight hours of sleep, that he is rested during the daytime and does not have any problems with daytime sleepiness. He denies any symptoms of narcolepsy or cataplexy. He does admit to some episodic initial insomnia, but I think this mostly relates to the fact that his sleep schedule is so convoluted that when he tries to go to bed earlier, he is just not tired and finds it difficult to fall asleep. John indicates that his plan is to take the high school graduate exit exams, and he tells me that he will be eligible to obtain a regular diploma, although I am not sure this is true.

John currently lives with his mother, Mrs. Joan Wise and his 22-year-old brother. His parents are divorced. His father is a 43-year-old disabled individual who has severe multiple sclerosis and has been wheelchair-bound for several years. Apparently, he is very ill and requires dialysis and chronic medical supervision. John frequently worries about him, and reports that this is his major stressor. He relates that his second highest stressor is that of worrying about making a good impression with his friends, which is followed by worrying about his mother "bitching" at him. John has worked in the past for a family plumbing business, as a busboy at Tony's, at Food Express, and at Dairy Queen. At least in some of these jobs, he apparently had some interpersonal conflicts which lead to him leaving. He holds a driver's license. He denies a history of legal difficulties or DWIs. Medical history is significant for minor injuries incurred in a four-wheeler accident in 1992, and then a car accident in 1996. He reports no loss of consciousness in these events, and I would anticipate no residual cognitive deficits based on the description of these accidents. He currently takes no medications. He was prescribed Ritalin in the ninth grade for what was believed to be possible ADD, but discontinued this about three months ago. According to his mother, Ritalin helped his focus. Mrs. Wise did not report a history of significant hyperactivity for John, but believes he has had a history of difficulties maintaining attention on tasks. About five months ago, he went to a counselor for about two months through the Family and Child Services. He says this was related to emotional difficulties he was having from conflicts at school, as well as worries about his father's illness. He has attended Family and Child Services for counseling off and on since his parents' divorce in 1993.

John has a history of psychiatric problems. He reports a history of depressive symptoms that have fluctuated over time. He states that he has been unhappy much of his life. At the age of 13, he says that he attempted suicide by tying a rope around his neck and jumping off of a porch. His sister came home, found him there, and took him down. He states that currently he does not perceive his mood as being significantly depressed or irritable, but he states that a couple of months ago he was more depressed. These fluctuations in his mood appear to be related to situational crises, including his father's illness and peer and family conflicts. Currently, he denies any suicidal ideation or homicidal ideation. He states that his appetite is up and down, but he reports no weight loss. He denies having any significant decrease in motivation, energy, or having excessive thoughts of hopelessness, helplessness, or low self-worth. He enjoys spending time with his friends, and states that many times he will go out to night clubs late at night and sneak into bars, and this apparently is why he is accustomed to staying up so late. He admits to drinking socially, but states that he has not gotten into any behavioral or legal problems secondary to this. He denies a history of illicit drug abuse. Although he has tried marijuana, he states that he does not use it frequently, and denies a history of using other drugs. John, although admitting to worry and episodically experiencing emotional crises, denies a pattern of chronic worry accompanied by significant psychophysiologic disruption. He also denies a history of social phobia, although he clearly does struggle with feelings of social alienation, interpersonal sensitivity, and feelings of rejection by some of his peers, which I suspect has some bearing in reality. He denies a history of panic attacks and agoraphobic avoidance. There is no indication from observation or in his report of the presence of current or past thought disorders, such as hallucinations or delusions. He denies a history of mania or hypomania.

John completed formal personality testing with the MMPI-2. Examination of validity indices suggests that he responded to items in a generally candid and straightforward fashion with no indication of significant exaggeration or minimization. The MMPI-2 was administered to him through the use of audiotape due to his severe reading difficulties. The resulting profile reveals an individual who, while having a history of episodic psychological disruption, appears currently to feel that he is coping generally well. Despite this, the profile does suggest the presence of chronic underlying difficulties which, when combined with acute stressors, lead to significant exacerbation of symptoms of anxiety, depression, and impulsive behavior. Individuals with a clinical profile similar to the one obtained by John tend to complain of feeling tense, worried, depressed, and alienated. Their behavior may be unpredictable and inappropriate at times. They are likely to be suspicious and distrustful of others and have difficulties making significant emotional attachments. They can be resentful when demands are placed on them. These individuals tend to have a strong need for support and dependency, but are not effective with regard to meeting these needs. Self-concept of these individuals tend to be quite poor, lacking in self-confidence, feeling inferior and insecure, and often times guilty. As you would anticipate, interpersonally these individuals are suspicious, emotionally distant, and prone to making poor judgments.

Examination of general intellectual abilities was accomplished using the WAIS-R. John obtained the following scores suggesting low-average to average intellectual abilities: VIQ = 85, PIQ = 97, and FSIQ = 89. He showed a relative weakness in the area of verbal comprehension relative to his perceptual-organizational skills. This pattern of VIQ-PIQ split has been reliably demonstrated across his developmental history and is commonly found among individuals with developmental learning disorders. Examination of his performance on tests of academic skills reveals clear evidence of a substantial learning disorder. On the WRAT-3, he obtained the following scores: Reading = SS 66, Spelling = SS 54, Arithmetic = SS 76. The discrepancy between his performance in basic academic skill areas relative to his general IQ is consistent with the diagnosis of reading disorder, mathematics disorder, and disorder of written expression.

Psychometric examination of language functions finds some mild difficulties with confrontational naming, but average to above average verbal fluency.

Examination of fine motor coordination and manual speed found no difficulties. Simple attention, concentration, and information processing speed are all within the generally average and expected range. When mental processing tasks involve performing mental operations which he is not good at, such as calculations, his performance drops off substantially.

Memory testing found that his ability to learn through the visuo-spatial format is within the average or better range, but his learning efficiency when given verbal information in an auditory verbal format is moderately deficient. Fortunately, with rehearsal, even his verbal learning curve improves substantially and at a 30-minute delayed recall is within the average range. This suggests that John's difficulties with regard to learning are not limited just to an orthographic-based dyslexia, which has been suggested in the past, but probably represents a developmental disorder with regard to phonological skills which effects both his reading ability and also his language processing whenever information is read to him. Fortunately, his performance on verbal learning tests suggests that, with rehearsal, his auditory verbal learning abilities do improve to within the average range and he has no difficulties with retaining information once appropriately encoded.

In summary, John Wise is a 17-year-old male who was referred for evaluation due to his history of learning difficulties and psychiatric problems. Testing and interview suggest that John does, in fact, have a significant learning disability in the areas of reading, math, and written expression. This occurs in the context of otherwise average to low average intellectual abilities. His deficit in language-based learning was also evident on tests of learning efficiency where he displayed average abilities with regard to the efficiency of learning visuo-spatial information, but substantial weaknesses with regard to quickly acquiring verbal information presented in an auditory-verbal format. With rehearsal, however, John was able to improve his verbal learning performance to within the average range on delayed recall. Our testing results are consistent with test scores from previous testing. From a psychiatric perspective, John has a long history of difficulties in emotional and behavioral adjustment. He reports being unhappy much of his childhood and has had episodic events where he appeared to be clinically depressed and has had suicidal ideation and at least one suicide attempt in the past. Currently, he does not appear to be significantly depressed, but does have episodic mood disturbance and anxiety consistent with an adjustment disorder with mixed features of anxiety and depression. He has been diagnosed with possible ADHD in the past, and I am not sure that this is an appropriate diagnosis, but it is worthwhile to keep this in mind as a working hypothesis.

John's combination of significant learning disorder and emotional difficulties pose substantial challenges for him with regard to being successful in his career pursuits. In talking with him, I got the impression that he was being a bit unrealistic with regard to his plans. He states that he would like to go to a four-year college and obtain a business degree. He states that if he does not go to college, he plans to open a nightclub. Both of these at this point appear to be unrealistic.

The following recommendations are given:

1. Due to John's fragile coping mechanisms, I think it would be appropriate to encourage him to become involved in long-term counseling. With the severe illness of his father and his chronic problems with learning and other stressors, he is at risk for having a relapse to more significant disturbance in mood in the future. If stimulant medication actually improved his functioning in the past, then he should be advised to consider using stimulant medications again.

2. I think it may be worthwhile to get John involved in an intensive reading program. My impression is that even though he has received LD services in the past, he feels that they were not very helpful. If he is willing and such a program can be found, I think it would be good to pursue an intensive reading program to see if he can improve his reading.

3. Given John's very poor reading level, he clearly will have difficulties even with a two-year college program even if he receives very good LD assistance. However, if he demonstrates strong commitment and perseverance with regard to pursuing a reading program, then I think it might be appropriate for him to try to take one or two courses at a community college. This reduced load would be a good first step and would provide an opportunity for him to learn to manage college-level work. If he fails at this, then of course this would be very informative with regard to future planning.

4. If John decides that he is not invested in putting forth the extensive work required for success in academic pursuits, then I think this may not be entirely unfortunate. He certainly has the intellectual abilities, practical judgment, and problem-solving skills, that would enable him to learn from observation skills taught in technical programs that require very little reading and writing skills.

Thank you for the opportunity to evaluate John and to participate in his care. Please let me know if I can provide additional information, or be of any further help.

Sincerely,

Frank A. Psychologist, Ph.D.
Assistant Professor, Neuropsychology

Sample Report 3: The Judicial System

March 25, 1997

George Hamlin
Hamlin, Groff, and Galbally
2362 Trend Avenue
Metropolis, SA 86428

RE: Neuropsychological evaluation of
Ron J. (DOB 3/25/51)

Dear Mr. Hamlin,

At your request, I had the pleasure of evaluating your client, Mr. Ron J of P.O. Box 86, Metropolis, SA 86428. As you know, he is a right-handed, 45-year-old, Caucasian, single male with a year 10 education who sustained a severe, diffuse head injury on May 21, 1994. My understanding is that you would like me to evaluate Mr. J with particular reference to the nature and severity of his deficits, the extent of care he would require, ability to work, personality functioning, and the likelihood of significant improvement.

On 2/20/97 I forwarded a packet of materials to be completed by Mr. J and his brother, Jeff J, which included the Patient Competency Rating (Patient and Relative Forms), Neuropsychological Symptom Checklist, Neuropsychological History Questionnaire, and the Sickness Impact Profile. Since Mr. J was unable to complete these materials unassisted, he was helped by his brother. I further evaluated Mr. J in person on 3/12/97 and 3/13/97 at which time I assessed him through clinical interview (60 minutes) and administered the Wechsler Adult Intelligence Scale-Revised (WAIS-R), Wechsler Memory-Scale Form II (WMS), Rey Auditory Verbal Learning Test, Bender, Bender Memory, Aphasia Screening Test, Finger Oscillation Test, Controlled Oral Word Association (FAS), Trail Making, and Beck Depression Inventory (BDI). Total face-to-face evaluation time was 5 hours. In addition, I have reviewed medical reports by Drs. Smith (11/2/94), Jones (11/3/94), Baskin (12/1/94), Fletcher (5/18/95), Anderson (5/29/95), and Pettinati (11/30/95).

Although Mr. J needed to be driven to both assessment sessions by his father, he was able to walk unassisted. However, he limped and, as he walked, his head was shaking back and forth. On many occasions he struggled to pronounce words correctly. He often drifted from one subject to the next and required continual reminding to keep focused on a topic. In addition, he continually repeated the events of the accident despite having previously provided the information. He also continually talked of how frustrated he felt at being unable to do simple things which he felt he should be able to do without difficulty. His test performance was typically quite slow and deliberate. For example, he took approximately 12 minutes to read and complete a self-report test having 21 items. Although there was a tendency to minimize some of his difficulties, particularly those related to psychosocial problems, he was generally cooperative and appeared to give his best effort to the tasks presented to him. Given the above observations, I feel the test results represent an accurate assessment of his current level of functioning.

Prior to Mr. J's injury he was employed doing various jobs such as driving trucks, cleaning houses, and mowing lawns. His best job seems to have been as a plant operator where he reported working for 2.5 years between 1984 and 1986. Mr. J's brother reported that Ron had been an average student. Although he was required to repeat year 4 because he evidently "had not grasped fundamental concepts," he did successfully complete year 10. His medical history prior to the accident was generally unremarkable with the exception of having poor nutrition as an infant, some difficulties with coordination, and petit mal seizures. The seizures occurred at age 18, were controlled with anticonvulsant medication, and, since age 30, he has neither had seizures nor required seizure medication. A further review of Mr. J's medical history indicated that he has not had unusually high fevers, previous head injuries, learning disabilities, substance abuse, exposure to toxic materials, or tumors.

On May 21, 1994, Ron J was a passenger in the front seat of a jeep that overturned resulting in him sustaining a severe head injury. I note numerous additional physical injuries in various medical records but will not repeat them here. He was initially transferred to St. John's hospital and the next day (22/5/94) flown to the St. Ann's Hospital Intensive Care Unit. Once he began to improve, he was transferred to St. Joseph's Rehabilitation Hospital on June 12, 1994, where he was eventually discharged on September 12, 1994, to the care of Metropolis General Hospital. Dr. Anderson's report of May 29, 1995, summarizes the severity of Mr. J's head injury by indicating that, during intake at Royal Perth Hospital, he scored only a 3 to 4 out of 15 on the Glasgow Coma Scale. Dr. Smith of St. Joseph's Rehabilitation Hospital further reported (11/2/94) that he had a 3-month period of post-traumatic amnesia. At St. Joseph's Rehabilitation Hospital he evidently made satisfactory progress but, upon discharge, ". . . there was still indications of significant cognitive deficits involving his memory, insight, judgment, and intellectual functioning. Emotionally there were still features of mood lability and occasional episodes of agitation" (p. 3).

Mr. J was evidently married for 2 years around 1977. At the time of the injury, he was involved in a de facto relationship. It was reported by his brother and sister-in-law that the relationship did not survive the stress of the injury and subsequent hospitalization. He does not have any contact with his previous partners. He is currently living with various family members, in particular his brother's family (Jeff and Elizabeth along with their three children). Jeff and Elizabeth J reported that Ron is able to perform basic tasks around the farm such as mowing lawns, sweeping, and checking on sheep. Ron's brother, Jeff, reported that he requires constant reminding even to continue simple, repetitive tasks. He is evidently easily distracted and has considerable difficulty following thought patterns in sequence. Mr. J's brother further reported that he has difficulty reasoning for himself and frequently misplaces things. He tires easily and needs to be continually stimulated. Ron repeatedly emphasized how frustrating simple day-to-day activities are and stated he can sometimes "flare up emotionally." Prior to the injury he used to enjoy fishing and working on his car. His only activities now are socializing with his family and attending the Lions' Social Club for Disabled People.

Noteworthy symptoms reported on the Neuropsychological Symptom Checklist include headaches, coordination problems, dropping things, muscle spasms, slowed thought processes, distractibility, trouble understanding other people, getting dressed, finding the right word, following conversations, reading, and writing. Despite the above restrictions in Ron's activities and significant deficits, the family has reported that it would be unacceptable for him to be placed in an institutional setting.

Assessment of *general intellectual ability* indicates that Mr. J is functioning overall in the lower 5% of the population (borderline mentally retarded range). There was little fluctuation between any of his scores which indicates an overall lowering in all his abilities. This is consistent with a severe diffuse head injury. Given his history and pattern of scores, I would estimate that his premorbid level of functioning would have been in the average to low average range (estimated lower 20% of the population).

Mr. J's *attention and speed of information processing* were within the mild to moderately impaired range. For example, he was only able to repeat a maximum of four numbers which were read to him. His brother also noted in the history that he needs constant reminding in order to complete something. The above indicates that he would have a difficult time responding quickly to instructions, concentrating for any length of time, and focusing on a task for very long.

Memory and learning functions were similarly in the moderate to severely impaired range. His overall memory "quotient" was in the lower .09% of the population (only 9 people in 10,000 would score this low). For example, he was unable to accurately reproduce from memory any of 9 simple designs even though he had worked with these designs for approximately 7 minutes. Even quite impaired persons can usually reproduce one or two designs from memory (and the average person will be able to reproduce 4–5 designs). Similarly, he could only recall 4 out of 15 simple words ("drum," "bell," etc.) which were read to him. Even after 5 practice trials his recall only increased to 5 out of the 15 words. In addition, his recall for words was easily interfered with by previous information he was required to work with.

Mr. J's *verbal functions and academic skills* indicate that he can adequately comprehend spoken information and he has an adequate fund of vocabulary words. However, he needs to absorb this information slowly, particularly if the information is even moderately complex. One particular difficulty is being able to come up with the correct word. When given 60 seconds to come up with as many words as possible beginning with the letter "f," he was only able to give "fish" and "fox."

Visuoconstructive abilities were in the mildly impaired range. In particular, he had difficulty putting together simple puzzles or reproducing simple designs. The designs he did draw were characterized by line tremor, overlapping, mild distortions, and drawing circles instead of dots. This test-related difficulty is consistent with the frustration he reported when he was unable to drive a truck through three consecutive gates on his brother's farm. He stressed that it was a simple task and knew that he should have been able to perform, but felt he was unable to do so.

Executive functions were assessed through history, behavioral observations, and clinical assessment and indicate that Mr J has difficulties initiating, monitoring, sequencing, and having awareness over his behavior. As stated previously, Mr. Paterson needs continual reminding to stay focused on a task. Clinical assessment indicated that he has a difficult time sequencing fairly simple behaviors (alternating between fist-palm-back of hand). In many areas Mr. J minimized the cognitive impact of his injuries. For example, Ron felt that he himself "can do with ease" the following: remembering what he had for dinner the night before, staying involved in work activities, participating in group activities, and scheduling daily activities. In contrast, Ron's brother rated each of these areas as Ron either being "unable" or "very difficult" for him to do.

As with the above cognitive abilities, review of *emotional and personality functions* indicates a general minimization or under reporting of psychological difficulties. For example, he endorsed very few items on a depression questionnaire related to being depressed; "I do not feel sad," "I don't cry any more than usual," "I don't get more tired than usual," and "I don't feel I look worse than I used to." I believe this is in part due to an optimistic outlook combined with a supportive, tolerant, patient family who are committed to taking care of him. His optimism was reflected in his statement that ". . . what's happened has happened . . . there's nothing that can change it . . . so there's no use getting upset over it." Minimization of psychological difficulties is also due to little awareness related to his deficits. Interestingly, he defined the word "evasive" as "running away from the truth all the time." Both minimization and poor awareness are adaptive in that they reduce the pain associated with fully attending to his deficits and the interpersonal and internal conflicts associated with his dependence on others. He is also likely to further adapt by perceiving himself as being important and therefore more deserving of the care which is given to him. However, there were more subtle signs of underlying but only minimally acknowledged depression and anger. He repeatedly seemed angry at how his life had been ruined. When asked to define the word "sentence" he replied "I've already been handed it" and "terminate" was defined as "when you try to get someone to kill you, when you've had enough of living." The above review of personality indicates that for some self-report measures there is very little psychological difficulties thereby suggesting a quite good level of adaptation. In many respects, I feel he has indeed made a quite good level of adjustment. However, more subtle behaviors, particularly some of the idiosyncratic responses on some of the items, indicate that, on a deeper level, there may be quite significant but only partially experienced difficulties.

Neuropsychologically it seems quite clear that Mr. J has sustained a severe, diffuse head injury. This is supported by the following:

1. Considerable depth of coma following the injury as noted on Dr. Anderson's report of 5/29/95.
2. Long period of post-traumatic amnesia (3 months) as noted in Dr. Smith's 11/2/94 report.
3. Documentation in my (as well as previous reports) that he is functioning at a level far below his premorbid level. Premorbidly he had been able to work independently, drive, take care of his finances, care for himself, and become involved in marriage or marriage type-relationships. Any of the above would now be extremely difficult or impossible for him to manage.
4. Overall, he is now functioning in the lower 5% of the population (borderline mentally retarded range). Relative strengths are fund of vocabulary words, general information, recognizing relevant from irrelevant details in his environment. However, the above areas are specifically those that are most likely to be resistant to decline following injury to the brain. In contrast, his performance on tests that are most sensitive to injury ("brain sensitive" tests) is where he demonstrated the most significant deficits. For example, his overall memory functions, which require intact attention and concentration, were in the lower .09% of the population which is in the moderate to severely impaired range (only 9 persons in 10,000 would score this low).
5. Not only the overall scores, but also the pattern of functions indicated by specific tests, indicate that many functions are in the impaired range. These include: poor concentration and attention, slowed thinking, difficulty learning new material, problems remembering relevant information, word finding difficulties, poor coordination, accurately perceiving and organizing spatial material, staying focused on tasks, initiating activities, and awareness of his deficits.

Given the extent and pattern of impairments documented above, Mr. J would need extensive care. While simple functions such as dressing himself, mowing lawns, or checking on sheep appear within his capability, more complicated ones would be beyond his reach. For example, it would be unsafe for him to cook for himself since he would be likely to leave the burners on. Similarly, he would not be able to focus on financial tasks such as balancing a checkbook, paying bills, or responding to postal inquiries related to his finances. Although he expressed the hope that he would be able to obtain his license again, this would certainly not currently be possible. At the most he might be able to live in a carefully supervised home for disabled persons and engage in work within the context of a sheltered workshop. His current situation with his family is ideal in that they provide much of the day-by-day supervision for someone with his degree of impairment. However, this depends on their continued good will (which at the present time seems both extensive and impressive) as well as their financial, physical, and psychological resources.

Given the above details of the injury and extent of current deficits, I believe that very little additional improvement in his neuropsychological functioning will occur. Typically, the vast majority of improvement occurs in the first 18 months post-injury. Currently nearly twice that length of time has elapsed. It should be further noted that depth of coma and length of post-traumatic amnesia are among the best predictors of degree of recovery following closed head injury; in Mr. J's case the coma was quite deep and the length of post-traumatic amnesia was extensive. Thus, the history of the injury along with the extent of deficits documented in the above report are entirely consistent with a pattern of continued and fairly extensive neuropsychological difficulties.

I hope the above information provides you with clear answers to the questions you had related to Mr. J. Should you wish further clarification or elaboration, please do not hesitate to contact me at your convenience.

Sincerely,

Gary Groth-Marnat, Ph.D.
Clinical Neuropsychologist
Senior Lecturer, Clinical Psychology

Commentary on Sample Report 2
(The Vocational/Rehabilitation Context)

The client was referred by a vocational rehabilitation counselor for a comprehensive neuropsychological evaluation to determine the presence, nature, and severity of psychiatric or learning disorders. The report was to be used by the counselor as an aid in making decisions about vocational training avenues for the client. Since learning disorders are developmental disorders, it is important to review past academic and cognitive testing records. These were reviewed and commented on in summary fashion. Past test scores were not included in the actual report because these records were already in the possession of the vocational counselor, making their inclusion in the report unnecessary. The client's history included evidence of significant psychological maladjustment which was viewed as pertinent to his potential for vocational functioning. Therefore, substantial space was given to this issue. Specific test scores from the current examination were selectively reported. Specifically, IQ scores and achievement test scores were reported in standard score format. Because the vocational counselor was appropriately knowledgeable of intelligence and academic achievement tests, the standard scores were helpful in concisely depicting important aspects of the client's ability level. Results from the other neuropsychological tests given were reported in summary fashion organized around specific cognitive domains (e.g., memory ability, concentration). In this case, coverage of neuropsychological domains in summary fashion was deemed to be most informative and least burdensome for the reader. Finally, recommendations were focused primarily on vocational issues because this was the primary purpose of the referral. While a recommendation was made for psychological treatment, specific treatment recommendations were avoided because this was judged to sufficiently fall outside of the realm of the goals for the evaluation.

Commentary on Sample Report 3 (The Judicial System)

The third report was written for an attorney who was requesting a report to determine the nature and extent of a client's disability as part of a personal injury claim. As a result, the report was relatively devoid of technical terminology. Consistent with this, most descriptions of symptoms were given with clear behavioral referents along with relevant history. For example, in the section on visuoconstructive abilities there is first the conclusion that the client was in the impaired range. This was then followed by a description of actual test behavior (line tremor, overlapping, distortions) along with a description of how the client had difficulty driving a truck through a gate. Presenting information in this way is likely to both make judgments related to client functioning, as well as concretely bring the client to life for both a professional as well as a lay reader. Another area of emphasis was a clear description of the referral question (nature and severity of deficits, extent of care required, etc.) at the beginning of the report. This was followed up at the end of the report by a detailed review of each of the referral questions. In the case of documenting that the client had sustained a "severe, diffuse head injury," each of the areas of evidence was numbered and summarized. In a more routine, clinical report, this degree of detail would probably not be included. In a forensic report where some of the crucial conclusions might be challenged (and significant compensation might be involved), it is often necessary to provide this level of documentation. The test interpretation material was also clearly organized around the domains of general intellectual ability, attention and speed of information processing, memory and learning, verbal functions and academic skills, visuoconstructive abilities, executive functions, and emotional and personality function. Each of these sections was highlighted to make them easier to identify. Finally, the report was written in a personalized letter format.

RECOMMENDED READING

Gass, C.G., & Brown, M.C. (1992). Neuropsychological test feedback to patients with brain dysfunction. *Psychological Assessment, 4,* 272–277.

Groth-Marnat, G. (1999). The psychological report. In G. Groth-Marnat, *Handbook of psychological assessment* (3rd ed. rev.) (pp. 619–670). New York: John Wiley & Sons.

Tallent, N. (1993). *Psychological report writing* (4th ed.). Englewood Cliffs, NJ: Prentice Hall.

Zuckerman, E.L. (1993). The clinician's thesaurus three: A guidebook for wording psychological reports (3rd ed.). Pittsburgh: Three Wishes Press.

REFERENCES

American Psychiatric Association. (1994). *Diagnostic and statistical manual of mental disorders* (4th ed.). Washington, DC: Author.

Boll, T.J., Williams, M.A., Kashden, J., & Putzke, J. (1998). Examination IV. Neuropsychological testing. In C.E. Coffey & R.A. Brumback (Eds.), *Textbook of pediatric neuropsychiatry* (pp. 221–252). Washington, DC: American Psychiatric Press.

Finn, S.E., & Tonsager, M.E. (1992). Therapeutic effects of providing MMPI-2 test feedback to college students awaiting therapy. *Psychological Assessment, 4,* 278–287.

Gass, C.G., & Brown, M.C. (1992). Neuropsychological test feedback to patients with brain dysfunction. *Psychological Assessment, 4,* 272–277.

Groth-Marnat, G. (1999). The psychological report. In G. Groth-Marnat, *Handbook of psychological assessment* (3rd ed. rev.) (pp. 619–670). New York: John Wiley & Sons.

Hannay, H.J., Bieliauskas, L., Crosson, B.A., Hammeke, T.A., Hamsher, K., & Koffler, S. (1998). Proceedings of the Houston conference on specialty education and training in clinical neuropsychology. *Archives of Clinical Neuropsychology, 13,* 157–249.

Matarazzo, J.D. (1990). Psychological assessment versus psychological testing. *American Psychologist, 45,* 999–1017.

Spreen, O., & Strauss, E. (1998). *A compendium of neuropsychological tests.* New York: Oxford University Press.

Stringer, A.Y. (1996). *A guide to adult neuropsychological diagnosis.* Philadelphia: Davis.

Tramontana, M.G., & Hooper, S.R. (1988). Child neuropsychological assessment: Overview of current status. In M.G. Tramontana & S.R. Hooper (Eds.), *Assessment issues in child neuropsychology. Critical issues in neuropsychology* (pp. 3–38). New York: Plenum Press.

Appendix A

Test Publishers

American Guidance Service, Inc.
Publisher's Building
Circle Pines, MN 55014-1796
1-800-328-2560
List includes: Kaufman Assessment Battery for Children, Kaufman Adolescent and Adult Intelligence Test, Kaufman Brief Intelligence Test

American Orthopsychiatric Association, Inc.
19 West 44th Street
New York, NY 10036
(212) 354-5770
List includes: Bender Visual-Motor Gestalt Test

Boston Neuropsychological Foundation
P.O. Box 476
Lexington, MA 02173
List includes: Stroop Color-Word Test (Comali/Kaplan version)

Consulting Psychologists Press
P.O. Box 10096
Palo Alto, CA 94303
(415) 857-1444
List includes: California Psychological Inventory

DLM Teaching Resources
P.O. Box 4000
One DLM Park
Allen, TX 75002
1-800-527-4747
1-800-442-4711
List includes: Test of Word Finding, Woodcock Johnson Psychoeducational Battery

Jastak Associates, Inc.
1526 Gilpin Avenue
Wilmington, DE 19806
1-800-221-WRAT
List includes: Wide Range Achievement Test

Lafayette Instrument Company
P.O. Box 5729
Lafayette, IN 47903
1-800-428-7545
List includes: Purdue Pegboard, Hand dynamometer

NFER-Nelson Publishing Co.
Darville House
2 Oxford Road
East Windsor
Berkshire 21A IDF, UK
List includes: National Adult Reading Test

National Computer Systems, Inc. (NCS)
5605 Green Circle Drive
Minnetonka, MI 55343
1-800-523-8805
List includes: Millon Clinical Multiaxial Inventory, Minnesota Multiphasic Personality
Inventory

Neuropsychology Laboratory
University of Victoria
P.O. Box 1700
Victoria, BC Canada
List includes: Paced Auditory Serial Addition Test, Stroop Color-Word Test (Victoria
version)

Psychological Assessment Resources
P.O. Box 98
Odessa, FL 33556
1-800-331-TEST
List includes: Adult Neuropsychological Questionnaire, Behavioral Assessment of the
Dysecutive Syndrome, Benton Visual Retention Test, Boston Diagnostic Aphasia Exam-
ination, Boston Naming Test, Cognitive Behavior Rating Scales, Children's Auditory
Verbal Learning Test, Color Trails Test, Dementia Rating Scale, Booklet Category Test,
Children's Category Test, Category Test (computer version), Grooved Pegboard, Hand
Dynamometer, Kaufman Short Neuropsychological Assessment Procedure, Memory
Assessment Scales, Neuropsychological Status Examination Rey Complex Figure and
Recognition Trial, Rivermead Behavioural Memory Test, Ruff Figural Fluency Test,
Stroop Neuropsychological Screening Test, Stroop Color and Word Test, Tactual Per-
formance Test, Test of Everyday Attention, Wide Range Assessment of Memory and
Learning, Wisconson Card Sorting Test.

Psychological Corporation
555 Academic Court
San Antonio, TX 78204
1-800-228-0752
List includes: Beck Depression Inventory, California Verbal Learning Test, Children's Category Test, Children's Memory Scale, Paced Auditory Serial Addition Test, Rorschach, Wechsler Adult Intelligence Scale, Wechsler Intelligence Scale for Children, Wechsler Preschool and Primary Scale for Children, Wechsler Memory Scale, Wide Range Test of Memory and Learning.

Reitan Neuropsychology Laboratory
2920 South 4th Avenue
Tucson, AZ 85713-4819
List includes: Halstead Reitan Neuropsychological Test Battery, Neuropsychological History Questionnaire

Riverside Publishing Co.
8420 Bryn Mawr Avenue
Chicago, IL 60631
(201) 729-6031
List includes: Stanford Binet

T.L. Stacks, Ph.D.
Hillcrest Hospital
P.O. Box 233
Greenacres, SA 5087 Australia
List includes: Stroop Colour-Word Test (five versions of the Dodrill version)

Stoelting Company
620 Wheat Lane
Wood Dale, IL 60191
List includes: Stroop Color-Word Test (Golden version)

Thames Valley Test Company Ltd.
7-9 The Green
Flempton, Bury St. Edmunds
Suffolk, IP28 England
List includes: Test of Everyday Attention

Western Psychological Services
12031 Wilshire Boulevard
Los Angeles, CA 90025
1-800-222-2670
List includes: Luria Nebraska Neuropsychological Battery, Rey Auditory and Verbal Learning Test, Symbol Digit Modalities Test

Glossary

Absence attack: Temporary loss of consciousness with minimal motor accompaniment, similar to the petit mal seizure.

Abulia: Loss or difficulties with motivation, will power, drive; difficulty sustaining a monologue or narrative.

Acalculia: Inability to perform mathematical operations, usually due to a lesion in the area of the angular gyrus within the left parietal lobe.

Achromatopsia: Inability to distinguish different hues despite normally pigmented cells in the retina, also referred to as cortical color blindness.

Agnosia: Deficit in the ability to recognize and name sensory stimuli.

Agraphia: Loss or decline in the ability to express thoughts into written words.

Akinetic mutism: A state characterized by the appearance of wakefulness but lacking impulse for speech and action, also known as coma vigil.

Alexia/Dyslexia: Inability to read, difficulty in visual recognition of words.

Aneurysm: A sac formed in the wall of an artery, a vein, or the heart caused by vascular dilations due to localized defects in vascular elasticity.

Angular gyrus: Important brain region in language functions, located in the inferior-parietal lobe, roughly corresponding to Brodman's area 39.

Anomia: Type of aphasia that affects the ability to name objects or recognize and recall their names.

Anosognosia: Real or pretended unawareness of the presence of bodily deficit or illness; usually associated with nondominant parietal lesions.

Anoxia: Shortage or absence of oxygen.

Anterograde amnesia: Inability to remember events subsequent to the onset of the amnesia.

Anton's Syndrome: Unawareness or denial of one's own blindness, often observed in cortical blindness due to bilateral infarction of the occipital lobes.

Aphasia: Deficit in expressing or understanding written or oral language.

Apperceptive agnosia: Deficit in the ability to organize distinct parts of symbols, obtained from sensory stimuli, into a perceptual whole.

Apraxia: Deficit or loss in the ability to perform purposeful movements in the absence of paralysis or paresis.

Aprosodia: Loss of production and/or comprehension of normal variations of pitch, rhythm, and emphasis in speech.

Arcuate fasciculus: A bundle of association fibers in the cerebrum connecting Wernicke's and Broca's areas.

Associative visual agnosia: Deficit in the ability to recognize what is seen.

Asterognosis: Inability to recognize familiar objects through touch despite intact tactile sensory function.

Astrocytoma: A slow-growing tumor of the brain resulting from the growth of astrocytes of the neuroglia.

Ataxia: Disordered muscular coordination, often resulting from lesion of one cerebellar hemisphere, especially in the anterior lobe.

Atherosclerosis: A degeneration of the arteries due to the formation of fatty deposits (atheromas) within the intima and inner media of large and medium size arteries.

Athetosis: A condition marked by involuntary slow irregular writhing movements especially in the hands and fingers.

Auras: A subjective sensation, perceptual experience, or motor phenomenon that precedes a paroxysmal attack.

Balint's syndrome: An agnostic syndrome characterized by cortical paralysis of visual fixation, optic ataxia, and disturbance of visual attention, caused by bilateral lesions of the parieto-occipital lobes.

Bilateral simultaneous stimulation: Simultaneous stimulation of both sides of the body using touch, hearing, or vision, to ascertain whether an individual imperceives the stimulus on one side or the other.

Broca's aphasia: An expressive aphasia, primarily a defect of speech resulting from a lesion to Broca's area.

Cerebral infarction: An area of coagulated dead tissue in a cerebral vessel which obstructs circulation, resulting in pathological changes in the area deprived of blood supply.

Chorea: Nervous condition marked by ceaseless occurrence of forcible, rapid, involuntary muscular movements of the limbs or facial muscles.

Clonus: Spasmatic contractions in response to maintenance of tension in a muscle.

Complex partial seizures: Alteration in the content of a person's consciousness (i.e., changes in smell or taste, sensory hallucinations, abnormal emotional experiences), associated with temporal-lobe epilipsy.

Constructional apraxia: An inability to perform simple well-rehearsed tasks due to a discontinuity between intent and outcome.

Contralateral neglect: Neglect of part of the body or space, the neglect is usually contralateral to a lesion to Brodman's areas 7 and 40.

Convulsions: Attacks of involuntary muscular contractions and relaxations.

Cortical dementia: Dementia resulting from dysfunction to the cortex (as opposed to dementia resulting from subcortical regions or pseudodementia resulting from depression).

Crystallized intelligence: Content aspect of intelligence, environmentally determined, past learning.

Cyanosis: A slate-like, bluish, gray discoloration of the skin due to the presence of abnormal amounts of reduced hemoglobin in the blood.

Dementia: Deterioration of intellectual and cognitive function, due to organic impairment of brain tissue.

Diplopia: Double vision, due to paralysis of the ocular muscles.

Double simultaneous stimulation: Simultaneous stimulation to both sides of a sensory area (visual, tactile, auditory), used to test for suppressions (see also bilateral simultaneous stimulation).

Dysarthria: Difficulty in articulation, poor phonation.

Dyslexia (also alexia):   Developmental learning disorder that results in difficulty interpreting written language despite normal vision and intelligence.

Dystonia: Abnormality of unusually excessive muscle tone or tension.

Edema: The localized or generalized presence of abnormal amounts of tissue fluid.

Embolism: Obstruction of a blood vessel of the brain by a foreign substance, blood clot, air bubble, fat deposit, or detached cell mass from a tumor.

Fasciculation: Small local involuntary muscle contractions due to the spontaneous discharge of a number of fibers stimulated by a single motor filament.

Finger agnosia: Inability to identify fingers.

Fluid intelligence: Intelligence related to new problem solving, closely tied to biological abilities, more susceptible to deterioration than crystalized intelligence.

Generalized seizures: Bilaterally symmetrical seizures without local onset.

Gerstmann's syndrome: Complex cluster of symptoms consisting of finger agnosia, agraphia, acalculia, and right left disorientation.

Glioblastoma: Highly malignant, rapidly growing tumor comprised of glial cells.

Grand mal seizures: Seizure or fit characterized by loss of consciousness and stereotyped, generalized convulsions.

Hemiparesis: Muscular weakness or partial paralysis affecting only one side of the body.

Hemorrhagic stroke: Rupture of artery causing bleeding into the brain, most frequent cause is hypertension.

Hypertension: Abnormally high blood pressure.

Hypoxia: Deficient oxygenation of the blood.

Ideational apraxia: Loss of ability to conceptualize how a movement is carried out, client cannot make proper utilization of an object.

Inattention: A defect of visual and tactile attention characterized by a loss of excitability to a previously adequate stimulus, usually due to parietal lobe lesions.

Infarct: An area of dead or dying tissue in an organ or part resulting from an obstruction of the blood vessels normally supplying the area.

Infiltrative tumors: Tumor which invades other tissue rather than being incapsulated in a specific region, they might destroy cells, occupy their place, or surround existing cells.

Intracerebral hemorrhage: Rupture of blood vessel resulting in bleeding into the brain.

Ischemic strokes: Local and temporary deficiency of blood supply due to functional constriction or obstruction of the circulation to a part of the brain.

Jacksonian march: The spread of clonic movements sequentially from one limb to another and the face, at which point consciousness may be lost.

Lesions: Any pathologically damaged body tissue.

Locked-in syndrome: Paralysis of all muscles except eye movements.

Meningioma: A slow-growing encapsulated brain tumor growing from the meninges.

Metastatic tumor: A tumor that develops via the transfer of tumor cells from one organ or part of the body to another not directly connected.

Moria: Euphoric mood.

Multi-infarct dementia: Dementia resulting from multiple small strokes (infarcts) due to arteriosclerosis.

Myoclonus: Sudden irregular twitching or clonic spasm of a muscle or group of muscles that does not normally generate movement of the appendage supplied by the muscle.

Neglect: Ignoring stimuli contralateral to area of brain damage.

Neologism: New often fragmented words, created by the patient that are meaningless or words he/she gives meaning without awareness of their normal connotations.

Obstructive strokes: Stroke caused by obstruction to the vasculature.

Ocular apraxia: Eyes turn to the opposite direction when the head is turned.

Optic ataxia: Deficit in perceptual motor coordination characterized by incorrect reaching for objects and locating stimuli in space such as past pointing.

Oxygen deprivation: See *Anoxia*.

Paraphasias: Aphasias characterized by production of jumbled unintended syllables, words, and word combinations during the effort to speak.

Partial seizures: Seizure activity that begins in a focal area of the brain and spreads to nearby areas but are still restricted to one hemisphere, characterized by inappropriate actions, feelings, or postural changes.

Perseveration: Persistent repetition of a word, phrase, idea, subject, or behavior after cessation of the causative stimulus.

Petit mal seizures: Brief generalized seizure characterized by brief loss of consciousness/awareness, minimal motor accompaniment, and a few blinks or jerks of eyelids or turning the head.

Pica: Excessive, persistent eating of nonnutritious material (i.e., dirt, wood).

Polydipsia: Excessive drinking of fluids.

Post traumatic amnesia (PTA):   Period of clouded consciousness following a head injury, typically occurs prior to the patient attaining full orientation and awareness.

Prosody: Changes in pitch, rhythm, and stress in speech which are essential in conveying different shades of meaning.

Prosopagnosia: A visual agnosia characterized by the inability to recognize familiar faces or identify unique properties or features of an object (but a familiar person may be recognized by their voice).

Pseudodementia: Reversible decline in cognitive performance and exaggerated indifference to one's surroundings associated with functional illness such as major depression.

Psychogenic unresponsiveness: Decrease in attention, arousal, alertness due to psychological causes.

Retrograde amnesia: Deficit in ability to recall events and situations prior to the onset of amnesia.

Semantic anomic aphasia: Aphasia in which general meaning is recognized but not the specific word (i.e., calling a "harmonica" a "piano").

Simple partial seizures: Seizures occurring in one portion of the brain (focal) which effect one specific sensory or motor area.

Simultanagnosia: Deficit in simultaneous form perception characterized by the inability to perceive more than one object at one time.

Somatoparaphrenia: Delusions regarding the ownership of one's limbs.

Stenosis: Obstruction or constriction of a passage or orifice.

Striate cortex: Primary visual cortex, area of brain responsible for the first stage of visual processing.

Subarachnoid hemorrhage: Bleeding into the sub-arachnoid space frequently due to aneurysms on vessels spanning the area.

Subcortical dementia: Dementia caused by impairment to subcortical regions, characterized by decreased initiation, slowing of responses, and specific deficits in memory (i.e., dementias associated with Parkinson's and Huntington's diseases).

Thrombosis: The formation or existence of a clot or thrombus within the vascular system formed by the coagulation of blood.

Tinnitus: Noise in the ear such as ringing, buzzing, ticking, roaring, clicking, etc.

Tonus: The partial steady constriction of muscle.

Transcortical motor aphasia: Aphasia caused by lesion in the pathway between the speech and other cortical centers, repetition of spoken language is intact but spontaneous speech is impaired (similar to Broca's aphasia), reading ability is intact.

Transcortical aphasia: Aphasia due to a lesion of a pathway between the speech center and other cortical centers, characterized by the ability to repeat words and name objects but unable to understand what is heard or repeated and may be unable to speak spontaneously.

Transcortical sensory aphasia: Restricted spontaneous speech, client may be fluent but paraphasic (like Wernicke's aphasia), may be unable to comprehend what is heard or repeated, likely caused by damage to the sensory association area thus words are not associated with other areas.

Transient ischemic attack (TIA):   Repeated temporary interference of blood supply to the brain area with complete recovery.

Visual agnosia: Inability to recognize objects due to difficulty combining visual impressions into complete patterns despite normal vision.

Wernicke's aphasia: Inability to comprehend or produce meaningful written or verbal speech resulting from lesions to the posterior cortex.

Author Index

Subject Index

Note: The bold numbers indicate primary information.